RACHMANINOFF
Composer, Pianist, Conductor

For Kate

RACHMANINOFF
Composer, Pianist, Conductor

BARRIE MARTYN

Scolar Press

Published by
SCOLAR PRESS
Gower Publishing Company Limited
Gower House
Croft Road
Aldershot
Hants GU11 3HR
England

Gower Publishing Company
Old Post Road
Brookfield
Vermont 05036
USA

British Library Cataloguing in Publication Data
Martyn, Barrie
Rachmaninoff: composer, pianist, conductor.
1. Russian Music. Rachmaninoff, Sergei 1873–1943
I. Title
780'.92'4

Library of Congress Cataloging-in-Publication Data
Martyn, Barrie
Rachmaninoff: composer, pianist, conductor / Barrie Martyn
  p. cm.
ISBN 0–85967–809–1
1. Rachmaninoff, Sergei, 1873–1943. 2. Composers—Soviet Union
Biography. I. Title.
ML410.R12M17 1990
780'.92—dc20
[B]   89–24085

ISBN 0–85967–809–1

Contents

List of plates

Between pages 400 and 401

Acknowledgements

I am indebted to the copyright holders of textual matter quoted with their permission:

Angus & Robertson (UK) (for extracts from *Duet for Three Hands* by Cyril Smith);

The BBC and Miss Phyllis Sellick (for a quotation from a broadcast by Cyril Smith);

Bertelsmann Music Group (for quotations from sleeve notes to RCA Red Seal recordings);

Jonathan Cape Ltd (for quotations from *My Many Years* by Arthur Rubinstein);

William Collins Sons & Co. Ltd (for a quotation from *Sir Thomas Beecham* by Neville Cardus);

Dobson Books Ltd (for a quotation from *Sergei Rachmaninov* by John Culshaw);

Faber & Faber Ltd (for a quotation from *Music Ho!* by Constant Lambert);

Victor Gollancz Ltd (for a quotation from *My Life of Music* by Sir Henry Wood);

Hallé Concerts Society (for a quotation from *Hallé*, No. 117);

Hamish Hamilton Ltd (for a quotation from *At the Piano* by Ivor Newton);

Harrap Ltd (for an extract from *The Selective Ego* by James Agate);

The Instrumentalist Co. (for quotations from *Clavier*, October 1973 – articles by Olga Conus, Gina Bachauer and Ruth Slenczynska);

Miss Constance Keene (for quotations from her late husband Abram Chasins' book *Speaking of Pianists*);

Alfred A. Knopf Inc., New York (for extracts from *The Other Side of the Record* by Charles O'Connell);

Macdonald & Co. Ltd (for quotations from *Chaliapin, An Autobiography as told to Maxim Gorky*, translated by Nina Froud and James Hanley, and *Horowitz, A Biography* by Glen Plaskin);

Macmillan & Co. Ltd (for an extract from Eric Blom's article on

Rachmaninoff in the fifth edition of *Grove's Dictionary of Music and Musicians*);

Miss Tanya Moiseiwitsch (for two quotations from radio broadcasts by her father Benno Moiseiwitsch);

The editor of *Musical Opinion* (for a quotation from an article by Clinton Gray-Fisk in the April 1943 edition of that magazine);

The editor of *New Statesman* (for a quotation from *NS*, 25 February 1966);

Orpheus Publications (for two quotations from *Music & Musicians International*);

Oxford University Press, Journals Department, New York, (for quotations from *The Musical Quarterly*, January and May 1944);

The editor of *Tempo* (for a quotation from an article by Serge Moreux in the Spring 1949 edition of that magazine);

University of South Carolina Press (for quotations from *The Amazing Marriage of Marie Eustis and Josef Hofmann* by Neil S. Graydon and Margaret S. Sizemore);

University of Minnesota Press (for a quotation from *Music and Maestros, The Story of the Minneapolis Symphony Orchestra* by John K. Shermann).

Thanks are due to those music publishers who have kindly given permission to reproduce extracts from their copyright scores:

Edwin Ashdown Ltd, London (Ex. 128b);

Boosey & Hawkes, Music Publishers Ltd (Exs. 4b, 8a–11, 17, 18b–20, 26b, 27, 36b, 41, 46–65, 81–83, 84, 85a, 86–104, 108, 109a, 110a, 111–117a, 118–128a, 129–131, 132b, 133b, 134b, 136–141, 146, 153b, 156b, 169b, 173b);

CPP/Belwin Inc. and International Music Publications for Belwin Mills Publishing Corp. (Filmtrax PLC), original copyright owner for the world (Exs. 105–107, 142–145, 154–156a, 157–162a, 163, 164c–168, 170–173a, 174, 175a, 176–190a, 191, 192);

Richard Schauer (Anton J. Benjamin), London and Hamburg (Exs. 42 and 43);

Rob. Forberg–P. Jurgenson, Musikverlag, 53 Bonn (Exs. 21–23a and 25b);

and William Elkin Music Services (ex. 164b).

Sources and permissions for the photographic illustrations are as follows:

Collection Author: 14, 24;

Kunstmuseum Basel (Depositum der Gottfried Keller-Stiftung): 10;

Novosti Press Agency: 1, 2, 6, 8, 9, 23;

Paul Popper Ltd: 21;

RCA Victor Red Seal: 17, 22;
Society for Cultural Relations with the USSR: 3–5, 7, 11, 13, 18, 19;
Topham Picture Library: jacket, 15, 16, 20.
Messrs. Boosey & Hawkes, Music Publishers Ltd, own the copyright
to the music illustrated in chapters 11 and 12.

Every effort has been made to contact all copyright holders of material
reproduced in this book. The publishers will be pleased to hear from
any whom they have been unable to locate and undertake to insert
any missing acknowledgements in future editions.

Introduction

Like all Gaul, the musical life of Sergei Vasilyevich Rachmaninoff was divided into three parts: composer, pianist and conductor; so too this book. The first and main part considers Rachmaninoff's activity as a composer, with a chronological survey of his output; the second and third parts comprise materials concerning his careers as a virtuoso pianist and conductor. In 1930, reviewing his life's work with characteristic modesty and scepticism, Rachmaninoff remarked:

> Today, when the greater part of my life is over, I am constantly troubled by the misgiving that, in venturing into too many fields, I may have failed to make the best use of my life. In the old Russian phrase, I have 'hunted three hares'. Can I be sure that I have caught one of them?

It is the author's contention that in each of his three careers Rachmaninoff not only caught his hare but achieved greatness.

Both as man and musician Rachmaninoff is a fascinating enigma and paradox, particularly for those of us in the West, where he spent the final twenty-five years of his life. During this time the enormous celebrity of his name as a composer reflected neither his reputation among generally hostile critics nor an admiring public's almost total unfamiliarity with most of his output. At the same time the place in musical history he seemed destined to be assigned alongside his country's nineteenth-century predecessors was manifestly irreconcilable with the chronology of the life of a man only one year older than Schönberg. In contrast with the extremes of emotion so powerfully and uninhibitedly expressed in his music, the private life that Rachmaninoff so carefully protected may now be seen, at least on the surface, to have been sober, even mundane, albeit with the trappings of material success and with endearing personal quirks, such as his typically twentieth-century passion for speed and the pleasure he evidently took in observing an intriguing game of poker or charades. Although in his music he wore his heart on his sleeve, except among intimates Rachmaninoff the man was always reserved, often aloof, sometimes unapproachable. Not only did his inscrutably impassive facial expression give nothing away about his inner feelings, but he lacked the vices of egotism and indiscretion that

xiii

might otherwise have broken down the barriers of reticence in his correspondence; even his wife never knew what he was composing, and this whole subject was taboo in the family circle. Although he had the world at his feet, the insecurity and self-doubt which had afflicted him near the beginning of his career after the traumatic failure of his First Symphony persisted not far below the surface throughout his life, belied by a towering physical presence and a commanding personality. At concerts he gave the impression of coming on to the stage only with the greatest reluctance and yet, at least in his later years, he used to declare that performing in public was his one satisfaction in life. No-one will ever know the price he must have paid for the battle within himself to present a front to the world that concealed his soul; the only clues are in the music, for it was here that Rachmaninoff expressed his innermost thoughts with absolute directness and sincerity.

In the years in which I grew up, immediately after World War II, Rachmaninoff perfectly epitomized the dichotomy of values that existed between the musical establishment and the concert-going public. While professional critics generally dismissed his music as second-rate and subversively reactionary, lay music lovers never ceased to respond enthusiastically to its powerful emotional appeal, finding in its continuance of nineteenth-century tradition an oasis in a desert of modernism. Since that time, with a wider and more representative cross-section of his output being heard in the concert hall and made available in recorded form, Rachmaninoff's popularity has steadily risen, and along with this has come a critical reappraisal and rehabilitation. Close intimacy with the composer increases rather than diminishes respect for his achievements; his music wears familiarity uncommonly well, as no art can without solid underlying virtues.

The reputation of Rachmaninoff the executant seems to have suffered the opposite fate to that of his music. Although his supremacy as a pianist was universally recognized during his lifetime, fashion in performance has changed so much since his death that the intrinsic merit of his art no less than the historical importance of his career both before the public and in the recording studio seems in danger of being neglected and unhonoured; it is here reasserted and examined in some detail. Rachmaninoff's work as a conductor, almost an unknown quantity in the West but a potent force for twenty years in his own country, has long since passed into forgotten history. It too, however, has been thought worth reconsidering here, not only for its inherent interest but also because his career and the repertoire he performed impinged on the central concern of Rachmaninoff's life – composition.

This Baedeker to Rachmaninoff is the product of one man's odyssey over many years. It makes no claim to be unprejudiced or nicely balanced: I have emphasized the aspects of Rachmaninoff's music and music-making that specially interest me, hoping that the reader may share my enthusiasms. Thus, in analysing the music, I have made much of the relationship between different works, for although there was no dramatic change in the composer's style over a creative life of more than half a century, the marks of gradual evolution often point the way to later developments. I have also explored in some depth the matter of outside musical influences and the fascinating if thorny topic of the literary and pictorial stimuli, acknowledged or presumed, which seem to have played a significant part in Rachmaninoff's composing process. It has been my general intention to fill in the more conspicuous gaps left in previous studies; conversely I have deliberately passed as lightly as possible over ground already well trodden elsewhere, in particular paring mere biography to the minimum necessary to shed light on his musical life. In this regard, since its publication well over thirty years ago, the admirable biography by Bertensson and Leyda has not yet been significantly supplemented, still less supplanted, by any later account in English.

The main literary sources for the book are listed on pp. 563–4. In compiling material I have drawn heavily on Rachmaninoff's own writings, mainly and most profitably his correspondence but also his articles and interviews, disappointingly few and for the most part unrevealing though they were, and on the Soviet anthology of reminiscences about the man and the musician by his friends and colleagues. For the Russian years of Rachmaninoff's career many interesting details are to be found conveniently assembled in the two most important Soviet musicological studies of the composer, by Bryantseva and Keldïsh; for the final twenty-five years abroad most of the documentary evidence resides in the Rachmaninoff Archive in the Library of Congress in Washington, where the author spent happy and fruitful days examining the materials deposited there by the composer's wife in 1951 and brought into order by his faithful confidante and sister-in-law, Sophie Satin (Sofiya Alexandrovna Satina). Meeting and corresponding with Miss Satin herself, whose memory remained astoundingly clear even into advanced old age, was particularly useful for illuminating certain aspects of Rachmaninoff's life. For his unstinting help with matters relating to the unfinished opera *Monna Vanna* I should like to place on record my special gratitude to Mr Igor Buketoff, who has put all admirers of Rachmaninoff in his debt for rescuing this important work from oblivion and bringing it out into the light of day. Thanks are due also to Mr Brian Rust, without whose assistance the discography could not have been completed.

In the vexed matter of the transliteration of Russian names from Cyrillic script I have made no attempt to be perfectly consistent. In the

1880s, when the young Rachmaninoff (strictly transliterated 'Rakhman-inov') was taught French and so presumably also the form of his own name in Roman characters, and in the 1890s, when the composer's name appeared in both Cyrillic and Roman letters on his first published works, and in the first decades of the twentieth century, it was the convention in Europeanizing Russian names to aim at close phonetic approximation in French forms rather than strict literal correspondence. Thus a Russian final –v (pronounced 'f') was generally rendered by –ff, resulting in the spellings Taneyeff, Liadoff, Tchekhoff, etc. As the century progressed, however, the fashion began to retain the –v ending, which has now long since become the universal form (as in Gavrilov, Nureyev), and had Rachmaninoff lived in a later era he would doubtless have followed suit. The consonant in his name represented by 'kh', which to Western European eyes has the appearance of an outlandish barbarism, happens to correspond phonetically with the more approachable Teutonic 'ch' (a sound heard in the Scottish word 'loch'), which therefore looks and sounds right in its stead. In this book I have chosen to adopt the spelling of his name that Rachmaninoff himself used and in the case of other familiar personalities their current Europeanized versions; I have, however, transliterated unfamiliar names more strictly.

Like most Russian composers of his time, Rachmaninoff gave many of his compositions French titles, but although some of these, for example *Polichinelle* and the coinage *Étude-Tableau*, clearly need to remain in that form, others – *Trio élégiaque, Morceau de fantaisie*, etc. – like *Casse-noisette* and *Sacre du printemps* seem to me to have no greater resonance or import in French than their less pretentious English equivalents, and they have therefore generally been anglicized here. Rachmaninoff's songs I have referred to by their customary English titles. The translations of the texts themselves in the English edition range from the quaint to the desperate, and it is pleasing that they seem at last to have passed unobtrusively away through the almost universal use now of the originals. Where a musical illustration has a text, for Russian-less readers I have transliterated it and provided an English version. I have left Russian dating unchanged. The Julian calendar operated in Russia until a couple of months after Rachmaninoff had finally emigrated from his homeland, at the end of 1917, setting dates before this either twelve or thirteen days behind our own, according to whether they refer to the nineteenth or twentieth century.

Part I
RACHMANINOFF THE COMPOSER

I Rachmaninoff and Russian Musical History

Rachmaninoff was born in 1873, one year before the first performance of *Boris Godunov*, forty years before *Rite of Spring*; Tolstoy was starting work on *Anna Karenina*. His close Russian contempories include Scriabin and Chaliapin, Diaghilev and Benois, Stanislavsky, Gorky, Rasputin and Lenin. The interval between the births of Glinka and Rachmaninoff – sixty-nine years – is almost the same as Rachmaninoff's own life-span: he died a few days before his seventieth birthday, in 1943, in which year Shostakovich composed his Eighth Symphony and Miaskovsky his Twenty-fourth; Prokofiev's Fifth Symphony appeared the following year. Thus the fundamental fact about Rachmaninoff's place in Russian musical history is that he stands Janus-like between the old Russia and the new, looking back to the flowering of Russian nineteenth-century 'classical' music as also ahead to the first generation of Soviet composers.

Although Glinka is traditionally cited as the founding father of Russian music, it in fact began to evolve many centuries before him.[1] The first Russian composer known by name seems to have been Tsar Ivan the Terrible (1533–1584), but both church and folk music, from which all Russian 'classical' music is ultimately derived, reach back for their origins much further still. A native church music, the counterpart of Western Gregorian plainchant, developed soon after the conversion of Russia to Christianity in 988, either out of imported Byzantine chant or, as many Soviet musicologists claim, from the ancient folk melodies of the Eastern Slavs. Curiously enough, although the origins of Russian folk music are archaic, it was not until the end of the eighteenth century that the first collections were made,[2] something that in retrospect was a hint that after so long a dormant period Russian music was at last about to take off.

The foundation by Peter the Great in 1703 of the city of St Petersburg inaugurated a century of unparalleled cultural development. The building and adornment of the new capital and the increasing brilliance of the Court attracted foreign craftsmen and creative artists in every

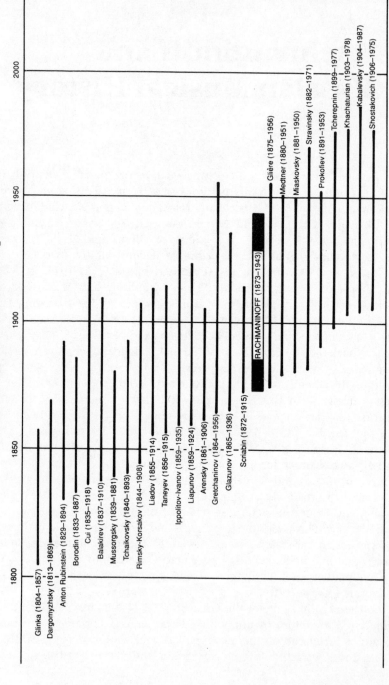

Chronology of Russian Composers

Glinka (1804–1857)
Dargomyzhsky (1813–1869)
Anton Rubinstein (1829–1894)
Borodin (1833–1887)
Cui (1835–1918)
Balakirev (1837–1910)
Mussorgsky (1839–1881)
Tchaikovsky (1840–1893)
Rimsky-Korsakov (1844–1908)
Liadov (1855–1914)
Taneyev (1856–1915)
Ippolitov-Ivanov (1859–1935)
Liapunov (1859–1924)
Arensky (1861–1906)
Gretchaninov (1864–1956)
Glazunov (1865–1936)
Scriabin (1872–1915)
RACHMANINOFF (1873–1943)
Glière (1875–1956)
Medtner (1880–1951)
Miaskovsky (1881–1950)
Stravinsky (1882–1971)
Prokofiev (1891–1953)
Tcherepnin (1899–1977)
Khachaturian (1903–1978)
Kabalevsky (1904–1987)
Shostakovich (1906–1975)

1800   1850   1900   1950   2000

sphere, especially during the reign of Catherine the Great (1762–1796). Many foreign musicians visited Russia or settled there, among whom Italians were particularly numerous, including such distinguished composers as Araja, Galuppi, Traetta, Manfredini, Sarti, Paisiello and Cimarosa, who created and then exploited in St Petersburg, as Handel had done in London, a vogue for Italian opera. But in music, as in the other arts, the assimilation of foreign influences itself sparked off indigenous talent, and by the end of the century Russian-born executants and composers had emerged in appreciable numbers. Native opera began to appear in the 1770s,[3] much of it containing Russian folk music, though arguably it was not until the early years of the nineteenth century that it acquired a distinct, national character, after the Napoleonic Wars had stimulated a feeling for nationalism in Russian art generally. As Pushkin (1799–1837) began a literary renaissance, so it was through Glinka (1804–1857) that Russian music at last emancipated itself and established its own identity. The first performance of *A Life for the Tsar* in 1836 is usually seen as the inaugural event in the process, and for Tchaikovsky *Kamarinskaya* (1848) was the 'acorn' from which the oak of Russian symphonic music grew.

Glinka's Russian feeling and the strong element of dilettantism in his musical make-up[4] made the self-conscious nationalism and inspired amateurism of his spiritual heir Balakirev and his circle of Cui, Mussorgsky, Rimsky-Korsakov and Borodin seem a natural succession, as indeed at first it was, but even before 'The Mighty Handful' had acquired their sobriquet[5] history changed course unexpectedly. With musical life in Russia now burgeoning, a demand was created for institutionalized academic and professional training, which was satisfied by the foundation in 1859 of the Imperial Russian Musical Society and subsequently of conservatoires in St Petersburg (1862) and Moscow (1866) under the direction of the brothers Anton and Nikolay Rubinstein. Their training in Berlin and, in Anton Rubinstein's case, Vienna too, made it inevitable that the new Russian academies should be modelled on the Austro-German pattern.[6]

Balakirev promptly condemned the St Petersburg Conservatoire as a conspiracy 'to bring all Russian music under the yoke of the German generals', and through his efforts in the same year as its foundation a Free School was opened in opposition. Vladimir Stasov, the great critic and inspirational force in the arts in Russia, cited what he claimed to be European opinion in support of him: 'Academies and conservatoires serve only as a breeding ground for mediocrities and help perpetuate deleterious artistic ideas and taste . . . [They] meddle most harmfully in the student's creative activity. They dictate the style and form of his works [and] impose their own fixed practices on him.'[7] As the supreme martinet, dogmatist and meddler in his colleagues' musical affairs proved to be Balakirev himself, these words from his apostle were ironical indeed.

Inasmuch as the conservatoires failed to tap new veins of creative talent or to do very much for their outstanding students, they realized the forebodings of their critics. Rachmaninoff was a case in point. Allowed as a young teenager at St Petersburg Conservatoire to fritter away his time, he had to be taken away and brought sternly to heel by the Moscow pedagogue Nikolay Zverev. At Moscow Conservatoire, according to his own admission,[8] he learned more about the nature of fugue from two chance lessons than from a whole year's classes with Arensky, and his course in counterpoint, despite the impeccable credentials of the teacher, Taneyev, the ultimate Russian authority on the subject, also proved ill-spent. Rachmaninoff survived on his own talent; his classmate Scriabin left the institution without even gaining a diploma in composition. Although predictably unsuccessful in catering for creative genius, the conservatoires nevertheless served a valuable function in providing a thorough professional training for executants, and they performed the useful incidental service of conferring on their graduates the status of 'Free Artist', a title originally created by Catherine the Great only for architects and painters; by putting their graduates on a par the conservatoires gave social respectability to a profession previously classified as proletarian.

The case against academic training was rather undermined at the outset by the towering stature of the first composer to emerge from St Petersburg Conservatoire, Tchaikovsky, pupil of the arch villain Anton Rubinstein, who himself, at least in some of his later works, such as the 'Russian' Symphony of 1880 and the orchestral fantasy *Russia* of 1882, could be self-consciously nationalist. Though Tchaikovsky had severe reservations about the work of 'The Mighty Handful' and their lack of professionalism, in some senses he might have been one of their number himself; he incorporated Russian folk music in his compositions, as in the Second Symphony; he was on friendly personal terms with the group – *Romeo and Juliet* was dedicated to Balakirev, *The Tempest* to Stasov; and, like all the others, he more than once accepted Balakirev's detailed criticism and advice (both *Romeo* and the 'Manfred' Symphony owed their genesis to him). Conversely, Balakirev and the others in their turn all came to use classical contrapuntal techniques in their work,[9] and all but Cui at least essayed a symphony, that symbol of classical tradition, as if this was the only way they could convince themselves they had musically come of age.

Even before Rachmaninoff's birth the gulf between professionalism and amateurism had been bridged by Rimsky-Korsakov, who had won

Pedagogic Genealogy of Russian Composers

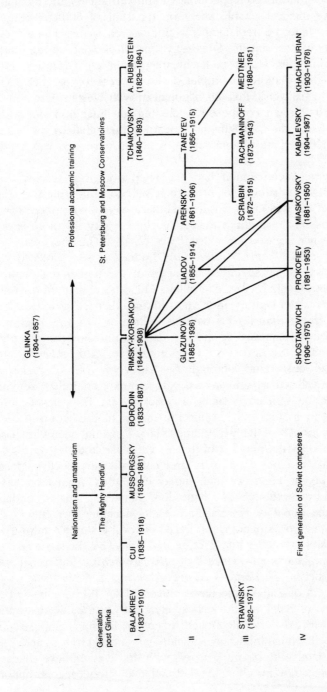

sufficient recognition and respectability to find an uneasy and incongruous niche in the musical establishment on the staff of St Petersburg Conservatoire, where he remained for thirty-seven years, mentor of the younger composers up to Stravinsky and Prokofiev, though not, to Rachmaninoff's later regret, of Rachmaninoff himself. Glazunov, protégé of 'The Mighty Handful', completed the process of reconciliation by combining in his music Russian nationalism with western tradition. After Glazunov all Russian composers, including Rachmaninoff but with the conspicuous exception of Stravinsky, learned their craft by the academic route and not the path of amateurism, which in retrospect was inevitably a dead-end.

By the time Rachmaninoff had graduated from the Moscow Conservatoire in 1892, whatever might once have been the collective identity and ideals of the nationalist group, and these were always more concepts in the minds of music critics than a practical reality for those involved, had long since ceased to exist. Two of their number were dead, Mussorgsky (1881) and Borodin (1887), and a new circle of lesser composers had emerged under the aegis of the timber millionaire and publisher Mitrofan Belyayev. The bilious Cui, who continued to compose for another quarter-century into ripe old age, then as now was known less for his music than for his writings (which include the much-quoted and notoriously damning review of Rachmaninoff's First Symphony). Balakirev, once the leader and driving force, had gone through a psychological crisis, and although he had come out of seclusion to resume musical activity and indeed was to enjoy an Indian summer as a composer, he was never again a major figure. Thus it was Rimsky-Korsakov who in the end became the doyen of the group.

The story of 'The Mighty Handful' is a fascinating one. Who has not been intrigued by the paradox of the cosmopolitan and westward-looking court capital, and not reactionary and culturally introspective Moscow, coming to be the centre of their movement? What imagination has not been stirred by the thought of a handful of pioneering amateur underdogs taking on the might of the state academic machine; by pictures of the striking oriental physiognomy of Balakirev or by Repin's unforgettable portrait of Mussorgsky in the Tretyakov Gallery; by the legendary post-humous completions of *Prince Igor*, *Khovanshchina* and other works; by the exoticism of *Boris Godunov*, *Tamara*, *Scheherazade*; by the double careers of Rimsky the naval officer, of Dr Borodin the Professor of Chemistry, of Balakirev the railway clerk, of Cui the military strategist, and of Mussorgsky the alcoholic? No other Russian composers, and certainly not Rachmaninoff, have so fairy-tale a background, and yet the widespread familiarity of music lovers with the lives of these charismatic personalities is not matched by their relatively modest contribution to the regular repertoire and average musical consciousness. Balakirev is remembered only by the piano spectacular *Islamey* and, though lip service is paid to *Tamara* and the First Symphony, these works are familiar not through concert performance but through the gramophone. The Lithuanian-Parisian Cui, in any case the odd-man-out in the group, is for all practical purposes a totally closed book; Mussorgsky is known only by *Boris Godunov*, *Pictures at an Exhibition* and a handful of songs; and Borodin by the Overture and *Polovtsian Dances* from *Prince Igor*, the Second Symphony and *In the Steppes of Central Asia*. Rimsky-Korsakov alone was truly prolific, but even of his output only a few colourful orchestral works are familiar to the average music lover: *Scheherazade*, *Russian Easter Festival Overture*, *Spanish Caprice*.

This focusing of interest in nineteenth-century Russian music on the nationalists has drawn attention away from their conservatoire colleagues. Anton Rubinstein, whose vast and undervalued output still awaits proper recognition, is the most glaring example of this neglect, but Rachmaninoff's teachers Taneyev and Arensky have fared little better. Rachmaninoff was two years under Taneyev studying counterpoint and five under Arensky studying harmony, fugue and free composition. The longer period of contact with Arensky left its mark on Rachmaninoff's early compositions, in which the style of his teacher is plainly discernible alongside that of his distant guiding star, Tchaikovsky.

Arensky (1861–1906) studied with Rimsky-Korsakov at St Petersburg and at the age of twenty-one was appointed to the staff of Moscow Conservatoire, where he remained for thirteen years, active as both teacher and composer. Songs, chamber, ballet and other orchestral music poured from his pen, as well as a vast quantity of piano music, much of which reveals a natural affinity with salon music. In 1890 his first opera, *A Dream on The Volga*, based on the same Ostrovsky play as Tchaikovsky's *Voyevoda*, was successfully launched in Moscow, and in 1895 he moved back to St Petersburg as Director of the Imperial Chapel Choir. Alas, his youthful success waned and, like Mussorgsky, he died in his forties, an alcoholic.

In lacking a distinct, individual musical personality Arensky was a more prolific Moscow counterpart to his equally neglected Petersburg contemporary Liapunov. Rimsky's vitriolic prophecy about the composer – 'He will soon be forgotten'[10] – has in time all but come true, though the charming Waltz from the First Suite for Two Pianos survives, and so too the Variations on a Theme by Tchaikovsky; Heifetz championed the Piano Trio and made a violin and piano transcription of part of the Violin Concerto as a recital item; Sir Henry Wood performed some of the orchestral pieces in early Promenade concerts, and in the 1905–6 season of Kerzin concerts in Moscow Rachmaninoff himself conducted the First Symphony. Written when Arensky was only 22, this fine work, with echoes of both Borodin (the Second Symphony) and Tchaikovsky, shows a promise that was never fulfilled. It also exemplifies the two dominant features of the composer's musical make-up: its obviously Russian character and its Tchaikovskian lyricism; both reappeared in the work of his pupil Rachmaninoff.

Taneyev (1856–1915) studied piano and composition at Moscow Conservatoire with Nikolay Rubinstein and Tchaikovsky, and after becoming the latter's close friend and the chief interpreter of his First Concerto, he gave the premieres of all his other works for piano and orchestra. Like Rachmaninoff, he won the conservatoire's gold medal at the age of nineteen. He returned as a teacher three years later, held the post of Director from 1885 to 1889, and finally resigned in 1905 to give himself more seriously to his careers as a pianist and composer. During his years at the conservatoire, when he viewed his own activity as a composer with sceptical indifference, a growing interest in Renaissance contrapuntal music by Josquin des Prés, Lassus and Palestrina set him off on a lifetime's study of the technique of counterpoint. Something at least of Taneyev's enthusiasm seems to have rubbed off on Rachmaninoff, whose Second Symphony, with its display of contrapuntal dexterity, was an eminently appropriate work to dedicate to his teacher.

It seemed self-evident to those who gasped in amazed reverence at Taneyev's gigantic feats of scholarship and endurance[11] that the music created by such an intellect could not be other than aridly academic; after all, did not Taneyev regard counterpoint as merely a branch of mathematics? Yet, though he never lost this stigma, in the main it is undeserved, just as it is by his pupil Medtner, of whom the same criticism has been made. It is true that Rimsky-Korsakov described Taneyev's early composition as 'most dry and laboured in character', but he also noted that from the nineties, when Taneyev devoted himself more to composition, things changed, and his opera *The Oresteia*, which might have been expected to turn out 'dry and academic', in view of all the contrapuntal exercises carried out on the material before composition proper was started, proved to be 'striking in its wealth of beauty and expressiveness.'[12] Nor did Rimsky live to hear the delightful Concert Suite for Violin and Orchestra (1909), which utterly confounds the charge; and the symphonies, songs and chamber music all prove Taneyev to be a real composer and not just a musical mathematician. Rachmaninoff once conducted the Overture to *The Oresteia*, and used to play the Prelude and Fugue in G sharp minor, Op. 29, in recital, but no-one since him has seriously taken up the piece.

Taneyev's influence on Rachmaninoff's musical upbringing probably extended to some transfer of his own sympathies towards western classical tradition and of the low opinion he had, at least in his earlier years, of the St Petersburg composers. On both counts this would have been very much in tune with the general musical philosophy already instilled into Rachmaninoff by Zverev. More than twenty years later Taneyev was still acting as his guru, with Rachmaninoff continuing to take his new compositions to him for approval right up to the time of the *All-Night Vigil* of 1915, the year of Taneyev's death.

The other influence on Rachmaninoff's musical personality, albeit an indirect one, was Tchaikovsky, whom the young composer first met at Zverev's when he was thirteen years of age. Already in his pre-conservatoire days Rachmaninoff's sister Elena had introduced him to Tchaikovsky's music through the songs, and Zverev, Tchaikovsky's friend, no doubt encouraged his enthusiasm. Although Rachmaninoff's music has sometimes been glibly categorized as 'like Tchaikovsky', except in the most superficial way this is quite untrue.

Certainly Rachmaninoff's upbringing as a composer in Moscow was at a time when Tchaikovsky was the city's musical hero; and it was Tchaikovsky, one of the examiners for Rachmaninoff's conservatoire graduation, who awarded him an unprecedentedly flattering mark. But Rachmaninoff was never his pupil, and there is no evidence that he sought his advice about any of his compositions. This is not to say that Tchaikovsky took no interest in what Rachmaninoff was doing; he made a public demonstration of support for the young composer at the premiere of his graduation opera *Aleko* and gave him advice about getting his work published. In the same year, 1892, the year before he died, Tchaikovsky gave an interview to a St Petersburg critic, to which Rachmaninoff refers in a letter to his friend Mikhail Slonov: 'Tchaikovsky tells the critic that he is being forced to give up composition and make way for young talents. To the question of whether they really exist Tchaikovsky answers, "Yes", and names, in Petersburg, Glazunov, and in Moscow, myself and Arensky. This was a real joy for me. Thanks to the old man for not forgetting me.'[13] These are certainly not the words of an infatuated protégé or chosen spiritual heir.

Tchaikovsky's premature death created a void in Moscow musical life that his disciples Taneyev and Arensky were not big enough to fill. This left the field open to the rising stars of the next generation, Rachmaninoff and Scriabin, who have the unexpected distinction of being the first international figures to emerge from Moscow Conservatoire. Their upbringing took place in what proved to be the last flowering of the old régime before music entered the no-man's land that preceded modernism, but whereas Scriabin's restless imagination led him along new paths, Rachmaninoff was happy to work within the traditions he inherited, already obsolescent though they were. This has often encouraged Western critics to the view that musically the composer belongs more naturally to the nineteenth than to the twentieth century, which in a sense, of course, he does. The contrast in the 1900s between the staid Rachmaninoff and the volatile and ceaselessly evolving Scriabin, Rachmaninoff's hardly concealed distaste for almost all contemporary music, his musical and physical isolation after the Russian Revolution, in which his sympathies and life-style linked him to a vanished age, the single-mindedly sour reception accorded his works by fashionable critics on the grounds of anachronism, even his performing repertoire – all this points to a man rooted firmly in the nineteenth century. But this simplistic view is misleading and has to be reconciled with the external facts of Rachmaninoff's personal life, which make him very much a man of his own time: he drove a car for thirty years, enjoyed speedboats, had a distinctly 1930s house built for himself, met Walt Disney, lived among movie stars in Beverly Hills, and died only two years before the dropping of the first atomic bomb on Hiroshima.

At the turn of the century Rachmaninoff's music must have sounded perfectly in keeping with the times. Indeed, in comparison with Glazunov's sparklingly scored but musically unadventurous Fifth Symphony and Scriabin's Chopinesque Piano Concerto, both of 1895, Rachmaninoff's First Symphony of the same year was daring enough to be vilified by Cui for its outlandish modernism. Tchaikovsky's 'Pathétique' Symphony had appeared only two years before, Brahms's Clarinet Sonatas the preceding year, and Dvořák's Cello Concerto the very same year; Sibelius's First Symphony and Elgar's 'Enigma' Variations were still a year or two ahead. But whereas Tchaikovsky, Brahms and Dvořák were then nearly at the end of their lives, Sibelius, Elgar and Rachmaninoff were near the beginning of their fame and creative careers, neither young enough nor temperamentally inclined to emancipate themselves from the past but beyond the point of being able to embrace the future. Thus, as time passed, they found themselves moving into a state of musical limbo, and by the 1920s all three had, to a greater or lesser degree, withdrawn from composition: Sibelius stopped abruptly after *Tapiola* and the Incidental Music to 'The Tempest', in 1926; Elgar after the Cello Concerto, in 1919; and Rachmaninoff after revising the First Concerto, in 1917, after which he wrote only six other works in the remaining twenty-five years of his life. In all three cases the pundits had facile explanations: Sibelius had said all he had to say; Elgar had been creatively paralysed by the death of his wife, Rachmaninoff by exile. Though these rationalizations were not without some foundation, the real underlying causes were much more complex, probably having much to do with the nature of the times and the attitudes of critics and public. A Sibelius vogue in the interwar years outlived its strength and petered out; Elgar, ignored by the arbiters of fashion, persuaded himself, not without cause, that no-one was interested in his music, an impression traumatically confirmed by the sparse attendance at his notorious seventieth birthday concert; and what would-be connoisseur of the 1920s and 30s, if he wished to consider himself abreast of fashion, would in those years have admitted to liking Rachmaninoff?

Rachmaninoff was not, therefore, a lone maverick atavist among progressive contemporaries, for one of the side effects of the revolution started by Stravinsky's *Rite of Spring* in 1913 was that a whole generation of conservative musicians found themselves stranded in a lost world, cut off from the mainstream of musical development. This was particularly true of those Russian composers who came to maturity during the last years of the nineteenth century. Some, such as Liapunov and Glazunov, left Russia for good at different times after the 1917 Revolution, but few of those who did so transplanted themselves successfully. In the West, Russian music was still something of a specialist interest and its lesser lights unknown or ignored. Those composers of the old guard who soldiered on, temporarily or permanently, in the Soviet Union, most notably Glière and Ippolitov-Ivanov, created a musical backwater.

Like Sibelius and Elgar, but unlike his contemporaries Scriabin and Stravinsky, Rachmaninoff continued to write in a style basically unchanged from first to last, so carrying over for forty years into the twentieth century the musical tradition he had inherited in the nineteenth. Starting his career in tune with the times, he finished it as a musical Canute. Nineteen years before the composer's death, the progressive Soviet critic Viktor Belyayev summed up Rachmaninoff's predicament in an article written as though his music was already in the past tense: 'It was Rachmaninoff's fate to live in the midst of this multitude of jostling and divergent currents in contemporary Russian music . . . In this concourse of circumstances we see the reason for the profoundest tragedy of his work – the tragedy of a great soul expressing itself in language and by methods which were antiquated, whereas under other conditions they would have harmonised with the times.'[14]

The death of Rimsky-Korsakov in 1908 left Scriabin, Medtner and Rachmaninoff as the three most distinguished living Russian composers. Scriabin survived only fifteen years into the twentieth century, and yet during that time he advanced in musical style along his own esoteric path no less far than did Schönberg, his junior by only two years, along his. At the same time as the latter progressed from the Wagnerian sumptuousness of *Verklärte Nacht* (1899) to the stark atonality of the Five Orchestral Pieces (1909), Scriabin left the still waters of the traditionally-anchored First Symphony for the uncharted chromaticism of the last piano sonatas. Yet, unlike Schönberg, Scriabin created a musical cul-de-sac, and his early death brought an abrupt halt to a still evolving style before it could establish itself as something durable or influential. As a result, Scriabin's reputation declined rapidly after his death, and, at least in the West, he still suffers shameful neglect.

In contrast with Scriabin, Medtner was stylistically fully-fledged at the outset of his career, and throughout his creative life he departed from the style of his first compositions as little as any composer in history. Like Rachmaninoff, with whom he was on the closest terms and who valued his work more than any other contemporary composer's, Medtner was uprooted from his native land, but unlike Rachmaninoff he brought with him no already-celebrated name. But for occasional concert appearances and recordings, Medtner devoted all his energy to composition, pursuing his vocation with almost religious fervour. Naturally he shared with Rachmaninoff a pathological distaste for modernism and he set down his creed on the artist's responsibilities in his book *The Muse and the Fashion* (1935), the last of the ten works published by Rachmaninoff's daughters' Paris publishing house Tair.[15] Medtner's almost complete lack of recognition except by a faithful band of acolytes and a handful of connoisseurs is a heinous crime against musical justice. His music, which has a strong vein of western classicism lacking in Rachmaninoff, is akin to his friend's in its beauty and fastidious craftsmanship, yet in no way derivative from it.

Like Medtner, Rachmaninoff left Russia after the 1917 Revolution and thereafter incurred the displeasure of those for whom anything that was not 'progressive' stank of dry rot. For some critics it was as if he lacked the respectability and importance conferred by death at the same time as being too old and too outmoded to merit the interest of the moment; for many music lovers, on the other hand, he represented the last bastion of musical civilization, under siege by the barbarian hordes of modernism. In the interwar period this schism was almost, but not quite, total.[16] A pointed but not unbalanced digest of the situation appeared in an article by Clinton Gray-Fisk[17] published to celebrate Rachmaninoff's seventieth birthday, in which a conspectus of critical comment was presented, with the perpetrators discreetly left anonymous:

> The most popular of all Rachmaninoff's works, the Second Piano Concerto, which has successfully survived every sort of performance for over forty years, was dismissed by one word, 'twaddle'. Another critic informed us that the same concerto '. . . is the sort of thing that any pianist and orchestra could extemporise by the yard.' The Fourth Concerto also received its fair share of abuse and after its first performance was immediately dubbed the 'Three Blind Mice' Concerto because of the slow movement's superficial resemblance to the tune. The superb Rhapsody, Op. 43, naturally came in for a chorus of critical cat-calls (with the honourable exceptions of Ernest Newman and Sorabji), such as 'lacks a

really musical foundation', 'trite to the verge of cheapness', 'just a concert piece for the composer's playing, and the day for that sort of thing is past', 'quite unimportant, very little distinction or originality', and 'even more threadbare than the Fourth Concerto; Rachmaninoff as a composer has not progressed one jot since his First Concerto, Op. 1'. The great Third Concerto, Op. 30, too, was soundly trounced; and our pundits described it as 'half-an-hour of padding', 'genteel vulgarity', 'definitely not highly distinguished music', 'not one of his most characteristic works', etc., the last movement being alleged to suffer from 'sectional form, inventive laziness and vamping'. The Second Symphony has been described as 'the best impersonation of good music I have heard'. The Third Symphony 'made an effect of purposelessness'. And of his work in general we read that 'one need not place Rachmaninoff's musical ideals higher than the literary ideals of a novelist of the second rank'; 'his invention failed him at the same time as the society into which he had been born crumbled under his feet'; 'he seems to have begun life with a large roll of effectively patterned musical material from which he has cut off so many yards for a concerto, even more for a symphony, and short strips for pieces'; 'a life-long failure to think of inspired and clinching ideas is unlikely to repair itself after the age of sixty'; and that 'it is synthetic music poured from a jug'. And to crown all this one writer goes so far as to prophesy: 'I doubt if posterity will rank him higher than Raff or Paganini!' (Can anyone imagine the possibility of a Raff or Paganini festival?) As for 'posterity', it is worth noting that in a recent plebiscite in America, when people were asked which living composers are most likely to be performed a hundred years hence, Rachmaninoff was given third place, the first and second being Sibelius and Strauss.

Rachmaninoff's apologists looked around in angry bewilderment for possible reasons behind such immoderate critical spite. Gray-Fisk himself probably hit the mark in putting it down to temperamental antipathy, pointing to Rachmaninoff's isolation from so-called fashionable modernist cliques; Rachmaninoff's biographer Riesemann had earlier argued that musicians with dual careers as composers and professional pianists, like Rachmaninoff, are viewed by critics with suspicion if not animosity,[18] a point already made by the Parsee composer and critic Kaikhosru Sorabji:

It is a cliché of the cheaper kind of criticism, especially in England and America, that a man cannot be a great interpretative and a great creative artist. When, like Liszt and Busoni, he is both, and in both respects of the highest order, the lie has to be bolstered up at all costs, and we see a deliberate campaign of denigration and belittlement set going against his creative work, which is dubbed 'virtuoso-music', 'pianist's music', and so on, quite regardless of honesty, fairness or truth.[19]

The term 'composer-pianist' used to be applied pejoratively to the great Romantic virtuosi of the nineteenth and early twentieth centuries, most of whom composed more or less trivial pieces to include in recital programmes otherwise given over to the works of other composers. From the distant past the names of Leschetizky, d'Albert and Chaminade come to mind, and of Rachmaninoff's great contemporaries those of Hofmann, Godowsky, Rosenthal, Levitzki and Friedman. Though by no means all their music was without merit (especially in the case of Godowsky), the stigma of the second-rate attaching to composer-pianists has never been entirely erased, and with varying degrees of justification composers such as Anton Rubinstein, Dohnányi, Paderewski and Busoni have arguably all received less than their deserts from critics. Yet it can easily be forgotten that Mozart, Beethoven, Schumann, Liszt, Debussy, Bartók, Prokofiev and Benjamin Britten, among others, were all also composer-pianists, and although they confined themselves almost totally to performing their own works, so did Rachmaninoff for the first forty-five years of his life, the period during which by far the largest part of his creative activity took place and his fame as a composer was at its height.

Whatever the reasons for Rachmaninoff's reputation among professional critics having sunk so low, it declined still further after his death. Sorabji devoted a whole chapter of a book to a counter-attack,[20] but prejudice, contempt and ignorance were all ingloriously combined in the patronizing and by now notorious article by Eric Blom in the fifth edition of *Grove's Dictionary*, appearing in 1954, which replaced an innocuous if ludicrously obsolete sketch by Rosa Newmarch in the fourth edition. Blom wrote:

> As a composer [Rachmaninoff] can hardly be said to have belonged to his time at all, and he represented his country only in the sense that accomplished but conventional composers like Glazunov or Arensky did. He had neither the national characteristics of the Balakirev school nor the individuality of Taneyev or Medtner. Technically he was highly gifted, but also severely limited. His music is well-constructed and effective, but monotonous in texture, which consists in essence mainly of artificial and gushing tunes accompanied by a variety of figures derived from arpeggios. The enormous popular success some few of Rachmaninoff's works had in his lifetime is not likely to last, and musicians never regarded it with much favour. The third pianoforte Concerto was on the whole liked by the public only because of its close resemblance to the second, while the fourth, which attempted something like a new departure, was a failure from the start.

The article in *Grove* is important because it remained holy writ for so long and enshrined prejudices and misconceptions that were rehashed in different contexts again and again over the years. However, it should be said that Blom, who also despised Mahler and Richard Strauss but, paradoxically, admired Medtner, was not putting forward merely his own paranoid viewpoint but reflecting a general opinion of the time, one which lingered on, at least in the English musical establishment, for a generation.[21]

Meanwhile, Rachmaninoff's music, far from suffering the long-expected demise, refused to lie down. In the 1950s and 60s, with the advent of long-playing records, there was an explosion of musical interest generally, and soon a Romantic revival was underway. Rachmaninoff's less familiar works, previously loved only by the faithful few, began to get an airing and gain wider acceptance; in particular, through the proselytizing efforts of conductors like André Previn, his symphonic music at last began to come into its own. A new generation of critics began to disinter 'masterpieces' which their predecessors had helped to bury. *The Bells*, the *All-Night Vigil* and other works of Rachmaninoff were reconsidered, and along with Elgar, Mahler and others, the composer began to win unwonted critical approval as well as public popularity.

The Rachmaninoff centenary in 1973 was celebrated modestly. In his own country a commemorative concert at Moscow Conservatoire with the USSR State Symphony Orchestra under Yevgeny Svetlanov included the *Symphonic Dances*; Eugene Ormandy and the Philadelphians performed *The Bells*; London contented itself with a chamber concert. There was a conspicuous lack of commemorative books and articles,[22] which, in an age obsessed with reappraisal, perhaps meant that Rachmaninoff had at last shed the accretion of clichés attached to him for so long by both detractors and apologists and had reached the stage when his work was accepted on its own merits.

References

1 For a succinct history in English of early Russian music see: *History of Russian Music, Vol. 1, From its Origins to Dargomyzhsky*, by Gerald R. Seaman, pub. Blackwell, Oxford, 1977. On a monumental scale the two classic accounts are: *Ocherki po istorii muzïki v Rossii s drevneishikh vremen do kontsa XVIII veka*, by Nikolay Findeisen, 2 vols., Moscow, 1928/29, and *Annales de la Musique et des Musiciens en Russie au XVIIIᵉ siècle*, by R. Aloys Mooser, 3 vols., Geneva, 1948 and 1951.

2 The first collection of authentic Russian folksong was the four albums of eighty songs compiled by Vasily Fyodorovich Trutovsky, published over the years 1776–1795. The collection of Ivan Prach, famous for being quarried by Beethoven for the 'Razumovsky' Quartets and by Rossini, appeared in 1790.

3 The first Russian opera by a native composer was *Anyuta* (1772), probably by V.A.Pashkevich (the music is lost); the first preserved intact is Zorin's *Pererozhdeniye* ('The Regeneration'), dating from 1777, which is based partly on folk melodies.

4 Except for a few months' study in Berlin with Siegfried Dehn, subsequently teacher of Anton Rubinstein, when he was 29 years of age, and again in 1856, the year before he died, Glinka had no serious professional music training.

5 The nickname 'The Mighty Handful' was coined by Vladimir Stasov in a review of a concert in Petersburg on 24 May 1867, conducted by Balakirev, at which the latter's *Overture on Czech Themes* and Rimsky-Korsakov's *Fantasy on Serbian Themes* were first performed.

6 At Petersburg the absence of Russian-born staff employed by the new conservatoire seemed deliberate policy; the famous Polish pedagogues Theodor Leschetizky (1830–1915) and Henryk Wieniawski (1835–1888) headed the piano and violin faculties; aesthetics, history, theory and composition were in the hands of English, German and Italian tutors.

7 *Vladimir Stasov, Selected Essays on Music*, translated by Florence Jones. Barrie & Rockliff, The Cresset Press, London, 1968, p. 83.

8 *Riesemann*, p. 68.

9 A good example of this paradox is the fugal exposition of the first movement of Balakirev's Piano Sonata.

10 *Rimsky-Korsakov*, p. 418.

11 Taneyev's study of counterpoint appeared in published form after twenty-two years' labour; his work on canon was unfinished after fourteen years, at his death. *Convertible Counterpoint in the Strict Style* has been translated into English by G. Ackley Brower, and published by Bruce Humphries, Boston, Mass., USA, 1962.

12 *Rimsky-Korsakov*, pp. 382 and 384.

13 R. to Slonov, 14 December 1892.

14 Victor Belaiev (*sic*): 'Sergei Rakhmaninov', in *Musical Quarterly*, Vol. 13, 1927, pp. 375–376.

15 *The Muse and the Fashion* was translated by Alfred J. Swan and published in 1951 by Haverford College Bookstore, Haverford, Pennsylvania, USA.

16 See, for example, the disdainful article on Rachmaninoff by Paul Rosenfield in *The New Republic*, 15 March 1919, pp. 208–210, or Edward Sackville West's dismissive review of the Second Symphony in *The Spectator*, 20 September 1924. For the other side see Richard Holt's appreciative article on Rachmaninoff in the January 1929 issue of *The Gramophone*, correspondence for and against after a review of *The Isle of the Dead* in the same periodical, November and December 1931, January 1932, and a letter from Robert Woodfield in the November 1938 issue, begging the question, 'Who is the greatest living composer?'

17 *Musical Opinion*, April 1943, pp. 221–222.

18 *Riesemann*, p. 247.

19 *Sorabji*, p. 59.

20 'Rachmaninoff and Rabies' in *Mi Contra Fa*, by Kaikhosru Sorabji, Porcupine Press, London, 1947.

21 When Geoffrey Norris's book on Rachmaninoff in the 'Master Musicians' series was reviewed in the *Musical Times* of December 1976, the review was given the patronizing title 'Master Rachmaninoff'.

22 The only commemorative review in English of the composer's work seems to have been 'Sergei Rachmaninoff, 1873–1943' by Stephen Walsh in *Tempo*, No. 105, June 1973.

Chronological Summary of Rachmaninoff's Principal Compositions

First Period

Student years

1890-91	First Concerto
	Elegiac Trio in G minor
1891	*Russian Rhapsody*, for two pianos
	'Youth' Symphony
	Prince Rostislav, symphonic poem
1892	*Aleko*, opera

Free Artist

1892	*Prelude* and *Oriental Dance*, for cello and piano, Op. 2
	Five *Fantasy Pieces*, for piano (including Prelude in C sharp minor), Op. 3
1892-93	Six Songs, Op. 4
	Fantasy-Pictures (First Suite), for two pianos, Op. 5
	Two *Salon Pieces*, for violin and piano, Op. 6
	The Crag, fantasy for orchestra, Op. 7
	O Mother of God Perpetually Praying, sacred concerto
	Six Songs, Op. 8
	Elegiac Trio in D minor, Op. 9
1893-94	Seven *Salon Pieces*, for piano, Op. 10
1894	Six Piano Duets, Op. 11
	Gypsy Caprice, for orchestra, Op. 12
1895	First Symphony, Op. 13
	Six Choruses, Op. 15
1896	Twelve Songs, Op. 14
	Six *Moments Musicaux*, for piano, Op. 16

Second Period

Moscow

1900-01	Second Concerto, Op. 18
	Second Suite, for two pianos, Op. 17
1901	Sonata for Piano and Cello, Op. 19
1902	*Spring*, cantata, Op. 20
	Twelve Songs, Op. 21
1902-03	Variations on a Theme of Chopin, for piano, Op. 22
1903	Ten Preludes (first set), for piano, Op. 23
1903-04	*The Miserly Knight*, opera, Op. 24
1904-05	*Francesca da Rimini*, opera, Op. 25
1906	Fifteen Songs, Op. 26

Dresden

1906-08	Second Symphony, Op. 27
1907-08	First Piano Sonata, Op. 28
1907	*Monna Vanna*, opera
1909	*The Isle of the Dead*, symphonic poem, Op. 29

Ivanovka

1909	Third Concerto, Op. 30
1910	*Liturgy of St John Chrysostom*, Op. 31
	Thirteen Preludes (second set), for piano, Op. 32
1911	Nine *Études-Tableaux* (first set), for piano, Op. 33
1912	Fourteen Songs, Op. 34
1913	*The Bells*, choral symphony, Op. 35
	Second Piano Sonata, Op. 36
1915	*All-Night Vigil*, Op. 37
1916	Six Songs, Op. 38
	Nine *Études-Tableaux* (second set), for piano, Op. 39
1917	Revision of First Concerto, Op. 1

Third Period

New World

1921-41	Various piano transcriptions
1926	Fourth Concerto, Op. 40
	Three Russian Songs, Op. 41
1931	Variations on a Theme of Corelli, for piano, Op. 42
	Revision of Second Piano Sonata
1934	Rhapsody on a Theme of Paganini, Op. 43
1935-36	Third Symphony, Op. 44
1940	Revision of four early piano pieces
	Symphonic Dances, Op. 45
1941	Revision of Fourth Concerto

2 Rachmaninoff's Composing Career and Musical Style

Rachmaninoff's life as a composer is divided naturally into three main periods, not by a once-statutory convention of music criticism but by two traumatic events: the disastrous premiere of his First Symphony and the Bolshevik Revolution. In terms of opus numbers, the first period, 1886–1897, covering his years as a student at Moscow Conservatoire and immediately after as a graduate 'Free Artist', stretches as far as the *Moments musicaux*, Op. 16; the second, 1897–1917, in which activity as a composer was divided between Moscow, Dresden and the beloved family estate of Ivanovka, runs from the time of the Second Concerto up to the second set of *Études-Tableaux*, Op. 39; the third, 1917–1943, the period of self-imposed exile, comprises Ops. 40–45.

Between 1886 and 1892, as a student at Moscow Conservatoire, Rachmaninoff essayed a wide range of composition. However, with few exceptions, these early pieces are to be seen merely as experimental exercises rather than as fully-fledged productions on their own; Rachmaninoff himself allowed only a few of the later of them to appear in print,[1] although virtually all of them were edited and published in the Soviet Union in the years immediately after World War II. They do, of course, reveal the early influences on the composer's creative evolution and the growing strength of his musical personality, but they are also interesting for the way in which the range of genres and instrumental combinations they cover defined the limits of growth for almost the whole of Rachmaninoff's subsequent development: the concertos, symphonies and other works for orchestra, the operas, songs and instrumental pieces of his maturity all have precedents in his student years.

Rachmaninoff's progress through the conservatoire was effortlessly brilliant and unfaltering. At the premiere of his First Concerto he confidently overruled the conductor, the fearsome martinet Safonov, who happened also to be the conservatoire's Director; twice he was granted special dispensation to bypass graduation regulations, as Scriabin was not; his graduation opera *Aleko* made his name famous overnight, and his music began to be published. In the history of Russian music only Glazunov had experienced such uninterrupted success so young, and at this stage in his life Rachmaninoff lacked the strength of character to cope with it. In his arrogance he was impervious even to constructive criticism from his elders and betters, whether from Arensky about *Aleko*, Rimsky-Korsakov about the First Suite for Two Pianos, or Taneyev about the First Symphony. Inevitably, sooner or later, nemesis was bound to strike. Just as he had cried like a spoiled child on finding his piano temporarily inaccessible when he wished to begin composing *Aleko*, so five years later he was psychologically devastated by the failure of the First Symphony. One wonders what Chaliapin made of him privately at this period, when they first met at the Mamontov Private Opera; the contrast between his own background of poverty, struggle and hardship and Rachmaninoff's easy success could hardly have been more stark.

Pampered from infancy by Grandmother Butakova, given free rein during boyhood by his parents after they were estranged, cosseted by friends and relations in his bohemian first years of manhood, Rachmaninoff had never needed, up to this point in his life, seriously to struggle, and this shows itself in the way in which works of the first period have a tendency to lapse into unsubtle dramatization and empty rhetoric, expressing emotions that seem contrived and not a direct reflection of personal experience. The *Elegiac Trio*, Op. 9, written as a memorial tribute to Tchaikovsky on his death in 1893, typifies this weakness: although the minor key is there and the appropriately sorrowful gestures, and although in this case the sincerity of feeling cannot be doubted, the overall effect is oppressive rather than moving. Other works of this period are facile and superficial (Piano Pieces, Op. 10), gushingly sentimental (*Élégie*, Op. 3, *Romance*, Op 10), or self-evidently not the product of any urgent internal creative need (Piano Duets, Op. 11). Some, however, are strikingly beautiful (certain of the songs), or show remarkable promise (*Aleko*); one of them (First Symphony) is a failed near-masterpiece.

The interim that followed the symphony's disastrous premiere marks the transition to Rachmaninoff's second and most productive period of composition. A comparison between works of similar genres composed before and after this time shows that the step forward in the quality of musical raw material transcends the development of technique that naturally went with it. For example, of the six piano *Moments musicaux* of 1896 Rachmaninoff himself played only one in public, the most effective, No. 2, in E flat minor; the five he disregarded, unmemorable and repetitive, have been all but ignored by other pianists too.[2] The

Preludes of 1903, on the other hand, have a much wider expressive range, more invention, more 'urge', and melodically are far more memorable (most notably those in G minor, B flat, D, E flat and G flat major). Similarly, the Second Suite for Two Pianos (1900–01) is much richer in material than its predecessor (1893), and the E minor Symphony (1906–08) is more affecting than the D minor (1895). In general it can be said that Rachmaninoff's later music explores depths of feeling touched earlier only in the best of the songs.

Rachmaninoff's enhanced powers of composition went along with an increased maturity and stability of character, helped, no doubt, by his marriage in 1902 to his cousin Natalya Satina. Artistic success and popular favour, both as composer and interpreter, resumed their brilliant course, a disagreeable if spurious rivalry with Scriabin, and bouts of melancholy self-doubt, casting occasional shadows. Although based in Moscow, but interrupting his career there for a three-year stay in Dresden in search of the peace and solitude he needed for composition, Rachmaninoff always found his greatest satisfaction and inspiration at Ivanovka, his wife's family's estate in Russia's southern steppe, where the majority of his output was either conceived or worked on. It was in these years that the composer wrote his most important music and the works most loved by the concert-going public and by which in the main his name lives today: the Second and Third Concertos, the Second Symphony, the bulk of the piano music and songs. Though no startling change in style can be observed over this period, after Rachmaninoff's return from Dresden a steady development did take place: the characteristically luxuriant lyricism begins to give way to a terser style, and there is a definite movement towards greater chromaticism in the writing. A comparison between the Preludes of 1910 and the two sets of *Études-Tableaux* (1911 and 1916), no less than between the two sets of songs, Op. 34 and Op. 38, immediately makes this clear. Another change of direction is the renewal of interest in religious music, hinted at before but at last coming to glorious fulfilment in two master-works, the *Liturgy* (1910) and the *All-Night Vigil* (1915).

In his professional career in the big cities Rachmaninoff was insulated from the harsh political and social realities of the Russia around him by the privileges of fame, and in his private world by life as a gentleman farmer. Ivanovka was Rachmaninoff's Cherry Orchard, a sanctuary in a maelstrom of change; thus, the boundary of his third and final period as a composer is marked by the Bolshevik Revolution of 1917. Uprooting himself from his homeland, he had to find a new means of supporting his wife and two young daughters. The role he found, as a concert pianist, brought him even greater material prosperity than before but only, from the point-of-view of posterity, at a high price. The physical links with the Russian land, people and culture, from which had come the stimulus to compose, were broken for ever, and his vital creative juices were somehow sapped by the pressures of a new career and an alien environment. The works of this period – only six major compositions in twenty-five years – reflect Rachmaninoff's changed circumstances and morale in exile. For all their many qualities and the abundant evidence they provide that his skill as a composer, far from diminishing in his last years, remained as masterly as ever, these works all lack something of the warmth of feeling so typical of his earlier, though not his final, Russian compositions. Qualities already hinted at in these last works are here much more evident: there are elements of brusqueness and astringency in the Fourth Concerto, austerity in the Three Russian Songs, emotional anaemia in the Corelli Variations; the *Paganini Rhapsody*, except for the famous Eighteenth Variation, is conspicuously unsentimental. The passages of bitter nostalgia in the Third Symphony and his swan-song, the *Symphonic Dances*, are backward glances at a vanished world.

In leaving Russia Rachmaninoff lost not only his sounding-board but also his pre-eminent place in his country's musical life. Abroad there was little incentive to compose, least of all when, in so short a time, he achieved a supremacy as an executant that was recognized throughout the musical world. Composers temperamentally different from him, such as Medtner and Gretchaninov, were able, even in exile, to add to the catalogue of specifically Russian music, such as songs and religious music, but not so Rachmaninoff. The Three Russian Songs (1926) were not original compositions, and the composer's only other attempts at song in the last twenty-five years of his life – three tiny sketches, two of which still await publication – were also merely arrangements. The one vocal recording in which he played the piano part was never issued commercially; the record company's apparent excuse, that there was no market for songs in an incomprehensible language like Russian,[3] must have been a powerful disincentive to further effort. As for church music, this was another area now closed to him because of its limited relevance and negligible potential audience abroad. The composition over a relatively brief period in Rachmaninoff's last years in Russia of his two major religious works, not to mention the sketching of two religious songs in the year before he left, perhaps hints that a blossoming interest in this direction may have been peremptorily stifled by the change in circumstances.

Apart from the Three Russian Songs, the kinds of work Rachmaninoff chose to write in exile are, without exception, international in appeal: a concerto, two sets of variations, two symphonic works, and some piano transcriptions, mostly of works by Austro-German composers who, at least in his Russian years, would have seemed very unlikely candidates for Rachmaninoff to choose – Bach, Kreisler, Mendelssohn, Schubert. It is significant that, unlike the vast majority of his Russian works, neither the *Paganini Rhapsody*, the Third Symphony, nor any of the transcriptions bears a dedication; it is as though, outside of the Philadelphia Orchestra, his compatriot Medtner and friend Kreisler,[4] he had no-one for whom he could write but himself, but this was not enough. 'For seventeen years,' he said in an interview in 1933, 'since I lost my country, I have felt unable to compose. When I was on my farm in Russia during the summers, I had joy in my work. Certainly I still write music – but it does not mean the same to me now.'[5]

It is of course true that the pressures of a full-time career as a concert pianist severely limited the time and energy Rachmaninoff might otherwise have devoted to composition, and he often claimed that he could cope with only one activity at a time. Like Mahler before him, he had to relegate composition to the summer months only, but in the early years of exile he had to use that time to work up piano repertoire. Even when he had achieved a position of financial security and artistic pre-eminence in his new career, he continued to need to add to that repertoire and to recuperate from the strain of concertizing. There are many references in Rachmaninoff's letters to his exhaustion at the end of a season, and he grew impatient and dissatisfied with himself for not composing, looking for excuses for having neglected what he felt was the responsibility of a creative artist. Nevertheless, his heavy annual concert schedules must have been made with his own connivance, or even at his express request; indeed, he once went so far as to describe his concerts as his 'only joy'.[6] 'I think,' wrote Alfred Swan, friend of Rachmaninoff in the later years, 'that if the urge to compose had been stronger and the lure of the concert platform not quite so strong, he would have overcome all the obstacles.'[7] The uncompromising Medtner in private put the matter more bluntly: 'He prostituted himself for the dollar;'[8] but then the high priest guarding the sacred flame was bound to see Rachmaninoff's withdrawal from composition and his temporal success as no venial sin.

Rachmaninoff was painfully aware of his own predicament:

Perhaps it is that I am lazy; perhaps the incessant practice and eternal rush inseparable from life as a concert artist takes too much toll of my strength; perhaps I feel that the kind of music I care to write is not acceptable today. And perhaps my true reason for adopting the life of an interpreter rather than that of a creator in recent years is none of these. For when I left Russia, I left behind me my desire to compose: losing my country I lost myself also. To the exile whose musical roots, traditions and background have been annihilated, there remains no desire for self-expression.[9]

There is a conspicuous lack of any mention of Rachmaninoff's self-imposed exile in his letters, and yet we know from the evidence of family and friends that the pain of the loss never left him. Although the wound could not be healed, it was periodically salved by contact with other Russians, but neither his continued association with Chaliapin, nor his contact with expatriate men of letters, such as the poet and novelist Ivan Bunin, nor his closer friendship with Medtner, acted as a creative catalyst. 'Perhaps no others can understand the hopeless home-sickness of us older Russians,' Rachmaninoff remarked in America in 1933;[10] 'even the air in your country is different. No, I cannot say just how.' But his predicament was no different from that of so many Russians abroad throughout history.

> The air of foreign lands does not inspire me, because I am a Russian, that is to say, the least suited man to be an exile, to be in an alien psychological climate . . . Look at those compatriots of mine who are living abroad; they are drugged with the air of their country. There's nothing to be done about it; they will never get it out of their systems . . . I must again immerse myself in the atmosphere of my homeland; I must once again see real winter and spring . . . I must hear Russian speech and talk to people of my own flesh and blood, so that they can give me back what I lack here, for their songs are my songs . . .[11]

It was Prokofiev who spoke these words, in the same year, 1933, and in a similar situation, but Rachmaninoff had just the same feelings.

The mark of Rachmaninoff's nationality is the most obvious single characteristic of his music. Rachmaninoff himself explained it very simply: 'I am a Russian composer, and the land of my birth has influenced my temperament and outlook. My music is the product of my temperament, and so it is Russian music.'[12] Ernest Newman put the point more forcefully:

> Superficially he is perhaps less national than the composers who coquet with Russian folk music. But in a deeper sense he is perhaps more national than they; his sombreness is the purest vintage of a wine that is to be found only in the more pessimistic of the Russian poets. He is more truly in the line of the pure Russian culture succession than Borodin or Rimsky-Korsakov, who often wrote as if Russian literature hardly existed.[13]

The peculiarly Russian quality of every bar Rachmaninoff wrote originates from within the music rather than being imposed from without by what Medtner dismissively used to call 'ethnographical trimmings'.[14] Rachmaninoff makes virtually no use of Russian folk music and yet, as Medtner again said, '[He] is so profoundly Russian himself that he has no need of folk music.'[15] Paradoxically, it is in the physiognomy of his lyricism that Rachmaninoff displays his nationality most obviously, particularly in the great, seemingly endless, arching melodies, which are so notable a feature of many of his works, from the 'big tune' in the last movement of the First Symphony of 1895 all the way to the saxophone melody in the first *Symphonic Dance* of 1940. Such extended melodies have enormous emotional power, though at least for some they are not without an element of enervation that is perhaps a legacy of the Moscow in which Rachmaninoff grew to adulthood and spent so much of his musical life, an ambience of which the critic Sabaneyeff gave a graphic if overblown description:

> [Moscow] was an artistically bohemian milieu with a strong bourgeois colouring. Moscow musicians gave themselves up to life's amusements considerably more than the musicians of St Petersburg. The famous Moscow restaurants, the no less famous gypsy choruses, the atmosphere of continuous dissipation in which perhaps there was no merriment at all but, on the contrary, the most genuine, bitter and impenetrable pessimism – this was the milieu. Music here was a terrible narcosis, a sort of intoxication and oblivion, a going off into irrational planes. Drunken mysticism, ecstatic sensations against a background of profound pessimism permeating existence. It was not form or harmoniousness or Apollonic vision that was demanded of music, but passion, feeling, languor, heartache. Such was Tchaikovsky's music and such also the music of Rachmaninoff developed into.[16]

Certainly Rachmaninoff did not emerge entirely unscathed from this debilitating environment, and his music does reflect the melancholy soul of someone preoccupied with the darker side of life. Rachmaninoff felt himself old and done for long before his time. In his correspondence, even in his twenties, morbid unhappiness and melancholy are recurrent themes. In his mid-thirties, having achieved success in all three of his musical careers and with material prosperity and a happy family life, he chose Böcklin's 'Isle of the Dead' as the subject of a tone poem. Not yet forty he complained urgently of ageing,[17] and his outward demeanour, reflecting this mental state, caused some of his younger contemporaries to nickname him 'starík', 'the old man'. In 1923 he wrote to his secretary: 'I take pleasure in deducting the passing days from my life's account'.[18] In his fifties, as a wandering emigré, having at last decided to build a permanent home in Switzerland as some kind of substitute for his beloved Russian estate, whilst writing to his sister-in-law a first, cheerful report about the progress being made by the builders, he could not forbear remarking that he had thought of a place where he could be buried.[19] In his last decade the spectre of death became still more insistent, the loss of Chaliapin particularly affecting him; Mrs. Rachmaninoff has described how the macabre graveyard scene at the beginning of the film 'Frankenstein' drove the composer in terror from the cinema.[20]

In keeping with this sombre view of life, it is not surprising that the medieval plainchant from the Requiem Mass, *Dies irae*, insinuated its way, in some form or another, into so many of his compositions. Before

Rachmaninoff, it had been used as a death motif by Liszt in the 'Dante' Symphony and as the basis of his *Totentanz*, a work which Rachmaninoff himself both conducted and once played. It also appears in the last movement of Berlioz's 'Fantastic' Symphony, another work which Rachmaninoff conducted and one which made a special impression on him during his first visit to America in 1909, in rehearsal under Mahler.[21] Among Russian composers who used *Dies irae* are Mussorgsky and Tchaikovsky, the former in his *Songs and Dances of Death* and in *Night on the Bare Mountain*, which Rachmaninoff several times conducted, the latter most notably in the fourth variation of the finale of the Third Suite for Orchestra, and less overtly in the middle of the last movement of the Fifth Symphony, two other works in Rachmaninoff's conducting repertoire.

It is probably true to say that *Dies irae* figures more prominently in Rachmaninoff's work than in that of any other composer, alive or dead, and yet Rachmaninoff himself left no clue about the reason for his apparent obsession. Even as late as 1931 he seems to have had only a hazy knowledge of its origin and significance,[22] though this is not altogether surprising in view of the fact that *Dies irae* came from the tradition of the Catholic and not of the Orthodox Church. Although Rachmaninoff associated *Dies irae* literally with death in a number of his works, most notably *The Isle of the Dead* and *The Bells*, its outline often occurs, like a natural mannerism, even when there is no obvious extra-musical connection.

Rachmaninoff's fascination with *Dies irae* naturally implies that his philosophy of life must have been fatalistic, and yet, while this is certainly true, his fatalism did not express itself in a morbid terror at the inevitability of death – for whether in *The Isle of the Dead*, *The Bells*, or the *Symphonic Dances*, death brings release and peace – so much as in the poignant realization that all human happiness is ephemeral. Significantly, this truism is the message of his song *Fate*, written in the fallow period after the disastrous failure of his First Symphony, when all his hopes for his future as a composer had been dashed; but then, as twenty years later, when fate struck again and he lost his native land, Rachmaninoff found within himself the strength of will with which to fight back. Moreover, at least in his last works, he came to treat *Dies irae* with even a certain degree of insouciance. In both the final movement of his swan-song, the *Symphonic Dances*, and the coda of his previous work, the Third Symphony, the manner of its setting is buoyantly confident, as though Rachmaninoff had at last come to terms with the implications of the motto which had haunted him for so long.

The apparent preponderance of minor keys in which Rachmaninoff chose to write is not the unequivocal evidence of a one-tracked melancholy mind it at first seems, for although it is true that all three symphonies, four concertos and the *Paganini Rhapsody* are in the minor key, not to mention fourteen out of seventeen *Études-Tableaux*, two sonatas for piano and one for cello and piano, one half of the Preludes and no fewer than thirty-four of the eighty-three songs in the Soviet collected edition are in the major key, and a further nine end that way. In his music as in his life Rachmaninoff could be slyly humorous (*Polka de W.R.*, *Paganini Rhapsody*), light-hearted (*Polichinelle*, *Oriental Sketch*), even exuberant (first movement of *The Bells*).

Although in his bohemian youth Rachmaninoff was probably little touched by the spiritual message of religion, the services in the cathedrals at Novgorod and St Petersburg, to which he was taken as a young boy by Grandmother Butakova, left an indelible mark on his music. The Orthodox Church laid down that, in order to avoid jarring intervals between adjacent notes, liturgical music should move by adjacent steps in the scale, and it is in the gently undulating contours of many of Rachmaninoff's most characteristic melodies – the mottoes of the Second and Third Symphonies, the opening themes of the Second and Third Concertos are but four of many examples – that its influence is most pervasive. The chanting of church choirs is imitated in the closing pages of both *Aleko* and the cantata *Spring*, and the ancient chants themselves provided the thematic material of the First Symphony. The composer's more serious view of religion in later life culminated in two major religious works of his own, and a passage from his *All-Night Vigil* was borrowed for use in the last of the three *Symphonic Dances*. But Rachmaninoff's consciousness was penetrated no less by the sound of church bells, which ring out in many of his compositions, whether written in Russia (First Suite for Two Pianos, Preludes, Op. 32, Second Sonata), Dresden (Second Symphony) or even Italy (*The Bells*).

Alongside the sounds of religion the incongruously contrasting music of gypsy singers also left a permanent impression on Rachmaninoff, as it did on so many Russian writers and musicians. The composer's friend Alexander Goedicke recalled how even in Rachmaninoff's daily life these two elements co-existed naturally:

> He loved church singing very much and quite often, even in winter, would get up at seven o'clock in the morning and hail a cab in the darkness, mostly to drive to the Taganka, to the Andronyev monastery, where he stood in the half-darkness of the enormous church through the whole of the liturgy, listening to the austere ancient chants from the *Oktoekhos*, sung by the monks in parallel fifths . . . It commonly happened that on the same evening he would go to a symphony concert . . . and then, more often than not, go on to have supper at the restaurant Yar or the Strelna, where he would stay late into the night, listening with great enthusiasm to the singing of the gypsies.[23]

These two elements, religion and gypsyism, can be heard juxtaposed in that pivotal work of Rachmaninoff's early career, the First Symphony.

The influence of gypsy music on Rachmaninoff is twofold. The element of pathos, heard in its most unrefined form in the overtly gypsy works, *Aleko* and *Gypsy Caprice*, but also in some of the early songs and piano music, becomes purified with time and assimilated into the composer's natural and deeper melancholy. It is interesting that in later life Rach - maninoff so much prized Chaliapin's recording of the popular song 'Black Eyes' precisely because of the affecting sob at the climax[24] – the feature above all others which epitomized the art of the gypsy singer. The other aspect of gypsy music that left its mark on the composer, its wild abandonment and excitement, is also heard in a raw and untamed state in the early works, such as the First Concerto, but more subtly and discreetly in the finales of the later concertos and symphonies.

Rachmaninoff's early works all proclaim their harmonic ancestry from Tchaikovsky, Arensky and Taneyev, but from the time of the Third Concerto (1909) hints began to appear in the more chromatic harmonies of the influence of the later compositions of Rimsky-Korsakov. Rachmaninoff's growing admiration for the composer was probably also responsible for the increased transparency of his orchestration in later years. In works of the first period it tends to be bright but unsubtle, and although the second period sees an added richness of sonority to complement the heightened emotional power of the music, in some places, as in the Second Concerto and Second Symphony, the textures tend towards denseness. Despite the still more massive orchestra used in *The Bells*, there is a welcome move in this work in the direction of greater clarity, which is yet more evident in the compositions of Rachmaninoff's last period, so that the third is the most transparently scored of all the symphonies, and the fourth orchestrally the least cluttered of the concertos.

In considering Rachmaninoff's style, it is important to remember that both domestically and musically he lived his life in a kind of ghetto. In his private world he was self-contained with his family and a small circle of friends, generally remaining aloof from social contact, whether at his isolated estate in southern Russia or back in Moscow, where his remoteness from everyday affairs allowed him to rewrite his First Concerto apparently oblivious even of the noise of the gunfire of revolution. The loss of his country in middle age and a change of career did not significantly change the manner of his private life after 1917 when, as a refugee, he was driven back still more on his powers of self-reliance. Musically he became even more isolated; except in his professional life, Rachmaninoff's meetings with other composers and performers were only casual social encounters and never occasions for serious musical discussion. The two well-documented meetings with Stravinsky in 1942 passed without a word spoken about their lives' main occupation, composition.[25] Even Medtner, whose work he admired so much, failed to break down the barriers of reticence.[26] With a temperamental abhorrence of all contemporary music from Prokofiev on, Rachmaninoff remained stylistically almost impervious to the musical world of the twentieth century, though he was by no means unaware of what was going on around him.

In an interview he gave less than two years before his death Rachmaninoff affirmed his creed as a composer:

> Composing is as essential a part of my being as breathing or eating; it is one of the necessary functions of living. My constant desire to compose music is actually the urge within me to give tonal expression to my feelings, just as I speak to give utterance to my thoughts. That, I believe, is the function that music should serve in the life of every composer; any other function it may fill is purely incidental. I have no sympathy with any composer who produces works according to preconceived theories or with the poseur who writes in a certain style because it is the fashion to do so. Great music has never been produced in that way – and I dare say it never will. Music should, in the final analysis, be the expression of a composer's complex personality. It should not be arrived at mentally, tailor-made to fit certain specifications – a tendency, I regret to say, all too prevalent during the past twenty years or so. A composer's music should express the country of his birth, his love affairs, his religion, the books which have influenced him, the pictures he loves. It should be the product of the sum total of a composer's experiences. Study the masterpieces of every great composer and you will find every aspect of the composer's personality and background in his music. Time may change the technique of music but it can never alter its mission.[27]

Practising such a philosophy so far into the twentieth century Rachmaninoff may justifiably be considered the last important composer in the Romantic tradition. In the circumstances of his life it is not surprising that he had no students or protégés, nor that his influence on other composers has been virtually nil. His music is *sui generis* and, in that the composer's personality establishes itself unmistakably within only a few bars, it unquestionably deserves the epithet 'original', even if not in the profound sense that applies to the seminal works of greater masters, such as Mussorgsky or Debussy. Living to become a relic from the past in an alien world, Rachmaninoff continued to give expression to personal feelings in his compositions in an age when, after Stravinsky, emotion in music had become unfashionable if not taboo. 'Music must first and foremost be loved,' he once said;[28] 'it must come from the heart and it must be directed to the heart. Otherwise it cannot hope to be lasting, indestructible art.' In the years since Rachmaninoff's death his music has triumphantly proved its durability, and it is a measure of his considerable achievement that in a troubled and changing world his distinctive message continues to strike home to music lovers of all ages everywhere, with undiminished effect and relevance.

References

1 *Aleko*, the First Concerto, Op. 1, the *Prelude* and *Oriental Dance* for cello and piano, Op. 2, and three of the Six Songs, Op. 4.

2 Medtner and Horowitz occasionally performed *Moment musical* No. 3, in B minor; Moiseiwitsch, No. 4, in E minor; Richter, No. 6, in C major.

3 Sofiya Satina, *VR/A* 1, p. 73.

4 The Three Russian Songs and *Symphonic Dances* are dedicated to Leopold Stokowski and to Eugene Ormandy and the Philadelphia Orchestra, the Fourth Concerto to Medtner, the Corelli Variations to Kreisler.

5 R. interview with H.E. Wortham in *Daily Telegraph*, 29 April 1933.

6 *Swan*, p. 186.

7 Ibid., p. 180.

8 Medtner in conversation with Wilfrid van Wyck.
   Medtner told Alfred Swan, 'If Rachmaninoff could only become a ne'er-do-well, if only for a short time, then he would again begin to compose. But he is tied hand and foot by his obligations; everything with him is measured by the hour.' *Swan*, p. 7.

9 'The Composer as Interpreter', R. interview by Norman Cameron in *The Monthly Musical Record*, November 1934, p. 201.

10 R. interview in *New York Evening Post*, 26 December 1933.

11 'Prokofiev, An Intimate Portrait', article by Serge Moreux in *Tempo*, No. 11, Spring 1949, pp. 5–9.

12 *Ewen*, p. 848.

13 Ernest Newman, quoted in *Hallé*, No. 117, 1960/61, pp. 11–12.

14 Nikolay Medtner, *VR/A* 2, p. 350.

15 Alfred J. Swan, *Russian Music*, John Baker, London, 1973, p. 172.

16 *Sabaneyeff*, pp. 105–6.

17 R. to Marietta Shaginyan, 8 May 1912.

18 R. to Yevgeny Somov, 27 January 1923.

19 R. to Sofiya Satina, 8 August 1931.

20 Mrs Rachmaninoff, *VR/A* 2, p. 320.

21 *Riesemann*, p. 160.

22 Conversation with Joseph Yasser, *VR/A* 2, p. 356; also quoted in *B/L*, p. 278.

23 Goedicke, *VR/A* 2, pp. 11–12.

24 See *B/L*, p. 233.

25 *B/L*, p. 374; Neil Turney: *The Unknown Country, A Life of Igor Stravinsky*, Robert Hale, London, 1977, p. 146.

26 *Swan*, p. 7.

27 *Ewen*, p. 804.

28 Ibid., p. 808.

The Rachmaninoff Family Tree

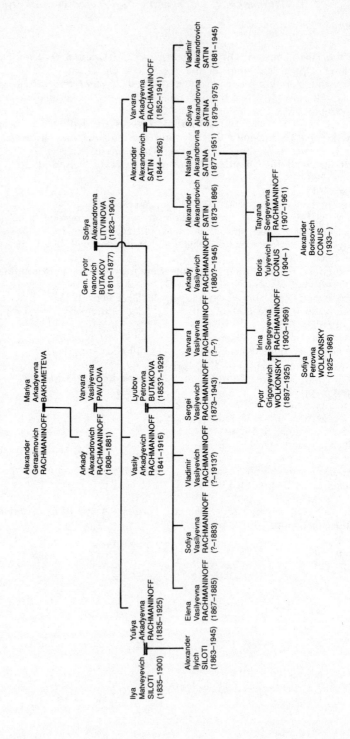

3 Student Years, 1886–1892

The case of Rachmaninoff helps to confirm the opinion of those who assert the importance of inheritance in the possession of musical gifts, for three generations of Rachmaninoffs on the composer's father's side were musically talented to an unusual degree. Rachmaninoff's great-grandfather Alexander Gerasimovich and his wife Mariya Arkadyevna, to whom the minor composer and Intendant of the Imperial Chapel Nikolay Bakhmetev (1807–1891) was related and who is said to have studied music 'with the best teachers of that time',[1] instituted a choir and orchestra on their Znamenskoye estate. Alexander Gerasimovich died young and Mariya Arkadyevna remarried, but the children of both marriages seem to have shared her musical talent. Her son, Arkady Alexandrovich Rachmaninoff, the composer's grandfather, was a devoted amateur musician, whose wealth deprived him of the necessity of turning his hobby into a profession. A pupil of John Field and a prolific composer of light piano pieces and songs, he played the piano every day of his life and often took part in charity concerts. Rachmaninoff dimly recalled once playing duets with him when he was four years old. The composer's father, Vasily Arkadyevich Rachmaninoff, was another enthusiastic pianist who may also have composed or at least improvised. One of his sisters wrote: 'He used to play the piano for hours, not familiar pieces but God knows what',[2] and Rachmaninoff himself carried away the mistaken impression that the polka by Franz Behr he had heard him play, and of which many years later he made a concert arrangement, the *Polka de W.R.*, was his father's own work. No-one, then, should have been altogether surprised when Rachmaninoff, like his sister Elena before him, showed a precocious talent in the family tradition.

Rachmaninoff's first music teacher was his mother. Despite being better placed than anyone to recognize her son's preternatural gift, she seems to have failed to do so, but when it was brought to her attention by the children's governess, she engaged a friend of hers who happened also to be a student of St Petersburg Consevatoire, Anna Ornatskaya, to give formal piano lessons. When the amiably feckless Vasily Rachmaninoff had squandered his wife's fortune, the family moved to St Petersburg, and for three years from 1882 Rachmaninoff continued his studies on a scholarship at the conservatoire. Although he worked hardly at all, his idleness at first escaped detection. He spent his summer holidays with his Grandmother Butakova, and it is in the final two halcyon summers of 1884 and 1885, at Borisovo, her estate near Novgorod, that the first glimmerings of the nascent composer may be discerned, for we are told that he improvised at the piano to entertain guests and ascribed the pieces to famous composers.[3] When his laziness as a student at Petersburg had at last been exposed and his musical training urgently reassessed, he was sent to Moscow to become a full-time boarding pupil of the renowned piano pedagogue Nikolay Sergeyevich Zverev. In 1886, after the first year, Rachmaninoff and his two fellow 'cubs', Matvey Pressman and Leonid Maximov, were taken for the summer holiday to the Crimea, where they were given lessons in basic harmony by a young teacher from Moscow Conservatoire, Nikolay Ladukhin, whose tuition may have been instrumental in prompting Rachmaninoff's first essay at composition, an *Étude* in F sharp, two pages long, which has not survived. Pressman, to whom Rachmaninoff dedicated his piece, sets the event during the Crimean holiday; Riesemann, presumably reporting the memories of the composer himself forty-four years on, puts it in Moscow the next year.[4]

In the autumn of 1886 Rachmaninoff entered Arensky's harmony class at the conservatoire and soon, quite independently, began to study his first orchestral score – Tchaikovsky's 'Manfred' Symphony, premiered in Moscow just six months before. Out of admiration for the composer Rachmaninoff decided to make a four-hand piano transcription of the work, and when it was completed Zverev gave him the opportunity to play it (with Pressman) in Tchaikovsky's presence. Although this juvenile act of homage did not survive, Rachmaninoff's close involvement with the symphony at this time may in retrospect explain the occasional apparent echoes of it in his own music, and the last movement almost certainly provided the young musician with his first encounter with what was to become the *idée fixe* of his creative life, the plainchant *Dies irae*. Moreover, Tchaikovsky's symphony may well have sown the seeds for Rachmaninoff's own orchestral work on the same Byronic subject four years later, and the study of orchestral scoring may at least have prepared the way for his own next work.

The Scherzo in D minor for orchestra is Rachmaninoff's earliest dated composition, the title page of the autograph score bearing the date '5–21 February 1888', with the year 'corrected' in an unknown hand to

'1887',[5] which improbably places the work only two or three months after the composer's initiation into the mysteries of orchestration. The heading on the manuscript, 'Third Movement', suggests at first sight that the Scherzo was at one stage earmarked as part of an unrealized larger project, presumably though not necessarily a symphony, but it may have been added later, and not even by Rachmaninoff himself. The musical material is as unsophisticated and derivative as is to be expected at this stage, and there is no hint in it of any of the characteristic features of the mature composer. In overall conception the work is all too obviously indebted to the Scherzo from Mendelssohn's incidental music to *A Midsummer Night's Dream* to stand by itself, and its main interest is its demonstration of the young composer's precocious ear for orchestral timbre.

The earliest surviving piano piece of Rachmaninoff is probably the so-called 'Song Without Words' in D minor, reproduced from memory by the composer in 1931 for Riesemann's biography and described there as one of ten written as an exercise for Arensky's harmony class at the end of the academic year 1886–87,[6] though the examination at the end of the course, at which Rachmaninoff played these pieces for Tchaikovsky, did not take place until a year later, in May 1888. Unlike the orchestral Scherzo, whose key it shares, far from having the Mendelssohnian overtones its title implies, the piece is imbued with Russian melancholy to a degree perhaps unnatural in a boy so young, though in retrospect this can be seen as a portent of the kind of emotional world the mature composer was to make so much his own:

Ex.1

Rachmaninoff's next extant compositions – the three piano Nocturnes, written between November 1887 and January 1888 – mark a striking advance on this juvenile academic exercise, though the models used by the young composer are all too clearly visible in their musical material and pianistic style. The first, in F minor, long and rhapsodic in structure, belies its name by reflecting not Chopin but Tchaikovsky and Rubinstein in its pronounced Russian character; the chordal climax of its bravura middle section, on the other hand, recalls the end of the first movement of Brahms's Second Piano Sonata, though this is doubtless fortuitous, as Rachmaninoff is most unlikely ever to have encountered the work.[7] The theme of the main section of the second, in F major, is reminiscent of the Intermezzo from Borodin's *Petite Suite*, whilst the third, in C minor, after an incongruous six-bar slow introduction, has an *allegro moderato* transition which thematically and pianistically re-processes Schumann. Like the other Nocturnes, though admirably written for the instrument, it is episodic, improvisatory and too long for its musical interest, but in its last and main part, before the music peters out (the last page of the manuscript is missing), Rachmaninoff succeeds in creating a genuinely tragic atmosphere. By any standards the depth of feeling expressed by a youth of only fourteen is surely astonishing, and Rachmaninoff's precocity must have severely startled an unsuspecting Zverev:

Ex.2

Another set of student piano pieces – *Romance, Prelude, Mélodie* and *Gavotte* – is also marked 1887 on the manuscript, though not in the composer's hand.[8] A later date is strongly suggested not only by the fact that Rachmaninoff himself at one stage thought them mature enough works to mark as his 'Opus 1', along with a group of songs positively dated 1889–90, but by the sheer extent of their musical superiority over the Nocturnes. Although there are growing hints of the individuality of the adult composer, the influences still at work are undisguised. The *Romance* in F sharp minor is reminiscent of a Chopin nocturne in its melodic line, whilst the *Prelude* in E flat minor is somewhat melodramatic, in the manner of the early works of Rachmaninoff's conservatoire contemporary Scriabin, with a rapid triplet figure making a third voice in the middle section, pointing forward to the polyphony of the mature composer. The *Mélodie*, not only sharing the title but anticipating the key of its better-known cousin from Op. 3 of 1892, has a fragrant Tchaikovskian plaintiveness. The final *Gavotte*, in 5/4 time, is high-spirited, and its insistent tonic chords hammered home at the end provide another link with Op. 3, reappearing as they do in minor form in *Polichinelle*. The characteristically Arenskian metre invites the thought that Rachmaninoff's teacher may have been an influence here, in particular his well-known *Basso ostinato* from the set of piano pieces Op. 5, written only a few years before:

Ex.3a   Rachmaninoff: *Gavotte* (1888?)

Ex.3b   Arensky: *Basso ostinato*, Op.5, No.5 (1884)

A composer who may just possibly be a distant influence on all these early pieces is the now forgotten Adolf Henselt (1814–1889), whose oratorical gestures, salon charm and melodramatic clichés, embodied most familiarly in two books of piano *Études*, so pleased nineteenth-

and early twentieth-century audiences. Since 1838 he had lived in St Petersburg, where he had become court pianist and earned a lucrative livelihood as a teacher. Zverev himself had been one of his pupils, and while there is no hard evidence that he singled out his teacher's music for the especial attention of his 'cubs', it was presumably at Zverev's suggestion that Rachmaninoff played Henselt's D major *étude* at a student concert in 1886. As more than thirty years later, when Rachmaninoff had taken up the career of a concert virtuoso, several items in his repertoire seem to have chosen themselves precisely because they were works he had played as a young student, his famous performance (and recording) of Henselt's *Si oiseau j'étais* may also reflect exposure to the composer during the years when his own early piano pieces were being written.

The only extant work that can be dated with certainty to the new academic year 1888–89 – though others that have not survived must surely have been attempted – is a six-page piano score of fragments from a projected opera set to an unidentified text based on Victor Hugo's dramatic novel *Notre Dame* and, like the setting Dargomyzhsky made of the same work in the 1830s, called *Esmeralda*,[9] after the gypsy girl rescued by Quasimodo. There is an introduction to Act 1, and sketches for three scenes from Act 3, dated 17 October 1888; an instrumental prelude followed by a recitative in which the priest, Claude Frollo (bass), tricks the old woman, Falourdelle (mezzo-soprano), into letting him look over her lodging house, where Esmeralda is to have an assignation with the rake Captain Phoebus; three lines of a theme evidently representing Frollo; and an entr'acte, probably depicting Notre Dame itself, in which for the first time in Rachmaninoff's music the ringing of bells sounds out clearly. There is nothing musically significant in any of these youthful sketches, but there is a surprising foretaste of the mature composer in the theme associated with Frollo, which unmistakably looks ahead to the Prelude in G sharp minor of 1910 (Ex. 4a and 4b).

In the spring of 1888 Rachmaninoff had moved on to the senior department of the conservatoire to continue his piano studies with his cousin Siloti, but in the end-of-year examinations in musical theory he was awarded the highest possible mark, a 5+, so effectively deciding for him that his future career in music would primarily be as a composer. Thus, in the autumn of 1889 he found himself joining Taneyev's class in counterpoint and Arensky's in harmony and orchestration.[10] Needing privacy for his work, he approached Zverev to ask for a room of his own, inexplicably prompting a furious argument.[11] Zverev arbitrarily severed relations, and a month later Rachmaninoff moved in with the Satin family, an event more momentous for his personal life than he

Ex.4a   *Esmeralda*

Ex.4b   Prelude, Op.32, No.12

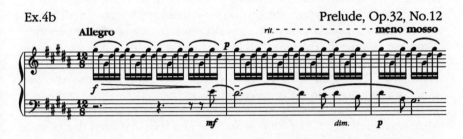

can ever have imagined at the time. It is interesting, if fruitless, to speculate on what might have been the outcome if at this stage in the life of the future composer and pianist he had acceded to his mother's request and returned to St Petersburg where, remote from Moscow and the orbit of Tchaikovsky and his followers, he might have studied composition with Rimsky-Korsakov and piano with Anton Rubinstein, who had resumed teaching at the conservatoire and whose pupil he might have become three years before Josef Hofmann.

In November 1889, about the time he joined the Satin household, Rachmaninoff set to work on a two-piano draft of the first movement of a piano concerto in C minor, which, however, he abandoned after a substantial fourteen pages. The opening theme is in the 'pathetic' vein of early Scriabin:

Ex.5

This is not far removed in mood from the opening of Rachmaninoff's 'official' First Concerto, in F sharp minor, begun only seven months later and demonstrating similar heroic gestures and youthful passion to these sketches. To judge from the numerous corrections and crossings-out, including no fewer than seven deleted pages of cadenza, the material proved intractable and the scope of the project beyond the capacity of the as yet inexperienced sixteen-year-old composer.[12]

Also dated 1889, albeit in the 'unknown hand', are two quartet movements in simple ternary form: *Romance* and *Scherzo*. Although Rachmaninoff left the quartet in this incomplete state, the fact that he allowed a performance of a version for string orchestra at a student concert two years later seems to show that he cannot have thought too badly of the two movements as they stood. However, even in the catalogue of Rachmaninoff's student works the quartet is something of an oddity, and the apprentice composer is unlikely to have undertaken it except as an assignment from Arensky, just as it was almost certainly at the prompting of Taneyev that he made a second and final attempt in the medium seven years later. In both cases the restraint of the writing for the unfamiliar, if not for him alien, combination of four stringed instruments alone seems somehow to have effaced the composer's personality, and the contrast between the restraint and lack of enterprise in Rachmaninoff's chamber writing and the rich sonorities and flamboyant gestures of his later piano and orchestral textures is stark indeed. The *Romance* unfolds a melody of drooping Russian melancholy to contrast with a plaintive Tchaikovskian theme in the middle section, the muting of the four instruments nearly throughout adding to the whimpering effect. In the *Scherzo*, the opening theme, reminiscent of the piano Gavotte of two years before, has a certain attractive vigour, but the sombre trio section, with violin and viola solos accompanied unvaryingly by plucked strings, is grey and uninteresting. There is no mistaking the influence of Borodin in the turns of phrase in the brief coda.

In the spring of 1890 the composer made his first surviving choral setting, a six-part motet of only thirty-one bars to a Latin text, *Deus meus*,[13] composed in two days under examination conditions as a graduation test-piece in counterpoint. Although the work was awarded a top mark of '5', Rachmaninoff himself had a low opinion of it, later even going so far as to describe it as 'trash',[14] a judgement, it has to be admitted, only mildly unkind to what was never more that an arid academic exercise. The motet was nevertheless performed the next year by the conservatoire chorus under the baton of the composer, making his conducting debut.

Rachmaninoff spent the summer of 1890 at the Satin family estate of Ivanovka, situated 250 miles south-east of Moscow near Tambov, the regional centre, conveniently on the main railway line from Moscow to Saratov. This was his first visit to what was to become his beloved summer retreat and an irreplaceable source of spiritual refreshment over the next twenty-seven years.[15] Among the many guests were Rachmaninoff's cousins, the three Skalon sisters, with whom he enjoyed an adolescent flirtation, and it was to the youngest, the fifteen-year-old

Vera Skalon, for whom he later came to entertain deeper feelings, that he dedicated his gravely melancholic *Romance* in F minor for cello and piano, written in August and the very first piece in what was to become a long catalogue of Ivanovka compositions. Rachmaninoff may also have written a more extended companion piece for the same instruments at this time, or at least 1890 is the date assigned to what has been entitled '*Mélodie on a theme by S. Rachmaninoff*', an arrangement by the conductor Modest Altschuler of a theme on a manuscript given him by the composer but lost long before its posthumous publication. The major works begun this summer, however, were the First Piano Concerto, whose slow movement, it has been fancifully suggested,[16] may also have been inspired by Vera Skalon, and a four-hand piano transcription of Tchaikovsky's *Sleeping Beauty*, Rachmaninoff's first paid musical commission, from the publisher Jurgenson. This work caused the young composer considerable trouble and had to be taken in hand by Siloti. Rachmaninoff's transcription, like others of its kind, languished even before the appearance of easily available gramophone recordings of the orchestral original made such versions redundant, though not before a commercial pianola roll had been made of the Waltz.

Returning in the autumn for the new term at the conservatoire, Rachmaninoff embarked on a suite based, like the Tchaikovsky symphony he had transcribed four years before, on Byron's 'Manfred'. We know from his correspondence with Natalya Skalon that the work made rapid progress and that by the beginning of January it had been orchestrated,[17] but all trace of it has unfortunately vanished. Indeed, outside of these letters there is no evidence for its ever having existed.

In 1890 and 1891 Rachmaninoff wrote two six-hand piano pieces for the Skalon sisters. The first, a brief *Waltz*, based on a theme composed by Natalya Skalon and dedicated to her, is no more than agreeable salon music, but the extended *Romance* of a year later is of a very different character, for this touching love song is the first example in Rachmaninoff's work of the kind of tender, lyrical outpouring that became characteristic of the mature composer. Moreover, it contains clear musical pointers to this later style, for not only is the introductory accompaniment figuration identical to the opening of the slow movement of the Second Concerto, written nine years later, in 1900–01, but a harmonic sequence in the coda was borrowed, not quite so literally, for the similarly named *Romance* of the Second Suite for Two Pianos, written at the same time as the concerto. It is interesting that some twenty years after the composition of these two pieces of juvenilia, when their existence was still known only to the dedicatees, the composer asked Natalya Skalon to return the manuscripts so that they could be destroyed, but the sisters kept them for sentimental reasons and the works were published only after Rachmaninoff's death[18] Perhaps Rachmaninoff, by then married to the formidable Natalya Alexandrovna, feared that the existence of what might be seen as a youthful musical love letter might be a source of embarrassment; we can only guess. Originally, possibly in imitation of the layout of Arensky's well-known Suite for Two Pianos, Op. 15, recently premiered by Taneyev and Siloti, which comprised a Romance, Waltz and Polonaise, Rachmaninoff apparently likewise intended to add to his two pieces a concluding Polonaise to make a three-movement suite,[19] but this was never written.

Nine Rachmaninoff songs in all appear to have survived from the time when the composer was a student at Moscow Conservatoire. The three best were later incorporated in his first published group, Op. 4; the others remained unpublished during his lifetime.

		Date on MS or copy	Text
1	*At the gate of the holy abode*	29/ 4/1890	Lermontov
2	*I shall tell you nothing*	1/ 5/1890	Fet
3	*In the silent night* (Op. 4, No. 3)	17/10/1890	Fet
4	*April (C'était en avril)*	1/ 4/1891	Pailleron
5	*Twilight has fallen*	22/ 4/1891	Alexey Tolstoy
6	*Do you remember that evening?*	16/ 7/1891	Alexey Tolstoy
7	*Again you leapt, my heart*	–	Grekov
8	*Morning* (Op. 4, No. 2)	–	Yanova
9	*Oh stay, my love, forsake me not* (Op. 4, No. 1)	26/ 2/1892	Merezhkovsky

Just as the early set of four piano pieces had been earmarked as 'Opus 1', so the title page of a bound copy of the autographs of the first six songs in the State Central Glinka Museum of Musical Culture in Moscow bears the superscription by Rachmaninoff's student contemporary and life-long friend Mikhail Slonov 'Songs of S. Rachmaninoff, Op. 1'. In view of Rachmaninoff's attraction to the Skalon sisters, it is not suprising that all these early songs are about love, though mainly, and perhaps for the composer already characteristically, an unhappy or unrequited love.

The three earliest songs all show the youthful composer's indebtedness to Tchaikovsky. In *At the gate of the holy abode*, from a poem by Lermontov, the singer compares the situation of a beggar who, seeking alms, is offered a stone with his own position as a rejected lover.

Although the bitter melancholy of the lyricism reflects the general mood of the poem, Rachmaninoff's setting fails to throw light on any psychological detail. Fet's poem *I shall tell you nothing*, about a lover who will not declare his love but keeps his feelings to himself, had been set by Tchaikovsky himself four years before.[20] Rachmaninoff's superficially pleasant but somehow characterless version inevitably invites unfavourable comparison.

April is something of a curiosity in that it was set to a French text. Although we know from the *Recollections*[21] that Rachmaninoff became quite proficient in the language even in his childhood, and he was later to make settings of both German and Ukrainian poems in translation, this is the only song of his not set in Russian. The poem, by the satirical dramatist Édouard Pailleron (1834–1899), about a lover who recalls a fresh April day when he and his beloved embraced, had been published only two years before. In the song's posthumous publication it was given a Russian translation by V. Tushnova, in which it is now invariably performed. The vocal melody is rather anaemic, and the only point of significant musical interest is the falling harmonic sequence at the climax half way through, which repeats the formula used in the same place in *In the silent night*. The song loses nothing in its arrangement, in Soviet times, as a salon piece for violin and piano.

Next come two settings of poems by Alexey Tolstoy (1817–1875). In *Twilight has fallen* the poet tells how there came to him a vision of his beloved. Whilst fresh and attractive on its own account, the music adds nothing to the poem, and much the same may be said of *Do you remember that evening?*, recalling an occasion when two lovers rode in silence by the sea, their sorrows forgotten. Rachmaninoff himself was particularly and perhaps unnecessarily cutting about this song: 'It turned out very unsuccessfully . . . one of the least of my compositions . . . Believe me, dear Akimïch, as far as this song is concerned I became mildly desperate,' he wrote to Slonov, with characteristic self-deprecation.[22] The undated *Again you leapt, my heart*, to a poem by Nikolay Grekov (1810–1866), describing the passion inspired in the heart of a lover, is also almost certain to be another of Rachmaninoff's earliest songs, judged purely on musical grounds, though the physical evidence of the ink and paper of the autograph suggests a date of 1893.[23] However, the unvarying right-hand quaver chords of the piano part throughout the whole piece (evidently representing the heart palpitating), the unsubtle gestures of the vocal line and the harmonies characteristic of Rachmaninoff's years at the conservatoire all proclaim this to be the work of the apprentice composer.

Rachmaninoff was later clearly right not to publish the six student songs he chose to withhold, and there is no evidence that any of them was ever performed even at student concerts. At the time of their composition he had insufficient experience of life or culture to enable him to make more than a superficial and generalized response to the words of his texts. Thus, while the songs reveal a natural feeling for the voice, and the piano accompaniment is invariably idiomatic, if unsophisticated and not very interesting, the music itself, though often beautiful, too easily inclines towards choking sentimentality (*At the gate*) or factitious melodrama (*I shall tell you nothing*), and it rarely illuminates the poems chosen for setting.

There is one other setting to be appended to this early group – an arrangement for voice and piano of the folksong *The Barge Haulers*, dated 10 September 1891 and dedicated to a piano teacher at the conservatoire, Adolf Yaroshevsky (1863–1910). The melody comes from a Russian folk music collection published twenty-one years before.[24] The simple text tells, with much repetition, how the barge-haulers shout and pull throughout the autumn night, straining their necks against the east wind. Unpublished during the composer's lifetime, Rachmaninoff's arrangement became available briefly in a Soviet edition of 1944 but, being omitted from the later Collected Edition, is generally unknown. In much the same vein as *The Volga Boat Song*, it must have made a fine vehicle for Chaliapin, who is said to have sung it to the composer's accompaniment more than once.

Russian Rhapsody

After completing the orchestration of his 'Manfred' Suite, Rachmaninoff wrote to Natalya Skalon on 10 January 1891 that he had begun a piece for two pianos he wanted to play later that week with Siloti. This was his *Russian Rhapsody*, completed with typical Rachmaninoff facility four days later[25] and subsequently given its one and only public performance in the composer's lifetime at a student concert the following October, by Rachmaninoff and Joseph Lhevinne. With two such astounding technicians at the keyboard it is curious that the manuscript has a number of simplified variant readings by the composer, and that the second part is distinctly subservient to the first. The Rhapsody is really a set of eight variations (the *Paganini Rhapsody*, forty-three years later, was to be similarly misnamed), and it may have been prompted by a visit Rachmaninoff and some student contemporaries made to a Moscow piano factory, recalled many years later by Rachmaninoff's friend Vladimir Wilshaw.[26] While trying out one of the instruments, Yury Sakhnovsky strummed a Russian song, to which Rachmaninoff, on another piano, responded with a variation on it; Sakhnovsky answered in kind, and between them he and Rachmaninoff improvised a whole set of variations. Whether or not Sakhnovsky's theme was the one Rachmaninoff used in the *Russian Rhapsody* we have no means of knowing; it is certainly not such as one would expect Rachmaninoff to use, still less invent, and indeed it is so aggressively nationalistic that it might very happily have found itself in the works of Glinka or any of 'The Mighty Handful' rather than a young Moscow upstart. The Rhapsody divides naturally into five sections of contrasting tempi, but Rachmaninoff rarely varies the outline of the theme itself. In the fourth variation, however, its guise bears a distinct if fortuitous resemblance to the folk tune from Novgorod, *U vorot*, that Tchaikovsky used in his '1812' Overture:

Ex.6a   Rachmaninoff, *Russian Rhapsody*

Ex.6b   Tchaikovsky, '1812' Overture

More interesting is the plangent sixth variation, *Meno mosso*, where the theme is varied rhythmically and the mood is more thoughtful, but in general Rachmaninoff concentrates throughout the work on dazzling decoration and pianistic effect, and as the theme chosen is short-breathed and repetitive the piece begins to outstay its welcome by the last.

An untitled canon in D minor, preposterously dated to 1884 in the Collected Edition but more reasonably to 1890–91 in the Glinka Museum catalogue,[27] is Rachmaninoff's first extant solo piano work since the two sets of three years before. Most likely an exercise given him by Arensky, the piece has the terseness of a Chopin prelude and says all it has to say in little more than a minute. The writing itself is pianistically more idiomatic and harmonically more interesting than in Rachmaninoff's earlier piano pieces, as in this characteristic sequence (Ex. 7).

In comparison, the gentle but unaffecting lyricism of the presumably roughly contemporary Prelude in F major, dated 20 July 1891, is rather tame. However, the composer later thought the piece worthy of publication, albeit in a version for cello and piano, as part of his Opus 2.

Ex.7

Concerto (No. 1) in F Sharp Minor

In 1890 and 1891 Rachmaninoff composed his first major work, the First Piano Concerto, known to concert audiences today only in the revised version made more than a quarter of a century later. To judge from the date on one of the sketches, the composer started work on the first movement at Ivanovka on 8 June 1890, but he seems not to have completed the second and third movements until the following July, although evidently they were already composed in his mind.[28] Rachmaninoff himself gave the first performance – of the first movement only – at a student concert at the Moscow Conservatoire on 17 March 1892, with the orchestra conducted by the conservatoire's Director, Vasily Safonov. At first Rachmaninoff was 'pleased' with the concerto,[29] but at least by 1899 he had become dissatisfied with it, for when he was invited that year in London to play the concerto on a return visit he turned down the suggestion and promised to compose another work in the same form, declaring that the First Concerto was not good enough to be played there.[30] Despite statements in biographies and programmes to the effect that Rachmaninoff became discontented with the work after performing it many times,[31] there is no evidence whatever that he ever played the work again in its original form after its part-premiere, though his cousin Siloti did. Rachmaninoff's publisher Gutheil printed the score only in the two-piano arrangement, for domestic consumption, and the work had to wait eighty years for publication of the original full score.[32]

Surprisingly few Russian piano concertos existed before Rachmaninoff's. Tchaikovsky's First Concerto (1874) had been preceded only by Rubinstein's five (1854–1874), of which the Fourth and Fifth were popular items in the concerto repertoire, Rachmaninoff himself performing the first movement of the Fourth in February 1891 at a student concert and again in September the following year at the Moscow Electrical Exhibition. But the Tchaikovsky marked a dramatic advance on Rubinstein's Mendelssohnian lyricism, establishing not only an authentic Russian voice but a new kind of bold grandiloquence that the composer did not quite recapture in his Second Concerto (1880). Rachmaninoff's teachers, Taneyev and Arensky, disciples of Tchaikovsky, had both tried their hand at writing a piano concerto. Taneyev's, dating from 1876–77, was never completed, but Arensky's, published in 1881 as his Op. 2, was one of the works which had launched him on his career as a composer, and he may well have suggested to Rachmaninoff that he should tackle the same musical form at this early stage in his own career; indeed, there may be just a hint of correspondence between the openings of the slow movements of the Arensky and Rachmaninoff concertos in their melodic lines and scoring. The Petersburg group of composers, on the other hand, preoccupied with opera, had avoided concerto form almost entirely. Balakirev in his youth had sketched out a piano concerto movement in Chopin style but proceeded no further with the work, which was published only in Soviet times; what we know as his Concerto in E flat, although begun in 1861, was incomplete at his death and not published until 1911. It was the unlikely Rimsky-Korsakov, with his nationalist concerto of 1882, who had produced the most recent of Rachmaninoff's Russian precedents. Interestingly enough, the concerto which arguably influenced Rachmaninoff most turns out to be not Russian at all: at Ivanovka throughout the summer of 1890 Siloti happened to be practising the Grieg concerto,[33] and both its Lisztian rhetoric and elements of its formal design left their mark on the Rachmaninoff work.

The concerto opens impressively with an imperious fanfare and a cascade of triplet quavers in double octaves for the soloist. The idea is not original, for not only the Grieg but also the Liszt in E flat and Schumann concertos open with similar flourishes, but Rachmaninoff's gestures are altogether his own. Nor are they empty gestures, for the descending triplet figure is closely integrated into the movement's fabric, prefiguring, as it does, the end of the first theme (Ex 8). The second theme is sparked off by the rising four-note figure it shares with the first theme (Ex. 9).

One other element is introduced into the musical discussion, appearing

Ex.8a

First Concerto, opening

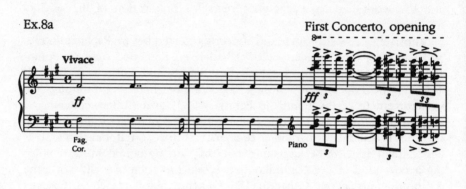

Ex.8b

1st theme

Ex.9

first in the development section and much used in the recapitulation –
a somewhat uninteresting figure of four descending semi-quavers, recalling
Chopin's A flat Polonaise in its insistent repetition:

Ex.10

Although this appears vaguely related to the piano figuration of the
transition, its appearance lacks the sanction of a proper connection with
the previous material. Before this section culminates in reference to the
concerto's opening, the four-note figure shared by the two themes is
worked up *poco a poco accelerando*, so that when the recapitulation
restates the first theme proper the transition has already perfectly
anticipated its opening. The cadenza to the movement is particularly
noteworthy. It neatly incorporates all the concerto's main material – the
descending quaver figure from the development and the two main
themes, in reverse order. It is prophetic of the mature composer in that
when the soloist comes to muse over the wistful second theme, the
music modulates to the calm of Rachmaninoff's so often favourite key
of D flat. If the piano writing is inevitably somewhat lacking in flexibility
and enterprise, seeming jejune in comparison with the composer's later
style, it nevertheless already demonstrates an intimate understanding of
the instrument's possibilities; musically, however, the grand gestures of
the coda are no more than empty rhetoric.

The second movement, an *andante cantabile* in D major, is a beautiful
nocturne, in mood at least again possibly showing the general influence
of Grieg's concerto. The melody is first sung by the piano and then
by the orchestra, while the soloist spins an exquisite decoration in the
triplet quavers that so often appear in Rachmaninoff's early works. The
direct lyrical appeal and simple structure of this movement make the
elaboration and striving after effect of the finale seem contrived. After
a tentatively quiet introduction in 12/8 time, the piano launches into a
wild dance in 9/8, in which added interest comes from the intriguingly
disjointed interjection of one bar of waltz rhythm back in 12/8. Two
other themes appear in the course of the movement: one, like its cousin
from the first movement, created from the repetition of a simple four-note
descending phrase emerging from the piano decoration, is not especially
interesting and comes to outstay its welcome, particularly through its
overuse at the end of the movement; the other, a pleasant lyrical theme,
usurps the role of a sonata development section and leads back directly
to a recapitulation of all the movement's musical material in the same

order as before. Rachmaninoff uses the lyrical third theme for the final grand climax, creating a precedent for the treatment of parallel themes in the same position in his later concertos. Here again he may have been influenced by the Grieg concerto, though, as is only to be expected with so youthful a work, his own melody does not yet contain within it either the emotional power or the expansive possibilities necessary for its pre-eminent role:

Ex.11

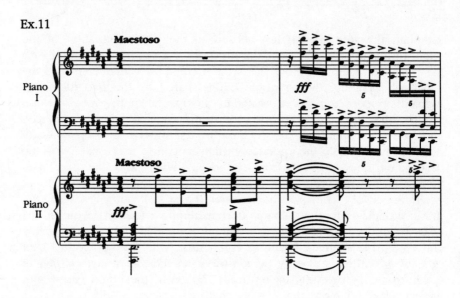

After this the soloist's double octaves continue relentlessly to the last bars, to bring the work to a suitably impressive conclusion.

Rachmaninoff's First Concerto is not only a remarkable achievement for a seventeen year-old, a work which can stand on its own feet and be judged on its own merits, but proof that the composer had come of age and that his own musical personality was emancipating itself from youthful influences. The nature of the concerto's themes, and particularly the 'pathos' of the main theme in the first movement, fixed a characteristically Rachmaninoff imprint on the work ten years before the Second Concerto confirmed the composer's image in the public's mind as a purveyor of sentiment and grand gesture. Though the revision twenty-six years later improved the work in every way (see pp. 277–286), the fact that Rachmaninoff returned to this youthful piece at all and retained most of the original material and structure is witness to the worth of the first version.

Elegiac Trio in G Minor

According to Sofiya Satina,[34] 1890–91 also saw the composition of the sombre and impassioned one-movement *Elegiac Trio* in G minor, though the manuscript bears the date 18–21 January 1892, possibly because it was touched up in preparation for the work's first public performance at the end of that month, in what was probably Rachmaninoff's first formal concert outside the conservatoire. The whole nature of the trio points to a less mature Rachmaninoff than the composer of the concerto, for there is a conspicuous lack of balance and judgement in both musical material and treatment. A sensitive and expressive opening is immediately undermined by the salon character of the second theme, and everywhere the power and brilliance of the piano part outbalances the uninteresting string writing. But the main problem is that the material is insufficiently substantial to sustain either the high emotional import attaching to it or, despite twelve changes of tempo, the repetition to which it is subjected, particularly as even the climax is unvaried in the recapitulation. Throughout the work the most important influence is still Tchaikovsky; the main theme is akin to that of his own *Elegiac Trio*, and a prominent string figure comes straight from the first movement of the 'Manfred' symphony:

Ex.12

The coda, marked '*Alla marcia funebre*', provides a pensive afterthought, as a funeral cortege seems to move away into silence. This seems to be merely a conventional musical gesture suited to the work's general nature rather than a personal reference, for there is no external evidence to substantiate the implication of the trio's title that the 'elegy' was for the loss of someone specific, as it was with Tchaikovsky's *Elegiac Trio* and with the second trio Rachmaninoff himself was to write only a year or two after this, to which he gave the same name.

'Youth' Symphony

In the autumn of 1890 a quarrel between Rachmaninoff's piano tutor, Siloti, and Safonov, Director of the Moscow Conservatoire, resulted in Siloti's resignation as from the end of the academic year, whereupon Rachmaninoff resolved to complete his piano course twelve months early, before Siloti left. He succeeded brilliantly in this, and returned the next year with the intention of doing the same in composition, compressing the final two years' study into one. Thus, what proved to be Rachmaninoff's final year at the conservatoire, 1891–92, was an intensive one, for in return for being allowed to graduate early Arensky required Rachmaninoff to submit a considerable number of compositions: a symphony, a number of recitatives and a complete opera. The symphony progressed with difficulty, but was eventually completed, at least according to the *Recollections*,[35] though all that survives is what appears to have been the first movement, in D minor. The manuscript is dated 28 September 1891, when Rachmaninoff was in Moscow with brain fever, but the movement was probably sketched at Ivanovka during the previous productive summer, when the First Concerto was completed, and at any rate some time after 10 August, when the composer wrote to Slonov to say that he had a new symphony in mind. If the *Recollections* are to be relied upon,[36] it was not until after his recovery that he asked Arensky to permit his accelerated graduation, in which case the movement we have could not have been written specifically for this purpose, though of course Rachmaninoff may have anticipated Arensky's demands. In Soviet fashion, like Balakirev's 'Youth Concerto', in its posthumous reincarnation in 1947 the movement was called 'Youth Symphony', to distinguish it from the official First Symphony, in the same key.

The movement is in traditional sonata form, with a *Grave* introduction based on three musical elements: a sombre motto on bassoons, cellos and basses, which looks back to Tchaikovsky's *Francesca da Rimini*; a menacing brass phrase, an idea which the composer re-used a few months later in slightly different form in his next work, the symphonic poem *Prince Rostislav*, as the Prince's motto; and a sinuous string figure, instinct with tragedy, which clearly anticipates the opening of the Second Symphony (see p. 182). Taken by itself this is all very impressive, but it turns out to have little to do with the rest of the movement. When the first subject arrives, it fails to measure up to the exalted mood of the introduction, and its line and scoring are the first hints of what becomes embarrassingly obvious as the movement proceeds, namely that Rachmaninoff was unable to emancipate himself from what was clearly the model for this work – the opening movement of Tchaikovsky's Fourth Symphony. The second theme has an ingratiating geniality, but when it reaches its final phrases, which are used as a pivot to introduce the development, further similarity to the Tchaikovsky work is revealed in the blatant borrowing of the dotted figure from its opening theme. The development itself, which also makes no attempt to disguise the model for its material and treatment, lacks direction and relies too much on factitious rising sequences; eventually, with nowhere to go, it peters out. The recapitulation starts abruptly, and at the end the brass fanfares that recall the scoring of the introduction curiously fail to refer to its material. The drama that concludes the movement is extorted unnaturally from the first subject, confirming the impression that the movement does not grow organically and that the musical argument lacks overall coherence. Indeed, the most impressive feature of the work may be said to be its idiomatic and assured orchestration, and it is therefore not surprising that this part of Rachmaninoff's graduation assignment satisfied neither Arensky, nor Taneyev, nor the young composer himself.[37]

Prince Rostislav

Much more successful and certainly deserving an occasional performance is the symphonic poem *Prince Rostislav*, which Rachmaninoff dedicated to 'dear Professor Anton Stepanovich Arensky'. Completed in December 1891, the work is based on a ballad of Alexey Tolstoy, and was perhaps prompted by a familiarity with the poet evidently acquired in the course of making song settings of two of his poems, 'Twilight has fallen' and 'Do you remember that evening?' earlier in the year. As with Rachmaninoff's work on *Manfred*, *Prince Rostislav* was first written in short score and orchestrated later,[38] a procedure which was to be the composer's regular practice throughout his life, right up to the time of the *Symphonic Dances*.

Rachmaninoff's poem divides into four clearly defined sections. The first depicts the eponymous hero of the ballad, a young prince who lies beneath the waters of the Dnieper, having been slain in battle;

Rachmaninoff gives him an appropriately melancholy and heroic brass motif against insistently surging triplets from the strings. In the second section, clearly influenced by earlier Russian musical watery legends – Rimsky-Korsakov's 'musical picture' *Sadko* and Balakirev's depiction of the Terek in his symphonic poem *Tamara*, published seven years before – a voluptuous Tchaikovskian theme depicts the nymphs who attend on the prince; they comb his golden hair and try to persuade him that he now irrevocably belongs to their realm. This motif already contains the seeds not only of the yearning main theme of *The Crag* of 1893 but even of the climax of *The Isle of the Dead* of 1909:

Ex.13

The third section opens dramatically with the prince's three cries of despair, given to strident trombones and tuba, as he calls to his young wife, his brother and the priests of Kiev. Against this motif the strings undulate in a vigorous dance rhythm, another appropriation from *Tamara*. This material is worked up into a great climax, culminating in a gong stroke, a gesture to be used again, five years later, at the end of the First Symphony. The fourth and final section brings back the prince's motif in a quiet and resigned form, against the strings playing a variation of the rippling water figure and with a last reference to the nymphs' theme. His appeals have gone unheard and he will rest forever in the Dnieper. The episodic nature of the story seems to have suited Rachmaninoff's organizational abilities at this stage better than symphonic structure, and the skilful and already characteristic way in which the orchestral forces are deployed to create darkly rich colours marks a significant step forward. Exhumed for a posthumous premiere in 1945, the work was played for the first time in Britain only in 1982.[39]

A number of fragments survive from Rachmaninoff's student dramatic projects, all of them undated, though, to judge by the nature of their musical material, they clearly come from the composer's last years at the conservatoire and thus possibly belong among the recitatives that Arensky demanded for graduation, even if only one strictly fits that definition – an impressively dramatic setting of Arbenin's Monologue from Lermontov's *Masquerade*, 'Night, spent without sleep', which requires a Chaliapin to do it justice. Then there is a fragment twelve bars long of a quartet from Pushkin's poem *Poltava*, which Tchaikovsky had set as an opera (*Mazeppa*) a few years before, and two monologues from the beginning of Pushkin's *Boris Godunov* which, in the declamatory writing for voice, clearly show the influence of Mussorgsky. In one, for bass voice, Boris addresses the patriach and boyars in the Kremlin as he accepts the crown of Russia – 'My soul is laid bare before you'; in the other, set for tenor, Pimen, the old monk, philosophizes as he writes his chronicles in his cell. The existence of three increasingly elaborate variants of the first monologue and two of the second suggests that Rachmaninoff reworked his material after tutorials with Arensky. In modern times, Pimen's Monologue has been given an overblown orchestration by V. Yurovsky, but even in this version the young composer's natural dramatic flair shines through. All these pieces promised well for the opera he was shortly to write.

As Seroff pointed out in his biography of Rachmaninoff,[40] gypsies were a vital element in Zverev's education of his protégés no less than in Russian culture generally, but their musical influence on Rachmaninoff has largely passed unremarked by commentators. Like many Russian musicians Zverev himself was greatly attracted by gypsy music, and in the course of preparing his 'cubs' for life he used to take them to the fashionable Moscow restaurants at which gypsy musicians played and stirred the Russian soul. Pressman describes a memorable party at Zverev's, attended by Maximov, Rachmaninoff and himself, at which a famous singer of gypsy songs, Vera Vasilyevna Zorina, entertained Zverev's guests, accompanied in turn by none other than Tchaikovsky, Taneyev, Arensky and Siloti.[41] In the years after leaving Zverev Rachmaninoff was often in the company of his one-time student contemporary Yury Sakhnovsky (1866–1930) – he lived with the Sakhnovsky family in the autumn of 1891, when he was ill – and it was through him that he was introduced, sometime in 1891 or 1892, to Pyotr Lodïzhensky and his gypsy wife Anna, whose sister Nadezhda Alexandrova was a well-known Moscow gypsy singer. This association had both personal and musical implications for the young composer, for naturally it not only exposed him even more widely to popular gypsy music but soon led to an infatuation with his 'darling Anna', as he called her, the first musical manifestation of which was the song he dedicated to her, *Oh stay, my love, forsake me not* (later published as No. 1 of Opus 4), in which there may be gypsy elements in the vocal line.[42] This piece was the last Rachmaninoff completed before his final and most important graduation task, the opera *Aleko*.

Aleko

In view of the natural leaning he had already shown towards dramatic setting, it is not surprising that Rachmaninoff was impatient to begin work on the opera as soon as the libretto was given him,[43] especially as it turned out to be on the congenial subject of gypsy life and was based on a work by his favourite poet, Pushkin; for the text was a version of Pushkin's dramatic poem '*The Gypsies*', compressed and otherwise modified by Vladimir Nemirovich-Danchenko (1858–1943), dramatist and co-founder with Stanislavsky of the Moscow Art Theatre, and distinguished producer under the Soviet regime.[44] 'The libretto has been done very well; the subject is marvellous. I don't know if the music will be marvellous!' remarked Rachmaninoff in a letter to Natalya Skalon on 23 March 1892. As with others of his early works, the composer wrote *Aleko* in an extraordinarily short time, evidently taking only twenty-four days to complete the entire orchestral score and leaving his two classmates and future life-long friends, Nikita Morozov and Leo Conus, far behind and still struggling with the assignment.[45] The subsequent award to Rachmaninoff of the conservatoire's Great Gold Medal, only the third in the history of the institution, became the happy occasion for his reconciliation with Zverev. Within a few months the vocal score of *Aleko* was published by Gutheil, and on 27 April the following year the opera was premiered at the Bolshoi Theatre in Moscow, alongside excerpts from operas by Glinka and by Tchaikovsky,[46] who was in the audience and whose ostentatious applause, Rachmaninoff later modestly maintained,[47] was largely responsible for the opera's success.

The single act in which the libretto is cast falls into thirteen separate numbers.

1 *Introduction.*
2 *Chorus.* The scene is a camp of Bessarabian gypsies late in the evening. The gypsies gather round their fires awaiting supper, celebrating the freedom of a nomadic outdoor life devoted to work and song.
3 *The Old Man's Story.* An old gypsy recalls how years ago his wife Mariula ran away with a young stranger from another tribe, leaving him alone and embittered with their young daughter Zemfira.
4 *Scene and Chorus.* Aleko, an outsider who joined the gypsies two years ago when he became Zemfira's lover, asks why the Old Man did not follow his wife and avenge her infidelity, as he himself would do in the same circumstances. Zemfira mocks him: 'Life must be free,' she argues; 'who can control love?' She tells her father that she is bored with Aleko, whose love is now repellent to her, and that she is attracted to a young gypsy. The latter boasts that he is not scared of Aleko, but the gypsies are by now weary of the story and turn instead to merry-making and dancing.
5 *Women's Dance.*

6 *Men's Dance.*

7 *Chorus.* The gypsies dampen their fires as the moon comes up.

8 *Duettino.* After kissing passionately the Young Gypsy and Zemfira arrange to meet again later; Aleko is seen lurking near. The Young Gypsy leaves and Zemfira returns to her tent, where she sits beside the cradle of her infant child.

9 *Scene by the Cradle.* Zemfira sings a song, ostensibly to her child, in which she taunts Aleko with being old; she despises him and loves another who is 'fresher than the spring and warmer than a summer's day'. 'But where is the pleasure of casual love?' asks Aleko. He tells her he has heard enough of her song.

10 *Aleko's Cavatina.* 'The whole camp sleeps.' As the moon rises Aleko recalls the passionate love that once existed between Zemfira and him; but now she is unfaithful and loves him no more.

11 *Intermezzo.* Daybreak.

12 *Song of the Young Gypsy.* Off stage the Young Gypsy serenades Zemfira, drawing a parallel between the motion of the moon and the fickleness of a young girl. Who will tell the moon to stop as she passes through the sky, spreading her radiance on all nature alike? Who will tell a young girl to be constant?

13 *Duet and Finale.* As it begins to grow light Zemfira is anxious to steal away immediately with the Young Gypsy before Aleko wakes up to find her gone, but the gypsy wants to stay to savour the moment and so they are surprised by Aleko, who bars their way. Zemfira tells him that he has grown hateful to her and that what has passed between them has gone forever. Despite appeals Aleko is mocked by his wife and her lover, and mad with jealousy he stabs his rival. Zemfira begs the dying man's forgiveness and laughs at Aleko's threats, whereupon Aleko stabs her too. The other gypsies arrive, disturbed by the noise. The Old Gypsy Woman instructs the men to go and dig graves and the women to file past the bodies and pay their last respects, while the Old Man declares that, although gypsies are savages with no code of laws or physical punishments, they cannot live with a murderer; they are timid and good people, whereas he is evil and daring. The gypsies steal away, and Aleko is left once again alone in the world.

Comparisons have been drawn between *Aleko* and Mascagni's *Cavalleria Rusticana*,[48] with which it has occasionally been staged,[49] another one-act work, written only three years before *Aleko* and staged at the Bolshoi Theatre in 1891 and in March 1892, just when Rachmaninoff was working on his opera. There are obvious parallels in the general themes of gypsy life and Sicilian village life, and in the crime of passion which forms the climax of both operas, but musically *Aleko* has nothing whatever in common with Mascagni's opera except for the use of an orchestral Intermezzo. Indeed in a sense *Aleko* should rather be seen as a distant relative of Bizet's *Carmen*; Mérimée, on whose novel *Carmen* was based, in fact translated and published Pushkin's poem along with his own work in 1846. Forty-six years later it can have been no easy task for Nemirovich-Danchenko to reconstitute 'The Gypsies' into material for a one-hour one-act opera suitable as a graduation exercise.[50] In compressing the already compact text into little more than one third of its original length, he excised its intellectual interest as a romantic poem – the implicit questioning of the values of so-called civilized society, where 'people are ashamed of love, persecute thought, barter their liberty, bow their heads before idols and beg for cash and chains', and the paradox of the Byronic hero Aleko himself, ardently espousing gypsy freedom but ultimately becoming its victim and proving himself incapable of bearing the full implications of sharing the life of a free community. Perhaps inevitably, the librettist conventionalized the drama by reducing it to a series of stock scenes, which the young composer then painted in primary colours.

Of thirteen items the Introduction is one of four for orchestra alone. It opens with two leitmotifs. The first, a forlorn theme on flutes and clarinets that reappears in the opera's final scene, depicts the gypsies. Its latter half, with its sinuous, eastern intonation, bears a distinct resemblance to Scheherazade's motif in Rimsky's orchestral suite, first performed three-and-a-half years before Rachmaninoff wrote his opera (Ex.14).

The other leitmotif, that of Aleko himself, a melodramatic phrase suggesting a character of turbulent passion, is used by Rachmaninoff almost indiscriminately, whenever Aleko appears or is mentioned (Ex. 15).

After a frenzied climax a third idea concludes the Introduction, a simple three-note phrase moving in repetition down the scale of D major, which has a wistfulness that looks back to the happier days of Aleko and Zemfira's love. A subtle point in the score is that it is this very phrase that Zemfira parodies in her song at the cradle, when she mocks Aleko (Ex. 16).

The other orchestral pieces are all attractive items in their own right. The two gypsy dances have rightly won an occasional place in ballet performance and the concert-hall, the Women's Dance for its seductive oriental appeal and the Men's Dance for its invigorating if unsubtle energy. Rachmaninoff noted in the score that the latter's theme was 'borrowed'. In fact it is an adaptation of a gypsy song called *The Golden Signet Ring*, which Gutheil had published in 1889. The Intermezzo perhaps best exemplifies the touches of bright orchestral colour to be

Ex.14

Ex.15

found throughout the score and which were no doubt influenced by the example of Arensky.

Each of the main characters has a set-piece, and these numbers contain some of the opera's best music: Aleko's *Cavatina*, which Chaliapin made so much his own; the *Old Man's Story*, profoundly Russian in its musical character; Zemfira's song in the *Scene at the Cradle*, powerful but somewhat relentlessly strident; the *Song of the Young Gypsy*, most attractive with its solo harp accompaniment; and the naively touching duet of the young lovers. Indeed, it can reasonably be argued that, despite their gaucheries, these pieces have a youthful freshness and ardour that Rachmaninoff never quite recaptured in his later music.

Ex.16a Introduction

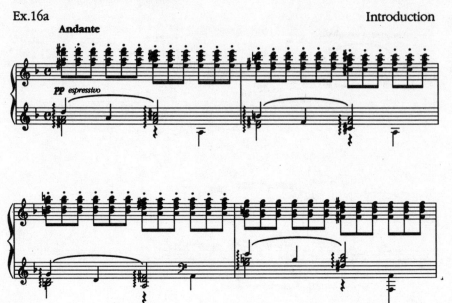

Ex.16b *Scene at the cradle*

[Old husband, grim husband, knife me, burn me.]

The last number, in which the dénouement is played out, is the longest in the score, but it compresses within its still modest compass a succession of situations that, in other circumstances and with a different libretto, might better have been expanded into a second act. The key of the Introduction, D minor, is re-established and much is made of the leitmotifs first heard there, of the gypsies and of Aleko. The incongruous appearance of a short *fugato* for the chorus suggests that the fondness for this technique Rachmaninoff showed later in the symphonies and elsewhere, doubtless acquired from Taneyev, was already implanted. The final choral dirge is clearly modelled on the monks' lament at the end of Mussorgsky's *Boris Godunov*, confirming the influence of that composer already evident in Rachmaninoff's settings of the monologues of Boris and Pimen. It is interesting that the very last line of the poem's epilogue (not in the libretto) warns us that against the fates there is no defence – almost a motto for Rachmaninoff's later philosophy of life.

Despite its auspicious launch and sporadic performances in the years before the close of the century, *Aleko* never gained a place in the regular operatic repertoire. Chaliapin, however, had a special affection for the opera,[51] his interest centering on the character of Aleko, behind whose mask he saw Pushkin himself (Aleko is a form of Pushkin's own name Alexander). At least in his later performances Chaliapin even appeared on stage dressed to resemble the poet, an interpretation thought inept by some, who were upset by the apparent absurdity of Pushkin killing Zemfira and the Young Gypsy. From Chaliapin's point of view, the opera needed altering to explain this anomaly and expanding to make an evening's entertainment by itself. His interest in the opera was renewed in the last years of his career, when he explained to Fred Gaisberg, HMV Recording Manager,[52] that he felt the work could be successfully revived if only Rachmaninoff added a prologue and second act. Chaliapin persuaded Gaisberg to relay this suggestion to the composer, with the promise that he would play the title role. Gaisberg did so, but Rachmaninoff dismissed the idea, adding that 'much water had run under the bridge since the days of *Aleko*'. In fact, it was not only in his later years that Rachmaninoff dismissed the opera as unworthy of him;[53] already by 1899 he had begun to forbid its staging.[54]

Gaisberg's unsuccessful efforts as an intermediary on Chaliapin's behalf most likely preceded the frontal assault on the composer the singer himself made in 1935. On what proved to be his last trip to New York Chaliapin disclosed to the conductor Mikhail Fiveisky the underlying reason for his current interest in *Aleko*: it was, he said, that he wished to finish his career at the same time as Rachmaninoff, just as they had begun it together. With celebrations afoot to mark the centenary of Pushkin's death in two years' time, he wished to sing Aleko for his farewell. He recalled, not without factual licence, that he had begun his career with it in St Petersburg. He would create the role in his accustomed way, reincarnating Pushkin. He maintained that the opera had been written in haste and that throughout the whole performance Aleko 'does nothing but grind his teeth. It's himself that Pushkin represents in the character of Aleko; for he really did associate with gypsies . . .'[55]

Chaliapin discussed the matter at length with Fiveisky, finally convincing him of the good sense of his idea of expanding the libretto to include two other tableaux, a prologue and an epilogue, to show that the story about Zemfira had been only a dream in the poet's mind. At Chaliapin's request Fiveisky's wife agreed to undertake the work, and when she had completed the prologue Chaliapin took it to the composer at Senar. Rachmaninoff, however, was unenthusiastic, pleading that his contracts for concerts did not permit him the necessary time. He was equally evasive to the Pushkin centenary committee, who asked for permission to present the opera in its original state in 1937: '*Aleko* is a work of youth,' he said: 'I intend to revise it . . . when I am free of my concerts . . .'[56] But Rachmaninoff was surely temporizing, and *Aleko* was to remain in the state in which he presented it to Arensky in April 1892.

References

1 Sofiya Satina, *VR/A* 1, pp. 13ff.
2 Sofiya Satina, *VR/A* 1, p. 15.
3 Sofiya Satina, *VR/A* 1, p. 18.
4 Pressman, *VR/A* 1, p. 156; *Riesemann*, pp. 55–56.
5 When there is cause for doubt about the chronology of early Rachmaninoff works, the 'unidentified hand' (or hands) that dated several of the manuscripts, possibly many years after they were written, seems invariably to have anticipated reality. The Scherzo is almost certainly a case in point.
6 *Riesemann*, p. 61. A facsimile of the manuscript appears on p. 253 of that work.
7 Russians of this time were neither very familiar with nor sympathetic to Brahms's work. Anton Rubinstein had excluded Brahms from his 'Historical Recitals' which Rachmaninoff had attended two years before, and there is no reference to Brahms during the whole of the composer's student years until he worked with Siloti on the Variations and Fugue on a Theme by Handel.
8 The identity of the person who dated the manuscript is not known (*Bortnikova*, p. 15, No. 52). According to *Tsïtovich*, p. 76, it was Goldenweiser, who, however, could only have guessed at the year, being too young to know Rachmaninoff at the time in question.
9 Further information about R's *Esmeralda* is to be found in the article by B. Dobrokhotov in *Tsïtovich*, pp. 89ff.
10 The chronology in *Riesemann* is confused. See *Keldïsh*, p. 38.
11 *Seroff* (pp. 31–32) gives a different account.
12 See *Bryantseva*, pp. 51–52.
13 *Deus meus, ad te de luce vigilo et in nomine tuo levabo manus meas. Alleluia.* These lines come from Psalm 63: 'O God, Thou art my God; early will I seek Thee . . . I will lift up my hands in Thy name.'
14 R. to Natalya Skalon, 10 January 1891.

15 The wing of the main house in which Rachmaninoff came to live when he stayed at Ivanovka has been reconstructed and opened as a museum. It is not yet accessible to foreign tourists.

16 *Bazhanov*, pp. 55–61.

17 R. to Natalya Skalon, 6 January 1891.

18 See *LN/A* 1, p. 503.

19 Ibid.

20 Tchaikovsky, Op. 60, No. 2.

21 *Riesemann*, pp. 24–25.

22 R. to Slonov, 20 July 1891.

23 *LN/A* 2, p. 413.

24 See *Bryantseva*, p. 87.

25 The autograph of the *Russian Rhapsody* is marked '12–14 January 1891', but the conclusive evidence of R's letter of 10 January that he had already started work on the piece sets the pattern for the dating of all his manuscripts, which invariably relates to the final version of a work and does not necessarily indicate when it was actually begun.

26 Wilshaw to R., 5 June 1934.

27 *Bortnikova*, p. 20, No. 75.

28 R. to Slonov, 26 March 1891.

29 R. to Slonov, 26 July 1891.

30 *Riesemann*, p. 110.

31 For example, *Norris*, p. 110.

32 The full score of the original version of Rachmaninoff's First Concerto, eds. I. Iordan & G. Kirkor, was published by Muzyka, Moscow, in 1971.

33 Vera Skalon, *VR/A* 2, pp. 435–436.

34 Sofiya Satina, *VR/A* 1, p. 23.

35 *Riesemann*, p. 78.

36 Ibid.

37 Op. cit., pp. 77–8.

38 R. to Natalya Skalon, 6 January and 7 December 1891.

39 The British premiere of *Prince Rostislav* was given in October 1982 by the Young Musicians Symphony Orchestra conducted by James Blair at a concert at London's Barbican Centre.

40 *Seroff*, pp. 22–23.

41 Pressman, *VR/A* 1, p. 180.

42 See *Bryantseva*, p. 99.

43 *Riesemann*, pp. 78–80.

44 Nemirovich-Danchenko had little contact with Rachmaninoff in the years after *Aleko*. In June 1916 he unsuccessfully tried to interest the composer in writing music for Blok's play 'The Rose and the Cross' (Lyubov Freidkina: *Dni i godi V l.I. Nemirovicha-Danchenko. Letopis' zhizni i tvorchestva*, Moscow, 1962, p. 323.).

45 Neither Morozov nor Conus made careers as composers, both instead becoming piano professors on the staff of Moscow Conservatoire. Conus subsequently left Soviet Russia and settled in Paris and later Cincinnati.

46 Glinka, *A Life for the Tsar*, Act IV, sc. 1; *Ruslan and Lyudmila*, Act III; Tchaikovsky, *Queen of Spades*, Act II.

47 *Riesemann*, p. 87.

48 *Riesemann*, p. 213; *Norris*, p. 136; Montagu-Nathan, *Contemporary Russian Composers*, Cecil Palmer & Hayward, London, 1917, p. 173.

49 *Aleko* and *Cavalleria Rusticana* were first staged as a double bill at Moscow's New Theatre on 21 September 1903.
50 See *Belza*, pp. 44–49, and 'Rakhmaninov's Student Opera', article by Geoffrey Norris in *The Musical Quarterly*, Vol. LIX, 1973, pp. 441–448.
51 During his career Chaliapin appeared in the role of Aleko ten times in all: first in the Petersburg premiere in 1899 as part of the celebrations of the centenary of Pushkin's birth, then in Moscow – three performances in 1903 and once under the composer's baton in 1905 – and finally five times in Petrograd in 1921. Although it was only in Russia that Chaliapin appeared in the opera, the *Cavatina* was a staple of his concert repertoire after he came to the West, and he recorded it twice.
52 See article on Rachmaninoff by Fred Gaisberg in *Gramophone*, August 1943.
53 'I am ashamed to have written such nonsense.' (1925) *B/L*, p. 241.
54 R. to Arensky, 17 April 1899.
55 Lidiya Nelidova-Fiveiskaya, *VR/A* 2, pp. 219–222.
56 Ibid.

4 Free Artist, 1892–1897

After the excitement of graduation from the conservatoire, the joy of reconciliation with Zverev, the satisfaction of fame and his good fortune in already having the support of a generous publisher, Rachmaninoff found the reality of everyday life as a 'Free Artist' a considerable anti-climax. His new-found celebrity brought him an invitation to spend the summer of 1892 on the estate of a wealthy landowner, Ivan Konovalov, in the Kostroma district, 200 miles north-east of Moscow, giving his young son a daily piano lesson. Despite the family's boundless kindness and the relief afforded by a brief visit from his mother, Rachmaninoff was bored and listless and, at least for the first two months, unable to get down to any new work. He did, however, correct the proofs of *Aleko* and of two salon miniatures for cello and piano, Op. 2, which were part of the publishing deal struck with Gutheil in May.

Prelude and Oriental Dance, for Cello and Piano, Op. 2

The precise date of the composition of these pieces is uncertain, as both the autographs are missing. The *Prelude* is a reworking of the F major piano prelude of July 1891, and its soulful melody undoubtedly sounds better when sung by the cello. Its premiere was given by Tchaikovsky's friend Anatoly Brandukov (1859–1930),[1] the dedicatee, and the composer on 30 January 1892, but the conspicuous absence from the same programme of its companion piece suggests that the latter may not yet have been written. However, that the *Oriental Dance* was contemporaneous with *Aleko* is strongly suggested by the striking similarity of melodic line and harmony in the conscious touches of eastern flavour in both pieces, a colouring that was to become a minor stylistic trait of the composer right up to the time of the D major *Étude-Tableau* and *Oriental Sketch* of 1917.

As Rachmaninoff had been so preoccupied with *Aleko*, it is not surprising that when he at last turned his thoughts to new composition it should be towards two natural sequels: on the one hand another work in the same genre, this time on a subject not unrelated to *Prince*

Rostislav, and on the other an orchestral work using gypsy themes. His operatic subject was the well-known story of *Undine*, by the German romantic writer Friedrich de la Motte Fouqué (1777–1843), known to Russians through Zhukovsky's verse translation. In Fouqué's tale the water nymph Undine, having married a knight and so acquiring a human soul, is deserted by her husband, whom she kills before his remarriage, thereupon turning into a fountain. As a subject for an opera the work already had an inauspicious history in Russia. Back in 1848 Vladimir Sollogub had made a libretto out of Zhukovsky's poem for Alexey Lvov (1798–1870), whose version of the opera, though achieving a revival in the 1860s, nevertheless then passed into irrevocable oblivion. In 1869 Tchaikovsky had used the same text for his own *Undine*, but his opera was rejected by the Imperial Theatres and he destroyed it four years later. In May of 1878 he toyed briefly with the idea of making another setting, this time turning to his brother Modest for a scenario, but the thought soon passed out of his mind. It was Modest too whom Siloti approached on Rachmaninoff's behalf in August 1892, asking if he were prepared to act as his cousin's *Undine* librettist.[2] Quickly agreeing, Modest completed a preliminary draft by March of the following year, but the work obviously revived thoughts in his mind of the earlier Tchaikovsky project, and instead of sending the scenario to Rachmaninoff directly he first passed it to his composer brother. But the cause was already lost: Tchaikovsky was not interested and returned the manuscript on 17 April, marking it 'For Rachmaninoff'. When Rachmaninoff at last received the scenario, he commented pointedly on the delay between its apparent completion and the date of his receiving it, but with Modest's work he was satisfied: 'In general I must say that I personally like everything very much and shall begin to write the opera with pleasure'.[3] Although Arensky, to whom Rachmaninoff had read the scenario, had misgivings, Rachmaninoff's one worry was that his opera might suffer the same fate as Tchaikovsky's in not being accepted by the Imperial Theatres and he wanted reassurance on this. None seems to have been forthcoming, however, and on 14 October 1893 he wrote to Modest asking him to stop work on the libretto as he was still 'in terrible doubt', and thus abruptly ended the whole project.

The orchestral work Rachmaninoff had in mind was the *Gypsy Caprice*, and this summer saw its drafting in two-piano form, though the work was deliberately laid on one side for orchestration later. Rachmaninoff marked the manuscript 'Opus 4', implying that he had already planned, or even begun, the group of five piano 'Fantasy' pieces which he completed back in Moscow in the autumn and which he published as his Opus 3. Rachmaninoff dedicated his new work, as he had *Prince Rostislav* two years before, to Arensky.

Five Fantasy Pieces for Piano, Op. 3

The first item in the set, the *Élégie* in E flat minor, has a languid and rather sickly sentimentality; the opening is reminiscent of 'September' from Tchaikovsky's *Seasons*, Op. 37. In its time the following *Prelude* in C sharp minor was, with Paderewsky's *Minuet*, the most popular contemporary piece in the whole piano literature. The furore started in 1898, when Siloti included the Prelude in his recital programmes in Europe and America, and subsequently, when Rachmaninoff became a concert pianist in the West, it became an inescapable encore. In 1910 the composer wrote a remarkably unrevealing article about the piece for an English music journal,[4] the most important part of which is reproduced in Seroff. [5] Though it seems that Clara Schumann did not approve of the Prelude, [6] Rachmaninoff's mentor Taneyev thought that the piece was very like her husband's *Novelletten*,[7] an odd judgement indeed, since those pieces are no less typical of Schumann than is the Prelude of Rachmaninoff. The sinisterly arresting opening and the insistent repetition of its three notes, always proclaiming a perfect cadence, the drama of the middle section, with its great chordal climax, the mournful tolling of bells in the gradual descent, and then the final sequence of eight chords, each held in suspense as the music gradually vanishes into the distance – all this makes the Prelude, in its own way, an astonishingly original piece, with a character and sonorities impressed with the mark of Rachmaninoff and no-one else.

The third piece in the set, *Mélodie* in E major, carries in the left hand a salon melody that could be from a song or opera, while the following *Polichinelle* nicely catches the gawky and aggressive exuberance of Mr Punch. There is a suggestion of the tinkling of a little bell in the decoration of Punch's theme, perhaps the bell on the puppet's hat:

Ex.17

According to Bertensson and Leyda,[8] the title '*Polichinelle*' was suggested by Slonov, but either he or Rachmaninoff himself must surely have taken it in the first place from the similarly-named movement of Arensky's Second Suite Op. 23 ('Silhouettes'), which was first performed in Moscow in its two-piano version by Taneyev and Paul Pabst on 11 November

1892,[9] at precisely the projected time of composition of the Rachmaninoff pieces. If so, the dedication of the set to Arensky was an especially appropriate gesture. Of sterner stuff, the *Serenade* in B flat minor, a favourite for many years of English teashop trios, harks back to the gypsy and eastern colouring of *Aleko*, to bring the set to an exotic and lively conclusion.

For the first published piano pieces of a nineteen-year-old, the Opus 3 set, with their idiomatic writing for the instrument and warm lyricism, are an impressive achievement. Even in later life Rachmaninoff seems to have entertained some affection for these early pieces, for he regularly programmed at least one or other of them in his concerts until the end of his career, as he did not with his later Op. 10 and Op. 16 sets; he made piano roll recordings of all five items, and he thought two of them, the *Mélodie* and *Serenade*, worthy of revision for fresh publication only three years before he died.

In the autumn of 1892 Rachmaninoff moved in with the Satins. He continued to earn a precarious subsistence income from piano lessons and occasional concert engagements, and his career did not pick up until the successful launch of *Aleko* at the end of April 1893. In May he paid a visit to Grandmother Butakova before joining Slonov for the summer at Lebedin, an estate near Kharkov belonging to a rich merchant called Lïsikov, whom he had met at his Kharkov concerts the previous winter. In the three-storeyed summer-house specially constructed for him[10] Rachmaninoff completed the six songs published as Op. 4, the suite for two pianos, Op. 5, the two pieces for violin and piano, Op. 6, the orchestral fantasy, Op. 7, and a three-movement church motet. For the quantity and variety of work, 1893 was the most productive year in Rachmaninoff's composing life.

Six Songs, Op. 4

In his original contract with Rachmaninoff, besides *Aleko* and the two cello pieces, Op. 2, Gutheil agreed also to publish a group of six songs.[11] In view of the absence of an opus number from the original version of the First Concerto, now known as Opus 1, and, as noted above, the designation of that number to the six student songs of 1890–91, these latter were possibly the songs for which Gutheil originally negotiated. In a letter to Slonov of 7 June 1892, Rachmaninoff mentions that his songs were expected to be published 'before the end of September', but within the next fortnight he had a change of heart about releasing them, describing them, on 20 June, with typical self-depreciation, as 'not worth publishing'. When, in the summer of 1893, he at last came to compile a set he felt worthy of him, it included only one of the early group of six, and this in a revised form, together with his song for Anna Lodïzhenskaya and four others written after his agreement with Gutheil.

The two opening songs most likely date from 1891. The first, Anna Lodïzhenskaya's *Oh stay, my love, forsake me not*, is an impassioned setting of a poem by Merezhkovsky in which a despairing lover begs his beloved not to leave him, a scenario perhaps with autobiographical overtones for the young composer. Although the manuscript is marked 26 February 1892, this almost certainly represents the date of the song's final recension before its first public performance three weeks later rather than of its original composition. The very first notes of the piano accompaniment are clearly an echo of the first phrase of the slow movement of the First Concerto, written in 1891, and some twenty-six years later Rachmaninoff himself dated this and the following song to that year.[12] *Morning* was most likely written in the autumn of 1891, when the composer was convalescing at Sakhnovsky's house in Moscow, for it is dedicated to his host then. In Yanova's charming poetic conceit there is an affectionate exchange of greeting between Dawn and Day, and Rachmaninoff's restrained setting aptly catches the delicacy of sentiment in the verses.

The third number, *In the silent night*, dedicated to Vera Skalon, is Rachmaninoff's first vocal masterpiece and deservedly one of his most popular songs still. The poem, by Afanasy Fet, tells of a lover seeing his beloved in his dreams and calling out to her. Most unusually in the composer's output, the original version of the song, dated 17 October 1890, has survived alongside its revision, made in the autumn of 1892, and the comparison this allows reveals just how much Rachmaninoff's technique advanced over these important two years in his development as a composer: a redistribution of the bar lines, added interest and variety in the opening, and fine changes to the rhythm of the more familiar shape of the melody later, all subtly enhance the original without detracting from its youthful freshness (Ex 18).

The piano accompaniment also plays a more subtle role than in the earlier songs. For example, the falling sixth of the singer's opening notes in the new version is prepared for in the introduction by pairs of minims falling the same interval, helping to create the mood of the silent, rapturous mystery of night (Ex 19).

At the climax of the song, where the lover seeks to rouse the night 'with the beloved name', the same falling interval of a sixth reappears in piano chords, as if crying out the name (Ex 20). This intense moment of ecstasy having passed, the singer repeats his melody, this time to a steadily receding piano accompaniment, as though the recollection of

Ex.18a — Original version, 1890

O, dol - go bu - du ya, v mol - cha-n'i no-chi tay - noy, ko - var - nïy le - pet tvoy, y - lïb - ku, vzor, vzor slu - chay - nïy,

Ex.18b — Revised version, 1892

[Lento]

O, dol - go bu - du ya, v mol-cha -n'i no - chi tay - noy, ko - var - nïy le - pet tvoy, y - lïb - ku, vzor, vzor slu-chay - nïy,

[Oh, long shall I be, in the silence of the secret night, [in banishing from my thoughts] your beguiling talk, your smile, your glance, your casual glance.]

the beloved is overtaken by sleep again. Thus, a characteristic outpouring of glorious lyricism is enhanced by greater structural subtlety and a closer reflection of the details of the text than hitherto in Rachmaninoff's songs.

Oh, never sing to me again is a Pushkin setting of high quality; dedicated to Natalya Satina, the composer's future wife, it probably dates from the beginning of 1893.[13] The poet begs a young girl not to sing songs from Georgia as they hold unhappy memories for him of a life and love now gone forever. In the piano introduction the element of oriental colouring evident in *Aleko*, the *Oriental Dance*, Op. 2, and the *Serenade*, Op. 3, here appears more subtly in the sinuous outline of the counterfeit Georgian melody. After his opening cry of appeal the singer tells of the painful memories evoked by the songs, and after a climax and another appeal the vocal line gradually and tearfully descends in wonderful arching phrases – demanding perfect breath control from the singer – as if sinking into the depths of misery, until it is taken over by the piano alone, muttering in its lowest register. Rachmaninoff's setting defers not at all to Balakirev's well-known version of 1863 of the same text, which happens earlier to have been set also by Glinka.

The last two songs are of lesser interest. In the fifth number, *The Harvest of Sorrow*, with words by Alexey Tolstoy and dedicated to Madame Lïsikova, wife of the composer's host this summer, a field of corn has been ruined, like the poet's dream of life. The picture of work on the land and the struggle against nature prompted in Rachmaninoff the, for him, unusual but unmistakable intonation of Russian folk song. By the end of the song, despite the beauty of its melody, its despair becomes oppressive. The final song, *So many hours, so many fancies*, with words by Count Golenishchev-Kutuzov (whose poetry Mussorgsky had used for his *Sunless* cycle and the *Songs and Dances of Death*) and dedicated to the Count's wife, to some extent recalls in style the songs of Glinka and Dargomyzhsky in its austere first half, in which the poet bemoans being separated from his friend, but becomes more typical of its composer at the end, depicting the happiness of two people reunited at last, where the music takes wing and a brief rhetorical piano coda brings to an effective conclusion a set that by its overall promise, and in some cases considerable achievement, is of a higher order than any of the unpublished student works in the same genre in both compositional technique and lyrical power. Rachmaninoff is here confirmed as a natural song writer, and he shows yet again that, far from being a mere epigone of Tchaikovsky, he was heir to a wide range of Russian musical culture, embracing the St Petersburg as well as the Moscow tradition.

Fantasy (First Suite) for Two Pianos, Op. 5

On 5 June 1893 Rachmaninoff wrote to Natalya Skalon: 'At the present time I am working on a fantasy for two pianos, consisting of musical pictures'. This was the work now generally known as the *First Suite for Two Pianos*, though its original title, 'Fantasy-Pictures', is more to the point, since the four movements are musical representations of poetic epigraphs printed in the score:

1	*Barcarolle*	'At dusk half-heard the dull wave laps beneath the gondola's slow oar . . .' (Lermontov)
2	*O Night, O Love*	'It is the hour when from the boughs the nightingale's high note is heard . . .' (Byron, in Russian translation)
3	*Tears*	'Tears, human *tears*, that pour forth beyond telling, Early and late, in the dark, out of sight . . .' (Tyutchev)[14]
4	*Easter Festival*	'Across the earth a mighty peal is sweeping Till all the booming air rocks like a sea . . .' (Khomyakov)

Since as a matter of policy Rachmaninoff almost never revealed publicly, nor indeed privately, the sources of his inspiration, the picture or poem that sparked off a work, the four epigraphs attaching to the Fantasy are in this respect most unusual. Although clearly not providing detailed programmes for the music, they obviously did inspire the general musical picture in each case.

The epigraph of the rapturous *Barcarolle* warns that the time for loving is brief and that passion never returns. It is thus linked in subject matter to the second movement, *O Night, O Love*, with its nightingale trills and passionate climax. In both, Rachmaninoff's skill in laying out the two piano parts in such a way as perfectly to complement one another is a particular delight. The last two movements are similarly paired, this time by the sound of bells. The debt to precedents in the works of the 'Mighty Handful' – the echoing of bells in Rimsky's *Sadko*, the Coronation Scene of *Boris Godunov* and at the end of the first act of *Prince Igor* – could not have escaped the notice of Rimsky-Korsakov and Liadov when Rachmaninoff played the work to them with Felix Blumenfield at one of Belyayev's Petersburg soirées later in the year. *Tears* was inspired by the bells of St Sofiya's Cathedral Novgorod, which the composer had heard as a young boy with Grandmother Butakova: in his own words, 'Four silvery sweeping notes, veiled in an everchanging accompaniment woven around them'.[15]

This hypnotically descending four-note phrase, used later also in his opera *The Miserly Knight*, rings out throughout the movement. The similarly insistent iteration of another bell motif in the last movement, *Easter Festival*, has been seen by critics from Rimsky-Korsakov onwards as overstepping tolerable limits,[16] a verdict which Rachmaninoff ignored at the time but with which he later agreed. The Easter message of victory over death is sung out in the chant 'Christ is risen', the bells tolling throughout, before, during and after the chant. Rimsky-Korsakov had used the same chant in his own *Russian Easter Festival Overture* but in Rachmaninoff's work felt that it should have been heard first alone and only the second time with the bells. It is interesting that the oscillating major second in the bell motif, anticipating the opening of the first movement of Rachmaninoff's choral symphony *The Bells*, which also depicts the joy of new life, has humble origins, namely *Polichinelle*, written the previous year (Ex. 17 above).

Rachmaninoff dedicated his Fantasy to Tchaikovsky, who promised to come to Moscow to attend the recital on 30 November 1893 by Paul Pabst at which he and the composer were to premiere the work, but in the event Tchaikovsky never heard it, for he died five weeks before.

Two Salon Pieces for Violin and Piano, Op. 6

Rachmaninoff's next opus was his two *Salon Pieces* for violin and piano, dedicated to his friend Julius Conus, another of the three Conus brothers who passed through Moscow Conservatoire in the 1880s and 90s. Both violinist and composer himself, Conus played in the premiere of Rachmaninoff's *Elegiac Trio*, Op. 9, and throughout the composer's life advised him on bowings in his orchestral works. In 1909 Rachmaninoff conducted his saccharine violin concerto, later taken up by Heifetz, and many years later Julius's son Boris would marry Rachmaninoff's daughter Tatyana. Rachmaninoff's two pieces share with the cello pieces of the previous year a slow and ruminative opening movement and a following more vigorous one in contrast. Both pieces live up to their 'salon' description in being entirely undistinguished musically: the *Romance* has an appropriately soulful melody, the *Hungarian Dance* a synthetic exoticism borrowed from *Aleko* and enormous energy, though the repetition of its slender musical material becomes tiring by the end.

The Crag, Fantasy for Orchestra, Op. 7

Rachmaninoff's most important work of the Lebedin summer was his Fantasy for Orchestra, *The Rock*, or *The Crag*, as it is generally known, though this title appears neither on the autograph nor on the published score, nor was the work programmed as such when the composer conducted it at the Queen's Hall during his first London visit in 1899. On the flyleaf of the score, however, Rachmaninoff wrote an ambiguously worded note: 'This fantasy was written under the influence of Lermontov's poem "The Crag" '. The composer has chosen the opening lines of the poem as epigraph for this composition:

'A little golden cloud slept the night
on the breast of a giant crag.'

The same epigraph had already been used by Chekhov at the head of his story 'On the Road' (1885), in which he restated Lermontov's allegory in human terms. The 'Cloud' and the 'Crag' are two travellers who meet in a deserted inn on Christmas Eve during a snow storm, a beautiful and compassionate young woman and a lonely and unsuccessful middle-aged man, who tells her his life-story; the woman listens sympathetically. The night passes, and next morning the man sadly watches the woman leave and resume her journey. As her sleigh disappears from view, the snow gradually covers him until he assumes the appearance of a giant crag. When the *Fantasy* was premiered in Moscow on 20 March 1894 under Safonov, Nikolay Kashkin, critic, conservatoire professor and friend of Tchaikovsky, revealed in a review[17] that Rachmaninoff had used the Chekhov story as the basis of his work, but that he had used the title 'Crag' because the opening of that poem of Lermontov's had served as epigraph for that story also. Later, when Rachmaninoff got to know Chekhov personally, he presented him with a copy of the two-piano version of the score with an inscription acknowledging his debt.[18]

The Crag can be considered a reworking of *Prince Rostislav* to a different scenario, and in following the outline of Chekhov's story Rachmaninoff uses again the procedure he adopted in the earlier work of characterizing the protagonists by contrasting leitmotifs and fleshing them in with varied orchestral timbres. The sombre opening, rising wearily from the lower register of cellos and basses, is capped by a bassoon melody of plaintively falling semitones, clearly representing the man's sad cry of resignation:

Ex.21

Immediately following, a flute solo[19] trips blithely down and up more than two octaves against the strings rising and falling a minor third; this gracious idea represents the vivacious young woman (Ex. 22).

Ex.22

The main burden of the work, however, is carried by a third theme, consisting of just two brief phrases. Full of yearning, this motif is an amalgam of the man's unrealized and unrealizable desires, his craving for affection, his regrets. It is clearly a development of part of the Nymphs' theme in *Rostislav*:

Ex.23a   *The Crag,* third theme

Ex.23b   *Prince Rostislav,* Nymphs' theme

This theme is repeated, perhaps to excess, in the ensuing dialogue with the Cloud's motif, but Rachmaninoff gives it various guises, tempi and orchestral colour. As in *Rostislav*, it eventually breaks out into a wild dance, reminiscent of Tamara's frenzied dance in Balakirev's symphonic poem of that name, and with its castanet punctuation also recalling the gypsy music of *Aleko*. Soon after, the Cloud's flute arabesques pause three times in expectation, tremolo strings stir mysteriously, and then the Cloud's theme is stated glowingly and compassionately against wistfully falling phrases on the strings. At this point it is tempting, as elsewhere in Rachmaninoff's music, to read an autobiographical element into the fantasy, since it is interrupted by the work's opening theme, the man's theme, in a restlessly anxious episode of growling strings and horns which pre-echoes the strange middle section of the slow movement of the First Symphony, dedicated to Anna Lodïzhenskaya. A despairing climax is reached, suggesting that the man finally realizes that nothing can come of this chance meeting. The yearning third theme is heard twice more, but each time dismissed by brusque interjections, and the work ends with two sighs of resignation on low strings.

On his return to Moscow in September Rachmaninoff showed *The Crag* to Tchaikovsky, who happened himself to have made a setting of the Lermontov poem for unaccompanied mixed chorus in 1887. Tchaikovsky was so pleased with Rachmaninoff's work that he promised to conduct it on his European tour the following year and also made arrangements for a performance in St Petersburg in January, but his unexpected death intervened. In January 1895 Rachmaninoff gave an inscribed copy of what was his first published orchestral score to Rimsky-Korsakov, and the skilful orchestral colouring, developed from *Prince Rostislav* and *Aleko*, must have especially pleased that master. It is interesting to note, however, that, except for this feature and the harmonization, when the work was first performed at St Petersburg under Glazunov on 20 January 1896, it failed to please César Cui, whose vitriolic strictures then were a foretaste of his devastating review of the First Symphony the following year:

> As a musical composition the *Fantasy* presents a kind of mosaic, consisting of small pieces without organisational relationship among themselves; the composer is always going somewhere but getting nowhere; in the whole composition it is clear that he is more concerned about sound than about music . . . Rachmaninoff is undoubtedly a talented man; he has taste and considerable technique but at the moment he has neither a sense of scale nor the ability to concentrate on an idea and its natural development.[20]

The Crag is generally dismissed by commentators as an immature work, and there is some justification for the view that it fails to live up to the promise of *Prince Rostislav*. Structurally the work is unsophisticated: as the three themes are all short-breathed and limited in their potential for growth, Rachmaninoff resorts to repeating them in varied form rather than to developing them organically. Nevertheless, in the interplay between the two characters Rachmaninoff manages to reflect more than a little of the psychological nuances of the Chekhov story. The varied and resourceful orchestration is impressive in itself, and the composer himself, always his sternest critic, was not ashamed to programme the work in his last ever Moscow concert, in January 1917, in the august company of *The Isle of the Dead* and *The Bells*.

O Mother of God Perpetually Praying, Sacred Concerto for Four-part Unaccompanied Chorus

If not the most important of Rachmaninoff's Lebedin works, then perhaps the most interesting, because so little known, is the motet, *O Mother of God Perpetually Praying*, the composition of which happened to fall at a time of renaissance in Russian church music after a chronic decline. During the nineteenth century, the monopoly which the Imperial Chapel authorities held over the setting of religious texts had excluded secular composers, and especially under the directorships of the mediocrities Lvov (1838–1861) and Rachmaninoff's remote relation Bakhmetev (1861–1883) the bland europeanized settings of the official court chants had adulterated the ancient tradition. It was Tchaikovsky who first broke out of the sterile straitjacket with his free setting of the *Liturgy of St John Chrysostom* of 1878, but more than two years' litigation was required for it to be allowed general circulation and public performance. His *All-Night Vigil* followed in 1882, based on themes from the *Obikhod*, the collection of daily canticles, and in 1885 he added to these pioneering works a free setting of Six Church Songs and in 1887 the chorus *An Angel Crying*. Of the Petersburg group of composers only Balakirev and Rimsky-Korsakov made any contribution to church music, and this a slender one, despite Balakirev's becoming Bakhmetev's successor as Musical Director of the Imperial Chapel, a post he held with Rimsky-Korsakov as his assistant for eleven years (1883–1894). Balakirev produced but a handful of anthems and Rimsky a few liturgical settings soon after his appointment, but neither of them recognized or at any rate was stimulated to act upon the shared ancestry of Russian sacred music and the folk music which so much preoccupied them. Then in 1889 the musical palaeontologist Stepan Smolensky (1848–1909) was appointed Director of the Moscow Synodal School and Professor of Church Music at the Conservatoire, where Rachmaninoff attended his class in the session of 1890–91. Under Smolensky's regime the standard of singing of the Synodal Choir was raised to new heights and interest was resuscitated in the long-neglected ancient chants. The arrival on the staff in 1891 of a composer with similar ideals, Alexander Kastalsky (1865–1926), completed the inauguration of what was to prove a golden autumn in the history of Russian church music.

It was at a Synodal Choir concert on 12 December 1893 that Rachmaninoff's Sacred Concerto was given its first and only performance in the composer's lifetime in a mixed programme of works by Tchaikovsky, Arkhangelsky, Sokolsky and Rimsky-Korsakov under the direction of the choir's regular conductor, Vasily Orlov. Rachmaninoff's motet, for which the most well-known Russian precedents are the sacred concertos of Bortnyansky (1752–1825), is set in the form of a classical three-movement instrumental concerto. The first movement, in G minor, is the most extended; it is largely based on a motif which, as Piggott pointed out,[21] unexpectedly anticipates a very different Rachmaninoff work, the finale of the Second Concerto (Ex. 24).

Ex.24

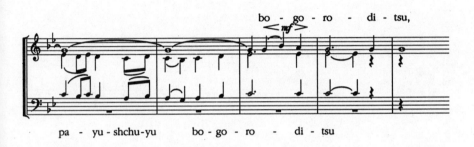

[Mother of God, ever awake in prayer.]

The short middle movement, in C minor, is a quasi four-part fugue, the theme of which Rachmaninoff re-uses, in transmogrified form, in the final movement. Its vague similarity to the opening theme of Prokofiev's First Concerto leads Bryantseva to wonder whether, during this Lebedin summer, Rachmaninoff was influenced by local Ukrainian singers as Prokofiev (born and brought up in the Ukraine) may also have been (Ex 25).[22]

In a cursory note about the work in a review of the 1893 performance, the critic Semyon Kruglikov berated Rachmaninoff for the freedom of his setting: although he found much beauty and talent in the work, he criticized the excess of youthful confidence, the superficiality of treatment and the insufficient penetration into the chosen religious text,[23] though in truth this is composed only of a few repeated devotional formulae. Nevertheless, despite the rebuff, Rachmaninoff's interest in religious music continued unabated. Sometime after the performance Smolensky seems to have proposed to Rachmaninoff that he write another concerto, possibly to a text chosen by himself, but Rachmaninoff replied that he was postponing the promised 'unfinished' work indefinitely.[24] We know that Rachmaninoff was still in close contact with Smolensky a year later,

Ex.25a   Rachmaninoff: *Mother of God,* third movement

Vo ut - ro - bu vse - li - vïy - sya pris - no -

dev - stven - nu - yu, pris - no - dev - stven - nu - yu

[Planted in the virgin womb]

Ex.25b   Prokofiev: First Concerto, opening (transposed)

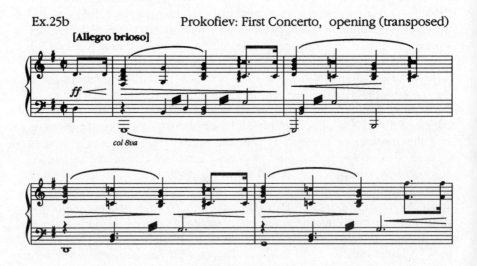

asking to be able to attend the rehearsal of one of the Synodal School's concerts,[25] and fifteen months after this Smolensky went so far as to invite Rachmaninoff to join the teaching staff,[26] but he declined. In 1897 Smolensky sent him the text of the Liturgy of St John Chrysostom,[27] but this arrived in the period of intense depression after the failure of the First Symphony and Rachmaninoff did not make his setting until 1910.

Rachmaninoff seems to have thought more highly of his Sacred Concerto than its obscurity suggests. In a letter to Arkady Kerzin thirteen years after its premiere he refers ruefully to its qualities as being 'quite decent but insufficiently spiritual'.[28] In the list of his compositions he sent to Boris Asafyev in his last year in Russia[29] Rachmaninoff recalls the performance of the Sacred Concerto in a note, the only one of his unpublished works he mentions. The truth is that, in the freedom of his setting, Rachmaninoff gave his music an independence outside the religious text which was bound to offend reactionary opinion, as indeed the *Liturgy* later did, but which in the present age ought all the more to encourage the work's revival and reconsideration on purely musical grounds.

Six Songs, Op. 8

Having returned to Moscow at the end of the summer of 1893, at an evening at Taneyev's on 18 September Rachmaninoff played through *The Crag* to an appreciative Tchaikovsky; a fortnight later the two composers met up again in melancholy circumstances at the burial of Zverev. A few days later still the Russian poet Pleshcheyev was buried in the Novodevichy cemetery, and this event may well have directed Rachmaninoff to his next work, another group of six songs, Op. 8, all settings of translations by Pleshcheyev of German of Ukrainian poems, which he completed in October while staying again at Lebedin in the course of fulfilling his engagement to conduct two performances of *Aleko* in Kiev.

The first two songs in the set are both from Heine. *The Water Lily* is a blithe and sensitive setting of a natural conceit, in which a water lily and the moon fall in love; like the setting of *The Barge Haulers* two years before, it is dedicated to Adolf Yaroshevsky. *Like blossom dew-freshen'd to gladness*, set earlier by Rubinstein, was written for Rachmaninoff's friend, copyist and confidant, Mikhail Slonov, himself a baritone. The poem is a simple blessing on a young child, and Rachmaninoff's setting is quietly attractive, matching the somewhat cloying sentimentality of the words. Siloti later made an arrangement of the song for piano solo, though the composer himself never played it.

The next pair of songs are both from poems by the national poet of the Ukraine, Taras Shevchenko, to whom Rachmaninoff's Lebedin hosts, the Lïsikovs, perhaps drew the composer's attention. *Brooding* is dedicated to Leonid Yakovlev, a baritone at the Maryinsky Theatre who had given the first Moscow performance of *Oh stay, my love, forsake me not*. Rachmaninoff did not like what he called his 'salon' performing style,[30] though, whether deliberately or unconsciously, he pandered to it with a melodramatic setting in which the self-indulgent gloomy introspection becomes oppressive. The theme of the text, the perpetual and losing struggle in life against fate, had already become Rachmaninoff's keynote. *The Soldier's Wife*, dedicated to Mariya Olferyeva, Rachmaninoff's father's common-law wife, tells of the tragic lot to be faced by a soldier's widow. The music combines a simple directness of utterance with a profound Russian melancholy, again evoking the world of folk song. At the end the vocal part is wordless, the first use in Rachmaninoff of a device the composer was later regularly to employ in his choral works and which he was to take to its logical conclusion in the wordless song *Vocalise*.

The opus concludes, as it began, with two more German settings. In *A Dream* (Heine) the poet conjures up thoughts of his native land and of past happiness there, but then realizes that it has all been only in his mind. The lyrical beauty of the vocal line and the restraint of the accompaniment make this the best song of the set, as Rachmaninoff himself saw,[31] and it is therefore not surprising that he chose to dedicate it to his close confidante Natalya Skalon. *A Prayer* (Goethe), is dedicated to Mariya Deysha-Sionitskaya, the soprano who was the first Zemfira in *Aleko*, and there is a passing musical reference to Aleko's Cavatina at the words *Ya muchus', ya bol'na dushoy* ('My spirit suffers deep disgrace', in the quaint authorized English version by Edward Agate). In the poem a girl begs forgiveness for having ignored a young lover and driving him to death from grief. Rachmaninoff's setting is melodically uninteresting and oppressively melodramatic, bringing to a somewhat disappointing end a group of songs that fails overall to live up to the promise of the Op. 4. set.

Two other songs probably belonging to the same summer[32] remained unpublished during the composer's life-time. *The Song of the Disillusioned* and *The flower has faded* are both settings of words by Daniel Rathaus (1869–1937), six of whose youthful poems Tchaikovsky had set as his Op. 73 in May of the same year; indeed, one wonders whether it was he who drew Rachmaninoff's attention to the poet. The first is an impassioned contrast of extremes of despair and hope for the future in the face of the ephemeral nature of life. The portentous repeated quaver octaves in the bass of the opening accompaniment resolve temporarily into the inevitable triplets of many of the early songs as the mood of optimism takes over, but the song poses at the end the impossibility of recapturing what has passed. *The flower has faded* similarly reflects the transitoriness of life, something to which Rachmaninoff was later to give maturer expression in another Rathaus setting, *All things depart*, Op. 26, No. 15; the spareness of the accompaniment points the way to a similar style in *The Little Island*, from Op. 14. Despite the beauty of the end, neither this nor the other Rathaus song has the lyrical power of the best of the songs published, and Rachmaninoff's unwillingness to release them for publication is perfectly understandable.

Elegiac Trio in D Minor, Op. 9

At 3 o'clock in the morning of 25 October 1893 Tchaikovsky died in St Petersburg, and later that day word reached Rachmaninoff, who had just returned to Moscow from Kiev.[33] The surprise news stunned all Russia, but Rachmaninoff was especially affected, for in the eighteen months since his graduation Tchaikovsky had become not only his chief professional mentor but a personal friend. If the dating on the manuscript is to be believed, it was on the very day of Tchaikovsky's death that Rachmaninoff began work on his *Elegiac Trio* for piano, violin and cello, appending the same dedication, 'In memory of a great artist', as Tchaikovsky himself had applied to the trio he had written twelve years before on the death of Nikolay Rubinstein. The musical form in which Tchaikovsky had cast his tribute in turn determined for Rachmaninoff the nature of his own gesture, and the close structural correspondence between the two trios shows the extent to which Rachmaninoff consciously copied his model. The Tchaikovsky work consists of two long movements only, the second of which, a set of eleven variations on a theme which Tchaikovsky and Rubinstein had heard together, is concluded by a coda marked *Allegro risoluto*, leading to a quiet and dignified final page. Rachmaninoff's trio follows the same scheme, except that the coda is replaced by a third movement, with the same marking and serving much the same function. The trio's composition cost Rachmaninoff much effort, occupying him for more than seven weeks. 'While working on it,' he wrote, 'all my thoughts, feelings, energies were devoted to it . . . As it says in one of my songs, "all the time I was tormented and sick in heart". I trembled for every phrase, sometimes crossed out everything and began again to think, think . . .'[34]

The first movement opens with the piano establishing a slow funeral

march, with two weary chords alternating with a despairing descending
four-quaver figure, over which the two stringed instruments sing a
lament. The second theme, which monopolizes the development section,
emphasizes the three notes of a falling minor third. Emotional outbursts
of piano rhetoric alternate with episodes of quieter elegiac anguish for
all three instruments, but these ideas are overworked before the recapitulation, in which the opening dirge is given to the piano, while the
strings continue to exploit the second theme. As in the Tchaikovsky
trio, the piano dominates throughout, overwhelming the uninteresting
string writing. Although the sincerity and depth of feeling expressed
are never in doubt, the musical material is too insubstantial to sustain
at length the emotionally powerful role it is given.

The second movement, a theme and variations, is musically more
compelling. The theme Rachmaninoff chose manages simultaneously to
be both an imitation of that used by Tchaikovsky at the same point
in his trio and a self-quotation. Its character is naturally different from
that of the theme Tchaikovsky uses, but, with the addition of a passing
note, its first eight notes coincide with the latter's first seven:

More obvious still is the quotation from Rachmaninoff's own work, for
the theme is unmistakably also a close relative of the 'yearning' motto
from *The Crag*, explicitly so in the very first variation, in which the D
minor harmony of the second bar requires a C sharp leading note (cf.
Ex. 23a above) (Ex. 27).

Ex.27

Tchaikovsky had chosen a theme with a personal significance for Rubinstein and him, a folk melody they had heard and enjoyed together on a day out in the country, and Rachmaninoff seems to have used the same autobiographical principle, for *The Crag* was closely associated with Tchaikovsky. Not only had he been enthusiastic about the work, volunteering to conduct what would have been its premiere, in St Petersburg in January 1894, but it was the very last composition Rachmaninoff ever showed him.

No-one has explained why in the original version of the trio Rachmaninoff apparently capriciously gave the initial statement of the theme optionally to the harmonium, though its bland solemnity sounds well enough on an instrument that seems mercifully to have been avoided by all other Russian composers, including Tchaikovsky. In the search for a source of inspiration for its use by Rachmaninoff in compositions by foreign composers containing a part for harmonium, only Dvořák's *Bagatelles*, Op. 47, seem in the least likely. At any rate, the movement's eight variations themselves are straightforward; predominantly in the major key, they alternate vigorous cheerfulness with episodes of pensiveness. The best is the third, *Allegro scherzando*, with fluttering piano figuration against pizzicato strings. The seventh variation, in D minor, interestingly anticipates the symphony in that same key written two years later in opening and closing with the same formula of an inverted turn.

In comparison with the expansiveness of the first two movements, the last seems a disproportionately brief post-script. After a massively rhetorical piano introduction, the four-note descending phrase of lament from the trio's opening is brought back in varied form (*Allegro molto*), and the strings fight an unequal battle to make their own anguished voices heard in the dramatic emotional outbursts which ensue. The opening of the whole work is finally recapitulated before the trio ends quietly, all emotion now spent.

Realizing that the trio was over-long, for a second edition in 1907 Rachmaninoff subjected it to revision and cuts, and for a performance in 1917 to further cuts, finally incorporated in the Muzgiz edition of 1950.[35] These tinkerings with an already published score are a manifestation of a striving after what Rachmaninoff was later to claim to be the most important and difficult of all goals in composition: saying what has to be said as succinctly as possible. However, following this admirable precept over-zealously was to lead him in later years to accepting a number of self-destructive cuts in his works and even to making complete revisions that were neither successful nor necessary. The revision of the trio, though not of this kind, is the first example in practice of what was to become a characteristic tendency.

The trio's first performance was given by the composer and his friends Julius Conus and Anatoly Brandukov in Moscow at the first, and for many years, only, all-Rachmaninoff concert, a modest chamber programme, on 31 January 1894. Unlike the Tchaikovsky trio, the Rachmaninoff work never became a favourite and it has been all but ignored outside of Russia. It is particularly vulnerable to performances less than totally committed, but not even the persuasive advocacy of Horowitz, Milstein and Piatigorsky in their chamber concerts in the early 1930s earned the work a place in the regular repertoire, and the situation has not changed since.

Seven Salon Pieces for Piano, Op. 10

At the same concert at which the *Elegiac Trio* was premiered, Rachmaninoff also performed for the first time the last four of his new set of seven piano pieces. As he had been totally absorbed in the composition of the trio until 15 December 1893, they must have been composed during the following six weeks or so. They are dedicated to Paul Pabst, pianist and professor at the Moscow Conservatoire, possibly out of gratitude for programming the premiere of the two-piano suite, Op. 5, at a concert of his on 30 November that year.[36]

The set opens with a *Nocturne* in A minor, which has a mixture of Chopinesque and Tchaikovskian melancholy in its main theme, and a rocking, chordal central section of no special distinction. The following *Waltz* in A major is also pleasant enough but entirely unmemorable. A manuscript sheet on which the composer had noted the melody of the Waltz was found after his death on a shelf near his piano, together with drafts for the 1940 version of the Serenade from Op. 3, one of four revisions of early pieces made at that time. This leads Threlfall and Norris to wonder[37] whether Rachmaninoff may have intended to rewrite the Waltz also, but since it had never been in his concert repertoire, as the other pieces all had, this seems unlikely.

The *Barcarolle* in G minor, one of the better items in the set, has an unsettled if not haunted atmosphere. The composer's 1919 Edison recording and the Ampico piano roll he made at about the same time reveal that he touched up the piece over the twenty-five years since publication, in particular heightening the mood of mysterious agitation at the end by a *tremolando* before the final cadence.[38] The fourth number, the *Mélodie* in E minor is noteworthy chiefly for the colourful decoration of the melody by arpeggiated chords above and below, while the *Humoresque* in G minor is as capricious in its harmony and rhythmic dislocations as its name suggests. It remained in Rachmaninoff's regular repertoire throughout his life and was one of the pieces revised, albeit only slightly, in 1940. The following *Romance* in F minor, marked *Andante doloroso*, is a tediously plangent love song, but the *Mazurka* in D flat makes a flamboyant end to the set – a kind of Russian equivalent to Scharwenka's famous Polish Dance in E flat minor. Whilst the form of the work is derived from Chopin, the characteristically robust piano writing is clearly not, and some amusing twists to the melody and coy passing runs show a vein of humour in Rachmaninoff that was later to be given mature expression in the *Polka de W.R.* However, agreeable music though they are, it must be admitted that overall the pieces mark no musical advance on the Op. 3 set of the previous year, and that their essentially second-rate character is aptly summed up by their 'salon' title.

Six Piano Duets, Op. 11

Despite its successful production in Moscow and Kiev, *Aleko* did not pass into the repertoire of either house and, after the double blow of the deaths of Zverev and Tchaikovsky and now without the latter's promotion of *The Crag*, Rachmaninoff's career as a composer seemed to have lost its impetus. He had been living alone for the first time in a flat in Moscow and, because his income was insufficient for the life-style to which he had become accustomed, he had been forced to give private piano lessons, which he loathed doing, and to teach music theory at a girls' school, the Maryinsky Academy. It was in this unsettled and uninspiring period in April 1894, that Rachmaninoff wrote the Six Piano Duets, no doubt with an eye on potential sales among amateur pianists. The composer did not think the set worthy of bearing a dedication, nor is there any record of his ever having played it, publicly or privately. The duets and Rachmaninoff's previous opus, the seven solo piano pieces, share certain common features: they both contain a Barcarolle in G minor, a Waltz in A major and a Romance, and as the products of economic necessity rather than artistic compulsion they both represent Rachmaninoff at his least inspired.

The six movements are appropriately diverse in style, though they are structurally unsophisticated, all relying over-much on simple varied repetition of their undistinguished material. The melancholy opening *Barcarolle* contrasts with a teasing *Scherzo*, which itself throws into relief the folk tune of the third piece, *Russian Theme*. This turns out to be the same as the song-arrangement *The Barge Haulers*,[39] on which Rachmaninoff had worked two-and-a-half years before. The graceful *Waltz* comes as light relief before a depressingly comfortless *Romance*. The last movement, *Slava*, makes a rousing finale. Its theme is well-known from the Coronation Scene of *Boris Godunov* but also occurs in Rimsky-Korsakov's opera *The Tsar's Bride* and Arensky's Second String Quartet. At the end, characteristically, the bells ring out insistently.

Another piano duet, a *Romance* in G major, though undated, clearly comes from the same period.[40] The fact that the piece is also laid out for piano duet, not to mention a similarity in the manuscript paper used for both, suggests that it is a parergon to the Op. 11 set. Those pieces are technically easy, particularly the *secondo* part, but the *Romance* is less demanding still, and shorter, and for these reasons does not quite fit as a discarded draft of a movement for the suite. Perhaps Rachmaninoff wrote it for use in his piano lessons, but, if so, why ennoble so anaemic a piece with the name 'Romance'? It is another of those very few pieces by the composer so lacking in originality as to defy recognition of its author by anyone unacquainted with it.

Rachmaninoff spent the summer of 1894 back on the estate of the Konovalovs giving more lessons, proof-reading *The Crag*, and making his second attempt at an orchestral work based on Byron; this time it was a section of the verse satire 'Don Juan' that captured his imagination. A shipwrecked Juan is washed ashore on an island in the Cyclades, ruled by Lambro, a cruel pirate king. Lambro's daughter, Haidée, finds Juan and becomes his lover. Lambro has long been away from the island and is presumed dead; however, he returns home unexpectedly and finds a feast in progress. He comes upon the unsuspecting lovers, has Juan beaten up by his men, placed in chains and sold as a slave. Haidée goes mad from grief and dies.[41]

As with his earlier 'Manfred' work, the only knowledge we have of this piece comes from the composer's correspondence, in this case just one letter to Slonov, dated 24 July 1894:

> I am not writing a symphony, though I have not given up Byron's 'Don Juan'. Doubtless it's a fine subject, but as it was impossible to make up a good programme, a good plan, I took one so-called 'episode' from it. This episode I am making into two scenes; the first of them is the feast, and second Don Juan and Haidée, Lambro and the death of Haidée. Because the action in these two scenes is completely different, I shall perhaps call it, à la Liszt, 'two episodes' – although as far as my music in them is concerned, there is something common to both. For the

moment the second part is not yet entirely ready. I have been composing it, and the first scene, since the 20th June. Terribly long! I have been terribly tormented and have kept rejecting more and more of what I have written; but worst of all, I may even reject what I have now. This 'episode' is not short; I think that if it gets completed it will last about forty minutes. Before 20th June, I wrote one other thing; . . . that piece is only for orchestra and will be called 'Capriccio on Gypsy Themes'. That composition is already complete in my head.

The juxtaposition of references at the beginning to the unwritten symphony and *Don Juan* suggests that the latter work was also symphonic. If the other work on which Rachmaninoff had been working was 'only for orchestra', it follows that *Don Juan* must have been for bigger forces still, perhaps for chorus and orchestra, or for soloists, chorus and orchestra, on the lines of Liszt's 'Dante' and 'Faust' symphonies, with the latter of which Rachmaninoff acquainted the Skalons and the Satins the following summer.[42]

Rachmaninoff had already worked on *Don Juan* for five weeks before writing his letter to Slonov. In contrast, his two previous orchestral poems were finished very rapidly: *Prince Rostislav* was completed in a week and *The Crag* was but one of several works written the previous summer. *Don Juan* was Rachmaninoff's biggest orchestral enterprise so far and it obviously caused him unusual trouble, and yet much must have been accomplished. If the second part was 'not yet entirely ready', by implication the first part was ready and the second part well on its way. Yet of all this industry there remains not a bar on paper. The existence of a page of undated manuscript containing sketches of two four-part vocal settings of *Don Juan* pieces – a gently wistful *Chorus of Spirits* and a *Song of the Nightingale* – is a misleading irrelevance, for the texts used here are from Pushkin and have nothing whatever to do with the Byron episodes.

Although on the evidence of his letter Rachmaninoff could well have composed *Don Juan* in his head, as he claimed to have done with the *Gypsy Caprice*, he already had his sketches for a two-piano version of that work from two years before, and it strains credulity to suppose that he worked for more than a month without once setting pen to paper. Clearly he did 'reject' what he had composed, because nothing more is heard of the project, but he did not necessarily 'throw away' his work, as some commentators misleadingly translate the word Rachmaninoff uses.[43] May it not be the case that the composer had in his mind, if not physically in his hands, his work on *Don Juan* when he later came to set to music another tale of illicit love and vengeance after an unexpected return, *Francesca da Rimini*?[44]

Capriccio on Gypsy Themes (Gypsy Caprice), Op. 12

It seems that it was not until after his return to Moscow, halfway through September 1894, that Rachmaninoff completed the orchestration of his *Gypsy Caprice*. He had admitted to Slonov a fortnight earlier, writing from Ivanovka, that he had not yet finished the work and that he was in no hurry to do so. He was in a state of depression over his money worries: 'This winter I shall probably content myself with my own finger, which I shall suck with imperturbable indifference. I am not writing. I have nothing to live on, nothing for a night out. Counting every kopek, that I cannot do . . .'[45] The *Caprice* was finished by the end of the year, in the Satins' apartment in Moscow, where Rachmaninoff had now resumed semi-permanent residence. The two-piano version was published in 1895 and the orchestral score in 1896, after a premiere under the composer's baton on 22 November 1894. Rachmaninoff consciously set out to write a gypsy counterpart to Tchaikovsky's *Italian Caprice* and Rimsky-Korsakov's *Spanish Caprice*,[46] and in doing so he had been prompted by his association with the Lodïzhenskys, a friendship close enough for him to dedicate not only the *Caprice* to Pyotr Lodïzhensky but his following work, the First Symphony, to the latter's wife.

Structurally the work divides naturally into three: an introduction, *Allegro vivace*, a long slow central section, and a contrastingly quick concluding part, all apparently made to grow out of one tiny germ cell, the insistent three-note descending phrase heard at the outset:

Ex.28

Allegro vivace

This motif turns out to have been extrapolated from the harmony of the main theme, one Nadezhda Alexandrova had sung for the composer,[47] which ushers in the central section in the guise of a funeral march:

Ex.29

The theme is subjected to many varied and wearisome repetitions, and there is much languor and sobbing despair before the final section is reached, in which the music at last takes off as a gypsy dance gets under way, the motto still clearly recognizable in the background:

Ex.30

The speed and excitement increases as the dance grows more frenzied, and the work is brought to a rousing if frankly vulgar and factitious climax.

Rachmaninoff's *Gypsy Caprice* cannot in any way be compared with its illustrious Tchaikovsky and Rimsky-Korsakov prototypes because it entirely lacks their geniality and the inherent attractiveness of their musical ideas. There is, however, a certain interest in the manner in which Rachmaninoff sought to impose a unity on the composition through economy of material and thematic transformation, a technique that was to become a feature of much of his later work. Rachmaninoff himself later dismissed the *Caprice* as unworthy of him. By 1908 it was one of three works that 'frightened' him and that he wished to revise (the others were the First Concerto and First Symphony),[48] and by 1930 it had become 'the only one of his children which the creator would prefer to disown'.[49] Since that time the composer's own antipathy and the work's innate weakness have kept it out of the concert hall. None, in fact, of the pieces Rachmaninoff completed in 1894 added lustre to his reputation: the mediocrity and affectation of their musical ideas was scarcely concealed by the sureness of technique with which they had been fabricated. It was as though the lull in the progress of his career had somehow debased his artistic aspirations. His next composition, however, was to be a quantum leap forward; it was also to prove the greatest failure of his life.

Symphony No. 1 in D Minor, Op. 13

It was in the Satins' apartment in Moscow in January 1895[50] that Rachmaninoff began work on his magnum opus, the First Symphony. Working with uncharacteristic slowness, he took the sketches with him to Ivanovka for the summer holiday, reporting with typical pessimism to Slonov on 17 July on the limited results of his daily regimen of seven hours' toil: 'Overall my work goes with difficulty. Let's say that so far my hope of completing what I had in mind has not entirely disappeared, but that is the only consolation there is for you and me in the meantime. Maybe, if God grants, I shall get to finish everything, although that's extremely hard, very hard . . .'. Yet six weeks later, by stepping up his workload to ten hours a day, Rachmaninoff had finished the composition of the symphony and had orchestrated it. He reported to Slonov: 'I am easy about the first three movements, though the first displeases me somewhat and I find several places that need changing.'[51] These changes occupied him for the next fortnight,[52] by which time he had also completed the four-hand piano transcription of that movement, finishing the other three before leaving Ivanovka on 25 September.

Still further alterations were to be made the following year, but in his letter of 2 September 1895 Rachmaninoff gave Slonov timings for the four movements as they were then, and these differ interestingly from a typical modern performance, thus giving some indication of the changes that must have taken place between the first draft of 1895 and the score as we now know it.

Movement	Estimates in Rachmaninoff's letter	Typical performance
1st	15+ minutes	13½–14 minutes
2nd	10	8½–9
3rd	6	9
4th	15	12½

Three of the four movements seem to have been subjected to typical Rachmaninoff pruning, particularly the last, but the slow movement has expanded by no less than 50 per cent. Can the original really have been so brief and, if it was, just how was it expanded to its present length? It is difficult to envisage what now seems so appropriate an interlude between scherzo and finale in a stunted form. Incidentally, from the evidence of the original orchestral parts, the conductor of the ill-fated first performance, Glazunov, seems himself to have made two further cuts in the work.[53]

With the symphony, for the first time in Rachmaninoff's career, there was a long hiatus – eighteen months – between composition and first performance. This was because Rachmaninoff had the chance of storming the musical citadel of St Petersburg by having his new work premiered there at one of Belyayev's concerts of Russian music. Belyayev had first met Rachmaninoff when he had visited Petersburg two years previously and was keen that Moscow's rising star should join his circle. In January 1896 *The Crag* received its Petersburg premiere at one of his concerts, conducted by Glazunov, and the symphony was eventually similarly scheduled for the new season, but not without a struggle. Now that the work seems a natural part of the Russian symphonic tradition, hindsight and the very notoriety of the premiere combine to give the impression that it could only have been Glazunov's reportedly inept performance that prevented public acclaim, but this is not necessarily so. Even before the premiere Russia's most famous musical figures all had misgivings. Taneyev, to whom Rachmaninoff played the symphony, was not enthusiastic about it: 'These melodies are flabby, colourless – there is nothing that can be done with them,' he said.[54] Possibly as a result of Taneyev's criticisms Rachmaninoff made further changes during the summer of 1896 at Ivanovka, more than a year after the symphony's completion. In reporting this to Belyayev on 26 October, Taneyev's unallayed reservations about the work are evident in his loyal attempt to pre-empt criticism:

Rachmaninoff has made alterations to the symphony but has not yet incorporated them in the score . . . I would greatly hope that the Committee [viz. Rimsky-Korsakov, Liadov and Glazunov] do not regard too severely the harmonic pretentiousness encountered in this work, which is undoubtedly a talented one. A man as richly gifted musically as Rachmaninoff will the more quickly come to his true path if he can hear his pieces performed. The shortcomings encountered in them are generally characteristic of our contemporary music and enthusiasm for them is understandable on the part of a young composer.

Taneyev sent another letter pressing Rachmaninoff's case three days later, and shortly afterwards he heard the news that the symphony had at last been accepted for performance.

Belyayev, who had already proved himself no mean musical judge in spotting the talent of Scriabin over the heads of his Committee, needed reassurance about Rachmaninoff's symphony. Taneyev wrote to him on 14 November making more excuses: 'If Rachmaninoff seems to you, as you put it, "conceited", this can be put down to his truly outstanding talent as a composer. If this talent has not yet revealed itself fully in his present compositions, then I profoundly believe that it will not be long before it does so in the future . . .' – a comment which clearly implies that Taneyev did not think that the symphony represented Rachmaninoff at his best. Nor was Glazunov exactly effusive in his praise; he approved of the symphony, 'on the whole',[55] though he did single out the orchestration for praise –

an ironical judgement in view of the fact that this was one of the features that Rachmaninoff himself subsequently found least satisfactory.[56] But Rimsky-Korsakov was frank in his dislike of the work, saying to the composer at the rehearsal, 'Forgive me but I do not find this music at all agreeable'. The omens for the premiere were not good.

Rachmaninoff's First Symphony was performed on the evening of 15 March 1897 at the Hall of the Nobility. Lyudmila Skalon wrote forty-nine years later:

> I see as if it were now the whole scene at the concert. Sitting in the hall were César Cui, Vladimir Stasov, Eduard Nápravník, other notable critics and musicians, and Mitrofan Belyayev. Seryozha hid on the spiral staircase [the fire-escape from the Gallery]. Glazunov stood on the conductor's rostrum phlegmatically and that was the way he conducted the symphony. He wrecked it. Cui shook his head and shrugged his shoulders the whole time. Stasov and Belyayev exchanged disapproving glances. We three [Skalon] sisters and Natasha [Satina] raged silently at Glazunov and the whole audience, who understood nothing. But our poor Seryozha was squirming on the staircase, unable to forgive himself for not conducting his composition himself and for having entrusted its performance to Glazunov.[57]

Whilst written evidence suggests on the whole that Glazunov was only a mediocre conductor – though, to judge from his only recording, made in 1929 of his *Seasons*, not that bad – the evidence of eyewitnesses is absolutely unanimous that the performance of Rachmaninoff's symphony was little short of disgraceful. Seven weeks after the event the composer gave his considered opinion to his friend Alexander Zateyevich: 'I am amazed how so talented a man as Glazunov can conduct so badly. I am not speaking now about conducting technique (it's no use expecting this of him) but about his musicianship. He feels nothing when he conducts; it's as if he understands nothing.'[58] In a postcard to Elena Kreutzer two days before the concert, inviting her to attend the general rehearsal, Natalya Satina wrote prophetically: 'You cannot imagine how abominably Glazunov conducts; I never expected it to be so bad it's quite impossible to recognise things.'[59] Many years later the same, not unbiased, eyewitness told the Swans that Glazunov was drunk at the performance.[60] Elena Kreutzer herself recalled:[61]

> As at the general rehearsal, so at the concert, I was struck by the monumental figure of Glazunov standing motionless on the conductor's stand and wielding the baton absolutely apathetically. Rachmaninoff obviously was very bothered and in moments of pause went up to Glazunov and said something to him, but he didn't manage to bring him out of a state of complete indifference . . . The estimate Rachmaninoff gives Glazunov as a conductor in his letter to Zateyevich wholly agrees with the immediate impression we received straight after the general rehearsal, after earlier having heard the composer's own interpretation.

Another eyewitness, the conductor and teacher Alexander Khessin, also puts the blame for the symphony's failure squarely on the inadequacy of the performance: 'The symphony was insufficiently rehearsed, the orchestra was ragged, elementary stability in tempi was lacking, many errors in the orchestral parts appeared uncorrected, but the main thing that wrecked the work was the lifeless, superficial, bland, matter-of-fact performance, with no flashes of animation, enthusiasm or brilliance of orchestral sound'.[62] The critic and musicologist Alexander Ossovsky, who attended both the general rehearsal and the concert itself, makes much the same comment:[63]

> The performance was raw, unthought-out, unfinished, and it produced the impression of a slovenly play-through and not of the realisation of a definite artistic idea, which the conductor clearly lacked. Rhythmic vitality, so essential in the works and performances of Rachmaninoff, withered. Dynamic shadings, gradations of tempo, nuances of expression – everything in which this music is so rich – disappeared. A kind of shapeless, turbid sound-mass dragged on interminably. The torpid character of the conductor completed the whole agonising ghastliness of the impression.

Ossovsky adds that Glazunov's inefficient use of rehearsal time was made still worse by having three first performances in one concert.[64] Rachmaninoff's symphony is certainly a demanding work to perform, and its American premiere in 1948 required no fewer than seven rehearsals with an orchestra as skilful as the Philadelphia, under a conductor as professional as Ormandy, both well attuned to the composer's idiom, as Glazunov temperamentally and intellectually was not, and that last fact doubtless lay at the root of the disaster.

Cui, who years before had savaged Tchaikovsky at the beginning of his career, was no less vitriolic about Moscow's latest star: 'If there were a conservatoire in Hell, if one of its talented students were instructed to write a programme symphony on "The Seven Plagues of Egypt", and if he were to compose a symphony like Mr Rachmaninoff's, then he would have fulfilled his task brilliantly and delighted the inmates of Hell',[65] Yet these remarks are not necessarily to be seen merely as the rantings of an arch Petersburg conservative but as a reflection of what was the general public sentiment at the concert. For whatever reasons, after the concert the audience was in turmoil. Ossovsky remarks that the work was 'misunderstood, unappreciated and rejected without ceremony . . . In all corners of the hall could be heard nothing but criticism, indignation, bewilderment, even rude language. Some shrugged their shoulders in astonishment at how so decadent a composition could have penetrated the polite programmes of the Belyayev concerts'.[66]

According to Sofiya Satina,[67] the now lost autograph of the full score of the symphony, like Tolstoy's *Anna Karenina*, bore the biblical epigraph 'Vengeance is mine, I will repay'. Though not appearing on the extant manuscript of the two-piano version, these words are to be found also on one of the orchestral parts used at the original performance.[68] The dedication of the work to Anna Lodïzhenskaya, discreetly referred to only by the initials 'A.L.', taken together with the epigraph, naturally prompts the thought that there may be auto-biographical overtones to the symphony relating to events in Tolstoy's novel (with which Rachmaninoff was of course familiar),[69] and that it may portray aspects of a liaison, actual or merely desired, between the young composer and the wife of his friend, Pyotr Lodïzhensky. To conceal the identity of the literary work underlying a musical programme by appropriating its epigraph was precisely what Rach-maninoff had done just two years before with *The Crag*, where the quotation from Lermontov had been calculated to mislead. While the reference to Tolstoy's novel would have been much less opaque, Rachmaninoff's private life was unknown and impenetrable to all except his closest confidants, and it would have been impossible to connect it with events in the novel. In her reminiscences[70] Lyudmila Skalon carefully emphasizes the 'platonic' nature of Rachmaninoff's love for Lodïzhenskaya, and one wonders why she felt this necessary at all, especially since she was outside the Lodïzhensky circle, unless it was for reasons of family discretion. At any rate, the extent of the appalling trauma Rachmaninoff suffered as a result of the failure of his symphony, from which he said he emerged 'a changed man', is surely most easily explained if, in the composer's mind, the words of the epigraph had been fulfilled and the work's failure seemed to him a form of divine retribution for moral guilt.

In the structure of its individual movements Rachmaninoff's First Symphony is relatively orthodox, though perhaps surprisingly its formal layout, in which the scherzo precedes the slow movement, follows Borodin and not Tchaikovsky. Where the work is truly innovative is in the high degree of integration and economy of musical material, something already seen on a smaller scale in the *Gypsy Caprice*. The composer states, rather misleadingly, that it was 'built up on' chants from the *Okteokhos*,[71] but none is used literally, despite the religious intonation of some parts of the work. The music also shows an unmistakable gypsy influence and the whole symphonic discussion is in a sense an interplay between two disparate elements so important in Rachmaninoff's upbringing and early manhood, religion and gypsyism.

The principal theme, stated at the very outset and present in one form or another on almost every page of the score, is a variant of the plain-chant *Dies irae*, which, although outside the Orthodox tradition, was familiar to Rachmaninoff through Tchaikovsky's 'Manfred' Symphony and probably also through some at least of the many other concert works in which it figures:

Ex.31

The Old Testament notion of a 'Day of wrath', a day of judgement when wrong-doers are brought to book, is a natural counterpart to 'Vengeance is mine, I will repay', and there could surely be no more fitting theme than *Dies irae* for the basis of a symphony with that epigraph. In the first movement it seems to represent the iron inexorability of fate, while in the second it takes on a wistful hue; in the middle of the slow movement it casts a menacing shadow across an interlude of tenderness, and in the finale, setting out as a festive march it appears at the end once more in its fundamental guise as implacable fate. After the traumatizing catastrophe of the premiere, it is hardly surprising that the symphony's musical motto was to haunt the composer throughout his life, appearing in his work with increasing insistence as he grew older and approached his own day of judgement.

There are just two other pieces of raw material in the whole fabric of the symphony. The curt inverted turn with which the work opens is used throughout as a linking device, not only between sections within movements but at their opening and close. It had already appeared in Rachmaninoff before in the seventh variation of the *Elegiac Trio*, Op. 9. The other is a rhythmic figure, occurring in the *Okteokhos*. A halting two-note motif, it underlies the opening of the main theme of the second movement and the last part of the third movement. It is first heard in the first movement second subject material (Ex. 32).

Ex.32

In stark contrast to the emotional world of *Dies irae*, the yearning melancholy of this motif is probably to be related to Lodïzhenskaya herself. Certainly the melodic shape of the sentimental preamble to this point has strong gypsy overtones and in fact a definite similarity to a popular Moscow gypsy song of the time.[72] It manages incidentally to incorporate not only the inverted turn but also, at the end, a gypsy sob:

Ex.33

The movement grows organically, with the momentum never sagging, and shows again how Rachmaninoff bridged the traditions of Petersburg and Moscow: the portentous opening is reminiscent of the start of Borodin's Second Symphony, melodically and instrumentally, while the development section, with its impetuous *fugato*, heralded by an orchestral crash, recalls Tchaikovsky's 'Pathétique' Symphony.

The delightful second movement, *Allegro animato*, is perhaps the best of the four. It has charm and a lightness of touch not always to be associated with its composer, and it has no obvious precedent among Russian symphonies; Rachmaninoff speaks with his own voice and with total confidence. The main theme of the *Larghetto*, a transformation of the first movement's second subject, is treated with sensitivity and restraint, its sentiment never being allowed to get out of hand. The movement's contrasting middle section, however, is a strangely menacing and growling episode, all but impossible to bring off successfully in performance. Perhaps it is one of those passages in Rachmaninoff's mind when he later described some parts of the work as 'strained'.[73] Shortly afterwards the gypsy sob reappears, as if to underline the link with Lodïzhenskaya:

Ex.34

The last movement, in which Rachmaninoff with great skill integrates all the previous material, opens with a festive variant of *Dies irae*, decked out in the brightest colours, with trumpet fanfares and a whole battery of percussion. Impetus is maintained into the development section, part of which, in its step-wise movement and rhythmic freedom, reproduces the intonation of religious chant:

Ex.35

In the middle of the movement appears the first 'big tune' in Rachmaninoff, derived from the first movement's second subject. In its position in the symphony, its high, arching line and its spirit of ecstatic outpouring, it anticipates the same moment in the Second Symphony twelve years on:

Ex.36a   Symphony No.1

Ex.36b   Symphony No.2

Whereas in the latter work sentiment is unfettered, particularly when the tune is brought back for the grand climax, in the First Symphony Rachmaninoff exercises much greater restraint, so pleasing those for whom an emotional wallow is anathema. As in the *Gypsy Caprice*, a vertiginous dance, with triangle and tambourine well to the fore, comes to a frenzied climax abruptly halted by a gong stroke. The movement has a heroic coda, which satisfactorily ties together all the loose ends, the work concluding, as it began, with the inverted turn.

Some critics rate Rachmaninoff's First Symphony his best.[74] At least at the time of its composition the composer himself thought he was

treading new musical paths, though later, with characteristic self-depreciation, he found in it 'much that is weak, childish, strained and
bombastic'.[75] Though in truth there are a few traces of all of these
qualities in the symphony, in the grandeur of its conception, its controlled
emotional intensity and its thematic integration it did unquestionably
mark a step forward for Russian music. To compare Stravinsky's uninteresting and already outmoded symphony of 1906–07, written at the
age of 24, with the 22-year-old Rachmaninoff's vastly more powerful
and advanced work of eleven years before, is to face a wry paradox:
Stravinsky was to be the arch-radical in music, and Rachmaninoff the
apostle of conservatism. After the First Symphony Rachmaninoff developed
as a composer only within the limits that work had defined. It was a
great leap forward that was never repeated; all that followed was
evolution along a fixed path. The disastrous premiere of a worthy
successor to Tchaikovsky's 'Pathétique' Symphony is all the sadder for
perhaps having permanently maimed its composer's creative spirit in
ways at which we can only guess.

Despite what commentators sometimes imply, it was never Rachmaninoff's intention to abandon his symphony. A few weeks after its
premiere, when he was already surprisingly cool and objective about
what had happened, he wrote, 'After leaving it on one side for six
months I shall look it through, perhaps correct it and perhaps publish
it – but perhaps by then my partiality for it will pass; then I shall tear
it up . . .'.[76] Though Gutheil had paid 500 roubles for the symphony,
he had not yet published it and tactfully never referred to the work
again. Twenty years on Rachmaninoff wrote to Boris Asafyev, 'I shall
not show the symphony, and in my will I shall forbid its inspection . . .',[77]
implying that he intended to keep the symphony by him until he died.
In fact the manuscript was locked away, 'under seven seals',[78] in his
Moscow flat, where it remained until he left Russia in 1917. Before his
departure he gave Sofiya Satina the key to his writing desk, showed
her the manuscript and asked her to look after it for him.[79] Miss Satina
had the desk moved to her own flat, in the same building, and there
it remained until she herself emigrated in 1921, when, along with other
Rachmaninoff materials, the manuscript passed into the care of the
faithful family housekeeper, Mariya Shatalina (*née* Ivanova). Its fate after
Shatalina's death in 1925 is unknown but, as all the other autographs
from Rachmaninoff's flat became state property and eventually found
their way into the archives of the Glinka Museum in Moscow, including
some sketches for the symphony and the complete two-piano version,
its mysterious disappearance suggests that it was appropriated by an
opportunist. Two years after Rachmaninoff's death the original band
parts were rediscovered in the Belyayev Archive in the Leningrad

Conservatoire, from which it was possible to reconstruct the whole orchestral score. The symphony received its second, and this time triumphant, performance at Moscow Conservatoire under Alexander Gauk on 17 October 1945, just forty-eight years after its premiere in St Petersburg.

Six Choruses for Women's or Children's Voices with Piano Accompaniment, Op. 15

The first work Rachmaninoff wrote in the interim between the composition of his symphony and its premiere, six short and undemanding choral pieces, seems by its nature to have been a by-product of his teaching post at the Maryinsky Academy. It is, at any rate, a work of humble artistic pretensions, the first five of the six choruses originally appearing at irregular intervals over a period of twelve months from January 1895 in the magazine *Dyetskoye chteniye* ('Reading for Children'), before the set was published complete the following year by Jurgenson, who had earlier published *The Crag* after the composer had had a temporary disagreement with Gutheil. Perhaps because of these pieces' unusual start in life they have always been the most elusive of all Rachmaninoff's works with an opus number, and their first public performance as a set seems not to have taken place before the Rachmaninoff centenary celebrations in 1973, with the Yurlov State Chorus under Yevgeny Svetlanov.

Throughout the set the chorus is divided into two parts, singing almost entirely at a third or in unison. In view of the straightforward nature of these songs, Rachmaninoff's comment that not a child would sing them[80] seems more than usually opaque. The first, *Be praised*,[81] was written at the end of 1894, at the time of the accession of the Emperor Nicholas II, to a patriotic hymn by Nekrasov. Rachmaninoff's setting, simple but imposing, reveals no characteristic fingerprints of its composer. On the other hand, *Night*, a fragrant setting of a poem by Vladimir Lodïzhensky, has some typically Rachmaninoff chromatics in the piano part at the end, where a new day rises while the weary earth still sleeps (Ex. 37).

The Pine Tree is a setting of a poem by Lermontov (after Heine). In the wild north a pine tree stands alone on a bare peak, wreathed in snow, dreaming of a beautiful palm tree growing in the hot desert. The vocal line is extremely simple, but there is considerable appeal in the wistful piano accompaniment to the static vocal line of the dream, where all the chorus except for two soloists intone wordlessly (Ex. 38). Lermontov's poem was also set, rather stolidly, by Balakirev, whose

Ex.37

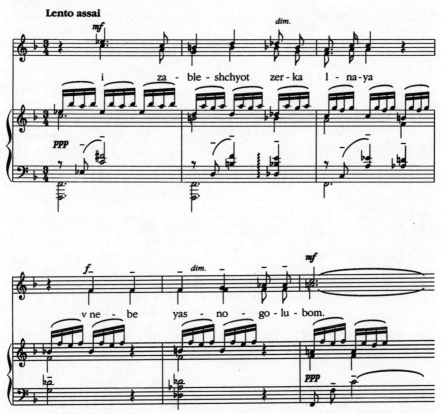

[It begins to shine crystalline in the clear blue sky]

song by chance was published by Jurgenson in the same year as the Rachmaninoff setting. *The waves dozed* is a delicate setting of a brief poem by Grand Duke Konstantinovich, describing how, as the moon lights up the sky, so joy brightens sorrow, while the title *Captivity* misleadingly conceals an unpretentious poem by Nikolay Tsïganov about a caged nightingale. When asked why he is so sad, the nightingale replies that his mate and nestlings are pining for him, whereupon he is released from captivity and sent on his way. Rachmaninoff echoes this naively touching tale sympathetically. The last song is the most extended, a sensitive setting of Lermontov's well-known poem *The Angel*, in which the poet tells how an angel sang a song in praise of God that surpassed all mortal songs. Rachmaninoff's setting echoes the mood

Ex.38

[It dreams of all that there is in the distant desert, where the sun rises.]

of Medtner's first published piano piece and song, based on the same text, composed at about the same time and also in E major, and in its restraint and dignity it makes a worthy conclusion to a set which, though having no claims to being a major discovery, deserves more than the total neglect it has so far suffered.

In the autumn of 1895 money worries drove Rachmaninoff to making a three-month recital tour of cities in Poland and the Baltic provinces with the Italian violinist Teresina Tua, but the gruelling schedule took its toll and eventually, exhausted both physically and mentally, he reneged on his contract and returned to Moscow. When he resumed composition, the first work he attempted was, of all things, a string quartet. Taneyev's diary for 22 March 1896 contains the entry: 'Friday, in the evening, Rachmaninoff came round. He is writing a quartet. We talked of quartet style and in particular of the C major Quartet of Mozart'. The project, however, was never completed. What survives is undated sketches for two movements: the exposition and fragments of the development of one sonata movement, lacking recapitulation and coda, and a second movement, more complete, with two versions of the opening, which the editors of the Soviet edition discreetly use to patch up the incomplete coda. Although Rachmaninoff's life-long friend the pianist and teacher Alexander Goldenweiser later recalled Rachmaninoff's speaking to him about writing a quartet at the time when he was working on *The Bells*,[82] that is, in 1913, the sketches are almost certainly to be identified with the 1896 work on stylistic grounds. Moreover, the fact that Taneyev dedicated his own Third Quartet to Rachmaninoff the following year may be not only a token of friendship but possibly also a memento of the efforts he may have made at this time to interest his one-time pupil in a form of composition which, though dear to himself, at least in retrospect seems somehow alien to Rachmaninoff.

The two movements of Rachmaninoff's new quartet mark a great advance on his juvenile effort of 1889 in terms both of the much more enterprising writing for the four instruments and of the musical material, whose stern and dark mood is recognizably Russian but which, being generally altogether uncharacteristic of its composer, is difficult to fit into the chronology of his work. However, in the impassioned first movement the last of the three themes introduced bears more than a passing similarity to the 'Cloud' motif in *The Crag* and the variation theme of the *Elegiac Trio* of three years before, confirming the 1896 rather than the 1913 date for its composition (Ex. 39). The earlier date is also confirmed by the nature of the final chords of the exposition, repeated at the end of the movement in the reconstructed score, in which the same harmonic sequence is used as at the end of the opening theme of the last movement of the First Symphony, written the previous year.

The second movement, in C minor, is mainly built on a ground bass, constantly rising step-wise to a fourth from the tonic note and then falling back again, in a sinister passacaglia of considerable power. An answering phrase, borrowed from the first movement, gives the two movements as they stand some structural cohesion. One wonders whether

Ex.39

it was Taneyev who persuaded his young friend to try his hand at an exercise in this very old musical form, which is otherwise unexampled in Rachmaninoff and rare indeed in Russian music generally.

Another musical exercise this year associated with Taneyev is a brief set of four improvisations for piano, a combined composition by Arensky, Glazunov, Rachmaninoff and Taneyev, obviously written only for their own amusement and perhaps given an impromptu performance at one of Taneyev's Wagner evenings so evocatively described by Sabaneyeff.[83] Each composer provided a few bars as a starting point for his three colleagues to continue in turn, before himself rounding off the improvisation. To Arensky's gently serious start Rachmaninoff's contribution was merely two modulatory bars, and to Glazunov's sprightly polka he added a brief counter theme. His own offering as a subject was four bars of an unsettled and rather mysterious *Allegro scherzando* in B flat minor:

Ex.40

Glazunov's continuation was abruptly and incongruously interrupted by some very un-Rachmaninoff hunting horn calls from Taneyev, before Arensky restored order and Rachmaninoff completed the improvisation in the vein in which it began. In the last improvisation, a contrast in dance rhythms started somewhat academically by Taneyev, Arensky incorporated a literal borrowing from The Women's Dance in *Aleko*, and Rachmaninoff added a few bars of march. One can imagine the four composers enjoying themselves enormously over these trifles, which alas musically amount to no more than a very odd curiosity.

Twelve Songs, Op. 14

The autumn of 1896 saw the composition of Rachmaninoff's third published set of songs, which, though varying considerably in quality, include several among his most popular. The texts are taken from a wide range of poets, and greater importance is given to the piano accompaniment than hitherto, but the rousing codas to some of the songs perhaps lack discretion. One such occurs in the opening song, *I wait for thee*, set to words by Mariya Davidova and dedicated to Lyudmila Skalon, which was held over for this collection from two years before. After a sensitively restrained vocal line in the first half, the depiction of the quickening feelings of the lover awaiting his beloved is made the excuse at the end for a gratuitous purple patch in the accompaniment, making all the more striking the contrast with the following song, *The Little Island*. Set to a free version by Konstantin Balmont of Shelley's poem *The Isle*, a picture of nature and tranquillity is reflected admirably in the gentle grace and purity of the musical setting, a perfect foil to its dedicatee, Sofiya Satina. Although such restraint is unique in this set, it has a precedent in Rachmaninoff's unpublished song *The flower has faded*, of 1893.

The next eight songs alternate between passionate expressions of love and grief. *How few the joys*, to a poem by Afanasy Fet about the pains of lost love, was dedicated out of affection[84] to Zoya Pribïtkova, the four-year-old daughter of Rachmaninoff's cousin; the setting is unattractively whimpering, but *I came to her*, by Alexey Koltsov and dedicated to Rachmaninoff's friend Yury Sakhnovsky, deftly catches the exhilaration of a love that is mutual, with its eager vocal line and arpeggiate accompaniment. Rathaus's *Midsummer Nights*, dedicated to Rachmaninoff's publisher Gutheil, is finer still. The composer captures perfectly the ecstasy and restless desire in the heart that is stirred by the fine nights of summer, a restlessness underlined by the alternating and uncertain tonality of the piano accompaniment (Ex.41). The sixth and seventh songs are both settings of poems by Alexey Tolstoy. *The world would see thee smile*, dedicated to a musician friend of Rachmaninoff's, A.N. Ivanovsky, describes a grief in the heart that destroys all pleasure in life; Rachmaninoff's setting is unrelievedly lugubrious. In contrast, *Believe it not*, dedicated to Rachmaninoff's cousin Anna Klokacheva, is the reaffirmation of a love that seems to have wavered. A blithe vocal line is supported by one of Rachmaninoff's typical triplet accompaniments, which runs gloriously amok at the end. Both Tchaikovsky (1869) and Rimsky-Korsakov (1897) set the same text, though much less exuberantly. The setting of Apukhtin's *O, do not grieve*, dedicated to the gypsy singer Nadezhda Alexandrova, Anna

Ex.41

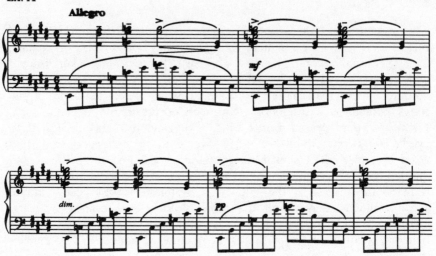

Lodïzhenskaya's sister, is redolent of gypsy pathos, echoing the text, in which a dead former lover tells his beloved not to grieve for him as he is close to her still. The next pair of songs are both settings of Nikolay Minsky (Valenkin) and both dedicated to the singer Elizaveta Lavrovskaya, whose contralto voice no doubt prompted Rachmaninoff to lay out the vocal part for the lower register. The subject of both is resignation in the face of a hopeless love, and both have an occasional oriental colouring in the melodic line that seems more a mannerism than a necessity, since it does not reflect the content of the poetry. The tranquil *As fair as day in blaze of noon* has an interesting rocking figure in thirds in the accompaniment, which anticipates the B minor and D flat *Moments musicaux*, written at about the same time. *Love's Flame*, a slow waltz, somewhat less sombre in mood, is the least memorable song in the group.

The last two songs of Op. 14 leave the self-indulgent sentimentality of the preceding numbers far behind. Rachmaninoff's setting of Tyutchev's *Spring Waters* rapidly became famous throughout Russia and justifiably retains its hold as one of the most attractive of all his songs. In it the composer catches perfectly the exhilaration of the awakening of spring in a marvellously buoyant melody for the voice, while the rushing piano part echoes the bubbling waters as the ice of a Russian winter begins its rapid thaw. Appropriately enough, Rachmaninoff dedicated this song to his first piano teacher, Anna Ornatskaya. Too good a tune to miss, it was later choreographed by Asaf Messerer as a *divertissement* for the

Bolshoi ballet company. In contrast, the final song, to a well-known poem by Semyon Nadson, *'Tis time*, is a powerful cry for help, in which the poet begs a prophet to come to help a struggling people before it is too late, a theme into which Soviet commentators naturally sometimes read political connotations. With a massive piano accompaniment to underline this message, the song brings the set to a powerful conclusion.

Six Moments Musicaux, Op. 16

The last of the works written before the premiere of the First Symphony was the set of six *Moments musicaux* for piano, dating from the autumn of 1896 and dedicated to Zateyevich. In these pieces Rachmaninoff's piano writing rises to new heights of virtuosity, and the composer finds his own personal manner of expression more distinctly than ever before. However, although they can be seen as immediate precursors of the Preludes, their melodic lines lack the character of these later works, and there is a tendency in them to monotonous repetition, which is almost certainly the reason why they have never won general popularity with either the public or professional pianists, few of whom have ever put the whole cycle into a recital programme.[85]

The set is arranged with the items alternately meditative and virtuosic, beginning with a plaintive *Andantino* in B flat minor, which recalls the style of the earlier piano pieces of Op. 3 and Op. 10, and in which the unremarkable main theme is subjected to a series of varied repetitions. The contrasting *con moto* middle section in the major key, in which the time signature changes ten times in seventeen bars, is a remarkable example of rhythmic flexibility and has a recitative feel about it. The following *Allegretto* in E flat minor is undoubtedly the best item in the set. Restlessly threatening and with an inexhaustible motoric energy that is calmed only in the last bars, the piece encapsulates in its elaborate piano figuration and urgent pathos all the essential characteristics of the piano writing of the mature Rachmaninoff, and it provides incontestable evidence that the composer was already taking Russian piano music forward. It is not surprising that it was this work and none other of the set that Rachmaninoff chose to play many years later in his years as a concert pianist, slightly revising it in the process. The changes in the second version (dated 5 February 1940) are confined to a new title, *Allegro*, minor improvements to the piano writing, the by now inevitable excision of a few redundant bars in the build-up to the central climax, and a slight change to the final cadence.

The third piece, an *Andante cantabile* in B minor, is a funeral elegy. It was a particular favourite of Medtner, who used to play it in his concert programmes in Russia and America.[86] Melodically it closely resembles the C minor *Étude-Tableau*, Op. 39, No. 7, of 1916, which Rachmaninoff himself admitted was a picture of a funeral, and the punctuated asymmetrical phrases are like mourners' spoken utterances of grief. The middle section, usually but not invariably repeated in performance, has a typically Rachmaninoff stepwise movement in plangent thirds, evoking a choir intoning:

Ex.42

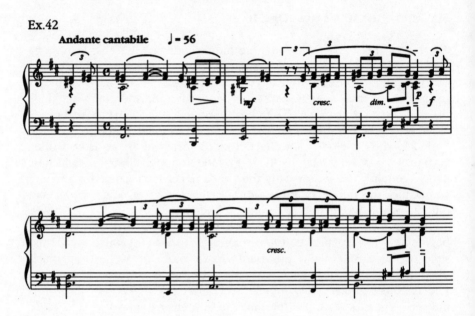

Later, staccato octave quavers in the left hand suggest a funeral march, and it therefore seems very likely that the composition was prompted by the death in September 1896 of Rachmaninoff's cousin Alexander Satin, with whom he had been on close terms.

The fourth piece, a tempestuous *Presto* in E minor, in which a short-spanned melody is relentlessly hammered home over a rapid figuration in the left hand, was perhaps unconsciously derived from Chopin's G major Prelude, Op. 28, No. 3. The demonic impetus never flags, and, as if to make up for the lack of tonal variety, interest is quickened by the metronome marking increasing twice before the end. It seems incredible that this dynamic piece could really have been written originally as a class exercise for Arensky four years previously, as Goldenweiser maintains.[87] In contrast, the fifth *Moment musical*, an *Adagio sostenuto* in D flat, is a tranquil barcarolle, with an agreeable

1 Nikolay Zverev with his 'cubs' (l.–r.) Maximov, Rachmaninoff and
Pressman. 1886

2 Arensky (sitting centre) with the three graduates of his composition class (l.–r.) Conus, Morozov and Rachmaninoff. 1892.

3 Rachmaninoff with his dog Levko on the banks of the River Khoper near Krasnenkoye. 1899.

4   Rachmaninoff and Levko. 1900

5 Rachmaninoff fishing in the River Khoper near Krasnenkoye.
Summer 1901.

6 Rachmaninoff in the study of his Moscow flat. 1904.

7 Rachmaninoff with the artists who took part in the premiere of
Francesca da Rimini: Georgy Baklanov (Lanciotto Malatesta) and
Nadezhda Salina (Francesca). January 1906.

8   Ivanovka. The wing of the house in which Rachmaninoff lived.

if undistinctive melody over a gently rocking triplet accompaniment. The sixth and last piece, in C major, labled *Maestoso*, is a grandiloquent pianistic *tour de force*, in which the composer demands not only the most agile of fingers but the most powerful of pianistic physiques with which to extract the maximum sonority from the instrument:

Ex.43

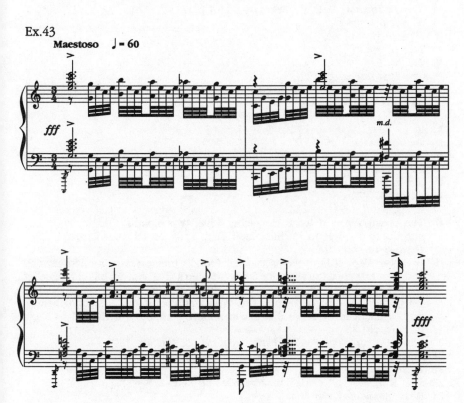

Rachmaninoff's most recent works – the First Symphony, the best of the Op. 14 songs and the *Moments musicaux* – all demonstrate how far he had come as a composer in only three years, since the time of the emotionally over-heated *Elegiac Trio* and the tepid piano pieces Ops. 10 and 11. They provide incontestable evidence that almost all of what we now think of as the *echt* features of Rachmaninoff's mature style had crystallized before the Second Concerto; only the soaring lyricism is missing, and this was to come in abundance in his next works. But first the disastrous premiere of the First Symphony had to be confronted and overcome, and that was to prove an almost intractable stumbling block for three years.

References

1 It was for Brandukov that Tchaikovsky, in 1887, wrote his *Pezzo capriccioso*, Op. 62.
2 Siloti to Modest Tchaikovsky, 25 August 1892.
3 R. to Modest Tchaikovsky, 13 May 1893.
4 *The Delineator*, Vol. 75, February 1910, p. 284.
5 *Seroff*, pp. 45–46.
6 *Piggott*, p. 28.
7 *B/L*, p. 49.
8 *B/L*, p. 51.
9 See *Bryantseva*, p. 129.
10 A photograph of the Lïsikov summer-house is to be found in *Piggott*, p. 34 and *Rudakova*, p. 45.
11 R. to Natalya Skalon, 10 June 1892.
12 R. to Boris Asafyev, 13 April 1917.
13 See *Bryantseva*, p. 139.
14 Set as a vocal duet, also in G minor, by Tchaikovsky (Op. 46, No. 3), and as a solo song by Taneyev.
15 R's dictated reminiscences, in *B/L*, p. 184.
16 *Swan*, p. 177.
17 *Artist*, April 1894, p. 248.
18 The inscription is dated 8 November 1898, two months after Chekhov had introduced himself to Rachmaninoff at a Yalta recital with Chaliapin. See *Bryantseva*, p. 151.
19 Bryantseva (p. 151) observes that the Cloud's theme shares its flute scoring and E major tonality with the Snow Maiden's first aria in the prologue of Rimsky-Korsakov's eponymous opera, first staged in Moscow on 26 January 1893, only six months before *The Crag* was composed. Although there is no documentary evidence that Rachmaninoff attended, it is more than likely that he did so.
20 César Cui in *Novosti i birzhevaya gazeta*, 22 January 1896.
21 *Piggott*, p. 46.
22 *Bryantseva*, p. 171.
23 S.N. Kruglikov in *Artist*, January 1894, pp. 176–177.
24 R. to Smolensky, 16 March 1894.
25 R. to Smolensky, 18 March 1895.
26 R. to Smolensky, 12 June 1896.
27 R. to Smolensky, 30 June 1897.
28 R. to Kerzin, 15 April 1906.
29 R. to Asafyev, 13 April 1917.
30 R. to Lyudmila Skalon, 23 March 1893.
31 Lyudmila Rostovtsova (Skalon), *VR/A* 1, p. 240.
32 For the dating of *The Song of the Disillusioned* see *LN/A* 2, p. 413.
33 In *B/L*, p. 62, following *Riesemann*, p. 92, it is stated that Rachmaninoff was still in Kiev at the time of Tchaikovsky's death, but it is impossible to reconcile this with the date on a surviving note from R. to Bertha Kreutzer (in Moscow) dated the day in question, 25 October, and saying that he would be coming that evening to give a piano lesson to her daughter, Elena, who later herself confirmed the date and recalled how upset R. was (*VR/A* 1, p. 255).

34 R. to Natalya Skalon, 17 December 1893.
35 Details in *T/N*, pp. 52–53.
36 In recitals during the previous two years Rachmaninoff had included in his programmes Pabst's 'Concert Paraphrases' of Tchaikovsky's most popular operas, *Eugene Onegin* and *Queen of Spades*.
37 *T/N*, p. 55.
38 Attention was first drawn to these revisions by Deryck Cooke in the last of his three broadcasts about piano rolls, 'The Late Romantic Piano' on the BBC Third Programme in 1964; they are also duly noted in *T/N*, p. 55.
39 *Threlfall and Norris* are mistaken in assuming (p. 56) that the theme has not been identified.
40 *B/L*, p. 407, places the work in '1893 or earlier'; *T/N*, p. 154, in '1894?'
41 Byron's 'Don Juan', cantos II–IV.
42 Lyudmila Rostovtsova (Skalon), *VR/A* 1, p. 240.
43 *B/L*, p. 64; *T/N*, p. 165.
44 The love duet of Paolo and Francesca, the first item of Rachmaninoff's opera to be composed, was completed six years after Don Juan, in July 1900.
45 R. to Slonov, 3 September 1894.
46 R. to Slonov, 2 August 1892.
47 Lyudmila Rostovtsova (Skalon), *VR/A* 1, p. 239. The theme has been identified as a variant of the dance-song *Vo sadu li, v ogorode*. See *Bryantseva*, p. 205.
48 R. to Morozov, 12 April 1908.
49 *Riesemann*, p. 217.
50 January 1895, according to Rachmaninoff's own not altogether reliably dated list of works sent to Boris Asafyev in April 1917.
51 R. to Slonov, 2 September 1895.
52 R. to Slonov, 15 September 1895.
53 Glazunov's cuts were of bars 276–289 in the first movement (followed by Kurt Sanderling in his 1950s recording) and, less certainly, a more substantial one of bars 302–340 in the second movement.
54 *B/L*, p. 70.
55 R. to Taneyev, 23 October 1896.
56 R. to Asafyev, 13 April 1917.
57 Lyudmila Rostovtsova (Skalon), *VR/A* 1, p. 242.
58 R. to Zateyevich, 6 May 1897.
59 Elena Zhukovskaya (Kreutzer), *VR/A* 1, p. 265.
60 *Swan*, p. 185.
61 Elena Zhukovskaya (Kreutzer), loc. cit.
62 Alexander Khessin, *VR/A* 1, p. 429.
63 Alexander Ossovsky, *VR/A* 1, p. 352.
64 Besides Rachmaninoff's symphony, the programme included the premieres of Tchaikovsky's symphonic poem *Fatum*, newly reconstructed and just published by Belyayev, and the *Valse-Fantaisie* of Nikolay Artsïbushev (1858–1937). It is sometimes stated (e.g. *Bazhanov*, p. 121) that Glazunov's Sixth Symphony was also premiered that evening, but this is due to a misreading of a note in *Rimsky-Korsakov*, p. 362.
65 Cui in *Novosti i birzhevaya gazeta*, 17 March 1897, p. 3.
66 Ossovsky, loc. cit.
67 Sofiya Satina, *VR/A* 1, p. 29.
68 Preface by the editors, I. Iordan and G. Kirkor, in the full score of the symphony, published by Muzyka, Moscow, 1977.

69 Lyudmila Rostovtsova (Skalon), *VR/A* 1, p. 237.
70 Op. cit., p. 239.
71 *Riesemann*, p. 96.
72 See *Bryantseva*, p. 220.
73 R. to Asafyev, 13 April 1917.
74 See specially Robert Simpson in *The Symphony, 2, Elgar to the Present Day*, Penguin Books, 1967, pp. 128–131.
75 R. to Asafyev, 13 April 1917.
76 R. to Zateyevich, 6 May 1897.
77 R. to Asafyev, 13 April 1917.
78 *Riesemann*, p. 100.
79 Conversation with the author, August 1973.
80 R. to Zateyevich, 7 December 1896.
81 Nekrasov's text 'Praise to our people, praise', was altered by the Imperial censor to 'Be praised he who grants freedom to the country', and it was this version that Rachmaninoff used. The original text is restored in the Soviet edition.
82 B. Dobrokhotov, *Tsitovich*, p. 119.
83 Sabaneyeff in *B/L*, p. 69, from his article *'Moi vstrechi: Rakhmaninov'*, in *Novoye russkoye slovo*, New York, 28 September 1952.
84 The dedication is an example of Rachmaninoff's love of children. See Z.A. Pribïtkova in *VR/A* 2, p. 58.
85 Lazar Berman is a notable exception to the rule.
86 See E. Dolinskaya, *Nikolay Metner*, Muzyka, Moscow, 1966, p. 17.
87 Goldenweiser, *VR/A* 1, p. 409.

5 Moscow, 1897–1906

> There are serious illnesses and deadly blows from fate which entirely change a man's character. This was the effect of my own symphony on myself. When the indescribable torture of the performance had at last come to an end, I was a different man.[1]

Thus did Rachmaninoff describe the effect on him of the disastrous failure of his symphony's premiere in St Petersburg on 15 March 1897. When he returned to Moscow, he was a psychological wreck. He told Riesemann that all his hopes, all belief in himself, had been destroyed,[2] and Boris Asafyev that he felt 'like a man who had suffered a stroke and for a long time had lost the use of his head and hands'.[3] There seemed to be no future for him as a composer, and few openings even as a performer. 'Agonising hours spent in doubt and hard thinking had brought me to the conclusion that I ought to give up composing. I was obviously unfitted for it, and therefore it would be better if I made an end to it at once . . . A paralysing apathy possessed me . . . I did not live; I vegetated, idle and hopeless.'[4] Sofiya Satina recounts how Rachmaninoff was at first not only demoralized about his work but also, on a more mundane level, bothered by financial worries:[5]

> Lying for days on end on a couch he kept gloomily silent, showing almost no reaction either to consolation or attempts to persuade him that he must take himself in hand or to the kindness with which those close to him tried to cheer him up. He kept saying only that he would be able to begin writing if he had a definite sum of money over a period of two or three years, which would allow him to forget about the necessity of earning money for a specified time.

In the event, three fallow years were to pass, during which occasional good intentions and even spasmodic work, inhibited either by self-criticism sharpened by the experience of failure or by a simple inability to break the grip of depression, all resulted in embarrassingly little concrete achievement.

Surprisingly, it seems that Rachmaninoff made his very first attempt to resume work only three weeks after the trauma of his symphony's premiere; more surprisingly still, the form of composition he chose was, of all things, another symphony. In this he was perhaps like an acrobat who has fallen off the high wire and who imagines that his confidence can be restored only by going straight back up. In this case, however, the self-imposed therapy failed to work. On the single page of manuscript Rachmaninoff left, containing 55 bars of a simple theme and its development, he wrote the sardonic comment: 'Sketches for my new symphony, which, by the look of them, will be of no special interest. S. V. Rachmaninoff, 5th April, 1897'.[6] His inability to proceed with the work can have done nothing but confirm his depression and morbid self-doubts.

Rachmaninoff's illness was psychosomatic,[7] as Lyudmila Skalon was later to recall: 'In the spring of 1897 Seryozha had sharp pains in his back, leg and arms from neurasthenia. He suffered a lot, and his doctor advised him to spend the summer somewhere in the country as quietly as possible, not working strenuously on the piano and not composing anything'.[8] Accordingly, at the end of May Rachmaninoff went with the Skalon sisters to spend the summer on their estate near Nizhni-Novgorod. Despite his doctor's advice, he used the time to earn 200 roubles by making a four-hand piano version of Glazunov's newly composed Sixth Symphony. When he returned to Moscow in September he received word from Slonov that Savva Mamontov, millionaire industrialist and opera impresario, had a vacancy for him as second conductor of his Private Opera. With the two Kiev performances of *Aleko* and one of his *Gypsy Caprice* as his only previous practical experience, Rachmaninoff boldy began a professional conducting career in October. The work took all his energy but provided much-needed income and no doubt usefully distracted him from self-indulgent introspection. The considerable artistic success and public acclaim Rachmaninoff achieved in his new role must surely have boosted his morale; no less important, as he admitted later,[9] was the fact that it brought him into contact with the genius who became perhaps his greatest friend and artistic stimulus, Fyodor Chaliapin.

Rachmaninoff left the season with the Mamontov company early and did not return. He had found, as he did again later, when he worked at the Bolshoi Theatre, that the demands of a conducting post allowed no time for any other activity, and although he had no immediate income except from piano lessons and the occasional concert engagement, he clearly intended at this stage to resume his career as a composer. In April 1898 he wrote to Zateyevich to say that although he had achieved nothing so far, he was 'getting ready',[10] and by June he had apparently been devoting a great deal of thought to a new piano concerto.

Goldenweiser, who was aware that Rachmaninoff was working on a concerto and had asked to be allowed to perform it at a Belyayev concert in St Petersburg, assumed that its realization was only a matter of time, but the composer quickly disillusioned him: 'Your desire to play my Second Concerto in Petersburg touches and gladdens my heart. But because I don't yet have this concerto and because all my intensive work on it has got nowhere, I want to ask for your permission to give you a final answer to your question in the middle of August'.[11]

The summer seemed promising for work. Far from moping in depression Rachmanioff seems to have enjoyed the time he spent on the estate of Tatyana Lyubatovich, Mamontov's prima donna, at Putyatino; indeed, Chaliapin even goes so far as to describe the composer at this time as 'full of vitality and vivacity, and excellent company'.[12] He helped Chaliapin to prepare a number of operatic roles, most notably Salieri in Rimsky-Korsakov's *Mozart and Salieri*, due to be premiered during the next season, and rehearsed Mussorgsky's *Boris Godunov* with the whole company. The work on *Boris* may have prompted Rachmaninoff to switch attention away from the concerto towards plans for an opera of his own based on Shakespeare, possibly on the not entirely dissimilar royal subject of *Richard II*,[13] with which he had been toying since Modest Tchaikovsky had suggested the idea in the spring. He wrote back to Tchaikovsky at the end of July enquiring about a possible libretto and remarking hopefully, 'If my affairs can be so arranged, I would expect to begin composition in about two or three month's time . . . If I am to write an opera, it will have to be written quickly'.[14] But Tchaikovsky now offered Rachmaninoff another libretto, *Francesca da Rimini*, from Dante, which he had originally written for Liadov in 1895[15] but which that composer, with characteristic procrastination, had so far done nothing with. The new subject immediately captured Rachmaninoff's imagination and he seems to have abandoned all other work. In an apologetic letter to Goldenweiser on 14 August he explained that he had not finished writing the concerto, and a fortnight later he wrote in detail to Tchaikovsky about changes he felt necessary to his *Francesca* scenario.[16]

In October, Rachmaninoff was at last free from outside commitment but still homeless. Fortunately Lyubatovich invited him back to Putyatino, where there was the solitude and freedom from disturbance so necessary for his work. But the composer was still not in the right psychological state to do more than rest and collect his thoughts. 'I have not composed anything yet but, with God's help, I hope to do so', he wrote to Zateyevich on 26 October. November was interrupted by medical treatment in Moscow, but the end of the year brought encouraging news from Siloti of the phenomenal success of the C sharp minor Prelude on his concert tour of Europe, England and America, and an invitation to Rachmaninoff to appear in London in April 1899 as conductor and soloist. Although the composer's energies now had to be channelled towards preparing for his first appearance abroad, he nevertheless managed to sketch out two piano pieces at this time. The first, a rippling *Allegro* in G minor, Rachmaninoff called 'Fantasy Piece', the title he had used collectively for the Op. 3 set. The single side of manuscript, dated 11 January 1899, bears the enigmatic inscription 'Delmo' or 'Lelmo'. Bryantseva wonders[17] whether this may not be an acronym of the Christian names of Leonid ('Lyola') Maximov and Matvey ('Motya') Pressman, who were cubs of Zverev along with Rachmaninoff and who often met up with Rachmaninoff after Zverev's death;[18] thus the work could be a celebration or reminiscence of the trio's studies with Zverev. A difficulty with this suggestion, however, is the urgently serious nature of the piece itself, which makes it a very odd remembrance of shared youthful studies:

Ex.44

Maximov left no formal reminiscences of his student years, dying when he was only thirty-one, but Pressman wrote an extensive article about life with Zverev,[19] in which he nowhere refers to the piece, as he surely would have done had he known about it or had some personal significance attached to it. Musically it is of no importance; its single idea moves to a climax, is recapitulated and then rounded off, evidently being incapable of further development, all within 45 seconds. The other piece, a *Fughetta* in F Major, dated 4 February 1899, is an even more striking testimony to Rachmaninoff's creative impotence. The composer seems to have absolutely nothing to say and simply has recourse to sterile academic gestures. No wonder Goldenweiser found it uninteresting when the composer played it through for him.[20]

On 30 March 1899 Rachmaninoff set out for London. In his concert at the Queen's Hall, on 19 April, he conducted his *Crag* and an aria from *Prince Igor*, and played the *Élégie* and *Prelude* from his Op. 3. As a result of his success Rachmaninoff was invited to return the next year and perform his concerto, this producing the confident reply that he would bring another and better one; and in a biographical sketch in the weekly magazine *Black and White*, published at the time of his London appearance, it was even announced that the composer was actually at work on a new opera. Both announcements were premature. When Rachmaninoff returned to Russia, he was annoyed to learn from

Arensky that *Aleko* was being staged in Petersburg on 27 May as part of the celebrations for the centenary of Pushkin's birth, but Chaliapin's superb performance in the title role and the favourable reception of the opera by the public banished his misgivings.

At the beginning of May Rachmaninoff joined the Kreutzer family for the first of three summers at Krasnenkoye in the province of Voronezh. According to Elena Kreutzer Rachmaninoff was by now feeling better in himself, encouraged by his London and Petersburg successes, and had begun to work intensively on composition.[21] In June Natasha Satina also came to stay with the Kreutzers and one day, while she and Elena were browsing through the library, Rachmaninoff joined them. By chance, he picked out an anthology containing a poem by Prince Vyazemsky, *Eperné*, celebrating the drinking of champagne, and read it out to them, making changes to the text as he did so to make Natasha the addressee. He announced that he would set the poem to music and the very next evening he accompanied himself in a performance of his new opus for the girls.[22] The heavy-handed jocularity of the text ('Were you hiccuping?') and the forced if not desperate gaiety of the music, with its fleeting references to Tchaikovsky's *Eugene Onegin*,[23] fail to disguise the banality of the incongruous setting. The superscription on the manuscript seems to be the composer's answer to Natasha's anxious questions about his creative activity – 'No! my muse has not died, dear Natasha. I dedicate to you my new song' – but the music can scarcely have reassured her.

Two other pieces were certainly completed that summer of 1899, despite the contrary evidence of the dates on the manuscripts: the cantata *Pantaley the Healer*, and the song *Fate*.[24] *Pantaley* is a short four-part unaccompanied chorus set to a satiric poem by Alexey Tolstoy, which Rachmaninoff found in the library at Krasnenkoye.[25] The text is an address to Pantaley, a kind of rustic deity who practises herbal medicine. As he walks around the field, greeted by the flowers, he shakes his knobbly stick at the poisonous herbs and collects the wholesome ones, which he uses for his healing work. The poet appeals to Pantaley to help those maimed in heart, soul and mind, and not spare his stick on unbelievers, who spurn such cures. The relevance of the poem to Rachmaninoff's own circumstances is all the clearer when it is remembered that his stay in the country among the flowers and scenic beauties of Krasnenkoye was itself an occasion for the healing powers of nature to work their cure. It must be admitted, however, that, though the choral writing is rich, the rather solemn musical material, with its ecclesiastical overtones, is not especially interesting, though profoundly Russian (Ex. 45).

The composer seems to have been pleased with his setting and frequently sang it that summer; subsequently Natasha (soprano), Elena

Ex.45

[Lord Panteley walks over the field]

(alto), Max Kreutzer (tenor) and Rachmaninoff (bass) performed it as a quartet. The work was published by Gutheil in 1901.

Fate has been much abused by musical commentators, but in fact it is a much better song than they allow. Apukhtin's poem, in which hopes for future happiness are forever wrecked by blows from a malevolent fate, must have gripped Rachmaninoff's imagination by its all-too-apt relevance to his own circumstances. Perhaps the use of the motto from Beethoven's Fifth Symphony to depict the knocking of fate on the door was a banal idea, but it works well in its context, and the middle section of the song, depicting the ephemeral rapture of ill-starred lovers, can make a haunting impression in the right hands. Whether *Fate* succeeds in performance or not depends critically upon the art of the singer. Many of Rachmaninoff's songs may satisfactorily be sung by more than one kind of voice, but only a bass will serve for this dramatic monologue, which demands theatrical as well as vocal skills of the highest order. Above all songs of Rachmaninoff, it is the one of which the lack of a recording by Chaliapin is most to be regretted: it was written for Chaliapin and it was he who gave the first public performance of it, on 9 March 1900, accompanied by the composer, in the Hall of the Nobility in Moscow, where its success led to its being encored.

Another powerful song, probably dating from the same time and on a not dissimilar theme, is *Night*, a Rathaus setting. The choice of poem may have been prompted by an event in Rachmaninoff's life glossed over by his biographers. In the autumn of 1899 Vera Skalon married. Since Rachmaninoff and she had first met at Ivanovka in 1890 their association had always been very close but, for whatever reason, it never reached the stage of formal courtship. Nevertheless, her sister was to recall that before her marriage Vera burned more than a hundred letters from the composer and that right up to her early death in 1909 Seryozha had a special place in her heart.[26] As with the circumstances of Rachmaninoff's courtship of Natalya Satina two years later, the total lack of any extant correspondence between the parties concerned frustrates the biographer, but Rachmaninoff was certain to have been saddened by a bright spirit in his past moving out of his life for good,[27] and Rathaus's poem must exactly have matched his mood:

> Once more sleep does not come to my tired eyes.
> I am alone . . . but in the dead silence
> Someone quietly sings to me mournful songs
> And tenderly bends over me.

Could that person, the poet wonders, be his 'dream of bygone childhood days'?

> My heart is weary of everyday cares,
> All ardour of desire is extinguished in my breast
> And a mocking fate has long since
> Closed all paths to happiness.

When he returned to Moscow Rachmaninoff was unable to shake off his depression. In November he sketched out a pleasant but insignificant arrangement for four-part unaccompanied chorus of a simple Ukrainian folk song, *Choboti* ('Shoes'), possibly at the request of Slonov, who had organized a concert of Ukrainian folk music in Moscow the previous year. The eight-bar tune repeats itself eight times, and Rachmaninoff is resourceful in varying its setting on each appearance, but the chasm between the triviality of this work and the high aspirations of the First Symphony must have been painfully self-evident. In comparison with the fecundity of earlier years the output of the summer had been ominously tiny.

To try to lift Rachmaninoff's spirits a friend of the Satins, Princess Alexandra Liven, arranged that he should visit Leo Tolstoy, who was then in Moscow. She had asked Tolstoy to speak encouragingly to the young composer, but when, on the night of 9 January 1900,[28] Rachmaninoff went to the house with Chaliapin, whom he accompanied in a number of songs, including his own *Fate*, the auspicious circumstances turned sour when the great man enquired what the point was of such music: 'Beethoven is nonsense, and so too Pushkin and Lermontov'. This must have seemed the final ironic blow of fate to Rachmaninoff, who may have been unaware that Tolstoy had only recently (1897) completed his book *What is Art?*, in which he had formulated his idiosyncratic aesthetic ideals, excluding from his definition anything that did not fit in with his own narrow social, moral and religious aims. Goldenweiser, who was also present at the meeting, said that Tolstoy called Apukhtin's poem 'abominable' and that he showed enthusiasm only for the simple folk song *Night*.[29]

Once again Rachmaninoff retreated to the Satins in Moscow in a state of total apathy, from which his by now desperate friends were unable to stir him. Drastic measures being required, he was inveigled into seeing a neurologist the family knew, Dr Nikolay Dahl, a specialist in hypnotherapy, and from January to April 1900 visited him daily.[30] The story of Dahl's success in reviving the composer's spirits through auto-suggestion is a famous one, and Rachmaninoff himself gratefully acknowledged his help by dedicating to him his Second Concerto, but although his depression appeared to be lifting there were no immediate tangible results, or at least none that he disclosed.

Towards the end of April Rachmaninoff moved with Chaliapin to a house on Princess Liven's estate in Yalta, where he remained until the beginning of June, renewing contact with Chekhov and members of the Moscow Art Theatre and making the acquaintance of the composer Vasily Kalinnikov, whom he had the consolation of helping materially shortly before his tragically early death from tuberculosis. Rachmaninoff's correspondence gives the impression that he was restless during his stay. Although it was ostensibly because he did not wish to tear himself away from his work that he turned down an invitation from Slonov to go and visit him, he admitted, 'I am not doing very much work but I am working regularly. I live restfully and quietly, and that's pretty boring'.[31] Chaliapin meanwhile had received an invitation to sing the title role in Boito's *Mefistofele* at La Scala (though he did not in fact do so until the next year), and Rachmaninoff decided to join him on a trip to Italy: 'I shall work on my music and in my spare time help you to work on the opera'.[32] Chekhov had thought of coming with Rachmaninoff [33] but was prevented by a fever. As it was, when Rachmaninoff arrived in Varazze before Chaliapin, his morale was low. Behind all the talk of work was the inescapable fact that there was still nothing to show on paper. On 14 June he wrote a frank letter to Modest Tchaikovsky:

> Two years have passed since I was with you at Klin, and in those two years, apart from one song, I have not composed a single note. Overall I have absolutely lost my facility to compose, so it seems, and all my thoughts are directed towards getting it back. Speaking frankly, I wanted this summer to try again to write *Francesca* and I hoped that maybe something would come, and that's why I want to ask you, if you think it is possible, to write to your candidate [Liadov] that Rachmaninoff is now abroad and that you will give him a reply about *Francesca* on his return, that is, in September, when, if still nothing comes, I shall have to abandon the subject. Say if this is impossible, and I shall send you back the libretto straightaway. Although you have not worked on the libretto specially for me, I daren't of course put you to the risk of again being without a composer for it.

Perhaps this uncharacteristically candid confession to an outsider helped to unburden Rachmaninoff's mind and steel his resolve. At any rate, only eight days later there were the first signs that the long-awaited breakthrough was imminent. While he was still waiting for Chaliapin to arrive, Rachmaninoff wrote to Morozov, who was also touring Europe, to tell him that he had decided not to travel to him because he 'wished to continue working regularly'.[34] Perhaps prompted by Tchaikovsky's agreement to defer a final decision about *Francesca* until September, and stimulated by the arrival of Chaliapin and the visit to Milan, in his final report from Italy he told Morozov that he would be leaving 'with enthusiasm and the firm intention of doing a lot of work on arriving home'.[35]

On returning to Russia Rachmaninoff had two immediate tasks: one was the composition of at least sufficient of *Francesca* to satisfy himself and Modest Tchaikovsky that the completion of the opera was a realistic possibility; the other was the writing of the concerto he had promised for London, though he had already lost his opportunity of appearing there that season. According to the composer's 1917 dated list of compositions,[36] the love duet from *Francesca* was written in July 1900, that is just before leaving Italy and immediately after returning home. At any rate, Rachmaninoff must have satisfactorily met the September deadline he set himself for returning the libretto, for we hear no more of a possible withdrawal from the project.

Concerto No. 2 in C Minor, Op. 18

Work on the long-awaited Second Concerto got under way at Krasnenkoye in the latter half of the summer and the autumn of 1900, the second and third movements reportedly being completed 'quickly and easily',[37] but the first causing Rachmaninoff much difficulty. Siloti eventually persuaded the composer to premiere the work in incomplete form, the performance taking place in Moscow on 2 December 1900. For Rachmaninoff that concert must have been a nerve-racking experience: the success of the concerto was obviously going to be critical for the restoration of his self-confidence as a composer, and the omens were not encouraging, for he had caught a bad cold and had been plied with inebriant remedies by his friends. Moreover, this was to be his first appearance with orchestra in eight years and only his fourth ever, and Siloti, who was directing the orchestra, was making his professional conducting debut.[38] Mercifully, however, all went well, and the two movements' great success with the audience must have been profoundly reassuring. It was at Goldenweiser's flat in April of the following year that Rachmaninoff at last produced from his case the manuscript of the first movement, and he premiered the work in its complete form at another Siloti concert, on 27 October. The public immediately took the concerto to their hearts and its fame soon became international after Siloti performed it at the Leipzig Gewandhaus under Nikisch in January 1902 and Sapellnikov in London in May of the same year.

Each of the three movements begins with a modulatory preamble. The famous and, be it said, unprecedented opening of the first movement, a sequence of swelling piano chords in F minor punctuated by bass octaves, is like the tolling of a bell, heard distantly at first but with each stroke more penetrating than the last. In his recorded performances Rachmaninoff gives impetus to the chords by sounding the bottom note first, one of the few places where he does not observe the printed score. Rachmaninoff may have derived this opening from his Prelude in C sharp minor by inverting the layout and dynamics of its final bars, where the bass octaves precede and not follow the chords:

Ex.46a

Prelude, Op.3, No.2, end

Ex.46b

Second Concerto, opening

The same prelude's three opening notes were probably the ancestors of the A flat, F, G, and C which join this introduction to the first subject and which play an important part in the development. The main theme itself is one of Rachmaninoff's typically long and sinuous tunes, moving step-wise and never straying far from the key note, its sombre strength, inexorability and iron control over sentiment belying its neu-rasthenic origins. Medtner described the profoundly Russian quality of the opening of the concerto:[39]

> The theme of [Rachmaninoff's] inspired Second Concerto is not only the theme of his life but always conveys the impression of being one of the most strikingly Russian of themes, and only because the soul of this theme is Russian; there is no ethnographic trimming here, no dressing up, no decking out in national dress, no folksong intonation, and yet every time, from the first bell stroke, you feel the figure of Russia rising up to her full height.

Critics have been perplexed by the supposedly out of sequence composition of the movements because of the possible stimulus for the concerto's opening theme, or at least the rocking first five notes of it, coming from the same figure in the last movement, in the 3/2 section after cue 29 and at 38.[40] But in fact the figure is merely a rhythmically dislocated version of the opening of the main theme of the last movement, as the manner of its orchestral restatement before the final *quasi glissando* piano cadenza confirms. Moreover, it is not unique to this concerto but reappears elsewhere in Rachmaninoff, notably in the accompaniment to the main theme of the first movement of the Third Concerto. In any case, the first movement of the Second Concerto, despite Rachmaninoff's later recollections to the contrary,[41] may already have existed, in embryonic state, either on paper or in the composer's mind, before the second and third movements were finalized. According to Goldenweiser,[42] it existed in several variants, and it was Rachmaninoff's inability to settle on a final version that led to the concerto being performed incomplete at its premiere.

Much more intriguing is the unanswerable question of origin, or derivation, posed by the second subject of the first movement. In that movement, it provides a gentle and wistful contrast to the main theme:

Ex.47

[Moderato]

In the second movement it appears in the first strain of the main theme, given to the flute:

Ex.48

[Adagio sostenuto]

Its derivation is made more explicit in the final piano chords of the movement:

Ex.49

[Adagio sostenuto]

Finally, in the last movement, it appears in the 'big tune':

Ex.50

[Moderato]

Such inter-movement references and economy of material are to be expected from the composer of the First Symphony, though they are rarely commented on.[43] The internal cohesion and general absence of musical superfluity is reflected in the lack of any need for a cadenza in the first movement; instead matters are brought to an exciting close by an ascending flourish, anticipating the opening of the *Tarantella* from the contemporaneous Second Suite for Two Pianos, and by three final emphatic chords reiterating the opening of the main theme.

The slow movement immediately picks up in its first modulatory bars the rising figure with which the previous movement concluded,[44] in a page which recalls the opening of the *Andante* of Tchaikovsky's Fifth Symphony. Rachmaninoff took the opening solo accompaniment figure of the movement almost literally from the *Romance* of 1891, written for the three Skalon sisters, and it is perhaps another backward glance at a part of his life now irretrievably past (after Vera Skalon's marriage, Rachmaninoff learnt in October of Lyudmila Skalon's engagement). Rhythmic ambiguity lends interest to the movement, Rachmaninoff splitting the four crotchets of the metre into twelve triplet quavers, which he variously treats as groups of three or four. The idea of a contrasting animated middle section, used also in the Third Concerto and much later in the Third Symphony, most likely comes from Tchaikovsky's First Concerto.

There are two curious features in the brief piano cadenza at the end of the passage. Firstly, the four arpeggios beginning 13 before fig. 26 are marked in the score as a *crescendo*, and yet, on the evidence both of those who remember Rachmaninoff's concert performances and of his two recordings of the concerto, the composer played these as a *diminuendo*, inverting the dynamics to striking effect. Then, the following piano flourish seems incongruously to imitate the sound of a cimbalon, perhaps an unconscious echo of a gypsy orchestra Rachmaninoff may have heard in a Moscow restaurant:

Ex.51

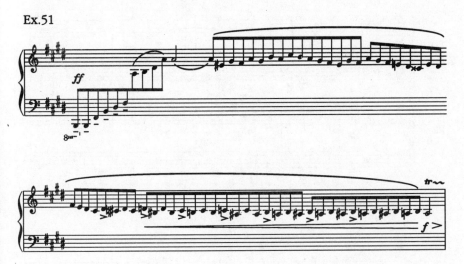

The movement ends with some of the most moving pages in the whole of Rachmaninoff, a sequence in which his unique brand of lyricism, set in glowing orchestral colours, is ideally complemented by a gentle rocking piano accompaniment, to weave an exquisite tapestry. It is not surprising that the beauties of this movement particularly touched Rachmaninoff's teacher Taneyev, who wept at a rehearsal performance and uttered the single word 'genius',[45] not an expression used lightly by the stern master or by Russians generally.

The beginning of the last movement contains two further tantalizing hints of the opening of the concerto. In the orchestral introduction there is a phrase from the principal theme of the first movement in its *alla marcia* form, and in the piano entry there is an echo of the harmonies of the introductory chords of the first movement, concluding with the A flat, F, G and C motif (Ex. 52). A surprising derivation in the movement is the opening theme, a direct borrowing from Rachmaninoff's own sacred concerto of 1893, *O Mother of God Perpetually Praying* (see p. 81). Its vigour and evident appropriateness for the keyboard entirely belies its origin, and it works well too in the brief *fugato*. As for the celebrated second subject, Sabaneyeff told Seroff [46] that it was given to Rachmaninoff by Nikita Morozov, but the tale is otherwise unauthenticated and it is curious, not to say suspicious, that Sabaneyeff does not mention the story himself in his book on Russian composers, in which he writes

Ex.52

at length about Rachmaninoff and the concerto.[47] The tune is heard three times in all, and it may be thought a weakness that, except for the increasingly elaborate presentation, it appears in the same guise each time. No doubt so marvellous a melody can bear such repetition, but Rachmaninoff managed things more subtly when faced with the same situation in the last movement of his Third Concerto, as indeed had Tchaikovsky in his First Concerto, the obvious model for this kind of finale.

The Second Concerto shows the reborn composer having triumphantly recaptured all of his former confidence and command. The whole work, and especially the first movement, has an admirable tautness of structure, and it entirely lacks the longueurs of, for example, the middle of the last movement of the Third Concerto, where the momentum is lost in repetitious passages of self-indulgent piano decoration. It is a true concerto in the sense that the orchestra plays as important a role as the soloist; indeed the only point over which Taneyev felt it perhaps merited criticism was the fact that the piano is rarely heard without the orchestra.[48] When the soloist does erupt into one of the cadential flourishes in the last movement, it is as if in the exhilaration at his own prowess Rachmaninoff were demonstrating just how far he had left behind his earlier years of depression. Gone forever is the melodrama of some of the earlier works, and even the most emotionally searing climaxes, at the end of the last two movements for example, are dignified and under perfect control. The greatest advance of all, however, is in the lyricism, which has demonstrated for nearly one hundred years the power to touch the hearts of each successive generation. The concerto and the works which followed it mark out Rachmaninoff as second only to Tchaikovsky in the list of Russian lyricists.

It is perhaps curious that at the very time of completing the Second Concerto Rachmaninoff should also have drafted his first solo piano transcription, of the Minuet from Bizet's *L'Arlésienne*. At any rate, if the date on the manuscript is to be believed, the transcription was completed on 13 September 1900, though even more curiously it seems not to have seen the light of day until after revision in 1922. The piece has no connection whatever with the concerto or the other works of this period, and the prompting for its creation seems to have been the simple fact that several times during 1900 Rachmaninoff had played two-piano works with Goldenweiser, both in public recitals and in private, and among the works they had performed was this Minuet in its two-piano form.[49] Rachmaninoff's arrangment for solo piano neatly reduces Bizet's orchestral textures to pianistic terms with little additional contribution except to the polyphony of the middle section, which was given a still more luscious treatment in the revision.

Second Suite for Two Pianos, Op. 17

In view of Rachmaninoff's close association with Goldenweiser at this time, it is not surprising that one of the first works to which he turned his mind when his creative powers revived should have been a new two-piano suite, which he dedicated to his colleague. Rachmaninoff sent him three of the four planned movements on 17 February 1901, and on 23 April the two played through the complete work at Goldenweiser's flat for the first time. Accepted for printing by Gutheil before any public performance, the Suite was published in October, some months ahead of the Concerto, so receiving the prior opus number, 17, while the Concerto became Opus 18, reversing the expected sequence.

The Second Suite for Two Pianos, the first work of Rachmaninoff to be published in the five years since the *Moments musicaux* of 1896, shows the composer in full lyrical flood. Indeed, Rachmaninoff seems to have had so much material on hand that the melodies in the middle of the first two movements get only a single hearing. The composer's sketches for the work suggest that he may originally have intended to open it with a fugal movement, and it may therefore have been the present, very different, *Introduction* that was missing when Rachmaninoff first sent Goldenweiser the incomplete work. As it is, the movement launches with the minimum of formality into a proud and energetic march, the richness of the piano writing contrasting with the simple statement at a bare octave of the second theme. When the march returns it reaches a climax of enormous sonority and then fades away, over a tonic pedal, like a procession passing on into the distance. The swirling and skittish *Waltz* has two heart-warming subsidiary themes, the second of which, beginning with the first four notes of *Dies irae*, reappears in the coda only to vanish into the night with the tinkle of troika bells. The *Romance* is another rapturous outpouring, decked out in the most exquisite tracery. As Keldïsh pointed out,[50] the theme, announced at the outset on the first piano, has a marked resemblance to Rachmaninoff's song *Lilacs*, Op. 21, No. 5, written in the same key and possibly exactly contemporary (Ex. 53).

Just as the six-hand *Romance* written for the three Skalon sisters in 1891 was quarried for the introduction to the slow movement of the Second Concerto, so here its final page provided the material for the conclusion of this *Romance*, before a last nostalgic look at the theme. The *Tarantella* is a splendidly exciting showpiece with which to end the suite. According to a footnote in the printed edition, the main theme was taken from a collection of Italian songs, though it has never been identified; presumably Rachmaninoff came across it on his visit to Italy. The composer imposes a Russian nationality on the tarantella, emphatic chords making it dramatic at one moment, and restlessly hovering *pianissimo* triplet decoration elsewhere giving it an air of quiet menace. Throughout, the dynamic impulse never flags, right up to the tumultuous and powerful conclusion.

The suite quickly became a cornerstone of the two-piano repertoire, and understandably; not only is it musically rich but it is great fun to play, and the interplay between the two soloists is a special delight. Unusually for him, Rachmaninoff provided indications of pedalling and fingering, perhaps for the benefit of the proficient amateurs who were

Ex.53a — Second Suite: *Romance*

Ex.53b — *Lilacs*

[I go in the fresh morning to breathe . . .
On the green branches . . .]

probably the principal buyers of Gutheil's handsome edition. Besides performing the work with Goldenweiser and Siloti, Rachmaninoff later played it also with the distinguished Polish pianist Alexander Michalowski during a visit to Warsaw in 1908, and though he never appeared publicly in two-piano performances after leaving Russia permanently, he played the suite privately with Horowitz, both at Senar and in California, and might have done so publicly had he lived longer and the joint recital which the two artists apparently discussed in 1942 actually taken place,[51] with the tantalizing possibility of a recording to follow.

According to the composer's own account, the 'joy of creating lasted during the next two years'.[52] Having triumphantly proved that his powers had been restored, Rachmaninoff was again preoccupied with seeking the financial independence he felt necessary for uninterrupted composition. It was fortunate for him that his cousin Siloti was not only a famous musician and propagandist for Rachmaninoff's work but also wealthy and generous. Siloti agreed to subsidize Rachmaninoff for a two-year period, and during this time, free at last from money worries, the composer produced his Ops. 19–23: the Cello Sonata, the cantata

Spring, a group of twelve songs, the Chopin Variations, and ten piano Preludes, dedicated to his benefactor.

Sonata for Piano and Cello in G Minor, Op. 19

The Cello Sonata, written in the latter half of 1901, was first performed in Moscow, on 2 December that year, by the composer and Anatoly Brandukov, to whom, like the earlier Op. 2 cello pieces, the work is dedicated. It is interesting that the manuscript bears two dates, one, 20 November, appearing just before the *vivace* coda to the last movement, and the other, 12 December, at the very end of the work. As the premiere intervened and as the manuscript has many corrections, it would seem that Rachmaninoff put the finishing touches to the work in the light of the experience of performing it, including the addition of the rousing final coda, considered by some a regrettable lapse of taste. In the exactly parallel conclusion to the Chopin Variations the composer makes the performance of the coda optional, and he might with advantage have done the same here, since, shorn of this accretion, the sonata would sink gently to rest over a tonic pedal, in a sunset glow.

The sonata shares a number of features with the two-piano suite. Like that work it has four self-contained, rhythmically contrasting movements. After the opening two-note rising semi-tone sob on the cello, used later in the development, the piano introduces the rhythmic leitmotif of the movement, ♪♪ ♩ ♪♪ ♩ , and the cello sings its two wistful songs. The exposition repeat, marked in the score but never these days observed in practice, would extend an already lengthy work unduly. It is interesting that the opening notes of the first theme, like the middle theme of the Waltz from the suite, have the shape of *Dies irae*, and that this outline reappears in the right-hand piano part of the final bars of the third movement, in neither case more than a coincidence, no doubt, but its occurrence showing how much this four-note pattern was now instilled into Rachmaninoff's consciousness (Ex. 54).

In the second movement the cello's first theme, with its gawky rhythmic figure, ♪♪ ♪ ♪♪ ♪ ♪♪ , contrasts with two lyrical melodies, again just as in the Waltz from the suite where, as here, the third theme gets only brief exposure. The best movement of the sonata is undoubtedly the *Andante,* whose opening for piano solo shows a growing characteristic of Rachmaninoff's melodies, a fondness for the interval of a fifth (Ex 55). This rapturous and heart-warming song expands and glows, with the cello weaving a sinuous decoration around it in the middle section. A definite advance on what Rachmaninoff had achieved at similar moments

Ex.54a   Cello Sonata: first movement

Ex.54b   Second Suite: Waltz

Ex.54c   Cello Sonata:
              third movement, conclusion

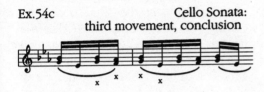

Ex.55

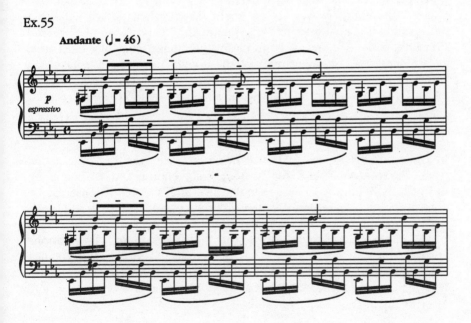

before is the climax, for which the composer reserves a further soaring expansion of the cello melody and an added richness in the piano part by using the whole range of the instrument (Ex. 56). As with the Waltz in the suite, a gentle tinkling of bells in the piano part sees the movement end.

After these heights, the last movement's cheerful and busy first theme seems rather non-descript, but the second has a dignity and strength that provides an appropriate counter-weight, and the two themes subtly interplay before the end. Rachmaninoff introduces an element of cyclical cohesion into the work by beginning the problematical coda with the cello taking a backward glance at the rhythmic leitmotif of the first movement.

The sonata is sometimes criticized for the overpowering role given to the piano, evidently confirming its prior position in the order of instruments in the work's title. Despite Brandukov's close association with the composer professionally and personally (he was soon, with Siloti, to be best man at his wedding), it must be admitted that the cello writing in the sonata is somewhat unenterprising, perhaps limited by the use to which Rachmaninoff employs the instrument almost throughout, namely to sing in its most soulfully lyrical vein; the piano part, on the other hand, is certainly laid out on a grand scale. Para-doxically, almost the only comment on record by the composer about the sonata is that the cello was not to dominate a performance but rather that cellist and pianist were to be equal partners.[53] It is plainly mistaken to assume that Rachmaninoff was unable to sublimate the piano – the songs prove that he could do so when he wished – but rather are the two parts, as with piano and orchestra in the Second Concerto, and voice and piano in the mature songs, musically integrated. At any rate, the lyrical warmth of the sonata has won it a favoured place in the cellist's repertoire, especially of Russian music, where, except for the sonatas of Rubinstein, it had no antecedents.

'Spring' Cantata, Op. 20

In January and February 1902 Rachmaninoff wrote his first large choral work, the cantata *Spring*, for baritone solo, chorus and orchestra, set to words by Nekrasov. Dedicated to Rachmaninoff's Moscow Conservatoire contemporary Nikita Morozov, the work received its first performance in Moscow very soon after completion, at a concert conducted by Siloti on 11 March. Although the soloist on that occasion was the baritone Dmitry Smirnov, the cantata was subsequently taken up by Chaliapin, who performed it three times: in Petersburg in 1905, Paris in 1906 – in which year the work won the composer the Glinka Prize – and Moscow in 1907.

Ex.56

Nekrasov's poem *The Verdant Noise* tells of a peasant who plans to kill his unfaithful wife but who relents at the arrival of spring, for the new season not only brings rebirth in nature but prompts humans to renew their own lives. The poem ends on a philosophic and quasi-religious note as the peasant recalls an old adage about the need for love, tolerance and forgiveness in life. Setting these verses must have been especially congenial to Rachmaninoff: we know that the composer was profoundly affected by nature, and he had already given musical form to the coming of spring in one of his best songs to date, *Spring Waters*; moreover the husband's dramatic narrative would make a fine vehicle for Chaliapin – for it must surely have been his friend's voice, rather than Smirnov's light baritone, that Rachmaninoff had in mind in composing his cantata. Although Rachmaninoff was later to agree with Rimsky-Korsakov's criticism of the work's orchestration that 'there is no sign of spring in the orchestra', and to profess a desire to 'alter the whole instrumentation',[54] the orchestral palette is nevertheless used with considerable subtlety, though the colouring is predominantly sombre, perhaps suggesting that the composer's prior interest in the text was not spring but the agonizing predicament of the peasant.

The cantata opens magically. A held E on the strings under which the opening spring motif is heard darkly on bassoons and basses, apparently in C major, turns out to be an inverted tonic pedal, and the music lifts brightly and hopefully to E major to start a gentle downward run of staccato harp notes, like the dripping of thawing ice as spring begins to stir. The motif itself, built around the intervals of a third and fourth, is complemented by a sinuous theme given to the cellos:

Ex.57a

Ex.57b

These two lyrical elements, which are developed and added to by the opening chorus and which form the basis of both the choral sections celebrating spring, contrast with the mainly declamatory ensuing narrative of the husband, whose music, beginning with a brusque orchestral introduction reminiscent of *Aleko*, is cast in an operatic mould. The use of the chorus to intone wordlessly in despairing descending minor thirds after the soloist's climax 'Kill, Kill, the faithless one', first tried out in the motet *O Mother of God*, looks forward to the chorus of lost souls in *Francesca* and the last movement of *The Bells*. With the words 'I prepared a sharp knife', the spring motif reappears in the orchestra and the chorus begins the build-up to the urgently insistent climax celebrating the return of spring. Although this climax is singularly lacking in the expected Rachmaninoff melodic sweep – 'startlingly foursquare and banal' is how one commentator describes it [55] – it is not a sudden and inexplicable failure but merely the emphatic reiteration of the major third interval from the spring motif, which Rachmaninoff had himself already used in the climactic affirmation of the return of spring in his song *Spring Waters*, Op. 14, No. 11:

Ex.58a   *Spring*

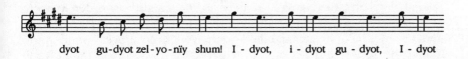

[It comes, it roars, the verdant noise!]

Ex.58b   Spring Waters

[Spring is coming!]

The glorious postlude is the purest distillation of vintage Rachmaninoff in his most affecting manner, the cello counterpoint perfectly catching the glowing mood. When the husband has relented, he sings what amounts to a solemn hymn: 'Love while you may; bear while you may; forgive while you may; and God will be your judge'. The repetition of these lines by the chorus has the fervour, and sound, of a church choir singing the Creed. Indeed, the manner in which the composer closely matches words and music impresses throughout the cantata, and there is no doubt that, as with the Three Russian Songs, Op. 41, it is only the large forces required to perform a work lasting little more than fifteen minutes that have militated against more frequent performance.

Twelve Songs, Op. 21

On 26 March 1902 Rachmaninoff conducted at a concert in Moscow at which Siloti appeared as soloist in the composer's Second Concerto, a reversal of their roles in the first performance five months before. Siloti also played Liszt's *Totentanz*, and acquaintance with that work, in which *Dies irae* plays so pervasive a part, no doubt instilled the plainchant more deeply than ever into Rachmaninoff's mind. With his marriage to Natalya Satina only a month away, Rachmaninoff needed a sum of money for the honeymoon. He wrote to Natalya Skalon on 1 April 1902: 'When I get to Moscow I shall have to tussle with priests for several days and then go off at once to the country in order to write at least twelve songs before the wedding to earn enough to pay them and to go abroad'. Rachmaninoff journeyed to Ivanovka on 6 April, drafted his songs, and returned to Moscow for his wedding on 29 April. On 17 June, while honeymooning at Lucerne, he wrote to Morozov: 'I am hanging on to the songs for the time being: they were written very hurriedly and are therefore quite unfinished and quite unbeautiful – rather like Malashkin or Prigozhy.[56] I shall probably have to leave them almost as they are as I don't have the time to tinker with them'. Despite this typical piece of self-disparagement, the songs show absolutely no signs of skimped craftsmanship, though undoubtedly some of the settings are more felicitous than others. In general the more dramatic settings, usually on morbidly introspective themes and mainly declamatory in the manner of several of the composer's earlier songs, are less successful than those in which Rachmaninoff's newly enhanced lyrical powers are given free rein.

To open the set Rachmaninoff used *Fate*, which he had held over from three years before and whose considerable length contrasts with the succinctness of all the new songs. The first of these, *By the grave*, without dedication, is one of two settings of poems by Semyon Nadson, whose *'Tis time* was the last song in Rachmaninoff's previous cycle, Op. 14. The poet broods obsessively on the hopelessness of a life without purpose and without love, and in its morbidity of theme and the composer's melodramatic treatment, emphasized by the soloist's declamatory part and the relentless repeated bass octave Es in the accompaniment, the song has much in common with *Fate*. Quite different is the third song in the set, *Twilight*, to words by Jean-Marie Guyot, translated by Ivan Tkhorzhevsky and dedicated to the coloratura soprano so much admired by Rimsky-Korsakov, Nadezhda Zabela-Vrubel, whom Rachmaninoff first met at the Mamontov Private Opera and whom he had just persuaded to sing a group of his songs at a fashionable Moscow soirée.[57] As night falls a radiant girl sits alone by her window, lost in thought. The purity and frailty of the girl is reflected in the chaste lyricism of the vocal part and the delicately simple piano accompaniment. As the girl appears haloed against the heavens, the music moves blithely into the major key, and over a hypnotically calm tonic pedal in the accompaniment the vocal line captures perfectly the rarefied atmosphere of a moment of elevated beauty. *The Answer*,[58] with words by Victor Hugo in Mey's translation and a dedication to Elena Kreutzer, in a different way is also one of the most successful settings. A group of men on the run put three questions to some women, who answer them laconically with three simple imperatives: How to escape to safety over the sea? – row! How to forget the sorrows of life? – sleep! How to attract women? – love! The urgency of the questions is reflected in the vigorous masculine arpeggio accompaniment, while, in contrast, for each of the answers the soloist lingers *pianissimo* over a graciously feminine phrase of three dotted quavers, always rising and falling back an octave but subtly changed harmonically each time. Particularly affecting is the final answer, in which the tonality wavers as the tongue-in-cheek reply is made:

Ex.59

["Love!" they answered.]

According to Goldenweiser,[59] *Lilacs*, with words by Ekaterina Be-ketova, dates from the fallow years after the failure of the First Symphony, though, like the other songs of the Op. 21 set, the manuscript bears the date April 1902. The poem combines a simple description of nature with the underlying theme of the unfulfilled search for happiness. The purity of the vocal line and the simple beauty of the gently rippling piano accompaniment mark out the song as one of Rachmaninoff's masterpieces and yet the marvellous melodic line is achieved by the simplest of means, being almost entirely a varied repetition of the three-note phrase with which the singer begins. Rachmaninoff dedicated *Loneliness* or *A Fragment from de Musset*, translated by Apukhtin, to Princess Alexandra Liven, no doubt in gratitude for her help during his years of crisis. The poem, about the anguish of loneliness, harks back to *Fate* in mood, but the setting is more subtle. As we hear from the clock chimes in the piano part, even before the singer tells us, it is midnight; the poet sits alone in terror and despair, in his confusion and hallucination awaiting he knows not what. Rachmaninoff effectively captures the melodrama of the strained and morbid atmosphere in the singer's declamatory phrases, and the climactic cry of despair, 'My God!' has its counterpart in the piano's self-indulgent *appassionato* coda. The contrast in style with the seventh song, *How fair this spot* could hardly be greater. Rach-maninoff took his text, as he did for the final song of the group, from a collection by the Countess Einerling, only just then published under the pseudonym Galina. Despite the mediocrity of the poetry, the sentiments expressed clearly fired the composer's imagination, for he never excelled these twenty-two bars of lyrical outpouring. The scene is some solitary retreat where the poet is alone except for nature, God and his dreams of his beloved. As with *Lilacs*, what is striking is the marvellous simplicity with which the whole melodic line grows, by a process of variation, out of the singer's opening phrase. The rising sequence in which it is incorporated is typical of the composer in works of this time and on, and the rapturous climax, reaching a *pianissimo* top A on the word 'thou', has a restrained and reverent beauty. As in the reflective piano postlude, it is the intensity of such moments that confirms the conviction that the essence of Rachmaninoff lies here rather than in the keyboard athletics beloved by the public.

The eighth song, *On the Death of a Linnet*, set to verses by the early nineteenth-century poet Vasily Zhukovsky, is dedicated to Rach-maninoff's aunt on his father's side, Olga Trubnikova. The poet tells the mock-tragic story of the death of a pet bird and his mate who could not live without him. In a sense Rachmaninoff's setting looks forward to the style of his later songs, in that most musical interest is in the elaborately contrapuntal piano part, which at one point clearly anticipates *The Pied Piper*, Op. 38, No. 4, of 1916:

Ex.60a *On the Death of a Linnet*

[Because of the loss he hid himself in the grave.]

Ex.60b *The Pied Piper*

[The lambs silently slumber, the fields sway gently.]

Melody, to words by Nadson, is dedicated to Natalya Lanting, a cousin of Rachmaninoff's wife-to-be, who does not otherwise appear in the composer's biography. In a romantic fantasy the poet expresses a desire to die 'on wings of rapture', amid the glories of nature, and to ascend to everlasting bliss in the world beyond. A seamless step-wise melody and a characteristic rising sequence for the singer to reach a climactic *pianissimo* top note are by now typical. The mood of ecstatic confidence is extended into the beautiful piano coda. The tenth song, *Before the image*, with words by Count Golenishchev-Kutuzov, is dedicated to the Satins' faithful maid Mariya Ivanova, who became the Rachmaninoffs' housekeeper when they married. The poem gives a picture of a pious woman standing in prayer before an ikon, and Rachmaninoff treats the vocal part as a series of declamatory phrases, catching the religious atmosphere with a respectfully discreet piano accompaniment. Shortly after an insistently repeated B flat in the piano part, like a bell tolling to summon the faithful, there is a moment anticipating the passage in *To the Children*, Op. 26, No. 7, written four years later, where the children are asked to pray. Like other composers, Rachmaninoff uses the same musical language within his work to express the same ideas (Ex 61).

In *No prophet I*, to words by Alexander Kruglov, the poet declares that although he may be no prophet, warrior or scholar, he too spreads God's word, through his song. Rachmaninoff emphasizes the certainty of the poet's belief in the power of song by the opening massive piano chords and the almost swaggering confidence of the singer's first phrases, which dissolve into glorious lyrical flight before the piano arpeggios of the coda, depicting the singer's lyre. The final song of the set, *Sorrow in Springtime*, dedicated to Natasha's younger brother, Vladimir Satin, is something of an anticlimax. The poem by Galina tells of the despairing desire that old age should come and bring peace to all passion, the return of spring awakening the old striving for the unattainable. The singer's declamatory phrases are paired with a restless accompaniment that burns itself out in an *appassionato* coda. *Sorrow in Springtime*, with its black and cheerless theme, much the same as in *By the grave*, seems an odd choice with which to finish a group of songs written when Rachmaninoff was in confident full flight artistically, and when his personal affairs – his marriage was but days away – should have been in their most hopeful and happy state; but then it was perhaps just because it does not reflect first-hand personal experience that its gesturing fails to convince.

Variations on a Theme of Chopin, Op. 22

After a three months' honeymoon abroad, including a month's stay in Vienna and a large dose of Wagner at Bayreuth – *The Ring, Flying*

Ex.61a

Before the image

[As if in silent langour she waited.]

Ex.61b

To the Children

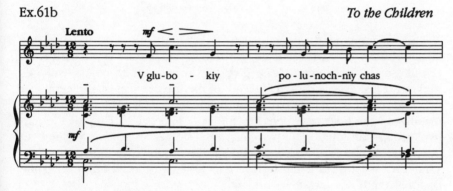

[At the late midnight hour.]

Dutchman, Parsifal – the tickets being a wedding present from Siloti, the newly-weds returned late in the summer to Ivanovka, where the composer began his first extended piano work, the Variations on a Theme of Chopin, Op. 22, and the group of piano Preludes, Op. 23. Composition was interrupted at the end of the year when, after much soul-searching over possible disloyalty to Siloti, Rachmaninoff agreed to return to Vienna to play his new concerto under Safonov on 27 December, but the Variations were ready for a first performance by their composer on 10 February 1903, at a concert in Moscow for the Ladies' Charity Prison Committee, of which Princess Alexandra Liven was chairman. Like Busoni's very much shorter set on the same theme, Rachmaninoff's Variations are based on Chopin's well-known C minor Prelude, Op. 28, No. 20, curiously enough not one of the dozen Chopin preludes which the composer chose to play as a set in his later years as concert pianist. Another minor mystery concerns the dedication of the work to the Vienna-based but Polish-born piano guru Theodor Leschetizky, professor at the St Petersburg Conservatoire during the 1860s and '70s, with whom Rachmaninoff seems to have had no dealings whatever. Perhaps Rachmaninoff met the great man in Vienna during his concert visit; Safonov may have effected the introduction as a Leschetizky pupil himself.

The variations are grouped in such a way as to form a continuous structure with the rough overall outline of a three or four movement sonata.

Movement	Variations
I	1 – 10
II (a)	11 – 14
(b)	15 – 18
III	19 – 22

As the variations tend to get longer as the work proceeds, there is also an impression of cumulative growth. However, despite the logic of the layout, some variations at least give the impression of being exercises in themselves, exploiting some aspect of the theme or of piano technique in isolation rather than as part of an integrated whole. The ten variations making up the first movement are the least interesting. They divide into two groups of four, with two relatively slower variations forming an interlude. All are in unvarying C minor. The sonorously imperious ninth variation itself makes a satisfactory conclusion to the group, leaving the optional tenth somewhat redundant.

A move to E flat and a change in mood, tempo and dynamics herald the second movement. The twelfth variation starts with a curiously academic and rather boring four-part fugue that sounds startlingly like Bach, as though Rachmaninoff were back in his days at Moscow Conservatoire, writing an exercise for Taneyev (Ex. 62). Matters improve only when Rachmaninoff casts off this strait-jacket and breaks out into a more characteristic free improvisation at the end. Variation 13 has an air of mystery about it, with uneasy fluttering decorations in the treble register, while the fourteenth is saturated with the sound of Rachmaninoff's beloved bells. The next four variations, in F minor, form a second sub-group within the movement, of which the centre piece is the sixteenth variation, the lyrical equivalent in this work of the famous eighteenth variation in the *Paganini Rhapsody* more than thirty years later, whose D flat tonality, despite the key signature, it shares. Now remote from the confines of the Chopin outline, the theme flowers into a beautiful lyrical melody, but, unlike its Paganini counterpart, before it can reach fulfilment it gets brusquely interrupted by the grimly tolling

Ex.62

funeral bells of the next variation and its appendage (17 and 18), in B flat minor.

The final group of four, more extended, variations, forming the last movement, begins with an abrupt change to the remote key of A major (19), as the bells ring out again, this time in festive celebration. After a display in 20 testing the suppleness of the right hand, variation 21, in D flat, is a delicate interlude of calm before the final and longest variation, which recapitulates in a kind of proud polonaise the mood of 19. The optional *presto* coda, almost invariably played in concert performances, is more obviously vulgar than that at the end of the Cello Sonata, on which it is modelled, but it successfully fulfils the same function of a final raising of excitement before the applause.

The large scale on which the Variations are laid out makes the work longer in performance even than the *Paganini Rhapsody*, and yet the original theme itself is only eight bars long (Rachmaninoff does not repeat the latter half), repetitive in its melodic line and unvaried rhythmically; moreover, it is self-contained, and within its tiny compass everything has been said. For all these reasons it is less malleable material for variation treatment than either the Corelli or Paganini themes to which Rachmaninoff turned later, and the composer was plainly not wholly satisfied with his work as it stood. More than anything, he was bothered by its length; he made performance of three of the variations – 7, 10 and 12 – and the coda optional, and in a note appended to the list of his compositions he sent Asafyev in 1917 [60] he remarked that he played the work 'in a shortened and altered form', and that he intended to include his corrections in a new edition (though nothing came of this). Sixteen years later, talking to Alfred Swan about what he saw as superfluities in some of his early works, Rachmaninoff mentioned the Chopin Variations as one of the pieces he had changed.[61] But mere pruning of the existing structure is not enough to solve its musical weaknesses, and the work inevitably lacks the assured continuity of progression of the Corelli and Paganini sets. It does, moreover, pose problems of programming, for it is too long to be an incidental item in a recital but, despite its obvious pianistic attractions and fine moments, it is musically insufficiently rewarding to make it a satisfactory centre-piece. It is thus likely to remain in the shadows.

Ten Preludes, Op. 23

At the same concert in February 1903 at which he premiered the Chopin Variations Rachmaninoff also played three[62] of his then incomplete new set of ten piano Preludes Op. 23. Seven years later he added a further thirteen, to make, with the early C sharp minor prelude, a set of twenty-four in all the major and minor keys, though the widespread dates of their composition – 1892 (Op. 3, No. 2), 1899, 1901, 1903 (Op. 23), 1910 (Op. 32) – suggest that they evolved into this form only with the completion of the final group, rather than originally being planned as such. In their published order of alternating major and minor keys, both the Op. 23 and 32 sets make effective and natural groups as they stand, though with Op. 23 some concert pianists, including the dedicatee Siloti, have preferred to end with the flamboyant Prelude in B flat major rather than the undemonstrative G flat. The logic of the sequence as it stands is in the musical substance rather than a fixed pattern of keys, such as the 'cycle of fifths'[63] used both by Chopin and by Scriabin in his Opus 11 set of 1895. In comparison with these composers' miniatures all of Rachmaninoff's Preludes are relatively long and complex works, well able to stand by themselves individually. It was their peculiarly Russian quality which particularly impressed the painter Ilya Repin, the eighty-year-old Vladimir Stasov, guiding spirit of 'The Mighty Handful', and Maxim Gorky, when Boris Asafyev first played through the Op. 23 set for them. Repin noted the Russian character and originality of the melodic line; Stasov the Rachmaninoff stamp in rhythm and intonation and the new bell sounds. Gorky said simply, 'How well he hears the silence'.[64]

After the *Sturm und Drang* of the youthful C sharp minor prelude Op. 3, the grave but reticent beauty of the Prelude in F sharp minor opening the Op. 23 set, with its simple melodic line set against a nervously undulating left-hand accompaniment, is in marked contrast.

Musical Letter to Ekaterina Alexeyevna Bakunina

'6th April, 1903. Moscow. I am very touched and sincerely thank you for the pineapple. (I waited long enough for it!) S. Rachmaninoff.'

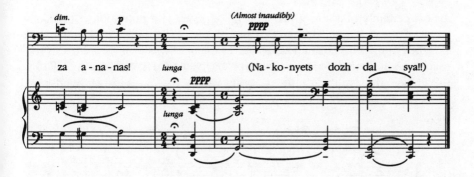

An element entirely new to Rachmaninoff is the stark dissonance of the agonized climax, representing the limit of Rachmaninoff's harmonic daring at this stage (Ex. 63).

No. 2 in B flat major is a powerful tour-de-force in Rachmaninoff's richest piano style, a solo 'Spring Waters' with the power of the C major *Moment musical*. Considered dispassionately the main theme is rather clumsy and unremarkable, and the contrasting lyrical middle section no more than a brief gesture, yet the enormous vigour and excitement of the piece sweeps away doubt. In this prelude Stasov 'saw originality in Rachmaninoff's bell-like rhythmic sound colours, their opulence and festiveness'.[65]

The third prelude in the set, in D minor, *Tempo di minuetto*, was

Ex.63

almost certainly first conceived as early as 1899. The notebook containing the draft of the *Fughetta* in F major, dated 4 February 1899, also has sketches of first the coda and then the opening of this prelude immediately following. It is therefore not perhaps by chance that the ending of the piece, like the twelfth of the Chopin Variations, has distinct overtones of Bach, in its tonic pedal:

Ex.64

The fourth prelude, in D major, is a gentle Chopinesque nocturne of quiet beauty, with a constantly flowing three-quaver accompaniment against two in the right-hand melody – 'a lake in spring flood', Repin called the piece.[66] The fifth in G minor, the famous *Alla marcia*, is always said, on no definite evidence, to date from 1901. The exciting vigour of the opening contrasts with the lyrical beauty of the middle section, which, as Riesemann rightly said,[67] conjures up pictures of the limitless Russian landscape. It is curious that in both his disc and piano-roll recordings the composer added two further gratuitous tonic notes to the last bar, not in the published version, and that in his later years Horowitz used to add one.

The next two preludes, as their keys suggest, inhabit the world of the Second Concerto. The sixth, in E flat major, is similar in mood to the first movement second subject, in the same key. Elena Gnesina once told the composer after a concert performance that the prelude seemed to her so radiant, joyous and exciting that it must surely have been composed on a very good day, to which Rachmaninoff replied, 'Yes, you are right: it really came to me all at once on the day my daughter was born',[68] that is on 14 May 1903. In contrast, No. 7 in C minor, a grim and relentlessly whirling exercise in rapid semi-quavers, first in the right and then the left hand, re-enacts the end of the exposition of the concerto's first subject. Though the corruscating piano writing and grimly tolling bells that underlie the decoration are quint-essentially Rachmaninoff, once more there are overtones of Bach in the mood of improvisation and the tonic pedal with which the prelude opens. This piece and the two following comprise a group of three studies. The eighth prelude, in A flat, beginning with three transitional bars, carries the melody in the left hand while the right is wholly preoccupied with rapid decoration. Elaboration is left behind in three final delightfully simple bars of Chopinesque coda:

Ex.65

The ninth, in E flat minor, is a technically cruel study in right-hand double fingering at an impossible metronome mark. Uniquely in this opus the composer marks fingerings. As Keldïsh was the first to point out,[69] this prelude was doubtless influenced by Chopin's G sharp minor *Étude*, Op. 25, No. 6. After the brilliance of the previous three pieces the epilogue, the Prelude in G flat, which returns in all but name to the tonality of the first prelude, carries in the left hand a gently tender melody reminiscent of the *Mélodie* from Op. 3, its low register and soulful tone doubtless being responsible for Brandukov's making an arrangement of it for cello. The mood of the concluding bars, in which the soloist as it were tiptoes away, is rather brusquely shattered by the two final dominant-tonic chords, marked '*forte*' in the published edition. In his recorded performance the composer plays these *piano* and characteristically voices the final chord more quietly than the preceding.

The Miserly Knight, Op. 24

Throughout most of the next two-and-a-half years Rachmaninoff was mainly preoccupied with opera, either as composer or conductor. The annual summer visit to Ivanovka in 1903 began inauspiciously with illness in the whole family, and it was not until the latter half of August that the composer was able to start work. Surprisingly enough, it was not the long-awaited completion of *Francesca* that Rachmaninoff had in mind but rather a setting of Pushkin's verse-drama *The Miserly Knight*, hitherto unmentioned by him. The work was finished in short score on 28 February 1904, though orchestration was not completed until June of the following year. In March of 1904 Rachmaninoff at last agreed to the proposal, first put to him in the autumn of 1901,[70] that he should conduct at the Bolshoi Theatre the next season; soon after, he took up *Francesca* again, completing the work in the summer at Ivanovka. Rachmaninoff expected that his two new operas would be staged in December 1904, during his season at the Bolshoi, but preparing the other operas he was to conduct there, seven in all, allowed him no time for the task of orchestration, which had to be deferred until the following summer. In the event, therefore, Rachmaninoff agreed to a second season at the theatre, 1905–06, during which he added only one new opera to his repertoire, Rimsky-Korsakov's *Pan Voyevoda*, besides his own *Miserly Knight* and *Francesca*, premiered as a double bill on 11 January 1906 and given five performances in all. As if all this activity were not enough, from November 1904 to December 1905 Rachmaninoff also conducted orchestral concerts, once for Siloti in St Petersburg and nine times in Moscow, mainly as a result of his growing friendship with Arkady and Mariya Kerzin, founders of the 'Circle of Lovers of Russian Music', whose all-Russian concerts of orchestral and other music had become a major feature of Moscow musical life. In the circumstances it is not surprising that in both *The Miserly Knight* and *Francesca da Rimini* Rachmaninoff gives special prominence to the role of the orchestra.

The Miserly Knight is one of four 'Little Tragedies' written in blank verse – 'Dramatic Fragments' the author also called them – which Pushkin wrote shortly before his marriage in 1830. All four were eventually made into operas by Russian composers, of whom Dargomyzhsky was the first, with *The Stone Guest* (1866–69), on the subject of envy. No doubt it was the conciseness of the text (all four poems are between 200 and 500 lines long) and the musicality of Pushkin's verses that prompted him to set the text as it stood. In his striving for 'truth and realism' through what he called 'melodic recitative', Dargomyzhsky created an exemplar for 'The Mighty Handful', which was not however imitated (except by Mussorgsky in his abortive setting of Gogol's *Marriage*) until Rimsky-Korsakov in 1897 set the second of these 'Little Tragedies', also on the theme of envy, *Mozart and Salieri*. It was this opera which Rachmaninoff studied in depth with Chaliapin during the summer of 1898, and there is no doubt that the manner of Rachmaninoff's own Pushkin setting was to be greatly influenced by this work. In 1900, after setting a string of French texts, Cui unexpectedly turned for his next opera to another of the Pushkin tragedies, *Feast in Time of Plague*, and this was staged next year in Moscow. Rachmaninoff is unlikely to have missed Chaliapin as the Priest in one of the opera's three performances put on at the New Theatre in November, particularly since it was paired with *Mozart and Salieri*. Only *The Miserly Knight* had not by now been set, and Rachmaninoff began work on it in 1904. There is no evidence that he was prompted by the thought that this too might be appropriated by some other composer, and the immediate source of inspiration was the artistry of Chaliapin; 'I composed the opera for him,' Rachmaninoff said later.[71]

Pushkin claimed to have based *The Miserly Knight* on a fictitious antique English original, 'Scenes from Trenston's Cavetous Knigth'[sic], befitting the setting of some unspecified time in medieval England. There are three scenes. The first is in the tower of the Baron's castle, where his son, Albert, complains to his squire of his father's miserliness. Despite his success in jousting he has no money even to replace his damaged helmet or to buy clothes in which to appear at the Duke's court. His squire has failed to persuade the Jewish usurer, Solomon, from whom Albert has borrowed before, to make him another loan, and so when Solomon enters Albert himself tries to extract the loan, with a mixture of cajolery and vituperation, but he has no security to offer; his father's inheritance may be many years away. Solomon remarks that the father could even outlive his son and hints tentatively that poisoning him would speed the legacy. When Albert grasps the full significance of the suggestion he is outraged and drives the usurer out. He determines to put his case before the Duke: 'Let him make my father keep me as his son, not as a mouse in his cellar'.

The second scene takes place in the castle vaults, where the Baron, adding some money to his treasure chests, expresses his delight in his wealth and the sense of power it gives him. It represents human sweat and tears: 'If all the tears, blood and sweat shed for everything that is saved here were suddenly to rise from the bowels of the earth, there would be a flood and I would drown in my faithful cellar'. The Baron confesses to experiencing the same ecstatic feeling when he unlocks his chests as a sadist murdering his victim. But who is to be heir to his kingdom? His spendthrift son? Not only will he squander his wealth but he will never know the pangs of conscience the Baron has suffered to acquire it.

The final scene is in the Duke's palace, where Albert tells the Duke that, because of his father's miserliness, he has suffered the shame of poverty. The Duke is sympathetic and says he will admonish the Baron. Albert retires when his father arrives. The Duke and the Baron at first talk as old soldiers but when the Duke suggests granting Albert an income the Knight is embarrassed and excuses his reluctance by accusing his son of being a vicious prodigal. He refuses to allow him to come to court to be educated, and when pressed by the Duke as to the reason he blurts out that it is because he wanted to kill him, or at least he tried to rob him. This is too much for Albert, who bursts in and calls his father a liar to his face, whereupon the Baron throws down his gauntlet. When Albert impetuously picks it up, so accepting the challenge, he cries mockingly, 'Thank you. This is my father's first present to me'. The Duke, appalled that Albert should be willing to fight his old father, banishes him from his sight, but when he rounds on the Knight, the old man has a seizure; the strain has been too much for him. He falls down dead, groping for the keys to his treasure chests.

Like his predecessors Rachmaninoff set Pushkin's text almost verbatim.[72] As with the other 'Little Tragedies', the number of characters is only small (five in all and all of them male), there are almost no ensembles (just one at the end of the opera), and there is no part for chorus. Faced with these limitations on the possible scope of the vocal writing, Rachmaninoff set the text in his own version of Dargomyzhskian melodic recitative, a style very different from the lyrical sweep of his other works of this period. However, at the same time he placed the main musical burden on the orchestra, using it to paint scene and character and to reflect the dialogue by means of a series of leitmotifs, deploying them with a flexibility and subtlety far removed from the tentative way in which he had applied the technique to *Aleko* or even to his cantata *Spring*. In this he may have been influenced by his musical experiences at Bayreuth during his honeymoon visit, though he both knew and admired Wagner's operas before this.[73]

The orchestral introduction to the opera contains most of the musical material for the whole work. It begins with the sinisterly rippling motif in the lower reaches of the orchestra, representing gold (Ex. 66). Against this the brass instruments play a slow and mournful counter theme, derived from the second group of ascending semi-quavers in [1]. Depicting the gloom and solitariness of greed, it is instinct with the doom that the gold will inevitably bring (Ex. 67). The sequence in the latter half leads naturally to another leitmotif, which Rachmaninoff had already used as the basis of the third

Ex.66   Leitmotif 1, 'Gold'

Ex.67   Leitmotif 2, 'Gloom and doom'

movement of his First Suite for Two Pianos and which he originally
derived from the bells of St Sophia's Cathedral, Novgorod, a descending
four-note phrase depicting the human tears and suffering that the gold
has cost to acquire:

Ex.68   Leitmotif 3, 'Tears'

A climax develops in which a snarling phrase appears first in strings
and then woodwind, a figure of four descending notes, later to be
recognized as representing greed (Ex. 69). At the climax there is reference
to the Baron, in a variation of the motif used in the second scene to
depict the cellars where he keeps his gold (Ex. 70). Finally, after another
chilling climax, in which the 'Tears' and 'Gold' motifs are combined,
the music modulates to E flat major as the first scene begins with
Albert's own music, springy, youthfully energetic, impetuous (Ex. 71).

One other character has his own motif in this scene: Solomon, the

Ex.69 Leitmotif 4, 'Greed' (Scene 2)

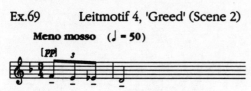

Ex.70a Baron

Ex.70b Leitmotif 5,'The cellars'
(Scene 2)

Ex.71 Leitmotif 6,'Albert'

Jewish money-lender, whose whining and wringing of hands is depicted by a sinuous descending figure (Ex. 72).

The subtle way in which Rachmaninoff uses the leitmotifs to illustrate the nuances of Pushkin's poem is impressive throughout the opera, but nowhere more than with the Moneylender, and it is not surprising that Taneyev singled out the portrayal of this character for especial praise.[74] When the Jew obsequiously tells Albert 'Your word, while you are alive, means very much indeed', the high register of the voice set

Ex.72   Leitmotif 7, 'The money-lender'

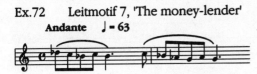

against woodwind gives the leitmotif an unpleasantly whining tone underlying his cringing hypocrisy; and when he speaks in general terms of the way in which reckless young men squander money, a snatch of Albert's motif tells us that it is the young knight of whom he is really thinking. When he hints at poisoning, his motif becomes much more sinister, with dark colouring from low clarinets and shivering strings. At the end of the scene, when Albert has thrown him out and decided to put his case before the Duke, the orchestral coda has a clear prospective reference to the Duke's motif. As it appears in Scene 3, it has a dignified quality and a feeling of benign authority about it:

Ex.73   Leitmotif 8, 'The Duke'
                                                                              (Scene 3)

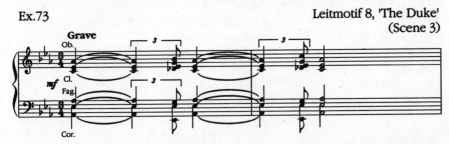

Scene 2, the Baron's monologue, is perhaps the finest part of the opera; not only is it a magnificent vehicle for a singer's vocal and dramatic skills, but it impressively demonstrates Rachmaninoff's imaginative use of the orchestra, with its close integration with the text. In the introduction the 'Cellar' motif is painted in the most sinisterly lugubrious tones with dark orchestral colour against snatches of the 'Greed' and 'Gold' figures. Later, when the Baron fantasizes about the palaces he will build in his gardens, with nymphs and muses in attendance, the orchestral writing takes on a sensuous glow, in contrast to the ugly stridency of the following passage in which the Baron ponders on the villainy also at his command. A great climax is reached, with the 'Tears' and 'Gold' motifs combined, as he thinks of the sum of tears, blood and sweat which his wealth represents. The rhythm becomes feverish as he anticipates opening his chests, and there is a typically Rachmaninoff sequence of mounting passion, rising to a peak of maniacal exaltation as the Baron surveys his gold and cries 'I reign'. (Ex. 74).

It was the tonality at this point in the opera that Rimsky-Korsakov

Ex.74

cited as proof of the validity of Scriabin's conviction about a link between key and colour, when they and Rachmaninoff happened to be discussing the matter in a Paris café a few months after the opera's premiere, for both Rimsky and Scriabin saw D major as golden brown. 'You see,' said Scriabin, 'your intuition has subconsciously followed the laws whose very existence you have tried in vain to deny.' 'I had a much simpler explanation of this fact,' declared Rachmaninoff years later.[75] 'While composing this particular passage I must unconsciously have borne in mind the scene in Rimsky-Korsakov's opera *Sadko*, where the people, at Sadko's command, draw the great catch of gold fish from Lake Ilmen and break into the jubilant shout, "Gold! Gold!". This shout is written in D major.' But Rachmaninoff was surely less influenced here by distant recollection of what is a very different operatic situation than by the tonal needs of the immediately following reference to the 'Cellar' motif, with which the scene started, in D major, and by the fact that all the rest of the scene is in D major/minor. Particularly nice touches in this latter half are the delicately bright snatches on the flute of the 'Gold' motif, after the climax, illustrating the glittering of the metal; the reference to 'Tears' when the Baron thinks of the weight on his conscience, and the ghostly, shadowy strings playing the 'Cellar' motif, when he remarks, 'If only I could appear from the grave', and the bleak low sound of clarinets and oboes which concludes the scene with the 'Greed' leitmotif, reminding the listener of the source of the Baron's agony of mind.

After the protracted conversation of the first scene and the psychological agonizing of the second, the last scene is somewhat short, as the composer recognized.[76] It brings the inevitable confrontation between father and son and completes the tragic triangle. Albert retires when the Baron arrives, and the quietly sinister reference to the 'Cellar' and 'Gold' motifs together with the halting rhythm cleverly suggests his frail old age and miserliness. When the Duke questions the Baron about his son, the music quickens uneasily, and the 'Gloom and doom' motif from the opera's introduction, ostensibly referring to Albert's disposition, hints ominously at the impending rift between them. Jagged rhythms and diminished harmonies suggest the Baron's growing uneasiness of mind, and when he is finally driven to saying that his son wants to kill him and tried to rob him, Albert angrily denies it all, with his motif, now in the minor key, exploding into a passionate outburst. After the Duke has quashed the challenge and the old man suffers a seizure, Rachmaninoff cleverly suggests his panting with snatches of the 'Greed' motif, twisting pairs of adjacent semiquavers. As the Baron cries out with his dying breath, 'Where are the keys? The keys, my keys!', the cellar motif sounds on vengefully strident brass. The opera concludes with the 'Greed' motif, emphasising the vice that has underlain the whole drama and which has brought down both its perpetrator and its victim.

Mystery has always surrounded the reason why Chaliapin never appeared in *The Miserly Knight* or in the other opera Rachmaninoff wrote at this time, *Francesca da Rimini*, when the parts of the Baron and of Lanciotto Malatesta seem so obviously tailored to his special vocal and dramatic abilities. He must certainly have been aware of the composition of these two works; after all, *Francesca* had its origins in Italy during Rachmaninoff's stay there with Chaliapin in 1900, and it is impossible to believe that Rachmaninoff never mentioned this opera or the *Knight* during his first season at the Bolshoi Theatre, when he had so much contact with the singer. According to the *Recollections*,[77] it was as late as the autumn of 1905 that the composer approached Chaliapin about taking on the parts, but the singer was enthusiastic at first and said that he was ready to study both parts. Rachmaninoff claims that out of modesty or some other reason he never played his opera through for him, and offers an unconvincing explanation of the reason for Chaliapin's change of mind: 'One day he surprised me by saying that the phrasing of my opera was faulty. I contradicted him, for I was not aware of having made a mistake. This was followed by a heated argument, and since then my operas have never been mentioned between us.' Goldenweiser, who was present when Rachmaninoff first showed his two operas to Chaliapin, gives a different account. 'Chaliapin sang the parts of the Miser and Lanciotto Malatesta, and made a great impression on us, despite the fact that he was sight-reading. Nevertheless, he didn't take the trouble to learn the part of the Miser, and for some reason the music was never given him and he declined to appear in these operas'.[78] Yet on 4 January 1906, exactly a week before the two operas' premiere at the Bolshoi Theatre, Chaliapin and some musical colleagues, including Glazunov and the Stravinsky family, gathered at the house of Rimsky-Korsakov in Petersburg for a run-through of *The Miserly Knight*. Felix Blumenfeld was at the piano, and one of the participants, Alexander Ossovsky, later recalled Chaliapin's comments,[79] which were that the connection between word and vocal melody in the opera was not so organic and indissoluble as in *The Stone Guest* and *Mozart and Salieri*; and that although Rachmaninoff magnificently expressed the general sense and the overall character of each dramatic situation through the orchestra, giving it a symphonic role, the vocal line lacked the 'fashioning of word in sound' which was so remarkable in Dargomyzhsky and Mussorgsky, and this made the singer's task in Rachmaninoff's opera a very difficult one. From these remarks it looks as though Chaliapin's attitude may have been coloured by his recent close association with the Petersburg musical world, and in any case he may have adjusted his comments to suit his listeners, who included Vladimir Stasov.

Rimsky-Korsakov's criticism of *The Miserly Knight*, not surprisingly, echoed Chaliapin's:

> There are very powerful and striking dramatic moments. The scene of the Baron, feasting his eyes upon the gold he has accumulated, is magnificent.[80] But as a whole, the almost unvaryingly thick texture of the orchestra overwhelms the voice. The composer's main attention is in the orchestra, and the vocal part is as it were adapted to it. This has resulted in a relationship the opposite of that in *The Stone Guest*, where the role of the orchestra is reduced to a minimum, as a straightforward support to the vocal part. Dargomyzhsky's orchestra, without the voice part, has no importance in itself. In Rachmaninoff the reverse applies: the orchestra absorbs almost all the artistic interest, and the vocal score, without the orchestra, is jejune. In the final analysis the ear misses the melody that is lacking. However, a final verdict about *The Miserly Knight* will only be able to be made after hearing the opera through in its orchestral version, with a stage setting.[81]

In truth there is some justification for Rimsky's criticisms, but Rachmaninoff had a formidable task in setting a libretto operatically so intractable, as contemporary critics were not slow to point out, and he created a work that cannot easily be categorized. It has been called a 'symphonic opera',[82] and it is interesting that the work falls into a four-movement key scheme:

Introduction:	E minor
Scene 1:	E flat major
Scene 2:	D major/minor
Scene 3:	E flat major/E minor

The nature of the opera makes it an ideal work to peruse or listen to at home, for the full subtlety of Rachmaninoff's craftsmanship can only reveal itself from study of the score, and in this sense the critic Yuly Engel was clearly right when he wrote that the opera is 'perhaps a *Kabinettstück* for those who can appreciate the subtle filigree work of its exquisite composition.'[83] Despite a revival at the Bolshoi Theatre in 1912, *The Miserly Knight* has so far failed to make any headway on the operatic stage, and that situation regrettably seems most unlikely to change.

Francesca da Rimini, Op. 25

As companion piece to *The Miserly Knight* Rachmaninoff at last completed *Francesca da Rimini*, using the libretto prepared by Modest Tchaikovsky, based on Canto V of Dante's *Inferno*. Two 'tableaux' are framed by a prologue and epilogue. The prologue opens in the First Circle of Hell, among the despairing souls of the damned. The ghost of the Roman poet Virgil leads Dante down to the Second Circle, where, he explains, the souls of adulterous lovers are tormented forever by a howling wind. When Dante asks two of them, Paolo and Francesca, how they have come to be there they reply, 'There is no greater sorrow in the world than to recall in misery a time of happiness'.

The first tableau is set in the Malatesta palace at Rimini. Having received a command from the Pope to support him in his fight against the Ghibellines, Lanciotto Malatesta declares his willingness to obey. He orders his men to prepare for battle, and after being blessed by the papal envoy summons his wife Francesca to say farewell. Before she arrives he broods on the unhappy circumstances of his marriage. His brother Paolo had courted Francesca on his behalf but because, at the suggestion of her father, he had not revealed that he was acting as his proxy, it was to Paolo that she had made her marriage vows; had there not been this deception, Francesca would have been a faithful wife to him. Nevertheless, it was Paolo she now loved, for he, Lanciotto, was lame and awkward, whereas Paolo was tall and handsome. He wishes to punish Francesca, but he hesitates in case his suspicions are founded on nothing more than jealousy. He must set a trap to find out the truth. Francesca then arrives. Lanciotto tells her that he is setting off to war and that, although she will be alone, his brother Paolo will be present to protect her. Francesca replies that she will do her duty, but her coldness of manner torments him. He desires not her obedience but her love, he says; fearsome to other men, before her he is powerless. He begs her to love him once, but she makes no reply, for she cannot tell a lie. Lanciotto says enigmatically that they will say goodbye later: 'Remember, I love you always and shall be waiting for you'. To Francesca's question of when he will return he answers, 'You will soon discover!'

The second tableau takes place in a room in the palace, where Paolo reads from a book of Arthurian legend the story of the adulterous love of Queen Guinevere and Launcelot. 'One day a knight appeared before Guinevere to seek an audience for Launcelot'. "Will she grant it?" asks Paolo. "Yes", replies Francesca; "I would not like her if she did not take pity on him". "And will you do the same for me?" "You must not ask such things", replies Francesca, flustered. Paolo resumes reading.

'The Queen blushed at mention of the name of Launcelot but granted the audience.' "How happy they must have been!" comments Paolo. 'Guinevere asked Launcelot what he wanted, but the latter could only look into her eyes in silent rapture.' At this point, as the parallel between fiction and the present reality begins to become too strong, Francesca begs Paolo not to look at her in the same way. Paolo asks how he can possibly continue to read of the lovers' surrender to passion, and he breaks down and falls tearfully to his knees. Francesca begs him not to weep, for happiness awaits them in the life hereafter; there she will be his forever. But Paolo answers that he is racked by desire; he would forfeit paradise itself for one kiss. Francesca protests that she is pledged to another, but Paolo reminds her that it was to him that she made her promises: "Before Heaven you are mine!" Though Francesca declares the torments of hell will await them, she finally surrenders to Paolo's embrace. "Where you are, there is everlasting bliss," they declare together. But at the very moment of their happiness Lanciotto enters and plunges a dagger into them both.

The epilogue returns to the fringes of Hell, the scene of the prologue, where the ghosts of the damned are tormented by the wind, Paolo and Francesca among them, who remark laconically that they read no more that day. The final word is given to the ghosts, who repeat the epigram from the beginning: 'There is no greater sorrow than to recall in misery a time of happiness'.

Most earlier operatic settings of the Francesca story had been based on the historical facts originally recounted by Boccaccio. This had been the case with the most recent setting, a five-act version by Eduard Nápravník, staged at the Maryinsky Theatre in Petersburg in 1902, in which the conductor/composer had used a libretto based on the newly-written tragedy by Stephen Phillips. In following Dante and setting the story within the framework of the torments of Hell, as his brother had done in his symphonic poem *Francesca da Rimini*, and as, for example, Ambroise Thomas had done in his opera on the same subject, Modest Tchaikovsky made a libretto already conspicuously lacking in dramatic interest even lamer operatically, since the roles of Dante and Virgil are very small and external to the action. Moreover, the broodings of Paolo in the first tableau and the reading of long excerpts from the story of Launcelot and Guinevere are dramatically inert and, worst of all, when the opera's climax is reached at last, it is brutally cut short.

Rachmaninoff himself was aware of deficiencies in the libretto. Already at the beginning of March 1904 he discussed with Taneyev possible changes[84] and told him of his intention to consult Modest Tchaikovsky about them.[85] On 26 March he wrote to Tchaikovsky, asking him drastically to prune the libretto by omitting the two first scenes altogether, including one with the Cardinal, and in the second tableau to rewrite sixteen lines and 'to add some completely new lines before the epilogue to give more space to the love duet'. Tchaikovsky complied with Rachmaninoff's request and in his letter of 8 June, before setting to work in earnest, the composer prematurely declared himself 'satisfied' with the changes, despite the fact that the additional material seems to have been nothing more than a pair of five short parallel lines – 'very banal', Rachmaninoff later described them.[86] In his next letter to Tchaikovsky, dated 3 August, written when the opera had already been completed, Rachmaninoff was more frank about the problems he had faced through shortage of text:

> This is felt most of all in the second scene, where there is a build up to the love duet, and a conclusion to the love duet but no actual duet. This shortage of words is all the more apparent because I do not allow myself to repeat words. But in *Francesca* I had to allow it; there were just too few words. The second tableau and epilogue last twenty-one minutes; this is terribly little. The whole opera lasts little more than an hour.

After he had completed the vocal score Rachmaninoff had a copy of the libretto sent to Modest for checking. When he got it back, he found that the corrections incorporated were so numerous that the two versions were incompatible and consequently had to be printed separately. Even at this eleventh hour Rachmaninoff slipped in a request for more material almost as an afterthought at the end of his letter to Modest of 7 September: 'I forgot one other request: could you write me an extra aria for Paolo? I am still afraid the second scene will be too short. Maybe I might still manage to compose it.' Three days later Rachmaninoff returned to the same subject, again unobtrusively at the end of a letter: 'I should like to put the extra aria in the duet and not at the beginning; my duet is short. Perhaps you could write some words for the duet; that would be better.' But by the time of his final letter to Tchaikovsky, dated 8 October, concerning details of the publication of the libretto, Rachmaninoff seems to have resigned himself to the inevitable and we hear nothing more of the matter. The pity is that he did not put his case more forcefully at the outset, when Modest was willingly making the other changes.

As with *The Miserly Knight*, Wagnerian influence is seen in the opera's dramatic continuity, emphasized by the lack of any division into separate numbers, certain turns of harmony, the use of leitmotifs and the dominant role assigned to the orchestra. The prologue, with its orchestral introduction and scene on the fringes of Hell, is fully one-third of the whole opera; yet, despite this imbalance, musically this is one of the most striking parts of the work. Seven years before, when Rachmaninoff had so enthusiastically first read through Tchaikovsky's libretto, he had appealed to his librettist to change the prologue by writing him thirty lines to give to the off-stage chorus, besides transferring to them the words of Virgil's Ghost, 'My son, now we are there'. 'Do you find this possible? I should very much like you to say "Yes", otherwise, although dissatisfied with only one phrase in the libretto to the point where my sighs are audible, I shall have to write a symphonic tableau only for orchestra, which is rather a pity since I have a choir too at my disposal once I write the opera. For heaven's sake, give me some of those words, Modest Ilyich!' [87] In fact Tchaikovsky did not fulfil either request, and in a sense Rachmaninoff did the very thing he had earlier wished to avoid, when he wrote the long orchestral preamble, and the use of the choir intoning wordlessly was not from choice but imposed upon him by the lack of text.

Rachmaninoff was clearly looking over his shoulder at the opening of Tchaikovsky's *Francesca da Rimini* when he composed the evocation of Hell, with its obsessive chromaticism. For the wailing of the damned and the swirling mists Rachmaninoff used a simple, plaintive descending semi-tone complemented by a rising three-note motif that is developed in the course of the introduction into a typical Rachmaninoff *fugato*:

Ex.75

As Dante and Virgil move to the Second Circle of Hell the music accelerates and becomes more lugubrious and diabolical still, with a clear foretaste of the third movement of *The Bells*, not only in the choral writing, the wailing, descending chromatic scales, but in musical material and orchestral scoring. When Dante asks 'Who are these two?', reference is made to the love music of Francesca and Paolo from the second tableau, a descending phrase used in a number of variants:

Ex.76

When the two lovers are asked by Dante to tell their story, they reply with a memorably direct and simple chant-like statement in unison of Dante's famous aphorism that sums up their predicament:

Ex.77

[There is no greater sorrow than to recall in misery a time of happiness.]

The first tableau, like the Baron's monologue in *The Miserly Knight*, was written as a vehicle for Chaliapin. The violent brusqueness of the orchestral introduction contrasts with the ethereal gloom of Hell. Lanciotto Malatesta himself is apostrophized by a persistent iambic rhythm (Ex. 78).

Ex.78

The transition to the second scene, in which Lanciotto broods on his unhappy love, introduces a second motif on trombones and horns over shuddering string tremolos, characterizing his despairing jealousy:

Ex.79

Lanciotto's soliloquy is declamatory, but the entry of Francesca marks a gentle lyrical contrast and Lanciotto's outburst ('It is your love I desire!') leads to a proper arioso, in which his motif of jealousy is used to marvellous effect to characterize a despairing and agonized passion. Rachmaninoff told Elena Kreutzer[88] that the latter half of Lanciotto's arioso is a reworking of an earlier unpublished piano prelude, the term 'prelude' suggesting a 1903 date. Without this knowledge the passage would appear to be derived closely from Lanciotto's leitmotifs with their characteristic dotted rhythm, but Rachmaninoff's statement implies that the arioso came first and that he excerpted the leitmotifs later:

Ex.80

When Francesca has left the scene, unable to make any response, there is an exquisitely poignant brief interlude before Lanciotto's final outburst, in which his dotted rhythm hovers ambivalently on flutes against *tremolo* strings, as though in the dark recesses of his tormented mind he cannot quite decide whether or not to take action; but then fatefully descending horn chords make it clear that the die has been cast, and he makes his last, sinister threats. The exciting orchestral climax with which the scene concludes anticipates the end of the first movement of the Second Symphony.

According to Rachmaninoff's 1917 list of his compositions,[89] the second tableau was written during or immediately after the composer's stay in Italy in 1900, and yet there is no sign of this in the sketches or the manuscript of the opera, where the scene appears in its proper order, though, unlike the prologue, first tableau and epilogue, undated. As a whole, however, the singing parts in the second tableau are more directly lyrical in Rachmaninoff's earlier vein than in the first, as the more extensive arioso passages show. The orchestral introduction, beginning and ending with a direct statement of the Francesca/love motif, develops variants of it against a hovering string accompaniment which marvellously captures the buoyant expectancy of love and which Rachmaninoff uses again when the lovers finally embrace. Paolo's initial reading from the book, 'The beautiful Guinevere ...', is a passage of melodic recitative, with the orchestra delicately capturing the gentle courtly modesty of the Queen, and by implication of Francesca herself. After appearing at the beginning and end of the orchestral preamble the Francesca theme wells up unresolved three further times, until at its sixth appearance Paolo breaks down and Francesca sings her arioso 'Weep not, my Paolo', with its taxing top B naturals, a glorious example of Rachmaninoff lyricism, and the only point in the whole opera where the voice carries the whole melodic line.

Another lyrical highspot is the two lovers' culminating arioso 'Where you are, there is happiness without end', at the end of which, with the reference to eternal ecstasy, comes a protracted peaceful afterglow, a portent of the very end of *The Bells*. The music of the swirling mists of the prologue returns, with a steady crescendo of intensity and with hints of the motif of Lanciotto's jealousy as a premonition of his imminent arrival and of his murder of the guilty but sympathetic lovers. The bankruptcy of Tchaikovsky's writing is all too evident in the trite lines of the lovers and in their simple cry 'Ah!' to Lanciotto's curse. The music at once accelerates as the tormented spirits of Hell return in the epilogue in another foretaste of the third movement of *The Bells*; the descending scales seem to mock the Francesca motif in cruel parody. The opera concludes with the chorus repeating Dante's aphorism, sung, as it was by Francesca and Dante in the Prologue, in stark and penetrating unison.

The same performing curse as blighted *The Miserly Knight* overhung *Francesca*. Not only was the opera put on without Chaliapin in the role of Malatesta – as in *The Miserly Knight* the then little-known twenty-four-year-old baritone Georgy Baklanov filled the breach – but Antonina Nezhdanova the distinguished soprano, then aged thirty-two, whom Rachmaninoff had ear-marked for the title role, also withdrew during rehearsals, perhaps because of Chaliapin, though ostensibly because she was also preparing the part of the Queen of the Night in *The Magic Flute* that same month and had been persuaded by the conductor and producer of that opera that she could not do justice to two such dissimilar roles at the same time.[90] Although Rachmaninoff offered the part to another young singer, she, apparently, found the part too high for her voice. Finally, in despair, the composer approached the forty-one-year-old soprano Nadezhda Salina: 'Nadezhda Vasilyevna, I've written the devil only knows what, which no-one can sing; for one it's too low, for another too high. I'll give you all the phrasing, everything you want; just try to sing it.'[91] Fortunately Salina worked hard at both the musical and dramatic aspects of the role and the production went without a hitch. In recognition of her qualities as a true professional, Rachmaninoff recommended her for a teaching post at the Music and Drama School of the Moscow Philharmonic Society, when Rachmaninoff's friend the cellist and conductor Brandukov became its Director a few months after the *Francesca* premiere.[92] Nevertheless, overall the performance of both operas seems to have left a lot to be desired. Baklanov's voice was not matched by his acting ability, an especial disadvantage in the Pushkin opera, where the tenor Bonachin too failed to make much of the character of Albert. The latter's difficulty with high notes detracted from his performance as Paolo, and for Francesca's part Salina lacked the essential freshness of youth.[93]

Francesca da Rimini, like *The Miserly Knight*, has never made its way in the operatic world. Even the timing of the two operas' launch was inauspicious, taking place under the cloud of political upheaval in Russia soon after the December 1905 uprising, when artistic life in

Moscow was in a state of suspended animation and the general public was staying firmly at home. It was announced in the press that the operas would be put on again the following season with Chaliapin,[94] but by then Rachmaninoff had resigned from his position at the Bolshoi Theatre. After its brief 1912 revival, it was not until fifty years after its first performance that *Francesca* was staged again at the Bolshoi Theatre,[95] and there is little prospect now that either of Rachmaninoff's mature operas will ever be known to more than the faithful few. In the Soviet Union, as in Rachmaninoff's Russia, it seems as though *Aleko*, greatly inferior musically, will continue to be the work by which his name as an opera composer is, if at all, known.

After the end of his second season at the Bolshoi Theatre Rachmaninoff retreated rapidly to Italy with his family for a rest and to escape from the political unrest at home. No sooner had he arrived in Florence than he began planning his next composition. Surprisingly, despite the mixed success of *The Miserly Knight* and *Francesca*, the work Rachmaninoff had in mind was another opera, though this time on a large scale. On 19 March 1906 he wrote Morozov a letter,[96] his longest extant, in which he gave a closely detailed programme for a possible four- or five-act scenario of Flaubert's novel of ancient Carthage, *Salammbô*, with a request that Morozov should approach Sakhovsky's friend Mikhail Svobodin and commission him to set a trial scene. Morozov was unenthusiastic about the project and Rachmaninoff's choice of Svobodin was an unhappy one; he seems to have made no attempt to respond to the commission and Rachmaninoff, who was bursting to begin work immediately, rapidly became desperate. After three weeks had gone by, the kindly Morozov sent Rachmaninoff an effort of his own, but the latter was still vainly hoping for something from Svobodin. Finally, he reluctantly turned to another friend, Mikhail Slonov, choosing him as his last resort rather than Modest Tchaikovsky, whom he had also considered originally. On 8 May, in the first of four letters over the next fortnight, he sent Slonov a long account of what he wanted, but despite Slonov's industriousness and the frank criticism and clear guidelines he received from Rachmaninoff, his verses too failed to satisfy the composer. Finally, on 24 May, Rachmaninoff wrote to Slonov: 'So far I have written absolutely nothing of *Salammbô*. I am testing and examining everything. But it's vital you complete the libretto quickly – and so much time has already gone by.' Two days later Rachmaninoff's daughter Irina fell dangerously ill, and with his wife also unwell for the previous fortnight Rachmaninoff was too preoccupied with domestic anxiety for composition and not a word more was ever heard of *Salammbô*. The impression that remains is one of astonishment that Rachmaninoff, with his prestige as by now the favourite of the Moscow musical world, should have had so much difficulty in finding a competent librettist. There was Svobodin, a minor poet who made a career as a journalist; Slonov, by profession a singer; Modest Tchaikovsky, whom Rachmaninoff had already found sadly wanting as a librettist; and his conservatoire friend Morozov: hardly a glittering pool of talent. Perhaps it was the composer's innate reserve and his preference for the familiar that prevented him from approaching anyone outside this group of literary dilettantes.

There was, however, to be one musical souvenir of the Rachmaninoffs' troubled stay in Italy. During the summer they were visited by their cousin Anna Trubnikova, who later recalled how an itinerant musician used to sing outside the house in Florence. 'A tiny donkey with very long ears pulled an upright mechanical piano on wheels and a cot with a baby in it was attached to the piano. The young man sang popular ballads and the woman wound the piano .... Our favourite number in their repertoire was a simple but quite melodious polka. Many years later, when I heard Rachmaninoff's *Italian Polka*, I knew where it had first entered his consciousness.'[97] The precise date of composition and publication of this cheerful piano duet is not known; Trubnikova's 'many years later' implies that it was written some considerable time after Rachmaninoff's Italian sojourn, and yet already by 1910 the piece had become popular enough for a transcription to be made for a military band, to which Rachmaninoff himself added some trumpet fanfares. Though these appear alongside the piano parts in the printed edition and though they may have worked well with band, they sound singularly ineffective with piano alone. Curiously enough, there are no tempo indications, and taken at too sedate a pace, as it frequently is, the piece can sound laboured; rather should it be played with the greatest vigour, as in the composer and his wife's sparkling 1938 party recording.

Fifteen Songs, Op. 26

Having at least succeeded in completing the corrections to *The Miserly Knight* and *Francesca* during his stay in Italy, Rachmaninoff returned to Ivanovka in July, where, with the health of his wife and daughter improving, he at last got down to composition. He laid on one side all operatic plans and turned instead to writing a group of songs for the Kerzins, a project he must have had in mind from the time of his arrival abroad, when Mariya Kerzin sent him copies of a number of poems she had selected as suitable for setting. 'I have quickly looked them through and find much that is suitable for music,' Rachmaninoff wrote encouragingly to her husband on 20 March, the day after his original letter to Morozov about *Salammbô*. But although a further selection was sent in May, on 2 August Rachmaninoff asked for others still. 'What could be taken from [the earlier collection] I have taken – but it is only little! Then in this little anthology of yours all the words demand the minor key. Is it impossible to find a few verses in a more major vein? Otherwise I shall sink into total apathy!' When, during August and September the composer completed his group of fifteen 'trifles', as he called them,[98] five of them turned out to be in the major key. Dedicated to the Kerzins, they were first performed as a set at one of their concerts in February the following year, when Rachmaninoff was abroad, by four different singers accompanied by Goldenweiser; the new songs, Rachmaninoff's Op. 26, made up the first half of the programme, a revival of the *Elegiac Trio* Op. 9 the second.

Characteristically, the profoundly serious subject matter of the first three songs embodies the melancholy philosophy of an old man rather than the optimism natural to a successful thirty-three-year-old composer with the world at his feet. *The Heart's Secret*, to a poem by Alexey Tolstoy, tells how thoughts in the hearts of men remain unexpressed, stifled by anxieties and life's vicissitudes. This sobering message is powerfully conveyed by the singer's sombre melodic line and the ponderous and measured steps in the accompaniment (the marking is *Adagio*). *All once I gladly owned*, from Tyutchev, is the briefest of the Op. 26 settings, a mere fifteen bars long. God has punished the poet by taking everything from him – health, strength of will, air, sleep – everything except his companion, the addressee, so that he might still pray to Him. The impassioned opening has the melodrama of some of the composer's early settings; the second half is more lyrical. The third song, *Come let us rest*, is taken from Sonya's concluding monologue in Chekhov's *Uncle Vanya*. We shall hear the angels and see the spangled heaven and see how all worldly evil and suffering is settled by compassion, and how life will become quiet, sweet and agreeable – that at least is her belief. This dark and declamatory setting of a prose text reminds us that five years before Chekhov once suggested to Rachmaninoff setting his *Black Monk* as an opera.

The fourth song, the most extended of the Op. 26 set and one of Rachmaninoff's most interesting, also has operatic overtones. *Two Partings*, from Koltsov, uniquely for Rachmaninoff is written for two voices, soprano and baritone, who do not however combine but engage in a dialogue. A man asks a young woman about her leave-taking from two lovers. The first, she says, was distraught by the parting, the latter indifferent. Asked which of the two she keeps in her heart, she answers that it is the first but that she loves the second. Rachmaninoff contrasts the two vignettes by making the first take the character of a quiet recitative against a chordal accompaniment, over a hypnotically repeated dominant pedal, whilst the second, in which the woman is incensed by the man's coldness, is more vehement. There are overtones of Mussorgsky in the passage where the second lover tells the woman that he is leaving:

Ex.81

[Look, I'm off for a short time.]

It is a pity that the forces required for performance make *Two Partings* the rarest of all Rachmaninoff's songs. *Beloved let us fly* is in complete contrast. It is a setting of a poem by Count Golenishchev-Kutuzov, who had provided the words for two of Rachmaninoff's earlier songs. The poet invites his beloved to leave the city and return to the beauties of the countryside in spring – a theme no doubt especially congenial to Rachmaninoff, who so often yearned to return to his beloved Ivanovka. The gentle lyrical beauty of the setting is enhanced by the restraint of the piano accompaniment.

The next three songs are among Rachmaninoff's finest. *Christ is risen* is a powerful setting of a poem by Merezhkovsky, in which the poet reflects that if Christ were to return among us he would weep in anguish to see all the evil in the world. The religious context is established at the beginning by two elements: first, the repeated chords of the Easter chant from the *Obikhod*, heard also in the last movement of the composer's own First Suite for Two Pianos, not to mention Rimsky-Korsakov's *Russian Easter Festival Overture*; and then the inverted turn in the opening bars of the piano part, echoing the beginning of Rachmaninoff's First Symphony, with its religious motto 'Vengeance is mine, I will repay' (Ex 82). The song gathers intensity as it moves inexorably towards a climax of overwhelming despair, as the Easter chant continues to sound, as if in mockery, after the singer's final words, 'He would weep'.

The much-loved *To the Children*, to a poem by Khomyakov, also

Ex.82

has a strongly religious atmosphere. The poem tells of a parent's sense of loss as the years pass and infant children grow up and leave home, and like the first songs of the set it reflects a view of life far in advance of the composer's years. At the time of its composition Rachmaninoff's daughter Irina was three years old and Tatyana not yet born. The simple chordal piano accompaniment moves only into arpeggios at the climactic cry of anguish 'Oh children!'; otherwise it is austerely simple, perfectly complementing the gently loving character of the vocal line.

Spring figures again in one of Rachmaninoff's most splendid settings, No. 8, *Thy pity I implore*, again from Merezhkovsky. The poet begs Spring not to awaken in him the feelings of suffering that have been dormant. Rachmaninoff's setting with its excitingly invigorating piano accompaniment has a marvellous urgency (the song is marked *Allegro con fuoco*) and an impetus which never flags. Performers should note that Rachmaninoff remarked that the song should be performed faster than his metronome marking. (♩ = 104).[99]

In his Op. 8 Rachmaninoff had set two poems by the Ukrainian national poet Taras Shevchenko, and the ninth song of the Op. 26 group is another, *Let me rest here alone*, in a translation by Ivan Bunin. The poet enthuses about the beauty of spring, but the lady with him is silent. Realizing that she is taking her farewell of him, he vehemently bemoans that he will again be alone. After the grandeur of the opening the setting is another that relapses somewhat into the melodramatic gestures of some of the early songs. *Before my window*, on the other hand, is one of Rachmaninoff's lyrical masterpieces. The words, by Galina, tell of a cherry tree, standing by the poet's window, which, by its fragrance and beauty, sings a wordless song of love. In its general musical character it bears a strong resemblance to the earlier Galina setting *How fair this spot*, which shares its key of A major; in both an exquisite vocal line is delicately echoed by a perfectly integrated accompaniment. For *The Fountains* the composer used the first stanza of a poem by Tyutchev, which describes a fountain rising into the sky against the sun (its subject is pluralized in the English version). The rising water is rather obviously represented by repeated surging arpeggios in the piano part and reflected by the singer's climactic octave leap to a top B flat on the word 'heights'; conversely at the end, where the poet remarks that the water must come back down to earth, the vocal line also descends. After this pleasant but commonplace setting *Night is mournful,* from Bunin's own work, is a distinct contrast. The poem is an expression of a passionate but despairing yearning for happiness; as the poet gazes out at night on the immensity of the steppe, he reflects on the sadness and love in his soul. To whom can he tell his trouble? The silent night is mournful, as are his dreams. Rachmaninoff himself remarked[100] that in this song, in which the piano part forms a delicate tracery in counterpoint to the vocal line, the 'singing' is more the prerogative of the accompanist than of the singer. Perhaps it was the polyphony of the setting that encouraged the composer to make an (unpublished) version, with Brandukov's assistance, for voice, cello and piano.

When yesterday we met (Polonsky), a favourite of Chaliapin's and sadly the only song of Rachmaninoff he recorded, is one of the composer's most subtle settings. The poem tells of the poet's chance meeting with the woman he once loved. He is amazed at how she has changed with time; her look of shame tells its own story. Although their parting must be for ever, she is still dear to him. Against the simplest of dotted accompaniments the vocal part is rhythmically free, with many pauses, and the music follows every nuance of the rapidly changing psychological moods of the story, as when the woman sings her simple goodbye. The unnaturally quiet falling phrases against the uneasy chords of the accompaniment catch perfectly the woman's tentative farewell and the strained atmosphere of the moment, whilst the following more robust crescendo emphasizes the man's mounting feelings as memories flood back and he is tempted to break his silence (Ex. 83).

The penultimate song, *The Ring,* to another poem by Koltsov, is less interesting. A woman casts into the flames a gold ring given her by a lover, since it has no point now he has gone. The restlessly twitching semi-quaver accompaniment at the beginning and end, for which, uniquely in a Rachmaninoff song, there is an *ossia* part, is like the fluttering of the flame of the taper. The cycle ends, as it began, in philosophic and quasi-religious reflection. *All things depart* (Rathaus) is a fatalistic comment on the transitoriness of life, a growing preoccupation of the composer. A few simple chords suffice to support the singer in the introduction, but as the poet lists examples of mortality, so the religious overtones become more marked, as the accompaniment assumes the same quaver/crotchet/quaver rhythm as in *Christ is risen.* The music builds to a powerful climax as the poet finally declares 'I cannot sing

Ex.83

['Goodbye, till next we meet!' But I wanted to say, 'Goodbye forever.']

joyful songs', an appropriate statement with which to finish a set of songs by a composer for whom, even at this stage in his career, the darker side of life provided the most natural material for musical expression.

References

1 *Riesemann*, p. 98.
2 *Riesemann*, p. 99.
3 R. to Asafyev, 13 April 1917.
4 *Riesemann*, p. 108.
5 Sofiya Satina, *VR/A* 1, p. 30.
6 *Bortnikova*, pp. 9–10, No. 27.
7 Faubion Bowers has an interesting if somewhat fanciful chapter on the widespread mental instability of Russian composers in his *Scriabin*, Kodansha International Ltd., Tokyo and Palo Alto, 1969, vol. 1, pp. 63–74.
8 Lyudmila Rostovtsova (Skalon), *VR/A* 1, p. 242.
9 *Riesemann*, p. 108.
10 R. to Zateyevich, 18 April 1898.
11 R. to Goldenweiser, 18 June 1898.
12 *Chaliapin*, p. 128.

13 Rachmaninoff does not refer to the 'Shakespeare subject' by name, and its identification with *Richard II* is the suggestion of *B/L*, p. 82.
14 R. to Modest Tchaikovsky, 28 July 1898.
15 Mikhail Mikhaylov, *A.K. Lyadov*, Muzyka, Moscow, 1985, p. 83.
16 R. to Modest Tchaikovsky, 28 August 1898.
17 *Bryantseva*, p. 267.
18 Pressman, *VR/A* 1, p. 204.
19 'A Small Corner of Musical Moscow in the 80s', by Matvey Pressman in *VR/A* 1, pp. 146–204.
20 Goldenweiser, *VR/A* 1, p. 407.
21 Elena Zhukovskaya (Kreutzer), *VR/A*, 1, p. 294.
22 Op. cit., pp.292–295. Kreutzer's evidence makes the date on the manuscript, 17 May, impossible, unless Rachmaninoff had prepared his joke beforehand.
23 See *T/N*, p. 169.
24 *Pantaley* is dated 4 May 1901 and *Fate* 18 February 1900. Elena Kreutzer, an eye-witness, is quite certain about the 1899 date of Panteley (*VR/A* 1, p. 311) and she is supported by Goldenweiser (*ibid.*, p. 407). *Norris* (p. 31) mistakenly follows *B/L* (p. 94) in placing the work in June/July 1900.
25 Elena Kreutzer, *VR/A* 1, p. 311.
26 Lyudmila Skalon, *VR/A* 1, p. 247.
27 See *Bazhanov*, pp. 150 and 161 for a romanticized account of these events.
28 There is some confusion about Rachmaninoff's visits to Tolstoy. The date comes from Chaliapin, 'Mask and Soul', in *Fyodor Ivanovich Shalyapin*, Iskusstvo, Moscow, 1976, vol. 1, p. 280. According to the Swans, Rachmaninoff said that he went twice, on the second occasion with Chaliapin, and that he never went again (*Swan*, p. 185); Riesemann implies that only one visit was made (*Riesemann*, p. 111), but Goldenweiser speaks of two (in *Vblizi Tolstovo*, Moscow and Leningrad, 1923, vol. 2, p. 379). A letter from Rachmaninoff to Goldenweiser, apparently to be dated 31 January 1900, concerning arrangements for a visit the following day, seems to contradict his statement to the Swans.
29 Goldenweiser, *op. cit.*
30 *Riesemann*, p. 111. Elena Kreutzer dates the consultations with Dahl to 1899 (*VR/A* 1, p. 293), and Apetyan in her commentary on the letters, confusing Rachmaninoff's doctors, puts them, still less probably, in the autumn of 1898 (*LN/A* 1, p. 547).
31 R. to Slonov, 10 May 1900.
32 *Chaliapin*, p. 145.
33 R. to Slonov, 10 May 1900.
34 R. to Morozov, 5 July 1900.
35 R. to Morozov, 18 July 1900.
36 R. to Asafyev, 13 May 1917.
37 Goldenweiser, *VR/A* 1, p. 415; Sofiya Satina in unpublished materials for a biography of Rachmaninoff, quoted in *B/L*, p. 95.
38 Rachmaninoff found himself in the same position seven years later, on 23 January 1908, when he played the concerto in Berlin at the concert at which Koussevitzky also made his first appearance as conductor.
39 Medtner, *VR/A* 2, p. 350.
40 *Piggott*, p. 47; *T/N,* p. 69.
41 *Riesemann*, p. 112.
42 Goldenweiser, *VR/A* 1, p. 415.

43 Attention is drawn to these points by *Bryantseva*, pp. 281–282.
44 See *T/N*, pp. 69–71.
45 Anatoly Alexandrov, *VR/A* 2, p. 162.
46 *Seroff*, p. 69.
47 *Sabaneyeff*, p. 105 et seq.
48 Taneyev's diary for 26 October 1901, quoted in *LN/A* 1, p. 563.
49 Goldenweiser, *VR/A* 1, p. 415.
50 *Keldïsh*, pp. 192–193.
51 Horowitz in conversation with Jack Pfeiffer, in sleeve note to his 1978 Golden Jubilee Concert recording of R.'s Third Concerto, on RCA RL 12633.
52 *Riesemann*, p. 113.
53 Rachmaninoff to Nadia Reisenberg after a radio performance with the cellist Joseph Schuster, in December, 1942, in *B/L*, p. 378.
54 *Riesemann*, p. 144.
55 *Norris*, p. 162.
56 Malashkin and Prigozhy were composers of popular songs.
57 R. to Nadezhda Zabela-Vrubel, 22 March 1902.
58 *The Answer* had already been set by Liszt as *Comment disaient-ils?*
59 Goldenweiser, *VR/A* 1, p. 407.
60 R. to Asafyev, 13 April 1917.
61 *Swan*, p. 8.
62 Rachmaninoff seems to have played the opening Prelude in F sharp minor, but which two others is unclear. Yury Engel's review in *Russkiye vedomosti*, 12 February 1903, quoted in *B/L*, p. 100, refers to the Preludes in D major (No. 4) and G flat (No. 10), whereas Apetyan, in her commentary on R. to Zabel-Vrubel, 6 February 1903 (*LN/A* 1, p. 573), quoting the published programme, lists those in B flat major (No. 2) and G minor (No. 5).
63 The 'cycle of fifths', in which each major key is followed by its relative minor, moves out from C major by adding a sharp to the key signature of each pair as far as B major, and then works back from G flat by subtracting flats.
64 Boris Asafyev, *VR/A* 2, p. 386.
65 Ibid.
66 Ibid.
67 *Riesemann*, p. 223.
68 Elena Gnesina, *VR/A* 1, p. 208.
69 *Keldïsh*, p. 247.
70 Riesemann's chronology in *R.'s Recollections*, p. 121, is wrong. See *LN/A* 1, pp. 579–580.
71 *Riesemann*, p. 130.
72 Rachmaninoff omitted forty lines and added two to Pushkin's text. See *Belza*, pp. 78–80.
73 Lyudmila Rostovtsova (Skalon), *VR/A* 1, p. 245.
74 Taneyev's diary for 5 March 1904, quoted in *LN/A* 1, p. 578.
75 *Riesemann*, p. 147.
76 R. to Morozov, 4 August 1904.
77 *Riesemann*, pp. 130–131. The year quoted on p. 130, viz. 1906, is an error.
78 Goldenweiser, *VR/A* 1, p. 419.
79 A.V. Ossovsky, *VR/A* 1, p. 359.
80 Chaliapin performed the Baron's monologue at a Siloti concert in St Petersburg the following year (3 February 1907).

81 A.V. Ossovsky, *VR/A* 1, p. 359.

82 *Seroff*, p. 77.

83 Yuly Engel in *Russkiye vedomosti*, 14 January 1906, No. 226, Vol. X, no. 2, quoted in *B/L*, p. 115.

84 R. to Taneyev, 29 February 1904.

85 Taneyev's diary for 5 March 1904.

86 R. to Morozov, 4 August 1904. The additional words supplied by Modest Tchaikovsky run from '*O svetlïy mig* ... to *V tebe blazhenstvo vechnoye!*'

> O joyous moment! O moment blessed!
> My heart's desire! ... I am yours forever!
> Dearest one ... All, all will I surrender!
> With you is bliss eternal! ...
> All, all will I surrender!
> With you is bliss eternal.

87 R. to Modest Tchaikovsky, 28 August 1898.

88 Elena Zhukovskaya (Kreutzer), *VR/A* 1, p. 311.

89 R. to Asafyev, 13 April 1917.

90 Antonina Nezhdanova, *VR/A* 2, pp. 29–30.

91 Nadezhda Salina, *VR/A* 2, p. 35.

92 R. to Brandukov, 19 June 1906.

93 See *Belza*, pp. 144–148.

94 Nikolay Kashkin in *Moskovskiye vedomosti*, 21 January 1906.

95 The 1912 Bolshoi production of the two operas (seven performances) was conducted by Emil Cooper, the 1956 production by Alexander Melik-Pashayev.

96 The letter is quoted extensively in *B/L*, pp. 117–120.

97 Anna Trubnikova in *Ogonyok*, 1946, No. 4.

98 R. to Slonov, 21 August 1906.

99 R. to Mariya Kerzin, 24 November 1906.

100 Ibid.

6 Dresden, 1906–1909

In Russia the continuing political unrest after the abortive 1905 Revolution was likely to extend, so Rachmaninoff learned from the publisher Jurgenson, even to possible interruptions to the forthcoming season's Moscow orchestral concerts, at which he was due to appear as conductor. Already unhappy about the burden of his commitments, and using this as an excuse for resigning from them all, Rachmaninoff decided to escape from Russia with his wife and three-year-old daughter in search of solitude in Dresden, where he hoped to devote himself to composition free from the distractions of celebrity and await the return of more settled times back home. With the exception of extended summer holidays, which continued to be spent at Ivanovka, from October 1906 until the spring of 1909 the family lived in a six-room villa with garden they rented in Dresden's Sidonienstrasse, and it was here that Rachmaninoff worked on the four compositions that comprise the output of this Dresden period, all of them having one feature in common, their largeness of scale: the Second Symphony, First Piano Sonata, the symphonic poem *The Isle of the Dead*, and his biggest operatic project, the ill-fated *Monna Vanna*. According at least to the *Recollections*,[1] the reason why Rachmaninoff chose the capital of Saxony as his retreat was principally its musical attraction; during a previous visit he had been impressed by the Dresden Opera's performance under Ernst von Schuch of *Die Meistersinger*, and as the city was within railway commuting distance of Leipzig, he could attend Nikisch's Gewandhaus concerts. However, the inexpensive living he also hoped for did not materialize, and Glinka prizes for the cantata *Spring* and for the Second Symphony, received during his stay, must have been doubly welcome.

Symphony No. 2 in E Minor, Op. 27

It is not generally realized that the origins of Rachmaninoff's Second Symphony date back to as early as 1902, when Siloti had embarked on a conducting career, directing the concerts of the Moscow Philharmonic Society. For the 1902–3 and again for the 1903–4 season, the premiere was announced of a new symphony by Rachmaninoff, to be given under the composer's baton. In view of Rachmaninoff's notorious reticence about progress on his compositions, that he allowed public an- nouncements to be made at all could be thought to suggest that the work may have been close to completion at this time,[2] though in June of 1903 Rachmaninoff wrote to Sofiya Satina, asking her to tell Siloti that he was not making progress on the symphony,[3] which fits in with the fact that musically it more looks forward to the Third Concerto of 1909 than back to the works of Rachmaninoff's rebirth as a composer, with which notionally it would be contemporary. At any rate, the symphony was completed in draft only in 1907, when Siloti was again responsible for prematurely circulating news of its completion. The composer wrote to Morozov on 29 January/11 February 1907:

> Not long ago I heard from Slonov that he had read in the press somewhere that I had finished a symphony. As you also may have heard something about it, I want to say a few words to you on the subject. A month or more ago I did indeed finish a symphony, but to this must be added the crucial words 'in rough'. I have not announced it to 'the world' because I wanted to finish it completely beforehand.
>
> While I was planning to put it in a 'tidy' state, it became terribly boring and repulsive to me. So I cast it on one side and took up something else. So 'the world' would not have known about my work for the time being, if Siloti had not come here and got out of me everything I have and am going to have. I told him that I *shall* have a symphony, and so I have already received an invitation to conduct it for him in the coming season and ... news of the symphony has flown everywhere. Speaking personally, I can tell you that I am dissatisfied with it but that it *will* come into existence, though really not before the autumn, because I shall begin to orchestrate it only in the summer.

According to plan, Rachmaninoff began the orchestration and working out of the drafts of his symphony in July 1907 back at Ivanovka, but the work went with difficulty at first. According to his own account,[4] he took three months to complete the first movement, three-and-a-half weeks the second, two weeks for the slow movement and a month for the finale. And so it was not until January 1908, during his second year in Dresden, that the work was completed, just in time for the first performance at a Siloti concert in Petersburg on 26 January. Rachmaninoff himself conducted, as he did at the Moscow premiere a week later. After the debacle of the First Symphony in Petersburg the successful launch of the Second Symphony in the same city must have been especially gratifying to him. He dedicated his most significant work so far to his old teacher Taneyev, though, according to Rachmaninoff,[5] Nikisch was expecting the work to be given to him.

The Second Symphony is laid out on the largest scale; indeed its epic length makes it, with the exception of Glière's *Ilya Muromets*, the longest Russian symphony of all before the Soviet period. Both in terms of emotional moods and the formal structure of its four movements, it parallels, albeit in a more profound, mature and subtle manner, the First Symphony, sharing with it the pervasive and varied use of a motto theme as a unifying agent in the symphonic structure and the fact that the outline of *Dies irae*, the motive force in the earlier symphony but almost entirely absent from the intervening works, is rarely far below the surface in some form or another.[6] It is as though in composing a replacement for the disastrous First Symphony Rachmaninoff was still haunted by the spectre of the earlier work. It is interesting that whereas in the earlier symphony and in the works following the Second Symphony the presence of *Dies irae*, when it occurs, is generally self-evident, in the new symphony, with the exception of the main theme of the scherzo, the references are so subtly disguised that most commentators are evidently unaware of their very existence. There is a homogeneity in the work's musical material, however, that is not all gain, and the second themes of the first, second and fourth movements are perhaps too similar in character. Moreover, the somewhat obsessive polyphony and the rather overloaded orchestration make for thick textures; Rachmaninoff was more discreet in his two other symphonies, *The Bells* of 1913 and the Third Symphony of 1935–6.

The most obvious advance of the Second Symphony over the First is in the emotional power of the lyricism. Melody, exemplified at its finest in the great song of the slow movement, seems to be the moving force in the symphony. The Soviet critic Konstantin Kuznetsov rightly described the work as the 'Russian Lyric Symphony' – 'so direct and sincere are its themes, and so naturally and spontaneously do they develop'.[7] It is this aspect of the work that has attracted concert goers and made the work, at least since the 1960s, into a popular favourite; but it had also been responsible earlier for the disdain of more classically oriented critics for whom overt emotionalism was anathema, and who could, perhaps justifiably, point to places – the same slow movement, for example – where the dynamic of the melody dictates the course of musical events at the expense of tautness of structure. Even so, the glory of the Second Symphony is that it is not only a moving masterpiece of natural and flowing lyricism but, for those who bother to investigate, intellectually satisfying as well in its organic growth. Rimsky-Korsakov's snap judgement[8] at the general rehearsal for the premiere in Petersburg, that there was no inner link between the movements, is demonstrably absurd.

It is intriguing that for the material for the opening of his new symphony Rachmaninoff should have gone back to a student exercise of 1891, the 'Youth' Symphony. The overall correspondence with the opening of that work, with its sombre motto and descending violin figure, is too close to be merely fortuitous:

Ex.84a — 'Youth' Symphony

Ex.84b — Second Symphony

The opening motto, a mere three bars of seven notes moving characteristically step-wise, appears to be the germ cell from which the whole symphony grows, but in fact it must have been drawn out of the material following. Although the shape of the two pairs of pivoting semitones is immediately echoed by the woodwind and horn fanfare and forms the basis of the introductory violin theme, this itself not only bears a resemblance to the earlier symphonic movement but turns out to be a very close relative of the Jewish moneylender's leitmotif in *The Miserly Knight.*:

Ex.85a   **Second Symphony**

Ex.85b   ***The Miserly Knight***

As in the First Symphony, the slow introduction leads to an *Allegro*, whose main theme is derived from the motto. At the end of the first subject clarinets and violas weave a counterpoint in sinuous semitones, hinting clearly at the outline of *Dies irae*.

Ex.86

The bridge passage not only anticipates the second subject in its triplet rhythm but in the three descending woodwind scales around figure 7 gives a foretaste of the bells of the finale. The apparently contrasting second subject itself also derives from the pivoting semitones of the motto. As it works to a typically Rachmaninoff culmination, *Dies irae* reappears:

Ex.87

In the development section the first subject is elaborated at length, interrupted by a dramatic reference on the brass to the opening horn fanfare. The second subject, not used in the development, is extended when it finally returns in the recapitulation, taking on an outline which looks forward to the opening of the slow movement:

Ex.88

Dies irae makes a fleeting reappearance on oboes and clarinets in the coda, which concludes with an impassioned restatement of the theme of the symphony's introduction.

In its most obvious form in the whole symphony, *Dies irae* becomes the opening theme of the marvellously unflagging scherzo, the best movement in the symphony, while the second subject forms a natural counterpoint to it:

Ex.89

The *fugato* in the middle section of the movement, an impressive demonstration of Rachmaninoff's contrapuntal dexterity, is also based on *Dies irae*, with snatches of the symphony's motto interwoven. At one point there are martial fanfares and a distant march is heard on the brass in another variant of the opening theme:

Ex.90

The recapitulation gives the composer an opportunity to superimpose on the main theme the ominous semitones of the motto, given to the brass, making clear the connection between it and *Dies irae*. The use of glockenspiel in this movement brings a welcome splash of colour to the symphony's generally thick orchestration.

The great romantic song of the slow movement is also derived, albeit at one remove, from *Dies irae*, the seamlessness of its lyricism stemming from the fact that the introductory motif turns out also to be a natural continuation of the clarinet melody and also later a counterpoint to it:

Ex.91a   Introduction

Ex.91b   Clarinet theme

In the middle of the movement occurs an interesting episode in which the cor anglais, clarinet and oboe exchange questioning phrases:

Ex.92

The opening phrases of the symphony are brought back for the climax and are strands in the texture for the rest of the movement, which ends with the same harmonies as at the conclusion of *The Heart's Secret*, the first song from Rachmaninoff's recently composed Op. 26 set, suggesting that this movement is indeed about the intimate secrets of the soul.

The fourth movement, like a celebration of some festival, opens with a whirling dance, yet another variant of *Dies irae*, already hinted at in the main theme of the scherzo (Ex. 93). The great second theme, of immense length, also has overtones of *Dies irae* (Ex. 94).

Ex.93

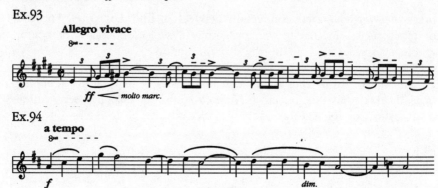

Ex.94

The theme of the slow movement and the motto are recalled before the development section begins with a reference to the slow movement's questioning phrases, when the motto and the rhythms of the opening theme are joined in celebration by a proliferation of descending bell scales. Nowhere else in his work did Rachmaninoff capture so effectively as here his beloved church bells. When, before the coda, the second theme is recapitulated (like that of the first movement it is omitted in the development), as at the end of the Third Concerto two years later Rachmaninoff applies an extra turn of the emotional screw, saved for this point, to cap his big tune. In the brief coda reminiscences of earlier thematic material in the symphony flash past in a heroic summation, and perhaps it was in moments like this that Rimsky-Korsakov saw the bombast he found disagreeable in the work;[9] but then he always had reservations about Rachmaninoff as a composer.

Rachmaninoff's Second, like Schubert's 'Great' C major Symphony, is a very expansive work and one that cannot satisfactorily be pruned without ruining the architecture. The first movement exposition repeat, evidently observed in the earliest performances,[10] is nowadays never followed, but during Rachmaninoff's exile in the West it became customary to make as many as seventeen cuts in the score, varying from 4 to 76 bars in length, making about 300 bars in all. This tradition, which lingered on well into the 1960s, ostensibly reduced the work to a more easily manageable and programmable length. According to Eugene Ormandy, these cuts were 'officially sanctioned' by the composer between 1933 and 1935, when Rachmaninoff's passion for excising anything redundant from his scores had reached its peak. As the symphony was at this time languishing in neglect, it is understandable that the composer reluctantly agreed to such pruning in order to have his work performed. Later, however, Rachmaninoff told Ormandy that he neither approved nor liked the cuts. Ormandy asked the composer whether some of the secondary development in the first movement might be cut.[11]

'Perhaps,' he replied. 'You come to me and I will help you.' So I went to him with the score. In the first movement, after the introduction, there are four bars vamp until the main theme begins. 'Oh, you can cut two bars there,' Rachmaninoff said. And that was all. That was the only cut he would allow. 'You don't know what cuts do to me,' he said; 'it is like cutting a piece out of my heart.'

Despite this, Ormandy continued until late in his career performing the work with cuts, including the two bars discussed. The only other cut for which there seems to have been some evidence for the composer's authority are the three bars before figure 73 in the finale, which Rachmaninoff is said to have allowed only with bad grace.[12] Nowadays, mercifully, with such barbarous traditions having passed into history and a greater respect being shown to texts generally, the symphony is always performed complete.

Piano Sonata No. 1 in D Minor, Op. 28

In December 1906, while still in the throes of composing the Second Symphony, Rachmaninoff wrote to his friend Morozov, who for some years had been teaching musical theory at Moscow Conservatoire, for advice on rondo form, ignorance of which he claimed was holding up his work.[13] He set down in some detail the outline scheme of the opening of a notional sonata movement and asked Morozov how it might be completed. For so eminent a composer at this stage in his career to seek postal tuition appears somewhat bizarre, but Morozov's advice seems to have been acted on, for none of the movements of the piano sonata which subsequently emerged during January and February 1907, after Rachmaninoff had received and digested his reply, corresponds to the torso the composer originally had in mind. At the beginning of May Rachmaninoff played a draft version of his new composition to Riesemann, but he was still working on it until he left Dresden for Paris, to perform at a concert on 26 May in Diaghilev's 'Russian Season'. Returning home to Ivanovka he stopped off in Moscow and at Vladimir Wilshaw's flat gave another reading to a group of colleagues, the composer Georgy Catoire, Leo Conus, the pianist and pedagogue Konstantin Igumnov and, new to Rachmaninoff's circle, Nikolay Medtner. Igumnov was overwhelmed, and subsequently wrote to the composer asking when the work would be printed. Rachmaninoff replied that it was still only in draft and that he wanted to shorten it further. In the autumn he sent Igumnov a copy, asking him for his opinion of the work, particularly its suitability for the piano, but it was not until April 1908 that Rachmaninoff completed his corrections, incorporating some, though not all, of Igumnov's suggestions.[14]

Rachmaninoff was characteristically disparaging about the original version of the sonata. He described it to Morozov[15] as being

> absolutely wild and interminably long – about 45 minutes, I think. I was lured into such length by the programme, or, to be more precise, by one guiding idea: that of three contrasting types from one outstanding literary work. Of course, there will be no programme given, although it does begin to occur to me that if I revealed the programme, the sonata would be clearer.

Yet he did not mention this literary inspiration even to Igumnov, who was to give the first performance of the work,[16] until three weeks after the premiere, by which time he had also played the sonata in Leipzig. However, when he did at last do so, Rachmaninoff was somewhat more specific, naming Goethe's *Faust* as the work and revealing that the first movement represented the eponymous hero, the second Gretchen (Margareta) and the third the flight to the Brocken and Mephistopheles. Thus the sonata follows the same scheme as Liszt's 'Faust' Symphony, a work with which we know Rachmaninoff had long been familiar.[17]

Although commentators customarily assume that the literary idea behind the composition is followed only in the most general terms musically, and though any attempt to match the musical content with Goethe's poem is bound to be a highly subjective and speculative process, there are nevertheless episodes in the sonata which, at least in the outer movements, are supernumerary to an already extended structure and whose presence is difficult to explain except by programmatic reasons.

The Faustian motto with which the sonata opens consists of two elements: the first starkly arches the interval of a fifth in quiet questioning; the second, marked '*forte*', peremptorily dismisses the preceding phrase and emphatically asserts a perfect cadence. The juxtaposition of abruptly contrasting dynamics and of doubt and certainty seems to reflect the struggle of opposing aspirations that goes on in the mind of Faust and Everyman:

Ex.95

Allegro moderato (♩ = 76)

The two brief but grave opening phrases of the second Faustian theme each end in chords held over the bar line before a rest, as if a pause for quiet thought; this is surely the pensive Faust, pondering on which course of action to take:

Ex.96

This second theme is worked up into a state of great agitation, perhaps representing the turmoil and hopelessness in Faust's mind as he seeks in vain the key to life. In Goethe's poem Faust's despair leads him to desire death, but the sound of Easter bells and a choir of angels checks him. It is therefore scarcely by chance that the third and final musical element in the movement, like so much of Rachmaninoff, has the intonation of an ecclesiastical chant:

Ex.97

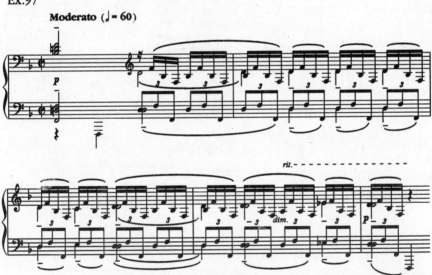

After the opening motto returns, two frenzied climaxes are built up, temporarily interrupted by the calming return of both halves of the motto and the chant. These two tumultuous sections may refer to the two degrees of devilment to which Faust is exposed in Auerbach's Cellar and the Witch's Kitchen. As the music reaches a peak of frenzy (*Allegro molto*), the piano writing seems to burst the limits of which even a modern concert grand is capable. It was surely this kind of passage of which Rachmaninoff was thinking when he told Morozov: 'At one time I wanted to make the sonata into a symphony, but that appeared impossible because of the purely pianistic style in which it is written':[18]

Ex.98

This climax, culminating in a group of furious trills, is resolved into peace by a reference to what turns out to be the Margareta theme from the following movement (Ex. 99). As this reference is gratuitous so far as musical structure is concerned, it surely represents events in the story, namely Faust's seeing in a mirror in the Witch's Kitchen a version of woman's beauty and his subsequent encounter with Margareta. A

Ex.99

serene restatement of the chant in D major and a final reference to the opening motto conclude a tumultuous movement in a mood of peace. Riesemann, who not only heard the sonata when newly written but who was in a unique position to question the composer about it twenty-five years later, suggests, very reasonably, that the composer's meaning here is 'that out of all man's disquietude and dark fear of death the way of deliverance leads to faith and God'.[19]

The second movement of the sonata is straightforward. The work's opening Faustian motif, emphasizing the interval of a fifth, forms the basis of the rocking triplet figure of the accompaniment, and a gentle but rather uninteresting diatonic melody reflects Margareta's simple and pure character. This is developed and elaborated into increasing ferment, perhaps reflecting the agitation in Margareta's heart, until it is resolved at last by an exquisite *veloce* flourish over the keyboard (Ex. 100). Some Scriabinesque trills intervene before the movement ends with hushed chords, in a spirit of calm resignation.

The last movement, a pianistic tour-de-force, depicts the witches' flight to the Brocken, Walpurgis Night and Mephistopheles. The opening material has enormous dynamism and rhythmic drive but a conspicuous lack of melodic interest, and in this respect the sonata established a pattern repeated in the last movements of many of Rachmaninoff's later works – the Third Concerto, Second Sonata, Fourth Concerto, Third Symphony (Ex. 101).

A second theme, with its obsessively repeated rhythm and three note

Ex.100

kernel, clearly representing the diabolism of Mephistopheles, draws once more on *Dies irae* (Ex. 102).

The extension of these ideas, just as vigorous but less forbidding, is followed by a contrasting lyrical melody, seemingly striking a more hopeful note but which derives from the descending Mephistopheles motif (Ex. 103).

An apparently confident and assertive climax is reached, but this mood changes rapidly with the unexpected appearance of Margareta's motto, which seems to mark the point at which Faust, while observing the events of the Witches' Sabbath on the Brocken, has a presentiment of her execution. His own pensive motto from the opening of the sonata intervenes before Margareta's theme is heard twice, at length, its mood now pathetic. Her forlorn song in prison is twice brusquely interrupted by Mephistopheles, as if trying to persuade Faust to get her out of his mind. At the second attempt he evidently succeeds; Margareta's theme sinks beneath his own insistent motto, and the music moves to a climax of diabolerie, with *Dies irae* pounded out by the left hand (Ex. 104).

The witchery that opens the movement is recapitulated, but in the coda the pensive Faust reappears, with one further reminiscence of Margareta before the demonic Mephistopheles takes command of the final overpowering climax. The last word is given to the chant from the first movement, hammered home in mighty chords, apparently in B flat major but returning inexorably at the last to the menacing home key of D minor, as if Rachmaninoff were emphasizing again that

Ex.101 **Allegro molto** (♩ = 100)

Ex.102

Meno mosso (♩ = 88)

Ex.103

Ex.104

redemption from sin can come only through an acceptance of God and religion, which Faust or any man ignores at his peril.

Although an extraordinarily interesting work, Rachmaninoff's First Sonata has made no headway in the concert world, as indeed the composer sardonically suspected would be the case: 'No-one will ever play this work because of its difficulty and length, and perhaps too – and this is the main reason – because of its dubious musical merits'.[20] Even Rachmaninoff himself made little effort in its cause, programming it only between 1909 and 1913, when it was supplanted in his performing repertoire by the Second Sonata, and again during 1916 and 1917; during his twenty-five years in exile as a concert pianist touring the world he played it not once. Although the sonata is a marvellous vehicle for a big technician, its considerable length and the frequency of passages in which maximum sonority is extracted from the instrument make it a difficult work to programme without overwhelming a whole recital. For the listener, on the other hand, what the sonata lacks in characteristically Rachmaninoff melodic appeal it undoubtedly makes up in excitement. What is needed for it to gain recognition is a daring virtuoso with not only the skill to conquer its technical challenges but the will to proselytize actively on its behalf, as Horowitz did with the Second Sonata.

Monna Vanna

In the years at the turn of the century several composers turned their attention to the works of the Belgian poet and playwright Maurice Maeterlinck (1862–1949). Fauré's incidental music to *Pelléas and Mélisande*, which appeared in 1898, seven years before Sibelius's similar work, met with Maeterlinck's delight and approval, but Debussy's opera on the same subject, staged in 1902, stirred the author to vehement fury; he disowned the production altogether and generally as a result became more wary in his choice of operatic collaborators. However, although he worked successfully enough with Paul Dukas, whose fine setting of *Ariadne and Bluebeard* was put on in 1907, unfortunately, as it proved, he assigned the Western European rights to *Monna Vanna*, which he had written in 1902, to Henri Février, an undistinguished pupil of Fauré and Massenet, whose version was eventually staged in Paris in 1909 and then sank without trace. Rachmaninoff was unaware of the copyright arrangement when he arrived in Dresden three years before this with the same Maeterlinck play in mind as a possible subject for an opera of his own.

Monna Vanna, a three-act historical drama of fifteenth-century Italy, had been staged in Russia from 1902 to 1904, the title role being played by the illustrious Vera Komissarzhevskaya, whom Rachmaninoff had got to know at this time, when she was staying with his cousins the Pribïtkovs in Petersburg.[21] We do not know whether Rachmaninoff saw the production but it is not unlikely that he did. At any rate he was familiar with the published Russian translation of the work by the time he arrived in Dresden, and in the very first sentences of his first extant letter from there, written even before he had moved into permanent lodgings, he asked Slonov to prepare in secrecy a blank verse version of half a dozen pages of the end of the first act for him to see how it went. 'It is possible that something may come of this; ... meanwhile, this is just a trial'.[22] Bearing in mind that one of the sticking points in the *Salammbô* libretto had been Slonov's rhymes, Rachmaninoff was at pains to emphasize again that they were unnecessary to him. Less than three weeks later, having received the test passage and been 'fully satisfied' with it, Rachmaninoff encouraged Slonov to continue,[23] but understandably Slonov wanted to know whether the work he had been somehow manoeuvred into undertaking was likely to result in anything concrete. Rachmaninoff prevaricated, while urging him to speed the completion of Act 1,[24] which in fact he had already finished a few days before, on 18 December 1906, incorporating the composer's suggestions. In the new year, sometime after completing the draft of the piano sonata in February, Rachmaninoff began work on the vocal score of the opera. Predictably, there is not a word about his work in the correspondence, but by 15 April 1907 he had completed Act 1.

The libretto of Act 2 proved a stumbling block. Already back in January Rachmaninoff had grave misgivings about its overall shape and particularly the climax for the two principal characters, Monna Vanna and Prinzivalle:[25]

The verses are good, but the scene itself scared me somewhat, so that I felt still more out of sorts. The declamation is in effect unbroken, but the main thing is, wherever is the culminating point in it? I don't find or sense one, and without one it's the end! It is essential to reach some extreme point; then all the foregoing is excused. Monna Vanna undoubtedly dampens Prinzivalle's ardour by her comments, that is to say, she apparently does not let him finish telling her his feelings. Of course her part can be shortened, but in his part too I can see no words on which it would be possible to construct an apotheosis for this scene.

Rachmaninoff suggested that they might reach a 'favourable result' by mutually agreed cuts and by giving Prinzivalle a chance to speak at greater length. Finally, he suggested that, if he thought it would help, Slonov might seek advice from Morozov, though in the event he did not, and Slonov's corrections to Prinzivalle's part over the next fortnight did nothing to assuage Rachmaninoff's misgivings.[26]

After several months, during which no more is heard about the libretto, Rachmaninoff reported to Morozov on 16 June that he had just received the second act and was shocked by its length – about 1,000 lines in comparison with 450 for the whole of *The Miserly Knight.* Though trying to cut this down, he was finding it extremely difficult. In what unexpectedly turned out to be his final letter to Slonov about the project six weeks later, Rachmaninoff remarked: 'I like the libretto, but it must be shortened – it is very long. Now I cannot attend to it before the autumn in Dresden'.[27] But the autumn found Rachmaninoff preoccupied with final corrections to the new symphony and sonata and with an increasing number of concert engagements well into the new year, which he had taken on to restore his finances. In the summer of 1908 Stanislavsky invited Maeterlinck to Moscow for the premiere of his *Blue Bird* at the Art Theatre, and on the basis of this acquaintanceship Rachmaninoff asked Stanislavsky, whom he had known since his meetings with Chekhov in Yalta, to use his influence with the playwright to secure the Russian and German rights to *Monna Vanna.* On the very day (22 December 1908) that he wrote to remind Stanislavsky of this, Maeterlinck answered: 'Unfortunately, as is the case in France, I had to conclude an agreement with the music publisher Heugel, unconditionally forbidding me to permit any composer except Février to write an opera on the subject of my play, and that is for all countries where copyright is recognised'. Although there is no documentary evidence to prove it, and although Riesemann, who was an intimate of Rachmaninoff during the Dresden period and who seems to have asked the composer about it during his Clairefontaine interviews in 1930, does not mention the copyright question in the *Recollections,*[28] it was almost certainly this unforeseen and insurmountable problem which caused the composer abruptly to abandon the whole project.

Though work on *Monna Vanna* halted and was never to be resumed, Rachmaninoff always kept his manuscript and Slonov's libretto by him, and at Ivanovka in the summer of 1913, untypically raising the veil of secrecy, he showed the work along with his newly completed *Bells* to the composer Alexander Goedicke.[29] The materials for *Monna Vanna* were among the few items he brought with him out of Russia in 1917, and in the 1930s he took them with him to Senar, his villa on Lake Lucerne, where they remained throughout the war. After the war they were brought back to the United States by Mrs. Rachmaninoff and in 1951 finally deposited in the Library of Congress as part of the Rachmaninoff Archive.

The 100-page vocal score of Act 1, incorporating Slonov's libretto, appears to be a final, pre-orchestration draft, with indications at several points over the piano part of string figuration to be transferred to the full score. The 1,010 bars of music, representing about 40 minutes in performance, consist of:

(a) Orchestral introduction (63 bars). The curtain goes up on ...

(b) Scene 1 (187 bars). The hall of the palace of Guido Colonna in Pisa. Under siege by the Florentines for more than three months, the town now has neither food nor ammunition. Guido, commander of the garrison, discusses with his lieutenants, Borso and Torello, the desperate situation.[30]

(c) Scene 2 (348 bars). Guido's father, Marco, returns from a mission to the mercenary general of the Florentines, Prinzivalle. Marco tells Guido that Prinzivalle is a humane and honorable man, being only the reluctant servant of the Florentines, who he knows are secretly accusing him of treachery because he has delayed sacking the city. Prinzivalle is willing to change sides and supply the Pisans with food and ammunition, but his price is that Guido's wife, Monna Vanna, should go to his camp and spend the night with him. Guido is appalled, but the town elders have already discussed the matter and decided to place the fate of Pisa in Vanna's hands; Marco believes she will make the sacrifice. The crowd outside is heard calling Vanna's name.

(d) Scene 3 (412 bars). Vanna enters. Guido expects her to have rejected the proposal but she has decided to go. Turning on her in helpless disbelief he first pleads with her, then renounces her, and finally threatens to kill her. Vanna begs him to understand but to no avail; with no more to be said, she leaves him to go on her mission.

In addition to Rachmaninoff's manuscript of the complete Act 1 and

Slonov's libretto of all three acts, the materials for *Monna Vanna* in the Library of Congress include quite extensive musical sketches for Act 2, comprising: section 1, eight pages, 144 bars; section 2, six pages numbered 1–7 (no. 2 is missing), 103 bars; section 3, one page, just 6 bars. Slonov's libretto for Act 2 (set in Prinzivalle's tent), with Rachmaninoff's corrections, is in two scenes:

1(a) 10 unnumbered sides – Slonov's first version of the opening of the act, omitting the very beginning of the original and changing it somewhat. Prinzivalle is alone and begins: 'It is 10 o'clock and Marco has not returned'. He infers that Vanna has decided to come.

(b) 15 sides – the second version of the scene, referred to in Rachmaninoff's last letter to Slonov dated 27 July 1907. This begins, as does Maeterlinck, with Vedio, Prinzivalle's secretary, announcing that a letter has come from one of the Florentine Commissioners about Prinzivalle's apparent dereliction of duty in not pressing the seige. He has one last day in which to do so or face arrest. The commissioner Trivulzio himself arrives. Prinzivalle tells him he has seen through the duplicity of the Florentines and has decided to save Pisa. Trivulzio tries to kill him but only succeeds in wounding him. Prinzivalle recognizes that they both have their loyalties and, magnanimously not taking revenge, keeps Trivulzio safe under guard.

2 43 sides of the second half of the act, beginning with Monna Vanna entering and saying to Prinzivalle: 'I have come, as you wished'. Prinzivalle sends food and ammunition off to Pisa, and then tells her that he has loved her ever since they were childhood friends. At that time his father took him away to Africa, and when he returned as a homeless adventurer he learned that Vanna was already betrothed to a Tuscan noble. He frankly admits that he has not risked his life to see her since he has already been condemned by the Florentines; Vanna appreciates his honesty. Vedio announces that the second Commissioner of Florence has come with six hundred troops, taking over the camp and declaring Prinzivalle a traitor; Prinzivalle must escape. Vanna invites him to return with her to Pisa, but he doubts whether her husband will believe that he has not touched her; he decides to go nonetheless. In the distance the bells of Pisa can be heard celebrating the arrival of the supplies from Prinzivalle. Prinzivalle and Vanna leave.

Act 3 is set in the hall of Guido's palace. When Vanna and Prinzivalle arrive, Guido, racked by shame at the price paid for raising the seige, refuses to believe his wife innocent and has Prinzivalle arrested. Vanna is shocked by the contrast between her husband's petty jealousy and Prinzivalle's magnanimity. Pretending she has lied and Guido has been right all along, she demands that he give her the key to the dungeon to dispose of Prinzivalle as she sees fit. But she whispers to Prinzivalle that when she opens the prison door, it will be to escape with him to a new life. In Rachmaninoff's extant correspondence there is no reference to Slonov's libretto of this final act, which is dated 18 March 1907, three months before the composer received Act 2 in June of 1907. As, unlike Acts 1 and 2, the text is totally uncorrected, it seems most likely that Rachmaninoff collected it when he was passing through Moscow in the summer but never worked on it.

The recent history of *Monna Vanna* is an extraordinary tale of mixed fortune: of successful rebirth and frustrated hopes. Near the end of her life Sofiya Satina suggested to the American conductor Igor Buketoff, who had known Rachmaninoff and her personally from the 1930s, that he should try to rescue the unfinished work from the oblivion to which it seemed to have been irredeemably consigned. Judging that the composer's sketches for the second act were too fragmentary to regenerate, Buketoff limited himself to the task of making an idiomatic orchestration of the vocal score of the completed Act 1, finding that the nature of the piano writing happily made it unnecessary to pad out the scoring with extraneous material. The rights to the opera, incorporating a translation of Slonov's libretto, were acquired by Belwin Mills, who then, however, like Rachmaninoff nearly half a century before, found themselves unable to negotiate a release from the original copyright ban from the lawyers of the Maeterlinck estate. Although copyright regulations in the United States were different from elsewhere in the world at the time of the original publication of Maeterlinck's work, the author's ownership continues to be protected in Great Britain and Western Europe generally until the year 2000, and in Germany and Austria until 2020, so currently hindering the work's publication and performance.

Unlike most rediscovered scores, *Monna Vanna* was not abandoned by its composer because of a failure to live up to expectations; indeed, Rachmaninoff went so far as to remark that it was the only one of his Dresden works to 'fully satisfy' him.[31] Its musical idiom is essentially a natural development of that he used in the favourite of his operas, *The Miserly Knight*, with its predominantly declamatory writing. In *Monna Vanna* the recitative is almost unbroken, but although this inhibits, as it had before, the use of long-breathed lyricism, there are nevertheless many characteristic Rachmaninoff melodic turns and sequences, unmistakably out of the same imagination as that which had just conceived the Second Symphony. As in the earlier operas, Rachmaninoff uses short leitmotifs to characterize personalities, psychological states and situations. Thus, a figure representing the desperate plight and imminent doom of the Pisans is heard at once in the bass register in the opera's dramatic introduction, an idea that may have its origin in Rachmaninoff's student operatic exercise *Esmeralda* (cf. Ex. 4a):

Ex.105

A simple falling fifth seems to be associated with Pisa itself, and this brusque gesture with the severe and implacable Guido:

Ex.106

Guido has overwhelmingly the most important and vocally taxing role in Act 1, not leaving the stage from start to finish. The small scope of Vanna's role here and the lack of even a single aria throughout the whole act prompts the speculation that Rachmaninoff may have intended to reserve his more expansive lyrical outpouring for later in the opera, for such moments, perhaps, as the meeting of Prinzivalle and Vanna in Act 2. However, everything would have depended on the suitability of the text: in the third scene, in imploring his wife not to sacrifice herself Guido apparently begins three different arias in succession, each tantalizingly cut short by the text's giving out.

In view of the turbulent sweep of much of the music, not to mention the sumptuous textures of the recent symphony, the marked austerity of some of the writing in *Monna Vanna* comes as a complete surprise. It is particularly striking in the music for Marco in the second scene, where he reports on his reception by the Florentines. Guido's father is a man of compassion and humanity, who, unlike his son, understands the human predicament. The starkly diatonic setting of the music associated with him, its ascetic harmonies and step-wise melodic line, are a clear foretaste of the style of the religious music that Rachmaninoff was to write in only a few years' time:

Ex.107

Khva-la Tvor - tsu! Nye var-va-rï o-ni. Po-chyot-nïm gos-tyem ya pri-nyat bïl u

nikh. Sam Prin-tsi-val - le chi-tal mo - i tvo-reni - ya; go-vo-

ril so mnoy o tryox Pla - to-na di-a-lo - gakh chto mno-yu nay-dye - nï...

[Praise be to God! They are not barbarians. I was received by them as an honoured guest. Prinzivalle himself had read my works; he spoke to me about the three dialogues of Plato that I had found...]

Monna Vanna certainly contains some of Rachmaninoff's best operatic moments. The finest of all is probably the transition to the third scene, where Guido's expression of bitterness at the apparent emptiness of his wife's love is interrupted by the crowd outside the palace repeatedly calling Vanna's name. The accompaniment, with an eerie rhythmic and harmonic independence from the chorus, wells up underneath with increasing anguish into a tremendous climax that not only echoes the maelstrom of Guido's feelings but, with its disconcerting overtones of foreboding, is also somehow a presentiment of the tragic turmoil that is to come. Guido's doubts are instantly swept away as he sets eyes on Vanna, and he reasssserts his faith in her love in one of Rachmaninoff's most glorious lyrical sequences, a passage certain to sweep any devotee of the composer off his feet. Scarcely less affecting are the final pages of the act, which are another example of Rachmaninoff's skill in following the psychological nuances of the text in a manner which is both musically satisfying and, it may well be imagined, effective on the operatic stage. With Guido now convinced that Vanna is betraying him by intending to go to Prinzivalle but not return, his disillusioned state is conveyed not by melodramatic bluster but by restrained cries of impotent bitterness. After a brief climax the music poignantly sinks down in the postlude into bleak and uncomprehending despair, the typically falling phrases bringing the act to a quiet but memorable close.

Whether *Monna Vanna* would have been Rachmaninoff's operatic masterpiece, if he had completed it, will always be an open question. The lack of a 'big scene' felt in Act 1, with its uninterrupted dialogue and discussion, would have been felt again in Act 2 if Slonov's libretto had remained unchanged, and the composer was clearly right to be anxious about the unsatisfied need for an 'apotheosis' in his text. As it stands, however, the completed act, coming from the period of Rachmaninoff's finest flowering, is entirely characteristic of its composer and should on every ground be included in the recognized catalogue of his work. The favourable public and critical reception of the first (concert) performance of *Monna Vanna* in 1984[32] raises hopes that, when legal difficulties have been overcome, rather than remaining an obscure curiosity this important work may at least achieve occasional performance as a concert cantata; only time will tell.

Although Rachmaninoff talked of other possible operatic subjects, *Monna Vanna* turned out to be his last attempt in the genre. According to the *Recollections*, Chekhov had frequently suggested working with Rachmaninoff on an opera,[33] in particular offering his own story *The Black Monk* and his adaptation of Lermontov's novel *A Hero of Our Time*, but the composer found Chekhov's manner of writing unsuitable for musical setting. He seems later to have toyed with Turgenev subjects – *The Lull, Spring Waters* and *A Song of Triumphant Love* – and there were rumours in the press of other projects under way: in 1907 *The Minstrel*, with a libretto by Chaliapin after Maykov, and in 1913 *The Secret Island*, a one-act opera to his own text.[34] In 1914 Rachmaninoff received a request from the committee organizing the 350th anniversary celebrations of the birth of Shakespeare for him to set a scene from *King Lear*, but nothing came of this.[35] Finally, and most improbably, as late as 1934, while composing the *Paganini Rhapsody*, Rachmaninoff was sent a three-act libretto based on Shakespeare's *Tempest*, by the writer Alexander Amfiteatrov (1862–1938). The libretto, dated 5 May 1934 –10 June 1934, was found posthumously among Rachmaninoff's papers and now resides in the Library of Congress. As the only two letters of Rachmaninoff to Amfiteatrov known to be extant are in private hands and unpublished, it has not been possible to verify whether or not the libretto was made at the composer's request, though one of the letters, dated only a month after the libretto was completed, must surely refer to it.[36]

1908 was an unproductive year for Rachmaninoff. Early on much time was taken up in concertizing, and later he had to put the new piano sonata in a final state for printing and proof-read the symphony, work on the four-hand piano version of which, for the first time with one of his own compositions, he contracted out (to his conservatoire friend Vladimir Wilshaw). The only musical memento of the year is the *Letter to Stanislavsky*, a solemn greeting in the form of a song, 'delivered' by Chaliapin on the occasion of the celebration of the tenth anniversary of the Moscow Art Theatre in October 1908, which Rachmaninoff could not attend personally because he had already returned to Dresden. The musical indications for the singer – 'with much feeling', 'majestically', etc. – are in Russian, perhaps emphasizing the informality of a setting outside the composer's 'serious' work. At the end of the first stanza at the words 'Blue Bird' Rachmaninoff makes reference in the vocal part to an ecclesiastical chant, 'Many years', incongruously combining it in the accompaniment with the ruffled dotted semi-quaver rhythm, also in the postlude to the song, of the Polka from Ilya Satz's incidental music to Stanislavsky's great success of that year, Maeterlinck's *Blue Bird*.[37] The incorporation at the end of the 'letter' of the date and a postscript from the composer's wife into an already prosaic text are agreeably light touches in a gracious gesture for a happy occasion.

The Isle of the Dead, Op. 29

For two years Rachmaninoff had been looking for a suitable subject for a symphonic poem. In November 1906 he had asked Morozov for help but had been unenthusiastic about his initial suggestions of 'In the Wild North', 'The Pine Tree and the Palm', a Heine subject already used in the Six Choruses, Op. 15, and 'North and South'. He asked him to try again, repeating his request more urgently two months later,[38] but Morozov seems to have had no other ideas. The problem at last solved itself when Rachmaninoff happened to see, perhaps in Paris in May 1907, a black and white reproduction of one of the five paintings of the then fashionable Swiss artist Arnold Böcklin (1827–1901) on the subject 'The Isle of the Dead'; it made a strong impression on him. In the winter of 1907-08 he made the acquaintance of a well-to-do Russo-German dilettante, Nikolay Struve,[39] and it may have been in the company of Struve that he later saw one of the original paintings, in Leipzig or Berlin.[40] At any rate, it was at Struve's suggestion that he used the Böcklin subject as the basis for his symphonic poem, writing it between January and March of 1909. The manuscript is dated 17 April of that year, one day before the first performance in Moscow, under the composer's direction, which suggests that he made corrections in the light of the orchestral rehearsals (the work was a last-minute substitution for the advertised *Spring* cantata). Further changes were made before the work was ready for printing in June 1909. 'I have made a great many corrections,' Rachmaninoff wrote to Morozov.[41]

> I have rewritten from scratch almost half. The alterations are mainly concerned with the orchestration, but I have changed the substance itself; and in one place, for the sake of the modulatory scheme, I have made a transposition. I'm afraid to vouch for it, but it does seem to me that now this composition is improved and will sound better. At least I now have the feeling that I would find no awkwardness anywhere if I performed it again.

The stark contrasts of the monochrome reproduction affected Rachmaninoff more than the colours of the painting itself. Many years later he recalled: 'The massive architecture and the mystic message of the painting made a marked impression on me, and the tone poem was the outcome... If I had seen the original first, I might not have composed [the work].'[42] However, from the nature of the Rachmaninoff work it is clear that Böcklin's painting served merely as an initial stimulus and point of departure, for the composer does not merely represent in music the physical details of the painting but also expresses the thoughts prompted by it, about death, and about life.

The musical raw material for *The Isle of the Dead* is typically economical. *Dies irae* must surely have chosen itself in Rachmaninoff's mind as the work's mainspring. Its first three notes are hinted at over the rocking 5/8 figure which forms the basis of the opening and which seems to represent the pull and return of the oars as Charon ferries the dead across the water; the fourth note is first added in the oboe part at figure 2. The whole of the opening grows inexorably to a climax of grim but noble power. En route a descending phrase is heard on the first violins, plainly depicting human lamentation and dejection of spirit:

Ex.108

A change of mood is reflected in a change of metre and a transition from A minor to E flat major, as Böcklin's picture is left behind and Rachmaninoff's imagination takes flight. In a letter of appreciation to Leopold Stokowski after a performance of *The Isle of the Dead* in 1925[43] Rachmaninoff wrote that he disagreed with his interpretation only in this part of the work: 'It should be a great contrast to all the rest of the work – faster, more nervous and more emotional – as that passage does not belong to the "picture"; it is in reality a "supplement" to the picture – which fact, of course, makes the contrast all the more necessary.' And then, added in pencil, are the words: 'In the former is death – in the latter life'. The opening of the 'life' section in *The Isle of the Dead* bears an intriguing resemblance in its overall feel to a passage in the middle of the second movement of Elgar's First Symphony, a work played first in Britain in December 1908 and then throughout Europe the following year. Was the concert at which Nikisch performed the work at the Leipzig Gewandhaus on 11 February 1909 one of those Rachmaninoff attended at the end of his Dresden stay, just when he was composing his symphonic poem? In both passages the melodic line hovers over a tonic pedal (Ex. 109).

Rachmaninoff's depiction of 'life' develops into an ecstatic outpouring about earthly joy and love, but as menacing shadows pass over the music, we are reminded that human happiness can never be more than transitory because of man's mortality. The music becomes more anguished and despairing until the orchestra sinks down rebuffed (at figure 19). It fights back, however, until the work's main climax is reached, ending in a group of decisive chords, like mortal blows. In the still aftermath *Dies irae* is stated more positively than at any point before, and the 'life' theme is heard once more, this time plaintively in the minor key. The ⅝ metre reasserts itself and, with a reference to the descending scales depicting human lamentation earlier in the work, Charon rows quietly away.

The Isle of the Dead is arguably Rachmaninoff's orchestral masterpiece and it was, incidentally, the only work of the composer's ever to be

Ex.109a

Rachmaninoff:
The Isle of the Dead

Ex.109b

Elgar, First Symphony,
second movement, figure 66

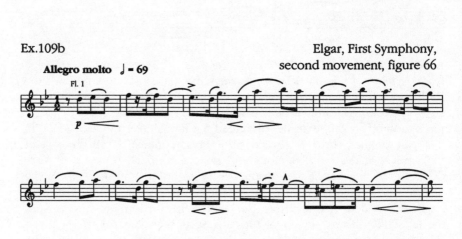

conducted by Toscanini,[44] who never concealed his low opinion of Russian music in general and of Rachmaninoff's in particular. The work is perfectly balanced as it stands, but when the opportunity came to record it in April 1929, Rachmaninoff subjected it to the by then almost inevitable pruning process, making cuts of 62 bars in all.[45] They were certainly not forced upon him by the technical exigencies of squeezing the music on to the five sides of the 78 r.p.m. records, as some have suggested,[46] especially since the last three sides are conspicuously short. On 28 January 1930 Rachmaninoff wrote to Gavriil Paichadze, who managed his musical affairs in Europe and was director of *Grandes Editions Russes*, about revisions to the score he wanted including in a proposed new edition of the work. 'I am sending you today in a separate parcel the score of *The Isle of the Dead*, with the cuts and corrections I have made in it. Please incorporate these corrections in the new edition of the score, and keep by you the copy I have sent you for comparison. Also, immediately, please incorporate these corrections in a clean copy of the score and send it to me, for I have to replace the copy of it I borrowed from the Philadelphia Orchestra Library.' The copy Rachmaninoff borrowed is no doubt the one he used for the recording (with the Philadelphia Orchestra), and the cuts he instituted then were naturally followed by that orchestra for fifty years, at least until Ormandy retired. Paradoxically, in the post-script to the letter, in which he lists the cuts incorporated in the score, Rachmaninoff mentions only the first four of the eleven made in the recording. But in 1932, when he was due to conduct the work in Detroit, Gabrilowitsch wrote to Rachmaninoff about the cuts, asking him whether they were to be observed in performance or not. The composer wired back, succinctly: 'Please use record cuts. Sincere thanks. Greetings'.[47]

References

1 *Riesemann*, p. 135.
2 Apetyan, *LN/A* 1, p. 574.
3 R. to Sofiya Satina, 23 June 1903.
4 R. to Morozov, 18 December 1907.
5 R. to Morozov, 11 December 1908.
6 The use of *Dies irae* in Rachmaninoff's Second Symphony has been analysed by David Rubin in an article in *The Music Review*, Vol. 23, May 1962, pp. 132–136.
7 'Rachmaninoff's Creative Life', article by Konstantin Kuznetsov in *Sovyetskaya Muzyka*, 1945, No. 4, p. 41.
8 Alexander Ossovsky, *VR/A* 1, pp. 357–358.
9 Ibid.
10 The critic Yuly Engel noted that the symphony's Moscow premiere took 68 minutes; a typical modern performance without the exposition repeat lasts rather less than an hour.
11 Interview by John Amis with Eugene Ormandy, BBC, 1970. See *Gramophone*, July 1970, p. 160.
12 David Wooldridge, *Conductor's World*, The Cresset Press, London, 1970, p. 272.
13 R. to Morozov, 10 December 1906 (quoted in *B/L*, pp. 132–3).
14 R. to Igumnov, 12 April 1908, and Igumnov in *Sovyetskaya Muzyka*, 1946, No. 1, p. 85.
15 R. to Morozov, 8 May 1907.
16 Igumnov premiered the First Sonata in an all-Rachmaninoff programme in Moscow on 17 October 1908.
17 Rachmaninoff introduced the Skalon sisters to Liszt's 'Faust' Symphony in 1895. Lyudmila Rostovtsova (Skalon), *VR/A* 1, p. 240.
18 R. to Morozov, 8 May 1907.
19 *Riesemann*, p. 231.
20 R. to Morozov, 8 May 1907.
21 Zoya Pribïtkova, *VR/A* 2, pp. 71–76.
22 R. to Slonov, 21 October 1906.
23 R. to Slonov, 8 November 1906.
24 R. to Slonov, 22 December 1906.
25 R. to Slonov, 11 January 1907.
26 R. to Slonov, 29 January 1907.

27 R. to Slonov, 27 July 1907.

28 *Riesemann*, pp. 140–141.

29 Alexander Goedicke, *VR/A* 1, p. 425.

30 A copy of the first page of this scene (Guido: 'The end of the Pisan Republic has come') appears in *B/L*, p. 208.

31 R. to Morozov, 31 March 1907.

32 The first performance of *Monna Vanna* was given in Saratoga, New York, on 11 August 1984, by Rachmaninoff's favourite orchestra, the Philadelphia, under Igor Buketoff, with Tatiana Troyanos as Monna Vanna, Sherrill Milnes as Guido, and John Alexander as Marco.

33 *Riesemann*, p. 151.

34 *Russkiye vedomosti*, 8 February 1907, No. 30, p. 4;
Obozreniye teatrov, St Petersburg, 1907, No. 53, p. 12;
Ranneye utro, 2 August 1913, No. 178, p. 4;
Teatr, 1913, No. 1314, p. 6.

35 R. to Marietta Shaginyan, 30 April 1914.

36 The two unpublished letters to Amfiteatrov are dated 13 September 1927 and 9 July 1934.

37 Constantin Stanislavsky, *My Life in Art*, Geoffrey Bles, London, 1924, p. 504.

38 R. to Morozov, 22 November 1906 and 29 January 1907.

39 For Nikolay Struve see *Riesemann*, pp. 137–138.

40 The notion that R. saw the monochrome version of 'The Isle of the Dead' in Paris in May 1907 seems to appear first in *B/L*, p. 156. According to the *Recollections*, p. 139, R. first saw the painting in the Leipzig gallery; according to an interview a few years before ('Rachmaninoff Remembers', in *The Musical Observer*, May 1927, p. 16) he saw the reproduction in Dresden and the original in Berlin.

41 R. to Morozov, 6 June 1909.

42 R. interview by Basanta Koomar Roy in *Musical Observer*, Vol. 26, May 1927, p. 16.

43 R. to Stokowski, 25 April 1925.

44 Toscanini conducted *The Isle of the Dead* at the Augusteum, Rome, in January and February 1916.

45 For details see *T/N*, p. 94.

46 Ibid.

47 Gabrilowitsch to R., 2 November 1932; R. to Gabrilowitsch, 4 November 1932.

7 Ivanovka, 1909–1917

Rachmaninoff was to live eight more years in Russia. During this time Ivanovka more than ever became the centre of his private life and the prime source of spiritual renewal, especially from 1910 onwards, when he came to share the day-to-day management of the estate. On the musical front, he appeared increasingly frequently both as a pianist and as conductor, though, except for conducting six performances of Tchaikovsky's *Queen of Spades* in St Petersburg in 1912, he abandoned the opera house. His activity as a performer soon began to define the annual pattern of his life, in which autumn, winter and spring were occupied by concertizing, and only the long summer holiday was free for composition. The output of this final Russian period may be divided into two groups. On the one hand, there are three works on the largest scale: the Third Concerto, Second Piano Sonata, and the choral symphony *The Bells*; on the other, there are the works in which pregnant musical ideas are concentrated into short forms: two sets of songs, three sets of piano pieces, and two groups of anthems that make up his great religious works, the *Liturgy of St John Chrysostom* and the *All-Night Vigil*, a brief but glorious flowering in an unexpected sphere.

On returning to Russia during April 1909, Rachmaninoff immediately fulfilled three conducting engagements within a fortnight, giving the first performance of *The Isle of the Dead* and twice standing in at Moscow Philharmonic Society concerts for the indisposed Nikisch. His still growing fame brought him the offer of the Vice-Presidency of the Imperial Russian Musical Society, an office he was willing to accept only on condition that it should be more than a nominal responsibility. At the beginning of May he retired to Ivanovka for the summer to recuperate.

Concerto No. 3 in D minor, Op. 30

At Ivanovka Rachmaninoff pondered his plans for the future. He reluctantly decided not to return in the autumn to the peace and quiet of Dresden, which his wife had found stultifying, but instead to take up the offer of a lucrative American concert tour, for which he intended to write a new concerto. At the beginning of June he reported to Morozov that he had begun to work, without saying on what.[1] Four months later, on 2 October, the day on which he left Moscow to begin his journey to the United States, he remarked in a letter to Pressman that he was working 'like a man doing hard labour' to finish his concerto – though the date at the end of the manuscript, 23 September 1909, is a week before this. The day before setting out he called on Taneyev, no doubt showing him his new composition, which he practised on a dummy keyboard on the boat coming over. He played the work for the first time in New York, with the New York Symphony Orchestra under Walter Damrosch, on 28 November 1909, repeating it two days later. A third and final New York performance took place on 16 January 1910 under Gustav Mahler, no less, whose management of the 'rather difficult' orchestral part caused Rachmaninoff immediately to set him next to Nikisch as the greatest conductor of his day. In contrast, when he came in April 1910 to prepare the work for its Moscow premiere, Rachmaninoff had no confidence in the scheduled conductor, his old friend Brandukov, who had turned from his cello to conducting the Moscow Philharmonic Society concerts. Having been dissatisfied with Brandukov two years before when he played the Second Concerto under his baton, he categorically insisted on having a different conductor on this occasion. Although there was little time left, another cellist-turned-conductor, Yevgeny Plotnikov, stepped in and learned the work in three days.[2] Of this first Russian performance the critic Grigory Prokofiev wrote:[3]

> The new concerto mirrored the best sides of [Rachmaninoff's] creative power - sincerity, simplicity and clarity of musical thought … It has a freshness of inspiration that does not aspire to the discovery of new paths; it has a sharp and concise form as well as simple and brilliant orchestration, qualities that will secure both outer success and enduring love by musicians and public alike.

The Third Concerto, one of Rachmaninoff's most completely integrated large-scale works, has a much more subtle structure than the Second. The themes of the first movement reappear in the second and third, and the dotted rhythmic motto which sets the work in motion is a unifying factor throughout. In the layout of its opening the Third Concerto is a direct antithesis to its predecessor: the latter has a chordal introduction for piano solo before the orchestra enters with the theme, decorated by the piano; whereas the new work opens with two bars for orchestra alone, after which the piano introduces the theme, in a simple octave throughout, accompanied by the orchestra. The theme itself, reminiscent of the minor key version of the religious motif of the first movement of the First Piano Sonata (in the same key) and of Marco's leitmotif in *Monna Vanna* (the phrases in the accompaniment in Ex. 107), typically moves step-wise over a limited span, pivoting around the tonic key-note of D. When the American musicologist Josef Yasser questioned the composer in 1935 about its possible ecclesiastical origin, Rachmaninoff replied that the theme was 'borrowed neither from folk song forms nor from church sources. It simply wrote itself! . . . If I had any plan in composing this theme, I was thinking only of sound. I wanted "to sing" the melody on the piano as a singer would sing it, and to find a suitable orchestral accompaniment or one that would not muffle this "singing". That is all!'[4] But the similarity of the chant from the Kiev area, ' Thy tomb, O Saviour, soldiers guarding', suggests that the theme may well be an unconscious reminiscence all the same:

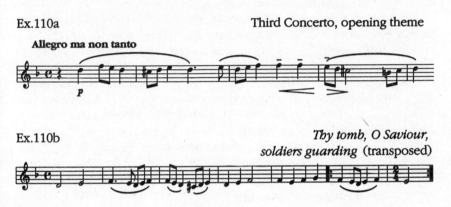

Ex.110a　　　　　　　　　　　　　Third Concerto, opening theme

Allegro ma non tanto

Ex.110b　　　　　　　　　　　　　　　　*Thy tomb, O Saviour,*
soldiers guarding (transposed)

The transition to the second theme is managed with great subtlety. After the opening theme has been developed, there are brief foretastes of the melody to come, first on horn and clarinets, then on trumpet and oboes, and again in the brief piano cadenza. The strings of the orchestra at last state without equivocation the kernel of the new theme, a staccato figure which proves to be a variant of the concerto's opening dotted rhythmic motto. Thus, although the movement's two themes are contrasted, the one grows organically from the other. After the second theme has taken lyrical flight the movement's rhythmic motto dominates, and the development section, one long *crescendo* and *accelerando*, concerns itself with the first theme. In the aftermath of the climax snatches on the piano and woodwinds show its kinship with the opening of the Second Symphony (Ex. 111)

Rachmaninoff wrote two cadenzas for the first movement, which coalesce in their latter half. The evidence of the original manuscript, now in the British Library,[5] is that what appears now as the *ossia* cadenza was written first, and that the shorter cadenza was a second

Ex.111

Allegro molto

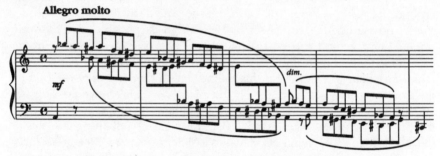

thought. Both are of unprecedented magnificence, though opinions differ about their musical merits. Rachmaninoff himself invariably played the shorter version and other pianists naturally followed his example. Gieseking (1939) seems to have been among the first to try the alternative, but it was not until the time of Van Cliburn and the Tchaikovsky Competition of 1958, when the young Texan re-established the uncut text of the concerto, that a fashion was started for the longer cadenza, with its massively chordal first half. Horowitz, the concerto's most famous exponent, shared the view of the majority in finding it to be on too large a scale: 'The alternative cadenza is like an ending in itself. It's not good to end the concerto before it's over!'[6] The fireworks and grandiloquence of either cadenza are thrown into relief by the movement's reticent conclusion, which also gives a measure of symmetry to its shape by matching the quiet opening.

The title 'Intermezzo' underlines the fact that the second movement is an interlude between two thematically interrelated movements. Its main theme, not picked up in either of the other movements, is, even by Rachmaninoff's standards, exceptionally sorrowful. How could Rachmaninoff write the harrowing music of the opening amid the contentment of his family at his beloved Ivanovka, remote from the turmoil of the world? After thirty bleak bars in the darkest orchestral colouring, the piano entry starts in anguished dissonance (Ex. 112).

The soloist finds his way to the remote but calmer waters of D flat, in which the theme itself is developed at length, briefly interrupted by a reference to the concerto's opening motto in a passage which treads water harmonically, marooned over an F for eighteen bars. After a great climax there is a change of key (to F sharp minor), mood and time signature (to 3/8) as a fast waltz breaks out (the middle section of the second movement of Tchaikovsky's First Concerto is the obvious precedent). The clarinet solo, over which the piano flutters delicately, turns out to be a variant of the concerto's opening theme, and even the piano embroidery has the same origin (Ex. 113).

Ex.112

Ex.113

The sad mood of the opening eventually returns, and the piano insistently reiterates a pair of tearful chords, as despairing descending chromatic phrases on the strings bring back the music of the movement's introduction. The piano then catapults the listener into the finale.

The last movement contrasts the rhythmic with the lyrical. The opening theme, based on the concerto's original rhythmic leitmotif, though exciting in itself by reason of its sheer energy, has no melodic interest. When the second theme is mooted, it too turns out to be built on the same rhythmic impulse and is not unrelated to the second theme of the first movement. It is hammered out *staccato* in massive piano chords (the marking '*Più mosso*' here and at its reappearance is reversed both times in the composer's recorded performance), but then immediately its bristly

outer clothing is removed to reveal pure Rachmaninoff lyricism underneath. In the *scherzando* episode, in which the piano weaves patterns
of elaborately ear-tickling decoration over four variations on the second
theme of the first movement, the pianistic delights help to conceal the
fact that the music has become becalmed over an E flat pedal in the
orchestra. This whole section concludes with a disappointingly ordinary
perfect cadence. When the pulse is regained, the two main themes are
recapitulated before the build up to the final climax. The extremely
percussive piano writing at this point, over a drum roll and growling
jabs from cellos and basses, must have struck early audiences as
altogether novel:

Ex.114

As the sequence develops, it becomes apparent that it has been derived
from the first movement cadenza. After this final gesture of integration
comes the apotheosis of the big tune, punctuated by the concerto's
rhythmic motto, one of the great moments in Romantic concerto literature.
It grandiloquently climbs one last emotional peak before Rachmaninoff
brings his most elaborate work in concerto form to a triumphant and
exhilarating conclusion. However, in developing for his Third Concerto
the characteristic features of its predecessor, and pushing them to the
very limits of expressive and virtuoso possibility, the composer may in
a sense be said to have created a problem for himself: along this route
he had reached a point beyond which he could not go. That, surely,
is the reason why his fourth and final concerto, conceived only five
years later, was necessarily to be so different in style.

The vexed question of cuts in Rachmaninoff crops up again with
the Third Concerto. Modern practice is to play the work entire, though,
at least during his years as a concert pianist in the West, the composer
seems never to have done so, and until the 1960s performers generally
followed his example. In view of Horowitz's special association with
the composer, his gramophone recordings are particularly valuable in
shedding light on how far the five cuts in Rachmaninoff's own recording
were definitive. Horowitz's first version of 1930 was made just under
three years after his arrival in America and his historic first meeting

with Rachmaninoff in Steinway's basement in New York, where he played the concerto with the composer and listened to his comments. Particularly as Horowitz was then awed by meeting his musical god, it is most likely that he would have taken away with him and observed, at least immediately after, any suggestions Rachmaninoff made, including those for textual changes.

Rachmaninoff: Third Concerto – Cuts Observed in the Recordings Made by the Composer and Horowitz

	Rachmaninoff 1939/40	Horowitz 1930	Horowitz 1951	Horowitz 1978
1st movement				
1 3 after 10 to 11	✓	—	—	—
2 9 and 10 before 19	✓	✓	✓	✓
2nd movement				
3a 4 after 27 to 28	—	—	✓	—
3b 6 after 27 to 8 after 28	✓	✓	—	—
4a 36 1 and 2	—	✓	—	—
4b 6 after 36 to 38	—	✓	✓	—
3rd movement				
5 45 to 4 before 47	✓	✓	—	—
6 2 after 52 to 54	✓	✓	✓	—

In the first movement, the first cut made by Rachmaninoff, and by him only, removes seven seconds of music. There seems little doubt that, as with the cuts in *The Isle of the Dead*, these few bars are excised not because they are obviously redundant but only because they are not strictly necessary. The second cut, common to Rachmaninoff and all Horowitz performances, removes two arguably redundant bars at the climax of the cadenza; Horowitz declared them musically 'absolutely impossible' and they certainly are a gratuitous rhetorical gesture in an already purple patch.

In the Intermezzo, Rachmaninoff observes only the first of the two cuts made by Horowitz nine years before. In both recordings the lost bars occur exactly between the two record sides given over to the movement, and the addition of what amounts to rather more than a minute's music at this point, with no obvious place for a pause, might well have caused technical problems.[7] The firm memory of those who heard the composer play the work in the concert hall is that he did not observe this cut. Jorge Bolet, for example, has recalled[8] that Rachmaninoff used to compress the semi-quavers in the triplet figure in the right hand (♪ ♩) in the passage. The two cuts in the finale, however, seem to be definitive. According to the pianist Gina Bachauer,[9] who knew the composer well and who heard him perform the work several times, Rachmaninoff always played the last movement as on his recording, which is textually the same as Horowitz's in 1930. He may, of course, have been led to make these cuts by his obsessive desire in later life for conciseness at all costs, but arguably there are rational musical grounds as well: the one cut removes the first lyrical statement of the 'big tune' and so avoids pre-empting its effect later; the other eliminates the third of the four variations in the *scherzando* section, improving the tautness of structure at a point where momentum sags. Rachmaninoff's recording, therefore, except in the Intermezzo, almost certainly reflects his final thoughts on the concerto in 1939, though that does not of course mean that his cuts should on that account necessarily be followed.

Rachmaninoff's Third Concerto has come to make a niche for itself in concert programmes as the ultimate in Romantic piano concertos. It combines lyricism and excitement with unparalleled pianistic virtuosity, and now that it has long rivalled, if not surpassed, the Second Concerto in public approval, it is difficult to realize that for the first twenty years of its life it was by no means a popular work. Although Rachmaninoff dedicated it to Josef Hofmann, that renowned artist never performed it. When Rachmaninoff first played it through to him, in November 1911, Hofmann, whose small hands would in any case have found some of the massive figurations of the piano layout difficult to handle, thought the work rather cut up – 'a short melody which is constantly interrupted with difficult passages; more a *fantaisie* than a concerto. Not enough form'.[10] Hofmann's extraordinary snap judgement meant that the work was not launched internationally as it otherwise would have been. Just as Chaliapin had withdrawn from *The Miserly Knight*, so Rachmaninoff must have been equally disappointed by Hofmann's response to the concerto. Of course, the composer frequently played it himself, both in Russia and abroad, over the next thirty years, but it was not until the advent of Vladimir Horowitz, who made the work his own, that the work took off. 'Without false modesty, I brought this concerto to light. I brought it to life, and everywhere! Rachmaninoff had not won the recognition with the concerto that he thought he deserved.'[11] Rachmaninoff told Horowitz that his only success with the concerto had been his performance with Mahler. Musicians loved it but not the audience or the critics. 'They thought it was too complicated.'[12] Many pianists besides Hofmann – Moiseiwitsch, Barere, Lhevinne, Rubinstein, even Richter – have steered clear of the work. Although these days it has become fodder for teenage starlets, mere virtuosity does it a profound disservice, and only great artists of the calibre of Horowitz or Gilels have revealed its true musical stature.

At the beginning of February 1910, shortly after returning from America, Rachmaninoff was deeply shocked to learn of the death from smallpox of Vera Komissarzhevskaya. Having in the previous year suffered the loss of his boyhood sweetheart Vera Skalon and of Grand-mother Butakova, he was prompted by this third blow to compose the song *So dread a fate*, to verses by Maykov expressing disbelief at the peremptoriness of death, which he held over for publication with the Op. 34 set. He escaped to Ivanovka earlier than usual for his summer break. With the retirement of his father-in-law Alexander Satin from management of the estate, Rachmaninoff took over the responsibility with his brother-in-law Vladimir Satin. From now until he left Russia permanently he was to devote much time, energy and money to improving the farm, but despite his new commitments he was nevertheless able this summer to complete two extended and contrasting works: the *Liturgy of St John Chrysostom* and a set of thirteen piano Preludes, to complete the cycle of twenty-four.

Liturgy of St John Chrysostom, Op. 31

It is often implied that Rachmaninoff was not a religious man, usually on the basis of the not very relevant story of the problems his irregular attendance at confession created when he wished to get married. It is true that for many Russian composers, right up to the time of Stravinsky, a lack of spiritual commitment has not precluded an attraction to the rituals of the Orthodox Church, but from the conviction apparent in his religious works, not to mention the firm evidence of his family,[13] it is clear that at least by the time of the *Liturgy* Rachmaninoff could indeed properly be called 'religious', at any rate in outlook, if not in strict practice. As with most aspects of his life, Rachmaninoff kept his religion to himself, but it is not without significance that the *Liturgy* is the first, but by no means the last, of his compositions to which he appended the pious epigraph 'Thanks be to God',[14] nor, as noted previously, that Smolensky, the guru of Russian ecclesiastical music, had sent Rachmaninoff the text of the Liturgy for possible setting as long ago as 1897. Although Rachmaninoff later fell out of love with his composition,[15] and commentators have little to say about this least known of all his major works, dismissing it as merely a trial run for the *All-Night Vigil*, in fact the *Liturgy* is outstandingly beautiful and musically satisfying in its own right.

Rachmaninoff sketched his *Liturgy*, which comprises twenty numbers for four-part unaccompanied chorus, in less than three weeks (3-21 June 1910) but spent a further two months in producing a final version. Evidently not very familiar with the service, he wrote to Slonov on 19 June to seek clarification about the texts of the antiphons and the meaning of 'prokimen' (a separate verse from a psalm). Although Rachmaninoff had looked up Tchaikovsky's setting of the Liturgy, this was of little help as these items had for the most part been omitted, whereas he himself intended to set the service in its entirety. Slonov could not reply immediately as he was in the Caucasus, and so Rachmaninoff turned for advice to Alexander Kastalsky, who had just succeeded Smolensky as Director of the Moscow Synodal School. Kastalsky answered Rachmaninoff's questions, looked through the manuscript and made a large number of suggestions many, though not all, of which Rachmaninoff incorporated in his final draft. He broke the news of his work to Morozov on 31 July: 'I have just finished a *Liturgy* (to your great surprise, probably). I have long thought about the *Liturgy* and I have long aimed at it. I took it up rather by chance and immediately got carried away. After that, I finished it very quickly. Not for a long time (since the time of *Monna Vanna*) have I written anything with such pleasure.'

The Liturgy of St John Chrysostom is the equivalent in the Eastern Orthodox Church of the Western Church's Communion service. It bears the name of the Bishop of the Byzantine Church who, according to tradition, revised the rite at the beginning of the fifth century and, like all Orthodox services, it is celebrated in Church Slávonic rather than vernacular Russian, rather as Latin used to be used in the Catholic Church. In church the first part of the Liturgy – the Proskomidia, the preparation of the bread and the wine – is performed privately at the altar by the celebrant, but the service itself is sung, a long responsorial dialogue between priest and congregation, punctuated by troparia (hymns)

and litanies, Glorias and broken verses from the Psalms, and culminating
in the Eucharist itself. The task Rachmaninoff set himself was not simply
to write a group of choral set-pieces for concert performance but to
compose a setting simple enough also to be used liturgically. In several
of the numbers this meant allowing for the integration of ritual incantations
for church use without disturbing musical coherence when not so used.
Moreover, variable elements would be incorporated into the service,
using traditional musical settings, and this need for musical uniformity
imposed strict restraints on the style of writing, in which no vestige is
to be found of the virtuosity of Rachmaninoff's piano pieces or the
excitement of the orchestral works; even his characteristic expansive
lyricism is nowhere to be found. Indeed, the contrast in style between
the adjacent works in the composer's catalogue, the Third Concerto and
piano Preludes that were begun within days of completing the *Liturgy*,
could hardly be greater. Rachmaninoff made no conscious use of
traditional chants, as he did four years later in the *All-Night Vigil*, but
he so assimilated the style of church music that his own identity as a
composer is almost always submerged, though his natural propensity
for step-wise melodic lines, itself clearly deriving from the influence of
church music and demanded by church music, must have made the
writing congenial. Structurally, the twenty items which go to make up
the setting are extremely simple; harmonically, while exercising great
restraint, Rachmaninoff somehow manages to inject a piquancy and
variety that makes the work musically satisfying outside its religious
context. The prohibition by the Orthodox Church on the use of musical
instruments in worship itself encouraged the development of colour and
variety in vocal writing and extended the range of sonority and variety
of effect of which Russian choirs, to this day, have traditionally been
capable, and one of the main pleasures in Rachmaninoff's setting is the
masterly use of the choral palette.

The first part of the service, the Liturgy of the Catechumens (the
unbaptised), opens with *The Great Litany*, the 'Kyrie eleison', which
alternates with the traditional intoning by the priest of the invitation to
prayer. Rachmaninoff's task is simply to provide great blocks of choral
harmony for the congregation's thirteen-fold repetition of the refrain
'Lord, have mercy'. In No. 2, the *First Antiphon*, a setting of what we
know as Psalm 103,[16] Rachmaninoff effectively contrasts a static alto
line with the bass-weighted tone of the full choir. In the service a brief
litany precedes No. 3, the Doxology, 'Glory be to the Father' (the
Second Antiphon), Rachmaninoff's lively setting of which is tolerably
well-known from occasional English church performances. Number 4,
the *Third Antiphon*, an elaborate setting of The Beatitudes, is laid out
for double choir (there is an alternative version for single choir). The

repetition of adjacent notes in the refrain has a hypnotically beautiful effect:

Ex.115

[Blessed are they which do hunger and thirst after righteousness.]

Number 5 is a brief invitation to worship, derived from 3, and No. 6, *The Trisagion*, 'Holy God, Holy and Mighty, Holy and Immortal, Have mercy upon us', is a rhythmically inspiriting hymn, notable for its choral refrains in 5/8 time. After what in church would be a reading of the Scriptures comes No. 7, *The Augmented Liturgy*, one of the high-spots of the whole work. The priest intones the prayer while the choir, alternating between minor and relative major, repeat in varied form, 'Lord, have mercy', over a haunting dominant pedal. The extreme beauty and reverence of the setting live in the memory. This part of the service is concluded by the *Litany of the Catechumens*, who, in the early church, were permitted to attend the Liturgy only to this point.

The Liturgy of the Faithful opens with the *Introit*. In church the celebrants would process to the altar with the bread and wine, and the choir would sing No. 8, the *Hymn of the Cherubim*. Like the Gloria, this beautiful piece is sometimes performed in English cathedrals. At the end of this hymn there occurs the only point of contact with one of Rachmaninoff's secular compositions, when the harmonies recall his prayerful song *To the Children*, Op. 26, No. 7 (Ex. 116).

Number 9, *The Suppliant Litany*, is a dialogue between priest and choir in which Rachmaninoff's contribution is mainly to provide harmony for the brief choral responses. This is followed by an elaborate setting of the *Creed*, where the repetition of one note in unison by a group of four sopranos, four altos and a tenor and later two tenors and two basses

Ex.116a

Hymn of the Cherubim

[Now let us lay aside all worldly care.]

Ex.116b
To the Children

against the rest of the choir makes an arresting contrast. Number 11, the joyful *Grace of Peace* (Eucharist), is followed by the prayer of thanksgiving, *To Thee We Sing*, a quiet and gently reverent setting for choir and soprano solo, which has been secularized in Soviet times into 'Quiet Melody'.[17] The quiet entry of the soloist above a cushion of hushed choral sound, a treasurable moment, calls to mind the opening of Klopstock's hymn in the finale of Mahler's 'Resurrection' Symphony, where the soprano soloist soars above the unaccompanied chorus (Ex. 117).

Number 13, *It is meet*, a hymn to the Mother of God, leads to the Eucharistic Prayer and a fervent setting for double choir of *The Lord's Prayer*. The opening plainchant phrase on which it is based is a much slowed-down version of the inverted turn with which Rachmaninoff opened his First Symphony, with its biblical epigraph. It is interesting that Elgar used exactly the same figure towards the end of Part 1 of his *Dream of Gerontius*, where the Chorus of Assistants, interceding on Gerontius's behalf, pray to God to rescue him 'in his evil hour'.[18] In view of a second possible echo of the Elgarian work in *The Bells*,[19] one wonders whether Rachmaninoff may have heard a performance of *Gerontius* during his Dresden sojourn.

The remaining six items forming a coda to the Eucharist, in general are of less interest musically. Number 15, *And to Thy Spirit and One is Holy*, announces the fulfilment of the Communion. Number 16, *Praise the Lord from Heaven*, in Rachmaninoff's setting is a delightful imitation of the tolling of bells, in which one by one the different voices join in the clangour. *Blessed is He that cometh in the name of the Lord*, No. 17, leads to the quietly fervent prayer *May Our Mouths Be Filled with Thy Praise*, in which the voices proclaiming in canon the final Alleluias again echo the tolling of bells. In No. 19, *Blessed Be the Name of the Lord*, the double choir sing with the fullest tone a succession of emphatic tonic chords in joyous thanksgiving, before the final brief *Glory to the Father and to the Son*.

Rachmaninoff's *Liturgy* was premiered on 25 November 1910 in a secular performance by the Synodal Choir conducted by Nikolay Danilin. As with Tchaikovsky's *Liturgy* thirty-two years before, the freedom of Rachmaninoff's setting met with hostility from the ecclesiastical authorities, and it is doubtful whether the work was ever performed in a religious context. Anna Trubnikova recalled that a teacher of religion at the school at which she worked described the music as 'absolutely wonderful, even too beautiful, but with such music it would be difficult to pray; it is not church music'.[20] Much the same judgement was passed when Rachmaninoff himself conducted the Chorus of the Maryinsky Theatre in twelve numbers from the *Liturgy* at a Siloti matinee concert at the Hall of the Nobility in Petersburg in March the following year:[21]

Ex.117a

Rachmaninoff: *To Thee we sing*

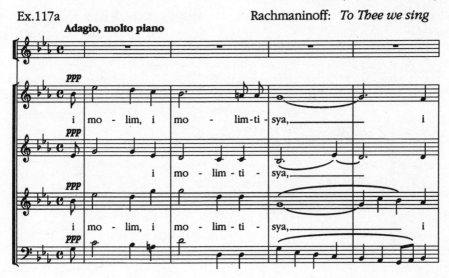

[And to Thee we pray, O our God.]

Ex.117b

Mahler: 'Resurrection' Symphony
last movement

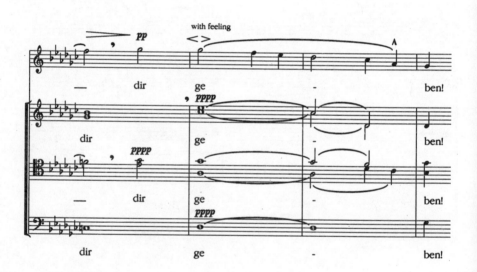

[He who has called you to Him will give you eternal life.]

In the praise heard afterwards there were many remarks about the music not being 'church music', that it contained apparent operatic nuances and symphonic refinements. Our impression is that the *Liturgy*, first and foremost, is written highly musically, and that it stands apart from the stylistic conditions of 'ecclesiastical formulae'. Obviously the composer never intended to fit his music into this convention. We leave it to the experts in church music to criticize him for not achieving what he did not set out to do.

It is indeed sad that religious difficulties both in Tsarist Russia and Soviet times, and the absence of any available printed edition since the original publication, have impeded circulation of Rachmaninoff's *Liturgy*, for it is clear not only that it was a great advance musically on Tchaikovsky's stylistically tentative pioneering effort but that it totally eclipses all later settings, most notably those of Arkhangelsky (1846-1924) and Gretchaninov (1864-1955), though, ironically enough, the latter's setting of the Creed, complete with heretical organ accompaniment, has been the only item in the entire service in any setting to achieve popular currency, thanks to Chaliapin's famous recording.

Thirteen Preludes, Op. 32

Rachmaninoff remarked later in life that the composition of small piano pieces cost him more trouble than large works. 'I am at the mercy of my thematic idea, which must be presented concisely and without digression ... After all, to say what you have to say, and to say it briefly, lucidly, and without any circumlocution, is still the most difficult problem facing the artist'.[22] The composer may well have had in mind his Op. 32 set of Preludes, with which he seems to have wrestled throughout most of the summer of 1910 after completing the *Liturgy*, though the two which became the most popular of the set, those in G major and G sharp minor, he had already played as encores at the first Moscow performance of his Third Concerto in April.[23] To Slonov on 13 July he reported that his work was spoiling his humour and stopping him 'breathing easily'; to Morozov on 31 July, 'The business of the small piano pieces goes worst of all. I don't like this occupation, and it goes with difficulty for me. There is neither beauty nor joy'. The manuscripts of the individual preludes are dated from 23 August to 10 September, as usual with Rachmaninoff indicating the completion of the final drafts. Despite, or because of, the effort spent, these Preludes are among Rachmaninoff's most perfectly shaped compositions, and they represent one of his most important and enduring achievements.

As with the earlier set, the preludes in the Op. 32 group are arranged to alternate major and minor, though not necessarily related, keys and to juxtapose contrasting moods. Most of them grow out of a simple, often brief, melodic or rhythmic idea, suggesting a pictorial association. Number 1, in C major, a corruscating aperitif, in a sense harks back to the C sharp minor Prelude in being based on the repetition of that piece's opening three notes, flattened submediant, dominant and tonic. The prelude's laconic final chords, *poco meno mosso*, lead perfectly into the second Prelude in B flat minor. This is the first of several numbers in the set dominated by the rhythmic figure ♩ ♫ . In this gravely beautiful and haunting piece, with its restlessly shifting harmonies, there seem to be profound and wistful undercurrents. In contrast, the following prelude, in E major, with its insistently regular pulse throughout, seems to call to mind a grand and colourful company of horsemen riding by. Trumpeters herald the cavalcade, which eventually moves away into the distance and out of sight (*poco a poco diminuendo*).

The next six preludes alternate drama and repose. In No. 4, in E minor, three repeated A's, in the same rhythmic pattern as the motif of No. 2 but four times slower, sound questioningly in bare octaves, only to be shouted down each time by phrases of hectoring chordal triplets. In its turn of phrase and even harmony the piece has been used variously by commentators to illustrate how Rachmaninoff was significantly influenced by Rimsky-Korsakov[24] (there are evident similarities with the opera *Kitezh*, premiered just three years before, a work which Rimsky himself once hoped Rachmaninoff would conduct at the Bolshoi), or by church music.[25] In the well-known fifth Prelude in G major a simple, rather stark, diatonic melody unfolds over an arpeggio accompaniment. The groups of demi-semi-quavers which punctuate the singing irresistibly call to mind a picture of a bird trilling on a bough:

Ex.118

Prelude No. 6 in F minor, dark, dramatic, full of torment, hurls defiance at the world. Like Nos. 1 and 8, it typifies the way in which Rachmaninoff was moving at this stage towards an increased interest in vigorous rhythmic patterns and very brief melodic ideas, in stark contrast to the long-breathed and, to some tastes, somewhat enervating lyricism of his earlier style. Prelude No. 7 in F major is a dialogue between a gentle song in the right hand and another in the left. The somewhat restless interjections of pairs of semiquavers into the accompaniment and the cold harmony never allow the piece to shake off its feeling of unease. Number 8 in A minor is sinisterly dramatic and, for its composer, harmonically relatively daring. There is a haunting ambivalence of feel, created by incorporating major elements in the minor tonality:

Ex.119

The gently wistful ninth prelude in A major seems to have come about as an improvisation on nothing more than descending and ascending diatonic scales in the left hand, and is another example of the composer's ability to create a characteristic piece out of the most simple material.

Prelude No. 10 in B minor is generally, and rightly, considered one of Rachmaninoff's masterpieces. In conversation with the composer the pianist Benno Moiseiwitsch discovered by chance that it was based on a Böcklin painting they both knew as 'The Return',[26] which is probably to be identified with one showing an old man looking thoughtfully from afar at a cottage to which he is evidently returning. Even more than with Böcklin's 'Isle of the Dead', Rachmaninoff's imagination takes him far beyond the confines of the immediate scene, for in the prelude it is undoubtedly a funeral and thoughts about man's mortality which are in the old man's mind. Rachmaninoff again employs the ♩. ♫ rhythmic motif, this time in a funeral chant, alternating with held chords which seem to pause for sombre reflection, and punctuated by the unremitting tolling of a church bell (x) (Ex. 120). From these tiny fragments the whole imposing structure is built up. As the music moves inexorably towards a massive chordal climax, the tolling of the bell becomes increasingly dominant, and even in the hushed aftermath (*L'istesso tempo*) it stills sounds as an insistent F sharp in the bass, until

Ex.120

the man's train of thought seems to run away in despairing confusion (*veloce*). The material of the opening is quietly recapitulated, and in the final three bars a pair of mournfully descending phrases of minor thirds in the right hand make a last tearful comment.

The eleventh prelude, in B major, grows entirely out of the same rhythmic motif as its predecessor, with which it also shares a certain religious atmosphere. The popular G sharp minor prelude, No. 12, has an outstandingly lovely melody in the left hand against an arpeggiate accompaniment in the right, reminiscent of tinkling bells; in layout it is thus the obverse of the earlier G major prelude. For the final number in the cycle, the Prelude in D flat, Rachmaninoff composed an appropriately solemn consummation on a scale epic both in terms of its range and in the manner of keyboard writing. To resort to making arpeggios out of its massive chords, as many pianists have to do, is a very unsatisfactory expedient in this prelude above all, and this technical problem may in part be responsible for its infrequent performance by those with less than enormous hands. The prelude is unlike any other in structure and in the nature of the different strands of material that go to make it up. The opening idea is based simply on the notes of the major tonic triad; the second makes brief reference to the ♩. ♫ rhythm of the earlier preludes as a conscious or unconscious reminiscence; the third, after a change of key (to A major), a descending four-note chromatic phrase, echoes the mournful end of the B minor prelude. A bridge passage leads to a *vivo* sequence of right-hand arpeggios, slowly climbing and then descending through another change of key (C sharp minor) before the final grand peroration, in which the motif of the tonic triad and the four-note descending phrase are combined in massive bell-like sonority, leaving nothing more to be said.

Following hints from Riesemann,[27] some commentators have shown great ingenuity in uncovering references in various places in this final prelude to the motto of the opening piece of the whole cycle, the Prelude in C sharp minor.[28] Yet no-one before seems to have looked in the most obvious place, the modulatory five bars before the final two pages, thoughtfully written in the required key, where Rachmaninoff even accentuates the notes of the motto to make matters perfectly clear:

Ex.121

To some ears even the descending chromatic phrase in the A major section near the beginning sounds suspiciously like an echo of the second theme of the earlier work, and it is certainly tempting to believe that it was not by accident that the composer held back the enharmonic major of the key of his original prelude for this final piece, and to infer that by doing so he was making a cyclical gesture. Nevertheless, such conclusions are probably unwarranted. The notional references are, to say the least, obscure, and the three-note motto of the C sharp minor prelude is a common-enough Rachmaninoff sequence anyway. It should therefore perhaps not surprise us to find it nearly as easily in the C major Prelude opening the Op. 32 set as in the D flat concluding it.

Rachmaninoff himself never played the Preludes as a complete cycle, and in recital always chose a small contrasting group taken from both Op. 23 and 32, changing them year by year. On the basis of being the most regularly performed, certain numbers were evidently his favourites: from Op. 23 – No. 2 in B flat major, No. 5 in G minor and No. 10 in G flat; from Op. 32 – No. 5 in G major, which he played far more frequently than any other after THE Prelude, No. 8 in A minor and No. 12 in G sharp minor. At the opposite extreme, four of the Preludes he seems never to have played in recital at all: from Op. 23, No. 7 in C minor and No. 8 in A flat; from Op. 32, No. 7 in F major, which he nevertheless recorded, and No. 9 in A major. One final curiosity: after its initial airing, the composer never played the magnificent final D flat Prelude in recital during the last thirty years of his life.

In September 1910 Rachmaninoff left for a concert tour of Europe, with twelve appearances in England, Austria, Germany and Holland, and fifteen besides in Russia, including the first of three seasons of conducting for the Moscow Philharmonic Society. Before the end of the concert season, however, he found time to complete a small piano work which has achieved lasting popularity, the *Polka de W.R.* The French title transliterates the initials of the composer's father, Vasily Rachmaninoff, who played this piece to his young son, leaving him with the mistaken impression that it was his own work. In fact the original polka was published by one Franz Behr (1837–1898) as his Op. 303, *Lachtäubchen* or *La rieuse – Polka badine*, which, to judge from the number of times it was reprinted, seems to have achieved great popularity in the 1870s, before gradually sinking without trace under the mountain of domestic light music published at the time. It surfaced again in 1957, when it was reprinted as an appendix to the Soviet collection of reminiscences about the composer.[29] Rachmaninoff's version of the naive tune is replete with the kind of succulent pianistic bonbons, not least in its three *ossia* passages, that must no doubt have delighted the work's dedicatee, the arch confectioner and transcriber Leopold Godowsky. It also contains in good measure a quality with which Rachmaninoff is not often credited and which not every performer of the piece succeeds in exploiting to the full – humour – from its teasingly protracted *rallentando* in the opening bars, to the sly conclusion, in which an apparently mistaken D natural brusquely obtrudes into the A flat tonality, only to lead back apologetically to another perfect cadence, with the final chord stretching both hands to an eleventh. Zoya Pribïtkova, no doubt reporting the composer's own account, has described how the young Rachmaninoff used to enjoy his father's performances of the original so much that he would choke with laughter.[30]

Nine Études-Tableaux, Op. 33

With his new responsibilities as an estate manager Rachmaninoff found life at Ivanovka in the summer of 1911 unusually tiring. Writing to Zoya Pribïtkova to congratulate her on her engagement he complained characteristically: 'Really, I have never had so strenuous, unrestful and fatiguing a summer. Moreover from tiredness (perhaps old age) I have become inexcusably forgetful … and every evening when I go to bed I am horrified when I remember how many things I have forgotten to do that day'.[31] Nevertheless, despite the difficulties he claimed to have suffered in composing the recent Preludes, only two days after this letter Rachmaninoff completed the final draft of the first of a new set of nine similar piano pieces, his Op. 33, finishing the last exactly a month later. If some of the Preludes of the previous year hinted at a pictorial inspiration, the connection is made explicit in the new pieces' title, *Études-Tableaux* – 'Study-Pictures' – a Rachmaninoff coinage, which he used again for a second set in 1916, though when he played three of them for the first time in Petersburg on 5 December 1911[32] they were programmed as 'Prelude-Pictures'. The 'study' element in these compositions is evident only occasionally; they are mainly concerned with creating a mood or with telling a story, in which the sound of bells often plays a part. As always, Rachmaninoff kept to himself the sources of inspiration of these pieces, though we know specifically that one represents a scene at a fair and another, like *The Isle of the Dead*, a Böcklin painting. A third depicts a Russian nature scene under a shower – a Russian *Jardins sous la pluie* – but the only clue to its identity is that it was not liked by Taneyev.[33] Throughout the set the emotions expressed are predominantly dark, with only two of the nine pieces not in the minor key.

The opening *Étude-Tableau* in F minor has a stern step-wise melody over a busy staccato accompaniment of dogmatic chords in the middle register and endlessly descending stamping scales in the left hand. The melody sets off determinedly but eventually begins to wander and finally peters out (*perdendo*). The accompaniment to the phrases which set it in motion again shows for the first time a mildly astringent element entering Rachmaninoff's harmonic language, a feature which was to become prominent in the final two sets of songs, Op. 34 and Op. 38:

Ex.122

On the last page, the composer toys with the tonic triad against the tinkle of bells, before the motto of the descending scale finally steals surreptitiously away. The second piece, in C major, is a miniature masterpiece. Its melody looks exceedingly unremarkable when viewed in isolation, and it is its setting which gives it a haunting feeling of wonder, of thoughts reaching out to remote areas, as the harmony shifts bar by bar away from the home key and then back, while yet still anchored by the repeated bottom C in the left hand. (Ex. 123). The theme is repeated obsessively as the music moves towards its climax, finally dissolving into a shimmering *veloce* flourish. The typical absence of any pedalling indication here sometimes misleads performers into crudely cutting this flourish short instead of pedalling the harmonies through into the following trill, as the composer does in his gramophone recording.

Ex.123

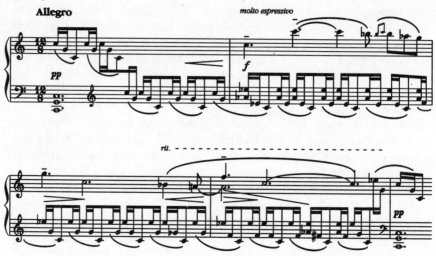

The next three pieces Rachmaninoff inscrutably chose not to publish. Number 4, in A minor, he kept back for inclusion in the Op. 39 set, but Nos. 3 and 5 he withheld altogether, keeping the manuscripts in the drawer of his desk in his Moscow flat, from where they eventually surfaced to be published in the Soviet Union for the first time in 1947. The decision not to publish cannot have been a rash one, since the original Gutheil edition of the separate *Études-Tableaux*, advertising all nine items and assigning them consecutive plate numbers, did not appear until 1914, three years after their composition. The same year, 1914, also saw the appearance in the press of rumours that Rachmaninoff was working on a new concerto, but when that Fourth Concerto finally saw the light of day so many years later, the latter half of the slow movement proved to contain a recast version of a page from the withheld third *Étude-Tableau* in C minor, though no-one could have appreciated the fact at the time. It is possible, therefore, to theorize that the reason why Rachmaninoff did not publish this *Étude-Tableau* was that he wished to use its material in his new concerto, which he started after the composition but before the printing of the piano pieces. It is by far the longest piece in the set. The feeling of mystery in the first half, which is evidently unrelated musically to the second, is emphasized by the brusque gestures of rising scales in the left hand followed by questioning chords with unsettling acciaccaturas. The music finally modulates to the calm of C major for the passage used also in the Fourth Concerto, where it appears in the same key; here it is decked out as a richly harmonized nocturne. There is no obvious reason why Rachmaninoff withheld the fifth *Étude-Tableau* in D minor, though musically it is perhaps the least interesting piece of the whole set. It does, however, demonstrate two features typical of the composer: the recourse to the interval of a fifth as a point of departure, and his inexhaustible obsession with the tinkling of bells.

The sixth *Étude-Tableau*, in E flat minor, is a virtuoso piece which fully lives up to its 'study' title; in the Soviet Union it is usually called 'Snow Storm'. There is a typical Rachmaninoff economy of material. Two pairs of questioning bare thirds descend to establish the tonic key – an opening freakishly similar to Debussy's Prelude, *Les tierces alternées*, written just two years after – triggering off a vertiginous flurry of *presto* semiquavers in the right hand, the impulse for which is the opening sinuous four-note pattern. The pianistic *diabolerie* proceeds unchecked throughout its chilly course, right to the end, when the descending thirds suddenly return and the music peters out with three final protesting references to the four-note pattern that started this devil's ride. Musical interest is mainly in the piece's prodigious vigour and brilliant pianism, and the same could be said of the next, very different, study, in E flat major, which we know represents a fair.[34] First, bells ring out celebration, calling people to enjoy the holiday, and then the composer's eye seems to focus on the antics of a clown or Punch and Judy. At least that is what the gawky phrases and misleading harmonies seem to suggest (Ex. 124). The bells continue to ring joyfully, and the music's unflagging impulse sums up the gay bustle and colourful activity of the scene.

The penultimate piece, No. 8, in G minor, exemplifies the increasingly laconic melodic style of both the last Preludes and the *Études-Tableaux*. A musical representation of a Böcklin painting on the subject of 'Morning',[35] it opens magically with arpeggios in the left hand providing delicate support for two brief singing phrases in the right, from the second of which, a simple five-note descending phrase, the whole study grows. The trouble in this case is that this short-breathed lyricism, having nowhere to go, is peremptorily disrupted by a dry virtuoso middle section (based on the second phrase and its inversion) which in turn comes to a sudden halt to allow the opening material to be recapitulated. The three-octave ascending rush up the piano with which the whole is rounded off is borrowed straight from the final page of Chopin's First Ballade, which happens also to be in G minor. The concluding *Étude-Tableau*, in C sharp minor, is a work of enormous and unrelenting power. The emotions expressed are so black, the piano writing so massive, that the limitations of the instrument can scarcely contain them. (Ex. 125)

Ex.124

Ex.125

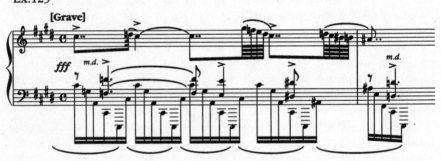

The insistent hammering home of juxtaposed major and minor chords near the beginning and again in the penultimate bars leads, inevitably in Rachmaninoff, to the triumph of the minor key in the overwhelming conclusion. Like the last of the Preludes, this study proclaims finality.

In the autumn of 1911 Rachmaninoff visited England to open an extensive new season of thirty-three appearances as soloist and conductor, which included, for the first time in many years, performances as soloist in a work not his own (Tchaikovsky's First Concerto) and six performances at the Maryinsky Theatre in St Petersburg conducting *The Queen of Spades*. 1911 also saw Scriabin's popularity reach new heights with the premiere, in March, of his *Prometheus*. Even Siloti began vigorously to espouse the composer's cause in his concerts. The press and popular rumour hinted at personal rivalry between Scriabin and Rachmaninoff, and there is no doubt that the allegiance of music lovers was divided between the two great Moscow musicians. Rachmaninoff was depressingly aware of the fact, and when he saw Josef Hofmann at the beginning of December Mrs Hofmann recorded in her diary that he told them so:[36]

> He was in a very dramatic situation in regard to his music and thought seriously of abandoning composing; for in Moscow no-one wanted to listen to his music anymore. He couldn't go on composing just for his wife, and if he went to a concert all the youth of Moscow gave him the cold shoulder. It is all that wretched Scriabin. He has demoralized them all with his crazy music ...

Nevertheless, not many days later Rachmaninoff was the conductor at a concert in which Scriabin played his own concerto, and this coming together of the two composers helped to confound popular opinion. However, it was opportune that a new stimulus and support entered Rachmaninoff's life at this time, in the person of the young poetess Marietta Shaginyan.

Fourteen Songs, Op. 34

Under the pseudonym of 'Re' (the note D), Shaginyan began writing to Rachmaninoff in February 1912. The relationship which developed through their correspondence and which lasted until Rachmaninoff left Russia was distant personally – perhaps he was put off by her close association with the 'clever' Medtner family – yet in his letters to Shaginyan Rachmaninoff revealed more of his intimate thoughts, his foibles, his innate lack of self-confidence than to any of his other correspondents.[37] Such was his frank trust in his new confidante that, already in his second letter, of 15 March, Rachmaninoff asked her to send him texts for songs. 'It seems to me that "Re" knows a lot in this field, nearly everything – perhaps everything. Whether the author is contemporary or dead makes no difference, provided that the piece is original and not a translation and no more than eight to twelve lines in length, or at most sixteen. And another thing: the mood should be sad, rather than gay; bright tones do not come easily to me.' This year

Rachmaninoff went early to Ivanovka (at the end of April), and on 19 June he was able to report to 'Re' that he had completed his new songs. 'In general I am satisfied with all the songs and am infinitely glad that they came to me easily, without great effort. May God grant that work continues in the same way in the future ...'

The fourteen new songs cover a wide range of texts, from Pushkin to Balmont; all but three are dedicated to singers. The first, *The Muse*, appropriately dedicated to 'Re', is from Pushkin, and tells how a singer was taught in childhood by the Muse to play and write music. In the following year Shaginyan submitted the same text to Medtner, who also made a setting which he likewise dedicated to Shaginyan.[38] Indeed, this period sees the beginning of a certain musical interaction between the two composers as well as a deepening of their personal friendship. Rachmaninoff's setting opens with the piano echoing the sound of the pipe in his favourite interval of a fifth. The mood of contemplation in the first stanza gives way to greater animation in the second, with a rapturous climax as the words tell of how sometimes the Muse herself would play, filling the musician with ecstasy. Medtner's setting ends in a mood of jubilation; Rachmaninoff's, as it began, with the sound of the pipe, the E minor tonality and the ascending octave in the piano right hand aptly reflecting the poet's reference to the Phrygian mode. The second song, *The Soul's Concealment*, by Apollon Korinfsky (1868-1937), the first of four dark settings in the group dedicated to Chaliapin, tells of the turmoil of emotional extremes in a man's soul, the sorrow that goes with love. Rachmaninoff's setting, with a declamatory and rather Mussorgskian part for the singer against a simple chordal accompaniment, has enormous power but needs a singer with Chaliapin's dramatic skills to bring it off convincingly.

The next three songs are the first of five in the set dedicated to the celebrated lyric tenor Leonid Sobinov (1872-1934). In No. 3, Pushkin's *Storm*, the poet tells of a maiden standing on a cliff top, silhouetted by lightning, with the sea, the wind and the storm raging about her. The menacing vigour of Rachmaninoff's setting excitingly conveys the violent fury of the scene, but perhaps the most delightful touch is the music's change of mood for the final two lines of the poem, when a temporary calm settles as the poet confides that for him the maiden on the cliff is a more beautiful sight than the forces of nature. The piano postlude brings back the violence of the storm and concludes with an unexpected modulation back from C minor to the home key of E minor. As in so many Rachmaninoff songs, the taxing piano part demands a virtuoso accompanist. The fourth song, *Day to Night comparing went the wind her way*, to words by Konstantin Balmont, is in great contrast. It is a setting of a poetic conceit in which at sunset the wind sadly whispers that Night is stronger than Day, but, as the sun rises on a new day, smilingly admits the reverse. Rachmaninoff's setting has great delicacy, and the hazy, languid harmonies are somehow redolent of the long summer evenings at Ivanovka. In the middle of the song, in the accompaniment, there is an interesting echo of the *Étude-Tableau* in C sharp minor of the previous year, though in a very different emotional context:

Ex.126a   *Day to Night comparing*

[The migrant wind passed over the swell]

Number 5, *Arion*, another Pushkin setting, tells how the Greek poet and singer was the lone survivor of a shipwreck. (In the familiar ancient Greek legend Arion's fellow sailors threatened to kill him, and he was saved by jumping overboard and riding to shore on the back of a dolphin which had been attracted by his singing.) Rachmaninoff's setting, with its modal main theme, has enormous energy and drama, and the high notes given to the singer at the climax of phrases and the busy piano part splendidly convey the struggle against the sea, though it must be admitted that Medtner's masterly setting of the same poem in his Op. 36 is more powerful still.

The sixth song, *The Raising of Lazarus*, dedicated to Chaliapin, is a setting of a religious poem by Khomyakov, in which the poet prays

Ex.126b

Étude-Tableau
in C sharp minor, Op.33, No.9

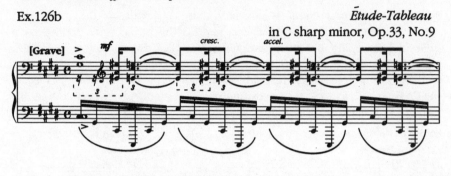

that his soul may rise again and praise the Lord. The austerity of the setting makes this perhaps one of Rachmaninoff's less appealing songs, and the peremptory sequence of harsh chords in the piano postlude sums up the composer's astringent new tone of voice (Ex. 127).

So dread a fate ('It cannot be') is set to words that the poet Maykov wrote on the death of his daughter. According to a note on the manuscript, the song we know today is a revision of an earlier version of March 1910,[39] made as an immediate response to the unexpected news of the death of Vera Komissarzhevskaya, to whose memory it is dedicated. Rachmaninoff's setting encapsulates all his skills as a song-writer, in particular his ability to follow musically every nuance of the text – the despairing cries of disbelief, the passionate but vain hope that the news of the loved-one's death is not true, the final hopelessness and quiet agony – in such a way as to enhance the original and at the same time achieve a satisfyingly coherent musical whole.

Number 8, *Music*, dedicated to P[yotr] Tch[aikovsky], has words by Yakov Polonsky. The poem tells how the artist is enveloped by the sounds of music that are in the air around him, the sounds of sorrow and joy. In the indefinite and disembodied feel of its harmonies and its flexible time signatures, Rachmaninoff's delicate setting aptly captures the ethereal mood of musical inspiration. The ninth song, *The Poet*, is a monologue taken from Tyutchev's poem 'You beheld him', which

Ex.127

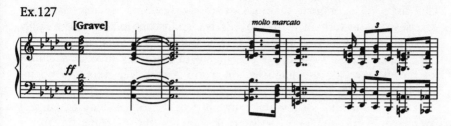

compares the gloom of a moody poet with the pallor and exhaustion of the moon in day-time; but just as the moon has its time for shining bright, so too the poet. As with the other Chaliapin songs, the dramatic style of the setting is obviously tailored to suit the manner of the singer, and it goes hand in hand with a certain lack of lyrical warmth, as the harsh and wayward harmonies of the piano introduction show. In No. 10, *The Morn of Life*, another Tyutchev setting, this time dedicated to Sobinov, the poet recalls the morning on which his beloved first declared her love to him, changing his whole world. Rachmaninoff's delicately lyrical setting has a touching simplicity. According to Nezhdanova, this was Rachmaninoff's favourite song in the group.[40] Number 11, *With holy banner firmly held*, is a setting of Fet's poem 'The Peasant', and tells of a crusader singing the praises of the Lord, confident of finally arriving at the gates of Heaven. The song is another powerful vehicle for Chaliapin, but its insistent trochaic rhythm becomes rather wearing by the end.

Number 12, *What wealth of rapture*, to a love poem by Fet and dedicated to Sobinov, is one of the very finest of all Rachmaninoff's songs, for the music faithfully reflects all the psychological subtleties of the poem within a framework of glorious lyricism. The opening quaver triplets in the accompaniment (*allegro con fuoco*) perfectly set the scene, capturing in one bar the racing of the pulse as the lover finds himself alone with his beloved. This is immediately contrasted with a feeling of wonder on seeing the night above them and the stars reflected in the river. The original tempo is abruptly resumed as interest again focuses on the turmoil in the lover's heart, and the excitement steadily mounts, the vocal part becoming increasingly strenuous, until, unable to contain himself any longer, he finally declares his love in a climax of the most passionate intensity, on a top A (the key note), saved for this moment. The elaborate piano postlude, which prolongs the mood of ecstasy, contains an intriguing instance of the universality of musical language in the similarity between its opening and a climactic phrase in Vaughan Williams's love song *Silent Noon*, written nine years before, of which Rachmaninoff surely cannot possibly have been aware (Ex. 128).

Number 13, *Dissonance*, is dedicated to another famous singer, the dramatic soprano Feliya Litvin (1861–1936), who happened to be related to Rachmaninoff's Grandmother Butakova. It has an unusually adventurous text by Polonsky, describing a woman's unrealized erotic fantasies; tired of her present lover she conjures up in her mind a picture of a romantic assignation. The setting of this dramatic monologue is the longest and perhaps most subtle of the whole group; it is notable for the musical freedom with which the composer closely follows the strained emotional undertones of the poem – there are six changes of key and thirty-three changes of time signature. In 1916 Litvin's pupil Nina Koshetz urged Rachmaninoff to orchestrate the song for concert performance but, although he seems to have agreed, nothing came of this.[41]

The final song in Op. 34, postdating the other settings by nearly three years, is the famous wordless *Vocalise*, dedicated to the coloratura soprano Antonina Nezhdanova. When the singer expressed her regret to the composer that there was no text, Rachmaninoff replied, flatteringly but uninformatively, 'What need is there of words, when you will be able to convey everything better and more expressively than anyone could with words by your voice and interpretation?'[42] But what is expressed in *Vocalise*? Just when the piece was written is not entirely certain, though the first draft was made before April 1915,[43] and the manuscript of the final version bears the words '21st September 1915, Moscow'. The pervasive feeling of mourning and loss in the music and the repeated references to the first four notes of *Dies irae* in the opening phrases suggest that it may have been written in response to a death or deaths, perhaps, like the setting for voice and piano *From St John's Gospel* Rachmaninoff had made a few months earlier, a reaction to the carnage of the Great War. In its great lyrical outpouring there is more than a suggestion of the baroque, and Rachmaninoff later responded enthusiastically to the suggestion that it should be performed like a Bach aria.[44] *Vocalise* quickly became the public favourite of all the songs in Op. 34, which have otherwise been neglected by performers, and the composer made an orchestral version at the suggestion of

Ex.128a   Rachmaninoff: *What wealth of rapture* (1912)

Ex.128b   Vaughan Williams: *Silent Noon* [D.G. Rossetti] (1903)

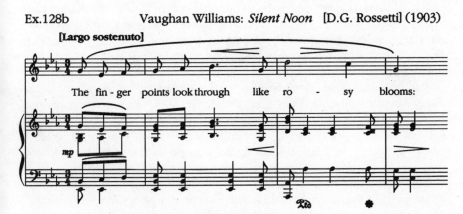

Nikolay Struve, after the highly successful premiere of the work by
Nezhdanova and himself at an orchestral concert by Koussevitzky in
January 1916. Although it was not the first specimen of a wordless
song in Russian music (it was preceded by Stravinsky's *Pastorale* of
1907), *Vocalise* was the forefather of Medtner's *Sonata-Vocalise* and
Suite-Vocalise, Op.42, and of such works as Glière's Concerto for
Coloratura and Orchestra, Op. 82.

The Bells, Op. 35

Back in Moscow after the summer, Rachmaninoff resumed his concert
schedule. Between 6 October and 1 December 1912 he conducted eight
concerts, five for the Moscow Philharmonic Society; in none of them
was his own music included. As he had neither conducted nor perhaps
even seen most of the programmed works before, intensive preparation
and effort was involved. For a concert hurriedly arranged as a tribute
to the recently deceased Ilya Satz (1875–1912), the now-forgotten com-

poser of incidental music for productions at the Moscow Art Theatre, Rachmaninoff not only conducted but helped Glière to put the manuscripts in order and to make the necessary choral and orchestral transcriptions.[45] All this frantic activity took a toll on his health. Already after the very first concert stiffness in his hands caused him to cancel an engagement in Petersburg on 17 November to play Tchaikovsky's First Concerto and, having finally decided to break away from this punishing routine altogether, Rachmaninoff withdrew from a sixth Philharmonic Society concert to leave on 5 December with his family for a month's recuperation in Switzerland, followed by eight weeks in Italy. In Rome, though the family put up at a boarding-house, for his work Rachmaninoff was able to use Modest Tchaikovsky's flat, where his composer brother had stayed and worked, and it was in this atmosphere of peace and seclusion, with the added stimulus of working at the same table as his master, that Rachmaninoff wrote both his choral symphony *The Bells*[46] and the Second Piano Sonata.

Rachmaninoff was not the first composer to be attracted to Edgar Allan Poe's poem 'The Bells', for already in 1906 the first performance had been given in Birmingham under Hans Richter, no less, of a setting for voices and orchestra by the English composer Joseph Holbrooke (1878–1958). In this same year Rachmaninoff had written to Morozov asking him to let him know if he came across a suitable text for a cantata he wished to write to follow his *Spring*,[47] and then, five-and-a-half years later, in the summer of 1912, he 'sketched a plan for a symphony'.[48] These two projects suddenly coalesced when, out of the blue, Rachmaninoff received from an unknown admirer[49] a typed copy of Balmont's free version of 'The Bells' (Poe was well-known in Russia in translation). Not only did the poem's general mood of fatalism match Rachmaninoff's own philosophy of life, but the subject matter gave an opportunity at last to give overt musical expression to the bell sounds which had obsessed him for so long. The use of three soloists and a chorus in addition to more massive orchestral forces than in any of his earlier works underlines the fact that with *The Bells* Rachmaninoff set out to write his most ambitious work. Sketched in Italy, the new work was orchestrated in the summer back at Ivanovka; Rachmaninoff dedicated it to Willem Mengelberg and the Concertgebouw Orchestra, with whom he particularly enjoyed playing.[50]

Each of the four stanzas of Poe's poem apostrophizes a different kind of bell, associated in turn with different stages in human life. Thus, silver sleigh-bells symbolize birth and youth, golden bells marriage; bronze is the metal of the fire alarum bells, the harbingers of terror, and the tolling of the iron funeral bell marks a man's last rites on earth. The scheme of the poem naturally suggested a four-movement musical structure, on which the order of events, two joyful, two sad, inevitably imposed a lugubrious finale; a Russian precedent for this of course already existed in Tchaikovsky's 'Pathétique' Symphony. How far, if at all, Rachmaninoff's plans for a purely orchestral symphony were incorporated into *The Bells* we have no way of knowing. It is true that in recreating the text in musical terms Rachmaninoff assigned a more important role to the orchestra than to the soloists and that, as in his earlier orchestral symphonies, there is a strong element of musical continuity between the movements. On the other hand, the remote relationship of the keys of the four movements – A flat, D major, F minor, C sharp minor – suggests four separate tableaux. Rachmaninoff called his work a 'choral symphony' – 'I would rather not call it a "cantata"'[51] – and when it was first performed in America it was billed as the composer's 'Third Symphony'. The scoring, though laid out on the most elaborate scale, avoids the opacity of parts of the Second Symphony, and its successful combination of richness and transparency proves unequivocally that the mastery which commentators have always recognized in the orchestral writing of the works of exile was already fully developed in Rachmaninoff by 1913, doubtless partly the result of his experience as a conductor.

The first movement, *Allegro ma non tanto*, opens with tremulous woodwind phrases, imitating the distant sound of tiny sleigh bells. Rachmaninoff makes a dramatic contrast between the tenor soloist's whispered entry on a held E flat, inviting us to 'listen', as a hush of expectation falls over the orchestral accompaniment, and the chorus's *fortissimo* response, excitingly augmented by the whole orchestra. Although the composer never wrote any music more exuberant than this movement, a shadow is cast by the soloist's reference to the 'universal slumber' which awaits men at the end of their days, reminding us that even the dawn of life and carefree youth are stages along the path to death. The use of the chorus hypnotically chanting a wordless funeral refrain at this point to shuddering macabre gestures on the strings is a particularly imaginative touch. The soloist and chorus blaze out again in a gloriously abrupt return to the major key and a rapturous climax ensues, but the soloist's last words are again of the final oblivion that even the silver bells foretell, and when the orchestra takes over for the concluding bars, there are more presentiments of man's mortality in the rocking string phrases, with their hints of *Dies irae*, a figure which occurs in each of the subsequent movements (Ex. 129).

The second movement, marked *Lento*, is for soprano and orchestra, with the chorus's role occasionally to interject the refrain with which the soloist opens: 'Hear the mellow wedding bells, golden bells'. The unhurried tempo allows a contrast between the adjacent faster movements

Ex.129

Meno mosso. Maestoso

but adds to the melancholy of Rachmaninoff's view of the golden wedding bells of marriage. The orchestral introduction picks up where the previous movement left off, with the bells quietly tolling the *Dies irae* figure. Before the chorus enters, gently and solemnly intoning the same figure, the trumpets briefly sound a menacing alarum, as though the composer were saying that even in the happiness of marriage man is still conscious of terror and mortality. As the movement develops, the figure of the rocking bells is complemented by mournful descending chromatic scales like those found in *The Isle of the Dead*. Indeed, the ecstatic climax built up at figure 42 before the entry of the chorus is very similar to the 'Life' section of that work, reminding us again that life and death co-exist and that love and marriage too are no more than transient stages in human existence; the poignancy of the falling orchestral phrases which follow the soloist's final words makes them among the most memorable in all Rachmaninoff. A lighter touch comes at the end of the movement when, as in Rachmaninoff's setting of 'Praise God in the heavens', No. 16 in *The Liturgy*, the chorus chant the bell figure from the beginning in such a way as themselves to imitate the sound of bells (Ex. 130).

The *Presto* third movement, which tells of the bronze alarum bells, is scored for chorus and orchestra only. As late as 1936, for a performance by Sir Henry Wood at the Sheffield Festival that year, Rachmaninoff simplified some of the choral writing because it had been 'found in previous performances that there were too many notes and words to be chorally effective,'[52] but in doing so arguably also removed some of the impact of the more strenuous original. The extended orchestral forces are deployed to exciting effect and the demonic momentum never falters. The horrors foretold by the fire bells are a metaphor for human fears and the destruction of a man's hopes and aspirations as he goes through life. In a first-rate performance the music conveys terror as convincingly as music ever can, yet again giving the lie to the notion that Rachmaninoff's fatalism was self-indulgent and submissive. In the introduction there is a rapid crescendo of tension as one by one bells join in to proclaim a warning of fire, the clash of different bells tolling irregularly against each other being brilliantly caught by the simple expedient of misplaced accents and pairs of dotted quavers in the horn, piano and cello parts against the three-beat rhythm of the rest of the

Ex.130

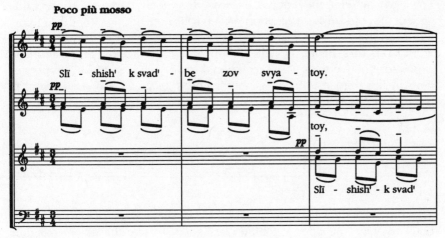

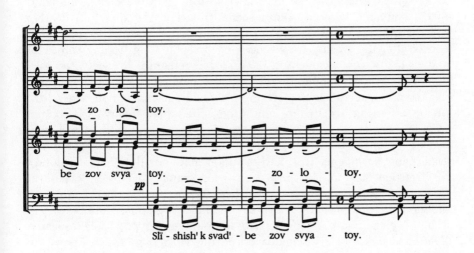

['Hark to the song of the bells, golden bells.']

orchestra. Much use is made throughout the movement of a sobbing descending chromatic phrase, 'How beseeching', and of the *Dies irae* figure, which first appears in the cellos at the beginning of the *Meno mosso* section at figure 64, before 'In afright now approaching', and again at 71 *Poco meno*, before 'Toll their frantic supplication', the chorus themselves articulating the first four notes at 83 with 'feebly ye compare'. Towards the end the chorus express their total despair: 'All is vain, and in hopelessness resignation', over four-note groups of descending thirds on cellos, a figure taken from the orchestral introduction to the work (1 before figure 1), where, full of life and joyful expectation, it expresses the very opposite emotional state. The figure as it appears here in the third movement is the same as Rachmaninoff uses again at the end of the last movement to depict man's final resignation in death:

Ex.131

The final movement, *Lento lugubre*, depicts the iron funeral bell. Not until the very end does a glimmer of light penetrate the gloom hanging over these pages like a pall. The plaintive sound of the cor anglais is used to introduce the main theme over a rocking string accompaniment of Rachmaninoff's favourite interval of a fifth. With the bleak monotone of his entry the baritone soloist seems frozen to the spot in a deathly still, before he launches into his comfortless threnody. The despairing climax after the words, 'heavy moaning their intoning waxing sorrowful and deep', which includes the inescapable reference to *Dies irae*, well demonstrates the sumptuousness and the typically meticulous dynamic markings of Rachmaninoff's scoring (Plate 12). Rachmaninoff's treatment of the following section, in which the spirit of the belfry is described as 'a sombre fiend that dwells in the shadow of the bells', is strikingly similar to Elgar's depiction of the demons in *The Dream of Gerontius*, confirming suspicions that Rachmaninoff had heard this work during his Dresden stay. A conscious borrowing from Tchaikovsky occurs at figure 105, 'Glad endeavour quenched forever in the silence and the gloom', made explicit by the note on the autograph of the score, 'P. Tch.'. Rachmaninoff obviously had in mind the hypnotically repeated tremulous figure of six semiquavers in the viola part, which opens the scene in the Countess's bedroom in the Second Act of *The Queen of Spades*, an opera he had conducted the previous year, and the falling phrase used at the end of the same scene when the Countess has died, which he slightly recast (Ex. 132).

In the quiet aftermath the descending four-note figure of resignation from the previous movement returns to the strings, this time sinking slowly down into apathy, as the chorus again intones the pairs of bell notes with mouths closed and the soloist too descends in a spirit of final submission and surrender: 'there is neither rest not respite, save

Ex.132a   Tchaikovsky:*Queen of Spades*, Act 2, sc.2

Ex.132b   Rachmaninoff: *The Bells*, 4th movement

the quiet of the tomb'. It is at this point that Rachmaninoff departs from the macabre gloom of his text and imposes his own less cynical philosophy on the final pages. The strings climb up to re-establish at last the calm and optimism of D flat with which the symphony started, a tonality as remote as possible from the despairing C sharp minor at the beginning of the movement. Rachmaninoff's music here has an unmistakable spirit of consolation and confidence, a mood of serenity in which resignation is untouched by despair, and a sweetness, almost to excess, which is beyond mortal care.

The first performances of *The Bells* in Petersburg and then Moscow in November and December of 1913 under the composer's direction aroused extraordinary public enthusiasm, and it is not clear why, unlike other Rachmaninoff scores of the time, the work was not published until 1920. In the autumn of 1914 Wood scheduled *The Bells* for performance at the Sheffield Festival, for which Fanny Copeland made the now-familiar English translation (quoted here), apparently from a German version of the Russian and so at three removes from the original.[53] However, the outbreak of the First World War and the consequent impossibility of obtaining copies of the still unpublished score caused this performance to be cancelled, and it was not until 1921 in Liverpool that Wood conducted the work for the first time. A remarkably similar thing happened in April 1938 when, after a twenty-one-year retirement from conducting, Rachmaninoff himself agreed to direct a performance in Vienna, only to be prevented from doing so by Hitler's *Anschluss*. He did however conduct the work in Philadelphia and New York in the 'Rachmaninoff Cycle' of 1939–1940, and twice in Chicago in 1941, his last appearances anywhere as conductor.

Piano Sonata No. 2 in B Flat Minor, Op. 36

Despite the serious illness of his two daughters, which cut short the family's stay in Rome, in the eight weeks he was there Rachmaninoff was able to sketch out not only his choral symphony but also the Second Piano Sonata, which he completed back at Ivanovka in August and September 1913. In a sense the two works can be said to share their inspiration, the sonata no less than the symphony deserving to be called 'The Bells', for it translates their language into piano sonority. Rachmaninoff dedicated the sonata to his boyhood friend Matvey Pressman, who had shared his life in the Zverev years and to whom he had dedicated his very first piano piece more than a quarter of a century before. Pressman's dismissal from his post as director of the music school of the Russian Musical Society at Rostov-on-Don had prompted Rachmaninoff to support him publicly by resigning from the vice-presidency of the Society in May 1912, and the sonata's dedication a year later was a further kind gesture after what must have been a difficult time.

The Second Piano Sonata not only takes its general tone and dramatic plan from the Third Concerto but shares with it a number of structural features, including: three musically interrelated movements; a contrasting pair of themes in the outer movements and a single idea freely treated in the middle; a quiet close to the opening movement and a precipitate launch into the last, where a rhythmic first theme is contrasted with a Rachmaninoff 'big tune' (not, however, a memorable example of the genre in the sonata), which is decked out in all its finery for its final appearance. Another unmistakable correspondence is the similarity between the second subjects of the respective opening movements in the way in which they were both evidently created by the composer improvising around the tonic chord (Ex. 133). Even the two bars which round off the initial statement of the theme in the second movement are, despite the differences of key and time signature, remarkably similar (Ex. 134).

A conspicuous difference between the two works, however, is the sonata's emotionally cooler and more objective lyricism, a tendency already seen in the Op. 34 songs. It was this feature which particularly

Ex.133a

Second Sonata

Ex.133b

Third Concerto

struck critics when the composer premiered the work in Moscow on 3 December 1913. ' The sonata,' wrote Boris Tyuneyev,[54] ' is the composition of a mature and great talent ... but you will find Rachmaninoff the lyricist in it in only a very small degree – rather the reverse: there is a certain inner reserve, severity and introspection. The composer speaks more of the intellect out of the intellect than of the heart out of the heart' – an opinion endorsed by Engel.[55] Certainly there is great interest in observing the composer's skill in integrating his musical material. For example, the imperious semiquaver-crotchet descending third at the beginning of the sonata's second bar not only informs the ensuing accompanying figure but influences the outline of the bell-like melody of the second movement, which itself predictably is also imprinted with *Dies irae* (Ex. 135).

Similarly, the descending figure of the opening motto of the sonata transmogrifies itself into the gently plaintive first movement second

Ex.134a

Second Sonata

Ex.134b

Third Concerto

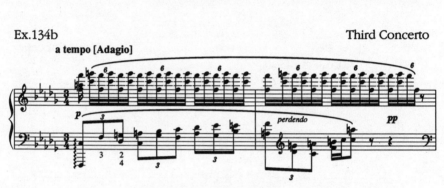

Ex.135

subject (Ex. 133a), is recalled in the middle of the second movement, shapes the descending semi-quaver flourish at the opening of the finale and appears at the end of the statement of that movement's first theme. The ingenuity Rachmaninoff shows in manipulating his material is reflected also in the complex polyphony, and this arguably excessive elaboration later caused him misgivings. In 1931, eighteen years after its conception, Rachmaninoff emasculated the sonata in an extensive revision (see pp. 320–323).

Another piano composition most likely dating from the time of the Second Piano Sonata[56] is Rachmaninoff's transcription of his song *Lilacs*, from Op. 21. Compared with the original, the writing in the new version is considerably more complex and polyphonic, the composer changing the time signature and adding cadenzas and a coda, to turn a simple song into a succulent recital item or encore.

The autumn of 1913 saw Rachmaninoff embark on his heaviest concert season yet, with eight appearances in England and thirty-six in Russia. Retiring to Ivanovka for the spring and summer of 1914, he received an invitation to make a setting for the Shakespeare 350th anniversary celebrations of the Scene on the Heath from *King Lear* ('Blow, winds, and crack your cheeks!'), but nothing came of this. Instead the composer spent some time corresponding with Goldenweiser, who was preparing for publication the vocal score of *The Bells*, and devoted much energy to farming. By the time he returned to Moscow in October, the Great War had broken out. Rachmaninoff's first musical response to these dark times seems to have been the brief setting for voice and piano of the well-known verse from St John: 'Greater love hath no man than this, that a man lay down his life for his friends',[57] which he wrote for an album published by Jurgenson in 1915 for war relief, to which other composers, writers and artists also contributed.[58] Although the publication reproduced in facsimile a date – 16 February 1915 – with Rachmaninoff's signature, in the chronology he drew up only two years later for Asafyev the composer himself assigned this piece to the previous autumn. It is no jingoistic statement of heroism; we know that Rachmaninoff was deeply affected by the war, and the dramatic descending scales in the accompaniment, the soloist's impassioned declamatory phrases and the music's harmonically ambivalent end, stranded and unresolved, like the conflict itself, all reflect a feeling of profound anguish.

The 1914–15 season's concert schedule – the proceeds of which were mainly devoted to war relief – was considerably lighter than the preceding year's, with Rachmaninoff making just nine appearances in all between October and March. The composer wrote to Siloti on 1 November that his work was 'at a standstill' but that he was nevertheless looking round for suitable material for composition:

I want to get hold of a subject for a ballet. Do you know Fokine or any of the Petersburg dancers, and would you ask around them about this? Fokine is best. For my part, I'll approach the Moscow dancers, though I don't know any of them and for some reason I'm afraid of them!... A few days ago this ballet idea suddenly entered my head. I believe that if someone were now to give me a good interesting theme which I liked I would start to write immediately.

The notion to write a ballet had first been sown that spring by a regisseur at the Maryinsky Theatre, Samuel Andrianov, but it was finally from Moscow that Rachmaninoff got help, when a young choreographer, Kasyan Goleyzovsky, using an idea given him by the Director of the Bolshoi ballet company, Alexander Gorsky, wrote a libretto after a poem of Balmont for a ballet called 'The Scythians'. There is tantalizingly little evidence for the whole episode, but it does seem that Rachmaninoff went so far as to make musical sketches for the ballet, for a fragment of the text still exists in the Rachmaninoff archive in Moscow, dated 22 April 1915, bearing the interesting note by Goleyzovsky: 'Tell Sergei that ——— [illegible] would like to listen to the sketches for the first scene and for the final symphonic dance'. A notice even appeared in the press about the project,[59] and later Goleyzovsky claimed – though there is no other evidence to substantiate the assertion – that Rachmaninoff completed 'a significant part' of the ballet and that he incorporated the music into his last work, the *Symphonic Dances*, written in 1940. The very title of that work seems almost a conscious re-use of the descriptive phrase 'symphonic dance' that Goleyzovsky had used twenty-five years before, presumably echoing the composer's own terminology.

A Rachmaninoff ballet at the Bolshoi in an intriguing notion indeed, and it is interesting to speculate on why the composer may have chosen not to complete *The Scythians*. He must have been aware of Diaghilev's successes in Paris, even of the definitive balletic study of paganism, Stravinsky's *Rite of Spring* of 1913. He may have come to hear also of Diaghilev's recent commission to Prokofiev to write *Ala and Lolly*, which finally emerged in 1915 as *The Scythian Suite*, the premiere of which in January 1916 he attended, and perhaps felt that the time was not opportune to set himself up in musical rivalry with the modernists by writing a third ballet on the same theme. At all events, not a note of the music survives. In March 1916 Rachmaninoff was again asked to write a ballet, this time by the famous stage director Vsevolod Meyerhold and the dancer Mikhail Mordkin. Marietta Shaginyan, to whom Rachmaninoff, with characteristic secrecy, breathed not a word about the Goleyzovsky project, agreed to try to find a suitable subject in the stories of Hans Andersen and wrote out notes for the composer on *The Little Mermaid*, *The Snow Queen* and *The Garden of Paradise*. According to her account,[60] Rachmaninoff was genuinely interested in

The Garden of Paradise, even going so far as to telephone to ask her to supply him with further details, but in the end nothing came of the project, and more than twenty years were to pass before Rachmaninoff's name was associated with ballet, when the *Paganini Rhapsody* was choreographed by Fokine, the very ballet-master he first had in mind back in 1914.

All-Night Vigil, Op. 37

In January and February 1915, in less than two weeks, Rachmaninoff wrote the fifteen unaccompanied motets that go to make up his religious masterpiece, the *All-Night Vigil*, commonly but mistakenly known in the West as the 'Vesper Mass'. No correspondence of Rachmaninoff survives from the period of its composition, but the composer spoke about the work at some length to Riesemann in 1930.[61] The immediate prompting to write another major religious work after the *Liturgy* was apparently a performance of that work, most likely the one he himself conducted in St Petersburg in February 1914, which seems to have convinced him that the style in which it had been cast was unsatisfactory. In setting the Vigil Rachmaninoff admitted to being influenced by Alexander Kastalsky, now Director of the Moscow Synodal School, but it was to the memory of his predecessor, Stepan Smolensky, that the new work was dedicated. Following his usual practice, Rachmaninoff took the *Vigil* for evaluation to his old teacher Taneyev, whose enthusiastic praise turned out to be the last he ever received before Taneyev's untimely death four months later.

Whereas in the *Liturgy* he had used wholly his own musical material, in the *All-Night Vigil* Rachmaninoff turned in the main to traditional ancient plainchants. Originally these are believed to have come to Russia with Christianity from Byzantium, though they doubtless soon assumed a Russian identity. For centuries they were passed on by oral tradition and only much later written down, not in Western notation but by a series of signs ('znameni'); hence the name 'znamenny' chant – the chant written in signs.[62] In the seventeenth century, in which the so-called Great Schism took place in the Orthodox Church, the znamenny began to be superseded by new and simpler chants, such as the Greek and Kiev chants, and by Western importations. The use of Western musical notation became standard practice, bringing with it the introduction of polyphony. During the eighteenth century the znamenny lapsed into disuse in the mainstream church but lingered on among the religious dissenters, 'The Old Believers', who clung to traditional practices. However, the transcription and publication of four books of the old chants by the Holy Synod in 1772 rescued the znamenny from general oblivion, though it was not until more than a century later that active interest in the ancient melodies was revived by Smolensky, whose classes in church music Rachmaninoff had attended at the Moscow Conservatoire, and by Kastalsky, who made settings of a number of the old chants and who had advised Rachmaninoff over the composition of the *Liturgy*. In making his version of the Vigil in 1882, Tchaikovsky had used only material from the *Obikhod*, the collection of the daily round of services made by the Director of the Imperial Court Chapel, Bakhmetev, in the 1860s, which included many of the later chants. Although Rachmaninoff eschewed this unadventurous approach, a composer was nevertheless obliged by the rules of the Church to incorporate certain of the traditional chants into any setting, and in four numbers of his own *Vigil* Rachmaninoff reworked material Tchaikovsky had already used. The chants Rachmaninoff chose are: five znamenny, two Greek, two Kiev, and six of his own invention, which he described as 'conscious counterfeits':[63]

Item	Text	Chant
VESPERS		
1 *Invitatory*	'O come, let us worship'	Original
2 *Verses from Psalm 104* (Psalm 103 in the Orthodox Church)	'Praise the Lord, O my soul'	Greek
3 *Verses from Psalms 1–3*	'Blessed is the man who walks not in the counsel of the wicked'	Original
4 *Vesper Hymn*	'O joyful light of the holy glory of the immortal Father'	Kiev
5 *Nunc dimittis*	'Lord, now lettest Thou Thy servant depart in peace'	Kiev
6 *Ave Maria*	'Hail, Mother of God, the Virgin Mary'	Original
MATINS		
7 *Gloria*	'Glory to God on high, and on earth peace, good will among men'	Znamenny

8	*Laudate Dominum –* verses from Psalms 135 and 136 (134 and 135 in the Orthodox Church)	'Praise ye the name of the Lord, alleluia'	Znamenny
9	*Resurrection Hymn*	'Blessed art Thou, O Lord; teach me Thy statutes'	Znamenny
10	*Veneration of the Cross*	'We have seen the Resurrection of Christ'	Original
11	*Magnificat*	'My soul doth magnify the Lord'	Original
12	*Gloria*	'Glory to God on high, and on earth peace, good will among men'	Original
13	*Resurrection Hymn*	'Today is salvation come unto the world'	Znamenny
14	*Resurrection Hymn*	'Rising from the tomb and bursting the bonds of hell asunder'	Znamenny
15	*Theotokion – Hymn to the Mother of God*	'To thee, O Virgin, the chosen guide'	Greek

In the pattern of worship of the Russian Orthodox Church the Vigil is the service observed on the eve of holy days. In churches it is celebrated on Saturday evening; in monasteries it begins at 6 o'clock on Saturday evening and finishes at 9 o'clock the following morning, and therefore embraces the offices of both Vespers and Matins.[64] In the service the fifteen numbers of Rachmaninoff's setting would not be sung consecutively but would be separated by prayers, litanies, readings and troparia (antiphons relating to particular feast days); the variable parts of the service would use traditional musical settings.

Since the *Vigil* demonstrates an absolute unity of style, Rachmaninoff's particular choice of chants is a subject of concern only to specialists; what is interesting to the layman is their treatment by the composer not as untouchable antiques but as thematic material to be moulded with the greatest plasticity. A feature of all Russian Orthodox Church music is the constant repetition of the melody of a piece, and in the *Vigil* the structure of each motet evolves naturally from the infinitely varied repetition of the brief diatonic substance of the chant, with subtle changes to outline, rhythm, harmony and vocal orchestration. To fit the sacred texts there is total rhythmic flexibility, eight of the numbers lacking a time signature altogether. Harmonically and contrapuntally Rachmaninoff is somewhat more enterprising than in the *Liturgy*, though the restraint exercised by the demands of the genre in which he was working effaces his public identity. He later admitted to being influenced in the manner of the setting by Kastalsky, 'the Rimsky-Korsakov of Russian choral music',[65] but he far surpassed his mentor, not least in the choral writing where, particularly by exploiting the fabled Russian basses, he created a range of vocal tonal effects to match any orchestral score. The texts Rachmaninoff treats as he would a poem for a song setting, closely echoing psychological nuances and dramatizing narrative. The solos are like brief character roles, and overall the *Vigil* often recalls Russian opera. The Church itself would almost certainly have looked askance at the dramatic treatment of the text, and the complexity of the choral writing would have made the setting impractical for regular church performance. The conscious musical contrast between the different numbers makes the work into a satisfying whole, and confirms the impression that Rachmaninoff saw his *Vigil* essentially in terms of concert, not church, performance, while at the same time being a personal expression of his own religious faith.

The *Vigil* opens with the *Invitatory*, one of Rachmaninoff's 'conscious counterfeits', a four times repeated summons to the faithful to come and worship God. After these sonorously fervent outbursts, the quietly reverent ending comes as a surprise but establishes at the outset what becomes a regular pattern throughout the work. The *Psalm of Intro- duction*, 'Praise the Lord, O my soul', had to incorporate the so-called Greek chant, given here to the alto soloist, who sings the narrative against the men's voices in a low register and throws into relief the interpolated choral refrains. The melody itself is not specially remarkable, but there is extraordinary beauty in the restrained choral accompaniment, with tenors and basses using Rachmaninoff's favourite choral device of humming with closed mouths. The descending scale for basses at the end of the piece, down to a bottom C, is only the first of several passages in the *Vigil* indissoluble from the unique growling timbre of Russian voices and making convincing performances by others so difficult. In the service there follows the *Great Litany* and then No. 3, a setting from the Psalter, 'Blessed is the man', in which the narrative, given mainly to altos and tenors, is interspersed with 'Alleluias' for the whole choir, underpinned by the sonorous weight of basses. The 'Alleluias' are fervently gentle, and although they rise in tone with each repetition, instead of the expected final climax, with glorious perversity they diminish to a memorably quiet end. In the service the *Small Litany* follows.

The Kiev chant which forms the basis of No. 4, the *Vesper Hymn*, is the simplest melody imaginable, a scale descending from the tonic a fourth and then climbing back again. The tenors start by singing the chant in its ancient form, in unison, and gradually all the other voices join in, Rachmaninoff finally dividing tenors and basses into three parts. The brief one-line tenor solo picks out for emphasis the essential purpose of this, or any other, hymn: 'We praise the Father, Son and Holy Ghost: God!' Then, in the church service come versicles, responses and prayers, until what was understandably Rachmaninoff's own favourite among the numbers in the *Vigil*, the *Nunc dimittis*, which the composer wished to be sung at his own funeral, although in the event this could not be arranged.[66] This is the only wholly solo number in the whole composition. The tenor sings a singularly beautiful melody over pairs of rocking choral chords, which evoke a distant echo of *Dies irae* and have a family relationship with the similar figure in *The Bells*. After the central climax the gentle descent by the basses down to a final subterranean B flat is one of the most memorable moments in the whole work. It is scarcely surprising that the first conductor of the piece doubted being able to find basses to cope – ' They are as rare as asparagus at Christmas!'[67] Readings and prayers precede the *Ave Maria*, in which the dynamics of Rachmaninoff's setting rise above *piano* only once and then only briefly, and on this quiet note of meditation the service of the *Great Vespers* ends, after the blessing.

Matins opens with a marvellous setting of the *Gloria*, which combines restraint of expression with an extreme richness of choral tone ringing out like the tolling of numerous bells. As Alfred Swan has pointed out,[68] the gorgeous decoration recalls Giovanni Gabrieli (Ex. 136). The end, in characteristic paradox, is quiet.

After a versicle comes No. 8, *Praise ye the name of the Lord*, which, like *the Great Litany*, has 'Alleluias' set between the verses. The dramatic contrasts Rachmaninoff creates in the choral writing of the *Vigil* are exemplified in the opening of this number, where sopranos in three parts and tenors in two, sing quietly in a high register against the deeper tones of altos and basses singing the znamenny chant *forte* and in unison (Ex. 137). The setting is remarkable for its rhythmic vigour and fervour, and at climaxes the intensity of tone demanded presses the limits of vocal resources.

Number 9, in which the chorus retells the story of the Resurrection, is one of the most elaborate items in the whole composition and illustrates the way in which Rachmaninoff uses countless rhythmic and harmonic variations and choral shadings of a brief chant for a whole narrative. Thus the same flexible formula serves both for the stern opening refrain for tenors and basses, 'Blessed art thou, O Lord, Teach me thy statutes' and, contrastingly slower, for the soprano and alto

Ex.136

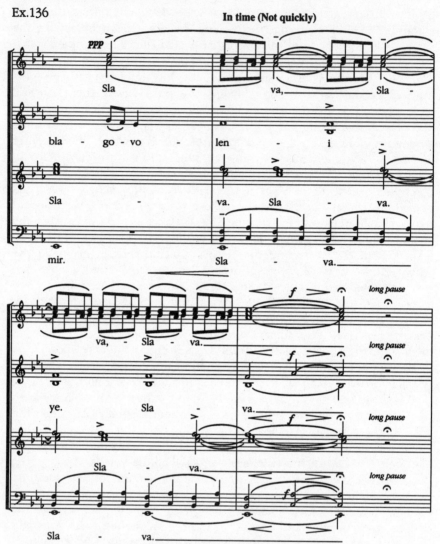

[Glory to God on high and on earth peace, good will toward men.]

statement of the angel host's amazement at finding Our Lord alive and for the angel telling the women to look at the tomb. With changed harmonies it assumes an air of plangency for the arrival of the women, weeping, at the tomb, and of compassion when the tenor soloist recounts how the angel told the women to cease their sorrow. Then, quiet but more animated and with elements of major tonality for the first time, it serves for the *Gloria* and later for the 'Alleluias', chiming out in celebration like tolling bells. A particularly delightful feature of this

Ex.137 **Not quickly**

[Praise the name of the Lord. Alleluia.]

piece is the way in which the different paragraphs are joined by a single held note, usually hummed. In the service the *Small Litany*, versicles and a Gospel reading would follow, before No. 10, *Veneration of the Cross*, a call to worship and praise. As so often in the work, after a blazing outburst, depicting joy at the Resurrection, the quiet ending is outstandingly beautiful. The shape of the 'counterfeit' chant closely resembles the opening theme of the composer's Third Concerto, whose key it shares. It is interesting that this theme too is first given out on the piano in unison, like a plainchant (Ex. 138).

In No. 11, the *Magnificat*, dramatic outbursts are contrasted with interludes of quiet meditation. The richly instrumented choral narrative

Ex.138a   *Veneration of the Cross*

Not quickly

[Having seen Christ's resurrection]

Ex.138b   **Third Concerto**

Allegro ma non tanto
commodo

contains within it a contrasting high refrain, in which the basses are omitted, venerating the Theotokos, Mother of God, 'Greater in honour than the Cherubim', so simple yet so hauntingly beautiful, as always in the *Vigil*, especially so at its final appearance. Further prayers precede No. 12, *Gloria in excelsis Deo*, appended to which are some verses from the 'Te Deum' and from Psalm 90, 'Lord, Thou hast been our dwelling place'. This provides another series of dramatic contrasts of choral tone, from a single part taking the melodic line against *pianissimo* held notes to eight-part writing of great blocks of sound at the fervent climax. The two penultimate numbers, 13 and 14, are both Resurrection hymns, emphasizing the significance of the event in the worship of the Orthodox Church. The latter hymn, in particular, is quietly redolent of the blissful peace Christ gave the world through His Resurrection. Finally, in radiant animation, the *Vigil* closes with the *Theotokion*, a brief hymn of joy to the Mother of God.

The *All-Night Vigil* was given its premiere by the Moscow Synodal Choir under Nikolay Danilin in March 1915, and such was its enthusiastic reception by public and critics alike that four performances were immediately arranged. However, the circumstances of war-time were inauspicious for the launch of any new work, and the outbreak of the October Revolution only two years later and the state's changed attitude to the Church perhaps prevented the work from achieving the recognition, and the performances, due to it. Nevertheless it began to enter the active repertoire of Russian choirs, and after settling in America Rachmaninoff himself learned of a performance in Kazan in 1922 and two in Moscow in 1926 by the Synodal Choir. Even so, Rachmaninoff's turned out to be a final but glorious contribution to a tradition interrupted by history. Outside Russia a supposedly authorized English version of the *Vigil*, published in America in 1920,[69] which diluted the vigour of the original by assimilating some of the short syllables in the translation, never got off the ground, and so for fifty years the work remained in general obscurity, though one Soviet commentator at least has expressed the view that the style of choral writing influenced later composers, such as Sviridov (b.1915) and Shchedrin (b.1932).[70] At any rate, in 1965, in changed circumstances, the State Academic Choir of Moscow under their conductor Alexander Sveshnikov made a definitive recording, and at last more than lip-service began to be paid to what by any standards is a formidable creative achievement, arguably, taking even Stravinsky's *Symphony of Psalms* into account, the supreme masterpiece of Russian sacred music.

Sometime before April 1915 Rachmaninoff sketched out *Vocalise*, but in April his routine was upset by his wife's falling ill with pneumonia and then by the unexpected news of Scriabin's death. Soon after the funeral he broke with his usual custom and for the summer took his family to Finland where, in June, he was shaken by the news of another death, Taneyev's. The war dragged on, and in August he had to attend a medical inspection, though he was not later called up for service. No compositions came from the summer holiday but instead Rachmaninoff prepared for a series of concerts he planned to give in memory of Scriabin. This meant learning a range of works new and clearly not altogether congenial to him, including the *Satanic Poem*, Op. 36, three *Études* from Op. 42 and the Fifth Sonata, Op. 53, of 1908, the most modern Scriabin work he was prepared to perform in public. And so in the 1915–16 concert season, in addition to touring Russian cities with his own Second and Third Concertos in aid of war charities, Rachmaninoff played the Scriabin concerto four times, and of twenty-four recitals devoted twelve to Scriabin's music wholly or in part. Though successful with the general public, they were received unfavourably by those who worshipped at the Scriabin shrine, which must have made them seem to Rachmaninoff something of an artistic disappointment.

Six Songs, Op. 38

The equivocal reception of the Scriabin recitals was but one element in Rachmaninoff's growing dissatisfaction with life and his consequent depression. What had started so many years before as joking about his 'old age' was fast becoming a psychological reality reflected even in his appearance. The self-doubts which had crippled his ability to compose after the failure of the First Symphony in 1897 and which, since his recovery, had been concealed by that famous, inscrutable hauteur of demeanour, had in fact never been far below the surface and now manifested themselves again. Tired and troubled by pains in his wrist, Rachmaninoff went for treatment in May of 1916 to the spa town of Essentuki in the Caucasus, where Shaginyan visited him at the sanatorium and found him giving way to terrible despair and self-pity.

> Rachmaninoff looked haggard and spent ... For the first time in my life I saw tears in his eyes. In the course of our conversation he several times wiped them away but they welled up again. I had never seen him before in such total despair. His voice broke the whole time. He said that he was not working at all, whereas before he always used to work at Ivanovka in the spring; that he had no desire to work and that what galled him was the awareness of being incapable of creative work and the impossibility of being anything more than 'a well-known pianist and a mediocre composer' ... 'If I had always been only that, and recognized it, it would be easier for me, but I did have a talent when I was young; I wish you knew how easily, casually, almost as a joke, I was able to sit down at the piano and turn out any piece, to begin composing in the morning and by evening have it finished. And I still have in me a need for creative work, but the desire to bring it out, the ability to bring it out – all this has gone forever!...' [Rachmaninoff admitted envying Medtner his purposeful and fulfilled life.] 'He lives but I do not and never have – till I was forty I had hopes, but after forty only memories, and that sums up the whole of my life.' He told me about his First Symphony ... He assured me that everything I was constantly writing to him about was already in it, but no-one had seen it. He cited the example of a tree; if you pinch its young shoot with a finger it stops growing, and that is how he was 'pinched' at his very dawn, when he was sending out his shoots ... Any would-be musician not ashamed to court failure in music got crowned with laurels as an innovator, was proclaimed 'advanced', 'original' and God knows what, but his own originality had been stifled in the bud ... He spoke of the impossibility of living in the state he was, and all this in a terrible dead voice, almost that of an old man, with his eyes lifeless and his face grey and ill.[71]

It was at this same meeting, after Rachmaninoff had calmed down, that Shaginyan handed the composer a notebook in which, at his request, she had copied out, as she had done four years before for his Op. 34, a selection of texts she felt suitable for song setting, with fifteen poems by Lermontov and twenty-six by contemporary poets. Who could have guessed on that black afternoon that Rachmaninoff would so soon recover his equilibrium and shortly set a group of these poems as his Op. 38, entirely free of the oppressive gloom of his inner thoughts? No doubt the composer was helped by Shaginyan's reassuring words, by the stimulus of meeting up with his old friends Chaliapin and Stanislavsky, who had also come to Essentuki, and later, when his physical condition was improving, by his moving away from the sepulchral silence of the sanatorium to the more cheerful atmosphere of near-by Kislovodsk. But above all Rachmaninoff's spirits were revived by the company of the twenty-two-year-old soprano whom he had first met at a party in Moscow the previous year and who was also a visitor to Essentuki, Nina Pavlovna Koshetz. Quickly becoming a soloist at Zimin's Private Opera in Petrograd after graduating from Moscow Conservatoire, she had also launched out on a recital career. Rachmaninoff had been impressed by her colourful voice and personality, and they had joined forces in March 1916 for a concert in which he accompanied her in some of his songs. At Essentuki Rachmaninoff made plans with Koshetz for another recital programme of his songs next season, among which was to be the new cycle, which he sketched out in August and September, when he returned to Ivanovka. He and Koshetz premiered the new songs in a recital in Moscow on 24 October, subsequently repeating the programme in Petrograd, Kharkov and Kiev.

The advance in the composer's style observable in the greater musical freedom of the new settings was, as critics of the first performances noted, no doubt prompted by the choice of texts, all of which Rachmaninoff unexpectedly took from contemporary poets associated with the symbolist movement and which in general were more self-consciously artistic than any he had used before. Rachmaninoff was notoriously conservative in his literary taste, and when Shaginyan had sent him a copy of 'An Anthology of Contemporary Russian Modernist Poets' in 1912, he told her he was 'horrified' by most of the verse,[72] and yet some of the poets in that collection were among those whose poems he set in the new cycle, which, for the first time with a group of his songs, he called 'Six Poems for Voice and Piano'. Rachmaninoff may consciously have appropriated the title that Medtner had come to use for all of his songs, or he may have intended to suggest by it that in the new settings he had deliberately made musical form subservient to the sounds and rhythms of the poetic texts. A further difference with his other songs, particularly with the last group, Op. 34, is that whereas each earlier set had been a collection of individual songs written with different singers in mind, the new Op. 38 settings were an integral group written for the singer, Koshetz, to whom they were dedicated.

The text of the first song, *In my garden at night*, a translation by Blok of a poem by Avetik Isaakian, tells of a weeping willow tree, a stock poetic symbol for a woman grieving, whose tears will be dried by the Dawn-Maiden. The shape of the vocal line in this haunting setting seems to be defined by the two simple chords at the outset of the accompaniment, and whether or not because the original poem is of Armenian provenance, there is a vaguely eastern air about the melody, emphasized by the C natural in the third bar:

Ex.139

Noch' - yu v sa-du   u me-nya   pla - chet pla-ku-cha-ya   i - va.

[At night in my garden the weeping willow weeps.]

The opening phrases are instinct with melancholy and lamentation, and between the two stanzas the piano accompaniment echoes this mood with a staccato phrase mournfully descending in semitones, an idea repeated in different form for the vocal climax, the cry 'bitterly', where the top note of each demi-semi-quaver group in the accompaniment also picks out the shape of *Dies irae* in a form familiar from the second movement of *The Bells:*

Ex.140

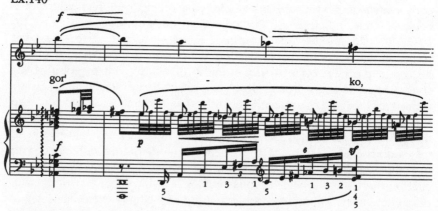

gor'   ko,

Rachmaninoff commented on the poem that the poet had a very musical feeling for nature: 'If they all wrote about nature as he did, we musicians would only have to reach out for the text and a song would be ready'.[73] Rachmaninoff follows the text with its varying lines of seven and eight syllables with total rhythmic freedom, and as in several of the items of the *All-Night Vigil* there is no time signature. So too in much, though not all, of the second song, a setting of an elusive poem *To Her*, by Andrey Bely, which tells of a lover who hears, or imagines he hears, his beloved call to him but waits for her in vain. The basic musical material in *To Her* is typically simple, consisting of the hauntingly repeated chromatic five-note phrase with which the piano part opens and a descending interval of a minor third which Rachmaninoff uses for the lover's despairing cries. The song sinks into a hazy calm of resignation at the end.

The third song, *Daisies*, a naive poem by Igor Severyanin, is one of Rachmaninoff's nature pictures. The poet sees daisies growing in profusion and asks the earth to nourish them. The calmly lyrical melody is given to the piano, with the voice adding its own counterpoint. It is significant that the song later evolved into a piano transcription with relatively little alteration to the piano part. Although the elaborate trills and sinuously chromatic turns in the accompaniment were described by Riesemann[74] as representing nightingale trills, the poetic text makes it plain that these are the flutterings of the silken petals of the daisies. The movement away from the overwhelming lyrical warmth of Rachmaninoff's earlier work towards a cooler and more dispassionate style is demonstrated in *Daisies* no less than in the other songs in this cycle, and the final piano flourish emphasizes this objectivity, with the warmth of the tonic chord eroded by the overlay of extraneous diatonic notes, a development of a trend which had begun with Rachmaninoff's piano transcription of *Lilacs*, made just two years before.

Valery Bryusov's poem *The Pied Piper* derives from the famous legend of the rat catcher of Hamelin, but the piper here lures only a lover, whom he intends faithlessly to abandon. Rachmaninoff's setting is quite unlike any other of his songs in its playful insouciance. The refrain of the pipe is not only vocalized by the singer but is made musically explicit by the spiky rhythmic figure with which the piano part opens and which is present in one form or another throughout the accompaniment. Although metrically free, the setting maintains throughout a regular jaunty rhythm in keeping with the swaggeringly fickle piper of the poem. This is the second of three poems in the group about the inconstancy of women, and the fascination with this theme perhaps adds credence to the view that the composer's association with Koshetz may have been more than merely musical. He is said to have told her that performing the song should come naturally to her since she herself was the pied piper.[75]

The date on the manuscript of the fifth song, *Dreams*, postdates the first public performance, showing yet again that such dates in Rachmaninoff indicate a final version rather than a simple date of composition. The somewhat pretentious poem by Fyodor Sologub describes the magic and unfathomable enchantment of a dream, and in his setting Rachmaninoff marvellously captures the disembodied mood by the simplest of means. The first two notes of the brief phrase in the piano right hand with which, like the call of a pipe, the song opens, B flat and A flat, are repeated and emphasized throughout the accompaniment in the first half, like the half-heard sound of a distant bell ringing, creating an effect of hypnosis in the listener, as the singer soars, entranced, over languid harmonies. The accompaniment then gathers momentum as the 'many mysterious pleasures' in the dream are musically concretized as the tinkling of myriad bells:

Ex.141

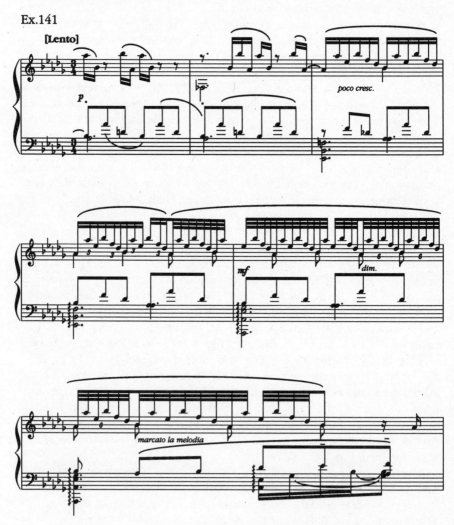

In the second half of the poem, in which the dream is described as having 'a pair of wide wings as light as the midnight mist', the first phrases of the vocal melody are each anticipated by the accompaniment, like a pre-echo from the unconscious mind. In keeping with Rachmaninoff's later style and with the nature of the text, the lyricism is gently dispassionate.

The last song in the group is *A-oo (The Quest)*, a setting of a poem by Balmont in which a lover, deluded by a girl's smile, would fly with her to the mountain slopes but does not know where she is; all he hears is the unanswered echo of his own voice calling to her. While the singer acts out the role of the lover, the psychological nuances of the poem are reflected in the accompaniment. The fluttering semi-quavers of the beginning reflect the lover's eager anticipation, the urgent dactylic rhythm which interrupts them, his bewildered impatience at not having his call answered, leading to an impassioned octave leap on the cries of 'A-oo'. The slackening of tension in the piano postlude *(Meno mosso)* emphasizes the lover's diminishing hopes, and the quiet, unresolved final cadence leaves a question mark, as though he is still listening to the echo, in the vain hope of a reply. It was this last song that Rachmaninoff told Riesemann was his preferred choice in the set,[76] but it is an amusing fact that he seems to have been as inconstant in his affection as the women in the poems he set, for he told Shaginyan that he thought *Daisies* and *The Pied Piper* the most successful songs in the cycle, but Nezhdanova *In my garden at night.*[77]

The notebook with Rachmaninoff's first drafts of Op. 38 contains not six but eight songs. Although the two additional settings were composed integrally with the others,[78] Rachmaninoff decided to withhold them from publication and they remained as sketches. He gave the notebook to Koshetz, who took it with her when she left Soviet Russia in 1920 and kept it until her death in 1965, the songs eventually being published only in 1973, to mark the centenary of the composer's birth.[79] Both are settings of religious poems, and the choice of such texts may be seen as further evidence of the composer's essentially religious disposition, even though at this stage in his life he was still unsure of his own belief. The first, *Prayer*, a naive appeal to God to teach man to lead the good Christian life, is by Grand Duke Konstantinovich, whose poem *The waves dozed* Rachmaninoff had set more than twenty years before as the fourth of his six Choruses, Op. 15. The whole song is built up from the varied repetition of the singer's opening phrase, which evolves out of the natural rhythm of the words and is unmistakably chantlike. The harmony, for Rachmaninoff, is distinctly adventurous, not only highly chromatic but tonally ambivalent, following the precedent of the setting *From St John's Gospel* two years previously. Thus, the plangent entreaty of the opening suggests the key of A flat:

Ex.142

[Teach me, God, to love Thee with all my understanding.]

But this is soon cut across by the second element in the song's musical material, a descending diminished seventh arpeggio in the accompaniment, in the distant key of G. This unsettled clash of tonality seems to lead the music out into distant regions, as though probing remote areas of the mind. Towards the end of the song the two conflicting elements are brought unequivocally together, when the soloist repeats the chant-phrase for the last time, as both the right and left hand of the accompaniment describe the arpeggio figure:

Ex.143

[Teach me, God, how to love.]

After this the song sinks to a submissive close on the chord with which it began, the ambiguous dominant seventh of G major.

The other religious song, *Glory to God*, is another Sologub setting. All things would sing the praises of the Lord, which men repeat from generation to generation. The opening arpeggio prefaces a fluttering accompaniment figure, prominent throughout, which is like the busy pealing of bells, as though they too were distantly ringing in praise:

Ex.144

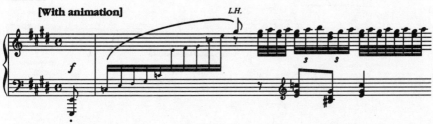

The melodic line in the opening and closing sections develops out of the assertive repetition of the notes of the tonic triad of the different keys through which the music passes – E major, C major, A flat major, A minor and back up to an unequivocal E major for the final page, always chromatically decorated. In the central *cantabile* section, Rachmaninoff's typically close attention to the nuances of the text is once again apparent as the vocal part repeats the line of the accompaniment as the words tell of men repeating word for word the praises they have heard. It is naturally at the words 'And their songs from age to age in varied harmonies they hear anew', that the chromaticism is seen at its extreme (Ex. 145).

Clearly these two religious songs would have sat incongruously among the secular settings of Op. 38, and one can understand Rachmaninoff's reluctance to publish them at the same time, though not his willingness apparently to abandon them; after all, he was not to know that both the circumstances conducive to writing songs, especially religious songs, and the Russian audiences for whom they might be written were soon to disappear from his life for ever. The publication of the two songs so many years after their composition seems to have passed unnoticed by the world at large, and sadly it seems unlikely that these two interesting but ill-starred experiments will be reinstated into the Rachmaninoff canon this late in the day.

Nine Études-Tableaux, Op. 39

When Rachmaninoff returned to Ivanovka from his cure in the summer of 1916, he learned that his father, who had been spending the summer with the family, had two days before suffered a heart attack and died. Though not close for many years, Rachmaninoff had nevertheless

Ex.145

entertained a real affection for the old man and the news must have
come as a painful shock; moreover, he seems for some time to have
been worried by general anxieties about human mortality.

On 5 November 1915, six months before his recent psychological crisis, Rachmaninoff had written to Shaginyan asking if he might see her the next day; the subject he wished to discuss with her turned out to be death itself.[80]

> He asked me in a very anxious and hesitant tone, 'What is your attitude towards death, dear Re? Are you afraid of death?' ... The occurrence of two deaths one after the other – of Scriabin and Taneyev – had affected him deeply, and he had come across a fashionable novel about death and had immediately become ill from terror of it. Before this he had been just a little afraid of robbers, thieves, epidemics, but these, for the most part, he could cope with. It was precisely the uncertainty of death which affected him. It was terrible if there was something after death. Better to rot, disappear, cease to exist: but if there was something else after the grave, that was terrible. What scared him was the uncertainty, the impossibility of knowing ... 'I have never wanted immortality personally. A man wears out, grows old; under old age he grows fed up with himself. I have grown fed up with myself even before old age. But if there is something beyond, then that is terrifying.' He immediately became rather pale and his face began to tremble ...

Though the songs on which Rachmaninoff worked this summer do not at all reflect this dark introspection, the piano pieces he also began to sketch out at this time – the second set of *Études-Tableaux*, Op. 39 – most certainly do. Eight of the nine pieces are in the minor key, and the majority of them feature *Dies irae* in one form or another. Although there is no proof whatever this was due to the death of Rachmaninoff's father, the obsessive recurrence of the chant throughout the set is likely to have come from something more than the usual mystical fascination it had for the composer. Rachmaninoff completed the *Études-Tableaux* back in Moscow in the autumn, giving the first performance (of eight of them) in Petrograd on 29 November 1916, though the dates on the manuscript of two of the pieces characteristically postdate this.[81] It was Rachmaninoff's intention to dedicate the set, like the songs, to Koshetz – she had graduated as a pianist from Moscow Conservatoire in 1911, playing Rachmaninoff's Second Concerto – but rumours of scandal beginning to circulate about their association made him decide otherwise and indeed in the summer of 1917 to sever their relations altogether.

According to Riesemann,[82] the first of the new set of *Études-Tableaux*, in C minor, was inspired by Böcklin's 'Waves', presumably '[The Play of the] Waves', the same picture as Reger had used four years before as the basis of the second of his *Four Tone Poems after Arnold Böcklin*, Op. 128.[83] The uncurbable and nightmarish momentum of the Rachmaninoff piece makes an arresting introduction to the set, its taxing technical demands putting it out of reach of all but the transcendental virtuoso. The sea depicted is turbulent indeed and notes, like sea spray, fly everywhere as the pianist pounds the keyboard as waves pound a beach.

Snatches of phrases in the bass part struggle under a welter of rapid semi-quavers in the right hand. There are only a few bars of contrasting calm in the middle, where *Dies irae* appears in the staccato quavers of the lefthand part just before the furious onslaught is renewed. The final bars seem to depict a giant wave rearing up and then, almost stationary at its apogee, gradually accelerating as it falls to smash itself to pieces.

Nothing could be further removed from the fury of the first than the calm of the second study, in A minor, another seascape, this time of the sea and seagulls.[84] The mournful cries of seabirds, in which Rachmaninoff's favourite interval of a fifth figures prominently, make a stark melody over a hypnotically repeated triplet quaver figure in the accompaniment that contains the outline of *Dies irae* and which recalls the tone-poem *The Isle of the Dead*. There are anguished cries in the middle section, and an anxious and unsettled air hangs over the whole piece, before it ends in an unearthly still.

Number 3 in F sharp minor, *Allegro molto*, is a demonic virtuoso study of restless semi-quavers, in which *Dies irae* menacingly informs the shape of the phrases which immediately answer the opening emphatic assertions of the tonic chord. A squall seems to be raging, and the music follows the oscillating contours of the howls of the wind, as here, where it temporarily subsides, with marks of accentuation in the left hand part, marking the gusts (Ex. 146). In a good performance the music acquires an apparently uncontrollable momentum before the central climax, in which three great howling blasts are followed irresistibly by a *veloce* flourish plunging down through five octaves. After this the dynamics gradually fine down, and by the concluding two bars the music is ready to tiptoe away, as though the squall has blown itself out and passed on elsewhere.

Number 4, in B minor, is a metrically free toccata, with an unflagging motoric rhythm. As with most of the set, the musical material for the whole piece is contained in the opening bars: an anapaestic rhythm, a group of five repeated tonic notes and a descending melodic minor scale. The mildly distorted outline of *Dies irae* can just be discerned in the response to this opening (Ex. 147). The skilful way in which Rachmaninoff exploits his unremarkable material is musically extremely satisfying. Structurally this study is unique in Rachmaninoff's piano pieces in repeating both the first and second of its three sections.

The fifth, in E flat minor, the central number of the set, is a full-blown romantic drama, a tale of anguished passion told entirely through the varied repetition of the typically Rachmaninoff lyrical melody with which the piece opens. Much of the piano writing is massively chordal, but the texture thins after the climax (*a tempo fff*), and the threatening tones of *Dies irae* are heard as the tension slackens into a quietly

9 Rachmaninoff correcting the proofs of his Third Concerto at
Ivanovka. 1910.

10 Böcklin's *The Isle of the Dead.*

11   Autograph of *Vocalise*, dated 21 September 1915.

12 *The Bells*: page from last movement.

13   Chaliapin and Rachmaninoff. 1916.

Sergei Rachmaninoff

(Pronounced Rack-man-e-noff)

THE SUPERB ARTISTRY of Rachmaninoff shows him to be one of the greatest pianists of all time, one who has received instant recognition from music lovers wherever he has appeared. Of special importance is this distinguished composer-pianist's playing of his own compositions. His noble "Preludes," the "Barcarolle," "Melodie," and other works, contributions of great value in the literature of the piano, are heard with every detail exactly as Rachmaninoff desires them known and played. To the student—to posterity—to present-day music lovers—the supreme art of one of the world's greatest figures is made alive through these recordings, which are played exclusively for the Ampico.

Played by SERGEI RACHMANINOFF

57604H BARCAROLLE, Op. 10, No. 3,
     G Minor   *Rachmaninoff* 2.00
Like all "Barcarolles," this delightful number offers a boat song, sombre in character, typically Russian and very beautiful. There is a delicious little figure heard throughout representing the rippling of the water. This recording offers the authentic playing of its distinguished composer.

60891H ETUDE TABLEAU, Op. 39,
     No. 6   .   *Rachmaninoff* 2.00
While Rachmaninoff calls this recording a "Study Picture," he does not disclose what

he had in mind in composing it. It has been suggested that it depicts the meeting of Little Red Riding Hood with the wolf. The wolf's savage growl is heard in the opening phrase as he moves stealthily into the road seeing the approach of the scarlet clad little lady. She responds with frightened protest which alternates with the panting and growling of the wicked animal, who cannot wholly conceal his evil purpose, try as he will.

He walks by her side and converses with her as pleasantly as he can, but he is a wicked, dreadful wolf and would eat her up then and there if he dared.

[146]

14   Page from Ampico catalogue. 1925.

15 Rachmaninoff in his London hotel. November 1929.

16 Rachmaninoff (with daughter Irina) at Le Bourget airport, Paris, after flight from London. March 1934.

Ex.146

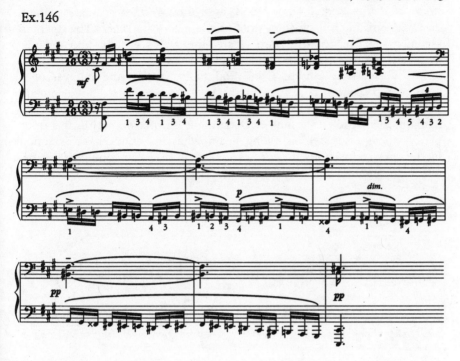

Ex.147

submissive conclusion. In this respect it differs from the otherwise similar outpouring of feeling in Scriabin's youthful D sharp minor *Étude*, Op. 8, No. 12, which Rachmaninoff had habitually used as an encore in his Scriabin recitals the year before and the playing of which may therefore have been the stimulus for his own composition, in what is effectively the same key.

Although Rachmaninoff preferred not to reveal the sources of inspiration for his compositions to the public at large, publicity attaching to the Ampico piano roll the composer made in 1922 of the sixth *Étude-Tableau* in A minor, coyly refers to the 'suggestion' that it depicts the story of Little Red Riding Hood and the Wolf, a scenario which Rachmaninoff himself privately confirmed eight years later.[85] The opening ascending chromatic scales are clearly the wolf's growls, and the tremulously agitated righthand semi-quavers – whose melodic element is simply a step-wise phrase rising and falling within the interval of a third – represent the terrified girl. As what seems to be a pursuit accelerates and reaches its climax, the music becomes increasingly daring harmonically, reaching a limit Rachmaninoff did not exceed in this opus or anywhere else, demonstrating again what his critics have so often in the past refused to accept, namely that he is a composer of the twentieth and not nineteenth century:

Ex.148

In the coda the girl's motif assumes a pathetically pleading character, but as the piece finishes, as it began, with two growls and a snap, we may conclude that the wolf eats her up. The innocent ear would find it hard to guess that so naive a story underlay such urgent and dramatic music, and the intellectual disparity is stark indeed between this programme and the esoteric philosophy behind Scriabin's late piano pieces, which happened to be contemporary with it, for this is the study that Rachmaninoff originally composed in 1911 as the fourth of the first set of *Études-Tableaux* Op. 33 but held over for inclusion here in slightly revised form. At the time of its composition, Rachmaninoff's daughters were aged eight and four, and although a nanny was on hand to bring up both the girls, we know that Rachmaninoff used to go in to see them every night before they went to sleep. He may therefore well have had occasion to read this tale to them, so putting in his mind the idea of setting it to music.

Number 7, in C minor, inhabits the same sound world as the B minor *Moment musical* and B minor Prelude. For once we have a detailed account by the composer of its programme.[86] He describes it as a 'funeral march ... the main theme is the march; the other theme represents the singing of a choir. In the section beginning with the movement in semi-quavers in C minor and shortly after in E flat minor I represent a fine, incessant and hopeless rain. The development of this motif reaches a climax in C minor, the ringing of church bells. At the end, the finale, the initial theme or march.' Although Rachmaninoff had presumably recently been present at his father's burial, it is likely that what is depicted here is his impression of Scriabin's funeral in Moscow, on 16 April 1915, which he also attended; for not only did that event take place on a bleak and rainy day, but Rachmaninoff himself later recalled the great effect the funeral had on him.[87]

The eighth *Étude-Tableau*, in D minor, seems to have been composed as an afterthought, for Rachmaninoff omitted it from his earlier perform-ances of the set and included it for the first time only on 21 February 1917 in a recital in Petrograd. The manuscript is unfortunately undated. The outline of *Dies irae* informs the shape of the opening figure, on which the whole piece is based, but which is nevertheless more whimsical than lugubrious.

The final *Étude-Tableau* in D major Rachmaninoff described as being like an oriental march and having the same character as the seventh *Étude-Tableau* in E flat major from his earlier Op. 33 set – a scene at a fair.[88] There are the same bell sounds and the same bustle and excitement, but a new ingredient is a contrastingly quicker central interlude, which wanders capriciously through oblique tonalities. In view of the known fairy-tale programme of No. 6, Rachmaninoff's more than passing interest in March and April 1916 in Shaginyan's suggestion of Hans Andersen's *Garden of Paradise* as a possible ballet subject and bearing in mind the tale's oriental reference, one wonders whether this very story may not be the underlying programme. It may be remembered that in the story the east wind visited China and danced round a porcelain tower 'so that the bells began to ring'. At all events, the D major *Étude-Tableau* brings to an energetic and, at last, cheerful con-clusion a set which, in the larger scale of its individual numbers and its often dauntingly virtuoso technical demands, advances that bit further the limits set by the earlier Op. 33 group.

The turbulence of the *Études-Tableaux* was echoed by the troubled political times in which they were written, but throughout Rachmaninoff continued his concert routine. On 7 January 1917 at the Bolshoi Theatre he appeared with enormous success for the last time as a conductor in Russia, in performances of *The Crag*, *The Isle of the Dead* and *The Bells*, and for the remainder of the month toured Russian cities with a recital programme. At the end of February he was in Petrograd for a recital at about the time of the general strike, which culminated in the February Revolution and the abdication of the Tsar. 'Freedom' was the watchword and, according to Sofiya Satina, the changed political circumstances were as much welcomed by Rachmaninoff as they were generally.[89] Back in Moscow Rachmaninoff played the Tchaikovsky concerto with Koussevitzky on 12 and 13 March, giving the proceeds to the Union of Artists with a note: 'Free artist S. Rachmaninoff donates his fee from the first performance in his henceforth free country to the needs of the free army.'[90] A week later Rachmaninoff performed Liszt's First Concerto with the same conductor for the first time, and on 25 March he appeared for the last time ever in Moscow in a charity performance of three concertos – his own Second and the Tchaikovsky and Liszt concertos – at the Bolshoi Theatre, with the orchestra conducted by Emil Cooper. The whole of the proceeds from this concert also went to army relief.[91]

The season over, in the second week of April Rachmaninoff left his wife and daughters in Moscow to go to Ivanovka for the spring sowing. The farm workers were naturally in a state of excitement over the events in Petrograd, and Rachmaninoff himself must soon have learned of Lenin's arrival there from abroad and of his demands for the redistribution of land to the peasants. As a landowner with most of his not inconsiderable income invested in Ivanovka, Rachmaninoff saw a bleak future, and some of the older workers on the estate advised him to 'get out of harm's way'.[92] He recalled later: 'The impressions I received from my contact with the peasants, who felt themselves masters of the situation, were unpleasant. I should have preferred to leave Russia with friendlier memories.'[93] However, Rachmaninoff later claimed to have made up his mind to leave Russia even before coming to Ivanovka. 'Almost from the very beginning of the revolution I realized that it was mishandled. Already by March of 1917 I had decided to leave Russia but was unable to carry out my plan, for Europe was still fighting and no-one could cross the frontier.'[94] In May he moved for a month's rest to the familiar surroundings of Essentuki, where Koshetz also happened to be staying and from where, on 1 June, he wrote a quietly despairing note to Siloti, asking him what he should do.

I have spent pretty well everything I have earned in my life on my Ivanovka estate; about 120,000 roubles are now invested there. I am writing this off and reckon another crash is on the way for me. Besides, the conditions of life there are such that, after spending three weeks there, I have decided never to return. I still have about 30,000 roubles. This is something, especially if I can work and earn ... But I fear another crash: everything around so affects me that I cannot work and I fear turning totally sour. Every circumstance advises me temporarily to leave Russia. But where and how? And is it possible? Could you possibly find a free moment with M.I.T[ereshchenko, Foreign Minister] and consult with him? May I count on getting a passport for my family and me to get away, if only to Norway, Denmark, Sweden? ... It makes no difference where! Anywhere! ... Could I get such a permit by July? Could I take with me any money I have left? Or a part? How much? Have a talk with him! Perhaps he will suggest something else? Seen from the mountain peak, his view may be clearer! Talk to him and answer me quickly.

Siloti, however, made no immediate reply, and after three weeks, on 22 June, Rachmaninoff repeated his urgent request for advice in similar panicky vein, adding the interesting sidelight that he had thought of giving Ivanovka to the 'citizens' but that even if he did he would still not be free from the outstanding debts on it. When Shaginyan met him for the last time, after a gala concert at Kislovodsk on 28 July,[95] he was depressed about the way the revolution was developing, afraid for his estate, the fate of his children and frightened of 'being left destitute'. He told her he was going abroad 'to wait for calmer times'.[96] In August (during which Kornilov's counter-revolutionary revolt failed), he moved with his family to the resort of Simeiz in the Crimea, near to the Chaliapins, and on 5 September made his final public appearance in Russia at Yalta, playing the Liszt concerto. After this he returned to his Moscow flat, still awaiting a means of escape. On 25 October the Bolsheviks seized power in Petrograd, and a week later in Moscow. He soon became uncomfortably aware of the new egalitarian order when he found himself a member of the house committee, doing night-watch duty in the block of flats with his fellow citizens, which must have been an uncongenial task not only because of his social background but his reclusive nature.

Concerto No. 1 in F Sharp Minor, Op. 1 (Revised version)

Unable or unwilling to begin anything new and with concerts suspended, Rachmaninoff decided to use the time on his hands to tackle the long-delayed revision of his First Concerto. For one who had always required quiet and solitude for his work, the turbulent circumstances made this an extraordinary time to choose, but work seems to have helped Rachmaninoff through the crisis.[97] 'I sat at the writing-table or the piano all day without troubling about the rattle of machine-guns and rifle-shots. I would have greeted any intruder with the answer that Archimedes gave the conquerors of Syracuse.'[98] When he was first contemplating the revision back in 1908 he explained to Morozov his reasons: 'There are so many requests for this concerto, and it is so frightful in its present form – that's the main thing – that I should like to work at it and, if possible, get it into shape. Of course, it will have to be written afresh, for the orchestration in it is worse than the music.'[99] Nine years later Rachmaninoff carried out his intention of drastic revision, totally rescoring the work in the light of his experience of more than a quarter of a century as conductor and composer. The original orchestration had been stolidly four-square, whereas in the revision it is infinitely more varied, flexible and clear, with much orchestral interplay and enterprising writing for solo instruments, though he used essentially the same forces, merely replacing the tuba by a bass trombone and adding triangle and cymbals for extra colour in the last movement only. The piano writing was recast to bring it into line with Rachmaninoff's current more elaborate and chromatic style, the same kind of process as can be seen, albeit in a rather less pronounced way, in the late revision of the early solo piano pieces – the Op. 3 *Serenade*, for example. The formal structure of the concerto, however, especially in the first two movements, was changed but little, and the youthfully fresh melodies not at all.[100]

ORIGINAL VERSION, 1890/91   *EQUIVALENT IN 1917 REVISION*

First movement

Bars		*Bars*	
1–15	*Vivace.* Opening fanfares and piano flourishes	1–15	
	EXPOSITION		
16–31	1st theme, *Moderato*	16–31	Fig. 2
32–48	Bridge passage, *Vivo con leggierezza*	32–47 (= –1)	*Vivace, leggiere*
49–59	2nd theme, *Meno mosso*	48–56 (= –2)	Fig. 5

ORIGINAL VERSION, 1890/91		EQUIVALENT IN 1917 REVISION	
60–77	Continued, *Allegro moderato*	57–70 (= –4)	Fig. 6 *Poco meno mosso*
78–81	Brief piano cadenza	71–74	5 after 7
	DEVELOPMENT		
82–112	*Moderato, Con moto, Più vivo.* Orchestra	75–124 (= +19)	*Vivace, Doppio movimento.* Into A minor
113–128	2nd theme, *Allegro moderato*	125–137 (= –3)	Fig. 14 *Moderato*
129–140	1st theme, clarinet	138–151 (= +2)	Fig. 16 1st theme, horn, back in F sharp minor. *Poco più mosso*
141–166	*Poco a poco accelerando*	152–171 (= +4)	2 after 17
	RECAPITULATION		
167–174	1st theme, *Moderato*	172–179	2 after 20
175–191	Bridge passage	180–191 (= –5)	Fig. 21 *Vivace. Scherzando*
192–202	2nd theme, F sharp major, *Meno mosso*	192–200 (= +2)	
203–224	Continued, *Allegro moderato*	201–214 (= – 8)	1 after 23 *Allegro*
225–230	*Moderato,* from opening of Development	215–224 (= +4)	*Vivace. Doppio movimento*
231–286	Cadenza, *Con agitazione*	225–277 (= – 3)	5 after 26
287–320	Coda, *Presto*	278–295 (= – 16)	*Vivace*

Second movement

1–9	*Andante cantabile.* Orchestral introduction	1–9	*Andante*
10–27	Theme, piano	10–27	

ORIGINAL VERSION, 1890/91		EQUIVALENT IN 1917 REVISION	
28–35	Continued. Counter theme, clarinet	28–35	Fig. 30 Counter theme, oboe
36–48	Piano solo	36–52 (= +4)	Piano with orchestra
49–66	Theme restated *a tempo*	53–70	4 after 33
66–70	Coda	70–74	

Third movement

1–6	*Allegro scherzando.* Introduction	1–9 (= +3)	*Allegro vivace*
	EXPOSITION		
7–31	1st theme, *Capriccioso*	10–37 (= +3)	*Con brio*
32–67	2nd theme, *Più mosso*	38–61 (= – 12)	2 after 42 *Allegro.* New counter theme, violins
68–76	Codetta	68–70 (= – 6)	Fig. 45
77–92	3rd theme, D major, *Andante espressivo*	70–86	E flat major, *Andante ma non troppo*
93–124	3rd theme developed, *Cantabile*	87–116 (= –2)	A tempo
	RECAPITULATION		
125–130	Introduction, *Allegro scherzando*	116–125 (= +3)	Fig. 51 *Tempo I*
131–149	1st theme	126–149 (= +5)	
150–155	Bridge passage	150–155	
156–171	2nd theme, *Più mosso*	156–171	6 after 54 *Allegro ma non tanto*

ORIGINAL VERSION, 1890/91		EQUIVALENT IN 1917 REVISION	
172–181	Piano solo	172–193 (= –39)	Fig 57 New counter theme, violins, from Exposition, *A tempo*
182–221	2nd theme developed, piano cadenza	—	
222–232	3rd theme, *Maestoso*	—	
233–240	Coda, *Più vivo*	194–208 (= +7)	Coda, *Allegro vivace*

In the first movement the most noteworthy departure is in the development section, where the original version introduces an apparently unconnected descending four-note quaver figure, which the revision more purposefully reshapes in triplets into a clear reminiscence of the concerto's opening piano flourish (Ex. 149). The revised version extends the orchestral opening of the development by 19 bars, while greatly adding to its dynamic vigour. En route the music modulates to A minor, whereas the original does not leave the confines of the home key until the cadenza, which, with the movement's coda, well demonstrates the total transformation of the writing which took place in the revision. The metre is changed from the original 3/4 to the 4/4 of the concerto's introduction, enabling the composer to recapitulate both the opening fanfares, ignored in the original, and the final chords of the piano preamble before the first theme. As in the development, Rachmaninoff dispenses with the original descending quaver figure and picks up instead the concerto's opening cascading flourish. The contrast between the piano writing of the 17- and the 44-year old composer is naturally here at its most obvious. For example, in the bars heralding the final restatement of the main theme, the conventional arpeggios of the original are now treated chordally (Ex. 150).

After the climax of the cadenza, the original version resumes limply *pianissimo* with rapid decorative figuration for the soloist and nothing at all of interest in the orchestra; even the final flourish of descending tonic chords is unaccompanied and the soloist adds an extra chord after he arrives at the bottom of the keyboard, to be followed by a conventional final orchestral *tutti*. In the revision, the coda begins furiously, *attacca subito*, and the momentum from the cadenza is sustained throughout, helped by cutting the coda's length by half. The end of the movement is made more effective by eliminating the redundant last two chords of soloist and orchestra, and instead by making the

Ex.149a

1890-91 version

Ex.149b

1917 version

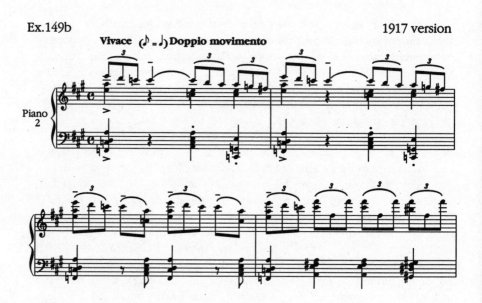

final descending piano torrent accelerate to the climactic last chord and by emphatically punctuating that chord with the orchestra.

The second movement has the opening rising three-note motif, given before to the clarinets, now a horn solo, and whereas the piano introduction was originally two simple chords of a spread dominant ninth and a dominant seventh arpeggio, the revised version has a typically mature Rachmaninoff chromatic musing, which integrates the three-note motif (Ex. 151). The theme and its treatment remain much the same, though scored differently, oboes replacing clarinets for the counter melody. The climax, however, a conventionally rhetorical piano solo in the original, now becomes a subtle interplay between soloist

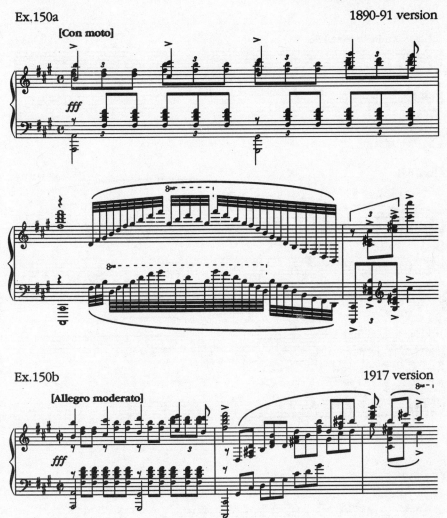

Ex.150a
1890-91 version
[Con moto]
fff

Ex.150b
1917 version
[Allegro moderato]
fff

and orchestra, in which the orchestra makes reference to the opening rising horn motif, previously a gesture unconnected with the rest of the movement but now integrated into the structure. After the orchestral restatement of the theme, with the piano decoration now more varied, an improved coda replaces the naive final bars of the original.

The last movement shows the most extensive revision. The original's tentative introduction gives way to a splendidly dynamic and rhythmically interesting opening emphasizing an octave leap, with alternating ⁹⁄₈ and 1²⁄₈ metre, to launch the energetically whimsical first theme. When the

Ex.151a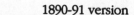

1890-91 version

Ex.151b

1917 version

Ex.152

second theme appears, a new counter theme naturally emerges, this being the only new thematic material in the whole revision (Ex. 152). The greater coherence of the new version is typified by the descending flourishes in the *tutti* which concludes this section and which reappear in the coda, for these are not imposed from outside but derive from the string interchanges with the piano in the opening theme (figure 40). Another instance is in the presentation of the contrasting third theme, previously in D major but now characteristically finding itself in the remote key of E flat. As Piggott was the first to point out,[101] the

Ex.153a

1890-91 version

Ex.153b

1917 version

melody is presented by the strings with a response from the soloist at
the end of each phrase which in the revised version is not mere
decoration but imitation in diminution of the theme itself (Ex. 153).
It is this theme which Rachmaninoff chose to deck out with rhetorical
double octaves in the original version as the movement's culminating
point. In his revision Rachmaninoff wisely excised this passage altogether,
and instead maintained momentum with a taut and purposeful coda
based on the descending *tutti* flourish.

Rachmaninoff finished the new version of his concerto on 10 November
1917 and sent the manuscript to his publishers before leaving Russia
the following month. Its first performance had to await Rachmaninoff's
arrival in the United States, and took place on 28 January 1919, in New

York, with the composer and the Russian Symphony Orchestra, conducted by Modest Altschuler. Although there were a number of performances in Rachmaninoff's first and last years in America, the work never caught on and, despite occasional performances today, much the same can be said of its present status as a poor relation of the Second and Third Concertos although, as the composer himself said of it, 'all the youthful freshness is there and yet it plays itself so much more easily'.[102]

In the five days after completing the revised version of the concerto Rachmaninoff made fair copies of three contrasting piano miniatures, all three untitled. The first, an unsettling *Andante ma non troppo*, in D minor, was infelicitously published posthumously as 'Prelude', a title indissolubly linked to the earlier set of twenty-four pieces, to which the new study is certainly no postscript stylistically. Its unrelieved blackness of mood fails to conceal the perfunctoriness of the material. Its grim message, the essence of which is contained within the first bar, is insistently reiterated, the repeatedly emphasized F's and later D's in the top line sounding out like an alarum bell:

Ex.154

Andante ma non troppo

The second piece, by far the most compelling of the three, though bearing the same date as the first, for some inscrutable reason was first performed by the composer only in 1931 and not published until seven years later. He then called it *Oriental Sketch*, though Fritz Kreisler, because of its motoric rhythm, gave it the nick-name of 'Oriental Express'. As with the D major *Étude-Tableau* of the previous year, the 'eastern' element seems to be confined to a certain spice in the harmonic colouring. It is a very surprising piece to have been written at so traumatic a time in Rachmaninoff's life, especially after the almost universal dark of the preceding *Études-Tableaux*, for it has a rather jaunty, bland air. Its relentless momentum culminates in the last bars in a splendidly exuberant descent in major and minor thirds over nearly four octaves.

The last of the three pieces, the so-called *Fragments*, is a perplexing anti-climax. It was first published under that name in 1919 in an

American music magazine,[103] its mere twenty-six bars being of convenient length nicely to fill a page. What other piece of Rachmaninoff is so short, so technically undemanding, so undistinctive? The plaintive idea in the outer sections is of the greatest simplicity and accordingly set in the plainest four-part harmony, while the middle eight bars, *più mosso*, of groups of six tremulous semi-quavers in the right hand against four in the left, are no more than the most trivial contrasting gesture. There are no conceivable circumstances in which Rachmaninoff might publicly have performed so brief and uncharacteristic a piece, and excusing it by its title begs the unanswerable questions: 'Of what is this piece fragments?' and 'Why bother to set them down in this form rather than leave them as jottings in a notebook?'

While still working on the revision of the First Concerto in November, Rachmaninoff was offered a solution to his immediate problems in the form of an unexpected invitation from neutral Scandinavia to appear in a series of concerts there. At the end of the month he went to Petrograd to obtain visas and was joined a few days later by his wife and daughters. From his desk in his Moscow flat he had taken with him all the materials to do with *Monna Vanna*, the new piano pieces, composing sketch-books, and a single score by another composer, Rimsky-Korsakov's *Golden Cockerel*. Rachmaninoff was painfully aware that he was leaving Moscow 'for a very long time, ... perhaps for ever'.[104] On 15 December a newspaper announced Rachmaninoff's imminent departure for a concert tour of Norway and Sweden 'lasting more than two months';[105] on 20 December Rachmaninoff received the visas, and in the company of Nikolay Struve the family left Russia on 23 December, never to return.

References

1 R. to Morozov, 6 June 1909.
2 Goldenweiser, *VR/A* 1, pp. 420–421.
3 Grigory Prokofiev in *Russkiye vedomosti*, 6 April 1910.
4 R. to Josef Yasser, 30 April 1935. Yasser deals with the whole matter at length in his article 'The Opening Theme of Rachmaninoff's Third Piano Concerto and its Liturgical Prototype', in *The Musical Quarterly*, Vol. 1v, 1969, pp. 313-328.
5 See *T/N*, p. 95.
6 Horowitz in conversation with Jack Pfeiffer, in notes with Horowitz's 1978 recording of R's Third Concerto.
7 Both Rachmaninoff's own and Horowitz's 1930 recording of the Third Concerto were made on nine record sides. Following standard practice, Horowitz's version was issued with a fill-up on the tenth side, Rachmaninoff's, most unusually, with the tenth side blank. Using this redundant space, as had been done with the shorter Second Concerto, where the nine sides of the original acoustic recording were spread extravagantly over a conveniently even ten sides in the electrical remake, would have

provided six and not five sides for the last two movements, with ample space for the restoration not only of the cut in the Intermezzo but of those in the finale too. The fact that so obvious a course was not followed strongly suggests that it was Rachmaninoff himself who did not wish the movements to be recorded uncut.

8 *Jorge Bolet Masterclass*, BBC television, 30 July 1983.

9 Conversation with the author, 1971.

10 *Hofmann*, Mrs Hofmann's diary.

11 *Horowitz*, p. 423.

12 *Op. cit.*, p. 112.

13 Author's conversation with Sofiya Satina, 1973.

14 'Thanks be to God' appears at the end of the manuscript of each of Rachmaninoff's last three works, the *Paganini Rhapsody*, Third Symphony and *Symphonic Dances*.

15 *Riesemann*, p. 176 and R. to Somov, 14 November 1934.

16 Psalm 103 is Psalm 102 to the Orthodox Church, whose numbering is out of step with the Western Psalter.

17 In *S. Rakhmaninov, Khorovïye proizvedeniya*, ed. A.P. Alexandrov, Muzyka, Moscow, 1976, p. 38.

18 'Noe from the waters in a saving home;
Job from all his multiform and fell distress;
Moses from the land of bondage and despair;
David from Golia and the Wrath of Saul.'

19 See p. 246.

20 Anna Trubnikova, *VR/A* 1, p. 133.

21 *Russkaya muzïkal'naya gazeta*, 3 April 1911.

22 *Ewen*, p. 848.

23 Goldenweiser, *VR/A* 1, p. 421.

24 See Vl. Protopopov in *Tsïtovich*, pp. 140-141.

25 See *Piggott*, p. 67

26 Moiseiwitsch's Rachmaninoff memorial article, *Gramophone*, May 1943, pp. 169-170.

27 *Riesemann*, p. 236.

28 *Culshaw*, p. 114; *T/N*, p. 103.

29 *VR/A* 2, pp. 467-471.

30 Zoya Pribïtkova, *VR/A* 2, p. 66.

31 R. to Zoya Pribïtkova, 9 August 1911.

32 *Études-Tableaux* in F minor (No. 1), E flat major (No. 7), C sharp minor (No. 9).

33 Marietta Shaginyan, *VR/A* 2, p. 158.

34 R. to Respighi, 2 January 1930; *Riesemann*, p. 237.

35 *Riesemann*, p. 247. Riesemann confuses the opus number with the later *Études-Tableaux*, Op. 39, but not the key or the number in the set.

36 *Hofmann*, diary for 2 December 1911.

37 Many of the Shaginyan letters are quoted in *Seroff* (pp. 115-138). At the end of her life Shaginyan wrote a detailed account of her relationship with Rachmaninoff, ridiculing Seroff's inference of a romantic attachment (*Novïy Mir*, January 1977, pp. 79-134).

38 *The Muse*, the first of a set of Pushkin settings, Medtner's Op. 29.

39 The original version of *So dread a fate* has not survived.

40 Antonina Nezhdanova, *VR/A* 2, p. 30.

41 See Koshetz's letter in *LN/A* 2, p. 408.

42 Nezhdanova, *VR/A* 2, p. 31.

43 A manuscript of a variant version of *Vocalise*, dated 1 April 1915, is in the Nezhdanova archive. The information about the date of *Vocalise* given in *T/N*, p. 110, is misleading. As Taneyev did not die until June 1915, the suggestion in *B/L*, p. 193, that *Vocalise* was written in memory of Taneyev is chronologically untenable.

44 R. to Modest Altschuler, 12 January 1918.

45 Ilya Satz, *Iz zapisnikh knizhek, Vospominaniya sovremennikov*, Moscow, 1968, pp. 102-103.

46 There is an interesting account by the composer of the genesis of *The Bells* in *Riesemann*, pp. 170-171. Articles about the music itself worthy of perusal are: by Robert Hull, in *The Monthly Musical Record*, October 1936, pp. 171-2; and by Stephen Walsh, in *The Listener*, 19 July 1973, p. 63.

47 R. to Morozov, 3 December 1906.

48 *Riesemann*, p. 171.

49 After Rachmaninoff's death the sender of Balmont's translation was revealed to have been a young cello student at Moscow Conservatoire called Mariya Danilova. See M. Bukinik in *VR/A* 1, pp. 225–226.

50 *Riesemann*, p. 170.

51 *Riesemann*, p. 171.

52 H.J. Wood, *My Life of Music*, Gollancz, London, 1938, p. 336.

53 'Famous Russian Musician Dislikes Cold Weather', Rachmaninoff interview with D.W. Hazen in *The Morning Oregonian, Portland*, 23 January 1937.

54 Boris Tyuneyev in *Russkaya muzïkal'naya gazeta*, 1913, No. 48, p. 1104.

55 Yuly Engel in *Russkiye vedomosti*, 5 December 1913.

56 The manuscript of the piano transcription of *Lilacs* is lost, but Rachmaninoff played the work for the first time in Kiev on 19 October 1913. The dating he later gave Asafyev, of December 1914, is doubtless that of the final revision before publication.

57 St John, ch. 15, v. 13.

58 See *T/N*, p. 172.

59 *Russkaya muzïkal'naya gazeta*, 1915, No. 15.

60 Marietta Shaginyan, *VR/A* 2, pp. 148–149.

61 *Riesemann*, pp. 176-178.

62 For a detailed account of the znamenny chant see Alfred Swan's article 'The Znamenny Chant of the Russian Church' in *The Musical Quarterly*, Vol. xxvi, 1940, April, pp. 232-243; July, pp. 365-380; October, pp. 529-545.

63 R. to Josef Yasser, 30 April 1935.

64 It should be noted that the All-Night Vigil has nothing whatever to do with the 'Mass' of the Western Church, which corresponds to the Orthodox Church's Liturgy of St. John Chrysostom, the service set by Rachmaninoff as his Op. 31. The fact that the Vigil embraces both Vespers and Matins makes the title 'Vesper Mass' doubly misleading.

65 *Riesemann*, p. 176.

66 According to Sofiya Satina (in a letter to the author, 4 January 1974), the *Nunc dimittis* from the *All-Night Vigil* could not be performed at Rachmaninoff's funeral because the choir was thought unable to cope and in any case the sheet music was not available at the time.

67 *Riesemann*, p. 177.

68 Alfred Swan, *Russian Music*, John Baker, London, 1973, p. 175.

69 *Songs of the Church. Fifteen Anthems for Mixed Chorus by Sergei Rachmaninoff Op. 37. Edited by Winifred Douglas*, pub. 1920 by the H.W. Gray Company Inc., New York (now part of Belwin Mills). Although the word 'authorized' appears on this edition, Rachmaninoff complained bitterly that he had not even had the chance of looking at it before it was published (his letter to H.W. Gray, written sometime after 15 January 1921).
70 *Sokolova*, p. 103.
71 Shaginyan, *VR/A* 2, pp. 151–152.
72 R. to Shaginyan, 19 June 1912.
73 Shaginyan, *VR/A* 2, p. 153.
74 *Riesemann* p. 241.
75 Koshetz's unpublished memoirs.
76 *Riesemann*, p. 241.
77 Shaginyan and Nezhdanova in *VR/A* 2, p. 153 and p. 30.
78 See *T/N*, pp. 121-122.
79 *Rachmaninoff: Two Sacred Songs*, pub. Belwin-Mills, 1973.
80 Shaginyan, *VR/A* 2, pp. 139–141.
81 Although the manuscripts of Nos. 5 and 9 of the Op. 39 group of *Études-Tableaux* are dated 17 and 2 February respectively, both pieces were performed at the Petrograd and Moscow premieres of the set, and specifically mentioned in Engel's review of the Moscow recital on 5 December 1916. Thus, the presumption in the note in *T/N*, p. 124, that the ninth number was not performed on that occasion is mistaken.
82 *Riesemann*, p. 237.
83 Reger's *Four Tone Poems after Arnold Böcklin* also contains a setting of *The Isle of the Dead.*
84 R. to Respighi, 2 January 1930.
85 *Ibid.*
86 *Ibid.*
87 *Riesemann*, pp. 180-181.
88 R. to Respighi, 2 January 1930.
89 Sofiya Satina, *VR/A* 1, p. 47.
90 R's note published in *Russkiye vedomosti*, 15 March 1917.
91 R. to editor of *Russkiye vedomosti*, 6 April 1917.
92 Mrs Rachmaninoff, *VR/A* 2, p. 298.
93 *Riesemann*, pp. 184-185
94 *Ibid.*
95 *B/L*, p. 203, is mistaken about the occasion of Shaginyan's final meeting with Rachmaninoff.
96 Shaginyan, *VR/A* 2, p. 155.
97 Mrs Rachmaninoff, *VR/A* 2, p. 299.
98 *Riesemann*, p. 185.
99 R. to Morozov, 12 April 1908.
100 The original and revised versions of the First Concerto are compared in Geoffrey Norris's article 'Rakhmaninov's Second Thoughts', in *The Musical Times*, Vol. cxiv, 1973, pp. 364-366.
101 *Piggott*, p. 43.
102 *Swan*, p. 8.
103 *The Etude*, October 1919.
104 *Riesemann*, p. 186.
105 *Dyen'*, 15 December 1917.

8 New World, 1917–1943

Rachmaninoff was destined to spend the entire latter half of his adult life away from his homeland. Although the time span of this self-imposed exile, twenty-five years in all, is as long as the whole of the period from his student opera *Aleko* up to his last Russian works, throughout this time Rachmaninoff's energies were so drained by his career as a performer that composition, previously the centre of his musical life, became relegated to being only an occasional occupation, and thus his final period as a composer is marked by only six major works. The first two, the Fourth Concerto and the Three Russian Songs, seem to be realizations of ideas already conceived, if not actually sketched out, in Russia; and although the Corelli Variations and *Paganini Rhapsody* were entirely new creations, the two final compositions, the Third Symphony and the *Symphonic Dances*, in the nature of their musical material again look back across the years to a homeland out of reach, to a Russia that had already ceased to exist even before Rachmaninoff's departure.

The Rachmaninoffs and Struve travelled first to Stockholm and then to Copenhagen, where Rachmaninoff gave his first concert on 15 February 1918, playing his Second Concerto. The twelve concerts in all he came to give in Scandinavia enabled him to pay off his debts and gave him a breathing space to think about his future. He faced two decisions: which of his three careers as composer, pianist and conductor he should choose as the basis of his livelihood in the changed circumstances of exile, and where that career should be based. According to Sofiya Satina: 'It became clear to him that he would have to give up composition for a long time, because he needed the financial means to provide a life for his family and to give his daughters an education'.[1] This pointed to a career as conductor or pianist, and in the summer of 1918 Rachmaninoff received offers from America of contracts in both capacities. However, conducting would have meant acquiring a catholic Western repertoire, an involvement in orchestral politics and an inevitable loss of autonomy; occasional guest appearances on the rostrum were one thing, the formidable pressures of a full-time contract were something else. In any case, the form Rachmaninoff's concertizing had taken in his last years in Russia already pointed to a pianist's career as the natural choice. Since directing a Liadov memorial concert in October 1914 he had conducted only once, whilst increasing the number of his public appearances as a pianist. Moreover, with his Scriabin concerts in 1915–16 Rachmaninoff had unconsciously taken the first steps in moving away from being merely a composer-pianist towards a career as a concert virtuoso performing works by composers other than himself. Even before this, in 1911, he had added the Tchaikovsky B flat minor Concerto to his repertoire, and more recently, in 1917, the Liszt E flat Concerto and some Liszt encores. Tiny and unbalanced though this repertoire was, it was on this slender foundation that Rachmaninoff decided, at the age of forty-four, to build his new life.

As to where to pursue his career, that decision too seems in retrospect to have been a foregone conclusion, for America had been in Rachmaninoff's mind even before he had left Russia. In the autumn of 1917 he had consulted the American Consul in Moscow, only to be told discouragingly, if understandably, that America was then more concerned about the war than about concerts.[2] Nevertheless, his American tour of 1909–1910 had been a great success and through it he had established a number of useful musical contacts. The arrival of the American offers of contracts, an auspicious omen, clinched matters. During the summer of 1918 Rachmaninoff worked on overhauling his piano technique and learning repertoire, using the first month of the new concert season in Sweden and Norway to try out the two recital programmes he had prepared. Then, with borrowed money, he booked a passage for himself and his family to the United States. Leaving Oslo on 1 November on board the Norwegian vessel 'Bergensfjord', the Rachmaninoffs arrived safely in New York nine days later. Installed in the Sherry-Netherland Hotel at the corner of East Fifty-ninth Street and Fifth Avenue, Rachmaninoff was visited by numerous musical acquaintances and well-wishers. He listened patiently to their advice about managers and contracts and then characteristically ignored it all, preferring instead to be guided by his own astute business instincts. In this he showed the same stubborn independence as had marked him out as a young boy, when the Trubnikovs nicknamed him *Ya sam* ('I myself') from his unwillingness to accept advice and a helping hand.

Although still recovering from an attack of Spanish 'flu which had stricken him and his daughters within a few days of their arrival, to pay off his debts Rachmaninoff had to start work as soon as possible, and his new American career opened on 8 December 1918 with a recital at Providence, Rhode Island, the first of 36 appearances in what was left of the season. The programme was the same as he had tried out in Scandinavia, with the addition of his own arrangement of *The Star-Spangled Banner* as a curtain-raiser. To call this last piece a 'transcription' is excessively to ennoble what is no more than a somewhat more sonorous version of an essentially untouched original. This restraint contrasts greatly with the flamboyance of some other versions, for example Godowsky's, and of the transcriptions Rachmaninoff himself came to make soon afterwards. There was little point in setting this 'arrangement' down on paper, and we know it only through the piano roll Rachmaninoff made of it.

At last Rachmaninoff's first concert season ended and the family moved to California for the summer holiday. The launch into a new career had been a great critical, popular and financial success: not only was Rachmaninoff able to pay off the money he had borrowed but he could look forward with confidence to an increasingly prosperous future. He had already signed lucrative gramophone and piano roll contracts which, in time, were to make him perhaps the wealthiest of all musicians in the United States, but only at the price of the exhausting routine of his new life-style, a strait-jacket from which he was only occasionally able to break out in his remaining twenty-four seasons on the concert platform. Whereas before, his summers at Ivanovka had given him an opportunity and stimulus for creative work, so now he had to use his holidays in an alien environment to work up new repertoire for the following season, leaving him little time and still less inclination for composition.

In 1921 Rachmaninoff was able to arrange for his wife's family, the Satins, to leave Russia and the following summer he met up with them in Dresden. When they asked the inevitable questions about his work as a composer, they learned in disbelief that in the intervening years all he had written was a cadenza to Liszt's Second Hungarian Rhapsody.[3] Rachmaninoff was of course by no means the first to add a cadenza to the Rhapsody, nor was he merely blindly following the tradition of the older virtuosi of his day. Liszt's invitation in the score *Cadenza ad libitum*, though generally ignored by performers today, is unequivocal enough, and Liszt himself composed a suitable, if brief, example to fill the bill. This, however, was not published until 1926, seven years after Rachmaninoff had premiered his own cadenza,[4] which, though sketched on paper, he evidently thought of insufficient importance to warrant publication. After the initial flourishes referring to the Rhapsody's opening section, the cadenza mainly concerns itself with reworking the material of the *friska*, subjecting its motif to a jaunty and mischievous distortion which gives new interest to one of the most hackneyed of all Liszt's pieces. As an expression of the tragic picture so readily but perhaps mistakenly conjured up in the mind's eye of the anguished composer, newly bereft of his homeland and cast out in the wilderness, the cadenza's shallow and insouciant air seems incongruous indeed.

Rachmaninoff's inactivity as a composer was not in fact quite as total as he had led the Satins to believe, since by 1922, besides the cadenza, he had made sketches of three Russian folk-song settings and completed a number of piano transcriptions. The songs date from 1920. *Luchinushka* ('The Little Splinter'), a favourite of Chaliapin's, was arranged for John McCormack, though there is no evidence that he ever performed it, and the copy of the manuscript in the Library of Congress has not seen the light of day since finding its way there. *The Apple Tree* was harmonized at the request of Alfred Swan for inclusion in a folk song anthology, [5] and Rachmaninoff's contribution, though consisting of little more than a few chords, lends a characteristically wistful melancholy to the simple tune. The third sketch, *Along the Street*, also probably dates from this same time and, like *Luchinushka*, has remained unpublished.

Work on the piano transcriptions began in the 1920–21 season, and the making of such arrangements continued to attract Rachmaninoff, albeit intermittently, until the end of his career. He was, of course, by no means a stranger to the medium. In 1900 he had made his first free solo piano transcription – of the Minuet from Bizet's *L'Arlésienne* – though he neither published it nor, so far as we know, publicly performed it. In 1911 he had metamorphosed Franz Behr's naive little polka into an elaborate concert encore, and in 1913 had done the same, though with much more restraint, to his own *Lilacs*. The transcriptions he made in exile are almost all of well-known pieces by other composers, and their *raison d'etre* was not, therefore, in the manner of Liszt, the popularizing of music undeservedly in the dark but rather the creation of what Horowitz used to call 'after-dinner peppermints', encores which extend and celebrate Rachmaninoff's own particular art as a pianist, that is, to recreate a work as though it were his own composition. Thus his transcriptions are always a delight to play, or to try to play, and they are among the composer's most interesting and enjoyable recordings. The ingenuity Rachmaninoff shows in the more elaborate of the transcriptions in the treatment of themes, in the harmonic and contrapuntal piquancy and the masterly exploitation of the instrument, places them alongside those of Godowsky and Busoni as the most important of the twentieth century.

The first of Rachmaninoff's new transcriptions[6] seems to have been his arrangement for piano solo, and subsequently for violin and piano, of the *Gopak* from Mussorgsky's opera *Sorochinsky Fair*, a favourite item in his orchestral programmes in Russia. Mussorgsky himself had made a literal piano transcription of the piece and Rachmaninoff too keeps closely to the text, though he does somewhat alter the ending.

His own enjoyment of the piece emerges clearly from his recording, in which, as in his *Polka de W.R.*, he teasingly exaggerates to the very limit the *ritenuto* at the end of the introduction before launching into the tune with enormous élan.

Fritz Kreisler had been among the first musicians to visit Rachmaninoff on his arrival in the United States, and their friendship and mutual admiration grew over the years. It was perhaps natural, therefore, that Rachmaninoff should make piano transcriptions of two of his most famous pieces – *Liebesleid* in 1921 and *Liebesfreud* in 1925 – a compliment which Kreisler returned by making violin arrangements of the theme from the slow movement of Rachmaninoff's Second Concerto and of his song *Daisies*. In his transcriptions Rachmaninoff adds introductions and codas, and so ingeniously elaborates the textures as to make the new versions more interesting musically than the originals, whose simple charm, after all, depended so much on Kreisler's own uniquely seductive playing. *Liebesfreud* is the more intricate of the two settings, indeed one of the finest of all Rachmaninoff's transcriptions. The manner in which the two themes in the piece are combined in labyrinthine polyphony is an unfailing source of musical pleasure. As in all his transcriptions, Rachmaninoff leaves an unmistakable impress of his own personality in the spicy harmonies with which he seasons Kreisler's naive tunes:

Ex.155

[Allegro]   Poco meno mosso e grazioso

Towards the end of *Liebesleid* Rachmaninoff inserts a *veloce* cadential flourish and in *Liebesfreud* he takes the process further, incorporating a full-blown cadenza in which, free from all external restraints, he builds up a climax of the most exuberant virtuosity.

Three other transcriptions date from Rachmaninoff's first years in the United States. The Minuet from Bizet's *L'Arlésienne*, which Rachmaninoff first played in January 1922, is a revision of the version he had made in 1900. The middle section, in which the second theme is elaborately decorated and passed from the right to the left hand, is especially attractive. The transcription of the composer's own *Daisies*, also probably dating from 1922, assimilates the song's vocal line into its texture but otherwise little alters the original accompaniment, which was already almost an independent work in itself. Finally, from 1925, comes Schubert's song *Wohin?*, from *Die Schöne Müllerin*, published under the title 'The Brooklet', in which the rippling accompaniment and Godowskian chromaticism rather overwhelm Schubert's simple diatonic tune.

For the first eight years of his life as an expatriate Rachmaninoff wrote not a single original composition. The apparent sudden drying up of his creative spring confirmed those who were antipathetic to his music in their view that he had written himself out, while profoundly saddening those who admired and loved it and who clung to it as to a life-raft in a hostile sea of modernism. In December 1922 Rachmaninoff's friend Morozov wrote him from Moscow: 'For a long time now I have been hearing, as I have myself long suspected, that you are not writing anything, and whenever I think about it I am greatly saddened by a feeling of irreparable loss, as much as though it were my own private affair... Thinking of your not writing one cannot remain calm and you too, I am sure, do not regard it with indifference'.[7] Morozov went on to propose a number of ideas for composition: a four-movement orchestral suite or symphony based on scenes from the four seasons, a biblical work about the creation of the world; an opera from Shakespeare, possibly Antony and Cleopatra; and, in view of his new career as a virtuoso, a group of piano studies. In a second letter Morozov added the idea of a set of orchestral variations,[8] but in his reply Rachmaninoff was frank in holding out little hope:[9]

> Your main question, encountered in all your letters, about my creative work I must answer as follows: whether from over-tiredness or lack of habit (it's five years now since I worked on composition) I am not drawn to it or only rarely drawn. The latter happens when I think about the two large compositions of mine I began not long before leaving Russia. When I think of these, I long to finish them. This seems to be the only possible way of shifting me from this dead-lock. To begin something new seems to me unattainably difficult. If I get a bit stronger and rest, I shall try to set about it this summer. So, your advice and new subjects will have to go for the time being into my portfolio and lie there until my 'awakening' or rebirth.

Rachmaninoff's letter poses an interesting unsolved question: what were the two 'large compositions' he longed to complete? One of them was certainly the Fourth Concerto, which we know he had begun to sketch out before leaving Russia, and as two of the major compositions of these later years – the *Corelli Variations* and *Paganini Rhapsody* – were undoubtedly entirely new works and as the composer left nothing else behind at his death, the choice for the other composition must be from among *Monna Vanna*, the Three Russian Songs, Third Symphony and *Symphonic Dances*. Although Rachmaninoff had brought the manuscript of his unfinished opera with him out of Russia and had been keeping it by him as though intending to do something with it, the time for its completion was surely past, and with Russia now closed to him and with the copyright restrictions still in force it would have made no sense to finish an opera that could not have been performed. The Three Russian Songs do seem to have had their origin, at least in part, in the Russian years, but they hardly qualify as a 'large composition'. This leaves the Third Symphony and the *Symphonic Dances* as the only possible candidates. In the case of the symphony there is one small but decisive piece of evidence, in the form of a musical quotation in one of Rachmaninoff's sketchbooks, that a fragment of the material in the work predates the composer's departure from Russia, but no other evidence, of any kind, of work on the composition itself. The notion that Rachmaninoff may have re-used material from his ballet *The Scythians* in his swan-song, the *Symphonic Dances*, depends solely on the unsupported claim of a single witness.

Concerto No. 4 in G Minor, Op. 40

After seven strenuous concert seasons Rachmaninoff decided to cut the eighth short and make 1926 a sabbatical year in order to complete his Fourth Concerto. Although he was characteristically secretive about the work and made no direct mention of it in his correspondence until he had completed it in August 1926, there is nevertheless the strongest evidence to support the presumption that it was conceived as early as 1913–14. The most interesting clues are musical ones. For the climax of the second movement of the concerto Rachmaninoff used a passage from the unpublished *Étude-Tableau* in C minor of 1911. The most likely explanation for its being withheld is surely that he had already earmarked it for use in the concerto, whose original conception, or at least whose slow movement, must therefore predate the publication in 1914 of the other *Études-Tableaux*. As will be seen later, there are other less obvious but nevertheless unmistakable similarities of melodic turn and general style between the concerto's outer movements and other works of the 1913–14 period, most notably the Second Piano Sonata of 1913.

The first public mention of the new work was in a musical periodical in April 1914,[10] which announced that Rachmaninoff was working on a fourth concerto. That year the composer went to Ivanovka unusually early, in March, and was not back in Moscow till October, and yet, unlike almost every previous summer, there was no tangible result in the form of a completed work to show for the holiday. However, there is no particular reason for supposing that Rachmaninoff broke his regular pattern of summer composition, and the apparent hiatus can conveniently be explained by work on the concerto, though this is neither supported nor refuted by Rachmaninoff's sparse and ambiguous extant correspondence. On 11 June the composer wrote to Goldenweiser that he had begun work the day before, but five days later contradictorily informed Slonov that he was not working and had not been. Then there is a gap until 1 November, when he told Siloti that since the war (*viz.* August) his work had been at a standstill.[11] Although the copious sketches of the concerto which survive in the Library of Congress are undated, part of the first and last movements are in a sketchbook also containing a draft of the setting *From St John's Gospel* that Rachmaninoff made in November of 1914 and which is thus likely to be of roughly the same date. Rachmaninoff almost certainly resumed work on the concerto the following year, after completing the *All-Night Vigil*. His comments to Goldenweiser,[12] if indeed they do refer to the concerto rather than to *The Scythians*, would help to explain its protracted and difficult gestation:

> We're already in Moscow in 'winter quarters'. The summer has passed and for me it passed badly. I was very busy until 15 June, but the whole time my work didn't get along; it didn't satisfy me, and by the time mentioned I had reached the point of being unable to control either the work or myself and so I gave up working. After a long period when work has not satisfied me this point always comes upon me. I began to pass the time in reading, walking, grumbling and falling into depression. I went to stay with Sasha Siloti, where I spent a whole week amusing myself. I led this sensible life until 15 July, when I again set to work. This time things seemed to be going well but then they turned bad. The grave news from the war, anxiety about our unfortunate choice of residence [in Finland], a new call-up for re-examination etc. – all this did not allow me to concentrate on work. And so I decided to escape to Moscow, hoping for something better for myself.

The following year, 1916, found Rachmaninoff preoccupied with the songs Op. 38 and the new *Études-Tableaux* Op. 39, but it is not impossible that in 1917, on his last visit to Ivanovka, he took with him his sketches for the concerto to work on that summer. At any rate, a note appeared in the musical press of the time announcing unequivocally that Rachmaninoff was currently working on the concerto.[13] Even in the first years after leaving Russia the composer must have continued working spasmodically on the sketches: a fragment of the last movement appears on the back of the draft of the cadenza to Liszt's Second Hungarian Rhapsody, which was first performed in January 1919, and other sketches, of parts of the first and third movements, appear in a sketchbook Rachmaninoff gave to Siloti, evidently dated 1921–22. In April 1924 Medtner met Rachmaninoff on several occasions in Florence, and asking in the course of their conversations the unaskable question of why he no longer composed received the not unambiguous reply: 'How can I compose without melody?'[14] Perhaps Medtner's remark stung Rachmaninoff into action, for two months later he told him that he had begun work,[15] and the next year Medtner was able to report to Goldenweiser that Rachmaninoff had actually played him portions of the concerto: 'He ran through different passages of his Fourth Concerto, which he had drafted in 1917 and which, at last, he is intending to take in hand this winter. It is of course the same authentic Rachmaninoff, but overall he played it too fragmentarily and too little of it to make a proper judgement.'[16]

In 1926, first in his New York apartment and then in Dresden, Rachmaninoff at last put the concerto into a state of completion, only to discover when he received a copy of the two-piano score that its 110 pages were more than he had anticipated. 'Out of cowardice I haven't yet tried it for time', he wrote to Medtner;[17]

> It will probably be performed like 'The Ring' on several evenings in succession. I recalled my conversations with you on the theme of length and the need to cut down, compress, and not to be long-winded, and I was ashamed! Apparently the whole trouble is in the last movement. I've heaped up something there! In my mind I've already begun to track down cuts. I've found one, but only of eight bars in all and that in the first movement, which is the one which has not scared me by its length. Moreover, I have already spotted that the orchestra is almost never silent, which I consider a big fault. That means that it is not a piano concerto but a concerto for piano and orchestra. I also noticed that the theme of the second movement is the theme of the first movement of Schumann's concerto. How is it that you didn't tell me this?

Medtner's long and earnest reply[18] seems not to have overcome Rachmaninoff's misgivings.

The premiere of the new concerto, dedicated to Medtner, took place in Philadelphia under Stokowski on 18 March 1927, and the performance was repeated twice more there before being taken to New York, Washington and Baltimore. The critics were unanimous in their attitude of withering scorn, condemning the work as a relic of the nineteenth century written out of its time, and one going so far as to describe it as 'long-winded, tiresome, unimportant, in places tawdry'.[19] During the following summer Rachmaninoff made considerable revisions, reducing the total length by 114 bars. 'After 1½ months of hard work I have finished the corrections to my concerto... The first twelve pages have been rewritten, as also the whole coda.'[20] In its revised state the concerto was at last published as the inaugural issue of his daughters' publishing house, Tair, in 1928. However, it was not until November 1929 that Rachmaninoff again tried out the work on a concert audience, with a single performance in London. The reception was as tepid as before, and achieving no greater success a year later when he played the concerto elsewhere in Europe, in The Hague, Amsterdam, Paris and in Berlin, he resigned himself to abandoning it as a lost cause. In the late thirties Rachmaninoff had notions of returning to work on it again, evidently still believing that its failure was mainly due to weakness in the structure of the third movement.[21] When he at last found time for the work, in the summer of 1941, he took the revisions of 1927 further, reducing the work by another 78 bars, concentrating particularly on the latter half of the last movement but also tinkering generally with minor details of piano and orchestral layout.[22] However, the reception accorded the revised version was as disappointing as before, and after seven performances in American cities the composer tried no more. The recording he made of the work in December 1941 was his last performance of it.

If ever a work of Rachmaninoff failed to live up to the promise of its opening, it is his Fourth Concerto. Expectations are raised at the outset by the exhilarating surprise modulation in the brief orchestral introduction, where, after D major has apparently been solidly established in the first four bars, at the last moment there is an abrupt switch to G minor for the piano entry. Then the soloist sets forth the first theme in massive chords, stepping out with a majestic confidence and in a pianistic style reminiscent of the climaxes of the earlier concertos. The overall arch shape of the melodic line seems to define much of the musical material throughout the work; the climax to the second movement and the development of the second subject in the last both have this configuration, and the outer parts of the outline, the gradual ascent and descent, also figure prominently by themselves. The material in between is based on a figure with so obvious a similarity to a phrase from *Vocalise* as strongly to suggest that the concerto's opening was conceived at the same time as that work, *viz.* 1914 (Ex. 156).

After the conviction of the opening the ensuing bridge passage, despite its energy, is musically flaccid; however, as in the Third Concerto, the arrival of the second theme is neatly heralded, here by presentiments

Ex.156a   Fourth Concerto, opening theme

Ex.156b   *Vocalise,* end

on cor-anglais and horn. The theme itself, at least in its opening phrases, is a close cousin of the F major Prelude of 1910. After it has taken wing in a typically glowing Rachmaninoff setting, an important four-note motif is heard, first on bassoons and then trumpet, a leap to an accented minor ninth resolving on the octave. Commentators generally imply that this figure is newly introduced here and apparently unconnected with what has gone before, whereas clearly Rachmaninoff created it merely by transforming the opening phrase of the second subject to show a very different, brusque, side of its nature (Ex. 157). This motif not only figures in the ensuing development section (the second subject as such does not) but also generates the opening theme of the finale, so playing an important part in the cyclical design of the whole work. When Alfred Swan noted a lack of spontaneity in the concerto,[23] he may well have

Ex.157a   First movement, second theme

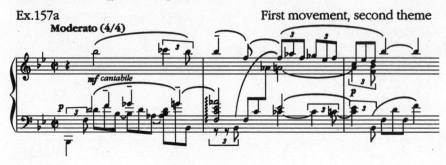

Ex.157b   First movement,
                      bassoon/trumpet motif

had the first movement development in mind, for though Rachmaninoff exploits his material with great ingenuity the musical effect is arid. In fact the music only takes off again when the main climax is reached and high strings play a variant of the *Vocalise* figure over rich piano chordal triplets to launch the soloist into an ecstatic frenzy. There is a passion and urge in the writing at this point, and in the no less admirable post-orgasmic aftermath, which far transcends the empty manipulation of notes that precedes them.

In the recapitulation, unusually for Rachmaninoff, the two themes appear in reverse order, a varied restatement of the concerto's opening bars heralding the final statement of the first theme, which is sung sweetly by the first violins against gentle piano arpeggios. Then the music seems gradually to exhaust itself, before a cry from the cor-anglais introduces the much-criticized coda. For these brief six bars Rachmaninoff changes the time signature from 2/2 to 3/4, a metre occurring nowhere else in the whole movement. This makes their attachment to what has gone before seem all the more abrupt, though their function is plain enough – to bring the music sharply back to heel from the remote tonal regions to which it has found itself wandering and to round off the movement with a reminiscence of its opening. Thus the coda shares with the concerto's introduction an *Allegro vivace* marking and a rising sequence establishing a major key (here E flat), which suddenly veers to the home key of G minor for the final chord.

The *Largo* middle movement is another enigma. The piano introduction, similar in style to the opening of the slow movement of the Second

Sonata of 1913, is derived from the opening theme of the previous movement with the omission of a passing note, another example of the high degree of integration of material evident in the concerto:

Ex.158

But was there ever a melody in Rachmaninoff so perfunctory or disappointing as the stunted motto of this movement, or one so different from its long-breathed predecessors? As if to emphasize its simplistic nature Rachmaninoff sets it in the key of C major. Marked '*misterioso*' in its initial appearance on the strings, its repeated three-note formula may perhaps derive from the final falling phrases of the first movement's main theme.

Ex.159

In the absence of melodic interest, attention necessarily focuses on the varied harmonic and rhythmic treatment to which the motto is subjected. Culshaw[24] seems to have originated the mistaken impression that the 'cries from the heart' in the middle section (*L'istesso tempo, ma agitato*) are a new element in the movement, whereas in fact they are merely a semitone version of the whole tones in the original theme, another instance in the concerto of Rachmaninoff's revealing startlingly different aspects of the same musical material. The sequence from the C minor *Étude-Tableau* of 1911 used as the climax of the movement was transferred quite literally and even keeps its original key – C major in the episode in question – raising the intriguing possibility that this, rather than the character of the three-note motto, may have dictated the movement's tonality. At any rate, the episode at least sounds like an organic part of the movement, its rising sequence being carefully prepared for by the groups of ascending quavers in the soloists' preceding bridge passage. In both the original version of the concerto and the *Étude-Tableau* from which it was borrowed this climax was given a rather florid piano decoration, which Rachmaninoff changed to advantage in 1941 to the same style of chordal triplets as in the first movement climax.

The coda of the *Largo* hints at the finale, the most complex movement of the concerto. Before the *attacca subito*, in an atmosphere of expectation, the horns sound in quiet warning the falling minor second from the first movement's four-note leaping motto, which the whole orchestra immediately repeats staccato, like the sneeze at the beginning of Kodály's *Háry János*. The reason for this gesture becomes clear when the soloist launches into the bustling first subject, for this turns out to be derived from the motto (or possibly vice versa!):

Ex.160

When the theme is passed to the full orchestra, the percussion section is augmented beyond the resources of all the earlier concertos by triangle, tambourine, snare drum, cymbals and bass drum. Then, as so often in Rachmaninoff, the second subject is subtly hinted at before it arrives, a sequence of rising chords from the piano (just before figure 49) anticipating the soloist's subsequent development of it. The theme itself turns out to be an old friend – *Dies irae* – in one of its most heart-warming guises:

Ex.161

The key of D flat is significant. In the original version the theme first appears as a romantic meandering for the soloist, decorated with trumpet fanfares, whereas in the revision the fanfares, now given to the piano, herald the theme, which emerges after presentiments of its shape on the horns. This compression, which undoubtedly eliminates a lull in the movement's momentum, points the way to Rachmaninoff's general approach in both revisions to solving the perceived problem of the last movement. Even in the original 1926 version this second subject played only a small part in the musical discussion since, because of Rachmaninoff's cyclical design, its usual function was usurped later in the movement by material from the concerto's opening. In 1927 Rachmaninoff pruned even the small part remaining, and in 1941 he took the process further, extinguishing all traces of the theme in the development section and coda. Thus the glowingly romantic sequence sparked off by *Dies irae*, in which the piano soars aloft in the manner of the Rachmaninoff of old, is reduced to no more than an isolated incident. In doing this the composer was perhaps consciously following the strategy he had already used in revising his First Concerto – between the time of the Fourth Concerto's conception and its completion – in which he similarly reduced the supernumerary third theme in the last movement to a single episode.

After the orchestra has begun the development section by restating the opening of the first subject, the piano picks up its final descending phrases in falling sequences of minor thirds, plumbing lugubrious depths before a final flourish. This is another passage proclaiming itself as among the concerto's earliest material, for it unmistakably recalls an episode in the original 1913 version of the Second Sonata, even sharing its key (Ex. 162).

In the development section Rachmaninoff contented himself in the final revision with removing just a few bars, so leaving almost intact the original exhaustive exploitation of the first theme, whose limited musical content is all too evident under the welter of empty decoration. To introduce the movement's final section the concerto's opening is literally recalled. It is perhaps a comment on Rachmaninoff's difficulty with the work that he should have resorted at this point to reusing a strategy he had adopted in the same place in the last movement of the very different Third Concerto, where, to set in motion the build-up to the final climax, he broke down the second subject into a series of staccato fragments. In the present work the syncopated jabs on piano and bassoon and the sequence they introduce also started life as a variant of the second subject, but it would be difficult to guess this from the revision, in which Rachmaninoff obliterated all hints of its pedigree by reducing the material still further to its rhythmic essentials and imposing a somewhat different character through a change of metre (Ex.163). The concerto's dénouement is provided by the reappearance of the first movement climax, which Rachmaninoff drives into tortured dissonance before a scurry of empty exhibitionism for the soloist that might better have been omitted and the final jaunty chords.

Despite all Rachmaninoff's attempts to improve it the Fourth Concerto remained, and remains, unloved. The reasons are not far to seek. In his Third Concerto the composer used again the proven style and form of

Ex.162a   Fourth Concerto, last movement

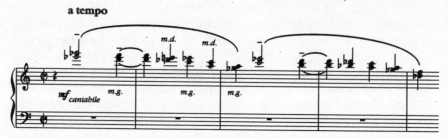

Ex.162b   Second Sonata, last movement

the Second, developing further the grandiloquent expression of melancholy and the element of gladiatorial combat between soloist and orchestra so successful before. All these ingredients the Fourth Concerto conspicuously lacks. As Sorabji wrote: 'After the splendour and richness [of its predecessor] the Fourth Concerto is a stark, rather bare and gaunt work, that comes in style and treatment rather within the domain of the *sinfonia concertante* than the concerto in the proper sense'.[25] Much of the work is characterized by an emotional aloofness reminiscent of the Second Sonata, with which its overall conception was probably contemporary. Thus the theme of the concerto's second movement seems to be in almost deliberate antithesis to the great sweeping melodies of earlier years, and the second subjects of the outer movements are both short-breathed and incapable of the

Ex.163a   1927

Ex.163b   1941

kind of climactic apotheosis so attractive in the Second and Third Concertos. Indeed, the First Concerto's only moderate success even in its revised form may have been due to the absence of just such a feature from its similarly lightweight finale. Even before the Fourth Concerto's first performance Rachmaninoff came to the opinion that the score needed further work, but the changes to which he subjected it were aimed specifically at improving its formal structure rather than its chances of public acceptability. What audiences expected and wanted was a wholly different concerto from the one Rachmaninoff wrote; what he gave them is a work of considerable originality in an unfamiliar vein, a work which, though uneven, has several memorable moments of real inspiration. When performed by an artist such as Michelangeli, the concerto seems scarcely to deserve its continued neglect.

Three Russian Songs, Op. 41

The concert in Philadelphia at which the Fourth Concerto was premiered also saw the first performance of another Rachmaninoff work, the Three Russian Songs, for orchestra and chorus, completed in 1926 and dedicated to the conductor of the Philadelphia Orchestra, Leopold Stokowski. It is implied in the *Recollections*[26] that Rachmaninoff's attention was drawn to the originals only after he had settled in America, but this is disproved by the existence of a notebook containing four pages of rough sketches for the work, dated 1916.[27]

Rachmaninoff had rarely before been drawn to folksong as such, *The Barge Haulers* (1891), the Ukrainian song *Shoes* (1899) and the three sketches of 1920 being the only precedents in the catalogue of his compositions. Each of the Three Russian Songs, like these earlier settings and like Russian and other folksongs generally, consists in essence of a brief and simple melody repeated many times, but, as Chaliapin above all so marvellously demonstrated on the stage, in his recordings, and on many occasions to Rachmaninoff in private, naive material can be a vehicle for high art when the interpreter uses to the full every source of expression available to him, necessarily including countless subtle differences in each presentation of the melody as the story unfolds. Rachmaninoff naturally followed a similar strategy, translating into orchestral and choral terms the artistry of the singers who had introduced him to the songs. On the one hand, he emphasizes the innate simplicity of the material by using only a modest choir of altos and basses and even then, in all but a few bars of the last song, in unison; on the other, to illustrate and comment on the dramas being enacted he employs an unusually large orchestra, larger even than in *The Bells*, but uses it with the greatest subtlety and variety to create textures notably more transparent than in that work. To impose an overall form on three disparate songs, Rachmaninoff so chooses and orders them as to create the structure and coherence of a miniature three-movement symphonic work: *Moderato* leading to *Allegro assai, Largo, Allegro moderato.*

There is some slight confusion over the source of the first song, *Over the River* ('See! a wooden bridge is jutting'). According to Sofiya Satina[28] Rachmaninoff had long been familiar with it from an unnamed folksong collection, and a Soviet commentator[29] has tracked down the melody as a round dance from the district of Vladimir, published in 1895, with different words, in an arrangement for voice and piano by Liadov. Whilst this collection may indeed be the original source, it is implied in the *Recollections*[30] that Rachmaninoff's attention was drawn to it by Chaliapin; at any rate, under the title 'The Drake', it was a regular part of that singer's public repertoire. The words of the song tell the pathetic tale of a drake escorting a grey duck over a bridge; the duck becomes frightened and flies away, leaving the drake forlorn and weeping. Rachmaninoff hints at this dénouement already in the orchestral introduction, which begins with a descending scale in thirds, like a disconsolate cry of despair. Rocking pairs of quavers on the strings seem to suggest the busy waddling of the two ducks, while a plaintive woodwind chord with an acciaccatura clearly represents their cry. These three elements Rachmaninoff weaves into the orchestral texture to illustrate the drama which the choral basses relate. Thus, when the duck forsakes her mate, the orchestra responds by making a great chromatic descent to reflect the depths of the drake's disappointment and the drake's plaintive cries are heard on woodwind against bleak violins. The despairing descending scale from the opening is recalled and the singers sing the refrain for the last time in measured and quietly sad tones as they describe the weeping drake. In the orchestral postlude (*Più mosso*) Rachmaninoff implies that the drake too flies despairingly away, uttering one last forlorn cry.

The second song, *O Vanka* ('O my Johnny, bold and headstrong') was from Chaliapin, who had learned it from his mother. It came to be one of the most popular folksong items in his repertoire, and Rachmaninoff may well have possessed a copy of one of the singer's two recordings of the piece, especially since the later two-sided issue was backed by *Aleko's Cavatina.*[31] The song is the bitter lament of a wife whose husband has been persuaded by his father to abandon her and spend the winter with him. The theme of desertion is thus common to both the first and the second songs, and Rachmaninoff imposes an element of musical coherence between them by making the point of departure of the second (in D minor) the same note, E, as that on which the first ends. This swells into bitter cries in the orchestra, in the shape of a repeated, falling four-note figure, a close cousin, appropriately enough, of the 'Tears' motif in the First Suite for Two Pianos (1893) and *The Miserly Knight* (1903–04), but whose direct line of descent is from one of Rachmaninoff's more recent compositions, *From St John's Gospel*, though the folksong setting *The Apple Tree*, perhaps fortuitously, has the same figure and similar harmony:

Ex.164a   *From St John's Gospel* (1914) - end

Ex.164b   *The Apple Tree* (1920) - opening

Ex.164c   *O Vanka* (1925) - opening

For this woman's lament Rachmaninoff naturally uses the altos; like the basses in the first song, they remain undivided throughout. With each repetition the refrain gains in intensity and bitterness, until the climax is reached and, in a passage harmonically reminiscent of parts of the third movement of *The Bells*, the singers wordlessly intone descending phrases of despair as the orchestra too sinks in chromatic scales down to a final recollection of the 'Tears' motif, in brief but exquisite solo phrases for violin, oboe, horn and finally clarinet, to bring this 'slow movement' to a sombrely impressive end.

The last song, *Powder and Paint* ('Quickly, quickly from my cheeks'), came from the singer Nadezhda Plevitskaya, a popular entertainer in pre-revolutionary Russia. When Plevitskaya emigrated to America she visited Rachmaninoff in his New York apartment and entertained him with some of her large folksong repertoire, this particular song especially attracting him because of its originality and the singer's interpretation.[32] Plevitskaya was a simple peasant woman from Kursk, from which this song comes. According to Sofiya Satina:[33] 'One could listen to the stories, both comic and sad, that she half-sang half-told and never grow tired of hearing them. She had almost no voice as a singer, and it was the way in which she delivered her songs, and their content, which was so good.' It seems that Rachmaninoff improvised an accompaniment to her singing and that in the case of this one song developed it into a formal setting. He persuaded the Victor Company to record Plevitskaya and him performing the song, which they promptly did, on 22 February 1926. The two artists received test copies but the record was not issued commercially until the days of LP, when the force of Plevitskaya's vibrant personality and Rachmaninoff's marvellously sympathetic accompaniment could at last be heard for the first time. It was this setting that Rachmaninoff orchestrated as the last of the three songs in his Op. 41.

The song is the humorous tale of an unfaithful wife who hurriedly removes the make-up from her face as she hears her husband unexpectedly returning home. Whilst he has been away, she has been flirting with a neighbour and now pretends not to know why her husband should return with a silken whip as a present for her. Of all three songs this has the simplest and most repeated refrain; not only does the music never modulate, but the most pervasive harmony implicit in the melody is nothing more exciting than the tonic triad. The setting therefore demonstrates most clearly Rachmaninoff's subtlety in using all his orchestral, choral and harmonic resources to avoid the monotony inherent in material musically so limited, and to create instead a continuously varied and artistically satisfying whole. For this song only, altos and basses are combined, and though they begin in unison they later divide into two or three parts. The orchestral forces also are heard in their most extended form, and for the first and last time in any score of his, Rachmaninoff employs a switch-stick in the elaborate percussion department.

Rachmaninoff was insistent that the song's indication of moderate tempo (*Allegro moderato, alla marcia*) should be strictly adhered to, and the conviction of his recording with Plevitskaya, at a speed which nowhere exceeds crotchet = 108, proves his point.[34] At the rehearsal for the premiere in the Academy of Music, Philadelphia, Rachmaninoff became restless at Stokowski's excessive speed. Pointing out the marking, he asked him for a slower tempo, but the conductor did not oblige. Rachmaninoff then turned to the chorus, begging them, in Russian, to sing more slowly, but they protested that they were unable to do so because of Stokowski's conducting. Finally, he turned again to the chorus, and noting that several of the basses sported clerical collars appealed to their religious feelings: 'I beg you, do not ruin a devout Russian Orthodox churchman. Please sing more slowly!'[35] However, Rachmaninoff's failure to write a metronome marking into the score has encouraged other conductors after Stokowski unduly to let out the reins and so turn a jaunty trot into a hasty scramble.

At their first performance in Philadelphia the Three Russian Songs were as much a success as the new Fourth Concerto was a failure, and when they were subsequently premiered in Moscow at the Bolshoi Theatre under Golovanov they created a similarly favourable impression and had to be encored. In a letter of appreciation to Rachmaninoff Stokowski wrote: 'The more I try to penetrate the inner essence of your new concerto and the Russian Songs, the more I love this music. For me these are two of your most wonderful works, and I am very proud that I am taking part in their performance and that the Russian Songs are dedicated to me, for there is so much of the beautiful ancient poetic spirit of Russia in them that I so greatly admire.'[36] Certainly the Songs are profoundly Russian in character, but their charm is universal; the melodies are inherently attractive, the settings varied, the orchestration masterly. The sole reason for the infrequent performances of these miniature masterpieces is undoubtedly the large and expensive forces required for a work lasting little more than ten minutes.

Two months after the first performance of the Three Russian Songs a Rachmaninoff interview appeared in the musical press[37] in which the composer philosophized interestingly about the nature of musical inspiration. From its substance it is clear that he was looking back to his Russian years rather than thinking of his two most recent works:

> It is most difficult to analyse the source of inspiration for compositions; so many factors work together in creative work. Love is certainly a never-failing source of inspiration; love inspires as nothing else does. To love is to gain happiness and strength of mind; it is the unfoldment of a new vista of intellectual energy. The beauty and grandeur of nature helps. Poetry inspires me much; of all the arts I love poetry best after music. Our Pushkin I find admirable; Shakespeare and Byron I read constantly in the Russian. I always have books of poetry around me.

Poetry inspires music – for there is so much music in poetry; they are like twin sisters. Everything of beauty helps... A beautiful woman is certainly a source of perpetual inspiration, but you must run away from her and seek seclusion; otherwise you will compose nothing. Carry the inspiration in your heart and mind; think of her, but be all by yourself for creative work. Real inspiration must come from within; nothing from outside can help. The best in poetry, the greatest of painting, the sublimest of nature cannot produce any worthwhile result if the divine spark of creative faculty is lacking within the artist.

Such rarefied views ill matched the unpleasant reality of the hostile reception accorded the Fourth Concerto, if not the Russian Songs, which must have banished from Rachmaninoff's mind any further thoughts of temporary retirement from the concert platform for the purposes of composition. The 1926 sabbatical had meant the expenditure of a great amount of time and effort, not to mention a financial sacrifice, unrewarded by commensurate artistic success, and over the next four years Rachmaninoff's only work on composition was the brief piano transcription of Rimsky-Korsakov's *Flight of the Bumble Bee*, completed early in 1929. Although the original is drastically pruned by eliminating its central episode altogether and making a synthesis of the beginning and end of the outer sections, Rachmaninoff otherwise keeps closely to Rimsky's text, while adding a small dash of harmonic spice. The airy texture of the orchestration is skilfully preserved on the keyboard to make a short but brilliant encore piece for the fleetest of fingers.

Back in 1922 Koussevitzky had commissioned Ravel to orchestrate Mussorgsky's *Pictures at an Exhibition*, bringing the work with him to America at the end of 1924 for his first season with the Boston Symphony Orchestra. Perhaps encouraged by the success of this work the conductor then turned his thoughts to the possibility of a similar exercise with another set of Russian piano-pictures, this time by Rachmaninoff. When the latter returned from Europe to New York in December 1929, he found Koussevitzky's proposal already awaiting him; it was that he should choose a group of his *Études-Tableaux* for orchestration by the Italian composer Ottorino Respighi, whose original compositions – eight operas, concertos, songs, chamber and orchestral works – include the colourful but musically empty trilogy of symphonic poems about Rome, brought to a triumphant climax earlier in 1929 with *Feste Romane*. Then as now these orchestral spectaculars eclipsed Respighi's more characteristic and profound works, but it was doubtless his reputation as a virtuoso orchestrator and arranger of other composers' works, such as the Diaghilev ballet *La Boutique fantasque*, from Rossini, and the suites *Ancient Airs and Dances* and *The Birds*, together with his impeccable credentials as a pupil, albeit only briefly, of Rimsky-Korsakov, that must have impressed Rachmaninoff, who gave the project his blessing.

In his initial letter to Respighi of 2 January 1930 Rachmaninoff listed the *Études-Tableaux* he had chosen and the programmes which had inspired them. He took one number from Op. 33 and four from Op. 39 to make a suite nearly twenty-five minutes in length, bunching the three most lively and noisy items together in the middle, and leaving the two slowest and most sombre to open and conclude the set. However, by the time Respighi had completed the orchestration in September, the order of the last four items had been changed to make a more contrasting sequence and at least to finish on a high note. On the work's rare outings in the concert hall subsequently, some conductors have taken this process further, sandwiching both slow numbers between livelier ones to create a more effective whole.

Rachmaninoff	Études–Tableaux	Respighi	Others
1	A minor, Op. 39, No. 2, *The Sea and Seagulls*	1	2
2	A minor, Op. 39, No. 6, *Little Red Riding Hood and the Wolf*	4	3
3	E flat major, Op. 33, No. 7, *Fair*	2	1
4	D major, Op. 39, No. 9, *March*	5	5
5	C Minor, Op. 39, No. 7, *Funeral March*	3	4

In one sense Respighi's task was more formidable than Ravel's in that Rachmaninoff's pieces, unlike Mussorgsky's, are pianistically so idiomatic, so totally the embodiment of the virtuoso at the keyboard, that to clothe them in any different dress might be thought inevitably to detract from their effect. On the other hand, the *Études-Tableaux* could also be said to be orchestral in conception, pressing the capacity of the concert grand to limits which beg the employment of greater resources. Respighi's orchestration turned out to be characteristically lavish, with a particularly fussy use of percussion at climaxes. This works colourfully enough in *The Fair* and *March*, but sounds garish and overdone in *The Sea and Seagulls* and *Red Riding Hood* and positively destroys the *Funeral March*, whose climax of tinkling bells turns a Russian funeral into a Roman festival.

In October 1930 Rachmaninoff sent a telegram to Respighi thanking him for his work and particularly for keeping so closely to the original texts, but later he seems to have been less than enthusiastic about what he called 'Respighi's Suite'. His reaction may have been soured by the careless editing, for when he came to see the first proofs he found to his horror some hundreds of errors. 'Never,' he wrote to Paichadze,[38] 'in my 38 years of being published have I seen such printing or such correction. Obviously the publication will be vile. Well, carry out your duty! But I personally have neither the time nor the desire to take part in a publication like this.' Although his recital schedule would have allowed him to do so, Rachmaninoff attended neither the rehearsals nor the premiere of the suite, though his wife did, of whose musical judgement she claimed he once said: 'What she says will be my opinion too'.[39] In two letters to Rachmaninoff Koussevitzky praised the orchestration – 'except for a few overloaded passages'[40] – but Mrs Rachmaninoff was displeased by the excessive speed at which she felt Koussevitzky took the first and last movements, and in writing again to Paichadze Rachmaninoff transferred his wife's unfavourable impression of Koussevitzky's interpretation to the suite as a whole: 'Sergei Alexandrovich [Koussevitzky] writes me vis-à-vis Respighi that his orchestration is magnificent. I think he scarcely believes this himself and says this as a consolation to me for not playing the work in New York, which is otherwise incomprehensible. My wife heard the performance in Brooklyn and was not pleased with it.'[41] Of Rachmaninoff's subsequent views of the suite, which was occasionally programmed in concerts at which he appeared as soloist in one of his concertos, we have no evidence.

Variations on a Theme of Corelli, Op. 42

In 1922, 1924 and 1928 Rachmaninoff had visited England, and from the 1928–29 season until the outbreak of war in 1939 he extended his annual concert itinerary to include Europe generally. In connection with this more widespread activity away from America he spent at least part of the summers of 1924–28 in Dresden and in 1928–1931 holidayed in France, where, in 1930, Riesemann interviewed him for his book *Rachmaninoff's Recollections*. Before returning to the United States for the new season Rachmaninoff paid a return visit to Riesemann in Switzerland, in the course of which he impetuously purchased a piece of land on the shores of Lake Lucerne on which to build the villa 'Senar'. In the summer of 1931, while construction work was underway on his new Ivanovka, Rachmaninoff spent his last French holiday at the villa 'Le Pavillon' at Clairefontaine, and it was here that he completed the only original solo piano work he was to write after leaving Russia, the *Variations on a Theme of Corelli*, Op. 42. He began work on the very day of his arrival at the villa, 27 May,[42] and in little more than three weeks had completed the composition.

Though Rachmaninoff was evidently unaware of it at the time, the theme he used in his new work was not in fact by Corelli at all but merely an ancient Portuguese dance melody called *La Folía*, Corelli being just one of countless composers to have used it as variation material in the course of its four-hundred-year history. Rachmaninoff himself probably first encountered the melody in Liszt's *Spanish Rhapsody*, a work he had added to his repertoire twelve years before, and he is surely most unlikely ever to have come across so obscure and, to him, stylistically so alien a work as the Corelli violin and harpsichord sonata[43] from which he might at first sight be thought to have appropriated the theme. Rachmaninoff's mistaken ascription to Corelli is perhaps to be explained by his dedication of the work to Fritz Kreisler, which may be not only a gesture of friendship and respect, particularly after their work together on three sonata recordings during 1928,[44] but also a recognition that the violinist may in some way have stimulated composition in the first place; for of all Rachmaninoff's friends Kreisler is obviously the most likely to have been familiar with the Corelli original, and Rachmaninoff may even have heard him play his own similarly entitled 'Variations on a Theme of Corelli (after Tartini)', based, though that work was, on a different Corelli melody.

Of all Rachmaninoff's works the *Corelli Variations* exemplifies in its most heightened form the more dispassionate and detached style already seen in the Second Sonata (revised this same summer of 1931), in some of the *Études-Tableaux* and in the recent Fourth Concerto. Although the sentiment so powerfully expressed in Rachmaninoff's music seems generally to have derived from internal forces within the composer rather than external circumstances, it is tempting to see the emotional aloofness of his new work as a reflection of one of his periodic depressions of spirit. In January he had broken his long vow of maintaining a discreet silence about political matters to add his signature to a letter of strong criticism of the Soviet regime published in the *New York Times*.[45] Two months later he learned that, in reprisal, a boycott had been called for on the performance and study of his music in what he still thought of as his homeland. Although Rachmaninoff claimed he was indifferent to this, the blow seems to have caused him at least temporarily to retreat into himself in emotional self-defence. This withdrawal was evidently noticeable even in his playing; of his last recital of the season, in Brooklyn on 27 March, one reviewer wrote: 'When [Rachmaninoff] is not at his best, as was the case last evening, he can be very dull. His emotional detachment then is translated into terms of indifference, and one feels that Mr Rachmaninoff has neither head nor heart for the task; nothing is expressed in his playing but weariness and lassitude of spirit.'[46]

In an unhappy letter to Sofiya Satina, penned a month after completing the *Corelli Variations* while he was still in the throes of revising the

Second Sonata, Rachmaninoff spoke of how he coped with external pressure: 'Not everything is bad, even for me; that is saying a lot. What saves me from "the bad", as always, is work. I've begun to work more so as not to be conscious of the bad.'[47] However, he thought work 'unimportant and trivial' in comparison with the world financial crisis and the worrying political situation in Europe. To his private secretary, Yevgeny Somov, he wrote the same day: 'The recent political events have burst on us like a thunder storm! It's no longer a good thing to be alive in this world! And it seems to me that worse times lie ahead...'[48] In an interview two years later he frankly admitted, as Elgar had, that so far as composition was concerned he had 'gone off the boil': 'Certainly I still write music, but it does not mean the same thing to me now'.[49] This disenchantment and emotional disengagement seem to underlie the *Corelli Variations*, in which Rachmaninoff goes through the formal processes of composition with no less skill than before but with little of the personal commitment of his Russian works. It could be called his most cerebral and least sentimental work.

So ascetic and consciously baroque a theme as the saraband-like *La Folía* seems at first sight entirely alien to Rachmaninoff's own earlier full-blooded romanticism, and yet it does bear a certain distant similarity to the opening theme of his Third Concerto, and, going still further back, the composer had used just such a naively solemn melody as the basis of a set of variations in the second movement of his *Elegiac Trio*. Unlike that example, however, the Corelli theme is all contained within the narrow interval of a perfect fifth and, as a result, is rather less interesting melodically.

Although Rachmaninoff's most recent work in variation form, the Variations on a Theme of Chopin, Op. 22, had been written nearly thirty years previously, the composer clearly took the pattern for his new work from the old, dividing the variations into three contrasting groups of 'movements', as he had before, to make a kind of sonata structure:

Movement	Description	Variations
I	*Allegro and Scherzo*, D minor	Theme; 1–13
II	*Adagio*, D flat major	14–15
III	*Finale*, D minor	16–20; Coda

The 'first movement' falls naturally into three parts. The statement of theme and the first four variations are all slow or moderate in tempo and modest in scope. The manner in which the theme is treated in the last of them is clearly reminiscent of the thirteenth Chopin variation, again emphasizing the relationship between the two works. Although the writing naturally becomes more complex as the work develops, perhaps in deference to the antiquity of the theme, the composer nowhere allows it to blossom into the rich fullness of his earlier style, and the relative pianistic simplicity and lean textures are paralleled only by the enigmatic and uncharacteristic *Fragments*. As Prokofiev commented, when he heard the composer play the work in Paris in March 1932, 'This is not the old Rachmaninoff of the Second and Third Concertos'.[50]

In the following three fast variations Rachmaninoff concentrates on the rhythmic possibilities of the theme. In variation 5 the brusque staccato and frequent metrical changes mark another and more obviously twentieth-century development in Rachmaninoff's style:

Ex.165 Variation 5

The *Adagio misterioso* which launches the last group of variations in the 'first movement', nos. 8–13, despite its strong musical sense of purpose, has an aimless feel about it, which reflects the psychological mood of the whole work. In it Rachmaninoff toys aloofly with the theme, as it wanders, effete and haunted, in a chill mist (Ex. 166).

After the Intermezzo between variations 13 and 14, with its baroque mordents sitting uncomfortably between romantic keyboard arpeggios, comes a restatement of the theme in D flat to prepare the way for the central focus of the work, the fifteenth variation or 'slow movement'.

Ex.166   Variation 8

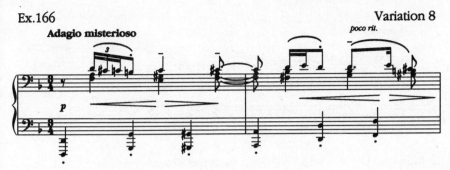

In its own terms it recreates the mood of the thirteenth Chopin variation, a romantic interlude before the final group of fast variations. The choice of key naturally arouses expectations of Rachmaninoff's warmest lyricism, but this variation too has an icy pallor, heightened by the diatonic chill in the harmony:

Ex.167   Variation 15

Who could have guessed from this that in the equivalent variation in the *Paganini Rhapsody* only three years later, the famous eighteenth, Rachmaninoff would recapture the warmth of his earlier style in all its glory?

The 'third movement', back in the home key of D minor, consists of a group of variations of increasing vigour and ingenuity, gathering momentum towards a sure climax. En route, in variation 19, *Agitato*, the ghostly swirls call to mind the same haunted mood as the last movement of Chopin's 'Funeral March' Sonata, with its visions of wind howling through a graveyard (Ex. 168). Then, after the climactic twentieth variation, as in the Chopin Variations, comes the after-glow of a pensive coda, the nearest thing in the whole work to 'the old Rachmaninoff'. The juxtaposition of a final snatch of the theme to bring the work to a close emphasizes the stylistic dichotomy between romanticism and the baroque that underlies the whole work.

The composer's few published comments about the *Corelli Variations* all seem to confirm an impression of indifference towards it. Playing it

Ex.168   Variation 19

Più mosso. Agitato

through to Alfred Swan, he dismissed the Intermezzo, in typical self-depreciation, with the words: 'All this mad rushing about is necessary in order to efface the theme'.[51] In the earliest public performances he seems capriciously to have omitted up to half of the variations according to the coughing response of the audience, explaining in his droll account to Medtner that playing his own music was 'so boring'.[52] Even in the published score three of the variations (nos. 11, 12 and 19) may optionally be omitted, though for no obvious musical reason. It is as though Rachmaninoff had put nothing of himself into the writing except technique and as though he felt no special affection for his new creation. After trying it out on audiences over the next three concert seasons, he never again returned to it.

Second Piano Sonata, Op. 36 [Revised version]

During his interviews with Riesemann in the summer of 1930 Rachmaninoff hinted that he was not satisfied with the original setting of his Second Sonata and that he wished to recast the work.[53] In conversation with Alfred Swan he explained why: 'I look at my early works and see how much there is that is superfluous. Even in this sonata so many voices are moving simultaneously and it is too long.'[54] Rachmaninoff set to work on the revision at the end of June 1931, immediately after completing the *Corelli Variations*, and it was ready for performance for the next concert season.

In considering the second version of the sonata commentators have concentrated on the apparent simplification of the piano writing. Certainly the lean style of the *Corelli Variations* rubbed off on the revision of the sonata, in which any note that could be declared not strictly essential was deleted. The opening bars are a case in point, where redundant repeated B flats are pruned from the semi-quaver groups (Ex. 169). This has been explained as a way of making the passage easier to play,[55] which not only is to misunderstand the psychology behind this and other Rachmaninoff revisions, where the desire to eliminate superfluity

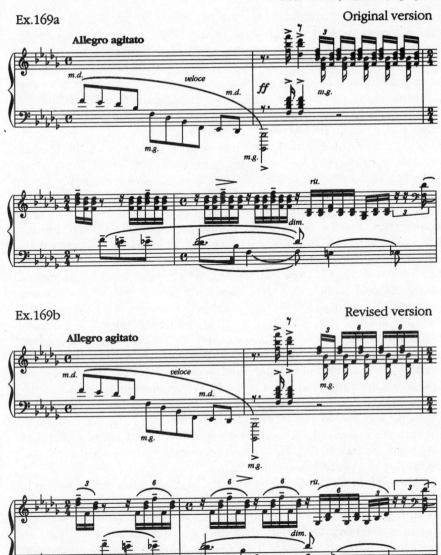

Ex.169a   Original version

Ex.169b   Revised version

at all costs became almost paranoid, but ignores the fact that even in its revised form the sonata requires a considerable virtuoso to do it justice. There is, however, a price to be paid for the greater clarity undoubtedly achieved in the new version, for whereas the leaner style of writing is appropriate to the restraint of the *Corelli Variations*, it is much less happy in the red-blooded rhetoric of the sonata, which loses some of its massive power in consequence.

More lamentable still, however, are the effects of the changes carried out in the revision to the structure of the sonata.[56] Some passages are deleted altogether, some are condensed, a few replaced – not always, incidentally, by material easier to play. Much of the sonata's substance is amputated, and it almost seems as though Rachmaninoff operated on the principle of retaining intact only those core parts of the work which had perhaps proved most effective in performance and of eliminating anything in the rest that was not strictly indispensable, a procedure recalling the cavalier attitude he showed to the integrity of the text in the first performances this same year, 1931, of the *Corelli Variations.*

In the first movement, after the appearance of the second subject, just where the descending scales of bells begin, ten bars (53–62, *Tempo I*) are eliminated, diminishing an elaborate and impassioned climax. Immediately after, a passage of considerable musical but no virtuoso interest is pruned (71–82, *Poco più mosso*), in which overlapping bells toll insistently, anticipating but not duplicating the magnificent descending bell scales of the development section, which echo the last movement of the Second Symphony. Here too a couple of bars (118–119) are peremptorily clipped off the end, and the restatement of the sonata's opening material (*Tempo I,* bars 122 ff.) drastically pruned. The recapitulation, like the exposition, has its climax amputated, and an anguished meditative afterthought of four bars (166–169) disappears before the coda. On the other hand, the final two bars of the movement are arguably improved in the new version by underpinning the final reference to the motto not by two simple tonic chords in B flat minor but by changing the first to the relative major, D flat, thus leaving explicit in the listener's mind the tension between the two tonalities that has underlain the movement. Most present-day performances of the original version at least incorporate this change.

The second movement loses its central section, a fine lyrical interlude (*Più mosso,* from bar 36), in which the prominence of the sonata's motto prepares the ground for the frenetic vortices of the main dramatic climax, which uses the same figure and which trimming reduces to an unrelated rhetorical gesture. The contrasting calm aftermath is also pruned, but it is to the last movement that Rachmaninoff made the most drastic alteration, cutting its length by a third. Besides minor excision and adjustments similar to those made in the previous movements, he left a yawning chasm by axing from the development section four whole pages (bars 116–199), with their bell sounds and dramatic echoes of the first movement. This not only impairs the balance of the movement but, leaving only the most fleeting reference to the work's motto immediately before the second subject, is a serious loss to the cyclic structure. Overall, indeed, one cannot but come to the view that, despite the occasionally more grateful piano writing and greater directness of the revised version, Rachmaninoff would have better stayed with his first thoughts for the sonata.

After a few seasons, in which Rachmaninoff was unsuccessful in his attempt to establish the revised sonata in the recital repertoire, the composer again abandoned it. Its subsequent resurrection was due to Horowitz, who had performed the work even in his Russian days, entertaining a special liking for it. He had been disappointed by the revision, feeling that what might have been gained in conciseness of expression had been outweighed by losses in pianistic sonority and drama. In 1940 he therefore approached the composer with suggestions for making a fusion of the most effective parts of both texts. Horowitz set to work with Rachmaninoff's agreement, and he eventually launched his new version, leaning heavily on the 1913 edition, in January 1943, only two months before the composer's death. As with the Third Concerto, it is little exaggeration to say that the sonata's survival owes a great deal to Horowitz's advocacy, which continued even into his later years on the concert platform, when he made a few further, but not advantageous, alterations, most notably to the last movement coda.[57] Impetus to the revival was also given by Van Cliburn, who was responsible for reintroducing the work to Moscow audiences. He too went back almost entirely to the original edition, in which form the work is usually played today.

For Rachmaninoff the summer of 1932 was mainly taken up with the business of overseeing the building of Senar, but in the course of the following concert season he introduced two important new piano transcriptions that presumably had been sketched out at this time. In January 1933 he premiered his arrangement of the Scherzo from Mendelssohn's incidental music to *A Midsummer Night's Dream*, which subsequently became the best known of all his transcriptions, despite the fact that relatively few concert pianists of the day took it up. Moiseiwitsch claimed[58] that Rachmaninoff, most untypically, approached Hofmann, Lhevinne and Horowitz to get them to add the piece to their repertoire, but none of them responded to his overtures. As for the transcription itself, so integral is the sound of the orchestra to the original that the work would seem incapable of having an independent existence apart from it, and yet the miracle of Rachmaninoff's writing is not only that the original text is more faithfully respected than in any other of his transcriptions but that the Scherzo's gossamer orchestral textures are somehow preserved intact on the keyboard.

The other transcription is very different. In March Rachmaninoff premiered an arrangement of the *Prelude* from Bach's E major Partita for unaccompanied violin, and probably during the summer worked also on the *Gavotte* and *Gigue*, to make a short suite of three contrasting movements.

He first tried out the work in its complete form in November, though he did not publish it until nine years later. Like the *Corelli Variations*, its creation may have been prompted by a performance of the original by Kreisler, who happened also to have published his own edition. In any case Rachmaninoff was by no means the first composer to attempt a piano transcription of the Partita, and he may already have been familiar with the somewhat four-square version made by his cousin Siloti.

Though Bach transcription has a long and honorable history, and though Bach himself was a great transcriber, tampering with holy writ has always offended musical puritans. Rachmaninoff, like Liszt and Busoni before him, uses his imagination and art to rework Bach's material in his own terms, using the very devices which Bach himself used but in a twentieth-century way. There is already considerable polyphony implicit in the original single line, which Rachmaninoff expands into a complex web, deriving counterpoint naturally from the melody. However, he does also inject a strong personal element, particularly into the harmony, at times giving the music an unmistakably hybrid air, as in this cadence from the Prelude:

Ex.170

A sequence from the Gavotte is another to which the expression 'Bachmaninoff' can well be applied (Ex 171).

Thus, despite the transcription's great pianistic clarity and restraint, an inability or unwillingness on the part of critics to accept Rachmaninoff's work on its own merits has, predictably enough, given it a bad press. However, those with less squeamish tastes have good reason to rejoice in the existence of so stimulating and inherently musical a work, which arguably should be set alongside Busoni's arrangement of the D minor Chaconne as the supreme Bach transcription of the twentieth century.

Rhapsody on a Theme of Paganini, Op. 43

Any hopeful prospects for composition in the summer of 1933 were blighted when the proofs of Riesemann's biography arrived at Senar

Ex.171

and Rachmaninoff realized with horror how embarrassingly unacceptable the book had turned out to be. He insisted on revisions – at his own expense – and, at least privately, throughout the rest of his life disowned the work. It was not until the following year that Rachmaninoff was at last to find the time and the inclination for composition. In April 1934, having completed his concert season with recitals in Paris and Liège, he drove to Switzerland for the holiday, clearly with his first Senar opus, the *Paganini Rhapsody*, already in mind. To judge from his repeatedly expressed anxiety about deferring a start to the work, he seems already to have had an idea of its large scale and so also, by implication, its form and subject matter. At first, however, he was preoccupied with preparations for undergoing a minor operation, this finally taking place on 23 May. On 9 June, back at Senar convalescing, Rachmaninoff noted anxiously in a letter to his former secretary Dagmar Rybner that he had still accomplished nothing, and then his wife persuaded him to take a short holiday in the Mediterranean. In a postscript to a letter to Sofiya Satina from Lake Como, dated 25 June, Rachmaninoff wrote: 'After returning home I shall begin to work seriously'.

Such confident talk of composition before the event is altogether untypical of Rachmaninoff, but he seems to have been determined this year to justify the purchase of Senar to his wife, if not to himself, by a tangible token of the stimulus it gave him. Doubtless he was excited at long last to be occupying the main wing of the house, with its studio in which to work and its new piano, a gift from Steinway's, and buoyed up by news from Moscow from the conductor Albert Coates and from Vladimir Wilshaw of the success there of his recent compositions. At any rate, as soon as he returned home he began to work intensively. Many years after the event Horowitz was to claim that while Rachmaninoff was composing the *Rhapsody* he telephoned him nearly every day to announce that he had a new variation to play for him.[59] Seven weeks after beginning work, Rachmaninoff was at last able to announce the successful completion of his new composition to Sofiya Satina:[60]

> I have not written to you for a long time, but from the very day of my return from Lake Como and Monte Carlo, that is 1 July, I've been hard at work 'from morning till night', as they say. The work is quite a large one and I finished it only yesterday, late in the evening. But this morning my first task has been to write to you. The piece I have completed is written for piano and orchestra and is about 20–25 minutes long. But it is not a 'concerto', and its name is 'Symphonic Variations on a Theme of Paganini'. I shall tell Foley [Charles Foley, Rachmaninoff's manager] to arrange for me to play it this season in Philadelphia and Chicago. If he does so, and I have little doubt that he will, then you will hear it. I am glad that I have been able to write this piece in the first year of living in the new Senar. It is some compensation for the many stupidities I allowed myself to commit in building Senar. True! So I think!

Rachmaninoff soon abandoned the original title of the new piece. Writing with news of the composition to Wilshaw three weeks later, he had already modified it to the still more cumbersome 'Fantasia for piano and orchestra in the form of variations on a theme of Paganini', but by the end of October he was referring to it simply by the title 'Rhapsody', by which it has always since been known.[61]

The theme Rachmaninoff uses in the *Rhapsody* – the last of Paganini's *24 Caprices* for solo violin, in A minor – had of course already attracted many composers before him as variation material, most notably, as Rachmaninoff himself was aware,[62] Liszt and Brahms, but after him, as though spurred by the *Rhapsody's* triumphant proof that this vein of musical ore was by no means exhausted, many others besides have taken up the challenge, beginning with Lutoslawski in 1941 and including practitioners of popular music as diverse as John Dankworth and Andrew Lloyd-Webber. The reason for the Paganini theme making such good variation material is surely its infinite flexibility:[63] it enshrines that most basic of musical ideas, the perfect cadence, literally in its first half and in a harmonic progression in the second, which itself expresses a musical aphorism; and the melodic line is made distinctive by a repetition of a simple but immediately memorable four-note semi-quaver figure (Rachmaninoff opens and closes the *Rhapsody* with it). Dividing neatly into two, with the second half developing the first before returning to where it began, the theme is generally of the same stamp as *La Folía*, which

Rachmaninoff had used in his *Corelli Variations*, and this may well have been one of its attractions when he first came to think in terms of composing a similar work in the same form but on a more elaborate scale with the added tone colours of the orchestra. Clearly, however, neither the Liszt nor the Brahms work was a conscious precedent. The essence particularly of the Brahms variations as a collection of individual technical studies is entirely different from the organic nature of Rachmaninoff's work; some pianists have varied the order of performance of the Brahms variations, something inconceivable with the *Rhapsody*. A more direct prompting, as with the *Corelli Variations*, may have come from Kreisler, who had himself produced an edition of the Paganini original, but the main inspiration for Rachmaninoff turns out to have been the story of Paganini himself, the artist and the man.

In 1935, a year after the *Rhapsody* and nineteen years after work on the abortive *Scythians* project, Rachmaninoff approached Fokine with a request for a ballet libretto, without mentioning any particular theme, but although keen to act on the composer's suggestion the choreographer had no suitable subject in mind at the time.[64] Two years later Rachmaninoff came to the view that the *Paganini Rhapsody* itself could be used for a ballet and proposed to Fokine a detailed scenario, based on the well-known nineteenth-century legends about the historical Paganini (1782–1840). Such was the speed and power with which Paganini could play the violin that rumours began to circulate in his lifetime that, in order to achieve so miraculous a technique, he had sold his soul to the Devil. He could play quiet melodies so affectingly that his listeners would often burst into tears, and some believed that the fourth string of his Guarnerius was made from the sinews of his wife, whom he was supposed to have strangled with his own hands. In real life he was a notorious gambler and philanderer, and his satanic appearance added to the legend, for he was extremely thin, with a pale, lined face, a hooked nose, an eagle eye and shoulder-length hair. People crossed themselves when he passed by. It is not surprising, therefore, that both musically and as a personality this Mephistophelean figure should have fired Rachmaninoff's imagination.[65]

About the *Rhapsody*, I wanted to tell you that I shall be very happy if you make something out of it. Last night I was thinking about a subject, and this is what came to mind: I give only the main outlines, for the details are still hazy to me. Why not recreate the legend of Paganini selling his soul to the Evil Spirit for perfection in art and also for a woman? All the variations on *Dies irae* represent the Evil Spirit. All those in the middle, from variation 11 to 18, are the love episodes. Paganini appears (for the first time) in the 'Theme' and, defeated, appears for the last time in the 23rd variation – the first 12 bars – after which, until the end, it is the triumph of his conquerors. The first appearance of the Evil

Spirit is the 7th variation, where at figure 19 there can be a dialogue with Paganini, when his theme appears alongside *Dies irae*. Variations 8, 9 and 10 are the progress of the Evil Spirit. The 11th variation is the transition to the realm of love; the 12th variation, the minuet, is the first appearance of the woman, up to the 18th variation. The 13th variation is the first appearance of the woman with Paganini. The 19th variation is the triumph of Paganini's art, his diabolical pizzicato. It would be good to represent Paganini with a violin, not a real one of course, but some kind of made-up, fantastical one. Another thing: it seems to me that at the end of the play some of the characters [representing] the Evil Spirit in the struggle for the woman and art should look like caricatures, absolute caricatures, of Paganini himself. And they must here have violins even more fantastically grotesque. You will not laugh at me?

Far from ridiculing Rachmaninoff's suggestions, Fokine used them as the basis of the surrealist Paganini ballet he subsequently created and which he staged with success in Covent Garden in 1939 and the following year in New York. However, although he adopted Rachmaninoff's general theme, he did depart considerably from the details of the composer's scenario.[66]

What is intriguing about Rachmaninoff's ideas for the ballet is that the music's programme is represented as having come into his mind after, and not before, its composition, and yet the nature of the work itself strongly suggests that the *Rhapsody* was always 'about Paganini' and never merely 'on a theme of Paganini', even though its formal framework harks back to the same design as the *Chopin* and more recently the *Corelli Variations*, the latter in retrospect perhaps to be considered a preparatory exercise for the greater work to follow. As with these two earlier sets of variations, the *Paganini Rhapsody* divides naturally into three sections, corresponding to the form of a sonata or concerto.

Opening movement	Variations 1–10, A minor.
	Variation 11 – transition to:
Slow movement	Variations 12–18, D minor, F major, B flat minor, D flat major.
Last movement	Variations 19–24, A minor.

The *Rhapsody* opens with a technical curiosity. After nine bars of stern introduction, the initial statement of the theme is preceded by the first variation. There is reason from the numbering of the pages of the autograph for believing that this was an afterthought on Rachmaninoff's part, the introduction originally leading directly into the theme, followed by variation 2,[67] but, if so, this change of mind was a most felicitous one. In the statement of the theme, in which the violins closely copy the Paganini original, the piano accompaniment merely picks out its rhythmic essentials, and it is these that Rachmaninoff exactly repeats, or rather exactly anticipates, in the first variation, for orchestra alone, a manner of treatment he had already exploited in the passages that prepare the ground for the final climactic statement of the second subjects of the last movements of the Third and more recently Fourth Concertos, and which Beethoven had used at the opening of the finale of his 'Eroica' Symphony. The contrasting styles of the first six variations, coupled with the mainly linear writing for the piano, suggests that Rachmaninoff is here recreating in pianistic terms different aspects of Paganini's playing.

At variation 7, in sonorous and chillingly menacing piano chords, Rachmaninoff introduces an alien second subject into the work, in the form of his old friend *Dies irae*, to which the Paganini theme happens to make a natural counterpoint:

Ex.172

Shortly after the composition of the *Corelli Variations* Rachmaninoff had at last tried to find out more about the theme which had never ceased to haunt him since the disaster of the First Symphony and about which, paradoxically, he was still ignorant, asking the musicologist Joseph Yasser about its origins, its full form (Rachmaninoff invariably quotes only its opening phrase) and its meaning, without giving him any clues as to why.[68] Its appearance three years later in the *Rhapsody*, whilst hardly in itself unexpected in view of Rachmaninoff's obsession with it, is nevertheless an intrusion on the music's formal structure. Its apparently random and niggardly scattering through the work (it appears only in variations 7, 10, 22 and 24) undermines any notion that it was introduced merely for the purposes of interplay with the Paganini theme – though of course it is so used – and makes real sense only by having a programmatic significance for the composer in the Paganini story. Thus, the four variations 7–10, bounded by the *Dies irae* motif, make a group which is demonic in character precisely because, from the time of the music's conception, they were always about Paganini and his dealings with the Devil.

There is a refreshing change of mood with the cadenza-like variation 11, whose virtuosic diabolerie ushers in the middle movement, passing through four different keys in a series of contrasting vignettes. First comes a graceful minuet, then a haughty and swaggering march, and with 14 a brighter interlude in the major key, based on an inversion of the theme. This idea is developed in the next variation, which launches the soloist into an exhibition of digital dexterity and whose ending, recalling both the opening and closing of the whole work with its unexpectedly quiet final chord, is especially delightful. Variation 16, with its delicate scoring, has a plaintive and anxious air, heightened by shuddering violin trills, and throughout 17 the theme struggles to raise itself out of the murky gloom of B flat minor into the sun of D flat for the middle movement's climax, the famous eighteenth variation. According to Horowitz, Rachmaninoff said of it: 'I have composed this one for my manager; well, maybe this will save the piece'.[69] While technically this too can be seen as merely a development of the inversion of the theme, one wonders whether among the ingredients for its happy inspiration was an unconscious recollection of the slow movement of Medtner's *Sonata–Fairy-Tale*, the only sonata of Medtner that Rachmaninoff ever played in public (Ex. 173).

The final group of variations, all back in the Paganini theme's home key of A minor, are increasingly virtuosic. The piano part in 19, marked *quasi pizzicato*, obviously depicts one particularly well-known aspect of Paganini's fabled technique and is thus another sure example of a programmatic element written into the Rhapsody long before the ballet was conceived. Variations 20 and 21 are diabolical in character, and in 22, as so often in Rachmaninoff but most similarly in the finale of the Second Symphony, the descending scales of church bells are heard, loud and insistent. This variation, Rachmaninoff admitted later,[70] was influenced by the American composer-pianist Abram Chasins' *Parade* (1930), a piece also dominated by the repetition of descending scales, though there representing marching feet. The bells at this point, against snatches of the Paganini theme and *Dies irae*, recall that in real life the Church persecuted Paganini for his alleged dealings with the Devil, and for five years after his death refused his interment in consecrated ground. But this warning fails to vanquish the mischievous Paganini theme, which sweeps blithely away for a further two variations, each of which concludes with a brief cadenza of truly Paganinian devilishness.

Ex.173a   *Paganini Rhapsody,* variation 18

Ex.173b   Medtner: *Sonata - Fairy-Tale,*
                                     Op.25, No.1, (2nd movement)

The twenty-fourth and last variation opens with another reference to
the real-life Paganini and his playing in the unmistakable imitation of
a violin figure. Even Rachmaninoff himself seems to have had some
difficulty in mastering its final skip (Ex. 174).* As this variation reaches
its climax, the forces of evil seem to triumph with a final brash
restatement of *Dies irae,* but this too the Paganini theme shrugs off.
As Strauss ends *Till Eulenspiegel* with the hero's indomitable motto, so
Rachmaninoff, in an apparent contradiction of his own scenario, where

---

* Moiseiwitsch was fond of telling a tale about Rachmaninoff and the
Paganini 'Variations'. One Saturday evening at a dinner party in London in
March 1935 Rachmaninoff told him he wanted his advice, 'with his tongue
in his cheek, I expect. He said he had just concluded a set of variations
on a theme of Paganini and one variation worried him. "When I wrote it
down it looked good on paper; when I played it on the piano it felt easy,
but now I've got to play it next Wednesday and I'm studying it seriously
and I cannot get the passage." So I said, "Why? What's wrong with the
passage?" He said, "Oh, the skips, and I can never get the right note –
the last note." He said, "What would you do?" At that moment a butler
came in with an array of beautiful liquers and everybody – we were about
sixteen men when the ladies left us – helped themselves to a drink, except

Ex.174   Variation 24

A tempo, un poco meno mosso

the forces of evil are finally victorious, ends the *Rhapsody* with a repetition of a gesture already made in the work's introductory bars – an unexpectedly suddenly quiet and tongue-in-cheek reference to the irrepressible Paganini theme.

The *Paganini Rhapsody* shows Rachmaninoff at the height of his powers. The tautness and coherence of its structure, the ingenuity and resourcefulness shown in the treatment of its musical material and the brilliance but discretion of its scoring command a respect not lessened by the over-familiarity the work's popularity inevitably creates. Every page proclaims a greater confidence, vigour and spontaneity than any of the earlier works of exile, and although rehabilitation had taken nearly twenty years, the *Rhapsody* is proof that Rachmaninoff had at last found himself again. In keeping with his policy of playing himself in for a concert season and first trying out new works to his repertoire at minor places, Rachmaninoff premiered the *Paganini Rhapsody* at Baltimore, on 7 November 1934, with the Philadelphia Orchestra under Leopold Stokowski. Its immediate and resounding success was repeated wherever he played the work that season – Washington, Saint-Louis, New York, Manchester and London – and he was immediately invited to record the work for the gramophone, which he did after only four public performances. The *Rhapsody* even excited the admiration of musicians, such as Bartók,[71] not usually sympathetic to Rachmaninoff,

---

Rachmaninoff. He waved it away; he said "No." So I said, "Sergei Vasilyevich, do have a look at that lovely bottle of crème-de-menthe." He said, "No, no, no, you know I never drink." So I said, "I know you don't but you know, if you have a glass of this, you'll be surprised how easily you'll get those skips that you're worried about!" He said; "You mean it?" So I said, "Of course." So he took a glass. Afterwards, when we joined the ladies, some friends prevailed upon him to play some of those variations, and he played just a few variations, including that skippy one. Absolutely note-perfect and brilliant – a wonderful performance. So afterwards, having congratulated him on this wonderful achievement, on this composition, I said, "What's wrong with those skips?" He said, "It must have been your crème-de-menthe." And ever since then, until the end of his days, whenever he played those "Variations", he always had a glass of crème-de-menthe! ' (BBC radio interview, c. 1958.)

and it was perhaps fitting that of his five concerted works it was with his *Rhapsody* that the composer was destined to make his last appearance with orchestra.

Symphony No. 3 in A Minor, Op. 44

Buoyed up by the success of the *Paganini Rhapsody*, which must have proved to him that at last, after seventeen years in exile, a new work of his could be popular with both critics and public alike, Rachmaninoff returned to Senar at the end of April 1935 with a still greater project in mind, nothing less than a large three-movement symphony. His good spirits and satisfaction with his new home were promising signs that he was in the right psychological mood: 'I always maintained that the only place to live would be Senar!' he wrote proudly to Dagmar Rybner on 4 May. Already on 15 May he announced to Sofiya Satina that he had done 'some work', and in the following weeks he got seriously to grips with the composition. However, a three-week cure at Baden-Baden in July and a further break of a fortnight in August put his work behind, and when, five days before leaving Senar at the end of the holiday, he reported to Sofiya Satina on his summer labours, without mentioning the nature of his composition, he was evidently somewhat dissatisfied with what he had achieved.

> I have finished two-thirds in clean form but the last third of the work in rough. If you take into account that the first two-thirds took seventy days of intensive work, for the last third – thirty-five days – there is not enough time. Travels begin and I must get down to playing the piano. So it looks as though my work will be put aside until next year.[72]

Towards the end of the following season, when recitals in Switzerland enabled him to pay a brief visit to Senar, Rachmaninoff evidently collected the score of the symphony from his study, for he had it with him for Julius Conus to mark bowings when he was in Paris in February 1936; but work on the last movement had to await his arrival at Senar, on 16 April, for the summer holiday. In his own words, composition went 'at a snail's pace'[73], and it was not until 30 June that he could write a final report to Sofiya Satina: 'Yesterday morning I finished my work, of which you are the first to be informed. It is a symphony. Its first performance is promised to Stokowski – probably in November. With all my thoughts I thank God that I was able to accomplish it!'[74] Rachmaninoff expressed these same feelings of pious gratitude also in a note on the manuscript, but, as with the *Paganini Rhapsody*, he left the work without a personal dedication.

With all but thirty years having passed since Rachmaninoff's last work in the genre, it is not surprising that the Third Symphony marks no less an advance in style over its predecessor than did the Second Symphony over the First Symphony. The changes that are apparent give the lie to the idea that the composer was merely repeating old gestures, and when he attended the London premiere Medtner even claimed to be bothered by what he called the work's 'modernism'. Abandoning the traditional four-movement structure of the earlier symphonies Rachmaninoff adopted the pattern of the Second and Third Concertos, in which the middle movement of three incorporates a scherzo. In terms of internal coherence, the Third is considerably less self-indulgent than the somewhat sprawling Second Symphony and its musical material more integrated, the whole work effectively growing out of the opening. Although the main theme of the first movement has all the sweep and emotional impact of the Rachmaninoff of Russian years, not only is much of the other melodic material conspicuously unsentimental and perhaps more consciously symphonic than before – the opening theme of the last movement is little more than an excuse for a fugal exercise – but, particularly at moments of tension, the harmonies are more astringent, modulations more abrupt, turns of phrase more unpredictable, than ever before. Rachmaninoff is sometimes criticized for an allegedly limited emotional range, but in this symphony he expresses a whole gamut of feeling, especially in the first movement, where extremes are encompassed in only a few pages. The brilliance yet clarity of the elaborate scoring marks a further step along the path set by the Three Russian Songs and *Paganini Rhapsody*, the whole symphony self-evidently being a virtuoso show-piece for the Philadelphia Orchestra, with whom the composer enjoyed a special relationship. But then all these stylistic developments can be seen as no more than a logical extension of the changes in manner evident in all the previous works of exile.

Like the two earlier symphonies, Rachmaninoff's Third Symphony opens with a motto, which appears as a unifying element at various significant points throughout the work. It makes a tentative, *pianissimo* entrance, strangely scored for muted solo cello, horns and two clarinets, though paste-overs in the manuscript suggest that it was originally given assertively to horns and trumpets, the instruments which mostly enunciate it elsewhere. Its guise here makes the symphony's opening seem as though some recollection from the remote past is stirring in the mind; Asafyev describes it as coming 'out of silence, out of the distance, out of contemplation'.[75] The motto itself, moving stepwise like an ancient religious chant and all contained within the narrow limits of a minor third, instantly suggests Mother Russia, and Protopopov was the first to draw attention to its close similarity to a theme from the Prologue to Borodin's patriotic historical epic *Prince Igor*,[76] an opera with which

Rachmaninoff was intimately familiar, having conducted it on ten occasions at the Bolshoi Theatre between 1904 and 1906:

Ex.175a   Rachmaninoff

Lento

Cl.,Cor.,Celli

pp   *dim.*

Ex.175b   Borodin

Allegro moderato

T.

B.

Po - day vam Bog po - be - du nad vra - ga - mi!

[May God grant victory over your enemies!]

As *Prince Igor* is set against a background of the struggle of Russia against the Tartar foe, so too in the Rachmaninoff symphony there is more than a hint of war. Thus the peremptory orchestral flourish which follows the motto, after a preparatory pause, is like a martial 'call to arms', and much of the movement's development is an angry combat. Not surprisingly, Soviet commentators see Rachmaninoff's Third Symphony, and particularly the first movement, as a musical reflection of the composer's thoughts about his country and its history, but when Sofiya Satina remarked on the work's Russian character to the composer he merely smiled, saying nothing either to confirm or refute the suggestion.

The first subject, given out in the bitter tones of oboes and bassoons accompanied by second violins, is set in mournful parallel thirds, an interval much used by Rachmaninoff throughout the work (Ex. 176). This theme contains much of the musical essence of the symphony, for not only does it form the basis of the whole of the first movement development section but it comprises a number of elements to be developed separately elsewhere. The three-note figure at the end of the opening phrase, (a), becomes a questioning motto at different moments in the first movement, whilst the accompanying quaver violin figure, (b), a characteristic Rachmaninoff motif found also in the Second Symphony, is picked up in the second movement, not to mention being destined to return again in the *Symphonic Dances*. Rachmaninoff also contrives to inflect the opening phrase at its repetition with the familiar shape of the opening of *Dies irae*, (c), a motif that plays a significant

Ex.176

part in the final movement. No less important is the answering phrase given to the violins, consisting of four descending notes, (d), to which the three-note questioning motto is attached, for this falling figure is to become the main theme of the second movement.

The second subject, with its noble sadness, defers not at all in lyrical power to the best of the melodies of Rachmaninoff's Russian period, though it is much shorter-spanned than those. Another of those tunes that seems to have started life as an improvisation on the tonic chord, it seems instinct with nostalgia for a life past and irrecoverable, and it is tempting, if almost certainly misleading, to see Rachmaninoff here looking back across the years on his own life and the country he left. To Russians the theme may be reminiscent of a wedding song;[77] to Western ears there is a hint of 'Shenandoah' in its opening (Ex. 177).

As the theme develops, it climbs out of its mood of resignation,

Ex.177

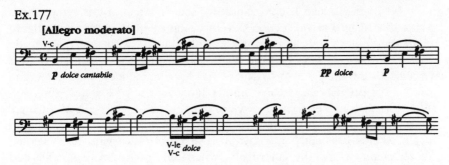

steadily gaining in assurance and impetus until it reaches an ecstatic climax, glitteringly scored. The repetition of the first movement exposition is a modern fashion, not followed by the composer in his 1939 recording nor, apparently, in his 1939/41 performances in Philadelphia, New York and Chicago, nor in subsequent performances by the Philadelphia Orchestra under Ormandy.

The development section shows Rachmaninoff at his most impressive as a symphonic writer. Confining himself to treating the first subject only, he takes his material through a diverse series of adventures which not only constantly shed new light on the material itself but which have the coherence of inevitable organic growth. The mood is one of increasing dark and tension. A three-note figure from the theme, given to oboe and cor anglais and then to violins, is transformed by repetition into a series of haunted cries. The increase of tempo to *allegro molto* marks still greater unease and then fury and violence, as fragments of the theme are hurled against each other in warring combat. The treatment here is strangely reminiscent of the middle of the first movement of Bax's Third Symphony, in its belligerent mood and its scoring – particularly the percussion effects – but most obviously in the strikingly similar manner in which the section is introduced, by a strongly rhythmic string figure on a repeated note, Bax's ⁶⁄₈ 𝅘𝅥 𝅘𝅥𝅮𝅘𝅥𝅯𝅘𝅥𝅯 | 𝅘𝅥 𝅘𝅥𝅮𝅘𝅥 𝅘𝅥𝅮| matched by Rachmaninoff's ²⁄₄ 𝅘𝅥𝅯𝅘𝅥𝅯 𝅘𝅥𝅯𝅘𝅥𝅯 𝅘𝅥𝅯𝅘𝅥𝅯 𝅘𝅥𝅯𝅘𝅥𝅯| 𝅘𝅥𝅮 . Although at first sight the Englishman might be thought unlikely to have influenced the Russian, there is evidence to suggest that Rachmaninoff may indeed have been familiar with the Bax symphony, even if the likely extent of that familiarity is debatable; for Medtner, who was impressed by Bax's talent, attended the concert in 1930 at which the work was premiered by Sir Henry Wood and so could well have drawn Rachmaninoff's attention to it. At any rate, an undated letter of Bax's survives in which he thanks not only Medtner but also Rachmaninoff for their interest in this symphony.[78]

As this *allegro molto* section develops, the descending arpeggio figure from the theme vainly tries to restore calm but is swept brusquely aside in the onrush towards conflict. Battle rages, and the metaphor of war implicit in the music at this point seems to be clinched by the sounding of the symphony's motto in trumpet fanfares (from 2 after figure 19). After ghoulish noises from the xylophone, all hell breaks out in a climax of dissonant fury unprecedented in Rachmaninoff, in which the motto again sounds insistently in a rhythm jarringly at odds with the din going on beneath it. In the aftermath, when the orchestra has collapsed defeated and prostrate, the motto prompts the strings gradually to heave themselves up for one last cry of unbearable pain, grief and bitter despair. Finally, with all passion spent, against woodwind sobs and quietly shuddering strings, the motto ushers in the recapitulation. In this last section of the movement Rachmaninoff restores the movement's balance by giving the first subject only a brief outing and now concentrating on the second, which receives a number of contrasting treatments, being rather anaemically harmonized and leanly scored for flute, harp and strings, and then richly and full-bloodedly laid out for the Philadelphia strings. Finally, as if to confirm that the events depicted come from a remote and unreal past, the first violins play the theme in ethereal harmonics. Rachmaninoff adds to the symmetry of the movement by bringing it back to where it began, with the motto, now in a spirit of calm resignation.

The opening of the second movement is another demonstration of organic growth, which even sympathetic commentators have managed to overlook.[79] It begins with the horn picking up the motto over a relaxed arching sequence of harp arpeggios first drafted in a sketchbook dating to 1916–17 and thus, so far as we know, unique among the material for the symphony in going back to Rachmaninoff's last years in Russia (Ex. 178).[80] As if taking its cue from the harp, the solo violin begins a series of descending arpeggios, languidly chromatic, a development of the answering phrase (d) of the previous movement's first subject. As with the violin solos in *Scheherazade*, it is as though we are being prepared for a story (Ex. 179). When in turn all the violins together begin the narrative over the same harp arpeggios, their line turns out to be based on the motto repeated in a step-wise rising sequence, with the addition of a pair of curiously uncharacteristic trills. When the violins finally descend, they come to rest on a semi-quaver figure which is to act as a pivot between the different parts of the movement (Ex. 180). Here it introduces a flute solo that may be thought of as a second subject, but the trill in the last phrase draws attention to the fact that it has really grown out of the violin sequence (Ex. 181).

Ex.178

Ex.179

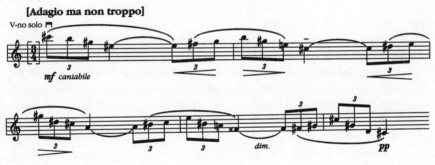

Ex.180

Two short episodes follow, joined by the semi-quaver linking figure, in which this opening material is further explored; the parallel thirds again contributing to the lushness of texture and harmony.

In an atmosphere of anticipation and mystery the linking figure now introduces the interpolated scherzo, *Allegro vivace*, which, being an exploration of the rhythmic elements of the two themes, is itself a development of what has come before. The inspiration for the colourful

Ex.181

[Adagio ma non troppo]

exhibition of orchestral virtuosity which follows was doubtless the 'Philadelphia sound' and the skills of the orchestra's individual players, but, as with the symphony's first movement, some pictorial or literary stimulus seems also to have been at work. In the colourfully fanciful introduction the pauses between the opening syncopated chords are like moments of expectancy on hearing, but not yet placing, sounds half-heard in the distance. Then a sudden flash of light sets the violins slithering down in an expansive gesture that seems to draw the mind's eye to the far horizon. Mysteriously isolated chords from harp and celesta and a breathless flurry from the woodwind are followed by trumpet fanfares to introduce the Rachmaninoff equivalent of the third movement of Tchaikovsky's 'Pathétique' Symphony, a virile march of enormous energy and impetus, based on yet another of the composer's 'tonic-chord' themes (Ex. 182).

As the march develops, proud and swaggering, its unflagging impetus is suggestive of cantering horses; it is as though in a fantastic dream a brilliantly caparisoned troop of cavalry comes into view and passes by. Trumpet fanfares and the gong add a blaze of colour at the climax, after which the procession moves away and passes quickly out of sight.

The return to the movement's opening material is handled most felicitously, with violins and then woodwind pivoting about C sharp in a compressed version of the symphony's motto. The semi-quaver linking phrase leads to an abbreviated recapitulation of the two opening themes and then the violin solo from the introduction, all in reverse order. A repetition of the motto proper, in the same guise as at the end of the first movement, quietly brings the music back to where it began.

As with the earlier symphonies, the last movement is perhaps the most problematic. Its material echoes the first movement, for the first subject is launched by a similar orchestral flourish and the theme itself, another of Rachmaninoff's tonic-chord improvisations, is a variant of the first movement's second subject (Ex. 183). In its high-spirited mood and its tinkling bells in the third and fourth bars it is not unlike *Polichinelle* or the D major *Étude-Tableau* of Op. 39, and like those pieces suggests the bustle of a fair. As the theme proceeds on its breezy way, it is difficult to realize at the time of hearing it that the following apparently carefree sequence, echoing a pattern from the first movement development

Ex.182

Ex.183

Ex.184

Ex.185

section but expressing an absolutely contrasting mood, conceals the figure of *Dies irae* (Ex. 184). The yearning lyrical melody which follows is miraculously created by reconstituting the tonic chord into arpeggios (Ex. 185).

At the end of this episode perky woodwind references to the original theme are brusquely swept aside by the menacing sound of the symphony's motto, to introduce the movement's central episode, an elaborate fugato, *Allegro vivace.*

Ex.186

Allegro vivace

The fugal subject, taken from the movement's first theme, includes within it the opening notes of *Dies irae*, and within its course that motif makes its presence felt first in the background and then more obviously (trumpets at figure 85), so not, as most commentators would have us believe, appearing out of nowhere but growing naturally out of the *fugato*. One curiosity of this section, however, is the gratuitous if brief reference to the second movement's second subject, which seems to have no place here in the musical discussion.

The *fugato* section comes to an end with a series of syncopated jabs that seem to swerve abruptly through remote keys before apparently settling into the comfortable stability of B flat major; but then, hardly having had time to catch its breath, the orchestra rushes off again to prepare for the recapitulation, the launching of which is heralded by the *Dies irae* motif brazenly undisguised. After the first and second subjects have made a reappearance, a bridge passage, based on *Dies irae*, sinister and uneasy in mood, leads to an unexpected and perplexing interlude. Doubtless with the Philadelphia's legendary William Kincaid in mind, Rachmaninoff gives to the solo flute a strangely touching but uncharacteristic pastoral melody which seems to have no musical connection with anything else in the symphony. Upon investigation, but by no means obvious to the innocent ear, it turns out to be merely a decorative superstructure under which the strings quietly voice the symphony's motto (Ex. 187). The musical point evidently being made is lost, especially as it is not the motto but *Dies irae* which dominates the ensuing coda, fighting for supremacy with the movement's opening figure, in a blazing riot of orchestral colour. Though *Dies irae* has the last word, it is, as it were, chased away in rout in the final two bars,

Ex.187

making the conventional *rallentando* that some conductors apply at this point disastrously inappropriate.

The Third Symphony was premiered in Philadelphia under Stokowski on 6 November 1936 and then taken the round of the major American cities. Its reception seems everywhere to have been only lukewarm. The public had doubtless been misled by the old-style romanticism of the eighteenth Paganini variation and were perplexed to find that Rachmaninoff had after all advanced beyond the 1900s; the critics on the other hand, condemned him just because they felt that he had not. Reviews spoke of the work's 'sterility' of 'chewing over again and again something that never had importance to start with'.[81] Writing to Wilshaw the following year Rachmaninoff reported:[82]

> It was played in New York, Philadelphia, Chicago, etc. At the first two performances I was present. It was played wonderfully. Its reception by both the public and critics was sour. One review sticks painfully in my mind: that I didn't have a Third Symphony in me any more. Personally, I'm firmly convinced that it is a good work. But...sometimes composers are mistaken too! Be that as it may, I am holding to my opinion so far.

Predictably, Rachmaninoff was led to make a number of 'corrections' to the work, that is mainly cuts,[83] which, although in total insignificant, led to a new edition of the symphony being brought out only two years after its original (1937) publication.

Although in truth the symphony's reception was not as unenthusiastic as Rachmaninoff suggested to Wilshaw – at the Philadelphia premiere, for example, the audience continued applauding at the end and would not leave the hall until the composer had returned on to the stage[84] – even when the symphony was performed in Europe it conspicuously failed to repeat the dramatic success of the *Rhapsody*. Rachmaninoff later ruefully commented: 'It has been heard once in every capital in the musical world; it has been condemned in them all. But it's quite possible that in fifty years' time it will be rediscovered like Schumann's Violin Concerto and become a sensational success.' [85] Where the symphony did achieve immediate acceptance, predictably enough, was in Russia, though the composer was not to know this, since the belated Moscow premiere took place only posthumously, on 11 July 1943. As this was only a few months after Rachmaninoff's death, and especially in view of his recent demonstrations of patriotism in his country's darkest hour, the Third Symphony was greeted with understandable rapture by critics and public alike, the conductor, Nikolay Golovanov, going so far as to hail it as 'the composer's greatest work'.[86] Its particularly Russian qualities were singled out for comment. The critic of *Pravda* called it 'a lyric poem about Russia, imbued with warm love for the fatherland, filled with the romance of youthful memories, and carried out with the experience and skill of the mature artist. The melodious and sweeping themes of the symphony, their clearly marked Russian nationalist character and colouring, the logic of their development, in short the structure of the movements and the composition of the work as a whole – all point to the fact that the symphony has its own poetic programme and at the basis of that programme lies a Russian subject...' [87] Asafyev called it a 'land-mark in the evolution of Russian nationalist symphonism'.[88]

Perhaps to some extent because of this Russian character, but mainly because of its technical difficulties, the Third Symphony is not an easy work to bring off in performance. The English premiere by Beecham in November 1938 was unidiomatic according to the composer's admirers – Medtner called the performance 'abominable', a word Rachmaninoff himself used to describe a later, 1939, broadcast performance by Sir Henry Wood, who had had the benefit of a detailed briefing by the composer the year before; 'the first time the symphony has not on the whole satisfied me (especially the first movement)'.[89] Rachmaninoff was clearly sensitive about the work's correct interpretation and he took special trouble to go carefully through the work not only with Wood but with Ormandy too. He was willing to conduct the Viennese premiere himself after a twenty-year absence from the rostrum, and only the *Anschluss* prevented its taking place (on 10 April 1938). He was also anxious to record the work, even going so far as to offer to pay for rehearsals.[90] Although the London recording scheduled for the beginning of September 1937 did not take place, as a spin-off from the festival of concerts in the 'Rachmaninoff Cycle' of 1939, he was at last able to set down his definitive interpretation. When, at the end of 1942, at the request of Vladimir Bazïkin, First Secretary of the Soviet Embassy in Washington, he passed to him the score and parts of the Third Symphony, he said: 'If the symphony is prepared for performance in Moscow, I would insist that you also send them the Victor recording of it. Hearing the recording will serve as the composer's instructions for the interpretation, in his absence.'[91] This advice is no less relevant to today's interpreters, for few recordings better illustrate the value of the gramophone in preserving historic performances for the instruction of posterity than Rachmaninoff's authoritative version of the symphony, which is a yardstick for all time against which all other interpretations can be measured but which few in practice can match.

As the success of the *Paganini Rhapsody* seems to have prompted the writing of the Third Symphony, so the symphony's relative failure seems to have curbed Rachmaninoff's impetus to compose. During the summer of 1937 he intended to revise the Fourth Concerto, but it did not take much persuading by friends for him to leave Senar for a three-week break in Italy and work was postponed. Clearly he was not in the right psychological state for composition. The day before leaving for Riccione he wrote a pessimistic letter to Sofiya Satina: 'My mood could change for the better if I wrote, if I composed something. That would be an advance that would help my general state. But this summer particularly I cannot work. I've had to begin my piano practice early,[92] but three hours of playing so fatigues me that I cannot even think of anything else.'[93]

In February 1938 Rachmaninoff gave a solo recital in Vienna. Next month Hitler occupied Austria, and Rachmaninoff cancelled the concert at which he was to return to the capital to conduct the Third Symphony and *The Bells*. 'We live as on a volcano,' he wrote.[94] In April Chaliapin died in Paris. Rachmaninoff visited him daily in those last days, and the shock of the loss of his friend, whose life, in many ways, had run parallel with his own, was profound and lasting. 'I'm not working. I read, I walk, I lie on the balcony,' he wrote dejectedly.[95] This summer he again expressed the intention of revising his Fourth Concerto but did not feel up to it. He spent a couple of weeks making final corrections to the Third Symphony but wrote to the Somovs in July: 'To write something new – I have no plans yet. My head is empty! I have always noticed that a desire for composition comes with physical cheerfulness, which I don't notice in myself just now'.[96] Sometime during the year, however, Rachmaninoff did manage to make a two-piano transcription of the notorious C sharp minor Prelude, in which the most noticeable difference from the original, apart from the expected amplification of sonority, is in the central *Agitato* section, where the writing is elaborated to good effect. Doubtless one consideration in making this version was financial, in that the work could be copyrighted, which had not been done with the original, with the result that the composer had missed out on a small fortune in royalties over the intervening forty-five years.

When Rachmaninoff returned to Senar in the spring of 1939, Europe was moving rapidly towards war; it was no longer a question of if, but rather when, it would break out. Worries about what it would mean for his daughter Tatyana, domiciled in France with a young son and with a husband (with French nationality) already in the army, added to the dispiritedness caused by the strain of concertizing, each year more demanding on his declining strength. A fall at Senar in July, resulting in lameness which prevented his attending the premiere of the ballet *Paganini*, was a further set-back. He wrote gloomily to Sofiya Satina on 3 August: 'As far as I'm concerned, I have been poorly. I cannot improve now, for I am unlikely to be able to compose anything again. I've grown altogether old, and I cannot say that the realisation of this comes easily to me.'

Having made his final appearance in Europe at the Lucerne Festival, Rachmaninoff left the Continent for the last time little more than a week before war was declared. Back in the United States the highlight of the 1939–40 season was the Philadelphia Orchestra's 'Rachmaninoff Cycle', in which a representative cross-section of his compositions was played in three concerts, the last of which he conducted himself. In connection with these concerts Rachmaninoff made a number of major recordings – the First and Third Concertos and the Third Symphony – and then, in the new year, an album of five records of his solo piano pieces. He seems to have used this opportunity to write down and subsequently to publish revised versions of the four earliest pieces he chose to record, for the revisions were completed in February and March 1940 and the recordings took place on 18 March.

The *Mélodie* and *Serenade* from Op. 3 and the *Humoresque* from Op. 10, all written nearly half a century before, received Rachmaninoff's greatest attention. In each the outline and structure of the work is left almost untouched but the piano texture is modified and in places thinned, whilst in general the pieces are brought into line with the composer's later more chromatic and tangy harmonic style. The revision process seems to have been one of continuous evolution over years of performance, since the 1922 and 1936 gramophone recordings of the *Serenade* mark intermediate stages between the original and the 1940 version; so too the 1920 piano roll of the *Mélodie*. The E flat minor

Moment musical of 1896, on the other hand, started life already as a fully mature piece, and Rachmaninoff's revisions are essentially minor retouchings.

Symphonic Dances, Op. 45

In May of 1940, after the concert season was finished, Rachmaninoff underwent a minor operation and in the summer went to recuperate on the estate at Huntington, Long Island, where he had already stayed briefly on his return to America the previous year. Here, despite fatigue and worry, and against every expectation, Rachmaninoff found the strength to write what proved to be his swan-song, the three *Symphonic Dances*. There is a hint that he may have begun the work before moving out to Huntington – 'I'm working a little,' he wrote from New York to a friend on 3 July, 'and undergoing an unpleasant course of treatment'.[97] Even so, on any reckoning the *Dances* were drafted exceptionally quickly. On 21 August Rachmaninoff wrote to Eugene Ormandy: 'Last week I finished a new symphonic piece, which I naturally want to give first to you and your orchestra. It is called "Fantastic Dances". I am beginning the orchestration. Unfortunately my concert tour begins on 14th October and I must practise intensively, and so I do not know whether I shall be able to finish the orchestration until November.' A week later, in another letter to Ormandy making arrangements to run through the work with him, Rachmaninoff had changed the title to its permanent form, *Symphonic Dances*. Later, in a newspaper interview, he declared: 'It should have been called just "Dances", but I was afraid people would think I had written dance music for jazz orchestras'.[98]

Alongside the orchestral score Rachmaninoff also worked on a two-piano version of the *Dances*, which stands in its own right as a concert piece and which, had he not died, he might well have performed publicly, as he did privately, with Horowitz. Mrs Rachmaninoff has told of the enormous daily effort Rachmaninoff made to complete all this work simultaneously with preparing for the new concert season:[99]

At 8 o'clock in the morning Sergei Vasilyevich drank coffee, and at half past 8 got down to composition. For two hours, from 10 o'clock, he played the piano, preparing for the concert season ahead. From 12 till 1 again he worked on the *Dances*. At 1 o'clock he had lunch and lay down to rest, but then from 3 o'clock onwards, with a break for dinner, he worked on composition until 10 in the evening. He wanted to finish the *Dances* for the beginning of the concert season, whatever the cost. Sergei Vasilyevich achieved his goal, but the whole time I was worried looking after him. In the evenings his eyes refused to focus because of the work of writing the score in his small hand. Afterwards too a lot of work was done when he was actually on his concert tour. At every large station at which we stopped the proofs of the *Symphonic Dances* awaited him, and Sergei Vasilyevich quickly got down to the correction of these green pages from the white sheets of music. How this tired his eyes! He carried on correcting both before and after the next concert.

It is interesting to speculate on the programme attaching to the *Dances*. According to Sofiya Satina,[100] Rachmaninoff originally intended to give the three movements the titles 'Noon', 'Evening' and 'Midnight', and though these appear neither on the autograph nor on the published edition, there is at least some internal musical evidence to suggest that, like *The Bells*, the work does indeed depict different phases of a man's life. Even so, as the original epithet 'fantastic' implies, these titles are nothing more than a starting point for a flight of the imagination. From the very beginning Rachmaninoff seems to have thought of the *Dances* in terms of material for a ballet, and even before showing the work to Ormandy he had played it through for Fokine, doubtless, as with the *Paganini Rhapsody*, revealing the kind of scenario he had in mind. However, Fokine's death in August 1942 brought an abrupt end to the project,[101] and no evidence remains as to what the scenario may have been, though the Fokine connection does support the claim that the work may contain material intended for the *Scythians* ballet of 1915 (see p. 252). The *Symphonic Dances* stand in the same relation to the symphonies as the *Paganini Rhapsody* to the concertos, and consequently some have suggested from their symphonic design that they deserve to be called the composer's 'Fourth Symphony', but the nature of their musical material, with its strongly accented rhythms, clearly makes the dance element paramount, and it is surprising indeed that the work has still not been made into a ballet.

The tempo marking of the first movement is *Non allegro*, which Rachmaninoff had used before only rarely: for the introductory two bars of the *Étude-Tableau* in E flat minor, Op. 33, No. 6, and the introductory seven bars of the slow movement of the Second Sonata, but also, more significantly, for two lively songs, *Dissonance* and *The Pied Piper*. In the absence of a metronome indication conductors sometimes take the marking at its face value and set a rather leisurely pace, but there is unequivocal evidence that this was not the composer's intention. On 20 November 1942 Dimitri Mitropoulos conducted the *Dances* at Minneapolis, at a concert in which Rachmaninoff played his Second Concerto. The music critic of *The Tribune* was present during the rehearsal of the *Dances* and later told how the composer, standing in the wings, kept frowning and snapping his fingers as if to accelerate the tempo. 'Stopping the orchestra Mitropoulos conferred with Rachmaninoff and it was quickly discovered that through some error the *Allegro* movement had been labelled *Non allegro* on the score. The '*non*' was promptly expunged, and the orchestra's leaden gait was changed to the proper quick-step'.[102]

The introductory bars of the first movement contain three important elements: at the outset, first violins establish the pulse in quadruple time that gives the movement its strongly motoric and insistent energy; then woodwinds sound the descending tonic triad motif that is to develop into the main theme; and simultaneously, second violins and violas diverge from the line of the first violins to fall gently in a chromatic scale that immediately provides the underlying basis for the brusque series of chords heralding the launch of the movement proper, first noted in a sketchbook dating back to no later than 1920–21.[103]

Ex.188

[Non Allegro]

This harmonic sequence recalls the famous motto of the Queen of Shemakha in Rimsky-Korsakov's *Golden Cockerel*, an opera whose harmonic daring greatly intrigued Rachmaninoff – 'the source of all the wretched modernism; but with Rimsky it is in the hands of genius'[104] – and the score of which was the only music not his own to be brought by him out of Russia in 1917, possibly for the very reason that it was already fertilizing the musical ideas he had in his mind. Rachmaninoff's harmonic colouring of this passage conceals the fact that the figure to which it is applied is none other than a contorted version of *Dies irae*, the composer's inescapable companion, which reappears in its regular form later in this movement and which dominates the last.

When the first subject has been developed in full, the tonic triad motif changes form to become a link to the movement's contrastingly reflective middle section and then the pattern of its accompaniment. The new theme is unexpectedly given to the alto saxophone, an instrument about which Rachmaninoff sought the expert advice of the well-known Broadway composer, Robert Russell Bennett. Whilst its use in this late work, the one and only Rachmaninoff composed in America, may reflect the influence on the composer of jazz or American 'big band' sound, the instrument already had a perfectly respectable history in serious music going back to Bizet's *L'Arlésienne*, and it is perhaps more likely that the stimulus to use it came from its more recent appearance in such works as Ravel's *Bolero* and his orchestration of Mussorgsky's *Pictures at an Exhibition*,[105] or in the Saxophone Quartet and Concerto of Glazunov, written in the early 1930s. In the autograph Rachmaninoff authorized the alternative of giving the melody to the cor anglais and the accompaniment to the first clarinet, but this note did not appear in the published score. The melody itself, strongly vocal in character, harks back to the Rachmaninoff of the 1900s, not only in its obviously Russian quality and emotional appeal but even in the matter of its considerable length. When repeated, it is dressed in a totally contrasting but no less unusual sound of strings accompanied by harp and piano. This time it is brought to an uneasy conclusion by the strings descending to murky depths through a sequence in which *Dies irae* rings out undisguised:

Ex.189

This leads naturally to a bridge passage, for lower woodwind and then strings, based on the *Dies-irae*-derived opening figure, stirring from the depths in mysterious staccato to rouse itself back to its original vigour and pulse, and culminating at figure 21 in an echo of the ninth and tenth bars of the E flat *Étude-Tableau*, Op. 33, No. 7, of 1911, and so just possibly hinting at an early date for the material in this section. Certainly the elemental, aggressive virility of this movement's outer sections makes it tempting to believe that here, if anywhere in the *Symphonic Dances*, Rachmaninoff may have used his abandoned *Scythians* material. After the recapitulation there is a reflective postlude, in which glockenspiel, piano and harp all ring out like bells, as the strings sing a benevolent version of *Dies irae*, seen by some commentators as a wistful self-quotation from the opening movement of the First Symphony, but possibly no more than another view of the motif that started the movement off, now tamed and quiescent.

The melancholy waltz which forms the second movement is introduced by sinisterly blaring fanfares, spectral woodwind arabesques and a haunted violin solo that makes a fearful glance back at the previous movement's opening. The waltz rhythm tries but fails three times to establish itself, and when at last the melody gets off to a quietly diffident start on the cor anglais, the metre alternates uneasily between 6/8, 3/8 and 9/8, and the waltz never succeeds in shaking off its mood of apprehension or the shudders and cries of ghosts that haunt it. Even the warmth of its middle section, an episode of romantic reverie, is rudely shattered by the fanfares to herald the waltz's return. The waltz itself is clearly by the same hand as the middle section of the slow movement of the Third Concerto but it shares the mood of strained disquiet underlying Ravel's *La Valse* or that same composer's *Valses nobles et sentimentales*, which Rachmaninoff had conducted in Moscow in 1914, the year before he worked on *The Scythians*. In the reprise the dance speeds up and, as in a nightmare, the dancers seem to be whirling vertiginously out of control. When order is at last restored, the pulse is momentarily upset by four bars, *poco meno mosso* (figure 54–55), that seem to drag their feet and which have occasionally been omitted in performance.[106] With helter-skelter woodwind figures over pulsating string pizzicatos, the dance breaks up in disarray.

The third movement is Rachmaninoff's last and definitive statement on *Dies irae*. It is impossible not to imagine him realizing, as he sat at his desk composing, that this would be his swan-song and that in this depiction of the last stage of man's existence as he faces death he was setting down in music his own philosophy. As in the first movement, in the introductory bars, *Lento assai*, the opening figure is a contorted version of *Dies irae*, descending chromatically in a series of weary and resigned sighs, but in this form the possible influence of the motto from *The Golden Cockerel* is even clearer than before:

Ex.190a   *Symphonic Dances*

Ex.190b   *Golden Cockerel*

This submissive mood is rudely shattered by two sneering shouts from demons and the twelve-times tolling of bells to launch a hectic and unflagging *Allegro vivace*, based on *Dies irae*. It is midnight and evil spirits are abroad. The gestures, the use of *Dies irae*, the demonic spirit of this last dance, and even the final chords, with their colourful use of the gong, all suggest the influence of that dramatic series of variations on the same motto, Liszt's *Totentanz*. Although Rachmaninoff was thoroughly familiar with the work from having conducted it three times in Russia, it is surely more than a coincidence that he had himself played it, for the one and only time in his life, as recently as a mere eight or nine months before beginning work on the *Symphonic Dances*.[107]

The central section, *Lento assai*, opens with a repetition of the movement's introductory motto and then the wailing of departed spirits, in spectral *glissandi* from violins, violas and harp. Like a man's pulse weakening and then ceasing to beat, the music's impetus seems temporarily to stop altogether, but this moment of suspended animation passes, and after a wistful interlude a powerful lament begins. Three-note cries swell tearfully and then fall in despair, but the reappearance of *Dies irae* offers uncharacteristic comfort:

Ex.191

Indeed, the manner in which this central episode finally resolves is reminiscent of the mood of contentment of the lovers in *Francesca da Rimini*, just before they are discovered.

The most significant influence on the final dance is that of Russian church music. At the end of the *Allegro vivace*, the *Dies irae* figure is assimilated into what is clearly a church chant, in a treatment that harks back to the finale of the composer's own First Symphony, written forty-five years before (cf. Ex. 35):

Ex.192

At its second appearance, at the end of the recapitulation, just before the coda, the chant is immediately followed by a literal self-quotation of the alleluias from the ninth number of the *All-Night Vigil*, at which point in the score, in Roman script but transliterated from the Russian, Rachmaninoff wrote the word 'Alliluya'.[108] This can be interpreted simply as a note drawing attention to the provenance of the theme itself, but is surely more likely to have been a devotional exclamation, prompted by the musical parallel with the earlier work but essentially referring to the text associated with it. For in the *Vigil* the alleluias bring to a close the story of Christ's Resurrection, and it was surely this event which the composer had in mind as he wrote the final, confident pages of the *Symphonic Dances*. On this interpretation, with the death motto *Dies irae* finally vanquished by the church chant, he was not only portraying the ultimate victory of Life over Death but making an affirmation of his own religious faith, which, for all the fears and scepticism of earlier years, had in the end led him to an unconditional acceptance of the reality of God, the Resurrection and a life hereafter. The words Rachmaninoff wrote at the end of his score, 'I thank Thee, Lord', may therefore be seen as not just a traditional expression of thanks on a work's completion but, as with the similar remark at the end of his two previous compositions, the *Paganini Rhapsody* and Third Symphony, a token of piety.

At the final rehearsal of the *Dances* before their premiere Rachmaninoff addressed the members of the orchestra: 'When I was a young man, Chaliapin was my great idol. Chaliapin is dead. Since then, everything I write is with the Philadelphia sound in my ears. Therefore, may I be permitted to dedicate my latest, and I think my best, composition to my beloved Philadelphia Orchestra and my friend', pointing to Eugene Ormandy.[109] Rachmaninoff's evaluation of the Dances as his 'best' work is especially interesting and confirmed by Sofiya Satina's account of his disappointment over not being able to record them and of his partiality for them:[110]

> Sergei Vasilyevich always viewed his compositions very severely and critically. He was often disappointed to find defects of one kind or another in them and tried to rework compositions already in print. His attitude to the *Symphonic Dances* was different. Till the end of his life he loved them, considering them probably his best composition, and he was delighted whenever he learned that this or that conductor wanted to perform them.

There is no doubt that the *Symphonic Dances* is technically a very difficult work to perform and one which cruelly exposes any weaknesses in individual departments of an orchestra, particularly the strings.[111] While this was obviously not a problem with the Philadelphia Orchestra, for other reasons the first performance of the work was inadequate. Rachmaninoff's new season opened with a recital in Detroit on 14 October, but it was not until a fortnight later that he was able to complete the orchestration of the final movement. With the premiere scheduled for 3 January and the composer correcting the proofs of parts until the last minute, there was insufficient time for orchestra and conductor to learn the work properly. The critics were probably unaware of this and in any case greeted the new work with predictable condescension. Even more than a year later the Philadelphia's performance of the work still did not meet with Rachmaninoff's approval. Writing of their concert at Ann-Arbor on 9 May 1942, he commented: 'Ormandy performed *The Isle of the Dead* badly and the *Dances* only in places tolerably well. Either he doesn't understand, that is, he doesn't feel the piece, or he knows it badly.[112] It was Mitropoulos whom Rachmaninoff most valued as an interpreter of the *Dances*, as also of the Third Symphony, and whose New York performances of the *Dances* in 1942 won the work a fresh critical appraisal.

The 1940–41 season came to an end in March with Rachmaninoff's last appearance as a conductor, in Chicago, repeating the programme of the Third Symphony and *The Bells* which he had conducted in the 'Rachmaninoff Cycle' in Philadelphia and New York fifteen months before. For the summer he returned to Huntington where, despite growing anxiety about Tatyana and the progress of the war, he was able at last to subject the Fourth Concerto to the revision he had intended so long and also to make his final piano transcription, of Tchaikovsky's *Lullaby*, Op. 16, No. 1. This simple, intensely Russian song Tchaikovsky himself had already transcribed for piano solo, but Rachmaninoff's version is considerably more florid, overlaying the innocence of the original with a sharp chromaticism and complex polyphony which imposes on it a sinister darkness and tormented introspection that doubtless reflected the composer's mood at the time.

The pattern of Rachmaninoff's last two concert seasons was unchanged from earlier years. He continued to the end to add new works to his repertoire and he also tried, unsuccessfully, to relaunch the Fourth Concerto. He publicly supported Russia in her fight against the Nazis and in 1942 decided to move to the kinder climate of California for the summer. In June he bought a house in Beverly Hills in readiness for a reluctant retirement the next year. He had a studio built in which to work, but no new compositions were to be written there; the *Symphonic Dances* had been his 'last flicker'. In Knoxville, Tennessee, on 17 February 1943, he played for the last time. Six weeks later he was dead.

References

1 Sofiya Satina, *VR/A* 1, p. 50.
2 R. to Altschuler, 12 January 1918.

3 *Riesemann*, p. 198.
4 Rachmaninoff played his cadenza to the Liszt Second Hungarian Rhapsody for the first time in Boston on 10 January 1919. It was later reconstructed from the composer's Edison recording by the Polish-American musicologist Jan Holcman and published by the Mercury Music Corporation, New York, in 1955.
5 Alfred J. Swan (ed.), *Songs from Many Lands*, Enoch & Sons, London, 1923.
6 Rachmaninoff made his first gramophone recording of the *Gopak* on 18 March 1921, which predates his other transcriptions of the period.
7 Morozov to R., 1 December 1922.
8 Morozov to R., 4 March 1923.
9 R. to Morozov, 15 April 1923.
10 *Muzïka*, 12 April 1914, p. 318.
11 R. to Siloti, 1 November 1914.
12 R. to Goldenweiser, 9 August 1915.
13 *Russkaya muzïkal'naya gazeta*, No. 17/18 of 1917, p. 353: 'At the present time S.V. Rachmaninoff is working on his Fourth Concerto'.
14 *Culshaw*, p. 161.
15 R. to Medtner, 20 June 1924.
16 Medtner to Goldenweiser, 17 September 1925.
17 R. to Medtner, 9 September 1926.
18 Medtner to R., 13 September 1926.
19 Pitts Sanborn in *The Evening Telegram* (New York), 23 March 1927.
20 R. to Yuly Conus, 28 July 1927.
21 R. to Somov, 19 July 1938.
22 Details of the differences between what amounts to three versions of the concerto are in *T/N*, pp. 126–133, expanding on Threlfall's original article, 'Rachmaninoff's Revisions and an Unknown Version of his Fourth Concerto', in *Musical Opinion*, 1973, pp. 235–237.
23 *Swan*, p. 3.
24 *Culshaw*, p. 94.
25 Kaikhosru Sorabji, *Around Music*, Unicorn Press, London, 1932, p. 75.
26 *Riesemann*, p. 199.
27 *Bortnikova*, p. 68, No. 145.
28 Sofiya Satina, *VR/A* 1, p. 73.
29 O. Sokolova, *Khorovïye i vocalno-simfonicheskiye proizvedeniya Rakhmaninova*, Moscow, 1963, p. 132. Liadov's collection was published as his Op. 43.
30 *Riesemann*, p. 199.
31 Chaliapin's recordings of *Eh! Vanka* were on HMV 022184 (1910) and 2-022019, DB 691 (1922). There is an interesting article on Chaliapin's performance of the song in *Fyodor Ivanovich Shalyapin*, ed. E.A. Grosheva, Iskusstvo, Moscow, 1979, vol. 3, pp. 186–189.
32 Sofiya Satina, *VR/A* 1, p. 73. It is uncertain whether Rachmaninoff had known Plevitskaya in his Russian days, but it is interesting that *Luchinushka* ('The Little Splinter'), one of the folksong settings he sketched in 1920, was in her active repertoire and among the items she recorded for Russian HMV around 1908 (record no. 023073), and that his association with her extended to publishing two volumes of her memoirs under the 'Tair' imprint.

33 Sofiya Satina to the author, 24 November 1973.
34 The marking supplied in the vocal score (♩ , =166–120) is absurd.
35 Story related by Igor Buketoff. See notes to his recording of the Three Russian Songs.
36 Stokowski to R., 17 March 1927.
37 'Rachmaninoff is Reminiscent', interview with Basanta Koomar Roy in *The Musical Observer*, May 1927, Vol. 26, p. 16.
38 R. to Paichadze, 28 October 1931.
39 Mrs Rachmaninoff, *VR/A* 2, p. 314.
40 Koussevitzky to R., 23 November and 16 December 1931.
41 R. to Paichadze, 19 December 1931.
42 R. to Dagmar Barclay, 27 May 1931.
43 Corelli, Sonata No. 12 in D minor, Op. 5, *La Folía*, for violin and harpsichord, written in 1700.
44 Despite stories to the contrary, Rachmaninoff and Kreisler never played together in public.
45 *New York Times*, 15 January 1931, letter headed 'Tagore on Russia', signed by Ivan Ostromislensky, Ilya Tolstoy, son of the author, and Rachmaninoff.
46 Edward Cushing in the *Brooklyn Daily Eagle*, 29 March 1931.
47 R. to Sofiya Satina, 16 July 1931.
48 R. to Somov, 16 July 1931.
49 *Daily Telegraph*, 29 April 1933.
50 S.S. Prokofiev, *Materialï, dokumentï, vospominaniya*, Moscow, 1961, p. 287.
51 *Swan*, p. 9.
52 R. to Medtner, 21 December 1931.
53 *Riesemann*, p. 171.
54 *Swan*, p. 8.
55 'Rakhmaninov's Second Thoughts', article by Geoffrey Norris in *The Musical Times*, Vol. cxiv, 1973, pp. 364–368.
56 See *T/N*, p. 116.
57 Commercial recordings were made of both Horowitz versions of the Second Sonata: of the earlier, in 1968, by CBS; of the later, by RCA.
58 Moiseiwitsch, BBC radio interview, c. 1958.
59 *Horowitz*, p. 186.
60 R. to Sofiya Satina, 19 August 1934.
61 R. to Wilshaw, 8 September 1934; R. to Swans, 25 October 1934.
62 R. to Wilshaw, 8 September 1934.
63 See 'A Theme of Paganini', article by Wadham Sutton in *Musical Opinion*, March 1971, pp. 187–188.
64 Fokine to R., 15 September 1935.
65 R. to Fokine, 29 August 1937.
66 For Fokine's scenario see *Mikhail Fokin, Protiv techeniya. Vospominaniya baletmeistera. Stat'i, Pis'ma*, ed. Y. I. Slonimsky, Moscow 1962, pp. 607–610, also reproduced in *LN/A* 3, pp. 305–308.
67 *T/N*, p. 140.
68 Joseph Yasser in *Pamyati Rakhmaninova*, ed. M.V. Dobuzhinsky, New York, 1946, quoted in *B/L*, p. 278.
69 *Horowitz*, p. 186.
70 R. to Chasins, 29 December 1934.
71 Bartók expressed a wish to have the score of the *Rhapsody* to hand when composing his Third Concerto.

72 R. to Sofiya Satina, 26 September 1935.

73 R. to Sofiya Satina, 1 May 1936.

74 R. to Sofiya Satina, 30 June 1936.

75 Boris Asafyev, *VR/A* 2, p. 399.

76 Protopopov in *Tsitovich*, p. 143.

77 *Bryantseva*, p. 56.

78 Bax's letter to Medtner is quoted in *Bax, A Composer and His Times*, by Lewis Foreman, Scolar Press, London, 1983, pp. 303–304.

79 For example, *Piggott*, p. 39.

80 See *T/N*, p. 17.

81 Edwin Schloss in the *Philadelphia Record*, 7 November 1936; B.G. Haggin in the *Brooklyn Eagle*, 7 November 1936.

82 R. to Wilshaw, 7 June 1937.

83 See *T/N*, p. 143.

84 *New York Times* review, 8 November 1936.

85 Ivor Newton, *At the Piano*, Hamish Hamilton, London, 1966, p. 156.

86 Golovanov in *Vechernaya Moskva*, 14 June 1943.

87 Georgy Khubov in *Pravda*, 26 July 1943.

88 Asafyev in *Literatura i iskusstvo*, 19 June 1943.

89 R. to Sofiya Satina, 3 August 1939.

90 F.W. Gaisberg, *Music on Record*, Robert Hale Ltd, London, 1946, p. 181.

91 R. to Bazïkin, 28 December 1942.

92 For the 1937–38 season, besides new solo items, Rachmaninoff learned Beethoven's First Concerto, the first concerto not his own that he had added to his repertoire since before leaving Russia.

93 R. to Sofiya Satina, 30 June 1937.

94 R. to Sofiya Satina, 15 March 1938; R. to Somovs, 27 March 1938.

95 R. to Sofiya Satina, 20 April 1938.

96 R. to Somovs, 19 July 1938.

97 R. to Yakov Weinberg, 3 July 1940.

98 E. Arnold in *New York World-Telegram*, 17 October 1940.

99 Mrs Rachmaninoff, *VR/A* 2, pp. 313–314.

100 Sofiya Satina, *VR/A* 1, p. 102.

101 Fokine, who was not himself a musician, was hampered by having no recording of the *Dances* to work from. The expected recording by Rachmaninoff never materialized.

102 William McNally quoted in *Music and Maestros, The Story of the Minneapolis Symphony Orchestra*, by John K. Sherman, University of Minnesota Press, Minneapolis, 1952, pp. 152–153.

103 See *T/N*, p. 17.

104 *Swan*, p. 178.

105 Glazunov commented on Ravel's use of the saxophone in *The Old Castle* in a letter to Rachmaninoff dated 19 December 1932, unenthusiastically calling it 'less successful as regards the blending of sonority than Bizet's use in *L'Arlésienne*'.

106 The omission of these bars was observed in the work's first commercial recording, by Eric Leinsdorf and the Rochester Philharmonic Orchestra, made by CBS around 1950.

107 Rachmaninoff performed *Totentanz* at Minneapolis on 3 November 1939, with the Minneapolis Symphony Orchestra under Dimitri Mitropoulos.

108 'Alliluya' appears at 1 bar after figure 99.

109 Eugene Ormandy, BBC interview, 1965.

110 Sofiya Satina, *VR/A* 1, p. 103.

111 Ormandy used to tell the amusing tale of how he visited Rachmaninoff at Huntington in connection with the *Dances*. This meant getting up at 5 a.m. and taking the train from Philadelphia to New York and thence to Long Island, where he arrived somewhat before midday to be greeted by an impatient maid. 'The master is waiting for you.' Shown into the studio, Ormandy found Rachmaninoff already at work. Rachmaninoff at once asked him, as a one-time violinist, his opinion of the bowings that had been marked into the score. Ormandy found that they were excellent for an individual artist but very difficult for a whole orchestral section. He asked the composer who had made them and received the laconic reply, 'Fritz' – that is Fritz Kreisler!

112 Rachmaninoff to Sofiya Satina, 10 May 1942.

Part II
RACHMANINOFF
THE PIANIST

Pedagogical Genealogy of the Most Famous Russian Pianists

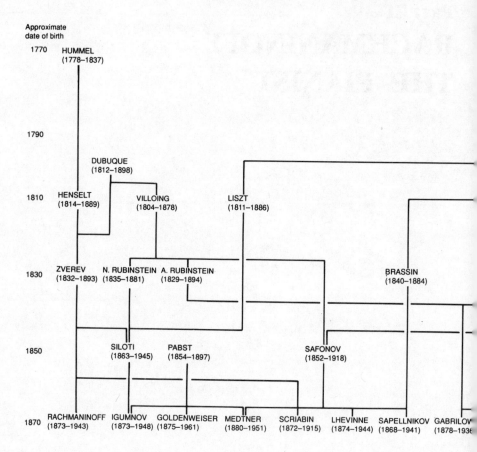

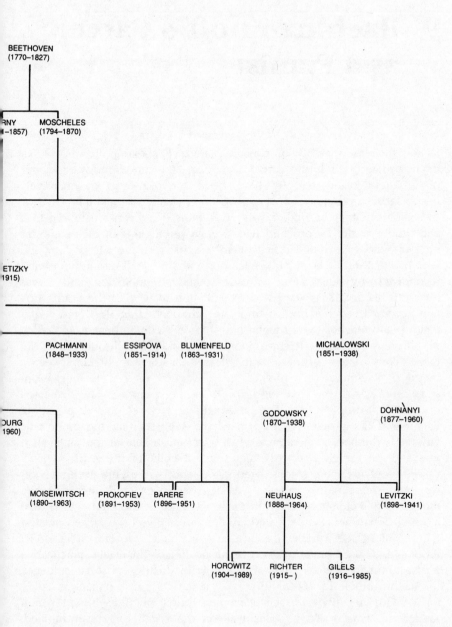

BEETHOVEN
(1770–1827)

RNY
(–1857)

MOSCHELES
(1794–1870)

ETIZKY
1915)

PACHMANN
(1848–1933)

ESSIPOVA
(1851–1914)

BLUMENFELD
(1863–1931)

MICHALOWSKI
(1851–1938)

OURG
1960)

GODOWSKY
(1870–1938)

DOHNÀNYI
(1877–1960)

MOISEIWITSCH
(1890–1963)

PROKOFIEV
(1891–1953)

BARERE
(1896–1951)

NEUHAUS
(1888–1964)

LEVITZKI
(1898–1941)

HOROWITZ
(1904–1989)

RICHTER
(1915–)

GILELS
(1916–1985)

9 Rachmaninoff's Career as a Pianist

Unlike the vast majority of concert pianists Rachmaninoff was not an infant prodigy. His future career as perhaps the most renowned pianist of his time could scarcely have been foretold from the relatively unspectacular progress he seems to have made in his infant years. Incredibly, neither his father, who was himself a keen amateur pianist and whose father before him had been a pupil of John Field, nor his mother, who gave him his first piano lessons from the age of four and who had apparently herself taken lessons with the great Anton Rubinstein,[1] recognized any outstanding pianistic aptitude in their son, and it was not until his sisters' governess drew attention to it, after the young boy had accompanied her from memory in Schubert's *Das Mädchens Klage*, that a piano teacher was brought in and formal training began. According to different accounts, Rachmaninoff was possibly still only four, but more likely seven, years of age.[2] The tutor the family employed, a friend of Rachmaninoff's mother and a student of St Petersburg Conservatoire, was Anna Ornatskaya, to whom the composer later dedicated his song *Spring Waters*. The conspicuous lack of anecdotes about Rachmaninoff's progress with Ornatskaya suggests that the embryonic virtuoso exhibited no greater level of accomplishment at this stage than was average for an obviously highly gifted child of his years.

The family's circumstances deteriorated, and by the time Rachmaninoff was nine years of age all their estates had been sold and they had moved to St Petersburg. Even in those days the conservatoire there had a junior department where gifted children were given specialized musical training alongside a general education – a practice developed in Soviet times – and, with private tuition being no longer financially practicable, it was fortunate that Ornatskaya was able to use her personal influence for Rachmaninoff to enter the conservatoire without payment to study piano with her own former teacher, a pupil of Henselt and Anton Rubinstein, Gustav Kross.[3] This was on the condition, never fulfilled, that he graduated successfully from a junior class taken by one of

Kross's students, Vladimir Demyansky, in which the unenterprising staple fare seems to have been the sonatinas of Kuhlau and Diabelli and the studies of Cramer and Kullak.[4] Demyansky seems to have spent most of his time on the least able students,[5] and Rachmaninoff was doubtless bored to tears by his classes. Against a background of unhappiness at home – his parents had by now become estranged – and a lack of discipline, Rachmaninoff often played truant, and he made only mediocre progress or worse in both musical theory and general academic studies. At the piano natural talent overcame lack of practice, and we are told in the *Recollections* that the Director of the Conservatoire, Karl Davydov, 'frequently paraded [Rachmaninoff] as a pianist', and that he was made to perform at all the student concerts.[6] We know from surviving programmes that, for example, on 30 January 1884 he performed a Berens sonata, on 16 October the Variations in C major by Beethoven, and on 5 and 19 February 1885 an *Étude* by Bagge, Bach's Two-Part Invention in E major and a Mozart *Rondo* – all very undemanding material for a student of his talent but perhaps further evidence of his modest achievement at this time.

For nearly three years Rachmaninoff frittered away his time and managed to conceal the truth from his mother, but in 1885, in the final spring examinations, he failed in all his general subjects, making it doubtful whether he would be allowed to continue at the conservatoire. Fortunately, in this crisis there was expert opinion within the family on which to draw in the person of Rachmaninoff's cousin, Alexander Siloti, who, at the age of twenty-two, had already embarked on a brilliant career as a virtuoso pianist. Siloti had never before heard Rachmaninoff play, and when the latter's mother asked him to do so, he first consulted Davydov for his opinion of the boy. Davydov declared that Rachmaninoff was gifted but very mischievous; he saw nothing special in his musical talent.[7] This unexpected judgement – Davydov was a cellist and not a pianist – nearly deterred Siloti from hearing Rachmaninoff play, and only the insistent pleas of Rachmaninoff's mother changed his mind. He found time to call in at the Rachmaninoffs' flat just briefly before catching a train back to Moscow, and, impressed when he heard the boy play, gave it as his immediate opinion that the man to instil discipline and to nurture and train his musical talent was his own former teacher in Moscow, Nikolay Zverev. The advice was taken, and in the autumn of 1885, after one final carefree summer with Grandmother Butakova, Rachmaninoff went to Moscow at last to begin training in earnest under his new teacher.

Nikolay Sergeyevich Zverev (1832–1893) was one of the most colourful personalities in Moscow musical life in the latter half of the nineteenth century. As with Rachmaninoff, the aristocratic family into which Zverev had been born had fallen upon hard times, and despite his musical inclinations he studied physics and mathematics for two years at Moscow University before launching into a career in the civil service, though at the same time took piano lessons in Moscow with the most fashionable teachers of the day, the expatriate Frenchmen Alexandre Dubuque and Léon Honoré. Dubuque (1812–1898), who, like Rachmaninoff's grand-father, had been a pupil of John Field, taught Alexandre Villoing (1804–1878), teacher of the Rubinstein brothers, Tchaikovsky's friends Kashkin and Laroche, and Balakirev, who used to claim that he owed all his technical ability to the ten lessons he had had with Dubuque when he was ten years of age. A few years later, when his work took him to Petersburg, Zverev studied with the Bavarian-born virtuoso Adolf von Henselt (1814–1889), who, like Field, spent most of his life in Russia, becoming court pianist when he arrived there from abroad in 1838. If Henselt is now remembered at all, it is as an undistinguished composer of piano music in the Romantic tradition (Rachmaninoff made a stupendous recording of one of his *Études*), but in his day he was known as a formidable virtuoso performer, admired even by Liszt. He seems to have tried to instil his own manic devotion to practice in his students – 'Henselt kills', was a current catch-phrase describing his method – and some of what Zverev must have observed, or even experienced, of his uncompromising rigour possibly rubbed off on his own teaching.

In 1867, when Zverev was thirty-five, Dubuque persuaded him to abandon his civil service career and to return to Moscow to become a piano teacher. Zverev's innate social talent gave him an introduction into the circles of Moscow's plutocracy, and tuition of the wealthy gave him a comfortable income with which to indulge his aristocratic taste for high living. Zverev mixed with Moscow's intellectual and artistic élite, and the luminaries of Moscow musical life came regularly to his house – Tchaikovsky, with whom he studied musical theory, Taneyev, Arensky – and visitors from St Petersburg, such as Anton Rubinstein. In 1870, Nikolay Rubinstein enrolled him as a piano teacher for junior students at Moscow Conservatoire, but Zverev continued to give his lucrative private lessons besides. It was also his habit, however, to bring a trio of young boys of outstanding talent into his own home and to give them board and to educate them at his own expense, a generous and altruistic patronage that, in view of Rachmaninoff's family's straitened circumstances, was fortunate indeed. The term Rachmaninoff arrived, one of the existing 'cubs', a certain Nikolay Tsvilenev, moved on for further study with Paul Pabst, so leaving a vacancy Rachmaninoff was able to fill. His two companions were Matvey Pressman and Leonid Maximov. Pressman (1870–1937), to whom Rachmaninoff dedicated his

very first composition, the lost *Étude* in F sharp, as well as his Second
Piano Sonata, later abandoned a concert career to become Director of
the Music Conservatoire of Rostov-on-Don; Maximov (1873–1904) died
from typhoid at the early age of thirty-one, from all accounts depriving
Russia of a great artist; Goedicke, at least, thought his playing like
Rachmaninoff's own.[8]

Zverev's regime proved to be not inhumane, as Rachmaninoff had
feared, but certainly rigorous: the 'cubs' had to be up at six in the
morning in turn to begin their three hours' daily practice, and during
the week, when Zverev was out of the house teaching, his sister kept
an iron grip on the boys to ensure that none of them escaped so much
as even five minutes of practice. Pressman recalled that when Rachmaninoff arrived at Zverev's, although what he played then was 'match-
less', he was not particularly well prepared technically.[9] In correcting
this weakness and insisting on technically perfect execution, through a
regime which inescapably imposed the discipline Rachmaninoff had so
far lacked and which had held back his development, Zverev instilled
a capacity for hard work and a routine of practice that was to last a
lifetime. Those who later marvelled at Rachmaninoff's playing little
realized the constant effort and mundane practice that went into maintaining a flawless technique, a prescription that went back to his days
with Zverev. In later life, Rachmaninoff's last words of advice to aspiring
young concert pianists were invariably, 'Work, work and work!'[10]

In an article in an American book published in 1913[11] Rachmaninoff
wrote about the rigour of the nine years' training which young pianists
received in Russian conservatoires and of the paramount importance
attached in these institutions to technique. During the first five years
the basic teaching material was Hanon, and in the final examination at
the end of the fifth year pupils were tested in both technical and artistic
proficiency; however, unless they passed the technical examination they
were barred from moving on to the higher course. A student would
be expected to know the Hanon studies so well that he could play
them by number and in any key and at predetermined speeds; later
he would move on to technical exercises by Tausig and Czerny. Although
Rachmaninoff presumably dictated the article during his American tour
of 1909–10, when his vice-presidency of the Russian Musical Society
involved his personally inspecting schools of music subsidized by the
Society's funds to check on their efficiency and when what became the
first generation of Soviet pianists were in their teens, he was doubtless
thinking of his own experience as a boy in Petersburg and Moscow.

According to Pressman, the most valuable point of technique Zverev
taught was hand training.[12]

Zverev was absolutely merciless if a pupil played with a tense hand and consequently played coarsely and rigidly, or if, through a tense wrist, a pupil rolled his elbows. Zverev gave many really elementary exercises and studies for perfecting different techniques. An extremely valuable feature of his teaching was that he introduced his pupils to music from the very beginning. To play unrhythmically, or without observing musical grammar and punctuation, was just not allowed by Zverev, and of course that is the whole basis of music, upon which it is not difficult to build even the biggest artistic structure.

In keeping with this general principle of putting music rather than mere piano playing at the centre of his educational method, Zverev required his 'cubs' to become familiar with the basic orchestral and chamber works of the Western classical tradition by playing them through in four-hand piano arrangements, either among themselves or with a lady pianist whom he employed specially for the purpose.

Rachmaninoff's progress under Zverev must have been exceptional. At the beginning of his second year with him he was awarded a 'Rubinstein Scholarship' and appeared regularly in student concerts. Thus in November 1885 he performed Bach's Prelude in A minor; in 1886 the *Étude* in D major by Henselt; and in two concerts at the end of 1887, the second and third movements of Beethoven's Sonata in E flat, Op. 31, and pieces by Chopin's pupil Julius Schulhoff (1825–1898) and Moskowski.

The extraordinary thing about Zverev as a teacher is that by the time Rachmaninoff came to him he had ceased to play altogether, so that he never demonstrated at the keyboard but taught his pupils by word alone. According to the *Recollections*,[13] no-one ever heard Zverev play the piano after he had become a teacher, but Pressman relates that his older students, Siloti, Sergei Remezov and Anatoly Galli, did hear him play, describing him as 'an outstanding, very refined and musical pianist, with a very beautiful tone'.[14] They specifically picked out his performance of Beethoven's 'Moonlight' Sonata as exceptionally fine. In any case, the efficacy of Zverev's teaching is proved by the keenness with which the teachers in the advanced classes, Safonov, Pabst, Taneyev, took his pupils and by the impressive roster of his protégés. Of the nineteen gold medallists to graduate from Moscow Conservatoire up to the year 1900, twelve were former pupils of Zverev, including such names as Siloti, Koreshchenko, whose career as a composer began so promisingly but never flowered and whose piano playing Rachmaninoff admired,[15] Rachmaninoff himself, Scriabin, Maximov, Samuelson, Koeneman (known now only as a minor composer – his song *When the king went forth to war* used to be generally familiar – and the arranger of Chaliapin's visiting card *The Volga Boatmen*, but also a fine pianist and a teacher at Moscow Conservatoire for thirty-three years) Igumnov and Bekman-Shcherbina.

Zverev took his 'cubs' to all the most notable Moscow concerts and operatic performances, but the most significant musical events during Rachmaninoff's time with him, so far as his future career as a pianist was concerned, were the seven 'Historical Recitals' given in Moscow in January and February 1886 by the legendary Anton Rubinstein. Rachmaninoff had first seen Rubinstein during his first autumn with Zverev,[16] and in his presence, at a student concert arranged in his honour, had played Bach's *English Suite* in A minor, a piece that was also to be on the programme of the very last concert he gave, in 1943. After the concert Rubinstein played Beethoven's Sonata in F sharp, Op. 78, a short work in two movements, the performance of which evidently made no special impression on Rachmaninoff, but the 'Historical Recitals', each of which Rachmaninoff attended twice, were an overwhelming musical experience for the twelve-year-old boy, one to which he constantly returned in reminiscence, in interview and conversation throughout his life.

After Liszt, Rubinstein (1829–1894) was generally considered the greatest pianist of his time. An infant prodigy who gave his first public recital at the age of ten, he was taken in 1840 by his teacher Villoing to Paris for further study, but an extensive European tour developed, during which he attracted the attention of Chopin and Liszt. Rubinstein began to copy Liszt's grandiose pianistic style, laying the basis of a reputation based on a colossal technique and a thunderous tone, which taxed to the very limit – and in his early days, beyond the limit – the resources of contemporary instruments. In 1844 he began to study musical theory in Berlin with Glinka's teacher, Siegfried Dehn, and to compose prolifically. After a period in Vienna when, like Rachmaninoff later, he found time to develop a third career as conductor, he returned to Russia to work and to teach. In 1854 he went back to Western Europe for a triumphal tour, and for the next forty years, particularly after Liszt had withdrawn from playing publicly, he dominated a golden age of piano virtuosos. In 1859 he founded the Russian Musical Society and three years later St Petersburg Conservatoire, of which he was also the first Director. In the seven 'Historical Recitals', which he gave not only in Russia but in America and throughout Western Europe, he made a chronological survey of keyboard music from the English virginalists Byrd and Bull, through German baroque and classical music up to Schumann, then Liszt and Chopin and finally the Russians. It was this group of recitals, which Rubinstein gave on consecutive Tuesday evenings in Moscow's Hall of the Nobility and repeated the following mornings in the German Club for the benefit of students, without charge, that Rachmaninoff, Maximov and Pressman attended with Zverev. Forty-four years later Rachmaninoff told Riesemann: '[His playing] gripped my whole imagination and had a marked influence on my ambition as a pianist'.[17]

The many words written about Rubinstein's playing by eye-witnesses form an overwhelming consensus of testimony to his pianistic genius. Pressman groped for superlatives:[18]

> He enthralled you by his power, and he captivated you by the elegance and grace of his playing, by his tempestuous, fiery temperament and by his warmth and charm. His *crescendo* had no limits to the growth of the power of its sonority; his *diminuendo* reached an unbelievable *pianissimo*, sounding in the most distant corners of a huge hall. In playing, Rubinstein created, and he created inimitably and with genius. He often treated the same programme absolutely differently when he played it the second time, but, more astounding still, everything came out wonderfully on both occasions. Rubinstein's playing amazed by its simplicity. His tone was strikingly full and deep. With him the piano sounded like a whole orchestra, not only as far as the power of sound was concerned but in the variety of timbres. With him, the piano sang as Patti sang, as Rubini sang.

Rachmaninoff himself was bowled over: 'It was not so much his magnificent technique that held one spellbound as the profound, spiritually refined musicianship, which spoke from every note and every bar he played and singled him out as the most original and unequalled pianist in the world'.[19]

The impetuous spontaneity and sheer artistry which infused whatever Rubinstein played more than compensated for the occasional sprays of wrong notes, for which he was notorious. When Rachmaninoff heard Rubinstein play Balakirev's *Islamey*, incomparably, as he always thought:[20]

> something distracted his attention and he apparently forgot the composition entirely; but he kept on improvising in the style of the piece, and after about four minutes the remainder of the composition came back to him and he played it to the end correctly. This annoyed him greatly and he played the next item on the programme [Tchaikovsky's *Chant sans paroles*, Op. 2, No. 3] with the greatest exactness, but, strange to say, it lost the wonderful charm of the interpretation of the piece in which his memory had failed him. Rubinstein was really incomparable, even more so perhaps because he was full of human impulse and his playing very far removed from mechanical perfection ... [but] for every possible mistake he may have made, he gave, in return, ideas and musical tone pictures that would have made up for a million mistakes. When Rubinstein was over-exact his playing lost something of its wonderful charm.[21]

Rachmaninoff heard Rubinstein only once more in the eight years before his death, but his playing left an indelible impression on him. It is surely not by chance that the two works which Rachmaninoff singled out as especially affecting him in Rubinstein's interpretation – Beethoven's 'Appassionata' and Chopin's 'Funeral March' Sonata – both became cornerstones of his own recital programmes. Shortly after he embarked on his career as a pianist in the West, he remarked in an interview: 'In my opinion, not one contemporary pianist even comes near to the great Rubinstein ... The possibilities of the piano are far from exhausted; until this happens, before pianists of the present and the future will stand a great goal: to be compared in their art with Rubinstein...'[22]

Four years later, after hearing in America the best the world had to offer, Rachmaninoff was unchanged in his opinion: 'The art of piano playing has not only not reached its limits, but it is very questionable whether the standards of attainment at the keyboard are anything like as high today as they were in the days of Anton Rubinstein. To my mind those performances transcended all that have appeared since that time.'[23]

In 1888, at the end of the lower piano course with Zverev, Rachmaninoff was ready to move on to the higher, graduation, class in the conservatoire, whose tutors at the time were Safonov (1852–1918), who had studied with Leschetizky in St Petersburg, and Paul Pabst (1854–1897), a Liszt pupil, to whom Rachmaninoff later dedicated his Op. 10 piano pieces. Both were excellent teachers, especially Safonov, among whose pupils were later to be numbered Lhevinne, Scriabin and Medtner, and whom Rachmaninoff would certainly have preferred as his piano supervisor in the critical final years before graduation, had he been given a free choice,[24] but this was not to be, for it so happened that for the new term Taneyev had invited Siloti to return to his *alma mater* as a teacher and to join Safonov and Pabst as a piano professor for senior students. Anxious to send only his best protégés to his former pupil, Zverev took the decision out of Rachmaninoff's hands and, to Safonov's annoyance, sent both Maximov and him to Siloti. Later they were joined by a third Zverev pupil, Konstantin Igumnov (1873–1948), a fine pianist in his own right but mainly remembered now as a teacher at Moscow Conservatoire for forty-nine years (Rachmaninoff's wife studied with him) and along with Goldenweiser chiefly responsible for handing on the tradition of Russian pianism to succeeding generations of Soviet pianists.

As a teacher Siloti was an unknown quantity; as a virtuoso pianist he was already, at twenty-five years of age, the brightest star among the young Russians. At the age of eight he had become one of Zverev's 'cubs' and at twelve had enrolled at Moscow Conservatoire to study piano with Nikolay Rubinstein. While there he studied musical theory with Tchaikovsky, whose friend he became (Siloti is known by name in the West almost exclusively as the perpetrator of the recasting of the slow movement of Tchaikovsky's Second Concerto). After graduating in 1881 with the conservatoire's gold medal for piano playing, he had a few lessons with Anton Rubinstein, who recommended that he should move to Weimar to study with Liszt. He did so in 1883, becoming one of Liszt's favourite pupils and remaining with the master until his death in 1886. He had been living for two years in Leipzig when he returned to Russia, his association with Liszt now helping to make him still more famous than before.

Siloti had a long and varied career. When he moved on from his brief spell of teaching at Moscow Conservatoire to return full time to the concert platform, he toured abroad for nine years, incidentally becoming more than anyone else responsible for bringing Rachmaninoff's name to the notice of Western Europe with performances of the First Concerto, and of America also when, on tour in the autumn of 1898, he everywhere played the C sharp minor Prelude, to astounding popular acclaim. Tempted, like some pianists of more recent times, to take up the conductor's baton, from 1901 to 1903 he directed the concerts of the Moscow Philharmonic Society. Having married into wealth – his wife was the daughter of the Moscow merchant Pavel Tretyakov, who founded the gallery still bearing his name – Siloti was able not only to act as Maecenas to Rachmaninoff in the difficult years at the beginning of the century but also to establish his own concert organization in St Petersburg, creating an orchestra and running a series of chamber and symphonic concerts under his name (1903–1917), at which many new works received their first performance, Rachmaninoff's Second Symphony and *The Bells* among them. When the Revolution came, he was unable to reconcile his conservative political principles with the new regime and he left Petersburg in 1920, settling first in Belgium and then England. Abandoning conducting, he sought to make a living from playing the piano, but being already sixty years of age he found it difficult to rebuild a career in postwar Europe. In the winter of 1922 he obtained a visa to go to the United States, and in 1926 he joined the staff of the Juilliard School of Music, New York, resuming the teaching career he had abandoned thirty-five years before. Although he made occasional public concert appearances, he is remembered now mainly as a respected figure in the Juilliard piano faculty, where he remained until his retirement in 1942, at the age of seventy-nine, three years before his death. He retained his affinity with Liszt to the end of his days, when, with his hooked nose, long grey hair and Lisztian warts, he even looked like his old master.

It is posterity's loss that Siloti left behind no gramophone recording and only a few dubious piano rolls on which to form an opinion about his playing.[25] At least at the time when he became Rachmaninoff's teacher he must have been a formidably powerful pianist, clearly proclaiming in his style the grand Lisztian tradition. Pressman recalled:

> Not only had I never heard anything like it, but such playing seemed
> to me altogether supernatural, magical. I was dazzled by his amazing

virtuosity and brilliance, charmed by the extraordinary richness and beauty of his tone and by his treatment of the best compositions of piano literature, interesting and full of the most subtle nuances ... I shall never forget how the whole audience, in amazement at the sound, rose from their places at the end of Liszt's *Carnival in Pest* (the Ninth Rhapsody), as if to verify whether it was being played by one man on the piano or a whole orchestra. Siloti's fascinating appearance and his exceptional pianistic mastery absolutely made him a public idol.[26]

What Siloti passed on to Rachmaninoff from his time with Liszt is a matter for speculation. Despite Siloti's enthusiasm for the old Abbé, for Rachmaninoff it was Rubinstein who never ceased to be his guiding light. Although Siloti seems to have been a successful teacher both at Moscow Conservatoire and at the Juilliard School, Rachmaninoff was too discreet ever to make any public statement about his cousin's playing or teaching. The only comment of his on record, dating from the early 1920s, when Siloti was marooned in London and hoping that Rachmaninoff would find him work in America, was the coldly dismissive enquiry to Arthur Rubinstein: 'Can one recommend Siloti as a pianist?'[27]

Even in his years under Siloti, Rachmaninoff's student contemporaries did not all recognize in him an outstanding talent for the piano. For them Rachmaninoff was a musician of remarkable gifts, a promising future composer, but 'as a pianist he impressed us less'.[28] Although Rachmaninoff continued to perform in student concerts, his appearances were on a much more modest scale than Scriabin's, whom Safonov was promoting, or indeed than those of his most famous pianistic contemporary, Josef Lhevinne, who at the age of fifteen made his public debut playing Beethoven's *Emperor* Concerto accompanied by Anton Rubinstein. When Rachmaninoff was the same age, in the autumn of 1888, his performances at two student concerts were limited to Bach's C major Prelude and Fugue and Rubinstein's F minor *Étude*, and to the first movement only of Beethoven's Sonata in D major, Op. 28 (*Pastoral*), and Liszt's B minor Ballade. Nevertheless, his blossoming pianistic prowess was beginning to attract attention. 'Whenever it became known that Rachmaninoff was going to play at a students' evening,' recalled Elena Gnesina, 'everyone would head for the hall to listen to him'.[29] Referring to his final years as a piano student, Goldenweiser maintained that by then Rachmaninoff 'played the piano with astounding perfection',[30] and he recalled the way in which he could learn even the most difficult pieces in an astonishingly short time: 'When I was studying with Rachmaninoff under Siloti, the latter once at a regular lesson (on Wednesday) told Rachmaninoff to learn Brahms's Variations and Fugue on a Theme of Handel – a difficult and very long work. At the next lesson that same week (on Saturday) Rachmaninoff played these Variations with absolute artistic perfection.'[31]

Rachmaninoff's study with Siloti was interrupted by two events. In the autumn of 1889 he broke with Zverev and moved out to live with his aunt Varvara Satina. Rachmaninoff's mother wrote to her son, urging him to come and join her in St Petersburg and transfer to the conservatoire there, where Rimsky-Korsakov taught composition and Anton Rubinstein had resumed teaching piano, but Rachmaninoff was too attached to Moscow to make the change. Then, towards the end of the following academic year, 1890–91, festering antipathy between Safonov and Siloti at last broke out into an open quarrel over Safonov's alleged pupil-poaching.[32] Siloti resigned, leaving Rachmaninoff the choice of moving to a new piano teacher with different methods for his final year's study, or of risking taking his final piano examination in only three weeks' time, a year early, and putting his fabulous speed of learning and preparing material to its severest test. Safonov, for his part, was not unwilling for him to do so, commenting, 'I know that your interest lies somewhere else', meaning composition.[33] The two main pieces set for the final examination were Beethoven's *Waldstein* Sonata and the first movement of Chopin's *Funeral March* Sonata;[34] Rachmaninoff's outstanding success was unexpected both to himself and to Siloti.[35]

With his piano training complete Rachmaninoff devoted the following, and what proved to be his final, year at the conservatoire to composition. However, he continued to make occasional appearances playing the piano, in his own works, as in the premieres on 17 October 1891 of his *Russian Rhapsody*, in which Goldenweiser considered that Rachmaninoff technically outshone even his illustrious partner, Josef Lhevinne,[36] and of his First Concerto, on 17 March 1892, with Safonov conducting, in a review of which, in contrast, a critic remarked that Rachmaninoff's virtuosity was not flawless.[37] At the first performance of his *Elegiac Trio* in G minor on 30 January 1892, in his first independent concert outside the conservatoire, Rachmaninoff played three groups of short items by other composers: the *Études* in A flat and C minor of Chopin from the Op. 10 set and his B minor Scherzo; a Liszt *Étude*, the *Valse-Impromptu* and his arrangement of the Waltz from Gounod's *Faust*; Tchaikovsky's Barcarolle from *The Seasons* and his Nocturne, Op. 10, No. 1: an *Étude* by Tausig and Godard's *En courant*.

After leaving the conservatoire Rachmaninoff embarked on a full-time career as a composer. Although his financial position was precarious, he made no attempt to build a parallel career as a professional pianist but, to supplement his income, gave piano lessons. He did, however, appear in September 1892 at the Moscow Electrical Exhibition, where he played the same first movement of Rubinstein's D minor Concerto that he had performed in February of the previous year at a student concert, this time with a group of solos: Chopin's *Berceuse*, Liszt's arrangement of the Waltz from Gounod's *Faust* (again), and the premiere of his own C sharp minor Prelude. The concerto performance was judged by the critic of the magazine *Artist* to have been 'beautiful, both technically and musically',[38] but a student contemporary recalled that although Rachmaninoff's playing was confident, 'technically the concerto was played rather badly. One got the impression that Rachmaninoff was not master of the instrument, and I believe that he had worked on it only a little. This appearance was a failure, particularly after the brilliant debuts of the young Josef Lhevinne'.[39]

In 1893, a year in which he composed prolifically, Rachmaninoff appeared as a pianist only in the premiere of his *Fantasy-Pictures* (First Suite) for Two Pianos, with Paul Pabst, on 30 November, but, though the lull in recital appearances continued during 1894, his reputation as a pianist was not forgotten. In 1895 the Warsaw impresario Langiewicz offered him a modest contract for a concert tour of Russia and Poland, not however as a solo recitalist but as accompanist to the twenty-nine-year-old Italian violinist Teresina Tua, who was making a come-back to the concert platform after a six years' absence following her marriage to an Italian count in 1889. It was simply the opportunity to earn some money, not the development of his career, that induced an otherwise reluctant Rachmaninoff to sign the contract.

The Contessa Teresina (real name Maria Felicità) Tua Franchi-Verney della Valetta (1867–1956) had left Paris Conservatoire as an infant prodigy in 1880 and then toured Europe and America. According to the first edition of *Grove's Dictionary*, published six years before the tour with Rachmaninoff, when she visited England in 1883, although her playing showed a delicacy of style, exquisite phrasing and refinement, despite a small tone, it was also marked by 'an obvious tendency to caricature the style of a great living artist [unnamed], which, though amusing, hardly added to the artistic qualities of Signora Tua's performance.'[40] In retrospect her main claim to fame seems to be that when she visited the Griegs at Troldhaugen in 1886 she inspired the composer to write his Third Violin Sonata, which Rachmaninoff himself, many years later, recorded so memorably with Kreisler.

Tua invariably began her programme with Beethoven's *Kreutzer* Sonata, following it with a group of violin sweetmeats in the form of pieces by Vieuxtemps and Sarasate. Although Tua was the star attraction, in each concert Rachmaninoff did play a substantial number of popular solo items – Chopin: Nocturne in C minor, Op. 49, No. 1, a Waltz and the *Berceuse*; Liszt: *Waldesrauschen*, *Valse-Impromptu* and the arrangement of Gounod's *Faust* Waltz, all from his programmes of three years before; Barcarolles by Rubinstein and Arensky; Pabst's Fantasy on Themes from Tchaikovsky's *Eugene Onegin*; and his own *Fantasy Pieces* Op 3.

Despite the success of the recitals, Rachmaninoff found little artistic satisfaction to compensate for the rigours of touring. The complaints in the *Grove* article of superficiality in Tua's playing seem to have been confirmed by Rachmaninoff's own experience; to his mind Tua's playing lacked true musicianship. Writing to Slonov on 9 November 1895, after the first recital, Rachmaninoff declared:

> She does not play especially well; her technique is mediocre. But then she plays wonderfully in front of an audience with her eyes and smiles. As an artist she is not serious, though undoubtedly she has talent. But the sweet smiles she gives the public, her breaks on high notes and her fermatas (like Mazzini [41]), I cannot all the same bear without irritation. Incidentally, I have discovered one other trait in her: she is very mean. With me she is charming; she is very afraid I shall run away.

Tua's fears were eventually realized. After twenty-three concerts and two months of intolerably gruelling travel, Rachmaninoff took advantage of the non-arrival of his fees by the due date to renounce his contract, abandon the tour and return to Moscow.

Rachmaninoff's financial problems continued throughout 1896, and March of the following year witnessed the disastrous premiere of his First Symphony. In the difficult times which followed Anton Rubinstein, even posthumously, played a part, for he appeared to Rachmaninoff in a dream, saying, 'Why are you not working, why are you not playing?'[42] Although this spiritual visitation made a profound impression, it was not to playing the piano that Rachmaninoff turned for a livelihood; Safonov's enmity towards Siloti was naturally directed also to himself, his cousin, and he was offered neither a teaching post at Moscow Conservatoire nor concert engagements with the Russian Musical Society, of which Safonov was Director. Instead, he became second conductor at Mamontov's Private Opera, so beginning his third career.

In the years at the turn of the century Rachmaninoff appeared several times as pianist in concerts of works by other composers put on in aid of the Ladies' Charitable Prison Committee, under the auspices of Princess Liven, either accompanying Chaliapin or playing works for two pianos with Goldenweiser. With the resurgence of creativity that began with the writing of the Second Concerto, however, and his consequently establishing himself as a major force among contemporary Russian composers, Rachmaninoff's appearances as a pianist began to be almost exclusively as the interpreter of his own compositions, though even here it was always in concerts or mixed recitals with other artists. Engagements abroad increased: 1907, Paris; 1908, Europe; 1909/10, America; 1910/11/12, Europe; January and February 1914, England. It later turned out to be prophetic that it was in America, at Northampton, Massachusetts, on 4 November 1909, that Rachmaninoff at long last gave his first solo recital; it was not until more than a year later that he did the same in Russia.

In 1911, for the first time in years, Rachmaninoff publicly played a composition by another composer. In Kiev, on 2 November, he performed Tchaikovsky's B flat minor Concerto, repeating the work at Tiflis and Kharkov before taking it to Moscow (18 December) and in the new year to Petersburg (28 January), the last two performances being conducted by Siloti, exchanging the roles Rachmaninoff and he had taken in a performance of the same work in 1904 and which they were to take again in two months' time when Siloti played the work under Rachmaninoff's direction at a Moscow Philharmonic Society concert. Despite his earlier familiarity with the work as conductor and three performances as soloist, three weeks before his Moscow appearance Rachmaninoff called in on Josef Hofmann (who was on tour in Russia at the time) for advice. 'He wanted Jef to hear him play the Tchaikovsky Concerto, which he has to play in Moscow. He says he has no conception how to play it and wants to take an hour's lesson. Jef told him he couldn't do it. He had too much admiration for him as an artist to be able to teach him anything ...' [43] This extraordinary request of Rachmaninoff's, doubtless made sincerely, not only sheds light on his innate diffidence and humility as an artist, qualities shown many times in his later years as a full-time pianist, but testifies to his enormous respect for the colleague whose playing, even then, he valued above any other living pianist's. Incidentally, in October 1912 Rachmaninoff conducted the concerto in Moscow for the third and last time in his career, with Hofmann as soloist, whose performance, despite the deft accompaniment, proved to be eclipsed in the mind of the public by the memory of Rachmaninoff's own interpretation the year before. [44]

In 1915 Scriabin died, and Rachmaninoff resolved to give a series of recitals of his former colleague's works not only in his memory but to raise funds for Scriabin's needy wife. In addition, he gave four performances of Scriabin's Concerto, a work in which he had accompanied the composer at a concert in Moscow in December 1911. The recital works Rachmaninoff chose to play were predictably mainly from Scriabin's unproblematical early and middle periods – eleven Preludes from Op. 11, the Second Sonata, Op. 19, *Fantasy*, Op. 28 and the *Poème* in F sharp from Op. 32 – but he also played the *Satanic Poem*, Op. 36, three *Études* from Op. 42 and most daringly of all, the Fifth Sonata, Op. 53, the last of Scriabin's sonatas to have a named key signature.

Public reaction to Rachmaninoff's Scriabin recitals was sharply divided according to personal allegiance to the one or the other composer. Scriabin's disciples were enraged by what they saw as Rachmaninoff's earth-bound vision of their master's lofty flights of imagination; Rachmaninoff's supporters, on the other hand, found his characteristically individual interpretations perfectly convincing. The composer Prokofiev, attending the Moscow recital of 18 November 1915, argued that Scriabin's way of playing his own music was not the only one possible, but Ivan Alchevsky, leading tenor of the Maryinsky Opera and arch-Scriabinite, was so incensed by Rachmaninoff's supposedly unidiomatic performance that he went round to the green room spoiling for a row. After Alchevsky had remonstrated with Rachmaninoff, Prokofiev, trying to pour oil on troubled waters, tactlessly offered his opinion: 'And yet, Sergei Vasilyevich, you played very well'. Rachmaninoff, taken aback by the apparent arrogance of the young upstart, replied acidly, 'And you probably thought I'd play badly?'[45]

Even those who generally admired Rachmaninoff as a pianist wavered in their loyalty over his Scriabin interpretations. Anatoly Alexandrov, composer and prominent teacher at Moscow Conservatoire, remembered:[46]

> In truth, even in this concert there were successes, for example the elegant interpretation of the F sharp minor Prelude from Op. 11 – I particularly remember the inimitably graceful *rubato* in the closing bars. However, the interpretation of the more important Scriabin works on the programme ... struck me as very strange and entirely failed to communicate the spirit of Scriabin's compositions. Particularly startling was his playing of the *Étude* in D sharp minor [Op. 8, No. 12 – an encore]. Scriabin was often criticised as a pianist for his lack of power; Rachmaninoff, on the other hand, played this *étude* with the utmost strength and temperament, but in the process all Scriabin's characteristic 'ecstatic' aspiration disappeared. Here I realised that the quality of Scriabin's pianism was fully in accord with the quality of his music, which does not need actual power at all but only imaginative power. Rachmaninoff's interpretation of Scriabin's Second, and particularly of his Fifth, Sonata, was just the opposite. Of course, everything was conditioned by the profound differences of personality of the two outstanding contemporaries and comrades.

This impression is confirmed by other eye-witnesses; the difference in piano style between the two composers was irreconcilable. The composer Yury Nikolsky wrote:[47]

> When [Scriabin] played, you didn't believe keys were involved; under his fingers sounds arose and melted away. From the first sounds of Scriabin's Second Sonata, I realised that, as always, Rachmaninoff was not submitting himself to the composer but the composer to himself. The whole programme was played not as Scriabin played and all the performers I heard imitating the composer in everything; Rachmaninoff played everything with an absolutely different sound, his own 'Rachmaninoffian' sound, and in my opinion this was very convincing. Rachmaninoff always delighted me by his way of playing, and so too on this occasion, but at the interval, in the lobby, I heard censure from the real 'Scriabinists'. I did not share their opinion, for I was delighted. At any rate, I never again heard an interpretation of Scriabin like this.

In preparing the Scriabin programme, Rachmaninoff's fabulous ability to learn difficult works in an incredibly short time was again demonstrated. Goldenweiser recalled:[48]

> Three or four days before the first concert Rachmaninoff was at my place. He said that the proposed programme seemed to him somewhat short, and he asked me to suggest some work or another which he might play. I asked him whether he knew Scriabin's *Fantasy* [Op. 28][49]. He replied that he did not. So I got a copy and showed him it. Rachmaninoff played it through. The *Fantasy* – one of the most exceptionally difficult of Scriabin's compositions – he liked a lot, and he decided to play it in his concert three or four days later.

Years later, speaking of the *Étude* in C sharp minor, Op. 42, No. 5, on the same programme, Rachmaninoff said: 'It's a difficult *étude* – it took me a whole hour to learn it'.[50]

In 1916 Rachmaninoff added another concerto to his repertoire, Liszt's First Concerto. As had been the case with the Tchaikovsky and Scriabin Concertos, he was already intimately familiar with it through having conducted it on three different occasions. He first played the concerto under Koussevitzky in Moscow in concerts on 19 and 20 March, then at a gigantic charity concert at the Bolshoi Theatre, accompanied by Emil Cooper, at which he also played the Tchaikovsky and his own Second Concerto, and again, in Yalta, on 5 September 1917, his final appearance before leaving Russia for good. Before his first performance of the concerto Rachmaninoff came with Koussevitzky to Goldenweiser's flat to rehearse the work.[51]

> He began to ask advice on what to play as encores. Whatever piece we named, he immediately played it as if he had specially prepared for it. We named a piece – *La Campanella*, Rhapsodies, *Études*. The study *Gnomenreigen* he did not know; he played it through from the music and decided to play it as an encore. At the concert he played it and the Twelfth Rhapsody with a perfection his alone. His performance of the Liszt Concerto [in part 2] that evening was phenomenal, but on this occasion he played his own Third Concerto [in part 1] in an unusually expressionless way, apparently because he was totally absorbed in his thoughts on the forthcoming performance of the Liszt Concerto.

When Rachmaninoff finally left Russia at the end of 1917 he spent the first half of 1918 fulfilling engagements in Scandinavia, playing his own solo piano music and Second Concerto but also the useful alternatives of the Tchaikovsky and Liszt Concertos. Before he left Moscow Rachmaninoff had been worried about dwindling exchange rates and the expected loss in the value of the money he could take with him out of the country. Pondering during the summer about his future career, he recalled the words of the Moscow University professor in whom he had confided: 'But, my dear Sir, you should be the last to worry about that; why, here you have your exchange!', pointing to Rachmaninoff's hands.[52] Thus, at the age of forty-five he decided to make piano-playing his principal musical activity and began to work at it with total dedication. He was about to embark upon a career for which he had all the qualities necessary to make him supreme, except for two things: a lack of repertoire and, at the very highest level, the lack of a background of rigorous daily practice necessary, as he thought, to consolidate and refine what was already a formidable technique. There was nothing that the single-minded application to work that he had learned from Zverev could not correct. His sister-in-law summed up his artistic creed: 'Sergei Vasilyevich always held that an artist must constantly go forward, constantly seek perfection, and that one who marks time is already going backwards'.[53]

During the summer of 1918 Rachmaninoff prepared the programmes for his first recital season as a full-time virtuoso pianist. Naturally he drew extensively on his own music, the main work being the Chopin Variations, to which he added a wide-ranging selection of shorter pieces from Ops. 3, 10, 23, 32, 33, and 39. He also used some of the items from his 1915 Scriabin recitals – the Second Sonata, a group of Preludes from Op. 11 and *Études* from Op. 42. Then he resurrected a number of short items which he had first played in the year of his debut, 1892, such as the Rubinstein Barcarolle, Chopin's A flat Waltz Op. 42 and Liszt's Twelfth Hungarian Rhapsody, and the *Troika en traineaux* from Tchaikovsky's suite *The Seasons*, which he had learned as a birthday present for Zverev as far back as March 1886. He prepared two major works – Beethoven's Sonata in D major, Op. 10, No. 3, and Chopin's Third Sonata, not, surprisingly, the *Funeral March* Sonata, which he had played for his graduation from Moscow Conservatoire and with which his name as a pianist was to become specially associated. For the rest, there were a number of shorter works of serious intent – the famous Bach-Busoni Chaconne, Beethoven's C minor and Haydn's F minor Variations, four short pieces by Medtner – and a range of pianistic bonbons – Godowsky arrangements of Dandrieu and Loeillet, the second (variation) movement from Mozart's A major Sonata, K. 331, two Scarlatti sonatas and two Strauss waltzes, all in arrangements by Tausig, and the two most well-known *Moments musicaux* of Schubert. Rachmaninoff tried out this material on audiences in Norway and Sweden during September and October, having in the meantime decided to stake his future on a career in the United States. He arrived there with his family on 10 November 1918.

In an age teeming with piano virtuosi, two names then dominated the stages of America and indeed the world: Josef Hofmann and Paderewski. Hofmann (1876–1957) had been a household word in America since his historic debut at the Metropolitan Opera House at the age of eleven, in 1887. After a period of retirement from the concert stage, during which he studied with Moriz Moskowski and with Anton Rubinstein as his only private pupil, he resumed his concert career in 1894, making his first appearance in Russia that same year and quickly being seen there as Rubinstein's natural heir. His popularity in Russia was enormous and so widespread that he was presented by the Tsar with a set of keys which literally and metaphorically opened every door on the entire Russian railway system. Because of his Russian connections, he was invited to play Scriabin's Concerto in the 'Russian Season' in 1905 in Paris, at which Rachmaninoff also appeared. Rachmaninoff always thought of Hofmann as the supreme pianist of his time. In 1911, after a performance of his Second Concerto by Hofmann in Tiflis, Rachmaninoff commented that his playing had revealed beauties in the work he had not known existed.[54] At another concert in the same city Hofmann made a special show of applauding Rachmaninoff's performance of his Third Concerto, a work which Rachmaninoff had dedicated to him but which Hofmann never played. This mutual admiration as pianists continued throughout their lives. In a letter to Rachmaninoff dated 15 January 1931, Hofmann referred to his friend as the 'Premier of Pianists', to which Rachmaninoff graciously reciprocated, referring to Hofmann's skill as 'incomparable'.[55] After attending a performance by Hofmann of Chopin's B minor Sonata Rachmaninoff remarked: 'Well, there goes one more composition out of my repertoire. Not since Anton Rubinstein have I heard anything like this. There's no use. It is the music itself and the only way to play it, and nobody else can do it.'[56] Two years earlier Rachmaninoff had added an inscription to a photograph of himself he sent Hofmann: 'To Josef Hofmann, my dear friend and constant teacher for many, many years'.[57] As Hofmann grew old and his life became complicated by personal problems, his attitude to public performance became increasingly capricious. Writing to Wilshaw in 1936 Rachmaninoff remarked: 'The best pianist, I dare say, is still Hofmann, provided that he is in the mood, or on form. If not, it's impossible even to recognise the old Hofmann.'[58] By 1942, when Rachmaninoff had moved to Beverly Hills and had Hofmann as a near neighbour, their relationship had cooled,[59] and when Arthur Rubinstein ventured to remark to Rachmaninoff that he must be glad to have Hofmann living nearby, Rachmaninoff merely shrugged his shoulders and answered, 'He has even lost his technique'.[60] But two years after Rachmaninoff's death Hofmann wrote a touching obituary on his old friend: 'Rachmaninoff was made of steel and gold; steel in his arms, gold in his heart. I can never think of this majestic being without tears in my eyes, for I not only admired him as a supreme artist, but I also loved him as a man. Josef Hofmann, Los Angeles, 16 May 1945'.

The other great pianistic luminary of the time, Ignacy Jan Paderewski (1860–1941), never crossed Rachmaninoff's path. A late starter as a pianist, he began a professional career immediately after graduating from Warsaw Conservatoire, but it was not successful and he returned for further study. At the age of twenty-four he at last went to Leschetizky, who despaired at his lack of technique. Undeterred, Paderewski worked like a slave and relaunched his career in 1887. Within a few years he had created a furore throughout Europe and America, as much by the force of his personality as his playing, which critics, though not the public, found increasingly fallible. Withdrawing from the concert platform to involve himself in the political affairs of his country, in the summer of 1919 he became premier of the Polish national government. Although he had resigned by the end of the year, Paderewski did not resume his piano career until 1921, meanwhile leaving his concert manager, Charles Ellis, who also handled Dame Nellie Melba, Geraldine Farrar and Fritz Kreisler, with a vacancy on his books just at the time when Rachmaninoff arrived in America. According to one source[61] it was Kreisler's wife, Harriet Kreisler, who enthusiastically recommended Rachmaninoff as a potential recruit to Ellis's roster of artists, but Ellis had already had dealings with Rachmaninoff the year before when, as manager of the Boston Symphony Orchestra, he had offered him a conducting contract he had not accepted. At all events, within a month of arriving in New York, Rachmaninoff had not only acquired Ellis as manager, but had made contracts for piano (Steinway), gramophone (Edison) and reproducing piano (Ampico). Ellis's organization (Charles Foley was to take over the management within the year) had helped to build the career from which Paderewski had made a fortune, and in the same way it was to make Rachmaninoff too a wealthy man.

Rachmaninoff began his American career with a recital in Providence, Rhode Island, on 8 December 1918, before his first major engagement, a week later, at Boston, and his return to New York's Carnegie Hall the week following, for the first time since his American tour of 1909–10.[62] The order in which he arranged the items on his programme created a precedent for the following twenty-five years as a recitalist. Working, like Rubinstein, within a chronological framework, the first half was given to pieces from the Austro-German classical tradition – the Mozart Variations and the early Beethoven Sonata he had prepared, that in D major, Op. 10, No. 3. The second half was made up of a Chopin group, some pieces of his own ('for the sake of appearance', he later said dismissively)[63] and Liszt's Twelfth Rhapsody, to provide an appropriately brilliant conclusion. In the new year Rachmaninoff used the other material he had prepared in the summer to form a second programme, but he kept to the same format – the Haydn and Beethoven Variations in the first half, and, in the second, a varied group of short pieces concluding this time with Liszt's Second Rhapsody (with his own newly-composed cadenza).

Every year without exception until the end of his life, Rachmaninoff introduced fresh repertoire into his programmes for the new season. He prepared his new material during the summer holidays and he did not vary this practice even if he was in the throes of composition, as in 1934–36, when he wrote the Paganini Rhapsody and Third Symphony. In this way Rachmaninoff not only satisfied his audiences and maintained their loyalty with different programmes each season, but in constantly regenerating and expanding his repertoire he ensured that his playing never lapsed into routine.

As for the nature of his repertoire, it is impossible to avoid the conclusion that it suited Rachmaninoff to accommodate himself to popular taste. Riesemann in the *Recollections* puts the matter rather naively:[64]

> [Rachmaninoff] recognised the necessity of following the laws sanctified by the greatest names in the pianistic world and of submitting to a taste in music which has remained unchanged through decades. So he played the music which was in demand, and luckily the wishes of the concert-goers coincided with his own. What the public wished to hear was, in the vast majority of cases, exactly what he wished to play – the masterpieces of classical music.

Riesemann's comments sound like an apology for a lack of enterprise, and a look through the list of his repertoire will quickly confirm that Rachmaninoff rarely ventured away from well-trodden paths but confined himself almost entirely to what he found not only temperamentally congenial but lying naturally under the fingers. This is why he loved Chopin, Liszt and Grieg,[65] and why of the Austro-German classics he played Beethoven and Schumann but almost no Brahms, which he found pianistically unidiomatic.[66] Mozart he all but ignored, and Schubert too (except in arrangements), being unaware even of the existence of the Schubert piano sonatas until 1928.[67] He of course felt no affinity at all with most twentieth-century music; although he found a place in his repertoire for Dohnányi's *Étude-Caprice*, this work belongs to the twentieth century only in the strictly chronological sense. From the French School he did play some of the more popular Debussy pieces dating from the beginning of the century – 'novelties' he called them[68] – though his unsympathetic recordings of movements from the *Children's Corner* Suite suggest that this composer's style was uncongenial to him and confirm his remarks to that effect to Harold Bauer in 1912.[69] He also played Ravel's *Toccata*, 'marvellously', according to eye-witnesses, and in the 1930s he took up Poulenc's First *Novelette* and his *Toccata*, describing the latter, which is dedicated to Horowitz, who presumably introduced him to these pieces, as 'distinguished by spontaneous inspiration and written for a musician of temperament'.[70] But these works apart, Rachmaninoff's repertoire might happily have been played, indeed was played, by Anton Rubinstein.

The only music unfamiliar to concert audiences which Rachmaninoff consciously tried to promote was that of his friend Medtner. In 1928 the critic of a Boston newspaper went so far as to refer to him as the 'champion of Medtner',[71] but in reality Rachmaninoff's programmes of those years included only a few of the shorter solo pieces, and in the 1930s the number of Medtner works in his active repertoire became fewer still. Though Rachmaninoff was generous in his praise of Medtner's music, he shied away from the great length of some of his sonata movements, and it is no coincidence that the one sonata he played in public (the *Sonata–Fairy-Tale* in C minor, Op. 25, No. 1), is the shortest of them all, though in truth also perhaps the most immediately attractive. Despite receiving the dedication of its companion piece, the great E minor Sonata, Op. 25, No. 2, as well as of the Second Concerto, Rachmaninoff made no effort to perform either work in public. Perhaps he realized, as other artists who have tried to espouse the Medtner cause, such as Horowitz and Gilels, have also discovered from practical experience, that, no matter what the advocacy, Medtner's art seems incapable of winning popular approval.

As regards concerto repertoire, after his first two seasons in America, in which he played the Liszt and Tchaikovsky concertos he had performed in Russia and Scandinavia, Rachmaninoff played only his own concertos and later the *Paganini Rhapsody* until 1937, when he took up Beethoven's First Concerto. In choice of repertoire, as in so many other aspects of his life, Rachmaninoff seems to have sought inspiration from his days in Russia; thus it comes as no surprise that this was the one Beethoven piano concerto he had conducted there, accompanying Josef Lhevinne in a performance in Moscow in 1914. He once described the work, which he performed without cadenza, as 'divine music',[72] and he told Barbirolli, with whom he played it in New York, that it was the only Beethoven concerto he would play because 'the rest are so boring for the pianist'![73] Single performances of Liszt's *Totentanz* (1939), another work he had conducted, and the Schumann Concerto (1941), seem to have been associated with projected but unrealized gramophone recordings.

Rachmaninoff was very demanding of the conductors with whom he played. His record producer, Charles O'Connell, remarked on his absolute unwillingness to submit his own will or his own conception of a work to the conductor's:[74]

He was invincibly convinced of the rectitude of his musical ideas, and with the most implacable determination would enforce them upon his colleagues. Where he could not do this with reasonable amiability on both sides, he simply wouldn't play. This, as he told me himself, was why he would not play with Toscanini, and I think it is fair to infer that the same reason accounts for the extreme rarity of his appearances with Koussevitzky. He preferred Ormandy to anyone, though he collaborated successfully and in the most friendly fashion with Stokowski.

Ormandy himself remarked of the partnership: 'He always seemed difficult, [but] he was not at all. He was a great artist, a great musician, and if anybody was attuned to his musical wavelength, so to speak, I can assure you he was the easiest, or one of the easiest, pianists to accompany.'[75]

Admiring professionalism above all, Rachmaninoff was naturally suspicious of what he considered dilettante English gentlemen conductors. Neville Cardus told the amusing story of how Rachmaninoff once confided to a friend that he was unhappy about a forthcoming concert: 'The conductor – so-and-so – he has no temperament. It is always so in England. Too many the English gentlemens.' 'But,' his friend pointed out, 'last year you said your concert with Sir Thomas Beecham was one of the best and happiest of your life.' 'Ah,' rejoined Rachmaninoff, 'but Sir Thomas is not one of your English gentlemens.'[76]

For Rachmaninoff, giving concerts was the stuff of life: 'If you deprive me of them, I shall wither away... It is best to die on the concert platform', he said. He admitted to being like an old grisette who could not bring herself to retire.[77] 'I am a stage artist', he wrote in a letter to Emil Medtner, 'that is, I love the stage and, unlike many artists, do not grow sick of it but from just one sound from the piano I get strength and inspiration for new and unexpected ideas and discoveries. For this there is just one essential condition – good acoustics; my playing varies according to the acoustics.'[78] Rachmaninoff's experiences were not always happy in this respect, especially in the improvised conditions of provincial auditoria.[79]

> I am well aware that my playing varies from day to day. A pianist is the slave of acoustics. Only when I have played my first item, tested the acoustics of the hall and felt the general atmosphere do I know in what mood I shall find myself at a recital. In a way this is unsatisfactory for me, but, artistically, it is perhaps a better thing never to be certain what one will do than to attain an unvarying level of performance which may easily develop into mere mechanical routine.

Rachmaninoff averaged about fifty concerts a year. For the first four years of his new career he confined himself to North America, but in May 1922 he gave two recitals in London, returning there for the first time since 1914. The following year he extended his American tour to Canada and Cuba, and from 1929 until the outbreak of the Second World War he included Europe in his annual itinerary. By the end of his career Rachmaninoff had made 1,457 appearances as a pianist, of which 1,189 were from the time of launching his career in America in 1918.

References

1   Boris Strelnikov, *LN/A* 3, p. 429.
2   The chronology of Rachmaninoff's earliest years is confused. According to a letter sent to Rachmaninoff on 5 September 1934, more than half a century after the event, by the children's then governess, Mme Defert, and quoted in *B/L*, p. 3, Grandfather Butakov came to Oneg to persuade Rachmaninoff's father to engage a piano teacher. If the given date of General Butakov's death, 1877, is correct, Rachmaninoff could not then have been more than four years old. On the other hand, it was only simple four- and five-note tunes that Rachmaninoff recalled playing with his grandfather Arkady on his visit to Oneg shortly before he died in 1881 (*Riesemann*, p.24). Moreover, Ornatskaya left St Petersburg Conservatoire only in 1882, when Rachmaninoff was nine years of age, which does not square with the composer's recollection (ibid.) that when she became his piano teacher she had only just graduated.
3   Kross, who taught at St Petersburg Conservatoire from 1867 until his death in 1885, was the soloist in the first Russian performance of Tchaikovsky's First Concerto on 13 November 1875.
4   *Riesemann*, p. 38.
5   S.M. Maykapar, *Godï ucheniya*, Moscow, 1938, p. 42.
6   *Riesemann*, p. 31.
7   Pressman, *VR/A* 1, p. 152.
8   Goedicke, *VR/A* 2, p. 4.
9   Pressman, *VR/A* 1, p. 152.
10 Advice to Cyril Smith, Gina Bachauer, etc. 'Interpretation Depends on Talent and Personality', R. interview in *The Etude*, April 1932, p. 240.
11 R. in *Great Pianists on Piano Playing* by James Francis Cooke, Theo Presser Co., Philadelphia, 1913, pp. 210–211. R. gave further details in an article 'New Lights on the Art of the Piano' in *The Etude*, April 1923, pp. 223–224.
12 Pressman, *VR/A* 1, p. 150.
13 *Riesemann*, p. 42.
14 Pressman, *VR/A* 1, p. 151.
15 *Swan*, p. 14.
16 In the *Recollections* (p. 49) Rachmaninoff associated this event with Rubinstein's coming to Moscow to conduct the hundredth performance of his opera *The Demon* at the Bolshoi Theatre, but this had taken place in St Petersburg on 1 October 1894 and it was not until 22 September 1896, after the 'Historical Recitals', that Rubinstein conducted the opera in Moscow.
17 *Riesemann*, p. 49.
18 Pressman, *VR/A* 1, p. 194.
19 *Riesemann*, p. 51.
20 Ibid.
21 R. in *Great Pianists on Piano Playing*, by James Francis Cooke, pub. Theo Presser Co., Philadelphia, 1913, pp. 218–219.

22 'National and Radical Impressions on the Music of Today and Yesterday', Rachmaninoff article in *The Etude*, October 1919, p. 615.
23 'New Light on the Art of the Piano', Rachmaninoff article in *The Etude*, April 1923, p. 223.
24 Sofiya Satina, *VR/A* 1, p. 20.
25 Siloti's piano rolls were made for Duo-Art in the late 1920s.
26 Pressman, *VR/A* 1, pp. 151–152.
27 *Rubinstein*, p. 112.
28 Mikhail Bukinik, *VR/A* 1, p. 214.
29 Elena Gnesina, *VR/A* 1, p. 205.
30 Goldenweiser, *VR/A* 1, p. 409.
31 Op. cit., pp. 405–406.
32 Siloti to Tchaikovsky, 31 May 1891.
33 *Riesemann*, p. 68.
34 *Riesemann*, p.69, and *B/L*, p. 33, deriving from it, are mistaken over the identity of the Chopin sonata through mistranslation from Riesemann's original German text of the music's key (*b-moll* in German being B flat minor and not B minor). Which Beethoven sonata Rachmaninoff played is less certain. In *Riesemann*, p. 68, and in *Swan*, p. 14, Rachmaninoff himself remembered it as the *Waldstein* Sonata, echoed by Sofiya Satina in *VR/A* 1, p. 22, but Goldenweiser in VR/A 1, p. 410, followed by *Norris*, p. 12, seems confident that it was the *Appassionata*.
35 *Riesemann*, p. 69.
36 Goldenweiser quoted in *Tsitovich*, p. 83.
37 Alexander Sirotinin in *Dnevnik artista*, Vol. 4, No. 1, May 1892, p. 39.
38 *Artist*, November 1892.
39 Mikhail Bukinik, *VR/A* 1, p. 218.
40 Article by Alex Chittis in *Grove I*, Macmillan & Co., London and New York, 1889, Vol. 4, p. 183.
41 Mazzini [sic]. Rachmaninoff's reference is to the Italian lyric tenor Angelo Masini (1844–1926), who was personally associated with the composer Verdi and who for many years appeared as leading singer of the Italian Opera in St Petersburg.
42 Mrs Rachmaninoff, *VR/A* 2, p. 312.
43 *Hofmann*, Mrs Hofmann's diary for 27 November 1911.
44 Grigory Prokofiev in *Russkiye vedomosti*, 24 October 1912.
45 S.S. Prokofiev, *Materiali, dokumenti, vospominaniya*, Moscow, 1961, p. 146.
46 Anatoly Alexandrov, *VR/A* 2, p. 163. Alexandrov's description of Rachmaninoff's performance of Scriabin's *Étude* in D sharp minor irresistibly calls to mind Horowitz's well-known and equally explosive interpretation of the piece many years later.
47 Yury Nikolsky, *VR/A* 2, p. 51.
48 Goldenweiser had given the premiere of the *Fantasy* in 1907.
49 Goldenweiser, *VR/A* 1, p. 411.
50 Olga Conus, *VR/A* 1, p. 229, and, in different form, in *Clavier*, October 1973, p. 18.
51 Goldenweiser, *VR/A* 1, pp. 411–412.
52 *Riesemann*, p. 187.
53 Sofiya Satina, *VR/A* 1, p. 50.
54 Nina Andrianova-Ryadnova, *VR/A* 2, p. 169.
55 R. to Hofmann, 19 January 1931.

56 *Chasins*, p. 15.
57 R's photograph is dated New York, 29 January 1929.
58 R. to Wilshaw, 15 April 1936.
59 R. to Greiner, 27 June 1942.
60 *Rubinstein*, p. 489.
61 Louis P. Lochner, *Fritz Kreisler*, Redcliff Publishing Corp. Ltd, New York, 1950, London, 1951, p. 265.
62 Appearing out-of-town first before more important engagements in the large musical centres, which allowed him to try out programmes and play himself in, subsequently became a hallmark of Rachmaninoff's tours.
63 R. to Wilshaw, 15 April 1936.
64 *Riesemann*, pp. 193–194.
65 R. 'New Lights on the Art of the Piano', in *The Etude*, April 1923, p. 223.
66 R., 'How Russian Students Work', in *The Etude*, May 1923, p. 298.
67 César Saerchinger, *Artur Schnabel, A Biography*, Cassell & Co., London, 1957, p. 192n.
68 Ruth Slenczynska, *Clavier*, October 1973, p. 15.
69 Harold Bauer, *His Book*, W.W. Norton & Co. Inc., New York, 1948, p. 213.
70 R. interview in *La Nation Belge*, 6 May 1933.
71 R. to Medtner, 29 March 1928.
72 R. to Wilshaw, 7 June 1937.
73 Michael Kennedy, *Barbirolli, Conductor Laureate*, MacGibbon & Kee, London, 1971, p. 144.
74 *O'Connell*, p. 168.
75 Eugene Ormandy, BBC interview, 1965.
76 Neville Cardus, *Sir Thomas Beecham*, Collins, London, 1961, pp. 61–62.
77 *Swan*, pp. 186–188.
78 R. to Emil Medtner, 19 December 1929.
79 'The Composer as Interpreter', R. interview with Norman Cameron in *The Monthly Musical Record*, November 1934, p. 201.

10 Concert Statistics

Season	Total	Notes
1888–1917	422	This period covers Rachmaninoff's student days at Moscow Conservatoire until his final departure from Russia in December 1917. During this time he made 351 appearances in Russia (178 in recital, 43 as orchestral conductor, 130 as opera conductor), 45 in western Europe (39 in recital, 6 conducting) and 26 in America, 1909–10 (19 in recital, 7 conducting).
1918	12	Rachmaninoff first moved to Scandinavia, where he gave 6 recitals (his own music), and 6 concerto performances (*Liszt 1* + *Rachmaninoff 2*, 2x; *Rachmaninoff 2* alone, 2x; *Rachmaninoff 2* + *Tchaikovsky 1*, once; *Tchaikovsky 1* alone, once).
1918–19	51	Rachmaninoff's first season as a concert pianist full time, first in Scandinavia and then in the United States, where he finally settled. Scandinavia: 14 recitals and 1 concerto performance (*Rachmaninoff 2* and *3*); North America: 22 recitals (2 shared), 13 concerto performances (*Rachmaninoff 1*, 4x; *2*, 8x), and 1 performance with Casals of the Cello Sonata.

New to Rachmaninoff's repertoire this season – BACH-BUSONI: Chaconne; BEETHOVEN: *Moonlight* Sonata, Sonata in D, Op. 10, No. 3, Thirty-two Variations in C minor; CHOPIN: Études in E major, Op. 10, No. 3, and C minor, Op. 25, No. 12, Nocturne in C sharp minor, Op. 27, No. 1, Polonaise in C minor, Op. 40, No. 2, Sonata No. 3, Waltz in A flat, Op. 42; DANDRIEU-GODOWSKY: *Le Caquet;* HAYDN: Variations in F minor; LISZT: Hungarian Rhapsodies 2 and 12;

Season   **Total**   **Notes**

LOEILLET-GODOWSKY: Gigue; MEDTNER: 3 Fairy Tales from Op. 20 and 26, Tragedy Fragment, Op. 7; MOZART: Andante from Sonata in A major, K. 331; RACHMANINOFF: Concerto No. 1 (revised version); RUBINSTEIN: Barcarolle and Polka; SCARLATTI–TAUSIG: Capriccio and Pastorale; SCHUBERT: Moments musicaux in C sharp minor and F minor; SCRIABIN: 3 Études from Op. 42, 8 Preludes from Op. 11, Sonata No. 2 (none of this strictly 'new', all of these pieces having been played by Rachmaninoff in the Scriabin memorial concerts in 1915); SMITH-RACHMANINOFF: Star-Spangled Banner; STRAUSS-TAUSIG: Waltzes: Forest Murmurs, One Lives But Once; TCHAIKOVSKY: Romance, Op. 5.

1919–20   69   North America: 42 recitals (2 shared), and 27 concerto performances (*Liszt 1*, 4x; *Rachmaninoff 1*, 3x; *2*, 6x; *3*, 13x; *Tchaikovsky 1*, once).

New to Rachmaninoff's repertoire this season – ALKAN: Étude: Comme le vent, Funeral March; BEETHOVEN: Sonata in D minor, Op. 31, No. 2; CHOPIN: Ballade in F minor, Op. 52, 8 Études, Impromptu in A flat, Op. 29, Polonaise in E flat minor, Op. 26, Scherzo in B minor, Op. 31, Waltzes in A flat, Op. 64, No. 3, and B minor, Op. 69, No. 2; LISZT: Campanella, *Faust* Waltz, Gnomenreigen: MENDELSSOHN: Bee's Wedding, Op. 67, No. 4, Rondo capriccioso, Variations sérieuses; RUBINSTEIN: Étude; SCHLÖZER: Concert Study, Op. 1; SCHUMANN: Carnaval, 2 Studies after Paganini.

1920–21   54   North America: 41 recitals and 13 concerto performances (*Rachmaninoff 2*, 6x; *3*, 4x; *Tchaikovsky 1*, 3x).

New to Rachmaninoff's repertoire this season – BACH: Prelude; BEETHOVEN: Sonata in E minor, Op. 90; CHOPIN: Ballade in G minor, Op. 23, Barcarolle, Op. 60, Mazurka in A flat, Op. 59,

Season	Total	Notes

No. 2, Nocturne in F sharp minor, Op. 48, No. 2, Waltzes in E flat, Op. 18, F major, Op. 34, No. 3, and G flat, Op. 70, No. 1; DAQUIN: Le Coucou; DEBUSSY: Children's Corner Suite (4 items only); GRIEG: Mountain Tune; LISZT: Spanish Rhapsody; MEDTNER: 2 Novellen; MENDELSSOHN: 8 more Songs without Words; MOZART: Sonata in A major, K. 331 (in full); MUSSORGSKY-RACHMANINOFF: Gopak; SCHUMANN: Papillons, Op. 2; SCRIABIN: Étude in D sharp minor, Op. 8, No. 12 (encore in 1915 Scriabin recitals); TCHAIKOVSKY: Waltz in A flat, Trepak; WEBER: Momento capriccioso.

1921–22 66 North America: 59 recitals and 5 concerto performances (*Rachmaninoff 1*, 2x; *2*, 2x; *2 + 3*, once); London: 2 recitals.

New to Rachmaninoff's repertoire this season – BEETHOVEN: *Pathétique* Sonata; BIZET-RACHMANINOFF: Minuet; CHOPIN: Ballade in A flat, Op. 47, Nocturne in D flat, Op. 27, No. 2, Polonaises in C sharp minor, Op. 26, No. 1, and A flat, Op. 53, Scherzo in C sharp minor, Op. 39; DOHNÁNYI: Étude-Caprice; GRIEG: Ballade in G minor, Op. 24; HANDEL: Air and Variations in B flat; KREISLER-RACHMANINOFF: Liebesleid; LISZT: Ballade in B minor, Grand Galop chromatique, Petrarch's Sonnet 104, Venezia e Napoli-Tarantella; MEDTNER: Fairy Tale in A minor, Op. 34, No. 3; RACHMANINOFF: Daisies; SCHUMANN: Novellette in F sharp minor, Op. 21; WEBER-TAUSIG: Invitation to the Dance.

1922–23 71 North America (69) and Cuba (2): 63 recitals and 8 concerto performances (*Rachmaninoff 2*, 6x; *3*, 2x).

New to Rachmaninoff's repertoire this season – BEETHOVEN: *Appassionata* Sonata; CHOPIN: Fantaisie in F minor, Op. 49, *Funeral March* Sonata, 3 Nocturnes; CHOPIN-LISZT: *Maiden's Wish*; LIADOV: Étude in A flat, Op. 5; MEDTNER: Improvisation, Op. 31, No. 1; MOSZKOWSKI: *La*

Season	Total	Notes

Jongleuse; STRAUSS-SCHULTZ-EVLER: *Blue Danube.*

1923–24   35   North America: 35 recitals.

New to Rachmaninoff's repertoire this season – BACH: English Suite No. 2 (first played for Rubinstein in 1886); CHOPIN: Nocturne in E major, Op. 62, No. 2; DELIBES-DOHNÁNYI: *Naila* Waltz; LISZT: *Funérailles*, Liebestraum No. 3; SCHUBERT-LISZT: *Ave Maria;* TCHAIKOVSKY: Theme and Variations, Op. 19; WAGNER-BRASSIN: Magic Fire Music, from *Walküre.*

1924–25   69   England: 6 recitals and 2 concerto performances (*Rachmaninoff 2*); North America: 57 recitals and 4 concerto performances (*Rachmaninoff 2*, 2x; *3*, 2x).

New to Rachmaninoff's repertoire this season – BACH: Prelude and Fugue in A minor (arr. Liszt), Prelude in D minor, from WTK; CHOPIN: Ballade in F major, Op. 38, Mazurka in E major, Op. 6, No. 3, Scherzo in E major, Op. 54; GLUCK-SGAMBATI: Mélodie; LISZT: Polonaise in E major, Sonata in B minor; SAINT-SAËNS: Caprice on a Theme from Gluck's *Alceste*; SCHUMANN: Sonata No. 2, in G minor, Op. 22; STRAUSS-GODOWSKY: *Artist's Life.*

1925–26   22   North America: 22 recitals.

New to Rachmaninoff's repertoire this season – BACH: Partita No. 4 in D major: Saraband; KREISLER-RACHMANINOFF: Liebesfreud; LISZT: Consolation in E major, *Eroica* Étude; MEDTNER: Fairy Tale in E minor, Op. 34, No. 2; SCHUBERT: Impromptu in A flat; SCHUBERT-RACHMANINOFF: *Wohin?* ('The Brooklet').

[1926–]27   34   North America: 28 recitals and 6 concerto performances (*Rachmaninoff 4*).

New to Rachmaninoff's repertoire this season – BEETHOVEN: Sonata in A flat, Op. 26; BRAHMS: Intermezzo in E flat minor, Op. 118, No. 6;

Season	Total	Notes

CHOPIN: Nocturne in F major, Op. 15, No. 1, Rondo in E flat, Op. 16, Waltz in E minor, Op. posth.; LISZT: Hungarian Rhapsody No. 15; MENDELSSOHN: Études in F major and A minor; RACHMANINOFF: Concerto No. 4; SCHUBERT-TAUSIG: Andantino and Variations; SCHUMANN: Symphonic Studies, Op. 13.

[1927–]28 32 North America: 31 recitals; London: 1 recital.

New to Rachmaninoff's repertoire this season – BACH-BUSONI: 2 Organ Preludes; CHOPIN: Étude in C major, Op. 10, No. 1, Waltz in D flat, Op. 70, No. 3; LISZT: *Dante* Sonata, Paganini Étude in A minor (Theme and Variations); MEDTNER: Sonata-Fairy-Tale in C minor, Op. 25, No. 1; SCRIABIN: Sonata No 4; STRAUSS-TAUSIG: Valse-Caprice No. 1; TANEYEV: Prelude and Fugue in G sharp minor, Op. 29.

1928–29 57 Europe: 24 recitals and 2 concerto performances (*Rachmaninoff 3*, twice in Berlin with Furtwängler); North America: 31 recitals.

New to Rachmaninoff's repertoire this season – BEETHOVEN: Sonata in E major, Op. 109; DEBUSSY: *Fille aux cheveux de lin, Jardins sous la pluie*; MEDTNER: Fairy-Tale in D minor, Op. 51, No. 1; MOZART: Sonata in D major, K. 576; RAVEL: Toccata from *Le Tombeau de Couperin*; SCARLATTI: 2 Sonatas; SCRIABIN: Étude in D flat, Op. 8, No. 10.

1929–30 54 Europe: 25 recitals and 5 concerto performances (*Rachmaninoff 2*, 4x in Holland and Berlin; *4*, once in London, with the LSO conducted by Albert Coates). North America: 24 recitals.

New to Rachmaninoff's repertoire this season – BEETHOVEN: Sonata in F sharp, Op. 78; CHOPIN: Fantaisie-Impromptu, Mazurka in B minor, Op. 33, No. 4, Nocturne in B major, Op. 32, No. 1; LISZT: Valse-Impromptu (not performed by R. since 1892); MEDTNER: Three Hymns in Praise of Toil; SCHUBERT-TAUSIG: Marche militaire;

Season	Total	Notes

WAGNER-LISZT: Spinning Song from *The Flying Dutchman.*

1930–31   46   Europe: 17 recitals and 5 concerto performances (*Rachmaninoff 4*, in Holland, Paris and Berlin); North America: 24 recitals.

New to Rachmaninoff's repertoire this season – BACH-TAUSIG: Organ Prelude in A major; BALAKIREV: Islamey; CHOPIN: Polonaise in F sharp minor, Op. 44, Scherzo in B flat minor, Op. 31; LISZT: Hungarian Rhapsody No. 9, Valse oubliée No. 1; MEDTNER: Funeral March, Op. 31, No. 2; SCHUMANN: Davidsbundlertänze.

1931–32   29   North America: 21 recitals and 6 concerto performances (*Rachmaninoff 2*, 2x; *3*, 4x); London: 1 concerto performance (*Rachmaninoff 3*) – at this concert Rachmaninoff received the Royal Philharmonic Society's Gold Medal; Paris: 1 recital.

New to Rachmaninoff's repertoire this season – BEETHOVEN: *Les Adieux* Sonata; BRAHMS: 2 Ballades from Op. 10; CHOPIN: Nocturne in G major, Op. 37, No. 2, Polonaise in A major; GLUCK-PAUER: Old French Gavotte; LISZT: Harmonies du soir; RACHMANINOFF: Oriental Sketch, Sonata No. 2 (revised), Variations on a Theme of Corelli.

1932–33   54   North America: 44 recitals and 6 concerto performances (*Rachmaninoff 2*, 3x; *3*, 3x); Europe: 3 recitals and 1 concerto performance (*Rachmaninoff 3*, in Rome).

New to Rachmaninoff's repertoire this season – BACH-RACHMANINOFF: Prelude; CHOPIN-LISZT: The Return: HAYDN: Fantasia in C major; MENDELSSOHN-RACHMANINOFF: *Midsummer Night's Dream* Scherzo; SCHUBERT: Impromptu in F minor; SCHUBERT-LISZT: *Ständchen* (Serenade); SCHUMANN: 3 Fantasiestücke, Nachtstücke, Op. 23; SCHUMANN-LISZT: Liebeslied (Widmung).

Season	Total	Notes

1933–34 **32** North America: 25 recitals; Europe: 7 recitals.

New to Rachmaninoff's repertoire this season – BACH-RACHMANINOFF: (Prelude), Gavotte, Gigue; BEETHOVEN: Sonata in G major, Op. 31, No. 1; BORODIN: Scherzo in A flat; CHOPIN: Tarantella; DEBUSSY: Suite Pour le Piano; LISZT: Hungarian Rhapsody No. 11, Petrarch's Sonnet 123; SCHUBERT: Rondo from Sonata in D major; SCHUMANN: 3 Albumblätter, Arabesque.

1934–35 **57** North America: 24 recitals and 6 performances of the new *Paganini Rhapsody*; Europe: 23 recitals and 4 concerto performances (*Rachmaninoff 2*, 2x; *Paganini Rhapsody*, 2x).

New to Rachmaninoff's repertoire this season – BACH-TAUSIG: Toccata and Fugue in D minor; BRAHMS: Ballade in G minor, Op. 118, No. 3; CHOPIN: Impromptu in F major, Op. 36, 2 Mazurkas; RACHMANINOFF: *Paganini Rhapsody*; SCARLATTI: 2 Sonatas.

1935–36 **59** North America: 26 recitals and 10 concerto performances (*Rachmaninoff 3*, 4x; *Paganini Rhapsody*, 6x); Europe: 17 recitals and 6 concerto performances (*Rachmaninoff 3*, 3x; *Paganini Rhapsody* 3x, once, Warsaw, combined with *Concerto 2*).

New to Rachmaninoff's repertoire this season – CHOPIN: Mazurka in A minor, Op. 68, No. 2; HANDEL: *Harmonious Blacksmith*; SCARLATTI: 2 Sonatas.

1936–37 **52** North America: 27 recitals and 12 concerto performances (all of *Rachmaninoff 2*); Europe: 11 recitals and 2 concerto performances (*Rachmaninoff 2*, once; *Paganini Rhapsody*, once).

New to Rachmaninoff's repertoire this season – BACH-LISZT: Fantasia and Fugue in G minor; CHOPIN: Mazurka in F minor, Op. 7, No. 3; FIELD: 2 Nocturnes; LISZT: Paganini Étude No. 2 (*Octave*), Valse oubliée No. 3.

Season	**Total**	**Notes**

1937–38 52 North America: 24 recitals and 10 concerto performances (*Beethoven 1 + Paganini Rhapsody*, 3x;
Paganini Rhapsody alone, 6x; *Rachmaninoff 1*,
once); Europe: 16 recitals and 2 concerto performances (*Beethoven 1 + Paganini Rhapsody*).

New to Rachmaninoff's repertoire this season –
BACH: Italian Concerto in F major; BEETHOVEN:
Concerto No. 1; CHOPIN: Mazurka in F minor,
Op. 63, No. 2; DEBUSSY: Suite Bergamasque;
LISZT: Wienen, Klagen, Sorgen, Zagen (after Bach).

1938–39 56 North America: 29 recitals and 10 concerto perfor-
mances (*Beethoven 1*, 2x; *Rachmaninoff 1*, 8x);
Europe: 13 recitals and 4 concerto performances
(*Rachmaninoff 2*, 2x – including the Henry Wood
Jubilee Concert; *Paganini Rhapsody*, 2x).

New to Rachmaninoff's repertoire this season –
BEETHOVEN: Sonata in C minor, Op. 111;
CHOPIN: 3 Études from Op. 25, 12 Preludes;
RAMEAU: Variations in A minor.

1939–40 42 Lucerne Festival, August 1939: 1 concerto performance (*Beethoven 1 + Paganini Rhapsody*); United
States: 21 recitals, 17 concerto performances (*Beethoven 1*, 2x; *Beethoven 1 + Liszt Totentanz*, once
– Rachmaninoff's only performance ever of the
Liszt, at Minneapolis, with Mitropoulos; *Rachmaninoff 1*, 2x; *Rachmaninoff 1 + Paganini Rhapsody*,
once; *Paganini Rhapsody* alone, once; *Rachmaninoff 2*, 7x; *3*, 2x; *2 + 3*, once), and 3 appearances
as orchestral conductor (2 in Philadelphia and 1
in New York, in *Symphony 3* and *Bells*).

New to Rachmaninoff's repertoire this season –
BACH: French Suite No. 6; LISZT: Totentanz;
POULENC: Novelette, Toccata; RACHMANINOFF:
Symphony No. 3 (conducting); SCHUBERT-LISZT:
Forelle.

1940–41 45 North America: 31 recitals, 12 concerto performances
(*Beethoven 1 + Paganini Rhapsody*, 2x; *Rachman-
inoff 1 + Paganini Rhapsody*, 2x; *Rhapsody* alone,
2x; *Rachmaninoff 2*, 2x; *3*, 4x), and 2 appearances

Season   **Total**   **Notes**

as orchestral conductor (in Chicago, in *Symphony 3* and *Bells*).

New to Rachmaninoff's repertoire this season – RACHMANINOFF: Humoresque, Op. 10, No. 5, and Moment musical in E flat minor, Op. 16, No. 2, in the revised versions.

1941–42   49   United States: 30 recitals and 19 concerto performances (*Rachmaninoff 2*, 7x; *4*, 7x; *Paganini Rhapsody*, 4x; *Schumann Concerto*, once, Rachmaninoff's only performance ever, at Detroit, with Victor Kolar).

New to Rachmaninoff's repertoire this season – CHOPIN: 2 Mazurkas; RACHMANINOFF: Concerto No. 4 (revised); SCHUMANN: Concerto; TCHAI-KOVSKY-RACHMANINOFF: Lullaby.

1942–43   22   North America: 17 recitals and 5 concerto performances (*Beethoven 1*, 2x; *Beethoven 1 + Paganini Rhapsody*, 2x; *Rachmaninoff 2*, once).

New to Rachmaninoff's repertoire this season – SCHUMANN: Faschingsschwank aus Wien.

1888–1943   1,643   This total includes 1,020 concerts in 221 cities in North America (United States and Canada) alone. The number of concerto performances given by Rachmaninoff is as follows:

BEETHOVEN: Concerto No. 1 in C major, Op. 15	17
LISZT: Concerto No. 1 in E flat, G. 124	10
LISZT: Totentanz, G. 126	1
RACHMANINOFF: Concerto No. 1 in F sharp minor, Op. 1 –	
original version	1
revised version	23
RACHMANINOFF: Concerto No. 2 in C minor, Op. 18	143
RACHMANINOFF: Concerto No. 3 in D minor, Op. 30	86
RACHMANINOFF: Concerto No. 4 in G minor, Op. 40 –	
original version	12
revised version	7
RACHMANINOFF: Rhapsody on a Theme of Paganini, Op. 43	46
SCHUMANN: Concerto in A minor, Op. 54	1
SCRIABIN: Concerto in F sharp minor, Op. 20	4
TCHAIKOVSKY: Concerto No. 1 in B flat minor, Op. 23	14

11 Rachmaninoff's Art as a Pianist

The pre-eminence as a pianist Rachmaninoff achieved so quickly after his arrival in America at the end of 1918 was recognized by audiences and fellow professionals alike. Even those who disliked Rachmaninoff's music – Stravinsky is the most extreme example – nevertheless acknowledged his genius at the piano. His colleagues were unanimous in their respect. It was not just for Hofmann that he was a 'supreme artist': for Horowitz he was a musical god whose memory never dimmed with the passing of the years, in retrospect 'surely the greatest of all pianists'; for Arthur Rubinstein, 'the most fascinating pianist of them all since Busoni'; for Claudio Arrau, 'one of the greatest pianists of all time and one of the very few truly worthy of immortality'.[1] Even artists not associated with the Romantic repertoire in which Rachmaninoff so excelled were no less respectful. For Gieseking Rachmaninoff was simply 'the greatest pianist of his time' and Artur Schnabel, in a posthumous tribute, wrote: 'I shall never forget the admiration I felt when I first heard Rachmaninoff play. His sovereign style, a combination of grandeur and daring, his naturalness and the giving of his whole self – all this was absolutely inimitable.'[2]

In analysing the reasons for Rachmaninoff's dominance in his career as a pianist, it is clear that, as with Paderewski, his awesome personality captured his audiences before he played a note. The English dramatic critic James Agate described a visit Rachmaninoff paid to the Savage Club in London in 1939, at the invitation of Benno Moiseiwitsch:[3]

> As I was sitting at an angle of the table within four feet of the chair, I had plenty of opportunity to study in Rachmaninoff that visual magnificence which comes naturally to great men like Irving and Chaliapin, to whose type this major artist belongs. It is an extraordinary mask, at once gentle and farouche, noble, melancholy and sardonic ... When the lean figure rose to leave, everybody in the room stood up. Apart from royalty, this has happened before at the Savage only in the cases of Irving and Lord Roberts.

When Rachmaninoff appeared, his audiences sensed that they were in the presence of a great man; in that respect he was like Liszt and Rubinstein, Busoni and Paderewski. Cyril Smith wrote of his entry on to the concert platform:[4]

> Those who were fortunate enough to hear him play will almost certainly remember this very tall, melancholy figure, with his greying hair in a crew cut and his deeply-lined face set in a sombre expression, walking unwillingly to the piano as though he hated the very sight of it. Slowly he would take his seat, gazing round at the audience with his gimlet eyes ... Such was the power of his personality that I have seen members of the audience cower down in their seats as his glance passed over them ... As he took in the stalls, the circle and the galleries, he would play a chord, *pianissimo*, then repeat it several times softer until it dwindled to less than a whisper. By then the audience would have quietened completely and Rachmaninoff was ready to begin his recital.

Once, at a Queen's Hall recital, there was an epidemic of sneezing and throat clearing. Rachmaninoff glanced around the hall, 'like a weary bloodhound' and the noise stopped dead.[5]

Rachmaninoff's demeanour at the keyboard was absolutely undemonstrative. He had the fewest physical gestures of any great pianist. Leonid Pasternak commented:[6]

> In general the character of a performer comes across in the way he sits at his instrument. Rachmaninoff sat at the piano with the same seriousness and simplicity as he must have sat down at his writing desk or at meals in front of a plate of soup, in as prosaic a manner, forgetful of how many eyes were fixed on him at that moment, on his hands, his fingers, his head, or the pedals. I remember him thus, bolt upright, his head slightly bent, his body rigid. All the strength of his touch was concentrated in his hands, his body apparently playing no part in his extraordinary *fortissimo.*

Unlike most virtuosos, Rachmaninoff had enormous hands, capable of stretching a twelfth and enabling him to grasp even the most rapid and wide-spread chords of his own compositions with total security. Jorge Bolet described shaking hands with Rachmaninoff as 'being enveloped in warm flesh – no bone, just meat'![7] and Rosalyn Tureck described the same experience in similar terms: 'His hands, which appeared bony and hard from a distance, were so large and soft that when I shook hands with him I lost mine in the cushions of his'.[8] Rachmaninoff suffered from neuralgia in his hands in later life and throughout his career complained of tiredness in them. In 1931, when he had played through the new *Corelli Variations* for Alfred Swan he looked at his hands: 'The blood-vessels on my finger-tips have begun to burst; bruises are forming. I don't say much about it at home. But it can happen at any concert. Then I can't play with that spot for about two minutes; I have to strum some chords. It is probably old age.'[9] As time went on, Rachmaninoff designed an electric muff with which to warm his hands before a concert.[10]

The technique which professionals held in awe and which enabled Rachmaninoff to ignore mere mechanical problems in whatever he chose to perform was achieved only by unrelenting toil and single-mindedness of purpose. Writing to Wilshaw in 1922 Rachmaninoff remarked on the intensive effort he had made since taking up the career of a virtuoso: 'For four years now I have been working hard. I make some progress, but actually the more I play the more clearly do I see my inadequacies.'[11] In 1925 in another letter to Wilshaw he picked up the subject again:[12]

> In France I shall again sit down at the piano and at the exercises for the fourth and fifth fingers. About five years ago Hofmann told me that our second finger is the lazy one! I devoted attention to it and began to 'pull it up'! Soon I noticed that the third finger has the same fault. And now, the longer I live the more I am convinced that both the fourth and fifth work unconscientiously. That leaves only the thumb and that also, probably, temporarily! So I have begun to look askance at that too! And so I have three months' preparatory work...

Rachmaninoff actually enjoyed practising, finding that it cheered him up.[13] From his Russian days his favourite technical studies were Czerny's Op. 740. Zoya Pribïtkova recalled that in the time immediately before a concert Rachmaninoff almost always played Hanon exercises in all keys and in different rhythmic patterns; then he would play two or three of the Czerny *Études*. 'Sergei Vasilyevich loved the Czerny *Études*, saying that they were unusually well and clearly written for the development of finger technique.'[14] Leo Conus's wife described Rachmaninoff practising these studies in the summer of 1928 at Villers-sur-Mer:[15]

> Every morning at least half an hour Rachmaninoff spent on Czerny *Études*, Op. 740 polishing his trill and arpeggio. Towards the end of that summer, Rachmaninoff played for a small group his new Fourth Concerto and also played a few *Études* of Czerny Op. 740. It was so beautifully done that all of us begged him to put them on his programme. The trills were really a big 'thrill' and the arpeggios were impeccably clear, with different expression, bravura, or light as a bird.

When, in July 1940, Boris Chaliapin painted his well-known informal portrait of Rachmaninoff at the keyboard (now in the Glinka Museum, Moscow), he sat in on his practising sessions.[16]

> Sergei Vasilyevich used to begin his exercises very slowly and, evidently, playing with one hand. Then the exercises became more complicated, speeded up and finally turned into a quick scattering of beads of sounds over the whole length of the keyboard, lingering in the low, middle or high register, or slipping down from top to bottom and then from bottom to top in an uninterrupted variety of scales. Then, after exercises, he chose some piece or another, often one of his own compositions on which he was working, and he continued to practise almost without stopping, playing them sometimes slowly, sometimes quickly. Sometimes he would play over one bar ten times or more.

Working through a piece incredibly slowly was a hallmark of Rachmaninoff's method of practising. Abram Chasins once had an appointment to see Rachmaninoff in Hollywood.[17]

> Arriving at the designated hour of twelve, I heard an occasional piano sound as I approached the cottage. I stood outside the door, unable to believe my ears. Rachmaninoff was practising Chopin's *étude* in thirds [G sharp minor, Op. 25, No. 6], but at such a snail's pace that it took me a while to recognise it because so much time elapsed between each finger stroke and the next. Fascinated, I clocked this remarkable exhibition; twenty seconds per bar was his pace for almost an hour while I waited riveted to the spot, quite unable to ring the bell. Perhaps this way of developing and maintaining an unerring mechanism accounted for his bitter sarcasm towards colleagues who practised their programmes 'once over lightly' between concerts.

Rachmaninoff showed Harriet Cohen a pocket metronome which he used. when he was practising. He would first set it to a slow speed and then when he had satisfied himself at that tempo, he would gradually speed it up, only setting it faster when he had achieved perfection at each stage.[18]

Arthur Hirst witnessed Rachmaninoff practising at Senar and elsewhere:[19]

> When he began to work on a new piece, first of all he learned the layout of each bar and decided on the fingering. In his opinion half the work was now done... Rachmaninoff played his exercises very slowly, and diligent pupils would have been heartened to hear at how slow a tempo this greatest of pianists used to practise, and with what painstaking attention he monitored the sound of each note and the work of each hand. Once I heard him playing like this from another room, and although each note of the piece he was practising was familiar to me, I could not recognise Liszt's *Waldesrauschen*.

Marietta Shaginyan described his routine in preparing for a concert as follows:[20]

> He used to take phrase after phrase from the piece he had to perform, change it into an arpeggio and run it up and down the whole keyboard over and over again. Quite often I sat next to him when he was practising like this and he would ask me to tell him stories, and I became terribly hungry to hear the piece in its entirety, for I felt as though from a familiar face he were giving first just the nose, then the chin, then the eyebrows, and so on. Once I couldn't bear it any longer and told him about it. He replied, half-jokingly, half-seriously: 'You must peer into every corner and take out every screw so that later it can more easily be put together into one complete whole'.

This was Rachmaninoff speaking not only as a pianist, with a profound understanding of his instrument, but as a composer, with an instinctive concern for musical structure and its component elements.

When composers play the piano, they possess the advantage of having an overall view of structure often denied mere pianists, who may be preoccupied with petty details and pianistic problems. Though Rachmaninoff was a perfectionist and worked hard to achieve an unerring technique, he used the piano primarily as a vehicle by which to achieve a realization of a particular view of a piece as he had seen it in his composer's mind. Thus, all his performances were compositions in themselves, deeply thought-out commentaries on the music he played, indelibly stamped with his own personality, and, as the invariably close similarity of different recordings of the same pieces made at different times proves, once he had 'composed' an interpretation, he remained faithful to it until the end of his days. In this respect he may be seen as the antithesis of his friend Josef Hofmann, whose apparently mercurial spontaneity created its own miracles.

In 1936 Rachmaninoff gave an interview in which he emphasized how important he felt it was for a performer also to be a creator:[21]

> If you are a composer you have an affinity with other composers. You can make contact with their imaginations, knowing something of their problems and ideals. You can give their works *colour*. That is the most important thing for me in my pianoforte interpretations, *colour*. So you can make music live. Without colour it is dead... The great interpreters in the past were composers in most instances. Paganini, so we understand, was a king of virtuosity... but he was a composer too. Liszt and Rubinstein; and in our time Paderewski and Kreisler. Ah! I know what you are thinking. But it doesn't matter. It makes no difference whether these are first- or fourth-rate composers. What matters is, they had the creative mind and so were able to communicate with other minds of the same order.

In an interview two years earlier Rachmaninoff had argued that the creator is necessarily endowed with greater imagination and sensitivity to colouring than a mere executant:[22]

> To my mind, there are two vitally important qualities innate in the creative artist which are not found, to the same degree, in the man who is solely an interpreter. The first is imagination. I do not suggest that the interpretative artist has no imagination; but it is safe to assume that a composer possesses the greater imaginative gift, because he must first imagine before he can create – imagine so powerfully that a concrete picture of his creation is vividly present in his mind before a single note is written. His finished composition is an attempt to recreate the essence of this picture in music. It follows that when a composer comes to interpret his own work, his own picture will be foremost in his mind, whereas every musician performing the work of another must imagine an entirely new picture for himself. Upon the vividness and extent of the performer's imagination the success and vitality of his interpretation largely depend; and, in this sense, it seems to me that the composer-interpreter, whose imagination is by nature so highly developed, may be said to possess an advantage over the purely executive artist.
> The second and even more important gift distinguishing the composer

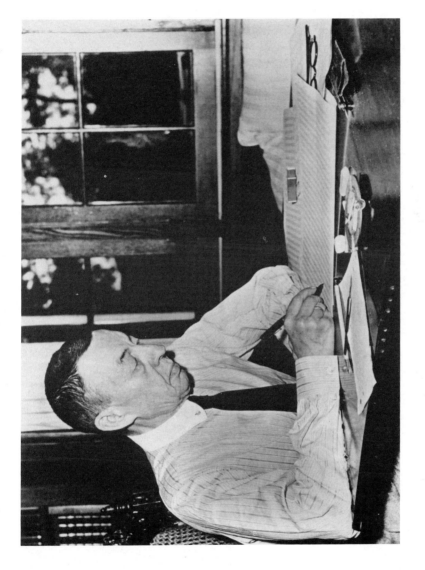

17 Rachmaninoff c. 1936.

18   Rachmaninoff at Senar. August 1938.

19 Rachmaninoff's study at Senar.

20 Rachmaninoff at the Sir Henry Wood Jubilee concert, Royal
Albert Hall, London, 5 October 1938.

21   Rachmaninoff and Medtner at Medtner's London house. 1938.

22　Rachmaninoff at Huntington, Long Island. 1940

23   Rachmaninoff at his house on Elm Drive, Beverly Hills. 1942.

24 Rachmaninoff's grave, Kensico cemetery.

from every other type of musician is an intensely refined sensitiveness for musical colouring. It was said of Anton Rubinstein that no other pianist produced such a dazzling wealth and variety of sheer musical colour from the keyboard. Listening to his playing, one might almost imagine he commanded the resources of a full orchestra, because Rubinstein, being also a great composer, possessed this intense feeling for colour which pervaded his interpretative as well as his creative work. Personally, I consider the possession of this acute colour-sensitiveness to be a composer's highest privilege. However fine a musician the executant may be, I think he can never acquire the talent for sensing and reproducing the full range of musical colour that is the composer's birthright.

Rachmaninoff's instinct as a composer led him to guide a performance to an inevitable climax or climaxes – the 'point', as he called it; to 'miss the point' meant that the whole interpretation had failed. Marietta Shaginyan was at a concert at which, unbeknown to the audience, this had happened:[23]

> During the interval, when there was a storm of wild enthusiasm in the hall and it was difficult to force one's way through the crowd, going to him in the green room we saw from Rachmaninoff's face that he was in a frightful state: he was biting his lip, angry, pale. Before we had a chance to open our mouths to congratulate him, he began to complain that he was most likely going out of his mind, that he was getting old and needed putting on the scrap-heap, that we had to prepare an obituary to the effect that there had once been a musician but that now nothing was left of him, that he could not forgive himself, etc. 'Did you really not notice that I missed the point? I let the point slip, you understand!' Later he told me that, for him, every piece he performed was a structure with a culminating point. One must so measure out the whole mass of sounds, give a depth and strength of sound in such frequency and gradation that this high point, which a musician must approach as if with the greatest naturalness though in fact with the greatest art, this point should sound and flash like the tape falling at the end of a race or glass breaking from a blow. Depending on the actual piece, this culmination may be at the end or in the middle; it may be loud or quiet, but the performer must know how to approach it with absolute calculation, absolute exactness, because if it slips the whole structure goes to pieces, the piece becomes disjointed and scrappy and does not convey to the listener what it should convey. Rachmaninoff added: 'I am not alone in feeling this; Chaliapin also feels the same thing. Once at a concert of his the public was wild with enthusiasm, but backstage he was tearing his hair out because the point had slipped.'

Rachmaninoff's composer's mind, his impregnable technique, the very nature of his hands, with their enormous stretch, the despotic authority of his personality, all these things in combination made him unique as a pianist. Unlike some of his contemporaries who were known for one or other aspect of their pianistic skill, Rachmaninoff possessed an art which was absolutely comprehensive. As Abram Chasins remarked:[24]

> One no sooner reflects that perhaps the most fabulous aspects of his

playing were his melodic eloquence and dramatic virtuosity than one remembers the unique rhythmic bite in sustained, short, or syncopated, accentuation, or his way of orchestrating chords with special beauty through individual distribution of balances and blendings. Rachmaninoff brought as much art to the performance of his own works and devotion to those of others as was brought to their creation.

Rachmaninoff's overpowering presence at the keyboard, on gramophone record as in life, is the antithesis of the faceless efficiency which characterizes so much contemporary pianism, and the passing years and changing fashion have created an apparently unbridgeable chasm between those who look back with reverence to what they see as a Golden Age of pianists, dominated by the genius of Rachmaninoff, and those who worship more modern musical gods and are unaware of his art altogether or who dismiss it as anachronistically self-indulgent, even unmusical. Of course, in recognizing the existence of different traditions of performance years ago, it is equally absurd to presume their inherent superiority as to prejudge them as invalid because a different ethos now operates; surely all that may sensibly be done is objectively to assess the evidence, in Rachmaninoff's case fortunately not only the written testimony and fallible memories of his contemporaries but the evidence of the recordings he left, which, unlike those of some of his most distinguished colleagues, Hofmann and Godowsky, for example, seem faithfully to represent his playing as it was in real life. As Rachmaninoff's performances of his own music, though by no means irreproachable in every detail and sometimes showing a surprising disregard for his own texts, have never ceased to be thought of as models for all time, it is perhaps most challenging to look at an area of his repertoire in which his interpretations, even in his own day, did not always win universal acclaim, namely Chopin, whose works he recorded more prolifically than those of any other composer next to his own.

Chopin had always been a composer very dear to Rachmaninoff's heart:[25]

> Chopin! From the time when I was nineteen years old I felt his greatness and I marvel at it still. He is today more modern than many moderns. It is incredible that he should remain so modern. His genius is so tremendous that not any composer of today is more modern in style, and he remains for me one of the greatest of the giants... Would that another Chopin might arise to bring new pianistic beauties to the world! Notwithstanding all the playing I do during the course of the year, I find myself continually playing Chopin at home, just for the sheer pleasure of the thing. There is a delight in letting one's fingers run through his perfectly moulded passages. Every note seems to be just where it belongs to produce the finest effect, and not one seems to be out of place. There is nothing to add and nothing to take away.

The general nature of Rachmaninoff's Chopin interpretations is something else which can be traced back to Anton Rubinstein. When in his American years he was once asked how Chopin should be played, Rachmaninoff replied: 'This is how we learnt to play in Russia. Rubinstein would give his historical concerts in St Petersburg and Moscow. I had the greatest good luck to attend them. He would come out on to the platform and merely say, "Every note of Chopin's is pure gold. Listen!" And then he played and we listened.'[26]

In an interview in 1932 Rachmaninoff firmly rejected the then current effeminate style of Chopin's interpretation:[27]

> With regard to Chopin there is in these days a tendency which I have observed among certain musical artists. They cite the letters of Chopin and the statements of his contemporaries to prove that he had little strength and that therefore he played everything *mezza voce*, delicately, never *fortissimo*. And it follows, they say, that all his compositions should be played in a subdued manner, with delicacy but never with robustness. This opinion is not sympathetic to me. I do not understand Chopin's music thus.
>
> Behind me and behind all the artists who play Chopin in the 'grand manner', the broader style, stands Rubinstein. He could play in all styles; he could have played Chopin in the subdued style if he had liked. But he did not choose to play it in that way. What a pity that there was in those days no mechanism for recording and preserving the playing of those artists!

Rubinstein's virile Chopin playing was heard at its best – and the same may be said of Rachmaninoff – in the *Funeral March* Sonata, and there is little doubt that Rachmaninoff, like Busoni before him,[28] modelled his own interpretation of the work on Rubinstein's performance, which Hanslick described so vividly:[29]

> His rendering of Chopin's B flat minor Sonata is indeed wonderful; he plays the first movement tempestuously, giving to it the atmosphere of passionate gloom; the funeral march is stern and sustained; the mighty *crescendo* at the beginning of the trio, and the gradual *decrescendo* after it, is a brilliant innovation of his own. But in the finale he takes such an astounding *prestissimo* that all accents are lost, and only a grey cloud of dust seems to hover before the dazed listener, who simply waits for the last note that he may open his eyes and draw a long breath of relief.

Rachmaninoff's performance of the sonata was generally held to be one of his most impressive achievements. In a famous review of Rachmaninoff's 1930 Carnegie Hall performance of the work W.J. Henderson, the critic of *The Sun*, wrote:[30]

> For one listener this interpretation of the B flat minor Sonata – in which even the Funeral March was played differently – closed itself with a magisterial *quod erat demonstrandum* which left no ground for argument.

The logic of the thing was impervious; the plan was invulnerable; the proclamation was imperial. There was nothing left for us but to thank our stars that one had lived when Rachmaninoff did and heard him, out of the divine might of his genius, recreate a masterpiece. It was a day of genius understanding genius. One does not often get the opportunity to be present when such forces are at work. But one thing must not be forgotten: there was no iconoclast engaged; Chopin was still Chopin.

Rachmaninoff gives the sonata's first subject a chillingly sinister impetus by minutely exaggerating the difference between adjacent long and short note values. This rhythmic 'snap', an extra accentuation of the beat, sometimes accompanied by a slight *crescendo* to it or by the clipping of the final note or notes of a group preceding it, is one of Rachmaninoff's most characteristic hallmarks as a pianist. The awkward left-hand part is played very lightly and the sustaining pedal used hardly at all. The second subject is contrastingly given a greater depth of tone and greater rhythmic flexibility, and, as the critic Edward Sackville-West pointed out long ago,[31] the second line of the theme is given extra tension by tiny hesitations in the scales:

Ex.193

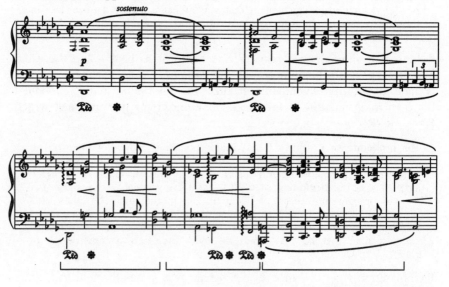

In the development section Rachmaninoff brings out the sinister implications of the first theme by emphasizing its rhythm in hammering bass octaves, which reach their logical culmination in the movement's final bars, where their syncopations are finally resolved. This amazing rhythmic sense is heard again in the second movement, where rhythmic tension is heightened by the extra impetus in the left hand from the characteristic 'snap'. As before, this powerful treatment throws into high relief the lyricism of the middle section, where the pulse is much more flexible.

It is not by chance that Rachmaninoff, the composer who was also a pianist, makes the Funeral March (composed two years before the rest of the sonata) the centre of his performance, since much of the material for the whole work is generated by it: the rhythm of the first movement's opening bars, *Grave*, anticipates it; that movement's first subject contains its rhythm in retrograde motion; and the finale is a *presto* reworking of the same motto. When playing this movement Rachmaninoff obviously had the same picture in his mind as Rubinstein: a funeral procession coming closer and then, after the meditation of the trio, passing on and out of sight. This is an image Rachmaninoff had already powerfully expressed in his own music, explicitly in the C minor *Étude-Tableau*, Op. 39, No. 7, and implicitly in the spiritually similar Prelude in B minor, Op. 32, No. 10, both of which, though lacking the quiet middle section of the Chopin movement, in like manner build slowly to a climax and then fade gradually away. The closeness of the musical parallel leads to the inescapable conclusion that, in recreating the Chopin work as an interpreter, Rachmaninoff had alive in his mind the same vision as had directed him as composer.

The march itself is played in very strict time, with the inexorably rocking chords of the left hand tolling like bells. In the trio section Rachmaninoff's melting and infinitely flexible *cantabile* is once again in evidence, as the theme seems to float disembodied from the strings of the piano, to create a natural and profound impression of pathos. Then, shattering the repose, comes the unexpected and unforgettably terrifying return of the march, *fortissimo*. Such cavalier treatment of holy writ now seems a wild anachronism, and yet it is by no means certain that the simple mark of repetition in the text necessarily implies a literal duplication of the dynamics of the original statement, especially since Chopin habitually made alterations to the dynamics of recapitulations wherever, because they were slightly varied, he wrote out the recapitulations in full. At all events, Rachmaninoff was by no means the only pianist of his time to follow Rubinstein: the same gesture can be heard in the recorded performances of Raoul Pugno (1903), Josef Hofmann (Duo-Art piano rolls, 1919), and even, to a lesser degree, of Percy Grainger (1928), but they all fade into insignificance in comparison with the titanic force of Rachmaninoff's vision. If one piece had to be chosen out of his whole recorded legacy to demonstrate his glorious and provocative daring at its most compelling, this movement would be it.

The drama enacted in the finale taxes any interpreter's imaginative power to the full. In Rachmaninoff's amazing performance Chopin's *sotto voce* marking gives way to an angry muttering with explosive accents, as gusts of wind blow across the graveyard. Here again he was assuredly following Anton Rubinstein, who, in Rachmaninoff's own words, in this movement used 'pedal effects that can never be described, but for anyone who remembers them they will always be treasured as one of the greatest musical joys, bringing to our mundane vision undreamt-of beauties'.[32] Rachmaninoff was always fond of quoting Rubinstein's dictum 'The pedal is the soul of the piano', and in the haze of half-pedalling in Rachmaninoff's performance of this final movement, in the great surges of tone, who can doubt that here, as elsewhere in the sonata, is the spirit of the great Anton Rubinstein, distilled through Rachmaninoff's own personality.

It was surely the powerful message of the music itself which made Chopin's B flat minor Sonata so congenial to Rachmaninoff's temperament, for what he most likely saw as at least part of its subject matter, the power of death to wreck human life and happiness, and a scene at a funeral, were recurrent themes in his own music, and it was never in the Sonata but always elsewhere in Chopin that Rachmaninoff's acolytes wavered in their faith. Abram Chasins remarked on the unexpected incongruity of some elements in his style of performance of this composer:[33]

> Rachmaninoff the pianist had a particular blind spot. Except for a handful of works, Chopin's language was alien to him. Somehow the sham heroics one finds in the unfledged composer of *the* Prelude, the gushing sentimentality that saturates his *Elegiac Trio*, brooded over most of his Chopin playing. I have a melancholy remembrance of his performances of Chopin's Twenty-four Preludes. Throughout there was an amazing absence of Rachmaninoff's distinctive strengths. His rhythmic precision deserted him. The lyrical pieces sounded whimpering, the bold ones inflated. The music and its interpreter both lost their essential traits. Later I heard Rachmaninoff play mazurkas, waltzes, nocturnes and *études* with a reckless loss of exactness and elegance. They did not emerge even as inspired misconceptions. They were stylistically artificial. I was pained and puzzled, unable to realise at the time how polarised were Rachmaninoff's Byronic romanticism and Chopin's poetic classicism.

Chasins's wholly unfavourable reaction seems more than a little out of proportion and is not justified by the evidence of Rachmaninoff's gramophone and piano roll recordings, though these do not, it has to be admitted, represent a balanced cross-section of his Chopin repertoire. The element of sentimentality in Rachmaninoff's music, to which he draws attention, is so conspicuously understated in all the composer's recorded performances as to make that a most unconvincing explanation of any vagaries of style in his Chopin playing: listening to Rachmaninoff's matter-of-fact delivery of the theme at the opening of the romantic slow movement of his First Concerto will quickly prove the point. Indeed, the composer Alexander Tcherepnin went so far as to describe Rachmaninoff's playing as being as cold-blooded as Prokofiev's: 'His playing of Chopin was not at all the "super-rubato" playing of many other great pianists, and my own impression was always that he was as it were barricading himself from the over-emphasising of the sentiment in the music he was playing; but the sentiment came not because of his underlining the sentiment but because of his having the sentiment.'[34]

Some of Rachmaninoff's Chopin performances strike the present-day listener as surprisingly straightforward (Nocturne in E flat, Op. 9, No. 2, Waltz in F major, Op. 34, No. 3), even ordinary (*Grande Valse brillante* in E flat, Op. 18); others (Waltzes in E minor, Op. posth. and in A flat, Op. 42, and the B flat minor Scherzo) are distinguished by unusually fast tempi. Some other signs of individuality are perhaps less acceptable. In the G flat Waltz, Op. 70, No. 1, Rachmaninoff adds an altogether uncharacteristic decoration a few bars from the end, in a manner more reminiscent of Pachmann than of himself. In the C sharp minor Waltz, Op. 64, No. 2, at the second time round in the *più mosso* section Rachmaninoff accentuates one of the quaver sextuplets in each bar to make a descending scale, as Godowsky also does in his 1928 recording:

Ex.194

In the *Minute* Waltz Rachmaninoff lingers inordinately on the top B flat quavers of the ascending scales in the opening tune, and in the middle section he not only picks out the repeated A flat *acciaccatura* for special highlighting but arbitrarily extends the sequence (Ex. 195).

Ex.195

In the opening of the C sharp minor Scherzo, Rachmaninoff dislocates the rhythm of the double octaves by a stuttering delivery of the descending scale (Ex. 196).

Ex.196

Rachmaninoff exchanges the note values of the quaver and the following crotchet in the seventh bar of the *Urtext* and the Paderewski edition. Russian performing tradition seems always to have been thus, at least to judge from the evidence of Balakirev's orchestral version of the Scherzo as the last movement of his *Chopin Suite* of 1910, where the same formula is observed. Rachmaninoff, however, goes further and also subjects the following bars to the same rhythmic aberration before the descending figure is heard a second time. To the modern listener, for whom the orthodoxy of Chopin interpretation established by Arthur Rubinstein is already part of history, such peculiarities will seem harmlessly eccentric mannerisms or objectionable distortions, according to taste. Yet, in contrast with this brusqueness, the choral tune is played with great sensitivity, and the descending flourishes between each section shimmer liquidly. Perhaps it is just this contrast that Rachmaninoff seeks to emphasize. As Rubinstein said of Rachmaninoff's Chopin (and Schumann) performances: 'Even if it was contrary to my own feelings, he could convince me by the sheer impact of his personality'.[35]

On the evidence both of eye-witnesses and of his recordings, in his own music and much of the Romantic repertoire Rachmaninoff was peerless, though his one recording of Scriabin (Prelude in F sharp minor, Op. 11, No. 8), in which he totally disregards the composer's marking *Allegro agitato*, playing the piece at about half speed, gives a clue to the adverse critical reception of his Russian Scriabin recitals by those who found his performances unidiomatically earthbound. Rachmaninoff removes all the Prelude's essential urgent restlessness, imposing on it an alien wistfulness.[36]

In the Austro-German classics, wilful though he was, Rachmaninoff convinced even sceptics through the sheer force of his intensely personal vision. Sir Clifford Curzon described his interpretation of Mozart: 'I used to go to his concerts mesmerised, rather like a rabbit in front of a snake. I remember him in Mozart's A major Sonata, wildly eccentric and in some senses ghastly, and yet ... one sat riveted by every note.'[37]

Others have described his large-scaled performances of the Beethoven sonatas, particularly of the *Appassionata* and the *Waldstein*, as incomparably grand. Even here Rachmaninoff stamped his own personality on the works he played, making them seem as if he had composed them himself. It is, of course, one of the tragedies of gramophone history that the nearest Rachmaninoff came to recording a Beethoven piano sonata was a series of attempts in his earliest recording sessions at just one brief movement (the finale of the F major Sonata, Op. 10, No. 2), which never saw the light of day. At least we may be thankful that he recorded the G major Violin Sonata with his friend Kreisler, a truly glorious example of duo playing; the reading itself is surprisingly straightforward. Rachmaninoff's somewhat idiosyncratic version of the famous Thirty-two Variations in C minor, however, possibly reveals more of his general approach to Beethoven. Rather than preserve a consistent tempo throughout, as in his own variation works Rachmaninoff gives each item its own independent life but so balances groups of variations as to make them into an integrated and coherent whole, in which contrasts of mood and colour stand out in sharp relief. This style of interpretation may be thought unclassical, but then, to so powerful a personality, the orthodoxy of received tradition was irrelevant: impresario Wilfred van Wyck recalled a performance at the Queen's Hall of the *Moonlight* Sonata, the last movement of which Rachmaninoff 'tore through at a pace you'd have thought he had to catch a train from Victoria [station] – which he probably did'.[38] One wonders whether here at work again was the spirit of the great Rubinstein, who had played this work in Moscow in 1886.

In some mysterious way Russians seem to have a special empathy with Schumann, a composer whose essence is so difficult to capture, and in recent years performances by Horowitz, Gilels and especially Richter have confirmed the impression left by earlier artists, such as Lhevinne and Moiseiwitsch. *Carnaval* was another work Rachmaninoff heard Rubinstein play, and, as with the *Funeral March* Sonata, Rachmaninoff's performance is absolutely inimitable, with the projection of the different characterizations so powerful that any other performance seems limp in comparison. Tempi are sometimes on the fast side – *Florestan, Estrella, Reconnaissance* – emphasizing the diversity in this heterogeneous series. In *Pause* (before *Davidsbündler*), the breathless pace suggests an impatience to move on to more important things. In contrast, the lyrical passages are played with great tenderness, as in *Pierrot*, which Rachmaninoff varies the second time by highlighting the bass quavers, *Chiarina*, Schumann's tribute to Clara, or in *Chopin*, where a memorable effect is achieved by subtle variations of dynamic and rubato. In *Sphinxes* Schumann makes explicit the three mottoes on which *Carnaval* is based: SCHA (for Schumann himself), ASCH (the town where Ernestine von Fricken lived), and ACH, in the notes these letters represent in German notation. Instead of leaving the Sphinxes' inscrutable mystery silent, Rachmaninoff, like Cortot, treats the notes as part of the musical score, decking them out in portentous tremolos. One naturally wonders again if this striking effect had its origin in Rubinstein.

It is significant that, just as Rachmaninoff became paranoid about cutting out superfluities in his own music, so in the performance of other composers' music his recordings consistently show (as did his concert performances) the omission of all optional repeats, whether, expectedly, in the first movement of the *Funeral March* Sonata or, less happily, of *Chopin* in *Carnaval*. Moreover, he was not unwilling to prune in order to accommodate music on to the available length of record sides, cutting out eight of the variations in Beethoven's C minor Variations, shortening the coda of the Liszt Polonaise, made at the same time, clipping a few bars from the Chopin-Liszt *Maiden's Wish* and even, at the end of his career, squeezing the remake of his own arrangement of Kreisler's *Liebesfreud* on to one record side, so requiring the omission of the splendid cadenza that is so notable a feature of the piece and a high point of the original recording.

Many of Rachmaninoff's contemporaries, but most notably Josef Hofmann, loved to bring out unexpected middle voices in polyphonic writing. As the examples of the two Chopin waltzes show, Rachmaninoff was not above doing this himself, but such indulgence was very rare; rather did he use the same skill miraculously to balance different parts in a musical dialogue. Even the pianist himself was satisfied with his recording of Sgambati's arrangement of Gluck's famous flute melody from *Orfeo*,[39] a once popular trifle now long since forgotten. Rachmaninoff voices the simple melody like a great singer, at the same time balancing against it the bass line and, independently, the gently undulating middle part in thirds. Here indeed is supreme pianism.

It would perhaps be unnecessary to draw attention to such a matter as mere digital skill in an artist of Rachmaninoff's calibre, were it not arguably a fact that he was not only unsurpassed in this respect by any other pianist of his own generation but is rarely if at all matched even in these days, when technical prowess is so ubiquitous that it is taken for granted in any artist on the concert platform. Three legendary examples of Rachmaninoff's transcendental technique are his performances of Mendelssohn's *Étude* in F major, his own *Moment musical* in E flat minor, Op. 16, No. 2, and Henselt's little study in repeated double notes, *Si oiseau j'étais*, a piece that was a relic from a bygone era (Rimsky-Korsakov recalled hearing it in 1856, when he was twelve years of age,[40] and it was later in one of the programmes of Rubinstein's 'Historical Recitals'). Rachmaninoff thought Henselt's studies 'so beautiful that they should be classed with pieces like the *études* of Chopin',[41] and his performance so elevates the music that we are persuaded to suspend disbelief in this provocative judgement.

Rachmaninoff once told Gina Bachauer: 'When performing at a concert a musician must always have the feeling that the particular work he is playing at that moment is the greatest music ever written'.[42] This ability to ennoble whatever he played, even when this was very much less than great music, is exemplified by his performance of Tausig's brilliant arrangement of the Strauss waltz, *One Lives But Once*. It is not so much the amazing pianistic colouring, such as the opening brass fanfares, that one remembers most, or the virtuosity, staggering though it is, but rather the slow middle section, with its pleasant though trivial sequences, which are so flighted that at the moment of their delivery they sound like the most beautiful music in the world.

Two minor quirks of Rachmaninoff's style need to be mentioned. As no pianist has made the pauses between long-held notes more pregnant with meaning than he, so none has prolonged a *ritenuto* to greater limits. A slyly humorous example occurs at the beginning of the Mussorgsky *Gopak*, where the pulse established in the introductory bars nearly, but not quite, gives out altogether before the tune begins; another typical instance is at the opening of the *Polka de W.R.* Then in the climactic closing bars of a piece Rachmaninoff would often play the final chord or chords unexpectedly quietly, as in Chopin's E minor Waltz, Op. posth., *The Maiden's Wish*, and Mendelssohn's *Spinning Song*. Incidentally, this last performance contains a peculiarity that was not Rachmaninoff's alone. In the introduction and elsewhere in the piece Rachmaninoff lengthens the final quaver in the bar just before the tune begins, interrupting the flow with a rhythmic hiccup, a mannerism which can be heard in different degrees also in the recordings of the piece by Pugno, Paderewski, Godowsky and Planté. Rachmaninoff told his biographer and writer of his English programme notes, Watson Lyle, that it represented the apparent pause in the spinning wheel's rotation as the connecting rod reaches its highest point.

After the days of his young manhood Rachmaninoff never gave formal piano lessons. He had very little interest in musical education generally and was unconvinced that teaching could produce anything of vital significance.[43] Occasionally he would go through pieces with young pianists, but none could in any way be called a 'pupil' of his. In the early 1920s, before being taken on as a pupil of Josef Hofmann, the young Shura Cherkassky was taken to see Rachmaninoff, who told him that he would become his teacher only on condition that he avoided concert appearances for three years and changed his finger technique.[44] One gets the impression that these conditions were deliberately intended to be unacceptable, though twelve years later Rachmaninoff did have a number of sessions in Paris with another infant prodigy, nine-year-old Ruth Slenczynska. Some of Rachmaninoff's comments on her playing during her visits to him, though mostly truisms, nevertheless do give an insight into some of the features which distinguished his own playing.[45]

> Big musical line, big musician; small musical line, small musician.

> Play for the man in the last row of the gallery; the real climax will reach him *after* the sound leaves the piano. The musical arch is shaped like an ocean wave which falls on the beach *after* it reaches its highest point.

> Never waste a single note; the tiniest ornament is part of the musical fabric.

> Never play a skeleton; even an 'alberti bass' contributes to the harmony.

> [A *pianissimo* climax is] more important [than a *fortissimo*; it is] as if you were confiding a secret.

> Invent a more musical fingering; that is what shapes your thought, your phrase.

> After a vacation, work on Scarlatti exclusively for two weeks until you regain your dexterity; in Scarlatti you find everything: trills, ornaments, jumps, arpeggios, crosshand passages, scales, changing fingers...

At about the same time, from 1933 to 1935, the young Bachauer occasionally played for Rachmaninoff during his European tours, and the great man listened and gave advice. When he told her that 'the performer must give the best that is in him, even if he is playing in the smallest town in the most terrible theatre, even if the audience is only one person – the doorman, holding the keys, waiting for the concert to finish as soon as possible, so he can lock the doors',[46] he revealed not only a sense of humour, but, underneath, the profound seriousness with which he approached his public appearances.

Cyril Smith told a wonderful story about Rachmaninoff's artistic humility. At a recital at the Queen's Hall Rachmaninoff was unhappy with his performance of his arrangement of Bach's E major Partita. Smith saw him afterwards in the green room.[47]

> Without wasting much time over greetings, he turned to me, demanding anxiously in his broken English, 'The Bach, the Bach, was it all right?' I said I thought his performance had been wonderful. Rachmaninoff went back to his other guests, obviously preoccupied, and a few minutes later he returned to me with the same question. I gave him the same answer. In the meantime, the artists' room had become very much more crowded, and before long the two of us were separated in the crush. But later, when I was least expecting it, he bore down upon me again, guided me into a corner where no-one else could hear us and whispered urgently, 'Really, the Bach, it was all right?' This was true modesty. He honestly believed that his own work was capable of much improvement and that I was a fit judge of it.

Smith was in his twenties at the time, Rachmaninoff his sixties.

When asked his opinion of contemporary pianists Rachmaninoff was fond of quoting the cynical comment Anton Rubinstein made when he was asked what he thought about the newly acclaimed Eugen d'Albert: 'Oh, nowadays everyone plays the piano well!' In an interview in 1919, in which he remarked that this was still the situation, Rachmaninoff added, 'But how rare, how few, are performers who even approach the great Rubinstein!'[48] If Rubinstein's comment seems just as applicable one hundred years later, towards the end of the twentieth century, when the world is saturated with pianistic talent of a very high order, then the thrust of Rachmaninoff's own remark is no less relevant, when brought up-to-date by the substitution of his name; for even today it can surely still be said that performers who even approach the great Rachmaninoff are rare and few indeed.

References

1 Horowitz in interview with Bryce Morrison, *Music and Musicians*, August 1975, p. 33; *Rubinstein*, p. 88; Arrau in *The Los Angeles Times*, 29 March 1943.

2 Artur Schnabel in *The New York World Telegram*, 3 April 1943.

3 James Agate, *Ego 4* (Diaries), entry for 11 March 1939; also in *The Selective Ego, The Diaries of James Agate*, ed. Tim Beaumont, Harrap, London, 1976, p. 116.

4 Cyril Smith, *Duet for Three Hands*, Angus and Robertson, London, 1958, p. 79, and in BBC radio interview.

5 Wilfrid van Wyck reminiscing, 1981.

6 Leonid Pasternak in 'Skryabin. Summer 1903 and after', article in *Musical Times*, December 1972, pp. 1169–1174, taken from *Noviy Mir*.

7 Jorge Bolet at lecture-recital, Wigmore Hall, London, 23 February 1982.

8 Rosalyn Tureck in *New Statesman*, 25 February 1966, p. 263.

9 *Swan*, pp. 8–9.

10 R. can be seen wearing this device in a photograph in *Seroff*, opposite p. 181.

11 R. to Wilshaw, 9 September 1922.

12 R. to Wilshaw, 2 July 1925.

13 R. to Somov, 20 February 1931.

14 Zoya Pribïtkova, *VR/A* 2, p. 60.

15 Olga Conus, 'Memories of a Personal Friend' in *Clavier*, October 1973, p. 17.

16 Boris Chaliapin, *VR/A* 2, p. 257.

17 *Chasins*, p. 44.

18 Harriet Cohen, BBC radio interview, c. 1964.

19 Arthur Hirst, *VR/A* 2, p. 345. Hirst, English by nationality, was a lecturer on the staff of the Stern Conservatoire, Berlin, before the war.

20 Marietta Shaginyan, *VR/A* 2, p. 157.

21 'Conversation with Rachmaninoff', article by Basil Maine in *Musical Opinion*, Vol. 60, October 1936, pp. 14–15.

22 'The Composer as Interpreter', R. interview with Norman Cameron in *The Monthly Musical Record*, November 1934, p. 201.

23 Marietta Shaginyan, *VR/A* 2, p. 156.

24 *Chasins*, p. 45.

25 Rachmaninoff articles: 'Interpretation Depends on Talent and Personality' and 'How Russian Students Work', in *The Etude*, April 1932, p. 240, and May 1923, p. 2.

26 *Swan*, pp. 175–176.

27 'Interpretation Depends on Talent and Personality', R. interview in *The Etude*, April 1932, p. 240.

28 E.J. Dent, *Ferrucio Busoni*, Oxford University Press, 1932, p. 106.

29 Hanslick, quoted in *Rubinstein: Autobiography*, translated by Aline Delano, Little, Brown and Co., Boston, USA, 1890, p. 165.

30 W.J. Henderson in *The Sun*, New York, 16 February 1930.

31 Edward Sackville-West, 'Rachmaninov', in the *Bulletin of the British Institute of Recorded Sound*, No. 4, Spring 1957, pp. 13–16.

32 R. in *Great Pianists on Piano Playing*, by James Francis Cooke, Theo Presser Co., Philadelphia, 1913, p. 214.

33 *Chasins*, pp. 59–60.

34 Alexander Tcherepnin, BBC radio interview, c. 1973.

35 *Rubinstein*, p. 88.

36 A similar view is taken by the Scriabin specialist Faubion Bowers in *The New Scriabin*, St Martin Press Inc., New York 1973, p. 203.

37 'Sir Clifford Curzon Talks to Bryce Morrison', article in *Music and Musicians*, February 1979, pp. 22–23.
38 Wilfred van Wyck reminiscing, 1981.
39 *Swan*, p. 12.
40 *Rimsky-Korsakov*, p. 6.
41 R. in *Great Pianists on Piano Playing*, by James Francis Cooke, Theo Presser Co., Philadelphia, 1913, p. 212.
42 'My Study with Rachmaninoff' by Gina Bachauer, in *Clavier*, October 1973, p. 12.
43 *Chasins*, p. 59.
44 'Practice Makes Perfect', Cherkassky interview with Edward Greenfield, *The Guardian*, 26 May 1980.
45 Ruth Slenczynska in *Clavier*, October 1973, p. 15.
46 'My Study with Rachmaninoff' by Gina Bachauer, in *Clavier*, October 1973, p. 12.
47 Cyril Smith, *Duet for Three Hands*, Angus and Robertson, London, 1958, pp. 77–78.
48 R. in *The Etude*, November 1919, p. 615.

12 Piano Repertoire

This list of repertoire includes every work Rachmaninoff played in public, from his debut in 1892 until his death in 1943, among them those in which he acted as accompanist but not those he played in private, of which only a few can now be established with certainty. Where a work was also recorded by Rachmaninoff, the index refers to the corresponding item in the discography (pp. 451–492) or the list of piano rolls (pp. 503–505). Dates given are of the earliest public performance or recording. Details of the additions which Rachmaninoff made to his repertoire each year can be found in the table of concert statistics in Chapter 10.

Title	Date	Discography	Piano Roll
ALKAN			
Étude, Comme le vent, Op. 39, No. 1	1919	—	—
Funeral March, Op. 26a	1919	—	—
ARENSKY			
Barcarolle, (?) in F major, Op. 36, No. 11	1895	—	—
Esquisse in F major, Op. 24, No. 1	1893	—	—
Esquisse in A flat, Op. 24, No. 3	1893	—	—
Song, *Night*, Op. 17, No. 4 (accompanying Vera Petrova-Zvantseva)	1903	—	—
BACH			
English Suite No. 2 in A minor, BWV 807	1923	—	—
Fantasia and Fugue in G minor, BWV 542 (arr. Liszt)	1936	—	—
French Suite No. 6 in E major, BWV 817	1939	—	—
Italian Concerto in F major, BWV 971	1937	—	—
Nun freut euch, Chorale Prelude, BWV 734 (arr. Busoni)	1928	—	—
Nun komm' der Heiden Heiland, Chorale Prelude, BWV 599 (arr. Busoni)	1928	—	—
Organ Chorale in A major (arr. Tausig)	1930	—	—
Organ Preludes in G minor and G major (arr. Busoni)	1928	—	—
Partita No. 2 in D minor for solo violin, BWV 1004 – Chaconne (arr. Busoni)	1918	—	—
Partita No. 3 in E major for solo violin, BWV 1006 – Prelude, Gavotte, Gigue (arr. Rachmaninoff)	1933	155,205,206	—
Partita No. 4 in D major, BWV 828 – Saraband	1925	84	26
Prelude (?)	1920	—	—
Prelude and Fugue in A minor, BWV 543 (arr. Liszt)	1924	—	—

Title	Date	Discography	Piano Roll
Prelude in D minor (from *The Well-Tempered Clavier*), BWV 851	1924	–	–
Toccata and Fugue in D minor, BWV 565 (arr. Tausig)	1934	–	–
Wienen, Klagen, Sorgen, Zagen – see Liszt			
BALAKIREV			
Islamey	1930	–	–
BEETHOVEN			
Concerto No. 1 in C major, Op. 15	1937	–	–
Sonata No. 6 in F major, Op. 10, No. 2 – third movement, Presto	1920	12	–
Sonata No. 7 in D major, Op. 10, No. 3	1918	–	–
Sonata No. 8 in C minor, Op. 13 (*Pathétique*)	1921	–	–
Sonata No. 12 in A flat, Op. 26	1927	–	–
Sonata No. 14 in C sharp minor, Op. 27, No. 2 (*Moonlight*)	1919	–	–
Sonata No. 16 in G major, Op. 31, No. 1	1933	–	–
Sonata No. 17 in D minor, Op. 31, No. 2 (*Tempest*)	1919	–	–
Sonata No. 23 in F minor, Op. 57 (*Appassionata*)	1922	–	–
Sonata No. 24 in F sharp, Op. 78	1929	–	–
Sonata No. 26 in E flat, Op. 81a (*Les Adieux*)	1931	–	–
Sonata No. 27 in E minor, Op. 90	1920	–	–
Sonata No. 30 in E major, Op. 109	1928	–	–
Sonata No. 32 in C minor, Op. 111	1938	–	–
Sonata No. 8 in G major, for violin and piano, Op. 30, No. 3 (accompanying Kreisler)	1928	99–102	–
Sonata No. 9 in A major, for violin and piano, Op. 47 (*Kreutzer*) (accompanying Teresina Tua)	1895	–	–

Title	Date	Discography	Piano Roll
Thirty-two Variations in C minor	1919	78–79	–
Turkish March from *The Ruins of Athens*, Op. 113 (arr. Rubinstein)	1925	98	29
BIZET			
Minuet from *L'Arlésienne* (arr. Rachmaninoff)	1922	51	14
BORODIN			
Scherzo in A flat	1933	157	–
BRAHMS			
Ballade in D minor, Op. 10, No. 1	1931	–	–
Ballade in D major, Op. 10, No. 2	1931	–	–
Ballade in G minor, Op. 118, No. 3	1934	–	–
Intermezzo in E flat minor, Op. 118, No. 6	1927	–	–
Liebeslieder Walzer, Op. 52 (accompanying, with Siloti)	1903	–	–
BRANDUKOV			
Three pieces for cello and piano (accompanying Brandukov):*Feuille d'album, Mazurka, On the Water*	1892	–	–
BUSONI			
See Bach (transcriptions)			
CHOPIN			
Ballade No. 1 in G minor, Op. 23	1920	–	–
Ballade No. 2 in F major, Op. 38	1924	–	–
Ballade No. 3 in A flat, Op. 47	1921	82–83	–
Ballade No. 4 in F minor, Op. 52	1919	–	–
Barcarolle in F sharp, Op. 60	1920	–	–

Title	Date	Discography	Piano Roll
Berceuse in D flat, Op. 57	1892	—	—
Étude in C major, Op. 10, No. 1	1928	—	—
Étude in E major, Op. 10, No. 3	1918	—	—
Étude in G flat, Op.10, No. 5 (*Black Keys*)	1920	15,16	—
Étude in A flat, Op. 10, No. 10	1892	—	—
Étude in C minor, Op. 10, No. 12 (*Revolutionary*)	1892	—	—
Étude in A flat, Op. 25, No. 1	?	—	—
Étude in F minor, Op. 25, No. 2	1920	21	—
Étude in F major, Op. 25, No. 3	1920	21	—
Étude in A minor, Op. 25, No. 4	1938	—	—
Étude in E minor, Op. 25, No. 5	1938	—	—
Étude in C sharp minor, Op. 25, No. 7	1938	—	—
Étude in G flat, Op. 25, No. 9 (*Butterfly*)	1920	15	—
Étude in C minor, Op. 25, No. 12	1918	—	—
Fantaisie-Impromptu, Op. 66	1929	—	—
Fantaisie in F minor, Op. 49	1922	—	—
Impromptu No. 1 in A flat, Op. 29	1892	—	—
Impromptu No. 2 in F major, Op. 36	1934	—	—
Mazurka in F sharp minor, Op. 6, No. 1	?	—	—
Mazurka in E major, Op. 6, No. 3	1924	—	—
Mazurka in A minor, Op. 7, No. 2	1934	—	—
Mazurka in F minor, Op. 7, No. 3	1936	—	—
Mazurka in A minor, Op. 17, No. 4	?	—	—
Mazurka in G minor, Op. 24, No. 1	1941	—	—
Mazurka in B minor, Op. 33, No. 4	1929	—	—

Title	Date	Disc-ography	Piano Roll
Mazurka in A flat, Op. 59, No. 2	1920	–	–
Mazurka in F sharp minor, Op. 59, No. 3	1934	–	–
Mazurka in F minor, Op. 63, No. 2	1937	–	–
Mazurka in C sharp minor, Op. 63, No. 3	1920	33	–
Mazurka in G major, Op. 67, No. 1	1941	–	–
Mazurka in A minor, Op. 67, No. 4	?	–	–
Mazurka in A minor, Op. 68, No. 2	1935	158	–
Nocturne in E flat, Op. 9, No. 2	1922	95	–
Nocturne in E flat, Op. 9, No. 2 (arr. violin and piano, Sarasate) (accompanying Teresina Tua)	1895	–	–
Nocturne in F major, Op. 15, No. 1	1927	–	27
Nocturne in F sharp major, Op. 15, No. 2	1922	56	–
Nocturne in C sharp minor, Op. 27, No. 1	1918	–	–
Nocturne in D flat, Op. 27, No. 2	1921	–	–
Nocturne in B major, Op. 32, No. 1	1929	–	–
Nocturne in G major, Op. 37, No. 2	1931	–	–
Nocturne in C minor, Op. 48, No. 1	1895	–	–
Nocturne in F sharp minor, Op. 48, No. 2	1920	–	–
Nocturne in F minor, Op. 55, No. 1	1922	–	–
Nocturne in E major, Op. 62, No. 2	1923	–	–
Nocturne in E minor, Op. 72, No. 1	?	–	–
Polish Songs, Op. 74 – *The Maiden's Wish* (arr. Liszt)	1922	52,210	19
Polish Songs, Op. 74 – *The Return Home* (arr. Liszt)	1932	211	–
Polonaise No. ?	1892	–	–
Polonaise No. 1 in C sharp minor, Op. 26, No. 1	1921	–	–

421

Title	Date	Discography	Piano Roll
Polonaise No. 2 in E flat minor, Op. 26, No. 2	1919	—	—
Polonaise No. 3 in A major, Op. 40, No. 1	1931	—	—
Polonaise No. 4 in C minor, Op. 40, No. 2	1918	—	—
Polonaise No. 5 in F sharp minor, Op. 44	1930	—	—
Polonaise No. 6 in A flat, Op. 53	1921	—	—
Prelude in C major, Op. 28, No. 1	1938	—	—
Prelude in A minor, Op. 28, No. 2	1938	—	—
Prelude in G major, Op. 28, No. 3	1938	—	—
Prelude in E minor, Op. 28, No. 4	1938	—	—
Prelude in D major, Op. 28, No. 5	1938	—	—
Prelude in B minor, Op. 28, No. 6	1938	—	—
Prelude in A major, Op. 28, No. 7	1938	—	—
Prelude in B major, Op. 28, No. 11	1938	—	—
Prelude in G sharp minor, Op. 28, No. 12	1938	—	—
Prelude in B flat minor, Op. 28, No. 16	1938	—	—
Prelude in E flat major, Op. 28, No. 19	1923	61	—
Prelude in G minor, Op. 28, No. 22	1938	—	—
Prelude in F major, Op. 28, No. 23	1938	—	—
Rondo in E flat, Op. 16	1927	—	—
Scherzo No. 1 in B minor, Op. 20	1892	—	—
Scherzo No. 2 in B flat minor, Op. 31	1930	—	35
Scherzo No. 3 in C sharp minor, Op. 39	1921	70–71	—
Scherzo No. 4 in E major, Op. 54	1924	—	—
Sonata No. 2 in B flat minor, Op. 35 (*Funeral March*)	1922	137,140–146	—
Sonata No. 3 in B minor, Op. 58	1918	—	—

Title	Date	Disc-ography	Piano Roll
Tarantella in A flat, Op. 43	1933	–	–
Waltz in E flat, Op. 18	1920	41	11
Waltz in F major, Op. 34, No. 3	1920	30	21
Waltz in A flat, Op. 42	1892	1	–
Waltz in D flat, Op. 64, No. 1	1892	24	–
Waltz in C sharp minor, Op. 64, No. 2	1920	34	–
Waltz in A flat, Op. 64, No. 3	1919	4,94	–
Waltz in A flat, Op. 69, No. 1	?	–	–
Waltz in B minor, Op. 69, No. 2	1919	13	–
Waltz in G flat, Op. 70, No. 1	1920	42	–
Waltz in D flat, Op. 70, No. 3	1928	–	–
Waltz in E minor, Op. posth.	1927	147	–
DANDRIEU			
Caprice, *Le Caquet* (arr. Godowsky)	1918	–	–
DAQUIN			
Le Coucou	1920	26	–
DARGOMYZHSKY			
Song, *The Paladin* (accompanying Chaliapin)	1900	–	–
Song, *The Old Corporal* (accompanying Chaliapin)	1900	–	–
DAVYDOV			
By the Fountain, for cello and piano (accompanying Brandukov)	1892	–	–
Farewell, for cello and piano (accompanying Brandukov)	1892	–	–

423

Title	Date	Discography	Piano Roll
DEBUSSY			
Children's Corner Suite – No. 1, Dr. Gradus ad Parnassum	1920	44	—
Children's Corner Suite – No. 3, Serenade to the Doll	1920	40	—
Children's Corner Suite – No. 5, Little Shepherd	1920	—	—
Children's Corner Suite – No. 6, Golliwog's Cakewalk	1920	25	—
Fille aux cheveux de lin	1928	—	—
Jardins sous la pluie	1928	—	—
Suite bergamasque	1937	—	—
Suite Pour le Piano	1933	—	—
DELIBES			
Naila Waltz (arr. Dohnányi)	1923	—	—
DOHNÁNYI			
Étude-Caprice in F minor, Op. 28, No. 6	1921	49	—
FIELD			
Nocturne No. 12 in E major (*Noontide*)	1936	—	—
Nocturne No. 18 in G major	1936	—	—
GLINKA			
Lark (arr. Balakirev)	1895	—	—
Song, *Jewish Song* (accompanying Chaliapin)	1900	—	—
GLUCK			
Mélodie (arr. Sgambati) from *Orfeo*, Ballet of the Blessed Spirits	1924	76	23

Title	Date	Disc-ography	Piano Roll
Old French Gavotte, from *Paris and Helen* (arr. Pauer)	1931	–	–
GODARD			
En courant	1892	–	–
GRIEG			
Ballade in G minor, Op. 24	1921	–	–
Lyric Pieces, Op. 12 – No. 2, Waltz	1920	14	–
Lyric Pieces, Op. 12 – No. 4, Elfin Dance	1920	11,14	–
Lyric Pieces, Op. 68 – No. 2, Grandmother's Minuet	1920	11	–
Scenes from Peasant Life, Op. 19 – No. 1, Mountain Tune	1920	–	–
Sonata No. 3 in C minor, for violin and piano, Op. 45 (accompanying Kreisler)	1928	103–108	–
Songs (accompanying Chaliapin):	1900	–	–
Ancient Song, Op. 4, No. 5			
Farewell, Op. 4, No. 3			
Swan, Op. 25, No. 2			
Verse for an album, Op. 25, No. 3			
You know not the waves' eternal motion, Op. 5, No. 2			
HANDEL			
Air and Variations in B flat	1921	–	–
Harmonious Blacksmith	1935	156	–
HAYDN			
Fantasia in C major	1932	–	–

425

Title	Date	Disc-ography	Piano Roll
Variations in F minor	1918	–	–
HENSELT			
Étude in F sharp, Op. 2, No. 6, *Si oiseau j'étais*	1923	60	20
IPPOLITOV-IVANOV			
Song, *Of what in the silence of the night* (accompanying Vera Petrova-Zvantseva)	1903	–	–
KREISLER			
Liebesfreud (arr. Rachmaninoff)	1925	88–89,209	25
Liebesleid (arr. Rachmaninoff)	1921	50	16
LIADOV			
Music Box, Op. 32	?	–	–
Étude in A flat, Op. 5	1922	–	–
LISZT			
Au bord d'une source, G. 160	1920	36	–
Ballade No. 2 in B minor, G. 171	1921	214	–
Concerto No. 1 in E flat, G. 124	1917	–	–
Concert Study No. 1 in A flat (*Il lamento*), G. 144	1922	–	–
Concert Study No. 3 in D flat (*Un sospiro*), G. 144	1892	–	–
Consolation in E major, G. 172	1925	–	–
Études d'exécution transcendante, G. 139 – No. 7, *Eroica*	1925	–	–
Études d'exécution transcendante, G. 139 – No. 11, *Harmonies du soir*	1931	–	–
Fantasia quasi Sonata based on Dante, G. 161	1928	–	–
Faust Waltz (from Gounod), G. 407	1892	–	–
Funérailles, G. 173	1923	–	–

Title	Date	Disc-ography	Piano Roll
Gnomenreigen, G. 145	1919	87	–
Grandes Études de Paganini, G. 140/1 – No. 2, *Octave*	1936	–	–
Grandes Études de Paganini, G. 140/1 – No. 3, *Campanella*	1919	20	–
Grandes Études de Paganini, G. 140/1 – No. 5, *La Chasse*	1922	–	–
Grandes Études de Paganini, G. 140/1 – No. 6, *Theme and Variations*	1928	–	–
Grand Galop chromatique, G. 219	1921	–	–
Hungarian Rhapsody No. 2, G. 244, with cadenza by Rachmaninoff	1919	5–7	–
Hungarian Rhapsody No. 9, G. 244	1930	–	–
Hungarian Rhapsody No. 11, G. 244	1933	–	–
Hungarian Rhapsody No. 12, G. 244	1892	–	–
Hungarian Rhapsody No. 14, G. 244	1893	–	–
Hungarian Rhapsody No. 15, G. 244 (*Rakoczy March*)	1927	69	–
Liebestraum No. 3 in D flat, G. 541	1923	69	–
Petrarch's Sonnet No. 104, G. 161	1921	–	–
Petrarch's Sonnet No. 123, G. 161	1933	–	–
Polonaise No. 2 in E major, G. 223	1924	80–81	–
Sonata in B minor, G. 178	1924	–	–
Spanish Rhapsody, G. 254	1920	62	–
Totentanz, G. 126	1939	–	–
Valse-Impromptu, G. 213	1892	–	–
Valse oubliée No. 1 in F sharp, G. 215	1930	–	–
Valse oubliée No. 3 in D flat, G. 215	1936	–	–
Venezia e Napoli, G. 162 – No. 3, Tarantella	1921	–	–
Waldesrauschen, G. 145	1895	–	–
Wienen, Klagen, Sorgen, Zagen – Variations after Bach, G. 673	1937	–	–

Title	Date	Disc-ography	Piano Roll
See also Bach, Chopin, Schubert, Schumann, Wagner (transcriptions)			
LOEILLET			
Gigue in E minor (arr. Godowsky)	1919	—	—
MEDTNER			
Fairy Tale in E minor, Op. 14, No. 2	1935	—	—
Fairy Tale in B flat minor, Op. 20, No. 1	1918	—	—
Fairy Tale in B minor, Op. 20, No. 2	1918	—	—
Fairy Tale in F minor, Op. 26, No. 3	1918	—	—
Fairy Tale in B minor, Op. 34, No. 1	1927	—	—
Fairy Tale in E minor, Op. 34, No. 2	1925	—	—
Fairy Tale in A minor, Op. 34, No. 3	1921	—	—
Fairy Tale in D minor, Op. 51, No. 1	1928	—	—
Funeral March, Op. 31, No. 2	1930	—	—
Improvisation, Op. 31, No. 1	1922	—	—
Novelle in G major, Op. 17, No. 1	1920	—	—
Novelle in C minor, Op. 17, No. 2	1920	—	—
Sonata–Fairy-Tale in C minor, Op. 25, No. 1	1928	—	—
Three Hymns in Praise of Toil, Op. 49	1929	—	—
Tragedy Fragment, Op. 7, No. ?	1918	—	—
MENDELSSOHN			
Étude in F major, Op. 104, No. 2	1927	92	—
Étude in A minor, Op. 104, No. 3	1927	93	—
Midsummer Night's Dream, Scherzo (arr. Rachmaninoff)	1933	184	—
Rondo capriccioso in E, Op. 14	1919	22	—

Title	Date	Discography	Piano Roll
Song Without Words No. 3 in A major, Op.19, No. 3 (*Hunting Song*)	1920	–	–
Song Without Words No. 4 in A major, Op. 19, No. 4	1920	–	–
Song Without Words No. 10 in B minor, Op. 30, No. 4	1920	–	–
Song Without Words No. 11 in D major, Op. 30, No. 5	1920	–	–
Song Without Words No. 17 in A minor, Op. 38, No. 5	1920	–	–
Song Without Words No. 32 in F sharp minor, Op. 67, No. 2 (*Lost Illusions*)	1920	–	–
Song Without Words No. 34 in C major, Op. 67, No. 4 (*Bee's Wedding*)	1919	35	10,36
Song Without Words No. 37 in F major, Op. 85, No. 1	1920	–	–
Song Without Words No. 47 in A major, Op. 102, No. 5 (*Joyous Peasant*)	1920	27	–
Song Without Words No. ?	1920	–	–
Variations sérieuses, Op. 54	1919	–	–
MOSZKOWSKI			
La Jongleuse, Op. 52, No. 4	1922	53	–
MOZART			
Figaro – Aria, *Husbands, open your eyes* (accompanying Chaliapin)	1900	–	–
Sonata No. 9 in D major, K. 311	1919	–	–
Sonata No. 11 in A major, K. 331	1920	–	–
1st movement, Theme and Variations	1918	2,202	–
3rd movement, Turkish March	1920	29	–
Sonata No. 17 in D major, K. 576	1928	–	–
MUSSORGSKY			
Gopak from *Sorochinsky Fair* (arr. Rachmaninoff)	1920	45	12
Songs:			

Title	Date	Discography	Piano Roll
Gopak (accompanying Vera Petrova-Zvantseva)	1903	—	—
Orphan, Puppet Show, Trepak (accompanying Chaliapin)	1900	—	—
PABST			
Fantasy on Themes from Tchaikovsky's *Eugene Onegin*	1892	—	—
Illustrations de l'opéra *La Dame de Pique*	1893	—	—
PADEREWSKI			
Minuet in G, Op. 14, No. 1	1920	38	28
POPPER			
Two pieces for cello and piano (accompanying Brandukov):	1892	—	—
Gavotte and Round Dance			
POULENC			
Novelette No. 1 in C major	1939	—	—
Toccata	1939	—	—
RACHMANINOFF (references to his recordings only)			
Barcarolle, Op. 10, No. 3	1919	9	6
Concerto No. 1 in F sharp minor, Op. 1	1939	160–165	—
Concerto No. 2 in C minor, Op. 18	1924	62–68,72–74	37
Concerto No. 3 in D minor, Op. 30	1929	109–118	—
Concerto No. 4 in G minor, Op. 40	1939	166–174	—
Daisies, Op. 38, No. 3 (piano transcription)	1941	194–201	—
Élégie in E flat minor, Op. 3, No. 1	1940	192	—
Étude-Tableau in C major, Op. 33, No. 2	1928	–	30
	1940	190	–

Title	Date	Discography	Piano Roll
Étude-Tableau in E flat major, Op. 33, No. 7	1940	191	—
Étude-Tableau in G minor, Op. 33, No. 8	1920	37	—
Étude-Tableau in B minor, Op. 39, No. 4	1929	–	32
Étude-Tableau in A minor, Op. 39, No. 6	1920	39,90	13
Humoresque, Op. 10, No. 5	1920	43,185	9
Isle of the Dead, Op. 29 (conducted by Rachmaninoff)	1929	119–123	—
Italian Polka (with Natalya Rachmaninoff)	1938	216	—
Lilacs, Op. 21, No. 5 (piano transcription)	1920	23,208	15
Mélodie in E major, Op. 3, No. 3	1920	184	5
Moment musical in E flat minor, Op. 16, No. 2	1940	186	—
Oriental Sketch	1940	193	—
Polichinelle, Op. 3, No. 4	1920	32	7
Polka de W.R.	1919	10,48	1
Prelude in C sharp minor, Op. 3, No. 2	1919	8,46,47	3
Prelude in G minor, Op. 23, No. 5	1919	18	4
Prelude in G flat, Op. 23, No. 10	1940	187	—
Prelude in E major, Op. 32, No. 3	1940	188	—
Prelude in G major, Op. 32, No. 5	1920	19	—
Prelude in F minor, Op. 32, No. 6	1940	189	—
Prelude in F major, Op. 32, No. 7	1940	189	—
Prelude in G sharp minor, Op. 32, No. 12	1920	31	—
Rhapsody on a Theme of Paganini, Op. 43	1934	148–154	—
Serenade in B flat minor, Op. 3, No. 5	1922	54,159	17
Song, *Quickly, quickly, from my cheeks* (accompanying Plevitskaya)	1926	91	—
Symphony No. 3 in A minor, Op. 44 (conducted by Rachmaninoff)	1939	175–183	—

Title	Date	Discography	Piano Roll
Vocalise, Op. 34, No. 14 (orchestral transcription cond. Rachmaninoff)	1929	124	–
See also: Bach, Bizet, Kreisler, Mendelssohn, Mussorgsky, Rimsky-Korsakov, Schubert, Tchaikovsky and Miscellaneous (piano transcriptions)			
RAMEAU			
Gavotte and Variations in A minor	1938	–	–
RAVEL			
Toccata from *Le tombeau de Couperin*	1928	–	–
RIMSKY-KORSAKOV			
Flight of the Bumble Bee, from *Tsar Sultan* (arr. Rachmaninoff)	1928	138	34
Songs (accompanying Chaliapin):	1900	–	–
O, if thou could'st for one moment, Op. 39. No. 1			
Prophet, Op. 49, No. 2			
Songs (accompanying Nadezhda Zabela-Vrubel):	1903	–	–
Look in thy garden, Op. 41, No. 4			
Nymph, Op. 56, No. 1			
RUBINSTEIN A.			
Barcarolle No. 2 in A minor, Op. 45	1892	–	33
Concerto No. 4 in D minor, Op. 70 – 1st movement only	1892	–	–
Étude in F minor, Op. 81, No. 1	1919	–	–
Polka bohémien, Op. 82, No. 7	1918	–	–
Song, *The Prisoner* (accompanying Chaliapin)	1900	–	–
RUBINSTEIN N.			
Valse et Tarantelle, for two pianos (arr. Langer) (with Goldenweiser)	1900	–	–

Title	Date	Discography	Piano Roll
SAINT-SAËNS			
Caprice on a Theme from Gluck's *Alceste*	1924	—	—
Danse macabre (arr. two pianos) (with Siloti)	1900	—	—
Swan, for cello and piano (accompanying Brandukov)	1892	—	—
Swan (piano transcription by Siloti)	1924	75	—
SARASATE			
Dance, for violin and piano (accompanying Teresina Tua)	1895	—	—
SCARLATTI			
Sonata in C major, (?) L. 105	1928	—	—
Sonata in D major, L. ?	1934	—	—
Sonata in D minor, (?) L. 422 (*Toccata*)	1928	—	—
Sonata in D minor, L. 413 (*Pastorale*) (arr. Tausig)	1918	3	—
Sonata in E major, L. 375 (*Capriccio*) (arr. Tausig)	1918	—	—
Sonata in E major, (?) L. 21	1935	—	—
Sonata in E minor, (?) L. 22	1935	—	—
Sonata in F minor, L. ?	1934	—	—
Sonata in G minor, (?) L. 338	1935	—	—
SCHLÖZER			
Concert Study in A flat, Op. 1, No. 2	1919	—	—
SCHUBERT			
Andantino and Variations in B minor (arr. Tausig)	1927	—	—
Ave Maria, D. 550 (arr. Liszt)	1923	—	—
Forelle, D. 950 (arr. Liszt)	1939	—	—

Title	Date	Discography	Piano Roll
Impromptu in 'A flat minor' (always thus on R's programmes), D.899, No. 4	1925	85	31
Impromptu in F minor, D. 935, No. 1	1932	–	–
Marche militaire, D. 733 (arr. Tausig)	1929	–	–
Moment musical No. 3 in F minor, D. 780	1918	–	–
Moment musical No. 4 in C sharp minor, D. 780	1918	–	–
Rondo for Violin and Piano in B minor, D. 895 (accompanying Teresina Tua)	1895	–	–
Rondo in D major (last movement of Sonata in D, D. 850)	1933	–	–
Sonata in A major for violin and piano, D. 574 (accompanying Kreisler)	1928	125–130	–
Ständchen (Serenade), D. 937 (arr. Liszt)	1932	212	–
Wandern, D. 795 (arr. Liszt)	1923	77	22
Wohin?, D. 795 (arr. Rachmaninoff) (*The Brooklet*)	1925	86	24
SCHUMANN			
Albumblätter, Op. 124 – Nos. 1–3	1933	–	–
Arabesque in C major, Op. 18	1933	–	–
Carnaval, Op. 9	1919	131–136	–
Concerto in A minor, Op. 54	1941	–	–
Davidsbundlertänze, Op. 6	1930	–	–
Fantasiestücke, Op. 12 – No. 1, Des Abends	1892	–	–
Fantasiestücke, Op. 12 – No. 2, Aufschwung	1892	–	–
Fantasiestücke, Op. 12 – No. 4, Grillen	1932	–	–
Fantasiestücke, Op. 12 – No. 5, In der Nacht	1932	–	–
Fantasiestücke, Op. 12 – No. 6, Fabel	1932	–	–
Faschingsschwank aus Wien, Op. 26	1942	–	–
Kontrabandiste, from *Spanisches Liederspiel*, Op. 74 (arr. Tausig)	1922	57,211	–

Title	Date	Discography	Piano Roll
Kreisleriana, Op. 16	1893	–	–
Liebeslied (Widmung), Op. 25, No. 1 (arr. Liszt)	1932	–	–
Nachtstücke, Op. 23	1932	–	–
Novellette in D major, Op. 21, No. 5	?	203–204	–
Novellette in F sharp minor, Op. 21, No. 8	1921	–	–
Papillons, Op. 2	1920	–	–
Prophet Bird from *Waldescenen*, Op. 82	1893	–	–
Sonata No. 2 in G minor, Op. 22	1924	–	–
Songs (accompanying Chaliapin):	1900	–	–
Aus meinen Tränen spriessen, from *Dichterliebe*, Op. 48			
Die alten bösen Lieder, from *Dichterliebe*, Op. 48			
Two Grenadiers, Op. 49			
Studies after Caprices by Paganini, Op. 3 –			
No. 2 in E major and one other	1919	–	–
Symphonic Studies, Op. 13	1927	–	–
SCRIABIN			
Concerto in F sharp minor, Op. 20	1915	–	–
Étude in D flat, Op. 8, No. 10	1928	–	–
Étude in D sharp minor, Op. 8, No. 12	1915	–	–
Étude in F sharp minor, Op. 42, No. 3	1915	–	–
Étude in C sharp minor, Op. 42, No. 5	1915	–	–
Étude in D flat, Op. 42, No. 6	1915	–	–
Fantasy in B minor, Op. 28	1915	–	–
Poème in F sharp major, Op. 32, No. 1	1915	–	–

Title	Date	Discography	Piano Roll
Prelude in C major, Op. 11, No. 1	1915	–	–
Prelude in G major, Op. 11, No. 3	1915	–	–
Prelude in B minor, Op. 11, No. 6	1915	139	–
Prelude in F sharp minor, Op. 11, No. 8	1915	–	–
Prelude in E major, Op. 11, No. 9	1915	–	–
Prelude in B major, Op. 11, No. 11	1915	–	–
Prelude in E flat minor, Op. 11, No. 14	1915	–	–
Prelude in F minor, Op. 11, No. 18	1915	–	–
Prelude in C minor, Op. 11, No. 20	1915	–	–
Prelude in B flat major, Op. 11, No. 21	1915	–	–
Prelude in F major, Op. 11, No. 23	1915	–	–
Satanic Poem, Op. 36	1915	–	–
Sonata No. 2 (*Sonata-Fantasy*) in G sharp minor, Op. 19	1915	–	–
Sonata No. 4 in F sharp major, Op. 30	1928	–	–
Sonata No. 5 in F sharp major, Op. 53	1915	–	–
STRAUSS J.			
Artist's Life, Waltz (arr. Godowsky)	1924	–	–
Blue Danube, Waltz (arr. Schultz-Evler)	1922	58	–
Forest Murmurs, Waltz (arr. Tausig as Valse-Caprice No. 3)	1918	–	–
Moth, Waltz (arr. Tausig as Valse-Caprice No. 1)	1928	–	–
One Lives But Once, Waltz (arr. Tausig as Valse-Caprice No. 2)	1918	96–97	–
STRAUSS R.			
Song *Sie wissen's nicht*, Op. 49, No. 5 (accompanying Nezhdanova)	1908	–	–
TANEYEV			

Title	Date	Disc-ography	Piano Roll
Prelude and Fugue in G sharp minor, Op. 29	1928	–	–
TAUSIG			
Étude	1892	–	–
Ungarische Zigeunerweisen	1892	–	–
See also: Bach, Scarlatti, Schubert, Schumann, Strauss, Weber (piano transcriptions)			
TCHAIKOVSKY			
Andante cantabile from Quartet No. 1 in D major, Op. 11 (arrangement for cello and piano) (accompanying Brandukov)	1903	–	–
Concerto No. 1 in B flat minor, Op. 23	1911	–	–
Humoresque, Op. 10, No. 2	1923	59	–
Iolanta – Iolanta's Arioso (accompanying Nadezhda Zabela-Vrubel)	1903	–	–
Lullaby, Op. 16, No. 1 (arr. Rachmaninoff)	1941	207	–
Maid of Orleans – Joan's Aria (accompanying Vera Petrova-Zvantseva)	1903	–	–
Mazeppa – Maria's Lullaby (accompanying Nadezhda Zabela-Vrubel)	1903	–	–
Mazurka (?)	?	–	–
Nocturne in F major, Op. 10, No. 1	1892	–	–
Piano Trio in A minor, Op. 50 (with Ysaye and Brandukov)	1901	–	–
Rêverie, Op. 9, No. 1	1894	–	–
Romance in F minor, Op. 5	1918	–	–
Seasons, Op. 37 – No. 3, March, *Song of the Skylark*	1892	–	–
Seasons, Op. 37 – No. 6, June, *Barcarolle*	1892	–	–
Seasons, Op. 37 – No. 10, October, *Autumn Song*	1892	–	–
Seasons, Op. 37 – No. 11, November, *Troika en traineaux*	1892	17	8

437

Title	Date	Discography	Piano Roll
Song, *I bless you, forests*, Op. 47, No. 5 (accompanying Chaliapin)	1900	–	–
Theme and Variations, Op. 19, No. 6	1923	–	–
Trepak, Op. 72, No. 18	1920	–	–
Waltz in A flat, Op. 40, No. 8	1920	55	18
VIEUXTEMPS			
Air varié, for violin and piano (accompanying Teresina Tua)	1895	–	–
Concerto No. 4 in D minor, Op. 31, arr. violin and piano (accompanying Ysaye)	1901	–	–
WAGNER			
Magic Fire Music, from *Walküre* (arr. Brassin)	1923	–	–
Spinning Song, from *Flying Dutchman* (arr. Liszt)	1929	–	–
WEBER			
Invitation to the Dance, Rondo brillant, Op. 65 (arr. Tausig)	1921	–	–
Momento capriccioso in B flat, Op. 12	1920	28	–
Perpetuum mobile (Rondo from Sonata in C major, Op. 24)	1931	213	–
Rondo in E flat, Op. 62 (*La Gaieté*)	?	–	–
WIENIAWSKI			
Fantasy on Themes from the Opera *Faust* (accompanying Teresina Tua)	1895	–	–
MISCELLANEOUS			
Folk Song, *Bublichki* (recording)	1931	215	–
God Save the King	1933	–	–
Star-Spangled Banner (arr. Rachmaninoff)	1919	–	2

13 Rachmaninoff and the Gramophone

Although the first recordings in Russia were made for the Berliner brothers in Petersburg as early as 1899, in its first years the Russian gramophone industry, like that of other countries at the time, was preoccupied with satisfying the demand for popular vocal music, the human voice then being technically the most successful musical instrument to record, and it neglected the piano totally. In the 1900s several of Rachmaninoff's songs were recorded by artists associated with the composer (Smirnov, Grïzunov, Alexandrovich, Labinsky, Zbruyeva), but right up to the time that he left Russia Rachmaninoff himself was never once invited to the recording studio, nor too were any of the other Russian virtuosos whose names we know today mainly on the basis of the careers and recordings they later made in the West.

When Rachmaninoff arrived in the United States at the end of 1918, he had an immediate need for money, and it was this which led him to make his first recordings, for the Edison Company, in April 1919. With records, as with other things, Edison was an individualist. Unlike his major competitors of the time, Edison recorded on the 'hill and dale' principle, and his 'Diamond Discs', as they were called, were thus technically incompatible with Victor, Columbia and other makes.[1] Ultimately this crucial disadvantage contributed to their commercial failure, but another reason was Edison's whimsical artistic policy, which padded the catalogue with dross. Even the 'label' – originally not made of paper, but merely pressed into the wax – concentrated on advertising the inventor's name and picture, with details of work and performer given lesser prominence.

Rachmaninoff's Edison recording sessions lasted a week and produced ten sides, with three versions or 'takes' of each side. Technically the records were not very satisfactory even for their time, the recording equipment being placed too far from the upright piano and the sound emerging indistinctly from a welter of surface noise created by the thick and heavy 'unbreakable' material Edison used for pressing. Contrary to

Rachmaninoff's wishes, Edison seems to have issued all three takes of each record, but those who diligently track down the alternatives will find only minute differences of performance. Rachmaninoff himself, however, was annoyed by the issue of recordings he had not authorized and by the lack of a satisfactory formal contract, and on 21 April 1920, a year almost to the day after he had begun work for Edison, he signed an exclusive five-year contract with the Victor Company to record twenty-five pieces, with a guaranteed annual advance against royalties of $15,000. Five days later Rachmaninoff was at work in Victor's Camden studio, beginning an association with the company that was to last uninterruptedly for twenty-two years.

The appearance of Rachmaninoff's first Victor records provoked the Edison Company into a burst of publicity hailing the superior merits of their own recordings. With a photograph of Rachmaninoff seated at a piano and with a jury behind a screen, the advertisement was a follow-up to the famous 'Tone Test' demonstrations Edison had conducted since 1915 in cities throughout North America, in which audiences were invited to compare live performances with Edison recordings. Under the picture was the caption: 'Hear Rachmaninoff on the New Edison. Now you can make a straightforward comparison and find out which is the best phonograph. Rachmaninoff himself, the great Russian pianist, gives you this opportunity. He has made recordings for one of the standard talking machines. We are glad he has done so. For now you can compare.'[2]

Both the Edison and early Victor recordings of Rachmaninoff were made acoustically, that is mechanically and not electrically, with strategically placed recording horns picking up the sound and funnelling it into the machine which cut the grooves on to the original master disc, from which the negative matrix stamper would be made. In essence the system was the same as that invented by Emile Berliner more than thirty years before. In recording Rachmaninoff the Victor engineers were more successful than their Edison counterparts in realistically capturing the sound of the piano, an instrument even in modern times notoriously difficult to record.

Rachmaninoff's acoustic Victor recordings, that is to say, all the recordings he made up to the end of 1924, number sixty-seven sides in all, of which thirty-two were issued, more than fulfilling the contractual quota. Of these records Rachmaninoff himself thought the best were the Grieg Waltz and the Mendelssohn *Spinning Song*.[3] Special interest, however, naturally attaches to the many unpublished recordings Rachmaninoff made in these years. Twenty-two sides were not approved for issue and never remade. Among these are such tantalizing items as a Beethoven sonata movement, the second item he recorded, some Chopin

Études, Liszt's *La Campanella*, *Au bord d'une source*, and *Liebestraum*, and, perhaps the greatest loss, his own G minor *Étude-Tableau*, Op. 33, No. 8. After his experience with Edison Rachmaninoff was scrupulous about having all copies of records he had not approved destroyed, which is why there are no copies in Victor's own archives, and why, unless an odd test pressing slipped through the net all those years ago, there is no possibility of any ever turning up.

Ten of his acoustic recordings Rachmaninoff subsequently remade electrically, and they were issued only in that form, but eight he marked to 'hold', that is not to reject but to keep until such time as he might decide to re-record them. This is why copies of five of them – Chopin's G flat Waltz and C sharp minor Scherzo, and the first two sides of his own Second Concerto – survived to be incorporated in the 1973 *Complete Rachmaninoff* LP reissue and why copies of the other three – his *Humoresque* (later recorded electrically), Chopin's E flat Prelude and part of Liszt's Spanish Rhapsody – must at least once have been in Victor's archives and may just conceivably some day turn up.

Rachmaninoff's acoustic recording of his Second Concerto is unusually interesting as providing an alternative performance to compare with the famous 1929 electrical remake. According to Victor recording books, for the benefit of the recording horns Stokowski's great Philadelphia Orchestra was reduced to seven first violins, four seconds, three violas, two cellos, two flutes, two bass, two clarinets, two oboes, four horns, one 'bass-baritone', one bass saxophone, contrabassoon, three trombones, two trumpets and 'taps'. In sessions lasting two days in Trinity Church, Camden, in December 1923 and January 1924 Rachmaninoff recorded the last two movements only, and then, when these records had already been issued, in December 1924 completed the work by recording the first movement, on three sides, two twelve-inch and one ten-inch, the smaller final side easily accommodating the remaining approximately two minutes and ten seconds of music (the 1929 recording divided the movement more evenly over its three twelve-inch sides). By this time double-sided records were the norm, and the published recording would therefore have oddly comprised one twelve-inch and one ten-inch record with fill-up. In the event, as Rachmaninoff did not approve any of the three takes of the final side, the recording was never issued.

Victor made their first electrical recordings in March 1925, and Rachmaninoff was soon in the studio taking advantage of the new process, which at least temporarily rescued the industry from the sudden decline into which it had fallen from competition with the newly arrived radio. Over the next five years he recorded the considerable total of eighty-three sides, of which fourteen were electrical remakes of earlier acoustic recordings. Only six of these records remained unpublished:

Chopin's A flat Ballade, the test recording with Nadezhda Plevitskaya, Rimsky-Korsakov's *Flight of the Bumble Bee*, the Scriabin Prelude, and a twelve-inch version of the opening of the first movement of the *Funeral March* Sc. ata, obviously made before it was decided to record the work in ten-inch format. All but one survived eventually to appear on LP, though only the two sides of the Chopin Ballade had not been rejected by Rachmaninoff.

In 1928 Rachmaninoff recorded three violin sonatas with his friend Fritz Kreisler. Years later Charles Foley, who was manager of both artists, described how this project came about:[4]

> The idea of collaborating for the sonatas was born in my house in New York City during a talk about music – what else? – between these two great men, and my house was the place selected for the rehearsal for reasons you might call 'social protocol'. Rather than have the rehearsals in Mr Rachmaninoff's house one day and Mr Kreisler's the next day, we decided on neutral ground. The two friends – they had become close friends by this time – were assembled at my house, and the only listener to their rehearsals was a manservant I had, a Korean, who admired both but was not very much interested in occidental music. He made coffee for them, which they gratefully and copiously consumed. There they felt free to discard their coats and waist-coats, discuss and sometimes argue about tempi, shadings, etc., and as you might say – let their long hair down.

The first work to be recorded was Beethoven's G major Sonata, but the success of the partnership quickly prompted the second recording, of the Grieg C minor Sonata,[5] completed six months later in Berlin and the only one of Rachmaninoff's recordings made outside America. Rachmaninoff later joked about the way in which his own nagging perfectionism had driven him to persuade Kreisler to record the whole work five times over:[6]

> Do the critics who have praised these Grieg records so highly realise the immense amount of hard work and patience necessary to achieve such results? The six sides of the Grieg set we recorded no fewer than five times each. From these thirty discs we finally selected the best, destroying the remainder. Perhaps so much labour did not altogether please Fritz Kreisler. He is a great artist, but does not care to work too hard. Being an optimist, he will declare with enthusiasm that the first set of proofs we make are wonderful, marvellous. But my own pessimism invariably causes me to feel, and argue, that they could be better. So when we work together, Fritz and I, we are always fighting.

The last of the recordings with Kreisler, the Schubert *Duo*, was made back in New York in December 1928. The tensions between Rachmaninoff the perfectionist, working towards realizing the ideal performance already worked out in his mind, and Kreisler, gloriously spontaneous, surfaced again during this recording, as Geraldine Farrar remembered:[7]

> Kreisler would come out of the studio in high glee, still aglow with the

beautiful music which he had helped to create. Rachmaninoff, on the other hand, emerged with his sad face, worried about this or that phrase which he thought had not quite come out as it should. He would continue to brood over the situation for days and finally decide that another recording ought to be made. His friend Fritz, however, thought only of the beauties of their ensemble effort and artfully dodged the issue of doing the whole thing over again. As Rachmaninoff put it to Miss Farrar in his slow deliberate way: 'Fritz – he is like a flea; one just can't put a finger on him'... It is no wonder that the efforts of the Victor management to get the Austrian and the Russian to record the entire series of Beethoven sonatas together did not materialise.

When he received the proofs of the Schubert recording, Rachmaninoff expressed his dissatisfaction with them to Kreisler:[8]

From the musical point of view all [the] records are good but the general impression of the whole *Duo* seems to me somewhat dull. Nevertheless, I consent to their release. It irritates me a little bit that in some places we do not play absolutely together. This is because we were too far away from each other. This defect is very small but you and I will notice it and that is why I am not satisfied with them.

In February of the following year, 1929, Rachmaninoff remade his Second Concerto. In contrast with the earlier acoustic recording, the new version had the Philadelphia Orchestra out in full strength, 106 musicians taking part in the two sessions, in the Academy of Music. The following week, with the same orchestra, Rachmaninoff took up the conductor's baton for the first time in twelve years to record his *Isle of the Dead* and *Vocalise*. At the same time Rachmaninoff also managed to fit in visits to the nearby Camden studio to record Schumann's *Carnaval* and three other items (35 takes in all), making this the most intensive fortnight's work of his entire recording career.

In February 1930 Rachmaninoff recorded Chopin's *Funeral March* Sonata and the E minor Waltz as a fill-up for the final side; these were to be his last recordings for nearly five years. In October 1929 the Wall Street Crash had all but wrecked the American record industry; radio, a cheaper source of home entertainment, seemed set finally to win the battle it had nearly won five years before. Already in January 1929 Victor had been taken over by the Radio Corporation of America, who lost no time in converting the Camden factory from gramophone to radio production. In 1930, making drastic cuts in recording and advertising, they allowed contracts with serious musicians on their 'Red Seal' label to lapse. Many of these artists, Heifetz, Rubinstein and Horowitz among them, subsequently signed up with Victor's English affiliate, HMV, whose recording ambitions in Europe were still expanding, but unfortunately Rachmaninoff did not join them.

Rachmaninoff's life-long suspicion of radio probably dates from these years. In an interview in 1931 he explained his views at some length:[9]

Not long ago I was asked to express my opinion as to the musical value of broadcasting. I replied that, to my mind, radio has a bad influence on art: that it destroys all the soul and true significance of art. To me it seems that the modern gramophone and modern methods of recording are musically superior to wireless transmission in every way, particularly where reproduction of the piano is concerned ... From what I have heard I cannot believe that the best performance imaginable would ever satisfy a sensitive artist. On this account alone, I deplore the present depression in the gramophone industry. It is a curious fact that when I began working for HMV [Victor] ten years ago business was excellent, though only indifferent records were available. Yet today, when we have first-class recording, business is worse than it has ever been. For this I can only think that the universal craze for radio is to blame ... To listen in great cities like London or New York when one could actually be present in a concert hall – to me that would seem sacrilege.

For Rachmaninoff a gramophone record, in contrast with an ephemeral radio broadcast, was a permanent artistic document, and he was therefore prepared to make recordings though intensely disliking the actual process. He told Alfred Swan: 'I get very nervous when I am making records, and all whom I have asked say that they get nervous too. When the test records are made, I know that I can hear them played back to me, and then everything is all right. But when the stage is set for the final recording and I realise that this will remain for good, I get nervous and my hands get tense.'[10] But, being a perfectionist, Rachmaninoff remade recordings repeatedly, until he was thoroughly satisfied with their musical worth, though he was entirely unconcerned about their sound quality. Charles O'Connell, who managed many of his Victor recordings, was surprised by this paradox:[11]

For a long time I flattered myself that I had his confidence in musical matters until eventually I realised that he was not in the least concerned with the technicalities of recording, and would take my word that a given record was a good record only because he was quite indifferent to its quality as a recording. He was concerned solely with his own performance, and rarely would permit the publication of any record in which his own playing was not flawless.

Rachmaninoff's reactionary attitude to radio seems also to have been coloured by the objectionable intrusions of advertisements into programmes on American commercial radio and the difficulty of picking up broadcasts from Moscow free from the distractions of atmospheric interference, whether in Switzerland or the United States. He was also concerned about the possible compression of musical dynamics in the hands of unmusical broadcasting engineers.[12] But more generally, in the facility which radio provides to turn on music like water from a tap, he saw a danger that it would remove the element of effort in listening and reduce the status of music to that of aural wallpaper; as Constant Lambert pointed out: 'The more people use the wireless, the less they listen to it'.[13] To the end of his life, almost alone with Fritz Kreisler, Rachmaninoff held out against allowing any of his live performances to be broadcast, despite the considerable financial inducements offered, and while this has unfortunately meant that there are no recordings 'off air' to supplement his discography, as mercifully there are in the case of his friend Josef Hofmann, there can be little doubt that he would have thought his worst fears amply realized, had he seen the extent of today's inescapable and omnipresent music broadcasting.

Sofiya Satina threw more light on Rachmaninoff's attitude to recording:[14]

He dreaded the process, often refused to record, or put it off as long as possible. Although he possessed exceptional self control at concerts and loved to appear before the public, Rachmaninoff used to get very nervous at a recording, despite the most courteous attention of everyone involved: technicians, engineers, etc. He was upset by interruptions when playing, compulsory stops, bells indicating when he had to start. In the end the bells were replaced with light signals, which for some reason troubled him less. Nevertheless he could not give himself entirely to his playing, to forget himself, as on the concert platform, and he missed the vital contact with the public he always felt so keenly in concerts. Always demanding of himself, Rachmaninoff became still more severe when he listened to a recording, vetoing and destroying test records mercilessly. Many of the rejected recordings were for the most part very good, but because of one chord or one passage which did not entirely satisfy him, they were there and then destroyed ... Rachmaninoff often used to say that the records he had made served as the best lesson and guide of what to avoid in performance.

Despite his dislike of the process of recording, Rachmaninoff stayed faithful to the medium and aloof from radio to the very end of his life, not to be swayed even by his esteemed colleague Leopold Stokowski, always an enthusiast for experiments in sound reproduction. It was Stokowski who persuaded Bell Telephone Laboratories (Western Electric) to install a studio under the stage of the Academy of Music at Philadelphia to experiment with ways of improving recording techniques. The engineers were linked by telephone line to the Bell laboratory in Manhattan, and on 3 December 1931 recordings were made in this way of Stokowski rehearsing the Philadelphia Orchestra. Rachmaninoff was in attendance (his Philadelphia concert was two days later), and at one stage in the proceedings he played two solo selections which were recorded by the Bell engineers: Weber's *Perpetuum mobile* and Liszt's B minor *Ballade*. Alas, copies of what would have been Rachmaninoff's only 'live' recordings, and of performances of works he otherwise did not record, have disappeared, and the one metal master which survives, of the *Ballade*, has irreparably rusted away.

Sales of records in America plummeted in the early 1930s, but 1933 at last saw an upturn, prompting RCA early in 1934 again to show interest in its 'Red Seal' catalogue. The instant success of the first performances of the *Paganini Rhapsody* in America in the autumn of 1934 encouraged the company to record the work immediately with the composer and his original partners, the Philadelphia Orchestra and Stokowski, the session taking place on the morning of Christmas Eve 1934. However, instead of taking advantage of the spacious sound of the orchestra's natural home and by now customary recording venue, the Academy of Music, Philadelphia, the engineers made the recording in 'Church Studio No. 2', an acoustically dead environment that gave the orchestral sound a hard and constricted quality. Another contrast with the recording of the Second Concerto made nearly six years previously is that the orchestral forces were considerably reduced (to 74 men only), a vein of economy which seems also to have applied to the session time available, for on the afternoon of the same day the orchestra was booked to record Sibelius's Violin Concerto with Heifetz. Two complete performances of the Rhapsody were recorded; for the published version Rachmaninoff chose the first performance in its entirety. Later he suffered his usual pangs of dissatisfaction; after playing the recording to Medtner in March 1935, he wrote to Sofiya Satina: '[Medtner] was very pleased! But I've only now realised how poor this recording is and how much better I play [the *Rhapsody*] now. I've just got to remake it.'[15]

A fortnight later Rachmaninoff was back in the studio in New York to record his two latest transcriptions, presumably to make a natural pairing on one record: the Scherzo from Mendelssohn's Incidental Music to *A Midsummer Night's Dream* and the Prelude from Bach's E major Violin Partita. However, the latter never saw the light of day, although, pending a remake, Rachmaninoff did sanction the holding of one of the takes, a copy of which survives; as might be guessed, the performance is strikingly similar to the well-known 1942 recording. The Mendelssohn Scherzo, on the other hand, became one of Rachmaninoff's most famous records, a marvellous example of orchestration at the keyboard, with an incredibly airy texture given by the very sparing use of the sustaining pedal. Rachmaninoff seems to have found it more than usually difficult to bring the piece off in the studio. The five versions made at the first session failed to satisfy him, and the recording had to be held over until his next visit to the studio, which was not until December 1935, nearly twelve months later, when he made two more versions, one of which he allowed to be published, though he was not happy about it.[16] For the other side of the record he set down his perhaps unexpectedly felicitous performance of Handel's *Harmonious Blacksmith*. In the same sessions three more ten-inch sides were recorded: Borodin's Scherzo, his own Serenade, and Chopin's A minor Mazurka, Op. 68, No. 2, this last remaining unpublished, like the Bach, having no other recording with which to pair it for commercial issue. This miserable sum of six items, two unpublished, comprises the only solo recordings Rachmaninoff made between 1930 and 1940.

Rachmaninoff's next opus, his Third Symphony, was two years (1935–36) in the writing, and the composer was naturally keen to have the work recorded as promptly as the *Rhapsody* had been. In March 1937, four months after its Philadelphia première, when Rachmaninoff was on tour in England, HMV recording manager Fred Gaisberg discussed with him the possibility of a London recording. Rachmaninoff evidently 'felt so touchy over [the work's] cool reception that he even offered to pay for rehearsals for recording it'.[17] By June, when Rachmaninoff wrote to Wilshaw, arrangements had been settled:[18]

> On September 5th I have to record my Third Symphony in London. For this they give me the Philharmonic Orchestra and three rehearsals, on the 2nd, 3rd and 4th. And because sales of such large works go badly and the orchestra is expensive and the Company loses on it, they have as it were bribed me also to record my First Concerto. As I am worried about my hands, which have got right out of the habit of conducting, I cannot make both recordings at the same time, and so I have decided to return home and come back again to London on the 21st and 22nd September.

The projected London recording never materialized. Gaisberg elsewhere relates that Rachmaninoff asked for a whole week's rehearsal and that he had to turn him down.[19] Plans seem not entirely to have been laid aside, however, for at a gramophone conference in November 1938 an official from HMV explained that the company was still willing to record the Symphony, but to balance the expense involved it had asked Rachmaninoff in return to make a recording of all twenty-four of his Preludes. This Rachmaninoff had refused to do.[20] And so the situation rested until the end of 1939, when, as part of the new concert season, the Philadelphia Orchestra, since 1936 under the directorship of Eugene Ormandy, devoted a series of three concerts in Philadelphia and New York exclusively to Rachmaninoff's music, the 'Rachmaninoff Cycle', in which the composer appeared publicly as conductor for the first time since leaving Russia. RCA used the opportunity at last to record the Symphony and also the First and Third Concertos, featured in these concerts. December 4 1939 was assigned for recording both concertos, but Rachmaninoff was dissatisfied with some of the takes and another session was arranged for 24 February 1940, in which four of the six sides of the First Concerto and two from the second and third movements of the Third Concerto were remade. Rachmaninoff, however, was still dissatisfied. In selecting the takes for issue he wrote to Charles O'Connell in his customary pessimistic vein: 'These recordings are far from being perfect, but the others are even worse. For God's sake, don't make any mistakes. This threatens to be my very downfall.' [21]

Sofiya Satina remarked that Rachmaninoff was less exacting about his recordings with orchestra than about his solo recordings, appreciating that extra sessions with his chosen orchestra, the Philadelphia, though artistically desirable in the quest for perfection, were a luxury that could not be afforded in the practical world of tight orchestral schedules and even tighter recording budgets.[22] However, it was arranged to record the symphony on the day after its Carnegie Hall performance, which in turn had immediately followed two performances in Philadelphia. Being so familiar to the musicians it was recorded economically in one session, with only two of the nine sides having to be taken a second time. The same might have been said of the unrealized but apparently promised[23] recording of *The Bells*, which had been programmed in the second half of the concerts, after the symphony, with Jan Peerce, Susanne Fisher and Mack Harrell as soloists, and the Westminster Choir. This was another project that seems likely to have been abandoned on straightforward financial grounds, as soon as the cost of the lavish forces involved had been realistically measured against the recording's potentially small sales.

In two sessions in March and April 1940 Rachmaninoff recorded a set of ten sides of his solo piano music. This went some way to repairing the neglect of earlier years, but the greater project of recording some of his recital programmes, apparently suggested by Rachmaninoff, was rejected.[24] Another disappointment occurred in the spring of the following year, when, at the end of the concert season, Rachmaninoff was to have recorded his newly composed *Symphonic Dances*, but the schedules of RCA Victor and the Philadelphia Orchestra apparently could not be reconciled and the project was deferred. Charles O'Connell later explained that he felt the *Dances* were neither an important work nor, more importantly from his viewpoint as a recording executive, a success with the public.[25]

> I discreetly postponed the matter until it was not only impracticable but impossible. A little later we engaged the Chicago Symphony to make 'Red Seal' records, and one of the first things on their programme that season was Rachmaninoff's *Symphonic Dances*, whereupon, conditions being quite different from those existing in Philadelphia, I proposed that the Chicago Orchestra record the *Symphonic Dances*. Rachmaninoff was not at all enthusiastic, and when it developed that Dr. Stock and not Rachmaninoff would conduct, the composer became actively resentful and things were rather uncomfortable between us for a time. When I was in a position to tell him the whole story, however, I was restored to his good graces.

Nevertheless, the 'postponement' proved fatal to the project, for after

31 July 1942 no new recordings were made in America for two years, as a result of a ban imposed by the American Federation of Musicians in a bitter and protracted pay dispute with the record industry.

Eight months before the ban came into effect, in December 1941, Rachmaninoff was able to record his newly revised Fourth Concerto, to complete the cycle of his concerted works, and towards the end of February 1942 he spent three days in RCA's Hollywood studios making what were to be his final recordings. Unfortunately they were spoiled by poor technical quality: the microphones were placed too close to the piano and the sound is uncomfortably distorted, the piano tone in the Schubert-Liszt Serenade in particular sounding uncharacteristically aggressive. All the records Rachmaninoff made on the first day of these sessions were scrapped at his request, and a note placed in the file saying that he would remake these selections 'at a later date'. As things turned out, he did not repeat two of these works – the variation movement from Mozart's A major Sonata, which he had recorded twenty-three years before for Edison, and Schumann's F sharp minor *Novellette*, which would have been an addition to his recorded repertoire. Of the other records, the Bach Prelude, though not the other two transcribed movements of the suite, already existed in a satisfactory version, and the remake of *Liebesfreud* was not only unnecessary but omitted the crucial cadenza, so striking a feature of the earlier recording.

Thus, Rachmaninoff's final recordings were a disappointing anticlimax to a career that varied between prolific activity in the 1920s, inactivity and tragic waste of opportunity throughout the 1930s, and a combination of substantial achievement alongside further glaring omissions in his last three or four years. Overall, in comparison with some of his famous contemporaries and predecessors, who recorded either tantalizingly little (Busoni), or profusely but unsatisfactorily (Paderewski), or in a way which failed to convey their real stature (Godowsky), Rachmaninoff recorded quite extensively and with a consistently Olympian level of musical excellence. His records represent his playing as it was in real life, and in conferring immortality on his pianistic genius the gramophone performed an inestimable service to posterity.

References

1 On the 'hill and dale' system the recording is cut in the groove vertically and not laterally as in conventional 78 and mono LP recordings. The combining of the two principles for stereo LPs means that Edison 'Diamond Discs' can be played satisfactorily with a standard stereo cartridge fitted with a suitable stylus.
2 *The Etude*, December 1920, Vol. 38, No. 12, p. 796, and elsewhere.

3 'Gramophone Celebrities XII – Sergei Rachmaninoff', by John F. Porte, in *Gramophone*, August 1925, p.128.

4 Charles Foley in sleeve note to RCA 1959 reissue of the Grieg and Schubert Sonata recordings, on LVT 1009 (RB 16154).

5 The Grieg Sonata, unlike the Beethoven and Schubert works recorded with Kreisler, was not new to Rachmaninoff, since, according to Lyudmila Skalon (*VR/A* 1, p. 238), he had played it, privately, with Nikolay Avierino as far back as the 1890s.

6 R., 'The Artist and the Gramophone' in *Gramophone*, April 1931, pp. 525–526.

7 Louis P. Lochner, *Fritz Kreisler*, Rockliff Publishing Corp. Ltd, London, 1951, pp. 265–266.

8 R. to Kreisler, 11 January 1929.

9 R., 'The Artist and the Gramophone', *Gramophone*, April 1931, pp. 525–526.

10 *Swan*, p. 11.

11 *O'Connell*, p. 167.

12 Sofiya Satina, *VR/A* 1, p. 109.

13 Constant Lambert, *Music Ho!*, Faber & Faber, London, 1937, p. 163.

14 Sofiya Satina, *VR/A* 1, pp. 108–109.

15 R. to Sofiya Satina, 29 March 1935.

16 'Although he always played [the Scherzo] perfectly in public, the very fact of waiting for the word "go" – four and a half minutes without a wrong note – it took him eleven [*sic*] records and he was not happy.' Benno Moiseiwitsch in BBC radio interview, c. 1958.

17 F.W. Gaisberg, *Music On Record*, Robert Hale Ltd, London, 1946, p. 181.

18 R. to Wilshaw, 7 June 1937.

19 Fred Gaisberg, 'The Last of the Three Giants of the Volga Has Departed', article in *Gramophone*, August, 1943.

20 Letter from Roy T. Budden in *Gramophone*, April 1939.

21 R. to O'Connell, 6 April 1940.

22 Sofiya Satina, *VR/A* 1, p. 109.

23 Op. cit., p. 103.

24 *B/L*, p. 371.

25 *O'Connell*, p. 168.

14 Discography

When an artist worked in a recording studio in the era of 78 r.p.m. records, it was the custom of the factory to give each side of music recorded a separate identifying number, and this was marked on the master from which commercial copies were pressed for sale to the public. These numbers, called 'matrix numbers', usually ran in a chronological series (as do the Rachmaninoff Edison and Victor recordings). On Edison records the matrix number was on and immediately below the impressed label, but on the Victor issues it was on the surround of the stamper, and so there was no visible evidence of it on the records themselves (except for a freak period of six months in 1928). HMV, on the other hand, who were affiliated to Victor throughout Rachmaninoff's recording career and who handled all his recordings in Great Britain, used the same matrix numbers as Victor, but imprinted them in the space around the run-in groove at the end of each side. If, as was usually the case, an artist made several attempts to record one piece, each of these recordings would be given the same matrix number but a different 'take' letter (Edison) or number (Victor). Edison included the take letter with the matrix number below the label; on Victor issues it is usually to be found in isolation around the run-in groove at the 9 o'clock position relative to the matrix number, and on HMV upside down at 3 o'clock. (Other numbers around the label are not significant.)

In the discography which follows, a take approved by Rachmaninoff for mastering is marked 'm'; one which he was ready to hold over, pending possible re-recording, is marked 'h'.

Victor matrix numbers

Prefix	Record size	Recording Process
B	10–inch	acoustic
C	12–inch	acoustic
BVE or BS	10–inch	electrical
CVE or CS	12–inch	electrical

HMV prefaced the matrix number of all its issues of Victor recordings with the letter 'A', standing for 'America'; the symbol Δ after the matrix number signifies an electrical recording. Victor changed to the electrical process in March 1925, beginning with matrix no. 32160. The following month Rachmaninoff made his first recording by the new system (item 76b in the discography).

Catalogue numbers of single-sided issues by both Victor and HMV were in a numerical series:

	Victor	*HMV*
12–inch	70000	05000
10–inch	60000	5000

In the early 1920s Victor and HMV followed the lead of other firms (including Edison) and abandoned single-sided records, reissuing their old recordings in double-sided form, with new catalogue numbers:

	Victor	*HMV*
12–inch	(V) 6000 onwards	prefix DB
10–inch	(V) 800 onwards	prefix DA

The catalogue numbers given refer only to the domestic issues of American Victor and English HMV. Many of the single-disc items Rachmaninoff made for Victor were published only in the United States, though they were often assigned an HMV number. An asterisk by a listing indicates a record that never found its way into the domestic catalogue.

Rachmaninoff's recordings have been reincarnated several times in the LP era, though it was not until 1973 that RCA gathered together all the published and extant unpublished recordings for a fifteen-record centenary reissue, *The Complete Rachmaninoff*, issued variously in five separate boxes or one set, the best pressings being those of the Japanese version (RVC 7617–31). Some of these recordings have already found their way on to Compact Disc, and it is to be hoped that the remainder will follow.

Rachmaninoff Discography

(a) Edison records, made in New York between 18 and 24 April 1919.

Item	Matrix no.	Recording date	Catalogue no. of issued 'take'	Title
1a	6731–A	18/4/1919	82197	CHOPIN – Waltz in A flat, Op. 42
b	–B		82197	
c	–C		82197	
2a	6732–A	18/4/1919	82197	MOZART – Sonata No. 11, in A major, K. 331: 1st
b	–B		82197	movement, Theme and Variations (see also item 202)
c	–C		82197	
3a	6735–A	19/4/1919	82170	SCARLATTI (arr. Tausig) – *Pastorale* (Sonata in D minor, L.413)
b	–B		82170	
c	–C		82170	
4a	6736–A	19/4/1919	82202	CHOPIN – Waltz in A flat, Op. 64, No. 3 (see also item 94)
b	–B		82202	
c	–C		82202	
5a	6739–A	23/4/1919	82169	LISZT – Hungarian Rhapsody No. 2 in C sharp minor
b	–B		82169	Part 1
c	–C		82169	
6a	6740–A	23/4/1919	82169	Part 2
b	–B		82169	
c	–C		82169	
7a	6741–A	23/4/1919	82170	Part 3
b	–B		82170	
c	–C		82170	

Item	Matrix no.	Recording date	Catalogue no. of issued 'take'	Title
8a	6742–A	24/4/1919	82187	RACHMANINOFF – Prelude in C sharp minor, Op. 3, No. 2
b	–B		82187	
c	–C		82187	(see also items 46 and 47)
9a	6743–A	24/4/1919	82202	RACHMANINOFF – Barcarolle, Op. 10, No. 3
b	–B		82202	
c	–C		82202	
10a	6744–A	24/4/1919	82187	RACHMANINOFF – *Polka de W.R.*
b	–B		82187	
c	–C		82187	(see also item 48)

(b) Victor records, made between 26 April 1920 and 27 February 1942.

Item	Matrix no.	Recording date	Victor	HMV	Title
11a	B 23956–1	26/4/1920			GRIEG – *Minuet* (? *'Grandmother's Minuet*, Op. 68, No. 2) and *Elfin Dance*, Op. 12, No. 4 (see also item 14)
12a	B 23961–1	26/4/1920			BEETHOVEN – Sonata No. 6, in F major, Op. 10, No. 2: 3rd movement, *Presto*
b	–2	3/5/1920			
c	–3				
d	–4	4/5/1920			
e	–5	17/5/1920			
13a	C 23962–1	26/4/1920			CHOPIN – Waltz in B minor, Op. 69, No. 2
b	B 23962–1				
c	–2	4/5/1920			

454

Item	Matrix no.	Recording date	Catalogue no. of issued 'take' Victor	HMV	Title
d	−3	3/11/1920			
e	−4	18/3/1921			
f	−5				
g	−6	2/4/1921			
h	−7				
i	−8				
j	−9	24/10/1923			
k	−10				
l	−11m		66202 V 972	5717* DA 593	
14a	B 23963−1	3/5/1920			GRIEG − *Waltz*, Op. 12, No. 2, and *Elfin Dance*, Op. 12, No. 4 (see also item 11)
b	−2				
c	−3	12/10/1921			
d	−4m		66105 V 815	5680* DA 371	
15a	B 23964−1	3/5/1920			CHOPIN − *Étude* in G flat, Op. 10, No. 5 (*Black Keys*) (see also item 16) and Op. 25, No. 9 (*Butterfly*)
b	−2	17/5/1920			
c	−3				
16a	B 23982−1	3/5/1920			CHOPIN − *Étude* in G flat, Op. 10, No. 5 (*Black Keys*) (see also item 15)
17a	C 23983−1m	3/5/1920	74630 V 6260	05653 DB 409	TCHAIKOVSKY − *Troika en traineaux*, No. 11 from *The Seasons*, Op. 37
b	CVE 23983 −2	21/3/1928			

Item	Matrix no.	Recording date	Catalogue no. of issued 'take' Victor	HMV	Title
c	–3				
d	–4				
e	–5	4/4/1928			
f	–6				
g	–7	11/4/1928			
h	–8m		V 6857	DB 1279	
18a	C 23984–1	3/5/1920			RACHMANINOFF – Prelude in G minor, Op. 23, No. 5
b	–2				
c	–3m	4/5/1920	74628	05652	
d	–4m	17/5/1920	V 6261	DB 410	
19a	C 23985–1m	3/5/1920	74645	05651	RACHMANINOFF – Prelude in G major, Op. 32, No. 5
			V 6261	DB 410	
20a	C 23986–1	3/5/1920			LISZT – La Campanella
b	–2	20/11/1922			
21a	B 24116–1	17/5/1920			CHOPIN – Études in F minor, Op. 25, No. 2, and F major, Op. 25, No 3.
b	–2				
22a	B 24117–1	17/5/1920			MENDELSSOHN – Rondo capriccioso in E, Op. 14
b	–2				
23a	B 24123–1	17/5/1920			RACHMANINOFF – Lilacs, Op. 21, No. 5
b	–2	24/2/1922			(see also item 208)
c	–3				
d	–4	24/10/1923			

Item	Matrix no.	Recording date	Catalogue no. of issued 'take' Victor	HMV	Title
e	–5				
f	–6				
g	–7h	25/10/1923			
h	–8	27/12/1923			
i	–9m		64906		
			V 1051	DA 666*	
j	–10	28/12/1923			
k	–11				
l	–12h				
24a	B 24192–1	2/7/1920			CHOPIN – Waltz in D flat, Op. 64, No. 1
b	–2				
c	–3m	2/4/1921	64971	5658	
d	–4	5/4/1923			
e	–5m		64971		
			V 815	DA 371	
25a	B 24193–1	2/7/1920			DEBUSSY – Children's Corner Suite – No. 6, Golliwog's Cake Walk
b	–2				
c	–3				
d	–4h	21/1/1921			
e	–5	18/3/1921			
f	–6				
g	–7	2/4/1921			

Item	Matrix no.	Recording date	Catalogue no. of issued 'take' Victor	HMV	Title
h	–8m		64980 V 813	5660 DA 369	DAQUIN – *Le Coucou*
26a	B 24635–1	20/10/1920			
b	–2m	21/10/1920	64919 V 812	5647* DA 368	
27a	B 24636–1	20/10/1920			MENDELSSOHN – *Song Without Words* (not identified)
28a	C 24637–1	20/10/1920			WEBER – *Momento capriccioso* in B flat, Op. 12
b	B 24637–1				
c	–2	21/10/1920			
29a	C 24638–1	20/10/1920			MOZART – Sonata No. 11, in A major, K. 331 – 3rd movement: *Turkish March*
b	B 24638–1				
c	BVE 24638–2	13/4/1925			
d	–3				
e	–4	14/5/1925			
f	–5				
g	–6m		V 1124	DA 719	
h	–7				
i	–8	14/12/1925	see 98a		
j	–9		see 98b		
30a	B 24639–1	20/10/1920			CHOPIN – Waltz in F major, Op. 34, No. 3
b	–2	21/10/1920			
c	–3	3/11/1920			

458

Item	Matrix no.	Recording date	Catalogue no. of issued 'take'		Title
			Victor	HMV	
d	–4				
e	–5	20/11/1922			
31a	B 24642–1	20/10/1920			RACHMANINOFF – Prelude in G sharp minor, Op. 32, No. 12
b	–2	21/10/1920			
c	–3	3/11/1920			
d	–4				
e	–5m	21/1/1921	64963 5657	V 812 DA 368	
32a	C 24643–1	20/10/1920			RACHMANINOFF – *Polichinelle*, Op. 3, No. 4
b	–2m	6/3/1923	74807	V 6452 DB 845*	
33a	B 24644–1	20/10/1920			CHOPIN – Mazurka in C sharp minor, Op. 63, No. 3
b	–2	21/10/1920			
c	–3	3/11/1920			
d	–4				
e	–5	21/1/1921			
f	–6				
g	–7	27/12/1923			
h	–8m		66248	V 1008 DA 613*	
34a	B 24645–1	20/10/1920			CHOPIN – Waltz in C sharp minor, Op. 64, No. 2
b	–2				

459

Item	Matrix no.	Recording date	Catalogue no. of issued 'take' Victor	HMV	Title
c	–3				
d	–4				
e	C 24645-1	31/12/1924			
f	–2				
g	CVE 24645-3h	13/4/1925			
h	–4				
i	–5	19/3/1927			
j	–6				
k	BVE 24645-5m	5/4/1927	V 1245	DA 894*	
l	–6				
35a	B 24646-1	20/10/1920			MENDELSSOHN – *Bee's Wedding (Spinning Song), Song Without Words*, Op. 67, No. 4
b	–2m	3/11/1920	64921 5648 V 814	DA 370	
c	–3				
d	–4				
e	BVE 24646-5	21/3/1928			
f	–6				
g	–7				
h	–8				
i	–9	4/4/1928			
j	–10				
k	–11				
l	–12	11/4/1928			

Item	Matrix no.	Recording date	Catalogue no. of issued 'take' Victor	HMV	Title
m	–13h				
n	–14				
o	–15h				
p	–16				
q	–17				
r	–18	25/4/1928			
s	–19h				
t	–20				
u	–21m		V 1326	DA 996	
v	–22				
36a	B 24649–1	21/10/1920			LISZT – Au bord d'une source
37a	B 24650–1	21/10/1920			RACHMANINOFF – Étude-Tableau in G minor, Op. 33, No. 8
38a	B 24651–1	21/10/1920			PADEREWSKI – Minuet in G, Op. 14, No. 1
b	CVE 24651–1	19/3/1927			
c	–2				
d	–3				
e	–4	5/4/1927			
f	–5m		V 6731		
39a	B 24652–1	21/10/1920			RACHMANINOFF – Étude-Tableau in A minor, Op. 39, No. 6 (see also item 90)
40a	B 24902–1	21/1/1921			DEBUSSY – Children's Corner Suite – No. 3, Serenade for the Doll
b	–2	18/3/1921			

461

Item	Matrix no.	Recording date	Catalogue no. of issued 'take' Victor	HMV	Title
41a	C 24903–1m	21/1/1921	74679	05669	CHOPIN – Waltz in E flat, Op. 18
42a	B 24904–1h	21/1/1921	V 6259	DB 408	CHOPIN – Waltz in G flat, Op. 70, No. 1
b	–2	18/3/1921			
c	–3	2/4/1921			
d	–4				
e	–5		66007*	5663*	
43a	C 24905–1h	21/1/1921			RACHMANINOFF – Humoresque, Op. 10, No. 5
b	–2	18/3/1921			(see also item 185)
c	–3	5/4/1923			
d	–4				
44a	B 24906–1m	21/1/1921	64935	5653	DEBUSSY – Children's Corner Suite – No. 1
			V 813	DA 369	Dr. Gradus ad Parnassum
45a	B 25108–1	18/3/1921			MUSSORGSKY (transcribed Rachmaninoff) – Gopak
b	–2	24/10/1923			from Sorochinsky Fair
c	–3				
d	–4	23/12/1923			
e	–5				
f	–6				
g	–7	30/12/1924			
h	–8m				
i	–9				
j	–10m	13/4/1925	V 1161		

Item	Matrix no.	Recording date	Catalogue no. of issued 'take'		Title
			Victor	HMV	
46a	C 25649–1	12/10/1921			RACHMANINOFF – Prelude in C sharp minor, Op. 3, No. 2
47a	B 25650–1	12/10/1921			RACHMANINOFF – Prelude in C sharp minor, Op. 3, No. 2 (see also items 8 and 46)
b	–2	14/10/1921			
c	–3m		66016 V 814	5672 DA 370	
d	–4				
e	–5	17/10/1921			
f	–6				
g	–7	25/10/1921			
h	–8				
i	–9				
j	–10	13/12/1921			
k	–11				
l	–12				
m	–13		66016*		
n	–14	24/2/1922			
o	–15				
p	–16h				
q	–17				
r	BVE 25650–18	13/4/1925			
s	–19	21/3/1928			
t	–20				

Item	Matrix no.	Recording date	Catalogue no. of issued 'take'		Title
			Victor	HMV	
u	–21				
v	–22	4/4/1928			
w	–23m		V 1326	DA 996	
48a	C 25651-1	12/10/1921			RACHMANINOFF – Polka de W. R.
b	–2m		74728	05691	(see also item 10)
c	CVE 25651-3	21/3/1928	V 6260	DB 409	
d	–4h				
e	–5h	4/4/1928			
f	–6m		V 6857	DB 1279	
g	–7				
49a	B 25652-1	12/10/1921			DOHNÁNYI – Étude-Caprice in F minor,
b	–2				Op. 28, No. 6
c	–3	14/10/1921			
d	–4				
e	–5	25/10/1921	66059		
f	–6m		V 943		
50a	C 25653-1h	12/10/1921			KREISLER (transcribed Rachmaninoff) – Liebesleid
b	–2	17/10/1921			
c	–3				
d	–4	25/10/1921			

Item	Matrix no.	Recording date	Catalogue no. of issued 'take' Victor	HMV	Title
e	–5m		74723	05690	
51a	B 26134–1	24/2/1922	V 6259	DB 408	BIZET (transcribed Rachmaninoff) – Minuet from
b	–2				*L'Arlésienne*
c	–3m				
52a	C 27108–1	1/11/1922	66085	5677	CHOPIN (transcribed Liszt) – *The Maiden's Wish*
b	–2	4/11/1922	V 816	DA 372	(see also item 210)
c	–3				
d	–4				
53a	B 27109–1	1/11/1922			MOSZKOWSKI – *La Jongleuse*, Op. 52, No. 4
b	–2				
c	–3				
d	–4	4/11/1922			
e	–5				
f	–6	20/11/1922	66154		
g	–7m	6/3/1923	V 943		
54a	B 27110–1	1/11/1922			RACHMANINOFF – Serenade in B flat minor,
b	–2				Op. 3, No. 5 (see also item 159)
c	–3				
d	–4	4/11/1922			

465

Item	Matrix no.	Recording date	Catalogue no. of issued 'take' Victor	HMV	Title
e	–5m		66129 V 816	DA 372	TCHAIKOVSKY – Waltz in A flat, Op. 40, No. 8
55a	B 27117–1	4/11/1922			
b	–2	20/11/1922			
c	–3m	5/4/1923	66138* V 972	5718* DA 593	
56a	C 27118–1	4/11/1922			CHOPIN – Nocturne in F sharp major, Op. 15, No. 2
b	–2	20/11/1922			
c	–3	6/3/1923			
d	–4				
e	–5				
f	–6				
g	–7	5/4/1923			
h	–8m	27/12/1923	74885 V 6452	DB 845*	
i	–9h				
j	–10				
57a	B 27119–1	4/11/1922			SCHUMANN (transcribed Tausig) – Der Kontrabandiste (see also item 211)
b	–2	20/11/1922			
c	–3				
58a	C 27732–1	5/4/1923			STRAUSS (transcribed Schultz–Evler) – The Blue Danube
b	–2				
59a	B 28690–1	24/10/1923			TCHAIKOVSKY – Humoresque, Op. 10, No. 2

Item	Matrix no.	Recording date	Catalogue no. of issued 'take' Victor	HMV	Title
b					
c	-2				
	-3h	27/12/1923			
d	-4m		V 1051	DA 666*	
60a	B 28691-1	24/11/1923			HENSELT – *Étude* in F sharp, Op. 2, No. 6, *Si oiseau j'étais*
b	-2				
c	-3h				
d	-4h				
e	-5m	27/12/1923	66249 5739* V 1008	DA 613*	
f	-6				
g	-7h				
61a	B 29223-1	27/12/1923			CHOPIN – Prelude in E flat, Op. 28, No. 19
b	-2h				
62a	B 29224-1h	27/12/1923			LISZT – Spanish Rhapsody
b	-2h				
c	-3				
d	-4	18/3/1924			
e	-5				
f	-6				
63a	C 29233-1	31/12/1923			RACHMANINOFF – Concerto No. 2 in C minor, Op. 18 (with Philadelphia Orchestra/Leopold Stokowski) 2nd movement, Part 1 (see also items 72–74 and 109–118)
b	-2				
c	-3	3/1/1924			

Item	Matrix no.	Recording date	Catalogue no. of issued 'take'		Title
			Victor	HMV	
d	–4m		89166* V 8064	05790* DB 747*	2nd movement, Part 2
64a	C 29234–1	31/12/1923			
b	–2				
c	–3m	3/1/1924	89167* V 8064	05791* DB 747*	2nd movement, Part 3
d	–4				
65a	C 29235–1	31/12/1923			
b	–2				
c	–3	3/1/1924			
d	–4m		89168* V 8065	05792* DB 748*	3rd movement, Part 1
66a	C 29236–1	31/12/1923			
b	–2				
c	–3m	3/1/1924	89169* V 8065	05793* DB 748*	3rd movement, Part 2
d	–4				
67a	C 29251–1	3/1/1924			
b	–2m		89170* V 8066	05794* DB 749*	3rd movement, Part 3
68a	C 29252–1	3/1/1924			
b	–2m		89171* V 8066	05795* DB 749*	

Item	Matrix no.	Recording date	Catalogue no. of issued 'take' Victor	HMV	Title
69a	C 29670–1	18/3/1924			LISZT – *Liebestraum* No. 3 in D flat
b	–2				
c	–3				
70a	C 29671–1	18/3/1924			CHOPIN – Scherzo No. 3, in C sharp minor, Op. 39
b	–2h				Part 1
71a	C 29678–1h	18/3/1924			Part 2
b	–2				
72a	C 31395–1h	22/12/1924			RACHMANINOFF – Concerto No. 2 in C minor, Op. 18
b	–2				(with Philadelphia Orchestra/Leopold Stokowski)
					1st movement, Part 1 (see also items 62–68 and 109–118)
73a	C 31396–1h	22/12/1924			1st movement, Part 2
b	–2				
74a	B 31397–1	22/12/1924			1st movement, Part 3
b	–2				
c	–3				
75a	B 31557–1	30/12/1924			SAINT-SAËNS (transcribed Siloti) – *The Swan*
b	–2				
c	–3				
76a	B 31558–1	30/12/1924			GLUCK (transcribed Sgambati) – *Mélodie* from *Orfeo*
b	BVE 31558–2	13/4/1925			
c	–3				
d	–4m	14/5/1925	V 1124	DA 719	

469

Item	Matrix no.	Recording date	Catalogue no. of issued 'take' Victor HMV	Title
e	–5			
77a	B 31564–1	31/12/1924		SCHUBERT (transcribed Liszt) – Das Wandern
b	–2			
c	–3			
d	BVE 31564–4m	14/4/1925	V 1161	
e	–5h			
78a	CVE 32506–1	13/4/1925		BEETHOVEN – Thirty-two Variations in C minor
b	–2	14/5/1925		Part 1
c	–3			
d	–4m		V 6544	
79a	CVE 32507–1m	13/4/1925	V 6544	Part 2
b	–2h			
80a	CVE 32508–1	13/4/1925		LISZT – Polonaise No. 2 in E major
b	–2m	14/4/1925	V 6504	Part 1
c	–3h			
81a	CVE 32509–1h	13/4/1925	V 6504	Part 2
b	–2m			
c	–3h	14/4/1925		
82a	CVE 32510–1h	13/4/1925		CHOPIN – Ballade No. 3 in A flat, Op. 47
b	–2h			Part 1
83a	CVE 32511–1h	13/4/1925		Part 2
b	–2h			
84a	CVE 34143–1	14/12/1925		BACH – Saraband from Clavier Partita

Item	Matrix no.	Recording date	Catalogue no. of issued 'take' Victor HMV	Title
b	-2			No. 4 in D, BWV 828
c	-3m	16/12/1925	V 6621 DB 1016	
d	-4			
85a	CVE 34144-1	14/12/1925		SCHUBERT – Impromptu in A flat, No. 4 from D.899
b	-2			
c	-3	29/12/1925		
d	-4			
e	-5m		V 6621 DB 1016	
86a	BVE 34145-1	14/12/1925	— —	SCHUBERT (transcribed Rachmaninoff) – *Wobin?* (*The Brooklet*)
b	-2	16/12/1925		
c	-4			
d	-5			
e	-6	29/12/1925		
f	-7m		V 1196 DA 939*	
g	-8			
87a	BVE 34146-1	14/12/1925		LISZT – *Gnomenreigen*
b	-2			
c	-3m	16/12/1925	V 1184 DA 827	
d	-4			
88a	BVE 34154-1	16/12/1925		KREISLER (transcribed Rachmaninoff) – *Liebesfreud* (see also item 209) Part 1
b	-2			
c	-3m	29/12/1925	V 1142 DA 786	

Item	Matrix no.	Recording date	Catalogue no. of issued 'take' Victor HMV	Title
89a	BVE 34155–1	16/12/1925		Part 2
b	–2			
c	–3m	29/12/1925	V 1142 DA 786	
90a	BVE 34156–1m	16/12/1925	V 1184 DA 827	RACHMANINOFF – *Étude-Tableau* in A minor, Op. 39, No. 6
b	–2			(see also item 39)
91a	BVE test–1	22/2/1926		RACHMANINOFF – Song, *Quickly, quickly, from my cheeks* Nadezhda Plevitskaya (mez-sop.) acc. by Rachmaninoff
b	–2			
92a	BVE 37453–1	19/3/1927		MENDELSSOHN – *Étude* in F major, Op. 104, No. 2
b	–2	5/4/1927		
c	–3			
d	–4m		V 1266 DA 925*	
93a	BVE 37454–1	19/3/1927		MENDELSSOHN -- *Étude* in A minor, Op. 104, No. 3
b	–2			
c	–3	5/4/1927		
d	–4m		V 1266 DA 925*	
e	–5			
94a	BVE 37455–1	19/3/1927		CHOPIN – Waltz in A flat, Op. 64, No. 3
b	–2			(see also item 4)
c	–4	5/4/1927		
d	–5			
e	–6m		V 1245 DA 894*	
95a	CVE 37465–1	5/4/1927		CHOPIN – Nocturne in E flat, Op. 9, No. 2

Item	Matrix no.	Recording date	Catalogue no. of issued 'take' Victor HMV	Title
b	-2			
c	-3m		V 6731	
96a	CVE 37466-1m	5/4/1927	V 6636 DB 1140	STRAUSS (transcribed Tausig) – *One Lives But Once,* Waltz, Part 1
b	-2			
c	-3	5/4/1927		Part 2
97a	CVE 37467-1			
b	-2			
c	-3m		V 6636 DB 1140	
98a	BVE 39387-1† = 24638-8m	14/12/1925	V 1196 DA 939*	BEETHOVEN (transcribed Rubinstein) – *Turkish March from Ruins of Athens*
b	39387-2 = 24638-9			
99a	CVE 41759-1	28/2/1928		BEETHOVEN – Sonata No. 8 in G major, for violin and piano, Op. 30, No. 3 (with Fritz Kreisler) 1st movement, Part 1
b	-2			
c	-3			
d	-4	29/2/1928		
e	-5			

† The anomaly of this isolated matrix number is explained by the recording's being ambiguously listed in the recording book as 'Turkish March' and hence confused with Mozart's *Turkish March*, which Rachmaninoff had recorded earlier (item 29). The two takes were thus wrongly listed as further versions of that work, and it was not until two years after the recording session that the error was discovered. A note in the files, dated 7 November 1927, assigned the recording a new matrix number, out of order from all Rachmaninoff's other recordings, under which it was at last published.

Item	Matrix no.	Recording date	Catalogue no. of issued 'take' Victor HMV	Title
f	−6			
g	−7	22/3/1928		
h	−8m	28/2/1928	V 8163 DB 1463	1st movement, Part 2
100a	CVE 41760−1			
b	−2			
c	−3			
d	−4m	22/3/1928	V 8163 DB 1463	
e	−5			
101a	CVE 41761−1	28/2/1928		2nd movement
b	−2			
c	−3	29/2/1928		
d	−4			
e	−5m			
f	−6	22/3/1928	V 8164 DB 1464	
g	−7			
h	−8			
102a	CVE 41762−1	28/2/1928		3rd movement
b	−2			
c	−3			
d	−4	29/2/1928		
e	−5			
f	−6			
g	−7m	22/3/1928	V 8164 DB 1464	

Item	Matrix no.	Recording date	Catalogue no. of issued 'take' Victor HMV	Title
h	−8			
103a	CL 4511-1	14 and 15/9/1928		GRIEG – Sonata No. 3, in C minor, for Violin and Piano, Op. 45 (with Fritz Kreisler)
b	−2			
c	−3			1st movement, Part 1
d	−4			
e	−5m		V 8112 DB 1259	
104a	CL 4512-1			1st movement, Part 2
b	−2			
c	−3			
d	−4			
e	−5m		V 8112 DB 1259	
105a	CL 4513-1			2nd movement, Part 1
b	−2			
c	−3			
d	−4			
e	−5m		V 8113 DB 1260	
106a	CL 4514-1			2nd movement, Part 2
b	−2			
c	−3			
d	−4			
e	−5m		V 8113 DB 1260	
107a	CL 4515-1			3rd movement, Part 1

Item	Matrix no.	Recording date	Catalogue no. of issued 'take'		Title
			Victor	HMV	
b	−2				
c	−3				
d	−4				
e	−5				
f	−6m		V 8114	DB 1261	3rd movement, Part 2
108a	CL 4516−1				Items 103–108 in Victor set M 45. Auto: V 8106–08, DB 7214–16
b	−2		V 8114	DB 1261	
c	−3				
d	−4				
e	−5m		V 8114	DB 1261	
109a	CVE 48963−1m	10/4/1929	V 8148	DB 1333	RACHMANINOFF – Concerto No. 2, in C minor, Op. 18 (with Philadelphia Orchestra/Leopold Stokowski) (see also items 62–68 and 72–74) 1st movement, Part 1
b	−2				
c	−3				
110a	CVE 48964−1m	10/4/1929	V 8148	DB 1333	1st movement, Part 2
b	−2				
111a	CVE 48965−1m	10/4/1929	V 8149	DB 1334	1st movement, Part 3
b	−2				
112a	CVE 48966−1m	10/4/1929	V 8149	DB 1334	2nd movement, Part 1
b	−2				
113a	CVE 48967−1	10/4/1929	V 8150	DB 1335	2nd movement, Part 2
b	−2				
c	−3m				

Item	Matrix no.	Recording date	Catalogue no. of issued 'take' Victor	HMV	Title
114a	CVE 48968–1	13/4/1929			2nd movement, Part 3
b	–2m		V 8150	DB 1335	
c	–3				
115a	CVE 48969–1m	13/4/1929	V 8151	DB 1336	2nd movement, Part 4
b	–2				
116a	CVE 48970–1	13/4/1929	V 8151	DB 1336	3rd movement, Part 1
b	–2m				
117a	CVE 48971–1	13/4/1929	V 8152	DB 1337	3rd movement, Part 2
b	–2m				
c	–3				
118a	CVE 48972–1	13/4/1929			3rd movement, Part 3
b	–2m		V 8152	DB 1337	
c	–3				

Items 109–118 in Victor set M 58.
Auto: V 8153–57, DB 7008–12 (up to 1933), DB 7205–09

RACHMANINOFF – *Isle of the Dead*, Op. 29
(Philadelphia Orchestra conducted by Rachmaninoff)

Item	Matrix no.	Recording date	Catalogue no. of issued 'take' Victor	HMV	Title
119a	CVE 48973–1	15/4/1929			Part 1
b	–2				
c	–3				
d	–4	20/4/1929	V 7219	DB 2011	
e	–5m				
120a	CVE 48974–1	15/4/1929			Part 2
b	–2				
c	–3	20/4/1929	V 7219	DB 2011	
d	–4m				

Item	Matrix no.	Recording date	Catalogue no. of issued 'take' Victor	HMV	Title
121a	CVE 48975–1	15/4/1929			Part 3
b	–2				
c	–3	20/4/1929			
d	–4m				
122a	CVE 48976–1	15/4/1929	V 7220	DB 2012	Part 4
b	–2				
c	–3				
d	–4	20/4/1929			
e	–5m			DB 2012	
123a	CVE 48977–1	15/4/1929	V 7220	DB 2012	Part 5
b	–2				
c	–3	20/4/1929			
d	–4m			DB 2013	
124a	CVE 48978–1	20/4/1929	V 7221	DB 2013	
b	–2		V 7221	DB 2013	
c	–3m		V 17430		
125a	CVE 49280–1	20/12/1928			1st movement, Part 1
b	–2				
c	–3				
d	–4	21/12/1928			
e	–5m		V 8216	DB 1465	
126a	CVE 49281–1	20/12/1928			1st movement, Part 2

RACHMANINOFF – *Vocalise*, Op. 34, No. 12
(Philadelphia Orchestra conducted by Rachmaninoff)
Items 119–124 in Victor set M 75.
Auto: V 7222–24, DB 7414–16

SCHUBERT – Sonata in A major, for violin and piano
(*Duo*), D.574 (with Fritz Kreisler)

478

Item	Matrix no.	Recording date	Catalogue no. of issued 'take' Victor	HMV	Title
b	–2				
c	–3				
d	–4	21/12/1928			
e	–5m		V 8216	DB 1465	2nd movement, Part 1
127a	CVE 49282–1	20/12/1928	V 8217	DB 1466	
b	–2m				
c	–3	21/12/1928			2nd movement, Part 2
128a	CVE 49283–1	20/12/1928			
b	–2				
c	–3				
d	–4m	21/12/1928	V 8217	DB 1466	
129a	CVE 49284–1	20/12/1928			3rd movement, Part 1
b	–2				
c	–3m	21/12/1928	V 8218	DB 1467	
d	–4	21/12/1928			
130a	CVE 49285–1	20/12/1928			3rd movement, Part 2,
b	–2				Items 125–130 in Victor set M 107.
c	–3				Auto: V 8213–15, DB 7205–07
d	–4m	21/12/1928	V 8218	DB 1467	
131a	CVE 51089–1	9/4/1929			SCHUMANN – *Carnaval*, Op. 9
b	–2				Part 1
c	–3	10/4/1929			
d	–4				

479

Item	Matrix no.	Recording date	Catalogue no. of issued 'take' Victor	HMV	Title
e	−5				
f	−6	12/4/1929			
g	−7m		V 7184	DB 1413	
h	−8				
132a	CVE 51090–1	9/4/1929	V 7184	DB 1413	Part 2
b	−2m				
c	−3	10/4/1929			
d	−4	12/4/1929			
e	−5				
133a	CVE 51091–1	9/4/1929			Part 3
b	−2				
c	−3m	10/4/1929	V 7185	DB 1414	
134a	CVE 51092–1	9/4/1929			Part 4
b	−2				
c	−3m	10/4/1929	V 7185	DB 1414	
d	−4	10/4/1929			
135a	CVE 51093–1	9/4/1929			Part 5
b	−2				
c	−3m	10/4/1929	V 7186	DB 1415	
136a	CVE 51094–1	9/4/1929			Part 6
b	−2				
c	−3m	10/4/1929	V 7186	DB 1415	
137a	CVE 51804–1	12/4/1929			CHOPIN – Sonata No. 2 in B flat minor, Op. 35

Items 131–136 in Victor set M 70.
Auto: V 7187–89, DB 7327–29

Item	Matrix no.	Recording date	Catalogue no. of issued 'take' Victor	HMV	Title
b	-2				(Funeral March) 1st movement, Part 1 (see also item 140)
138a	BVE 51805-1	16/4/1929			RIMSKY-KORSAKOV (transcribed Rachmaninoff) – Flight of the Bumble Bee, from Tsar Sultan
b	-2				
c	-3				
d	-4				
e	-5				
139a	BVE 51806-1	16/4/1929			SCRIABIN – Prelude in F sharp minor, Op. 11, No. 8
b	-2				
140a	BVE 59408-1	18/2/1930	V 1489	DA 1186	CHOPIN – Sonata No. 2 in B flat minor, Op. 35 (Funeral March) (see also item 137)
b	-2m				1st movement, Part 1
c	-3	19/2/1930			
141a	BVE 59409-1	18/2/1930	V 1489	DA 1186	1st movement, Part 2
b	-2m				
c	-3	19/2/1930			
142a	BVE 59410-1	18/2/1930	V 1490	DA 1187	2nd movement, Part 1
b	-2m				
143a	BVE 59411-1	18/2/1930	V 1490	DA 1187	2nd movement, Part 2
b	-2m				
144a	BVE 59412-1	18/2/1930	V 1492	DA 1189	4th movement
b	-2m				
145a	BVE 59413-1	18/2/1930	V 1491	DA 1188	3rd movement, Part 1
b	-2m				

Item	Matrix no.	Recording date	Catalogue no. of issued 'take' Victor	HMV	Title
146a	BVE 59414–1m	18/2/1930	V 1491	DA 1188	3rd movement, Part 2
b	–2				Items 140–147 in Victor set M 95. Auto: V 1493–96, DA 7004–07 (up to 1933), DA 7027–30
c	–3				
147a	BVE 59415–1	18/2/1930	V 1492	DA 1189	CHOPIN – Waltz in E minor, Op. posth.
b	–2				
c	–3m				
148a	CS 87066–1m	24/12/1934	V 8553	DB 2426	RACHMANINOFF – Rhapsody on a Theme of Paganini, Op. 43 (with Philadelphia Orchestra/Leopold Stokowski) Part 1
	–1A				
b	–2				
	–2A				
149a	CS 87067–1m	24/12/1934	V 8553	DB 2426	Part 2
	–1A				
b	–2				
	–2A				
150a	CS 87068–1m	24/12/1934	V 8554	DB 2427	Part 3
	–1A				
b	–2				
	–2A				
151a	CS 87069–1m	24/12/1934	V 8554	DB 2427	Part 4
	–1A				
b	–2				
	–2A				

Item	Matrix no.	Recording date	Catalogue no. of issued 'take'		Title
			Victor	HMV	
152a	CS 87070–1m	24/12/1934	V 8555	DB 2428	Part 5
	–1A				
b	–2				
	–2A				
153a	CS 87071–1m	24/12/1934	V 8555	DB 2428	Part 6
	–1A				
b	–2				Items 148–153 in Victor set M250.
	–2A				Auto: V 8556–58, DB 7812–14
154a	CS 87283–1	8/1/1935			MENDELSSOHN (transcribed Rachmaninoff) – Scherzo
b	–2				from *A Midsummer Night's Dream*
c	–3				
d	–4				
e	–5				
f	–6m	23/12/1935		DB 3146	
g	–7				
	–7A				
155a	CS 87284–1	8/1/1935			BACH (transcribed Rachmaninoff) – Prelude from Partita
b	–2				No. 3 in E major for Solo Violin, BWV 1006
c	–3h				(see also item 205)
d	–4				
e	–5	10/1/1936			
	–5A				
f	–6				

Item	Matrix no.	Recording date	Catalogue no. of issued 'take' Victor HMV	Title
g	−6A			
	−7			
	−7A			
h	−8			
	−8A			
156a	CS 98393−1	23/12/1935		HANDEL – Suite No. 5, Air and Variations
b	−1A	3/1/1936		(*The Harmonious Blacksmith*)
	−2			
	−2A			
c	−3m		DB 3146	
	−3A			
157a	BS 98394−1m	23/12/1935	V 1761 DA 1522	BORODIN – Scherzo in A flat
	−1A			
158a	BS 98395−1	23/12/1935		CHOPIN – Mazurka in A minor, Op. 68, No. 2
	−1A			
159a	BS 98396−1	23/12/1935		RACHMANINOFF – Serenade in B flat minor, Op. 3,
b	−1A			No. 5 (see also item 54)
	−2	3/1/1936		
	−2A			
c	−3m		V 1762 DA 1522	
	−3A			
d	−4			
	−4A			

Item	Matrix no.	Recording date	Catalogue no. of issued 'take' Victor	HMV	Title
160a	CS 045621–1	4/12/1939			RACHMANINOFF – Concerto No. 1 in F sharp minor, Op. 1 1st movement, Part 1
	–1A				
b	–2m		V 18374	DB 5706	
	–2A				
c	–3	24/2/1940			
	–3A				
161a	CS 045622–1	4/12/1939			1st movement, Part 2
	–1A				
b	–2				
	–2A				
c	–3m	24/2/1940	V 18374	DB 5706	
	–3A				
162a	CS 045623–1	4/12/1939			1st movement, Part 3
	–1A				
b	–2m		V 18375	DB 5707	
	–2A				
163a	CS 045624–1m	4/12/1939	V 18375	DB 5707	2nd movement
	–1A				
164a	CS 045625–1	4/12/1939			3rd movement, Part 1
	–1A				
b	–2	24/2/1940			
	–2A				

Item	Matrix no.	Recording date	Victor	HMV	Title
c	−3m		V 18376	DB 5708	3rd movement, Part 2
	−3A				
165a	CS 045626−1	4/12/1939			
	−1A				
b	−2				
	−2A				
c	−3m	24/2/1940	V 18376	DB 5708	
	−3A				Items 160–165 in Victor set M 865. Auto: V 18377–79, DB8806–08.
166a	CS 045627−1m	4/12/1939	V 17481	DB 5709	RACHMANINOFF − Concerto No. 3 in D minor, Op. 30 (with Philadelphia Orchestra/Eugene Ormandy)
	−1A				1st movement, Part 1
167a	CS 045628−1m	4/12/1939	V 17481	DB 5709	1st movement, Part 2
	−1A				
168a	CS 045629−1m	4/12/1939	V 17482	DB 5710	1st movement, Part 3
	−1A				
169a	CS 045630−1m	4/12/1939	V 17482	DB 5710	1st movement, Part 4
	−1A				
170a	CS 045631−1m	4/12/1939	V 17483	DB 5711	2nd movement, Part 1
	−1A				
171a	CS 045632−1	4/12/1939	V 17483	DB 5711	2nd movement, Part 2
	−1A				
b	−2	24/2/1940			
	−2Am		V 17483	DB 5711	

Item	Matrix no.	Recording date	Catalogue no. of issued 'take' Victor	HMV	Title	
172a	CS 045633-1m	4/12/1939	V 17484	DB 5712	3rd movement, Part 1	
	-1A					
173a	CS 045634-1	4/12/1939			3rd movement, Part 2	
	-1A					
b	-2	24/ 2/1940				
	-2A					
c	-3m		V 17484	DB 5712		
	-3A					
174a	CS 045635-1m	4/12/1939	VS 17485	DBS 5713	3rd movement, Part 3	Items 166–174 in Victor set M 710. Auto: V 17486–90, DB 8809–13
	-1A					
175a	CS 045636-1	11/12/1939			RACHMANINOFF – Symphony No. 3 in A minor, Op. 44 (Philadelphia Orchestra conducted by Rachmaninoff) 1st movement, Part 1	
	-1A					
b	-2m		V 17426	DB 5780		
	-2A					
176a	CS 045637-1m	11/12/1939	V 17426	DB 5780	1st movement, Part 2	
	-1A					
177a	CS 045638-1	11/12/1939			1st movement, Part 3	
	-1A					
b	-2m		V 17427	DB 5781		
	-2A					
178a	CS 045639-1m	11/12/1939	V 17427	DB 5781	2nd movement, Part 1	
	-1A					
179a	CS 045640-1	11/12/1939			2nd movement, Part 2	

Item	Matrix no.	Recording date	Catalogue no. of issued 'take' Victor	HMV	Title
b	−1A −2m −2A		V 17428	DB 5782	
180a	CS 045641–1m −1A	11/12/1939	V 17428	DB 5782	2nd movement, Part 3
181a	CS 045642–1m −1A	11/12/1939	V 17429	DB 5783	3rd movement, Part 1
182a	CS 045643–1m −1A	11/12/1939	V 17429	DB 5783	3rd movement, Part 2
183a	CS 045644–1m −1A	11/12/1939	V 17430	DBS 5784	3rd movement, Part 3
184a	BS 048174–1	18/3/1940			RACHMANINOFF – *Mélodie* in E major, Op. 3, No. 3
b	−2				
c	−3	9/4/1940			
d	−4 −4Am				
185a	BS 048175–1 −1A	18/3/1940	V 2123	DA 1787	RACHMANINOFF – *Humoresque*, Op. 10, No. 5 (see also item 43)
b	−2m	9/4/1940	V 2123	DA 1771	
c	−3 −3A				
186a	BS 048176–1m	18/3/1940	V 2124	DA 1771	RACHMANINOFF – *Moment musical* in E flat minor, Op. 16, No. 2
b	−2				

Items 175–183 and 124 in Victor set M 712.
Auto: V 17431–35.
Items 175–183 only on auto DB 8844–48

Item	Matrix no.	Recording date	Victor	HMV	Title
	–2A				
187a	BS 048177–1m	18/3/1940	V 2124	DA 1772	RACHMANINOFF – Prelude in G flat, Op. 23, No. 10
	–1A				
188a	BS 048178–1m	18/3/1940	V 2125	DA 1772	RACHMANINOFF – Prelude in E major, Op. 32, No. 3
	–1A				
189a	BS 048179–1	18/3/1940	V 2125	DA 1787	RACHMANINOFF – Prelude in F major, Op. 32, No. 7, and Prelude in F minor, Op. 32, No. 6
b	–2m				
	–2A				
190a	BS 048182–1	18/3/1940	V 2126	DA 1788	RACHMANINOFF – Étude-Tableau in C major, Op. 33, No. 2
b	–2m				
	–2A				
191a	BS 048183–1	18/3/1940	V 2126	DA 1788	RACHMANINOFF – Étude-Tableau in E flat major, Op. 33, No. 7
b	–2m				
	–2A				
192a	BS 048184–1	18/3/1940	V 2127	DA 1789*	RACHMANINOFF – Daisies, Op. 38, No. 3
	–1A				
b	–2m				
	–2A				
c	–3	9/4/1940			
193a	BS 048185–1	18/3/1940	V 2127	DA 1789*	RACHMANINOFF – Oriental Sketch
b	–2m				
	–2A				

Items 184–193 in
Victor set M 722

Item	Matrix no.	Recording date	Catalogue no. of issued 'take' Victor	HMV	Title
					RACHMANINOFF – Concerto No. 4 in G minor, Op. 40 (with Philadelphia Orchestra/Eugene Ormandy)
194a	CS 071277–1	20/12/1941			1st movement, Part 1
b	–2m		V 11–8611	DB 6284*	
	–2A				
195a	CS 071278–1	20/12/1941			1st movement, Part 2
b	–2m		V 11–8611	DB 6284*	
	–2A				
196a	CS 071279–1	20/12/1941			1st movement, Part 3
	–1Am		V 11–8612	DB 6285*	
197a	CS 071280–1	20/12/1941			2nd movement, Part 1
	–1Am		V 11–8612	DB 6285*	
b	–2				
	–2A				
198a	CS 071281–1m	20/12/1941	V 11–8613	DB 6286*	2nd movement, Part 2
	–1A				
199a	CS 071282–1m	20/12/1941	V 11–8613	DB 6286*	3rd movement, Part 1
	–1A				
200a	CS 071283–1	20/12/1941	V 11–8614	DB 6287*	3rd movement, Part 2
	–1A				
201a	CS 071284–1m	20/12/1941	V 11–8614	DB 6287*	3rd movement, Part 3
	–1A				

Items 194–201 in Victor set M 972.
Auto: V 11–8615–18

Item	Matrix no.	Recording date	Catalogue no. of issued 'take' Victor	HMV	Title
202a	PCS 072124–1	25/2/1942			MOZART – Sonata No. 11 in A major, K. 331; 1st movement, Theme and Variations (see also item 2)
203a	PCS 072125–1	25/2/1942			SCHUMANN – *Novellette* in F sharp minor, Op. 21, No. 8
204a	PCS 072126–1	25/2/1942			Part 1
205a	PCS 072127–1	25/2/1942			Part 2
b	–2	26/2/1942			
c	–3m	27/2/1942	V 11–8607		BACH (transcribed Rachmaninoff) – Partita No. 3 in E major for Solo Violin, BWV 1006
206a	PCS 072128–1	25/2/1942			Prelude (see also item 155)
b	–2m	26/2/1942	V 11–8607		Gavotte and Gigue
c	–3				
207a	PCS 072131–1	26/2/1942			TCHAIKOVSKY (transcribed Rachmaninoff) – *Lullaby*, Op. 16, No. 1
208a	PCS 072132–1	26/2/1942			RACHMANINOFF – *Lilacs*, Op. 21, No. 5 (see also item 23)
209a	PCS 072133–1m	26/2/1942	V 11–8728		KREISLER (transcribed Rachmaninoff) – *Liebesfreud* (see also items 88–89)
210a	PCS 072136–1m	27/2/1942	V 11–8593		CHOPIN (transcribed Liszt) – *The Maiden's Wish* (see also item 52)
211a	PCS 072137–1m	27/2/1942	V 11–8593		SCHUMANN (transcribed Tausig) – *Der Kondrabandiste* (see also item 57) and CHOPIN (transcribed Liszt) – *The Return Home*
212a	PCS 072138–1m	27/2/1942	V 11–8728		SCHUBERT (transcribed Liszt) – *Ständchen (Serenade)*

Item	Matrix no.	Recording date	Catalogue no. of issued 'take' Victor HMV	Title
Other recordings				
213a	Bell Telephone	3/12/1931		WEBER – *Perpetuum mobile* (*Rondo* from Sonata in C major, Op. 24)
214a	Bell Telephone	3/12/1931		LISZT – Ballade No. 2 in B minor, G.171
215a	Private	1933		FOLK SONG: *Bublichki* (Rachmaninoff accompanying friends at a party)
216a	Private	1938		RACHMANINOFF – *Italian Polka* (with Natalya Rachmaninoff, at a party)

Recording sessions

Session	Venue	Date	Items recorded
EDISON			
1	New York	18/4/1919	1a, 1b, 1c, 2a, 2b, 2c
2	"	19/4/1919	3a, 3b, 3c, 4a, 4b, 4c
3	"	23/4/1919	5a, 5b, 5c, 6a, 6b, 6c, 7a, 7b, 7c
4	"	24/4/1919	8a, 8b, 8c, 9a, 9b, 9c, 10a, 10b, 10c
VICTOR			
5	Camden	26/4/1920	11a, 12a, 13a, 13b
6	"	3/5/1920	12b, 12c, 14a, 14b, 15a, 16a, 17a, 18a, 18b, 19a, 20a
7	"	4/5/1920	12d, 13c, 18c
8	"	17/5/1920	12e, 15b, 15c, 18d, 21a, 21b, 22a, 22b, 23a
9	"	2/7/1920	24a, 24b, 25a, 25b, 25c
10	"	20/10/1920	26a, 27a, 28a, 28b, 29a, 29b, 30a, 31a, 32a, 33a, 34a, 34b, 34c, 34d, 35a
11	"	21/10/1920	26b, 28c, 30b, 31b, 33b, 36a, 37a, 38a, 39a
12	New York	3/11/1920	13d, 30c, 30d, 31c, 31d, 33c, 33d, 35b, 35c, 35d
13	"	21/1/1921	25d, 31e, 33e, 33f, 40a, 41a, 42a, 43a, 44a
14	"	18/3/1921	13e, 13f, 25e, 25f, 40b, 42b, 43b, 45a
15	"	2/4/1921	13g, 13h, 13i, 24c, 25g, 25h, 42c, 42d, 42e
16	"	12/10/1921	14c, 14d, 46a, 47a, 48a, 48b, 49a, 49b, 50a
17	"	14/10/1921	47b, 47c, 47d, 49c, 49d
18	"	17/10/1921	47e, 47f, 50b, 50c
19	"	25/10/1921	47g, 47h, 47i, 49e, 49f, 50d, 50e

Session	Venue	Date	Items recorded
20	"	13/12/1921	47j, 47k, 47l, 47m
21	"	24/2/1922	23b, 23c, 47n, 47o, 47p, 47q, 51a, 51b, 51c
22	Camden	1/11/1922	52a, 52b, 53a, 53b, 53c, 54a, 54b, 54c
23	"	4/11/1922	52c, 52d, 53d, 53e, 54d, 54e, 55a, 56a, 57a
24	"	20/11/1922	20b, 30e, 53f, 55b, 56b, 57b, 57c
25	"	6/3/1923	32b, 53g, 56c, 56d, 56e, 56f
26	"	5/4/1923	24d, 24e, 43c, 43d, 55c, 56g, 58a, 58b
27	"	24/10/1923	13j, 13k, 13l, 23d, 23e, 23f, 45b, 45c, 59a, 59b
28	"	25/10/1923	23g
29	"	24/11/1923	60a, 60b, 60c, 60d
30	"	23/12/1923	45d, 45e, 45f
31	"	27/12/1923	23h, 23i, 33g, 33h, 56h, 56i, 56j, 59c, 59d, 60e, 60f, 60g, 61a, 61b, 62a, 62b, 62c
32	"	28/12/1923	23j, 23k, 23l
33	Trinity Church, Camden	31/12/1923	63a, 63b, 64a, 64b, 65a, 65b, 66a, 66b
34	"	3/1/1924	63c, 63d, 64c, 64d, 65c, 65d, 66c, 66d, 67a, 67b, 68a, 68b
35	Camden	18/3/1924	62d, 62e, 62f, 69a, 69b, 69c, 70a, 70b, 71a, 71b
36	Trinity Church, Camden	22/12/1924	72a, 72b, 73a, 73b, 74a, 74b, 74c
37	Camden	30/12/1924	45g, 45h, 45i, 75a, 75b, 75c, 76a
38	"	31/12/1924	34e, 34f, 77a, 77b, 77c

Session	Venue	Date	Items recorded
ELECTRICAL RECORDINGS			
39	Camden	13/ 4/1925	29c, 29d, 34g, 34h, 45j, 47r, 76b, 76c, 78a, 79a, 79b, 80a, 80b, 81a, 81b, 82a, 82b, 83a, 83b
40	"	14/ 4/1925	77d, 77e, 80c, 81c
41	"	14/ 5/1925	29e, 29f, 29g, 29h, 76d, 76e, 78b, 78c, 78d
42	New York	14/12/1925	29i (=98a), 29j (=98b), 84a, 84b, 85a, 85b, 86a, 86b, 87a, 87b
43	"	16/12/1925	84c, 84d, 86c, 86d, 87c, 87d, 88a, 88b, 89a, 89b, 90a, 90b
44	"	29/12/1925	85c, 85d, 85e, 86e, 86f, 86g, 88c, 89c
45	"	22/2/1926	91a, 91b
46	"	19/3/1927	34i, 34j, 38b, 38c, 38d, 92a, 92b, 93a, 93b, 94a, 94b
47	"	5/4/1927	34k, 34l, 38e, 38f, 92c, 92d, 93c, 93d, 93e, 94c, 94d, 94e, 95a, 95b, 95c, 96a, 96b, 96c, 97a, 97b, 97c
48	"	28/2/1928	99a, 99b, 99c, 100a, 100b, 100c, 101a, 101b, 102a, 102b, 102c
49	"	29/2/1928	99d, 99e, 99f, 101c, 101d, 101e, 102d, 102e, 102f
50	"	21/3/1928	17b, 17c, 17d, 35e, 35f, 35g, 35h, 47s, 47t, 47u, 48c, 48d
51	"	22/3/1928	99g, 99h, 100d, 100e, 101f, 101g, 101h, 102g, 102h
52	"	4/4/1928	17e, 17f, 35i, 35j, 35k, 47v, 47w, 48e, 48f, 48g
53	"	11/4/1928	17g, 17h, 35l, 35m, 35n, 35o, 35p, 35q
54	"	25/4/1928	35r, 35s, 35t, 35u, 35v
55	Berlin	14/9/1928 and	103a, 103b, 103c, 103d, 103e, 104a, 104b, 104c, 104d, 104e, 105a, 105b, 105c, 105d, 105e, 106a, 106b, 106c, 106d, 106e, 107a, 107b, 107c, 107d,
56	"	15/9/1928	107e, 107f, 108a, 108b, 108c, 108d, 108e

Session	Venue	Date	Items recorded											
57	New York	20/12/1928	125a,	125b,	125c,	126a,	126b,	126c,	127a,	127b,	128a,	128b,	128c,	129a,
			129b,	129c,	130a,	130b,	130c							
58	"	21/12/1928	125d,	125e,	126d,	126e,	127c,	128d,	129d,	130d				
59	Camden	9/4/1929	131a,	131b,	132a,	132b,	133a,	133b,	134a,	134b,	134c,	135a,	135b,	136a,
			136b											
60	Academy of Music, Philadelphia	10/4/1929	109a,	109b,	109c,	110a,	110b,	111a,	111b,	112a,	112b,	113a,	113b,	113c
61	Camden	"	131c,	131d,	131e,	132c,	133c,	134d,	135c,	136c				
62	"	12/4/1929	131f,	131g,	131h,	132d,	132e,	137a,	137b					
63	Academy of Music, Philadelphia	13/4/1929	114a,	114b,	114c,	115a,	115b,	116a,	116b,	117a,	117b,	117c,	118a,	118b,
			118c											
64	Camden	15/4/1929	119a,	119b,	119c,	120a,	120b,	121a,	121b,	122a,	122b,	122c,	123a,	123b
65	"	16/4/1929	138a,	138b,	138c,	138d,	138e,	139a,	139b					
66	"	20/4/1929	119d,	119e,	120c,	120d,	121c,	121d,	122d,	122e,	123c,	123d,	124a,	124b,
			124c											
67	"	18/2/1930	140a,	140b,	141a,	141b,	142a,	142b,	143a,	143b,	144a,	144b,	145a,	145b,
			146a,	146b,	146c,	147a,	147b,	147c						
68	"	19/2/1930	140c,	141c										

BELL TELEPHONE

69	Academy of Music, Philadelphia	3/12/1931	213a,	214a
	[Party	1933	215a]	

Session	Venue	Date	Items recorded
VICTOR			
70	Trinity Church, Camden	24/12/1934	148a, 148b, 149a, 149b, 150a, 150b, 151a, 151b, 152a, 152b, 153a, 153b
71	New York, Studio No.2	8/1/1935	154a, 154b, 154c, 154d, 154e, 155a, 155b, 155c, 155d
72	"	10/1/1935	155e, 155f, 155g, 155h
73	"	23/12/1935	154f, 154g, 156a, 157a, 158a, 159a
74	"	3/1/1936	156b, 156c, 159b, 159c, 159d
	[Party	1938	216a]
75	Academy of Music, Philadelphia	4/12/1939	160a, 160b, 161a, 161b, 162a, 162b, 163a, 164a, 165a, 165b, 166a, 167a, 168a, 169a, 170a, 171a, 172a, 173a, 174a
76	"	11/12/1939	175a, 175b, 176a, 177a, 177b, 178a, 179a, 179b, 180a, 181a, 182a, 183a
77	"	24/2/1940	160c, 161c, 164b, 164c, 165c, 171b, 173b, 173c
78	New York, Studio No.2	18/3/1940	184a, 184b, 185a, 186a, 186b, 187a, 188a, 189a, 189b, 190a, 190b, 191a, 191b, 192a, 192b, 193a, 193b
79	"	9/4/1940	184c, 184d, 185b, 185c, 192c
80	Academy of Music, Philadelphia	20/12/1941	194a, 194b, 195a, 195b, 196a, 197a, 197b, 198a, 199a, 200a, 201a
81	Hollywood	25/2/1942	202a, 203a, 204a, 205a, 206a
82	"	26/2/1942	205b, 206b, 206c, 207a, 208a, 209a
83	"	27/2/1942	205c, 210a, 211a, 212a

15 Rachmaninoff and the Reproducing Piano

The reproducing piano, obsolete but not extinct for more than half a century, is an instrument with which few musicians today are really familiar, and yet not only was its use once quite widespread, but most of the virtuosos active in the first decades of the twentieth century, including Rachmaninoff, recorded for it. Its grandiose title distinguished it from the humbler player-piano or pianola, from which it was developed and with which it shared the basic principle of playing back music recorded on a perforated paper roll through a system of pneumatics in the piano action. At the turn of the century Edwin Welte perfected a mechanism which automatically reproduced not only the notes but also the speed, dynamics and pedalling of the original performance, so at last making the machine a serious musical instrument. At a time when the few gramophone records of the piano being made sounded tinny and unlifelike, many important pianists were attracted to Welte's studio at Freiburg-im-Bresgau to record their art for posterity on the 'Welte-Mignon' system, among them the Russians Essipova and Rachmaninoff's contemporaries Scriabin and Lhevinne. Rachmaninoff himself, however, made no piano rolls until he came to settle in America,by which time the two other principal makes of reproducing piano had been developed and now shared the market: the Aeolian Company's 'Duo-Art' and, most sophisticated of all, the American Piano Company's 'Ampico'.

Josef Hofmann used to joke that, when Rachmaninoff arrived in America, he ignored his musical friends' earnest advice, based on their experience of American business and musical life, and stubbornly went his own way – to his considerable financial advantage, as matters turned out.[1] Thus on disc Rachmaninoff recorded for Edison and Victor, whilst Hofmann appeared on the Columbia and Brunswick labels; and whereas Hofmann recorded for Welte-Mignon and later Duo-Art, when Rachmaninoff came to sign a contract to record for the reproducing piano, it was with the relatively small and only recently established Ampico Company. In this, however, he probably did take notice of the advice of a friend, Fritz Kreisler, who had already made a number of rolls for Ampico in his capacity as pianist. The story is that at Kreisler's suggestion Rachmaninoff made four test rolls, and that when he came to hear the proofs he sat impassively, smoking. At the end he got up and went to the door, still saying nothing. Then he turned and calmly remarked: 'Gentlemen, I have just heard myself play'. This one comment supposedly triggered off a sensational rise of Ampico stock on Wall Street.[2]

There is no doubt that Ampico were desperate to add Rachmaninoff's name to their roster of artists. Most famous pianists were already contracted to one or other rival system at the time, and their catalogue contained little material that was really first-rate. Later they leavened their lists by leasing from the firm of Hupfeld isolated examples of early rolls by such artists as Grieg and Saint-Saëns, reissuing them recut to suit their own system, but capturing Rachmaninoff was a major coup, and they were not slow to make the maximum publicity out of it. On 27 April 1919 Rachmaninoff appeared with Heifetz at the Metropolitan Opera House in a function to sponsor the Victory Liberty Loan. Rachmaninoff performed his arrangement of *The Star-Spangled Banner* and Liszt's Second Hungarian Rhapsody, and Heifetz played three items. Both artists auctioned their encores to the highest bidder, in Rachmaninoff's case his Prelude in C sharp minor, which was 'sold' for the astounding sum of one million dollars. The 'purchasers' turned out to be none other than Ampico, who achieved enormous publicity, and business, from this strategem for promoting one of their artists.

Rachmaninoff visited the Ampico New York studio to record his current repertoire on and off over a period of ten years, making thirty-five published rolls in all (one issued in duplicate), though he may have made others: an unpublished and otherwise unknown roll of the slow movement of his Second Concerto survived to be given its first public hearing in America in 1983. Twenty-nine rolls are of pieces which he also recorded for the gramophone, and not the least valuable aspect of this legacy is the overwhelming corroborative evidence it provides of the amazing consistency over the years of his 'composed' interpretations. A comparison between the dates in the discography and the list of piano rolls shows that in general Rachmaninoff recorded the same items for the two media at roughly the same period, but even when the interval between recordings is very considerable, as in the eighteen years between the 1924 piano roll and 1942 gramophone recording of the Chopin-Liszt *Maiden's Wish*, the same remarkable similarity in interpretation can be heard.

Even more than with the gramophone of the period, piano roll repertoire had to be aimed at the tastes of the persons who typically could afford the considerable expense of a reproducing piano, solid well-to-do citizens with often unsophisticated musical taste. Rachmaninoff recorded thirteen of his original compositions, eight of his transcriptions, and fourteen popular items by other composers. The nature of the repertoire is shown clearly by an analysis of the rolls of Rachmaninoff's own works, of which the early salon pieces are best represented – all five items of Op. 3 and two from Op. 10 – and the more substantial and demanding later works least well – only three out of thirty-eight Preludes and *Études-Tableaux.* On the other hand, we can be grateful for the six items he recorded for this medium but never for the gramophone: *The Star-Spangled Banner,* Chopin's Nocturne in F major, Op. 15, No. 1, and the B flat minor Scherzo, Op. 31, Rubinstein's Barcarolle, his own *Élégie* from Op. 3 and, perhaps above all, the B minor *Étude-Tableau,* Op. 39, No. 4.

As a medium for recreating a musical performance the reproducing piano had inherent limitations that still cause debate among musicians. One relevant to the Rachmaninoff rolls was its arguable inability, despite technical improvements in the 1920s, to record and reproduce subtleties of half-pedalling and the independent dynamics of different fingers. Thus, although Rachmaninoff's rolls are in general of excellent quality, the individual shadings which the pianist gave to different strands in a polyphonic dialogue are somewhat levelled out when heard on a reproducing piano. Rachmaninoff on piano roll is still recognizable from any other pianist, but not so obviously as he is on disc. On the other hand, the frequently-made criticism of the system that editing a roll could remove defects from the original performance and make it unnaturally perfect is no more or less valid than of the editing of tape before the manufacture of a modern recording. Nevertheless, a 78 r.p.m. record does have the advantage, whatever its sound quality, of representing three or four minutes' continuous performance as it actually was, even though the published version may be, and in Rachmaninoff's case usually was, only the best of several takes.

The reproducing piano always remained the preserve of a monied minority, and it could never hope to be a medium of mass entertainment. In the early 1920s radio arrived and in 1925 electrical recording, with its improved sound quality. Both radio and gramophone brought into the home not only famous pianists but every kind of instrumentalist and orchestra as well, for but a fraction of the cost of a good reproducing piano. For the industry, the Wall Street Crash of 1929 dealt the final blow. Though Ampico lingered on for a few years after this, Rachmaninoff made only one more roll, and the company was eventually forced to merge with its rival, Duo-Art, before ceasing to trade altogether. Henceforth, obtaining rolls and maintaining the complex and temperamental reproducing mechanism, depending, for perfect operation, on the correct functioning of hundreds of delicate valves, bellows and fine rubber tubing, became steadily more difficult. Instruments fell into disuse and decay, and the reproducing piano seemed to have passed into history.

In their day reproducing pianos were enthusiastically endorsed by performers, including Rachmaninoff, as an entirely faithful means of recreating an original performance. Artists of the calibre of Cortot and Moiseiwitsch (though not Rachmaninoff) appeared in concerts at which live performances could be compared with re-enactments by the reproducing piano; critics of the eminence of Ernest Newman declared themselves unable to tell when the machine and when the artist was playing. However, after its demise in the 1930s, for serious musicians the reproducing piano became an object of suspicion and then ridicule: the few instruments which remained were generally sadly out of adjustment, and on the evidence of their performance piano rolls seemed to offer only a very approximate and musically unsatisfactory recreation of the great pianists of the past.

The first major transcription of piano rolls to LP was made about 1950 by American Columbia, who published a set of five records (ML 4291-5) entitled *Great Masters of the Keyboard*. It was perhaps unfortunate in the first place that the Welte system should have been chosen rather than the more sophisticated Duo-Art or Ampico, but the issue was more seriously flawed by the poor technical quality of the recording and by the use of an inferior instrument out of adjustment. This fatal combination, unhappily repeated in several subsequent issues, inevitably persuaded those with short memories generally to deny any reliability in the evidence of piano rolls about the playing of the great pianists of the past. Over the ensuing years several of Rachmaninoff's own rolls were transcribed in America, just as unconvincingly, but in 1964 a series of three programmes was broadcast by the BBC in which the critic Deryck Cooke analysed Romantic pianism with the help of a properly restored Ampico piano and a range of Ampico rolls, including some by Rachmaninoff. Cooke argued that what had been heard before on record had been wholly unrepresentative of the medium, and the broadcast and the three gramophone records, drawn from the broadcasts, which subsequently appeared[3] did much to rehabilitate the reproducing piano among musicians as an instrument to be taken seriously. Enthusiasts who for years had been hiding in corners gradually emerged into the light, and the reproducing piano was posthumously resurrected and restored to respectability. Finally, in 1978, all Rachmaninoff's rolls were set down using, for the first time on records, a full-size concert grand. The results achieved were definitive.[4]

References

1 Sofiya Satina, *VR/A* 1, p. 53.
2 Ampico advertising literature and Arthur W.J.G. Ord-Hume, *Player-Piano*, George Allen & Unwin, London, 1970, p. 97.
3 *The Golden Age of Piano Virtuosi*, on Argo DA 41-43.
4 *The Ampico Recordings, Sergei Rachmaninov*, on Oiseau-Lyre 414 096, 414 099 and 414 122.

Numerical List of Ampico Rolls made by Rachmaninoff

Item	Roll no.	Publication Date	Title
1	57275	1919	RACHMANINOFF – *Polka de W.R.*
2*	57282		SMITH (arr. Rachmaninoff) – *Star-Spangled Banner*
3	57504		RACHMANINOFF – Prelude in C sharp minor, Op. 3, No. 2
4	57525	1920	RACHMANINOFF – Prelude in G minor, Op. 23, No. 5
5	57545		RACHMANINOFF – *Mélodie* in E major, Op. 3. No. 3
6	57604		RACHMANINOFF – Barcarolle, Op. 10, No. 3
7	57905		RACHMANINOFF – *Polichinelle*, Op. 3, No. 4
8	57914		TCHAIKOVSKY – *Troika en traineaux*, No. 11 from *The Seasons*, Op. 37
9	57965		RACHMANINOFF – *Humoresque*, Op. 10, No. 5
10	59661	1921	MENDELSSOHN – *Bee's Wedding* (*Spinning Song*), *Song Without Words*, Op. 67, No. 4
11	59743		CHOPIN – Waltz in E flat, Op. 18
12	60641	1922	MUSSORGSKY (transcribed Rachmaninoff) – *Gopak* from *Sorochinsky Fair*
13	60891		RACHMANINOFF – Étude-Tableau in A minor, Op. 39, No. 6
14	61601	1923	BIZET (transcribed Rachmaninoff) – Minuet from *L'Arlésienne*
15	61761		RACHMANINOFF – *Lilacs*, Op. 21, No. 5
16	62103		KREISLER (transcribed Rachmaninoff) – *Liebesleid*

503

Item	Roll no.	Publication Date	Title
17	62441		RACHMANINOFF – Serenade in B flat minor, Op. 3, No. 5
18	62531		TCHAIKOVSKY – Waltz in A flat, Op. 40, No. 8
19	62803	1924	CHOPIN (transcribed Liszt) – *The Maiden's Wish*
20	62971		HENSELT – *Si oiseau j' étais*
21	63311		CHOPIN – Waltz in F major, Op. 34, No. 3
22	64561	1925	SCHUBERT (transcribed Liszt) – *Das Wandern*
23	64921		GLUCK (transcribed Sgambati) – *Mélodie* from *Orfeo*
24	65771	1926	SCHUBERT (transcribed Rachmaninoff) – *Wohin? (The Brooklet)*
25	66143		KREISLER (transcribed Rachmaninoff) – *Liebesfreud*
26	66483		BACH – Saraband from Clavier Partita No. 4 in D, BWV 828
27*	67673	1927	CHOPIN – Nocturne in F major, Op. 15, No. 1
28	68283		PADEREWSKI – Minuet in G, Op. 14, No. 1
29	68771	1928	BEETHOVEN (transcribed Rubinstein) – *Turkish March* from *The Ruins of Athens*
30*	69253		RACHMANINOFF – *Élégie* in E flat minor, Op. 3, No. 1
31	69373		SCHUBERT – Impromptu in A flat, No. 4 from D.899
32*	69593	1929	RACHMANINOFF – *Étude-Tableau* in B minor, Op. 39, No. 4
33*	69893		RUBINSTEIN – Barcarolle No. 2 in A minor, Op. 45
34	70301		RIMSKY-KORSAKOV (transcribed Rachmaninoff) – *Flight of the Bumble Bee*

Item	Roll no.	Publication Date	Title
35*	71173	1933	CHOPIN – Scherzo No. 2 in B flat minor, Op. 31
36	71521		MENDELSSOHN – *Bee's Wedding (Spinning Song), Song Without Words*, Op. 67, No. 4
	(same as Item 10)		
37†	–	?	RACHMANINOFF – Second Concerto, Op. 18: 2nd movement

Ampico later reissued twelve of Rachmaninoff's recordings on long-playing rolls, each containing four items: roll no. 100055 contained items 21, 10, 19, 13; no. 100075, items 17, 3, 15, 11; no. 100095, items 22, 8, 4, 20.

* Not duplicated by an Edison or Victor gramophone recording.

† This unpublished roll received its first performance at a concert in the Bismarck Pavilion Theatre, Chicago, by the American Chamber Symphony Orchestra conducted by Robert Frisbie, on 16 July 1983.

Part III
RACHMANINOFF
THE CONDUCTOR

16 Rachmaninoff's Career as a Conductor

While the legend of Rachmaninoff the pianist has been kept alive by the recordings he left, sadly his career as a conductor has passed forgotten into the history books; yet all the evidence points irresistibly to the conclusion that his artistry expressed itself as distinctively and successfully in this role as at the keyboard.[1]

Rachmaninoff became a conductor, as he later became a professional pianist, by force of circumstances rather than by choice. In his years at Moscow Conservatoire there was no class in conducting to attend, even had he wished to do so, and during this time he seems to have taken up the baton only once, in 1891, to direct a student choir in a performance of his motet *Deus meus*. However, following the success of his graduation opera *Aleko* at the Bolshoi Theatre in Moscow, he was invited to Kiev in October 1893 himself to conduct two performances of the same work there. In view of his total inexperience, to be embarrassingly exposed at his first rehearsal as a professional opera conductor four years later, the apparent success of the Kiev production perhaps owed more to the attractiveness of the music than to the ill-prepared performance. On the first night the Young Gypsy and Zemfira lost their way altogether in their duet, so wrecking one of the most important numbers in the opera. Whether this was due simply to the singers' forgetting their parts, as a critic assumed,[2] or at least in part to the twenty-year-old conductor's ineptitude, is a moot point. Two years after this, while touring with Teresina Tua, Rachmaninoff made another brief appearance as conductor when he conducted the premiere of his own *Gypsy Caprice* in Moscow, at a mixed concert in which he appeared also as accompanist, but he can be said effectively to have begun his conducting career only after the failure of his First Symphony, when he was led temporarily to seek an alternative career to that of composer by joining Mamontov's Private Opera as assistant conductor.

The railway magnate Savva Mamontov had founded his opera in 1895 to inject new life and fresh talent into the unenterprising Moscow

509

opera scene. For principal conductor he had engaged an Italian expatriate, Eugenio Esposito, who, though artistically altogether uninspiring, was nevertheless efficient in the routine performance of his duties; in hiring the untried Rachmaninoff as Esposito's assistant Mamontov had taken a calculated risk that seemed at first not to pay off. For his debut Rachmaninoff was assigned Glinka's *A Life for the Tsar*, as it was familiar to orchestra, chorus and soloists alike; however, though he knew every note of the score, through inexperience he did not realize that a conductor needs to give cues to singers as well as orchestra, and the rehearsal had to be abandoned because of the chaos resulting: 'In my ignorance and innocence I had imagined that an artist who walks on to the stage to sing an opera is bound to know it as well as the conductor. Why should I give him a cue? I had no idea of the astonishing lack of musical understanding that characterises most singers, who know nothing of an opera except their own part.'[3]

Rachmaninoff's last remark is probably more significant than it appears at first sight. In the previous season Mamontov's company had been joined by a young singer on the threshold of a legendary career, Fyodor Chaliapin. Rachmaninoff and he quickly became friends, and they studied many operatic roles together, beginning, during the summer of 1898, with Boris Godunov, for which Chaliapin worked through all the parts, both male and female.[4] The singer found this comprehensive study so useful that he subsequently applied the practice to all his other repertoire, quite possibly prompted in the first place by what Rachmaninoff may have said to him about the inadequacy of the average opera singer's blinkered view of the works in which he performed. Thus Rachmaninoff's elementary discovery, stumbled upon through inexperience, may have played a part in setting genius on its course.

Rachmaninoff made his postponed conducting debut at the Private Opera on 12 October 1897, with *Samson and Delilah* by Saint-Saëns. Esposito had taken over the Glinka opera in which Rachmaninoff had failed, conducting it successfully without a rehearsal. By watching his performance closely Rachmaninoff saw where he had gone wrong: 'The experience I was able to gather during this performance conducted by Esposito enabled me to rehearse the opera *Samson and Delilah* without difficulty and to perform it without a hitch. The audience and the press seemed satisfied with me, for they always greeted my appearance at the conductor's desk with demonstrations of friendliness.'[5] As might be guessed, the self-critical composer, pianist, and now conductor, dismissed his performances as 'mediocre.'[6] From the point-of-view of his subsequent conducting career, it is interesting that what one critic at least singled out for comment in his review of the first night was that Rachmaninoff had quite changed the sound of the orchestra,[7] an ability showed by all conductors of genuine talent. Esposito must have sensed the threat to his own position; at any rate, as perhaps befitted a novice assistant, Rachmaninoff was assigned all the lesser productions: performances of Verstovsky's *The Tomb of Ashkold* and Serov's *Rogneda*; Sunday matinees for children; four scattered performances of *Carmen*; a single performance of Gluck's *Orfeo*, taken over when Esposito was indisposed, and one of *Mignon* by Thomas, both works most unlikely to have been congenial to his musical temperament.

As far as artistic satisfaction was concerned, for Rachmaninoff the most significant productions during his Mamontov season were undoubtedly the two major Russian operas in which he worked with Chaliapin: Dargomyzhsky's *Rusalka* and Rimsky-Korsakov's *May Night*, though the latter, with Chaliapin singing the part of the Mayor for the first time in his career, received mixed reviews. In January of the new year there had been a fire in the Solodnikov Theatre, to which the company had recently moved, necessitating yet another change of venue. The stage of the new building, the International Theatre,[8] was not only inadequate for the proper mounting of an opera but the acoustics of the auditorium were bad. In the improvised circumstances it is not surprising that the production had evident weaknesses; even so, Rachmaninoff's part was greatly praised: 'Even now Rachmaninoff leads the orchestra one hundred times better than Esposito... In the management's position I would not dare to give Russian operas to the talentless Esposito when I had such an excellent musician as Rachmaninoff...'.[9]

Rachmaninoff's initial enthusiasm for his new post soon waned when he experienced for himself the chaos and pressures under which the company operated: the absurdly inadequate rehearsal time; the musical incompetence of many of the company; the ineffective management; the gruelling schedule of operas programmed. Although it was mainly because of his collaboration with Chaliapin that in retrospect at least he considered his apprenticeship with the Mamontov company worth while,[10] the opportunities given him of working with the singer were in fact few: a proposal of his to stage Schumann's *Manfred* with Chaliapin, although at first accepted, was not proceeded with, and despite the verdict of the critics it was Esposito, not he, who was given most of the principal Russian operas to conduct in which Chaliapin appeared: *A Life for the Tsar*, *Prince Igor*, *The Maid of Pskov*, *Khovanshchina* and *Sadko*. In the end Rachmaninoff was glad to leave the company; not only did he never return but he did not stay even for the last two months of the season, in St Petersburg.

The year after leaving the Mamontov company Rachmaninoff was invited to London, thanks to Siloti, to conduct his orchestral fantasy *The Crag* at a concert at the Queen's Hall. It is clear from reviews that

Rachmaninoff's authoritative yet undemonstrative demeanour, which critics were to single out for comment during the 'Rachmaninoff Cycle' concerts at the end of his career thirty years later and which was the counterpart of his impassivity at the keyboard, was already also the hallmark of his conducting style: 'His command was supreme', remarked the critic of *The Times*; 'his method, quietness idealised'.[11] In 1902 and 1903, in concerts in Moscow and St Petersburg, he accompanied Siloti, twice in Liszt's *Totentanz* and once in his own newly completed Second Concerto. These appearances were no more than occasional forays, however, and it was not until the autumn of 1904, when he made his debut at the Bolshoi Theatre, that Rachmaninoff at last began definitely to establish himself as Russia's most talented conductor.

Since 1898 the Director of the Bolshoi Theatre, and later of all the imperial theatres, had been a former colonel in the Imperial Cavalry, Vladimir Telyakovsky (1861–1924). Proving himself an energetic administrator, he had begun to stir the organization out of its lethargy and was on the look-out for fresh and invigorating talent. His first coup had been to attract Chaliapin away from Mamontov to join the Bolshoi in 1899, and it was perhaps at the singer's suggestion that he subsequently sought Rachmaninoff himself as conductor. Rachmaninoff, however, was unenthusiastic: having recently fully recovered from the depression brought on by the failure of his First Symphony, he was now unwilling to dam the stream of compositions flowing from his pen. It took eighteen months of negotiations to persuade the reluctant composer to accept the appointment on offer, though the contract he signed initially was for five months only (1904–05); later he extended it to a second season. According to the *Recollections*,[12] it was the artistic opportunities the post offered, and in particular the prospect of working again with Chaliapin, which finally persuaded Rachmaninoff to accept.

The one-time dominance in Russia of Italian music and musicians lingered on in pockets throughout the nineteenth century, being especially evident in the sphere of conducting, where native talent either failed to appear or lacked the opportunity for nurture. As Esposito was principal conductor of the Mamontov Opera, so his more prestigious opposite number at the Bolshoi Theatre was also an Italian, Ippolit Karlovich Altani (1846–1919), who had premiered Rachmaninoff's student opera *Aleko* in 1893. According to Telyakovsky, echoing the opinion of Rimsky-Korsakov: 'Altani was a good musician but not very gifted as a conductor. He was not distinguished in temperament, although some operas, particularly foreign ones, he conducted well... As a director of opera Altani was significantly weaker than as chief *Kapellmeister*.'[13] Although Altani's seniority was respected in Rachmaninoff's contract, the new younger conductor was given extraordinary powers, and it is a reasonable guess that the management may have hoped to groom him as his successor (Altani retired in 1906), but in this they were to be disappointed.

Not everyone was pleased by Rachmaninoff's appointment. Rachmaninoff himself always held the view that being a strict disciplinarian was the most important prerequisite for success as a conductor, and the reputation he must have established as a martinet at Mamontov's Private Opera had obviously gone ahead of him. According to Sofiya Satina, circles at Moscow Conservatoire, headed by Ippolitov-Ivanov, felt that no-one would get on with him: 'He was too demanding, severe and unbending'.[14] Nor were these fears groundless: from the outset Rachmaninoff sought to remedy the slackness of discipline among the orchestral musicians that had developed in Altani's later years, and in doing so he showed himself quite uncompromising. His attitude was made clear from the start, when he stopped members of the orchestra leaving the pit for a smoke during performances, as had been their traditional practice, threatening them all with instant dismissal if they persisted.[15]

Those who hoped that Rachmaninoff would bring a breath of fresh air to stir the stale atmosphere of routine which had pervaded the theatre for so long were quickly vindicated. Of the several beneficial changes of practice he instituted, the most obvious was to move the conductor's stand back from its nineteenth-century position between stage and orchestra pit so as to face both orchestra and singers; during his honeymoon visit to Bayreuth two years before Rachmaninoff had seen for himself the practical advantages of what in retrospect seems the only logical layout, though it was not Altani's perverse adherence to an obsolete tradition so much as the low level of professionalism among singers, with which Rachmaninoff was already all too familiar, that had created and maintained the need for conductors to be in a position where they could give their main attention to the singers rather than to the orchestra. To improve the performance of singers and to ensure that both they and he shared the same aims, he established at the Bolshoi the successful practice he had followed at the Mamontov Opera of working on roles with soloists, accompanying them in their parts on the piano. A more short-lived but no less sensible innovation was his attempt to create opportunities for young Russian conductors to be trained within the theatre's organization, in the hope of injecting an element of native talent into what still seemed to be a foreign preserve.

Rachmaninoff made his debut at the Bolshoi Theatre on 3 September 1904 with Dargomyzhsky's *Rusalka*, one of the works he had conducted at the Mamontov Opera seven years before, when he had worked with

Chaliapin on the role of the Miller. Although Chaliapin appeared also in the Bolshoi production, it was not with this opera that he first renewed his collaboration with his friend, for he did not appear in it until six weeks after the season had begun, in what proved to be the first of only five of the sixteen performances that Rachmaninoff in all conducted. As the production had already been staged the previous year, critics had all the more reason for concentrating their attention on its orchestral and general musical aspects. They were unanimous about the refinement and sensibility of the interpretation and about the difference Rachmaninoff's presence had made. Kashkin commented: 'From the very first bars [the performance] breathed freshness and high spirits; the conductor's lively and rich temperament revealed itself clearly.'[16]

The next productions were *Eugene Onegin* and *Prince Igor*. According to Kashkin, in Rachmaninoff's hands Tchaikovsky's opera was 'rejuvenated';[17] in the Borodin work, despite the presence of Chaliapin as Prince Galitsky, the attention of critics was focused on the orchestral sound, which had suddenly assumed a new fullness, brilliance and subtlety, without ever being allowed to overwhelm the singers.[18] It was plain that in terms both of his freshness of approach, and even of mere technical competence, Rachmaninoff was amply vindicating Telyakovsky's faith in him; he was moreover demonstrating that he could establish his musical will no less characteristically with an orchestra than when playing the piano.

Rachmaninoff's appointment to the Bolshoi in 1904 coincided with the centenary of the birth of Glinka, and it was originally planned to mark the opening of the season with an entirely new production of 'the first Russian opera', *A Life for the Tsar*. Balakirev had edited the work for publication in 1881, and at first the committee set up to organize the production floated his name as possible conductor; however, foremost authority on Glinka though he undoubtedly was, he had effectively abandoned conducting some years before because of his weak heart, and Rachmaninoff was nominated instead. Even the critic Kruglikov, who in 1897 had become Mamontov's musical consultant and who may possibly have recommended Rachmaninoff for the Private Opera, felt that protocol required that historically so important a production should, failing Balakirev, be given to the long-serving and vastly more experienced Altani and not to the new appointee,[19] but Rachmaninoff it was who took up the baton on the night of 21 September. With its new sets and costumes to designs by Korovin, the opera had not been ready for the opening of the season, but, with an all-star cast of Chaliapin as Susanin, Nezhdanova as his wife Antonida, Zbruyeva as his adoptive son Vanya and Rozanov as Sobinin, the first night attracted all musical Moscow. In the glowing critical reviews which followed,

Rachmaninoff was 'the hero of the evening' and hailed as an inspiration to singers and orchestra alike, who had swept away the accretion of sterile tradition with which the work had become encrusted over the years, a judgement which confirms that in the Bolshoi production Rachmaninoff was able to realize the very intentions he had been unable to carry into effect at the Mamontov Opera.[20]

In Rachmaninoff's repertoire for this season were three more operas new to him as a conductor. The first two were by Tchaikovsky, *The Queen of Spades* and *The Oprichnik*. Especially memorable must have been the performance of *The Queen of Spades* on 26 October 1904, the one-hundredth to be put on at the Bolshoi Theatre and with a starry cast, including Chaliapin in the role of Tomsky and also, on this occasion, in the tiny part of Pluto. *The Oprichnik* received less favourable reviews, partly at least because of the composer's allegedly overpowering orchestral scoring or Rachmaninoff's failure to curb it in performance.[21] Then in January came *Boris Godunov*, with Chaliapin in the title role, a titanic combination of vocal and conducting talent that must have created an overwhelming impression on those fortunate enough to be present. Finally, in a charity performance of operatic excerpts, put on for war relief, Rachmaninoff conducted his own opera *Aleko*, for the third and final time in his career.

Wishing to see into production his two new operas, *Francesca da Rimini* and *The Miserly Knight*, Rachmaninoff returned to the Bolshoi for a second season, but after the achievements of his first year he now experienced only anti-climax. Political unrest was sweeping through the country; already at the beginning of 1905 Rachmaninoff himself had signed a declaration by thirty-two of Russia's most famous musicians demanding political reform, and as the year passed strikes and political disturbances disrupted life in Moscow. On 27 September 1905 Rachmaninoff premiered Rimsky-Korsakov's *Pan Voyevoda*. The performance had not been widely advertised because of a printing strike, and the work itself proved to be musically weak and not destined to enter the regular repertoire. Rimsky nevertheless declared himself well-pleased with Rachmaninoff's part in the performance, though both he and the critics found less satisfaction with the singers.[22] According to the composer at least, it was the December Presnya uprising in Moscow which brought about the opera's premature withdrawal.

As the autumn wore on, unrest among the workers at the Bolshoi reached a point were Telyakovsky was obliged to travel from St Petersburg to Moscow to try to contain the situation,[23] and with the deterioration in discipline Rachmaninoff found his own position as conductor increasingly untenable. It was in these inauspicious circumstances that in January and February of 1906 he conducted five performances of his two operas. He had already suffered a double disappointment in the withdrawal of both Chaliapin and Nezhdanova from the cast, and now came the further blow of a tepid reaction by the public. At the end of the season he left the theatre, never to return there again as conductor except once, eleven years later, in a programme of his own symphonic works.

In his two seasons at the Bolshoi Theatre Rachmaninoff proved himself a natural operatic conductor: the virtually unanimous critical success of all the productions in which he was involved and the eloquent testimony of artists who worked with him, not least of Chaliapin, is proof enough of his outstanding talent. Nevertheless, he clearly lacked, and would have found it impossible to bring himself to acquire, the catholicity of taste in repertoire demanded of the typical professional opera-house conductor. He was appointed to conduct, and doubtless found it most congenial to conduct, Russian opera exclusively, and it is difficult to imagine his tackling *Don Giovanni* or *Traviata* with equal sympathy and success. Even so, 1904 to 1906 were golden years in Moscow operatic life, and Telyakovsky was ready to give Rachmaninoff supreme powers if he would agree to continue at the Bolshoi. However, the disappointments of the last year and the impossibility of taking the draconian measures necessary, as Rachmaninoff saw it, to restore discipline in the theatre ruled out his return; in any case, he wished to move abroad for peace and quiet in which to resume his work as a composer. Except for six guest appearances at the Maryinsky Theatre in February 1912, when he again conducted *The Queen of Spades*, Rachmaninoff's career as an operatic conductor was by now over.

Even while in his first term at the Bolshoi Theatre Rachmaninoff began to make appearances also in orchestral concerts. In this area, as in opera, there had been a dearth of native talent. In the latter half of the nineteenth century concerts were still mainly in the hands of foreign conductors, such as Nápravník (1839–1916), a Bohemian who assumed Russian nationality and who worked mainly but not exclusively in the opera house, and Max Erdmannsdörfer (1848–1905), Leipzig-trained, remembered now for having premiered some of Tchaikovsky's works, but always, it seems, more at ease with the Austro-German repertoire. Russian-born conductors tended to be composers who tried their hands at the art only as a side-line to their main activity – Rubinstein, Balakirev, Rimsky-Korsakov, Glazunov, Liadov, Liapunov, Tchaikovsky – and the same may be said of Rachmaninoff himself, but none before him had shown any great natural talent. The first two Russian conductors not to fall into this pattern were both primarily pianists – Safonov and Siloti. Safonov began his conducting career in Moscow in 1887 at the age of thirty-seven, appeared with the New York Philharmonic in 1904 and after a period as their permanent conductor (1906–1909) returned to Russia in 1911 to direct concerts in St Petersburg. Siloti also began his conducting career late, by taking over the Moscow Philharmonic Society concerts (1901–1903) when he was already thirty-eight, though of course this was not his first conducting experience. From 1903 until 1917 he proved himself an efficient and enterprising conductor of his own 'Siloti Concerts'. Koussevitzky, on the other hand, who had been principal double bass in the Bolshoi orchestra under Rachmaninoff, arrived as a major talent on the Russian scene only in 1909, and thus with Safonov abroad and Koussevitzky not yet launched on his career, the emergence of Rachmaninoff as a great new Russian conductor created all the more striking an impression.

On 30 November 1904 Rachmaninoff accompanied Siloti in a programme of three works for piano and orchestra at St Petersburg, and in the new year began to appear in Moscow both at the symphony concerts put on by the Kerzins and at those sponsored by the Moscow Philharmonic Society. The former, concentrating on Russian music, were parochial so far as the artists who performed in them were concerned; the latter, catholic in repertoire, provided a platform not only for the most famous Russian musicians but for international artists of the top rank. In these concerts Rachmaninoff not only established himself as an unrivalled interpreter of Russian symphonic music but invited comparison with the greatest European conductors of the day. His reputation grew by the year, until critics began to use the word 'genius' of him. After a performance of Grieg's *Peer Gynt* Suite on 22 October 1912 Yury Engel declared: 'Rachmaninoff, a real conductor, by the grace of God (and one who impresses both public and orchestra equally), may be the only Russian conductor to be compared with such names in the West as Nikisch, Colonne and Mahler.'[24]

Engel was not alone in placing Rachmaninoff among the greatest of conductors. Yury Nikolsky wrote:[25]

> I had the opportunity of hearing concerts under the direction of such titans as Artur Nikisch, Willem Mengelberg, Felix Weingartner, Felix Mottl and others. However excellent they were in their various ways, Rachmaninoff also, in his fashion, in his Rachmaninoff way, was great and incomparable. His appearance at the conductor's stand as it were electrified the whole atmosphere. The orchestra pulled itself up, became rejuvenated and compliant. Every musician became an artist on a high plane and each one played his part just as well as he could. All this was under the command of the magic baton in the masterful hand of Rachmaninoff, who, with niggardly but expressive gestures, seemed to create the sounds.

Rachmaninoff's restrained manner of conducting reflected an internal calm and balance. In an interview in 1934 he remarked:[26]

> Of all musical gifts, conducting is in a class apart – a personal talent

which cannot be acquired. To be a good conductor a musician must possess tremendous powers of restraint. He must have the strength to be quiet. And by 'quiet' I do not mean placid and unmoved. The full intensity of musical emotion must be there, but at the heart of it is the quietness of perfect mental poise and power controlled. When I conduct, I experience much the same feeling as when I drive my car – an inner calm that gives me complete mastery of myself and of the forces, musical or mechanical, at my command.

Rachmaninoff's gestures to an orchestra were simple and unpolished. In the opinion of a contemporary:[27]

The peculiarities of Rachmaninoff's figure, tall, rather angular and very slightly stooped, did not allow him to enslave an audience by the elegance and plasticity of his movements and gestures when conducting. However, Rachmaninoff's apparently inflexible hands produced signals of such irresistible will, cogency and expressiveness as to cause the group performing (orchestra, choir) to submit to him completely and utterly.

The same writer continues:

Rachmaninoff was very exacting, persistent and even imperious with regard to the group under his direction. At rehearsals he made many criticisms and imposed great demands. In his rehearsal work Rachmaninoff was greatly helped by his absolute pitch and an astoundingly precise and fine ear. Rachmaninoff really did hear the whole score being performed in its entirety and in all its details. He detected and placed not only the usual kind of mistakes by performers but even the slightest chance inconspicuous imprecisions, no matter how heavy the weight of orchestral sound, tenaciously securing their correction.

Rachmaninoff's verbal directions to an orchestra were made in an imperious tone which brooked no argument, and contemporaries have suggested that this was acceptable only because of the general recognition of his towering musical authority, which also more than made up for any lack of conducting technique. The conductor Nikolay Malko felt that there was even an advantage in Rachmaninoff's lack of background of professional routine and in what he saw as technical weaknesses, for 'Rachmaninoff never exhibited the unfortunately all-too-common characteristic of professional conductors of resorting to a formalised, soulless performance, concealed by the gloss of so-called technique'.[28]

According to Goldenweiser, Rachmaninoff's performances as a conductor were stricter than as a pianist.[29]

Rachmaninoff was no less a genius of an interpreter as conductor but, strangely, his individuality as a conductor was somewhat different from that as a pianist. His piano performances were distinguished by great rhythmic freedom; he quite often adopted a *rubato* that seemed somewhat paradoxical and in no way lent itself to imitation. With his interpretation of this or that work, particularly when he was not playing a piece of his own, one might in places disagree, because the imprint of his personality was too clear, especially so far as the rhythmic freedom of his performance was concerned; but it masterfully subjugated the listener, preventing him from being able to take a critical view. As a conductor Rachmaninoff was much more strict and restrained rhythmically. His interpretations were distinguished by the same strength of temperament and power over the listener as when he played the piano, but they were much more strict and straightforward. Nikisch was as graceful and theatrical in his gestures as Rachmaninoff was miserly – I might even have said 'primitive', as though he were simply counting off the bars – and yet his power over an orchestra and audience was absolutely irresistible. His interpretation of such works as Mozart's G minor Symphony, Tchaikovsky's *Francesca da Rimini*, Scriabin's First Symphony, his own Second Symphony and many others, made an absolutely unforgettable impression.

The enthusiastic response to Rachmaninoff's appearances as conductor in Russia was repeated abroad, where he no less convincingly demonstrated his ability to transform an orchestra and to draw his own particular sound from it. During his American tour of 1909 Rachmaninoff conducted in Philadelphia, Chicago, Boston and New York. His final appearance, at Carnegie Hall on 27 January 1910, where he conducted his *Isle of the Dead*, was not with the illustrious New York Philharmonic or Symphony, with each of which he had earlier played his Third Concerto, but with his friend Modest Altschuler's Russian Symphony Society, a less than first-rate ensemble, which nevertheless 'under the inspiration of the composer's baton ... developed qualities of sonority and precision which it has hitherto given little evidence of posssessing'.[30] Before his American tour was over, and on the basis of only two appearances with them as conductor, Rachmaninoff was invited to take over the conductorship of the Boston Symphony Orchestra in succession to Max Fiedler, but he turned down the offer.[31]

Rachmaninoff made appearances as a conductor, both at home and abroad, each year up to 1914. Outside Russia it was exclusively as a propagandist for his own music, particularly the Second Symphony and *The Isle of the Dead*, that he took up the baton, and although in Russia also he frequently conducted his own compositions, his participation in the general programme of the Moscow Philharmonic Society meant that his repertoire steadily expanded over the years; with rare exceptions, however, most obviously a concert in February 1914, in which works by Franck, Debussy, Roger-Ducasse and Ravel incongruously preceded his own choral symphony *The Bells*, he avoided performing compositions uncongenial to him. For reasons of temperamental incompatibility or the sheer pressure of time, some of the novelties advertised for his programmes – such as Strauss's *Heldenleben* and Ravel's *Spanish Rhapsody* – were not in fact performed in his concerts. Possibly because of other commitments Rachmaninoff passed over the first Moscow performance of Elgar's *Enigma Variations*, following its Russian premiere in October 1904 at a Siloti concert in Petersburg.

This seems all the more regrettable as the work would surely have ideally suited him.[32]

Rachmaninoff's spiritual kinship with the music of Tchaikovsky gave his performances of that composer's works a special authority. His interpretation of the Fifth Symphony, which he conducted on three occasions, became particularly famous, the climaxes, a contemporary remarked, the 'points', being quite unforgettable: 'They appeared with such justification and arresting clarity that they seemed perfectly logical and absolutely inevitable'.[33] Of this interpretation Medtner wrote:[34]

> Until Rachmaninoff it so happened that we heard this symphony mainly from Nikisch and his imitators. Nikisch, it used to be said, rescued the work after its complete failure at the hands of its composer. Nikisch's brilliant interpretation, his distinctive style of expression, his sentimental slowing of tempi, became as it were the law for Tchaikovsky performance and were straightaway adopted by the uncultured self-styled conductors who blindly and unsuccessfully imitated him. I shall never forget how suddenly, with Rachmaninoff's first beat, all this imitative tradition fell away from the composition and we once more heard it as if for the first time. Particularly striking was the shattering impetuosity of the finale as a counterbalance to Nikisch's pathos, which had rather impaired this movement.

Those of us who attended Mravinsky's no less revelatory performances of the same work with the Leningrad Philharmonic Orchestra in Edinburgh and London in 1960 experienced similar feelings, and again it was the finale, with its breath-taking *Allegro vivace*, that was specially memorable. Mravinsky exposed the fact that Nikisch's performing tradition had lived on in the West undisturbed; it had taken another fifty years and another great Russian conductor to open Western ears as Rachmaninoff had done in Russia so long ago.

However, in Rachmaninoff's conducting, as in his composing, Tchaikovsky was no more than one of a range of Russian composers with whom he revealed a natural affinity, for he seems to have conducted the works of the nationalist composers no less magnificently. His interpretation of Balakirev's *Tamara* was hailed as the first to reveal to Moscow audiences the proper stature of this masterpiece; his Borodin's B minor Symphony and Mussorgsky's *Night on the Bare Mountain* likewise won rave notices; his performance of Rimsky-Korsakov's *Battle of Kerzhenets*, from the opera *Kitezh*, was acknowledged as one of genius. He was frequently compared with Nikisch, the conductor he himself most admired, even in works which might be thought stylistically alien to him, such as Strauss's *Till Eulenspiegel* and *Don Juan*. One critic, writing of Rachmaninoff's interpretation of *Till Eulenspiegel* on 15 April 1909 found that 'it was capable of making one forget even the most felicitous moments of Nikisch's appearances as conductor'.[35] Another, speaking three years later of *Don Juan*, found it impossible to choose between Nikisch's and Rachmaninoff's performances: 'If one noticed a certain special brio in Nikisch's interpretation, Rachmaninoff's struck one by its nobility, its elegant masculinity and ardent conviction.' [36] Such encomia regularly followed Rachmaninoff's appearances as conductor throughout his Russian years.

Rachmaninoff's excursions into the older Austro-German repertoire were more controversial. As with his interpretations of Mozart piano sonatas years later, so his conducting of Mozart's Fortieth Symphony was found unidiomatic by some critics. Grigory Prokofiev remarked: 'The conductor took some slow tempi and treated the undertaking rather formally.' [37] Sabaneyeff declared: 'The Mozart Symphony was not for Rachmaninoff; ... it came out inflated, it lost its lightness and simplicity.'[38] But other commentators disagreed: 'It was performed strictly and stylishly. Its "classicism" was carefully and attentively observed. The orchestral sound was lightened; it caressed the ear with its gentleness and transparency.' [39] In Medtner's view, Rachmaninoff's interpretation revealed the work in a fresh light:[40]

> I shall never forget this Mozart of Rachmaninoff, coming upon us unexpectedly, pulsating with life but authentic all the same... I shall never forget the alarm of some individuals at the resuscitated 'deceased', the joyful amazement of others, and finally the sombre, gloomy dissatisfaction with himself of the interpreter, who declared after the performance, 'It's still... this... or that...' In other words, what had seemed to us the highest achievement had for him been merely one step towards it.

Rachmaninoff made his final appearance in Russia as a conductor in 1917, after a three years' hiatus, in a concert of his own works at the Bolshoi Theatre. How his conducting career might have developed in his own country, had he chosen to stay on, or abroad, is another of those intriguing but unanswerable questions that prompt all kinds of futile speculation. After the Revolution Rachmaninoff was invited to return to the Bolshoi Theatre as supremo there, but, already having other plans and with unhappy memories of his last term of office, he firmly turned down the offer. While in Scandinavia in 1918, pondering his future, he received two offers of conductorships in America, at Cincinnati and, for a second time, at prestigious Boston, where the finances, administration and artistic direction of the orchestra were all at a critical turning point: its conductor, Karl Muck, had been arrested in a frenzy of anti-German hysteria at the end of the Great War, and the board were desperate for a replacement who could maintain the position of what was then, as now, one of America's finest orchestras. However, learning that the annual programme was for no fewer than one hundred and ten concerts in thirty-six weeks, a schedule far more exacting than anything he had undertaken before, and warned by Josef Hofmann that the power politics of American orchestral organization would plague his life, Rachmaninoff declined the offer. Had he accepted, the exigencies of orchestral concert planning would have brought him into contact with a much wider range of musical experience than did the self-imposed dictates of piano recitals, and this exposure to fresh external influences might have rubbed off on his own creative work – or perhaps have left him no time at all for it. In any case, it is difficult to imagine Rachmaninoff being sympathetic to conducting the general orchestral repertoire, Ravel or Brahms, say, let alone *The Rite of Spring*, and no doubt this was a consideration in his mind in coming to a decision. But musical history could so easily have been significantly different: it might just have been Rachmaninoff, not Koussevitzky, at Boston.

During his years in America, of all conductors Rachmaninoff most respected Stokowski and Ormandy, whose great professionalism was reflected in the superb quality of the Philadelphia Orchestra; at the end of his life he also came to think highly of Mitropoulos. Koussevitzky he disliked on personal grounds; Furtwängler because of the incompatibility of their contrasting musical personalities. Toscanini he seems to have admired from afar, but his well-known contempt for Russian music, including Rachmaninoff's own, was an unbridgeable temperamental chasm between them.

Rachmaninoff found conducting tiring, and once having embarked on his career as a pianist in America he decided to reserve all his strength for his piano playing. After leaving Russia, Rachmaninoff conducted on only seven more occasions in the remaining twenty-five years of his life, and these appearances were invariably planned for the end of a season or before a substantial break. In all, there were two recording sessions, in 1929 and 1939, and five concert appearances, when he conducted *The Bells* and his Third Symphony during 'The Rachmaninoff Cycle' of 1939 with the Philadelphia Orchestra, in Philadelphia and New York, and again in Chicago in 1941, just two years before his death. Several other schemes, however, were mooted: concerts in New York (1919, 1929), Philadelphia (1936, 1938) and Vienna (1938), and most interesting of all, a project to get Rachmaninoff back in the opera house, with a production of Tchaikovsky's *Queen of Spades* at the Metropolitan, New York, in 1926.

Rachmaninoff retained all his authority over an orchestra right to the very end of his career. This is perfectly clear from the three recordings he made, in which the Philadelphia Orchestra play with a commitment no less intense than in any of their great recordings under Stokowski, and in which Rachmaninoff's characteristic rhythmic punch and flexible phrasing is as evident as in his piano playing. Reviews of his conducting appearances in 'The Rachmaninoff Cycle' unanimously make the same point: 'There is no doubt that he knew exactly the effects he desired and how to get them...' [41] 'Grave, scholarly, earnest and utterly devoid of all ostentation or excesses on the podium, the tall intense Russian gave his cues yesterday in clear-cut fashion, using score throughout in his own music...' [42]

> Mr Rachmaninoff, on the rare occasions when this writer has heard him lead an orchestra, has proved as masterly in his control, musicianship and projective power as he is when he plays the piano. And the styles of the pianist and of the conductor are of a piece. There is the same complete lack of ostentation, the same artistry and apparent reserve, the same commanding evocative power. From the first down-beat last night his mastery was obvious, as also the response that he secures from the singers and players. The Philadelphia Orchestra is famous for the quick sensitiveness of the players to the wishes of the functioning leader, whoever he may be. But what Mr Rachmaninoff secured is only obtained when the players know and obey instinctively the wishes of a master whose presence and power are indisputable. In fact there were places last night when Mr Rachmaninoff, the conductor, outshone in significance the composer of the music...' [43]

Musical history has many examples of musicians with dual careers, such as the composer-conductors Strauss and Mahler and all the composer-pianists from Bach on, but few have spread their energies at all extensively or successfully in three directions; only the names of Liszt, Dohnányi and Benjamin Britten come readily to mind alongside that of Rachmaninoff. It is tantalizing to know that Rachmaninoff was assuredly one of the truly great conductors – together with Koussevitzky and Mravinsky the greatest yet produced by Russia – and yet to find that, because of the unusual course it took, his conducting career is by now no more than a historical curiosity. The copious recordings left by most of his great contemporaries can at least still provide evidence of their claim to fame; in Rachmaninoff's case, the three works of his own he recorded, though impressive in themselves, are scarcely representative of a conducting activity that must have been as exciting and musically illuminating as his piano playing. As Medtner said, 'Yes, Rachmaninoff, without doubt, besides everything else, was also the greatest Russian conductor'. [44]

References

1 There is a general survey of Rachmaninoff's career as conductor by Vasily Yakovlev in *Tsitovich*, pp. 176–193; quotations from reviews of many of Rachmaninoff's Russian conducting appearances are to be found in *Keldïsh*.

2 Viktor Chechott in *Artist*, 1893, No. 12, p. 179.
3 *Riesemann*, pp. 106–107.
4 *Chaliapin*, p. 128.
5 *Riesemann*, p. 107.
6 R. to Natalya Skalon, 19 October 1897.
7 'Teatr i muzïka', article in *Moskovskiye vedomosti*, No. 283, 14 October 1897.
8 The Solodnikov Theatre is now the Moscow Operetta Theatre on Pushkin Street; the International became the Mayakovsky Theatre on Herzen Street.
9 'Muzïkal'naya zhizn' Moskvï', article by Ivan Lipayev in *Russkaya muzï- kal'naya gazeta*, February 1898.
10 *Riesemann*, p. 108.
11 *The Times*, 21 April 1899.
12 *Riesemann*, p. 119.
13 Vladimir Telyakovsky, *Vospominaniya*, Moscow, 1965, pp. 116–117; *Rim- sky-Korsakov*, p. 327.
14 Sofiya Satina, *VR/A* 1, p. 35.
15 *Riesemann*, p. 124.
16 Kashkin in *Russkiy listok*, 4 September 1904.
17 Kashkin, 'Yevgeny Onegin' in *Russkoye slovo*, 11 September 1904.
18 See *Keldïsh*, p. 213.
19 Semyon Kruglikov, article 'Bolshoy Teatr' in *Novosti dnya*, 5 September 1904.
20 *Riesemann*, p. 107.
21 See *Keldïsh*, p. 217.
22 *Rimsky-Korsakov*, p. 415.
23 Seroff has a colourful account of this period in his Rachmaninoff biography, pp. 72–89.
24 Yury Engel, 'Symphony Concert' in *Russkiye vedomosti*, No. 245, 24 October 1912.
25 Yury Nikolsky, *VR/A* 2, pp. 48–49.
26 Rachmaninoff interview 'The Composer as Interpreter', in *The Monthly Musical Record*, November 1934, p. 201.
27 Mikhail Bagrinovsky, *VR/A* 2, p. 39.
28 Nikolay Malko, *VR/A* 2, p. 227.
29 Alexander Goldenweiser, *VR/A* 1, pp. 422–423.
30 Unsigned review (by Richard Aldrich) in the *New York Times*, 28 January 1910.
31 *Riesemann*, p. 158. Fiedler was in charge at Boston in an interregnum (1908–1912) between two periods when the orchestra was under the direction of Karl Muck.
32 *Palmieri* (p. 85) is mistaken in including the Elgar Variations in Rachmaninoff's repertoire.
33 Mikhail Bagrinovsky, *VR/A* 2, pp. 40–41.
34 Medtner, *VR/A* 2, p. 350.
35 Grigory Chereshnev, 'Filarmonicheskoye obshestvo' in *Moskovskiye vedomosti*, 17 April 1909.
36 Mikhail Bagrinovsky in *Utro Rossii*, 4 December 1912.
37 Grigory Prokofiev in *Russkiye vedomosti*, 24 October 1912.
38 Leonid Sabaneyeff in *Golos Moskvï*, 21 October 1912.
39 Mikhail Bagrinovsky, *VR/A* 2, p. 41.
40 Medtner, op. cit.

41 Samuel L. Lacia in *The Ledger*, Philadelphia, 9 December 1939.
42 Review in *The Philadelphia Inquirer*, 9 December 1939.
43 Olin Downes in *New York Times*, 11 December 1939.
44 Medtner, op. cit.

17 Conducting Repertoire

Alphabetical List Of Works Conducted By Rachmaninoff

(*Item* refers to the chronological list of Rachmaninoff's conducting appearances on pp. 532–562)

Title	Item
ARENSKY	
Symphony No.1 in B minor, Op.4	124
Variations on a Theme by Tchaikovsky, Op.35a	176
BACH	
Prelude from Cantata No.35	187
BALAKIREV	
Overture on Three Russian Themes	94
Tamara	117
BEETHOVEN	
Concerto No.1 in C major, Op.15	187
Egmont, Overture, Op.84	96
Jena Symphony	168
Violin Concerto in D major, Op.61	168
BERLIOZ	
Fantastic Symphony, Op.14	175
Temptation of Faust, Op.24 – 2 excerpts	180
BIZET	
Carmen (4 times)	12, 13, 21, 28
BORODIN	
Prince Igor – Aria	38
Prince Igor (10 times)	44, 49, 63, 76, 77, 89, 114, 123, 131, 137
Song, *Romance* (orch. Glazunov)	188
Symphony No.2 in B minor (twice)	94, 182

Title	Item
BRAHMS	
Tragic Overture, Op.81	160
Variations on a Theme by Haydn, Op.56a	187
CONUS	
Violin Concerto in E minor	146
DARGOMYZHSKY	
Rusalka (22 times)	7, 8, 11, 15, 27, 31 (Mamontov); 41, 43, 45, 48, 54, 72, 81, 92, 104, 105, 108, 112, 126, 129, 135, 139 (Bolshoi)
DAVYDOV	
Cello Concerto No.2 in A minor, Op.14	167
DEBUSSY	
Martyrdom of St Sebastian	185
DVOŘÀK	
Cello Concerto in B minor, Op.104	182
FRANCK	
Chasseur maudit, Symphonic Poem	185
GLAZUNOV	
Ballet Suite, Op.52	175
Finnish Fantasy, Op.88	160
From the Middle Ages, Suite, Op.79	167
Lyric Poem, Op.12	124
Prologue, *In Memory of Gogol*	149
Seasons, Op.67 – *Winter*	94
Spring, Musical Picture, Op.34 (twice)	128, 182
Symphony No.6 in C minor, Op.58	188
Violin Concerto in A minor, Op.82	145
GLINKA	
Kamarinskaya	80
Life for the Tsar (11 times)	46, 50, 52, 53, 56, 69, 78, 88, 98, 100, 102
Life for the Tsar. Finale only (twice)	95, 97
Night in Madrid	117

Title	Item
Violin Concerto No.3 in G major, K.216	168

MUSSORGSKY

Boris Godunov (4 times)	82–84, 86
Boris Godunov – Inn Scene	87
Night on the Bare Mountain (7 times)	94, 143, 145, 148, 150, 151, 167
Sorochinsky Fair – *Gopak* (3 times)	124, 149, 166
– Introduction (twice)	124, 149

RACHMANINOFF

Aleko (3 times)	2, 3, 87
Bells, Op.35 (8 times)	183, 185, 190, 192 –194, 196, 197
Concerto No.2 in C minor, Op.18 (3 times)	39, 124, 183
Crag, Op.7 (4 times)	38, 159, 161, 190
Deus meus	1
Francesca da Rimini, Op.25 (5 times)	132–134, 136, 138
Gypsy Caprice, Op.12	4
Isle of the Dead, Op.29 (11 times)	148, 152–157, 162, 183, 190, 191
Liturgy of St John Chrysostom, Op.31 (twice)	163, 186
Miserly Knight, Op.24 (5 times)	132–134, 136, 138
Miserly Knight, Op.24 – Baron's Monologue	166
Spring, Cantata, Op.20 (twice)	140, 160
Symphony No.2 in E minor, Op.27 (15 times)	141–146, 148, 150, 151, 157– 159, 161, 162, 189
Symphony No.3 in A minor, Op.44 (6 times)	192–197
Vocalise, Op.34, No.14	191

RAVEL

Valses nobles et sentimentales	185

RIMSKY-KORSAKOV

Antar (Symphony No. 2), Op.9	117
Christmas Eve – Aria and Suite	149
Invisible City of Kitezh – *Battle of Kerzhenets*	182
May Night (5 times)	32, 34–37
May Night – Levko's Song	149
Pan Voyevoda (6 times)	107, 109, 111, 113, 116, 120
Russian Easter Festival Overture, Op.36	188
Sadko, Musical Picture, Op.5	80
Scheherazade, Op.35	128

Title	Item
Tsar's Bride – Aria	142
ROGER-DUCASSE	
Interlude, *Au Jardin de Marguerite*	185
SAINT-SAËNS	
Cello Concerto in A minor, Op.33	184
Samson and Delilah (5 times)	5, 6, 9, 10, 19
SATZ	
Blue Bird, Suite	181
Drama of Life, Suite	181
Fanfares and Chorus, *On the Death of Hamlet*	181
Goat-Footed, Dance	181
SCHUBERT	
March (arr. Yury Sakhnovsky)	180
Wanderer Fantasy (Liszt's version for piano and orchestra)	68
SCRIABIN	
Concerto in F sharp minor, Op.20	165
Symphony No.1 in E major, Op.26	147
SEROV	
Hostile Force – Act 2 (3 times)	22, 25, 26
Rogneda	16
STRAUSS	
Don Juan, Op.20 (twice)	146, 165
Till Eulenspiegel, Op.28 (twice)	147, 179
TANEYEV	
Oresteia, Overture	167
TCHAIKOVSKY	
Concert Fantasia for Piano and Orchestra, Op.56	80
Concerto No.1 in B flat minor, Op.23 (3 times)	68, 164, 176
Eighteen-Twelve, Overture, Op.49 (twice)	150, 151
Eugene Onegin (16 times)	42, 47, 59, 65, 66, 70, 73, 75, 91, 99, 110, 115, 118, 121, 125, 127
Eugene Onegin – Act 1 only	87
Francesca da Rimini, Op.32 (twice)	96, 128

Title	*Item*
Marche slave, Op.31 (twice)	95, 97
Moscow, cantata – Arioso, *To me, O Lord*	188
Oprichnik (5 times)	57, 60, 61, 67, 74
Perevichki – Polonaise	149
Queen of Spades (21 times)	51, 55, 58, 62, 64, 71, 79, 85, 90, 101, 103, 106, 119, 122, 130 (Bolshoi); 169– 174 (Maryinsky).
Symphony No.2 in C minor, Op.17 (*Little Russian*)	164
Symphony No.4 in F minor, Op.36 (twice)	165, 184
Symphony No.5 in E minor, Op.64 (3 times)	80, 93, 179
Tempest, Fantasy, Op.18	164
Theme and Variations, from Suite No.3 in G, Op.55	184
Voyevoda, Symphonic Ballad, Op.78	124

THOMAS
Mignon	17

VERSTOVSKY
Tomb of Ashkold (7 times)	18, 20, 23, 24, 29, 30, 33
Tomb of Ashkold – Act 3 only (3 times)	22, 25, 26

VIVALDI
Concerto in D minor (arr. Siloti)	187

WAGNER
Lohengrin – Prelude to Act 3	93
Siegfried Idyll	147
Walküre – Wotan's Farewell and Magic Fire Music	179
Wesendonk Lieder – 3 items	178

WEBER
Invitation to the Dance (arr. Weingartner) (twice)	168, 187
Oberon, Overture	176

18 Chronological List of Performances

Item	Date	Work	Place	Notes
1	24/2/1891	RACHMANINOFF – *Deus meus*	Moscow Conservatoire	Rachmaninoff's conducting debut, at a student concert
2	18/10/1893	RACHMANINOFF – *Aleko*	Kiev Opera	In the course of his career Rachmaninoff was to conduct just one other performance of *Aleko*, at the Bolshoi Theatre, Moscow (item 87)
3	21/10/1893	RACHMANINOFF – *Aleko*	"	
4	22/11/1895	RACHMANINOFF – *Gypsy Caprice*, Op.12	Moscow	In concert with violinist Teresina Tua
5	12/10/1897	SAINT-SAËNS – *Samson and Delilah*	Mamontov Private Opera, Moscow, Hermitage Theatre	Chaliapin in the part of the Old Jew (also in 6 and 9). In the 1897–98 season Rachmaninoff appeared 33 times, in 9 operas, 5 of them with Chaliapin

532

Item	Date	Work	Place	Notes
6	15/10/1897	SAINT-SAËNS – *Samson and Delilah*	"	2nd of 5 performances
7	19/10/1897	DARGOMYZHSKY – *Rusalka*	"	1st of 6. Chaliapin as the Miller (also in 8, 11, 15, 27, 31)
8	29/10/1897	DARGOMYZHSKY – *Rusalka*	"	2nd of 6
9	30/10/1897	SAINT-SAËNS – *Samson and Delilah*	"	3rd of 5
10	16/11/1897	SAINT-SAËNS – *Samson and Delilah*	Moscow, Solodnikov Theatre	4th of 5
11	26/11/1897	DARGOMYZHSKY – *Rusalka*	"	3rd of 6
12	28/11/1897	BIZET – *Carmen*	"	1st of 4
13	2/12/1897	BIZET – *Carmen*	"	2nd of 4
14	3/12/1897	GLUCK – *Orfeo*	"	1 performance only, taken by Rachmaninoff because of the indisposition of Esposito
15	7/12/1897	DARGOMYZHSKY – *Rusalka*	"	4th of 6
16	11/12/1897	SEROV – *Rogneda*	"	1 performance only. Chaliapin as the Pilgrim
17	12/12/1897	THOMAS – *Mignon*	"	1 performance only
18	21/12/1897	VERSTOVSKY – *The Tomb of Ashkold*	"	1st of 7

Item	Date	Work	Place	Notes
19	22/12/1897	SAINT-SAËNS – *Samson and Delilah*	"	Last of 5
20	26/12/1897	VERSTOVSKY – *The Tomb of Ashkold*	"	2nd of 7
21	27/12/1897	BIZET – *Carmen*	"	3rd of 4
22	28/12/1897	SEROV – *Hostile Power*, Act 2 / VERSTOVSKY – *The Tomb of Ashkold*, Act 3	"	1st of 3 children's matinées
23	30/12/1897	VERSTOVSKY – *The Tomb of Ashkold*	"	3rd of 7
24	31/12/1897	VERSTOVSKY – *The Tomb of Ashkold*	"	4th of 7
25	2/1/1898	SEROV – *Hostile Power*, Act 2 / VERSTOVSKY – *The Tomb of Ashkold*, Act 3	"	2nd of 3
26	3/1/1898	SEROV – *Hostile Power*, Act 2 / VERSTOVSKY – *The Tomb of Ashkold*, Act 3	"	Last of 3
27	4/1/1898	DARGOMYZHSKY – *Rusalka*	"	5th of 6
28	15/1/1898	BIZET – *Carmen*	"	Last of 4
29	18/1/1898	VERSTOVSKY – *The Tomb of Ashkold*	"	5th of 7

534

Item	Date	Work	Place	Notes
30	25/1/1898	VERSTOVSKY – *The Tomb of Askbold*	Moscow, International Theatre	6th of 7
31	27/1/1898	DARGOMYZHSKY – *Rusalka*	"	Last of 6
32	30/1/1898	RIMSKY-KORSAKOV – *May Night*	"	1st of 5. Chaliapin as the Mayor (and in 34, 35, 36, 37)
33	2/2/1898	VERSTOVSKY – *The Tomb of Askbold*	"	Last of 7
34	3/2/1898	RIMSKY-KORSAKOV – *May Night*	"	2nd of 5
35	8/2/1898	RIMSKY-KORSAKOV – *May Night*	"	3rd of 5
36	12/2/1898	RIMSKY-KORSAKOV – *May Night*	"	4th of 5
37	15/2/1898	RIMSKY-KORSAKOV – *May Night*	"	Last of 5
38	7/4/1899	BORODIN – Aria from *Prince Igor* RACHMANINOFF – *The Crag*, Op.7	London, Queen's Hall	Soloist: Mlle Andray. Rachmaninoff also played his *Élégie* and *Prelude* from Op.3. Sir Alexander MacKenzie conducted Beethoven's Fifth Symphony to end the programme

535

Item	Date	Work	Place	Notes
39	26/3/1902	RACHMANINOFF – Concerto No.2 in C minor, Op.18 LISZT – *Totentanz*, G.126	Moscow Philharmonic Society	Soloist in both works: Alexander Siloti, who also conducted the other items in the programme
40	13/12/1903	LISZT – *Totentanz*, G.126	Petersburg, Siloti Concert	Soloist: Alexander Siloti. In the same programme Brahms's *Liebeslieder Walzer* were performed, with Siloti and Rachmaninoff accompanying
41	3/9/1904	DARGOMYZHSKY – *Rusalka*	Moscow, Bolshoi Theatre	1st of 16 performances. In all, Rachmaninoff conducted at the Bolshoi 50 times in the 1904–05 season, and 39 times in 1905–06, in 11 different operas
42	10/9/1904	TCHAIKOVSKY – *Eugene Onegin*	"	1st of 16
43	15/9/1904	DARGOMYZHSKY – *Rusalka*	"	2nd of 16
44	17/9/1904	BORODIN – *Prince Igor*	"	1st of 10 Chaliapin as Prince Galitsky (and in 49, 76, 77, 123, 137)
45	20/9/1904	DARGOMYZHSKY – *Rusalka*	"	3rd of 16
46	21/9/1904	GLINKA – *A Life for the Tsar*	"	1st of 11 Chaliapin as Susanin (and in 50, 52)

Item	Date	Work	Place	Notes
47	22/9/1904	TCHAIKOVSKY – Eugene Onegin	"	2nd of 16
48	23/9/1904	DARGOMYZHSKY – Rusalka	"	4th of 16
49	28/9/1904	BORODIN – Prince Igor	"	2nd of 10
50	30/9/1904	GLINKA – A Life for the Tsar	"	2nd of 11
51	1/10/1904	TCHAIKOVSKY – The Queen of Spades	"	1st of 15
52	4/10/1904	GLINKA – A Life for the Tsar	"	3rd of 11
53	5/10/1904	GLINKA – A Life for the Tsar	"	4th of 11
54	12/10/1904	DARGOMYZHSKY – Rusalka	"	5th of 16. Chaliapin as the Miller (and in 81, 104, 105, 112)
55	15/10/1904	TCHAIKOVSKY – The Queen of Spades	"	2nd of 15
56	21/10/1904	GLINKA – A Life for the Tsar	"	5th of 11
57	25/10/1904	TCHAIKOVSKY – The Opricbnik	"	1st of 5
58	26/10/1904	TCHAIKOVSKY – The Queen of Spades	"	3rd of 15. Special celebratory 100th perfomance of the opera at the Bolshoi, with an all-star cast. Chaliapin's first appearance anywhere as Tomsky and his only appearance ever as Pluto

Item	Date	Work	Place	Notes
59	27/10/1904	TCHAIKOVSKY – *Eugene Onegin*	"	3rd of 16
60	28/10/1904	TCHAIKOVSKY – *The Opricbnik*	"	2nd of 5
61	9/11/1904	TCHAIKOVSKY – *The Opricbnik*	"	3rd of 5
62	15/11/1904	TCHAIKOVSKY – *The Queen of Spades*	"	4th of 15
63	17/11/1904	BORODIN – *Prince Igor*	"	3rd of 10
64	18/11/1904	TCHAIKOVSKY – *The Queen of Spades*	"	5th of 15
65	22/11/1904	TCHAIKOVSKY – *Eugene Onegin*	"	4th of 16
66	25/11/1904	TCHAIKOVSKY – *Eugene Onegin*	"	5th of 16
67	26/11/1904	TCHAIKOVSKY – *The Opricbnik*	"	4th of 5
68	30/11/1904	TCHAIKOVSKY – Concerto No. 1 in B flat minor, Op. 23 SCHUBERT-LISZT – *Wanderer* Fantasy LISZT – *Totentanz*, G. 126	Petersburg, Siloti Concert	Soloist in all three works: Alexander Siloti
69	6/12/1904	GLINKA – *A Life for the Tsar*	Moscow, Bolshoi Theatre	6th of 11

538

Item	Date	Work	Place	Notes
70	8/12/1904	TCHAIKOVSKY – *Eugene Onegin*	"	6th of 16
71	15/12/1904	TCHAIKOVSKY – *The Queen of Spades*	"	6th of 15
72	21/12/1904	DARGOMYZHSKY – *Rusalka*	"	6th of 16
73	22/12/1904	TCHAIKOVSKY – *Eugene Onegin*	"	7th of 16
74	27/12/1904	TCHAIKOVSKY – *The Opricbnik*	"	Last of 5
75	29/12/1904	TCHAIKOVSKY – *Eugene Onegin*	"	8th of 16
76	30/12/1904	BORODIN – *Prince Igor*	"	4th of 10
77	3/1/1905	BORODIN – *Prince Igor*	"	5th of 10
78	10/1/1905	GLINKA – *A Life for tbe Tsar*	"	7th of 11
79	14/1/1905	TCHAIKOVSKY – *The Queen of Spades*	"	7th of 15
80	16/1/1905	TCHAIKOVSKY – Symphony No. 5 in E minor, Op. 64 RIMSKY-KORSAKOV – *Sadko*, Musical Picture, Op. 5 TCHAIKOVSKY – Concert Fantasia, Op. 56 GLINKA – *Kamarinskaya*	Moscow, Kerzin Concert.	Soloist: Sergei Taneyev

Item	Date	Work	Place	Notes
81	19/1/1905	DARGOMYZHSKY – *Rusalka*	Moscow, Bolshoi Theatre	7th of 16
82	21/1/1905	MUSSORGSKY – *Boris Godunov*	"	1st of 4. Chaliapin as Boris in all four performances.
83	24/1/1905	MUSSORGSKY – *Boris Godunov*	"	2nd of 4
84	27/1/1905	MUSSORGSKY – *Boris Godunov*	"	3rd of 4
85	28/1/1905	TCHAIKOVSKY – *The Queen of Spades*	"	8th of 15
86	30/1/1905	MUSSORGSKY – *Boris Godunov*	"	Last of 4
87	2/2/1905	TCHAIKOVSKY –*Eugene Onegin*, Act 1 RACHMANINOFF – *Aleko* MUSSORGSKY – *Boris Godunov*, Inn Scene (Act 1)	"	1 (charity) performance only. Chaliapin as Onegin (the only time ever), Aleko and Varlaam
88	4/2/1905	GLINKA – *A Life for the Tsar*	"	8th of 11
89	23/2/1905	BORODIN – *Prince Igor*	"	6th of 10
90	25/2/1905	TCHAIKOVSKY – *The Queen of Spades*	"	9th of 15

Item	Date	Work	Place	Notes
91	26/2/1905	TCHAIKOVSKY – *Eugene Onegin*	"	9th of 16
92	27/2/1905	DARGOMYZHSKY – *Rusalka*	"	8th of 16
93	14/3/1905	TCHAIKOVSKY – Symphony No. 5 in E minor, Op. 64 WAGNER – *Lobengrin*, Prelude to Act 3 GRIEG – *Peer Gynt*, Suite No. 1, Op. 46 MOSZKOWSKI – Violin Concerto	Moscow Philharmonic Society	Soloist: Karl Grigorovich
94	18/3/1905	BORODIN – Symphony No. 2 in B minor BALAKIREV – Overture on Three Russian Themes GLAZUNOV – *The Seasons*, Op. 67: *Winter* MUSSORGSKY – *Night on the Bare Mountain*	Moscow, Kerzin Concert	
95	27/3/1905	GLINKA – *A Life for the Tsar* – Finale	Moscow, Bolshoi Theatre	Part of a charity concert

Item	Date	Work	Place	Notes
96	28/3/1905	GRIEG – *Anitra's Dance* and *In the Hall of the Mountain King*, from *Peer Gynt* TCHAIKOVSKY – *Marche slave*, Op. 31 BEETHOVEN – *Egmont*, Overture, Op. 84 TCHAIKOVSKY – *Francesca da Rimini*, Op. 32 LISZT – Concerto No. 1 in E flat, G. 124 MENDELSSOHN – Incidental Music to *A Midsummer Night's Dream*, Op. 21/61	Moscow Philharmonic Society	Soloist: Frieda Kwast-Hodapp
97	29/3/1905	GLINKA – *A Life for the Tsar* – Finale	Moscow, Bolshoi Theatre	Part of a charity concert
98	30/8/1905	GRIEG – *Anitra's Dance* and *In the Hall of the Mountain King*, from *Peer Gynt* TCHAIKOVSKY – *Marche slave*, Op. 31 GLINKA – *A Life for the Tsar*	Moscow, Bolshoi Theatre	9th of 11

Item	Date	Work	Place	Notes
99	1/9/1905	TCHAIKOVSKY – Eugene Onegin	"	10th of 16
100	5/9/1905	GLINKA – A Life for the Tsar	"	10th of 11
101	6/9/1905	TCHAIKOVSKY – The Queen of Spades	"	10th of 15
102	8/9/1905	GLINKA – A Life for the Tsar	"	Last of 11
103	12/9/1905	TCHAIKOVSKY – The Queen of Spades	"	11th of 15
104	16/9/1905	DARGOMYZHSKY – Rusalka	"	9th of 16
105	21/9/1905	DARGOMYZHSKY – Rusalka	"	10th of 16
106	22/9/1905	TCHAIKOVSKY – The Queen of Spades	"	12th of 15
107	27/9/1905	RIMSKY-KORSAKOV – Pan Voyevoda (premiere)	"	1st of 6
108	29/9/1905	DARGOMYZHSKY – Rusalka	"	11th of 16
109	3/10/1905	RIMSKY-KORSAKOV – Pan Voyevoda	"	2nd of 6
110	5/10/1905	TCHAIKOVSKY – Eugene Onegin	"	11th of 16
111	6/10/1905	RIMSKY-KORSAKOV – Pan Voyevoda	"	3rd of 6
112	10/10/1905	DARGOMYZHSKY – Rusalka	"	12th of 16

Item	Date	Work	Place	Notes
113	12/10/1905	RIMSKY-KORSAKOV – *Pan Voyevoda*	"	4th of 6
114	14/10/1905	BORODIN – *Prince Igor*	"	7th of 10
115	27/10/1905	TCHAIKOVSKY – *Eugene Onegin*	"	12th of 16
116	28/10/1905	RIMSKY-KORSAKOV – *Pan Voyevoda*	"	5th of 6
117	30/10/1905	RIMSKY-KORSAKOV – *Antar* (Symphony No. 2), Op. 9 BALAKIREV – *Tamara* LIADOV – Intermezzo in C major, Op. 8 LIADOV – *Baba Yaga*, Op. 56 GLINKA – *Night in Madrid*	Moscow, Kerzin Concert	
118	31/10/1905	TCHAIKOVSKY – *Eugene Onegin*	Moscow, Bolshoi Theatre	13th of 16
119	2/11/1905	TCHAIKOVSKY – *The Queen of Spades*	"	13th of 15
120	9/11/1905	RIMSKY-KORSAKOV – *Pan Voyevoda*	"	Last of 6
121	16/11/1905	TCHAIKOVSKY – *Eugene Onegin*	"	14th of 16

544

Item	Date	Work	Place	Notes
122	18/11/1905	TCHAIKOVSKY – *The Queen of Spades*	"	14th of 15
123	23/11/1905	BORODIN – *Prince Igor*	"	8th of 10
124	26/11/1905	ARENSKY – Symphony No. 1 in B minor, Op. 4 GLAZUNOV – *Lyric Poem*, Op. 12 TCHAIKOVSKY – *The Voyevoda*, Symphonic Ballad, Op. 78 RACHMANINOFF – Concerto No. 2 in C minor, Op. 18 MUSSORGSKY – *Sorochinsky Fair*: Introduction and Gopak	Moscow, Kerzin Concert	Soloist: Konstantin Igumnov
125	30/11/1905	TCHAIKOVSKY – *Eugene Onegin*	Moscow, Bolshoi Theatre	15th of 16
126	2/12/1905	DARGOMYZHSKY – *Rusalka*	"	13th of 16
127	6/12/1905	TCHAIKOVSKY – *Eugene Onegin*	"	Last of 16

545

Item	Date	Work	Place	Notes
128	18/12/1905	RIMSKY-KORSAKOV – *Scheherazade*, Op. 35 GLAZUNOV – *Spring*, Musical Picture, Op. 34 TCHAIKOVSKY – *Francesca da Rimini*, Op. 32	Moscow	Also in this concert – Arensky's Suite No. 2, Op. 23 (*Silhouettes*), arr. two pianos, played by Sergei Taneyev and Alexander Goldenweiser
129	28/12/1905	DARGOMYZHSKY – *Rusalka*	Moscow, Bolshoi Theatre	14th of 16
130	3/1/1906	TCHAIKOVSKY – *The Queen of Spades*	"	Last of 15
131	4/1/1906	BORODIN – *Prince Igor*	"	9th of 10
132	11/1/1906	RACHMANINOFF – *Miserly Knight* (premiere) RACHMANINOFF – *Francesca da Rimini* (premiere)	"	1st of 5
133	13/1/1906	RACHMANINOFF – *Miserly Knight* RACHMANINOFF – *Francesca da Rimini*	"	2nd of 5
134	16/1/1906	RACHMANINOFF – *Miserly Knight* RACHMANINOFF – *Francesca da Rimini*	"	3rd of 5

546

Item	Date	Work	Place	Notes
135	17/1/1906	DARGOMYZHSKY – Rusalka	"	15th of 16
136	19/1/1906	RACHMANINOFF – Miserly Knight	"	4th of 5
		RACHMANINOFF – Fran-cesca da Rimini		
137	26/1/1906	BORODIN – Prince Igor	"	Last of 10. The last operatic performance with Chaliapin conducted by Rachmaninoff
138	7/2/1906	RACHMANINOFF – Miserly Knight	"	Last of 5
		RACHMANINOFF – Fran-cesca da Rimini		
139	12/2/1906	DARGOMYZHSKY – Rusalka	"	Last of 16. Rachmaninoff's last appearance at the Bolshoi Theatre as an opera conductor
140	26/5/1907	RACHMANINOFF – Spring, Cantata, Op.20	Paris, Grand Opera	Soloist: Chaliapin. Rachmaninoff also played his Second Concerto, conducted by Camille Chevillard. Rest of programme: Glazunov's Second Symphony; Balakirev's

Item	Date	Work	Place	Notes
				Tamara, and the Prelude to Mussorgsky's *Kbovansbcbina*. This concert was one of five in the 'Russian Season' organized by Diaghilev.
141	26/1/1908	GRIEG – Concerto in A minor, Op.16 RACHMANINOFF – Symphony No.2 in E minor, Op. 27 (premiere)	Petersburg, Siloti Concert	Soloist: Alexander Siloti
142	2/2/1908	RACHMANINOFF – Symphony No.2 in E minor, Op. 27 RIMSKY-KORSAKOV – *The Tsar's Bride*: Aria	Moscow Philharmonic Society	Soloist: Antonina Nezhdanova. Rachmaninoff also played his Second Concerto, conducted by Brandukov, and accompanied a group of songs
143	14/3/1908	RACHMANINOFF – Symphony No.2 in E minor, Op. 27 MUSSORGSKY – *Night on the Bare Mountain* TCHAIKOVSKY – *The Queen of Spades*: Lisa's Aria LIADOV – Scherzo in D major, Op.16	Warsaw	Soloist: Yanina Korolevich. Rachmaninoff also played his Second Suite for Two Pianos with Alexander Michalowski and accompanied two of his songs

Item	Date	Work	Place	Notes
144	9/11/1908	RACHMANINOFF – Symphony No.2 in E minor, Op.27	Amsterdam	
145	27/11/1908	RACHMANINOFF – Symphony No.2 in E minor, Op.27 MUSSORGSKY – *Night on the Bare Mountain* GLAZUNOV – Violin Concerto in A minor, Op.82	Antwerp	Soloist: Mischa Elman. Rachmaninoff also played his Second Concerto
146	3/1/1909	RACHMANINOFF – Symphony No.2 in E minor, Op.27 CONUS – Violin Concerto in E minor STRAUSS – *Don Juan*, Op.20	Moscow, Russian Musical Society	Soloist: Karl Grigorovich. Rachmaninoff also played his Second Concerto, conducted by Emil Cooper.
147	15/4/1909	SCRIABIN – Symphony No.1 in E major, Op.26 STRAUSS – *Till Eulenspiegel*, Op.28 WAGNER – *Siegfried Idyll* LISZT – *Tasso*, Symphonic Poem, G.96	Moscow Philharmonic Society	
148	18/4/1909	RACHMANINOFF – Symphony No.2 in E minor, Op.27	Moscow Philharmonic Society	

Item	Date	Work	Place	Notes
		RACHMANINOFF – *The Isle of the Dead*, Op.29 (premiere)		
		MUSSORGSKY – *Night on the Bare Mountain*		
149	27/4/1909	GLAZUNOV – Prologue, *In Memory of Gogol*	Moscow Conservatoire	Soloists: Avreliya Dobrovolsky (s.) and Dmitry Smirnov (t.). Gogol centenary concert
		RIMSKY-KORSAKOV – *Christmas Eve*: Aria		
		TCHAIKOVSKY – *Perevechki: Polonaise*		
		MUSSORGSKY – *Sorochinsky Fair*: Introduction and Gopak		
		RIMSKY-KORSAKOV – *May Night*: Levko's Song		
		RIMSKY-KORSAKOV – *Christmas Eve*: Suite		
150	26/11/1909	MUSSORGSKY – *Night on the Bare Mountain*	Philadelphia	Rachmaninoff's first appearance with the Philadelphia Orchestra. He also played three of his Preludes
		RACHMANINOFF – Symphony No.2 in E minor, Op.27		

550

Item	Date	Work	Place	Notes
		TCHAIKOVSKY – *Eighteen-Twelve*, Overture, Op. 49		
151	27/11/1909	MUSSORGSKY – *Night on the Bare Mountain*	"	Rachmaninoff also played three of his Preludes
		RACHMANINOFF – Symphony No.2 in E minor, Op. 27		
		TCHAIKOVSKY – *Eighteen-Twelve*, Overture, Op.49		
152	3/12/1909	RACHMANINOFF – *The Isle of the Dead*, Op. 29	Chicago	Theodore Thomas Orchestra. Rachmaninoff also played his Second Concerto, conducted by Frederick Stock
153	4/12/1909	RACHMANINOFF – *The Isle of the Dead*, Op. 29	"	"
154	17/12/1909	RACHMANINOFF – *The Isle of the Dead*, Op. 29	Boston	Boston Symphony Orchestra. Rachmaninoff also played his Second Concerto, conducted by Max Fiedler
155	18/12/1909	RACHMANINOFF – *The Isle of the Dead*, Op. 29	"	"
156	27/1/1910	RACHMANINOFF – *The Isle of the Dead*, Op. 29	New York	Russian Symphony Society. Rachmaninoff also played his Second Concerto, conducted by the orchestra's founder, Modest Altschuler

Item	Date	Work	Place	Notes
157	4/4/1910	RACHMANINOFF – Symphony No.2 in E minor, Op. 27 RACHMANINOFF – *The Isle of the Dead*, Op. 29	Moscow Philharmonic Society	Rachmaninoff also played his Third Concerto, its Russian premiere, conducted by Yevgeny Plotnikov
158	13/10/1910	RACHMANINOFF – Symphony No.2 in E minor, Op. 27	Leeds	
159	28/11/1910	RACHMANINOFF – *The Crag*, Op. 7 RACHMANINOFF – Symphony No.2 in E minor, Op. 27	Moscow, Kerzin concert	Rachmaninoff also played his Third Concerto, conducted by Emil Cooper
160	15/1/1911	BRAHMS – *Tragic Overture*, Op. 81 GLAZUNOV – *Finnish Fantasy*, Op. 88 RACHMANINOFF – *Spring*, Cantata, Op. 20	Moscow Philharmonic Society	Soloist: Vasily Petrov (bass), with the Bolshoi Theatre Choir. Rachmaninoff also played his Third Concerto (not Second, as in *B/L*, p.171), conducted by Yury Pomerantsev
161	21/1/1911	RACHMANINOFF – Symphony No.2 in E minor, Op. 27 RACHMANINOFF – *The Crag*, Op. 7	Kiev	Rachmaninoff also played his Second Concerto, conducted by G. Khodorovsky
162	12/2/1911	RACHMANINOFF – Symphony No.2 in E minor, Op.27	Petersburg, Siloti Concert	Rachmaninoff also played his Third Concerto, conducted by Siloti

Item	Date	Work	Place	Notes
163	15/3/1911	RACHMANINOFF – *The Isle of the Dead*, Op. 29 RACHMANINOFF – *Liturgy of St John Chrysostom*, Op.31	Petersburg	Choir of Maryinsky Theatre
164	29/3/1911	TCHAIKOVSKY – *The Tempest*, Fantasy, Op. 18 TCHAIKOVSKY – Concerto No.1 in B flat minor, Op.23 TCHAIKOVSKY – Symphony No.2 in C minor, Op.17 (*Little Russian*)	Moscow Philharmonic Society	Soloist: Alexander Siloti
165	10/12/1911	TCHAIKOVSKY – Symphony No.4 in F minor, Op.36 SCRIABIN – Concerto in F sharp minor, Op.20 STRAUSS – *Don Juan*, Op.20	"	Soloist: Alexander Scriabin
166	15/12/1911	RACHMANINOFF – *The Miserly Knight*: Baron's Monologue GRIEG – *Peer Gynt*, Suite No.1, Op.46	Moscow	Soloist Georgy Baklanov (bar.), who organized the concert for the benefit of needy students. Baklanov was the Baron in the original production of *The Miserly Knight*

Item	Date	Work	Place	Notes
167	7/1/1912	MUSSORGSKY – *Sorochinsky Fair: Gopak* (arr. Liadov) GLAZUNOV – *From the Middle Ages*, Suite, Op.79 TANEYEV – *The Oresteia:* Overture DAVYDOV – Cello Concerto No.2 in A minor, Op.14 MUSSORGSKY – *Night on the Bare Mountain*	Moscow Philharmonic Society	Soloist: Casals
168	14/1/1912	BEETHOVEN – *Jena Symphony* MOZART – Violin Concerto No.3 in G, K.216 BEETHOVEN – Violin Concerto in D major, Op.61 WEBER – *Invitation to the Dance* (arr. Weingartner)	"	Soloist: Eugene Ysaye
169	13/2/1912	TCHAIKOVSKY – *The Queen of Spades*	Petersburg, Maryinsky Theatre	1st of 6 performances
170	15/2/1912	TCHAIKOVSKY – *The Queen of Spades*	"	2nd of 6

Item	Date	Work	Place	Notes
171	17/2/1912	TCHAIKOVSKY – *The Queen of Spades*	"	3rd of 6
172	20/2/1912	TCHAIKOVSKY – *The Queen of Spades*	"	4th of 6
173	22/2/1912	TCHAIKOVSKY – *The Queen of Spades*	"	5th of 6
174	23/2/1912	TCHAIKOVSKY – *The Queen of Spades*	"	Last of 6 Rachmaninoff's farewell as an opera conductor
175	6/10/1912	BERLIOZ – *Fantastic Symphony*, Op.14	Moscow Philharmonic Society	Soloist: André Hekking
		LALO – Cello Concerto in D minor		
		GLAZUNOV – Ballet Suite, Op.52		
176	20/10/1912	MOZART – Symphony No.40 in G minor, K.550	"	Soloist: Josef Hofmann
		TCHAIKOVSKY – Concerto No.1 in B flat minor, Op.23		
		ARENSKY – Variations on a Theme by Tchaikovsky, Op.35a		

Item	Date	Work	Place	Notes
		LISZT – Concerto No.1 in E flat, G.124		
		WEBER – *Oberon*, Overture		
177	22/10/1912	GRIEG – *Peer Gynt*, Suites 1 and 2, Ops. 46 and 55	Moscow	Soloist: Mark Meychik. Concert to mark the 5th anniversary of Grieg's death
		GRIEG – *Lyric Suite*, Op.54		
		GRIEG – Concerto in A minor, Op.16		
178	27/10/1912	MENDELSSOHN – Symphony No.3 in A minor, Op.56 (*Scotch*)	Moscow Philhar-monic Society	Soloist: Ilona Durigo (m-s.)
		WAGNER – *Wesendonk Lieder*: *Schmerzen* (orch. Mottl) *Im Treibhaus* (orch. Mottl) *Traume* (orch. Wagner)		
		GRIEG – *Lyric Suite*, Op.54		
		LISZT – *Mazeppa*, Tone Poem, G.100		
		GRIEG – *Last Spring* (*Elegiac Melodies*, Op.34)		
		LISZT – *Lorelei*, G.273		

Item	Date	Work	Place	Notes
179	3/11/1912	TCHAIKOVSKY – Symphony No.5 in E minor, Op.64 WAGNER – *Walküre*: Wotan's Farewell and Magic Fire Music STRAUSS – *Till Eulenspiegel*, Op.28	"	Soloist: Georgy Baklanov (bar.), who also sang Rachmaninoff's *Spring Waters*, Op.14, No.11, and *Fate*, Op.21, No.1, accompanied by the composer
180	11/11/1912	SCHUBERT – March (arr. Yury Sakhnovsky) BERLIOZ – *Temptation of Faust*: two excerpts LISZT – *Hungarian Rhapsody No.1* (= piano No.14)	Moscow	Soloist: Antonina Nezhdanova, who also sang a group of Rachmaninoff songs, accompanied by the composer
181	23/11/1912	SATZ – *On the Death of Hamlet*, Fanfares and Chorus SATZ – *Blue Bird*, Suite SATZ – *Drama of Life*, Suite SATZ – *Goat-Footed*, Dance	Moscow Art Theatre	Memorial concert on the death of Ilya Satz (1875-1912), composer and musical director at the Moscow Art Theatre
182	1/12/1912	BORODIN – Symphony No.2 in B minor GLAZUNOV – *Spring*, Musical Picture, Op. 34	Moscow Philharmonic Society	Soloist: Casals

Item	Date	Work	Place	Notes
		DVOŘÁK – Cello Concerto in B minor, Op.104 RIMSKY-KORSAKOV – *Invisible City of Kitezh: Battle of Kerzhenets*		
183	30/11/1913	RACHMANINOFF – *The Isle of the Dead*, Op. 29 RACHMANINOFF – Concerto No.2 in C minor, Op.18 RACHMANINOFF – *The Bells*, Op.35 (premiere)	Petersburg, Siloti Concert	Soloist: Alexander Siloti. Soloists in *Bells*. Elizaveta Popova (s.), Alexander Alexandrovich (t.), Pavel Andreyev (b.bar.), with the Choir of the Maryinsky Theatre
184	14/12/1913	TCHAIKOVSKY – Symphony No.4 in F minor, Op.36 TCHAIKOVSKY – *Theme and Variations* from Suite No.3 in G, Op.55 SAINT-SAËNS – Cello Concerto in A minor, Op.33	Moscow Philharmonic Society	Soloist: Casals
185	8/2/1914	FRANCK – *Chasseur maudit*, Symphonic Poem DEBUSSY – *Martyrdom of St Sebastian*	"	Soloists: Elena Stepanova (s.), Alexander Bogdanovich (t.), Feofan Pavlovsky (bar.), with the Choir and Orchestra of the Bolshoi Theatre

Item	Date	Work	Place	Notes
		ROGER-DUCASSE – Interlude, *Au Jardin de Marguerite* RAVEL – *Valses nobles et sentimentales* RACHMANINOFF – *The Bells*, Op. 35		
186	24/2/1914	RACHMANINOFF – *Liturgy of St John Chrysostom*, Op.31	Petersburg	Choir of the Maryinsky Theatre
187	1/3/1914	BACH – Prelude from Cantata No.35 VIVALDI – Concerto in D minor (ed. Siloti) BEETHOVEN – Concerto No.1 in C major, Op.15 BRAHMS – Variations on a Theme by Haydn, Op.56a LISZT – Concerto No.1 in E flat, G.124 WEBER – *Invitation to the Dance* (arr. Weingartner)	Moscow Philharmonic Society	Soloist: Josef Lhevinne
188	22/3/1914	GLAZUNOV – Symphony No.6 in C minor, Op.58	"	Soloist: Evgeniya Zbruyeva (con.), who also sang a group of songs not accompanied by Rachmaninoff

Item	Date	Work	Place	Notes
		BORODIN – Song, *Romance* (orch. Glazunov)		
		TCHAIKOVSKY – Arioso, *To me, O Lord, within Thy power*, from the cantata *Moscow*		
		RIMSKY-KORSAKOV – *Russian Easter Festival Overture*, Op.36		
189	25/10/1914	LIADOV – *From the Book of Revelation*, Op.66	Moscow	Concert to mark the recent death of Liadov
		LIADOV – *Baba Yaga*, Op.56		
		LIADOV – *Kikimora*, Op.63		
		LIADOV – *Enchanted Lake*, Op.62		
		LIADOV – *Nénie (Dirge)*, Op.67		
		LIADOV – *Eight Russian Folk Songs*, Op.58		
		RACHMANINOFF – Symphony No.2 in E minor, Op.27		
190	7/1/1917	RACHMANINOFF – *The Crag*, Op.7	Moscow, Bolshoi Theatre	Soloists: Elena Stepanova (s.), Andrey Labinsky (t.), Sergei Migay (bar.),

Item	Date	Work	Place	Notes
		RACHMANINOFF – *The Isle of the Dead*, Op. 29 RACHMANINOFF – *The Bells*, Op. 35		with the Bolshoi Theatre Orchestra and Chorus. Rachmaninoff's conducting farewell to Russia
191	20/4/1929	RACHMANINOFF – *The Isle of the Dead*, Op. 29 RACHMANINOFF – *Vocalise*, Op.34, No.14	Philadelphia, Academy of Music	Recording session with Philadelphia Orchestra. A preliminary session had taken place on 15/4/1929
192	8/12/1939	RACHMANINOFF – Symphony No.3 in A minor, Op.44 RACHMANINOFF – *The Bells*, Op.35	"	Soloists: Susanne Fisher (s.), Jan Peerce (t.), Mack Harrell (bar.), with the Westminster Choir and Philadelphia Orchestra
193	9/12/1939	RACHMANINOFF – Symphony No.3 in A minor, Op.44 RACHMANINOFF – *The Bells*, Op.35	"	"
194	10/12/1939	RACHMANINOFF – Symphony No.3 in A minor, Op.44 RACHMANINOFF – *The Bells*, Op.35	New York, Carnegie Hall	" The last of three concerts in a 'Rachmaninoff Cycle', celebrating thirty years of concert appearances in America
195	11/12/1939	RACHMANINOFF – Symphony No.3 in A minor, Op.44	Philadelphia, Academy of Music	Recording session

561

Item	Date	Work	Place	Notes
196	13/3/1941	RACHMANINOFF – Symphony No.3 in A minor, Op.44	Chicago	Soloists: Jean Fairbank (s.), Jan Peerce (t.), Mack Harrell (bar.), with the Apollo Music Club and Chicago Symphony Orchestra
		RACHMANINOFF – *The Bells*, Op. 35		
197	14/3/1941	RACHMANINOFF – Symphony No.3 in A minor, Op.44	"	"
		RACHMANINOFF – *The Bells*, Op. 35		Rachmaninoff's farewell as conductor

Notes

The literary sources most often quoted or referred to in the text have been given the following abbreviations in the References:

Bazhanov – Bazhanov, Nikolai: *Rachmaninov*, English version, Raduga Publishers, Moscow, 1983.

Belaiev – Belaiev, Victor: 'Sergei Rakhmaninov', in *The Musical Quarterly*, Vol. 13, July 1927, pp. 359–376.

Belza – Belza, I.F. (ed.): *S.V. Rakhmaninov i russkaya opera* [Rachmaninoff and Russian opera], Moscow, 1947.

B/L – Bertensson, Sergei, and Leyda, Jay: *Sergei Rachmaninoff, A Lifetime in Music*, New York University Press, 1956; George Allen & Unwin Ltd, London, 1965.

Bortnikova – Bortnikova, E.E.: *Avtografi S.V. Rakhmaninova v fondakh gosudarstvennovo tsentral'novo muzeya muzïkalnoy kulturï imeni M.I. Glinki: katalog-spravochnik* [Autographs of Rachmaninoff in the archives of the State Central Glinka Museum of Musical Culture: reference catalogue], 2nd ed., Moscow, 1980.

Bryantseva – Bryantseva, V.N.: *S.V. Rakhmaninov*, Moscow, 1976.

Chaliapin – Froud, Nina, and Hanley, James: *Chaliapin, An Autobiography as told to Maxim Gorky*, Macdonald & Co. Ltd, London, 1968.

Chasins – Chasins, Abram: *Speaking of Pianists*, Alfred A. Knopf Inc., New York, 1957.

Culshaw – Culshaw, John: *Sergei Rachmaninov*, Dennis Dobson Ltd, London, 1949.

Ewen – Ewen, David: 'Music Should Speak from the Heart', Rachmaninoff interview in *The Etude*, No. 59, December 1941, pp. 804–848.

Hofmann – Graydon, Neil S., and Sizemore, Margaret D.: *The Amazing Marriage of Marie Eustis and Josef Hofmann*, University of South Carolina Press, Columbia, 1965.

Horowitz – Plaskin, Glenn: *Horowitz, A Biography*, William Morrow & Co. Inc., New York, and Macdonald & Co. Ltd, London, 1983.

Keldïsh – Keldïsh, Y.V.: *Rakhmaninov i evo vremya* [Rachmaninoff and his times], Moscow, 1973.

LN/A – Apetyan, Z.A. (ed.): *Sergey Rakhmaninov: Literaturnoye naslediye* [literary legacy], 3 vols, Moscow, 1978, 1980. (A new edition is due in 1992)

Norris – Norris, Geoffrey: *Rakhmaninov*, J.M. Dent & Sons Ltd, London, 1976, 'Master Musicians' series.

O'Connell – O'Connell, Charles: *The Other Side of the Record,* Alfred A. Knopf Inc., New York, 1947.

Palmieri – Palmieri, Robert: *Sergei Vasil'evich Rachmaninoff: A Guide to Research*, Garland Publishing Inc., New York, 1985.

Piggott – Piggott, Patrick: *Rachmaninov Orchestral Music*, BBC Publications, London, 1974.

Riesemann – Riesemann, Oskar von: *Rachmaninoff's Recollections*, George Allen & Unwin Ltd, London, 1934.

Rimsky-Korsakov – Rimsky-Korsakov, Nikolay: *My Musical Life*, translated by Judah A. Joffe, Alfred A. Knopf Inc., New York, 1923.

Rubinstein – Rubinstein, Arthur: *My Many Years*, Alfred A. Knopf Inc., New York, and Jonathan Cape Ltd, London, 1980.

Rudakova – Rudakova, E.N. (compiler): *S.V. Rakhmaninov*, Moscow, 1982.

Sabaneyeff – Sabaneyeff, Leonid: 'Rachmaninoff' in *Modern Russian Composers,* translated by Judah A. Joffe, pp. 103-120, Martin Lawrence Ltd, London, 1927.

Seroff – Seroff, Victor: *Rachmaninoff,* Cassell & Co, Ltd, London, 1951.

Sokolova – Sokolova, O.I.: *Sergey Vasilyevich Rakhmaninov*, Moscow, 1983.

Sorabji – Sorabji, Kaikhosru: *Around Music,* Unicorn Press, London, 1932.

Swan – Swan, Alfred and Katherine: 'Rachmaninoff: Personal Reminiscences', in *The Musical Quarterly*, Vol. 30, January 1944, pp. 1–19, and May 1944, pp. 174–191.

T/N – Threlfall, Robert, and Norris, Geoffrey: *A Catalogue of the Compositions of S. Rachmaninoff,* Scolar Press, London, 1982.

Tsitovich – Tsïtovich, T.E.: *S.V. Rakhmaninov: sbornik statey i materialov* [collection of articles and materials], Moscow, 1947.

VR/A – Apetyan, Z.A. (ed.): *Vospominaniya o Rakhmaninove* [Reminiscences about Rachmaninoff], 2 vols, 5th ed., Moscow, 1988.

Index of Rachmaninoff's Works

565

Index of Persons and of Works Referred to in the Text

Printed in Great Britain by
Billing & Sons Ltd, Worcester